SUMMARY OF AMERICAN LAW

BY

ROBERT T. KIMBROUGH

Former Editor-in-Chief of
The Lawyers Co-operative Publishing Company
Member of the Bars of Kentucky and New York

Based on AMERICAN JURISPRUDENCE
First and Second Editions

1974

THE LAWYERS CO-OPERATIVE PUBLISHING CO.
Rochester, New York 14603

BANCROFT-WHITNEY CO.
San Francisco, California 94107

LCP BW

Library of Congress Catalog Card Number 73–88586

FOREWORD

The plan of the present work is to present, under chapters or divisions based upon the traditional law school topics of law, a concise statement of the fundamental principles of modern American law. As the same few basic principles are involved in the numerous aspects and applications of the law, the plan adopted for this work reduces to a minimum the necessary repetition and duplication.

This Summary is based upon the monumental and authoritative encyclopedia, AMERICAN JURISPRUDENCE, First and Second Editions. The aim of the author has been to reduce to its quintessence the vast literature of the law and to state only the basic principles which govern all situations. Although the nature and scope of this work required that minute detail and exhaustive illustrations of the application of principles be dispensed with, care has been taken to make clear, sometimes by specific examples and in other instances by categories, the kind of cases and circumstances to which the principles are appropriate.

There can be no doubt of the need for a brief outline of our law. The need was felt even before the court decisions interpreting the law increased to millions. The trend toward specialization in practice and in teaching does not lessen the requirement of familiarity with all branches and aspects of law. The law school student needs something to illuminate and coordinate the case book system of teaching and to make the lectures more understandable. The Code and the Pandects or Digest of Justinian, exhaustive and vast as they were, emphasized rather than dispensed with the need of a brief summary, by both practitioner and student; hence, the one-volume Institutes was very successful. The present work is also designed for use in review and preparation for bar exams. And it should be useful as an elementary and understandable reference book for laymen and scholars in other fields who seek knowledge of law.

Following each section heading of this work are references to the specific sections of Am Jur and Am Jur 2d on which the text is based. This will enable the student to explore each point in more detail. It will also afford the practicing lawyer or judge an elementary orientation, a starting point from which to pursue further research, and an additional means of entry into the Am Jur system.

*

SUMMARY OF AMERICAN LAW

AGENCY

I. NATURE AND CREATION OF AGENCY

II. AUTHORITY AND ACTS OF AGENT

COMMERCIAL PAPER; BILLS AND NOTES

CONFLICT OF LAWS

CONSTITUTIONAL LAW

CONTRACTS

CORPORATIONS

I. GENERAL MATTERS: INCORPORATION, ORGANIZATION, AND NATURE

II. CAPITAL STOCK

III. STOCKHOLDERS

IV. POWERS, FUNCTIONS, AND LIABILITIES OF CORPORATION

V. DIRECTORS, OFFICERS, AND EMPLOYEES

VI. FOREIGN CORPORATIONS

CRIMINAL LAW

DAMAGES

DOMESTIC RELATIONS AND PERSONS

EQUITY

I. NATURE AND BASIS OF EQUITY JURISPRUDENCE

EVIDENCE

EXTRAORDINARY REMEDIES

PARTNERSHIP AND OTHER UNINCORPORATED ORGANIZATIONS

I. PARTNERSHIP

II. JOINT VENTURES

III. BUSINESS TRUSTS

IV. OTHER FORMS OF ORGANIZATION

PERSONAL PROPERTY

I. IN GENERAL; NATURE AND CLASSES OF PERSONAL PROPERTY

II. ACQUISITION AND OWNERSHIP

PRODUCTS LIABILITY

REAL PROPERTY

XI. RECORDING OF TITLE INSTRUMENTS: REGISTRATION OF TITLE

XII. ADVERSE POSSESSION

XIII. LIENS

XIV. REMEDIES TO PROTECT PROPERTY RIGHTS

RESTITUTION, QUASI-CONTRACTS AND IMPLIED CONTRACTS

I. IN GENERAL

II. RECOVERY FOR WORK, SERVICES, AND MATERIALS

III. RECOVERY OF PAYMENTS

SALES

TORTS

I. GENERAL CONSIDERATIONS

II. NEGLIGENCE

III. AUTOMOBILES AND OTHER MOTOR VEHICLES

XVIII. TRADE OR BUSINESS PRACTICES

XIX. OTHER WRONGS AND INJURIES INVOLVING WILFUL ACT OR VIOLATION OF LAW

TRUSTS

WILLS, DESCENT, AND DECEDENTS' ESTATES

I. WILLS

A. IN GENERAL; TESTAMENTARY CHARACTER AND VALIDITY

B. FORMAL REQUISITES; EXECUTION, ATTESTATION, AND PUBLICATION

C. REVOCATION OR CHANGE

†

AGENCY

I. NATURE AND CREATION OF AGENCY

I. NATURE AND CREATION OF AGENCY

§ 1:1. Generally.

Am Jur 2d References: Agency, §§ 1–8, 23.

The term "agency" is defined as a fiduciary relationship arising where one party, known as the "principal," confides to another person, known as the "agent," the management of some business or the performance of some trans-

1

action by the agent in the principal's name and on his account, and by which the agent assumes to transact the business or do the act and to render an account of it. The term "agency," in its legal sense, imports commercial or contractual dealings between two parties through the medium of another.

The agent is a substitute or deputy appointed by the principal with power to do certain things which the principal could do. The agent is the representative of the principal and acts in the place of the principal and subject to the latter's control. Whatever an agent does in the lawful prosecution of the transaction or business entrusted to him is the act of the principal.

According to the nature and extent of their authority, agents are classified as general, special, or universal. A general agent is usually authorized to do all acts connected with the business or employment in which he engaged. A special agent is authorized to do only one or more specific acts under particular instructions or with restrictions implied from the act to be done. A universal agent is authorized to transact all the business of his principal of every kind and to do all delegable acts for him.

Another type of agent is the "attorney in fact," appointed by a written instrument called a "power of attorney," and given authority to perform certain specified acts or kinds of acts on behalf of the principal. The power of attorney may be general, special, or partly general and partly limited or special.

§ 1:2. Capacity of parties.

Am Jur 2d References: Agency, §§ 9–16, 24.

Any person who is sui juris and has capacity to affect his legal relations by the giving of consent to a delegable act or transaction may authorize an agent to act for him with the same effect as if he acted in person. The principal may be either a natural person or an artificial entity. And ordinarily any person having capacity to appoint an agent may confer upon another the power to act as his attorney in fact.

The capacity of certain classes of persons, such as infants and mental incompetents, may be limited or qualified. The authorities are not in accord on the question whether the appointment of an agent by an infant, and the acts of the agent under such appointment, are absolutely void or merely voidable and subject to ratification or repudiation by the infant. Some courts make no distinction between the appointment of an agent and other acts or contracts of an infant, holding that the infant's appointment of an agent or attorney and the acts of the latter are merely voidable. On the other hand, there is authority to the effect that an infant's appointment of an agent or attorney, and the acts under such appointment, are not merely voidable, but absolutely void, on the theory that the agent cannot confer upon others a power which he does not himself possess.

A person who is not mentally competent to contract cannot appoint an agent, although a court may do so for him.

The fact that a person is under legal disability or incapacity of such nature that he cannot appoint an agent to act for him, does not prevent him from acting as agent for another and binding the latter by contracts on his behalf. Thus, an infant may act as agent. And according to some, but not all, authorities, the act of a mental incompetent, acting as agent for another, may be binding upon the latter.

§ 1:3. Creation of agency.

Am Jur 2d References: Agency, §§ 17–22, 25–27; Brokers, §§ 30–53.

The relation of principal and agent is ordinarily created by agreement of the parties. As between principal and agent, there must be a meeting of the minds in establishing the agency, and the consent of both parties is necessary, although such consent may be implied. An implied agency is an actual agency, the existence of which is established by inferences from the facts and circumstances of the case, such as a prior course of dealings of a similar nature between the parties. As between the principal and third persons, agency may be inferred from appearances and from the operation of principles of estoppel (infra § 1:8). Under rare and compelling circumstances, liability has been predicated upon a relationship, analogous to that of principal and agent, called agency by necessity or by operation of law.

Generally, a person may appoint an agent to perform the same acts which he might legally do himself, unless public policy or contractual obligations of the principal require that he perform the acts in person.

A power of attorney, appointing an attorney in fact, is a written instrument, and in certain instances, as where it involves dealings in real estate, the instrument is required to be acknowledged and recorded.

A broker is an agent and his employment is ordinarily governed by the same principles as apply to agency generally. A contract for the purchase or sale of real estate need not be in writing, unless a writing is required by statute or the broker is to acquire an interest in the property itself. However, statutes in some states require that contracts for the employment of a broker to negotiate a purchase or sale of real estate be in writing.

§ 1:4. Duration and termination.

Am Jur 2d References: Agency, §§ 34–50; Brokers, §§ 54–64.

The time or duration of an agency is governed by the agreement between the parties, or, if no time is specified, by the expiration of a reasonable time or the accomplishment of the purpose of the agency. If the agency is not coupled with an interest (as to which, see § 1:6, infra), and no third-party rights are involved, either the principal or the agent may revoke or terminate the agency at any time for any reason, or without reason. This, however, is a power and not a right, and either the principal or the agent may be liable in damages to the other for a revocation or renunciation of the agency in violation of the agreement between them. Either party may cancel the agency for good cause without liability to the other party.

As against third persons dealing with the agent, the principal's power of revocation is not so absolute. The acts of an agent may bind a principal as against third persons who, without notice of the revocation of the agent's authority, rely upon its continued existence. In other words, the agent's acts, within the apparent scope of his authority, are binding on the principal as against one who formerly dealt with him through the agent and who had no notice of the revocation. And the principal's conduct after the revocation of an agent's authority may estop him to deny the agency.

§ 1:5. — Termination by operation of law; death.

Am Jur 2d References: Agency, §§ 51–59; Brokers, § 63.

An agency may be terminated by operation of law. Thus, it is a well-established general rule that the death of the principal effects an instantaneous and absolute revocation of the agent's authority or power, unless the agency is one coupled with an interest. The estate of the principal is not bound by any act done by the agent after the principal's death. The same rule applies where there are two or more joint principals and one of them dies. And the same rule applies to powers of attorney. Similarly, the death of an agent, or of one of several joint agents, will revoke a simple agency not coupled with an interest.

There is a conflict of authority on the question whether the termination of an agency by the death of the principal is dependent upon notice of his death. Many cases take the view that the principal's death terminates the agency although the agent and third persons are ignorant of the death. Other authorities hold that as to a third person dealing with the agent in good faith and in ignorance of the principal's death, the revocation of the agency takes effect only from the time of notice of the death.

The authority of an agent may also be terminated by the mental incompetency of the principal or by his bankruptcy. The complete loss or destruction of the subject matter of the agency, or the termination on the principal's interest therein, is held to terminate the agent's authority to deal with reference to it, at least where it is not possible to substitute other material for that lost or destroyed.

§ 1:6. — Irrevocable agency; power coupled with interest.

Am Jur 2d References: Agency, §§ 60–67; Brokers, § 59.

The general rule is well settled that if the authority or power of an agent is coupled with an interest, it cannot be revoked by the act, condition, or death of the principal, in the absence of an agreement to the contrary. This rule applies to an agency or power of attorney given as security. To come within the rule of irrevocability, however, the interest of the agent must be in the subject matter of the power rather than in the proceeds to arise from the exercise of the power. Thus, if the agent's interest is merely his right to receive, by way of compensation, a certain amount or percentage from the proceeds of a sale or collection to be effected by him, the agency is not coupled with an interest; but if he receives some kind of interest or title, legal or equitable, in the subject matter of the agency, his power with reference to the subject matters is coupled with an interest and may not be revoked.

4

II. AUTHORITY AND ACTS OF AGENT

§ 1:7. Generally.

Am Jur 2d References: Agency, §§ 68–72, 77, 83.

The authority of the agent to act for and bind the principal is the very essence of the principal and agent relationship. This authority may be either actual authority (which includes both express and implied authority) or apparent or ostensible authority (as to which, see § 1:8, infra).

Implied authority of an agent is that which the principal is deemed to have intended the agent to possess, although not expressly granted, and it includes authority to do whatever acts are incidental to, or necessary, usual, and proper to accomplish or perform, the main authority expressly delegated to the agent.

The principal may, of course, limit the authority of his agent, and if such limitation is brought to the attention of the party with whom the agent deals, the power to bind the principal is defined and limited thereby. And a third person dealing with a known agent must use reasonable diligence to ascertain whether the agent is acting within the scope of his powers. One who deals with a special agent or an agent having only special authority, acts at his peril and must ascertain the extent of the agent's authority. In the case of a general agent, however, a third person is not obliged to inquire whether there are secret limitations or private instructions limiting the agent's authority.

Persons dealing with an agent must take notice of the rule that an agency cannot be used for the benefit of the agent himself or of any person other than the principal, adversely to the principal's interests.

§ 1:8. Ostensible authority; estoppel.

Am Jur 2d References: Agency, §§ 73–76.

The liability of the principal for the acts and contracts of his agent is not limited to such acts and contracts as are expressly authorized or necessarily implied from express authority. So far as concerns a third person dealing in good faith with an agent, the agent's authority also includes that which has apparently been delegated to him. This apparent or ostensible authority may be thus stated: if a principal acts or conducts his business, either intentionally or through negligence or by failing to disapprove of the agent's act or course of action, so as to lead third persons to believe with justification that the agent possesses authority to act or contract in the name of the principal with regard to particular matters, the principal is bound by the acts of the agent within the scope of that apparent authority as to any person who, upon the faith of such holding out, believes with justification that the agent has such authority, and in good faith deals with him.

In order to invoke the doctrine of apparent or ostensible authority, it must be established (1) that the principal has manifested his consent to the exercise of such authority or has knowingly permitted the agent to assume the exercise thereof; (2) that the third person knew of the facts and, acting in good faith, had reason to believe, and did actually believe, that the agent possessed such authority; and (3) that the third person, relying on such appearance of authority, has changed his position and will suffer injury or loss if the transaction executed by the agent does not bind the principal.

The apparent authority of an agent is to be determined by the acts of the principal and not by the acts of the agent. The mere fact that an agent assumes or represents the existence of authority does not give rise to an apparent authority. Another limitation upon the doctrine of apparent authority is that it cannot be so extended as to permit the agent to depart from the usual manner of accomplishing what he is employed to effect.

Although the general statements of the doctrine of apparent authority may not include all of the elements of equitable estoppel or estoppel in pais, there is little if any diffence between the two doctrines as they are applied by the courts. And the rule of apparent authority is frequently attributed to the general principles of estoppel, and to the doctrine that where one of two innocent parties must suffer for the wrongful act of another, the loss should fall upon the one who, by his conduct, created the circumstances which enabled the third party to perpetrate the wrong and cause the loss.

§ 1:9. Authority in particular matters.

explain

Am Jur 2d References: Agency, §§ 84–148; Brokers, §§ 65–80.

The power of an agent to bind his principal by his contracts or acts in the latter's behalf depends upon the authority expressly, impliedly, or ostensibly conferred upon the agent by the principal, and this depends upon the circumstances of each particular case. Generally, authority to make a specified contract contemplates a contract in the usual form and with usual terms and to do other acts which are usually incidental thereto or reasonably necessary for making the contract.

The power of an agent to make or execute a contract does not include the authority to vary an agreement after execution, or to waive its conditions or otherwise diminish or discharge the obligations of the third person.

The powers of an agent acting as general agent or general manager are particularly broad, and he may generally bind his principal by any contracts that he deems reasonably necessary for the protection of the interests of his principal or to keep the property in repair and the business a going concern.

The authority to borrow money on the credit of the principal is among the most important and also most dangerous powers which a principal can confer upon an agent, and such authority will not be inferred unless it is expressly conferred or necessarily implied by the scope and character of the authority expressly given. Even a general or managing agent or one employed to carry on a business has not, ipso facto, power to borrow money unless such action is a necessary incident to the business. The power to borrow may, however, be implied from the conduct of the principal or from a previous course of dealings.

The authority of an agent to purchase or sell the personal property of his principal depends upon the scope and purpose of the agency. The same is true with reference to the agent's authority to fix the price, to purchase on credit, and to give negotiable instruments in payment.

The general rule is that mere authority in an agent to sell or find a market for commodities does not carry implied authority to receive or collect payment therefor; but there may be apparent authority to do so and such authority may be imported from the course of dealing, the very nature of the agency, or from all of the circumstances of the particular case.

There is a conflict of authority on the question whether the principal will be bound by the agent's agreement, in selling personal property, for the return, repurchase, or resale of the property. The weight of authority, at least in cases involving personal property other than stocks, bonds, and other securities, appears to support the view that the agent engaged in the sale of personal property is not authorized to agree, contemporaneously with the sale, that the purchaser may return the property purchased, or that the property will be repurchased from, or resold for, him by the principal.

Authority to warrant goods sold by an agent may be expressly given or may exist as an implied or incidental power or under the doctrine of apparent authority. The rule followed by most courts is, however, that authority to sell a particular kind or article of personal property includes authority to warrant the title, quality, or condition of the thing if, and only if, such warranty is usual or customary in such a transaction and is reasonably necessary to transact the business entrusted to the agent. Where a warranty arises by operation of law, regardless of any intention of the seller to create it, such a warranty will be imported into a sale negotiated by an agent.

Where the power to sell the principal's real estate is not expressly conferred upon an agent, the courts are very reluctant to imply such power. And express authority to sell land does not ordinarily give the agent power to convey the property, nor does authority merely to find a purchaser authorize the agent to execute a contract to convey. Where an agent is employed to sell the principal's real estate, his authority to fix the terms of the sale depends, of course, upon the agency agreement. There is a difference of opinion as to whether an agent employed to sell or convey real estate may bind his principal to convey by a deed containing covenants of warranty. Even assuming such authority, it does not extend to unusual covenants.

In the absence of express authority, an agent has the power to mortgage or pledge the principal's property only when such action is necessary for the execution of the duties actually delegated to him.

The authority of an agent to collect or receive payment on behalf of his principal is peculiarly dependent upon the terms, scope, and purpose of the agency. Mere authority in an agent to sell real estate or to find a purchaser does not ordinarily, according to the prevailing view, give the agent authority to receive the purchase money or any part thereof, in the absence of special circumstances.

Authority in an agent to make or issue, indorse, or transfer commercial paper will not be lightly inferred, but must be clearly shown; and where given, the authority must be strictly construed and strictly pursued.

§ 1:10. Delegation of authority by agent; subagency.

Am Jur 2d References: Agency, §§ 7, 149–159; Brokers, §§ 81, 82.

Where the principal expressly authorizes his agent to delegate the authority conferred on him, the subagent represents the principal as if directly appointed by him. And such authority may be implied when the nature of the business is such that it must be contemplated by the principal that the authority conferred on the agent will be exercised through subagents. Unless he has either express or implied authority to delegate his powers, or the circumstances are such as to invoke the doctrine of apparent authority, the agent cannot confer upon another powers entrusted to him by the principal.

Where personal trust or confidence is reposed in the agent, and especially where the exercise of the power is made subject to his judgment or discretion, the agent's authority cannot be delegated to another without the consent of the principal. The performance of purely ministerial or mechanical acts, however, may be delegated by an agent under ordinary circumstances. And if by established custom or usage of the business to which an agency pertains, an agent may appoint subagents, the principal is presumed to have acted with reference to that usage in the appointment of the agent.

The principal is bound by the acts of an authorized subagent to the same extent as if they had been performed by the agent. If he has used due care in the selection of a subagent, the agent is not generally liable for the acts or defaults of the subagent. Where the delegation of authority to the subagent is not authorized, however, the principal is not liable to third persons for any act or contract of the subagent. In such cases, the agent and not the principal is responsible. Similarly, where an agent makes an unauthorized delegation of powers to a subagent, it is the agent and not the principal who is liable to the subagent for his compensation.

§ 1:11. Ratification.

Am Jur 2d References: Agency, §§ 160–186; Brokers, §§ 68, 82.

An unauthorized act of one purporting to represent a principal may be ratified by the latter so as to be binding upon him. This doctrine applies to the ratification of the act of an agent in excess of his authority and also to the act of one who purports to be an agent but actually is not. Such a ratification relates back and supplies the original authority to perform the act. The ratification may be express, as by spoken or written words, or implied, resulting from the conduct of the principal. The ratification of an unauthorized act must be in the particular mode or form necessary to confer authority in the first place. Thus, where the original authorization would be required to be in writing, the ratification must be in writing.

In order to have an effective ratification, there must be an intention on the part of the purported principal to ratify the act in question, although this intention may be inferred from the surrounding circumstances.

If the principal elects to ratify any portion of an unauthorized transaction of his agent, he must ratify the whole of it, and his ratification of a part results in a ratification of the entire transaction. He cannot avail himself of such acts as are beneficial to him and repudiate those which are detrimental. The principal's failure to repudiate an unauthorized act of his purported agent within a reasonable time, may give rise to an inference that the principal has ratified the unauthorized act. He cannot, by waiting, have the benefit of the unauthorized act or contract if it should turn out to be profitable, and yet retain a right to repudiate it otherwise.

In order to bind a principal by ratification of prior acts of his agent, a knowledge of the material facts must be brought home to the principal; he must have been in possession of all of the material facts and must have acted in the light of such knowledge. Thus, the acceptance or retention of the benefits derived from an agent's unauthorized act does not amount to a ratification of such act if the principal does not have knowledge of all the material facts surrounding the transaction.

III. RIGHTS, DUTIES, AND LIABILITIES AS BETWEEN PRINCIPAL AND AGENT

§ 1:12. Obligations of agent to principal.

Am Jur 2d References: Agency, §§ 198–219; Brokers, §§ 83–85, 81–99.

The duties of an agent toward his principal are always to be determined by the character of the agency, the scope of authority conferred, and the fundamental obligations of fidelity to the interests of the principal. The agent is under a duty to act only as authorized, and if he exceeds his authority he generally becomes liable to his principal for any loss or damage naturally resulting from his unauthorized acts.

An agent is a fiduciary with respect to matters within the scope of his agency, and he is required to exercise the utmost good faith, loyalty, and honesty toward his principal. The fiduciary relationship between an agent and his principal may be compared to that which arises upon the creation of a trust. As a fiduciary, an agent is under duty to make full disclosure to his principal of all material facts relevant to the agency.

An agent owes to his principal the duty to use such skill as may be required to accomplish the object of his employment, and he may be held responsible for damage resulting to the principal for his failure to exercise reasonable care, diligence, and judgment. Perfection is not required. Reasonable care and the skill ordinarily possessed by persons of common capacity engaged in the same occupation or business, are the standards by which the agent's duty is measured. Mere errors of judgment not due to want of care or diligence do not render the agent liable to his principal.

An agent who holds himself out as having special skills and talents in a particular field assumes an obligation to exercise such care and skill as would characterize his counterparts in the same field, superior to the diligence or capacity of the ordinary citizen.

It is the duty of an agent to obey all reasonable instructions and directions of the principal, except that he may, exercising prudence and good faith, adopt such course as seems to be necessary where he is faced with an unprovided for and unforeseen emergency. But even here he should deviate from his instructions only so far as is necessary. If the agency is coupled with an interest, the agent has the right to deviate from his instructions in order to protect his own interest in the subject matter of the agency, and even to disregard unreasonable instructions detrimental to his own interests.

§ 1:13. — Duty not to act adversely.

Am Jur 2d References: Agency, §§ 220–237; Brokers, §§ 86–88.

It is fundamental that an agent cannot act adversely to the interest of his principal by serving or acquiring any private interest of his own in antagonism to the principal. An agent will not be permitted to deal in the agency matter on his own account or for his own benefit without the consent of his principal, freely given with full knowledge of all details which might affect the transaction. Nor, without the consent of the principal, may the agent engage in competition with the latter or gain any unfair advantage or secret profit in an agency transaction. And the agent is under duty not to furnish to others or use for himself, in opposition to his principal's interests, any information confidentially given him by the principal or acquired by him in the course of his agency.

An agent employed to sell the principal's property may not, without the latter's full knowledge and consent, become the purchaser of the property. This rule applies regardless of any positive fraud or unfairness perpetrated by the agent upon the principal. The rule also applies to an indirect or collusive sale or transfer as well as to a direct sale or transfer to the agent. Similarly, an agent employed to buy property cannot become the seller of his own property to the principal without the knowledge and consent of the latter. And an agent employed to purchase property for his principal may not purchase the property for his own account or benefit without the principal's full knowledge and consent.

It is clear that an agent may not act in an agency transaction for a party whose interests are adverse to those of his principal, although such double agency may be proper where the principal consents to it after full disclosure. Where there is no conflict of interest between the principal and a third party, the agent may in certain circumstances be permitted to act for both parties.

§ 1:14. Obligations of principal to agent.

Am Jur 2d References: Agency, §§ 238–260; Brokers, §§ 100, 157 et seq.

The main duties of the principal to the agent are those arising from the contract of agency or from the quasi-contractual duty to compensate, reimburse, and indemnify the agent for services rendered or money expended in the agency transaction. The principal must not interfere with the consummation of the agency or thwart the effectiveness thereof.

The law implies a promise by the principal to indemnify the agent for damages resulting proximately from the execution of the agency, as well as reimbursement for necessary expenses incurred by the agent to consummate the agency, so long as the acts of the agent have been properly within the scope of the agency. The amount or basis of the agent's compensation for his services is usually fixed in the contract of employment. In the absence of such an agreement, the law implies a promise on the part of the principal to pay the fair and reasonable value of the agent's services.

In the absence of any stipulation to the contrary, an agent on commission basis is entitled to commissions on a bona fide sale to a solvent purchaser, notwithstanding the principal's refusal to fill the order, and notwithstanding the refusal of the customer to receive the goods or to pay for them; but the agency contract may reserve to the principal the right to reject orders, and the agent is not entitled to his commission on orders so rejected. The agent is not entitled to his compensation where the order is cancelled or rejected by the buyer in accordance with the terms of the order itself, or where the sale was made by the agent to a purchaser not meeting the standards of financial responsibility prescribed in the agency agreement.

The agent may lose his right to compensation if he is guilty of fraud or bad faith toward his employer or if he disregards his obligations to the principal or acts in a manner inconsistent with the agency contract or his fiduciary obligations.

Unless there is an exclusive agency, an agent employed to sell the principal's property is not entitled to commissions on sales of which he was not the procuring cause, and it is immaterial whether the actual sales are made by the principal or another agent. Where the agent or broker is given the exclusive right to sell certain property, however, or to sell in a designated territory, he is ordinarily entitled to his commission on sales made by the principal or another person.

The agent may have a lien on property or funds of the principal in his possession for necessary expenditures, advancements, or liabilities incurred on behalf of the principal and for commissions and services.

IV. RIGHTS, DUTIES, AND LIABILITIES AS BETWEEN PRINCIPAL AND THIRD PERSONS

§ 1:15. Duties and liabilities, generally.

Am Jur 2d References: Agency, §§ 261–272.

It is so fundamental in the law of agency as to be a matter of definition, that the principal is bound by and liable for the acts which his agent does on his behalf within the actual or apparent scope of his authority from the principal, or which the principal legally ratifies. The extent of the agent's authority, which determines the principal's liability to third persons, has been discussed in earlier sections (§§ 1:7–1:11) of this topic. The principal is liable for the tortious acts of his agent which are done within the course and scope of the agent's employment. However, this rule is not grounded on principles distinctive to the agency relationship, but upon a principle applicable alike to all servants and employees, viz., the doctrine of respondeat superior. This aspect of the agency relationship is treated in this work under the topic TORTS.

§ 1:16. Imputation to principal of agent's knowledge.

Am Jur 2d References: Agency, §§ 273–286; Brokers, § 89.

A principal is, as a general rule, chargeable with and bound by the knowledge of or notice to his agent received by the latter while he is acting as such within the scope of his authority. As this is a form of constructive notice, the fact that it is not actually communicated to the principal will not prevent the operation of the general rule. This general rule is applicable only to matters relevant to the agency. Knowledge acquired by an agent which does not relate to the subject matter of his employment and which relates solely to matters outside the scope of his agency is not chargeable to the principal unless actually communicated to him.

Knowledge acquired by an agent prior to the existence of the agency may, under some circumstances, be chargeable to the principal, unless the agent is under a duty to some other person not to divulge such information. Imputation of knowledge in such cases, however, is very cautiously applied and by some courts denied altogether.

There is an exception to the general rule that knowledge of an agent will be imputed to his principal, in situations where the conduct and dealings of the agent are such as to raise a presumption that he will not communicate to the principal the facts in question, as where the agent is in reality acting in his own business or interest or fraudulently or adversely to the principal. This qualification may not apply, however, where the agent is the sole representative of the principal in the transaction and the principal seeks to retain the benefits thereof.

§ 1:17. Third person's duties and liability to principal.

Am Jur 2d References: Agency, §§ 287–292.

The principal is entitled to the rights and benefits resulting from the agent's authorized acts on his behalf. Where the principal is named as the contracting party, a third person is bound by a contract made by an agent in the name of the principal and is liable to the principal to the same extent as if he had contracted with the principal in person, subject to any defenses based on the fraud or other wrongful act of the agent.

A third person who knowingly causes an agent to abandon his duties to the principal may be liable in tort to the principal. Money or property entrusted to an agent and wrongfully diverted or misapplied by the latter may be followed into the hands of, and recovered from, a third person who participates in the agent's fraud or has knowledge thereof.

§ 1:18. Undisclosed agency.

Am Jur 2d References: Agency, §§ 307–316, 322–327.

The liability of an undisclosed principal and his agent to a third party with whom the agent deals is an alternative liability: after the third party becomes aware of the agency and of the identity of the principal, he is put to an election to hold either the agent or the principal liable; he cannot hold both. The third party has a reasonable time in which to decide whether he will hold the principal or the agent responsible in the transaction. After he makes such an election, however, he must abide by it even though there is no satisfaction of his claim.

When an agent makes a contract for his principal, but proceeds as though he were the principal and does not disclose the fact that he is an agent, the principal may appear in his true character and claim all the benefits of the contract from the other contracting party, subject to certain qualifications.

The third person does not become liable to an undisclosed principal on a contract where the specific terms of the contract, or the circumstances under which it is made, exclude liability to any undisclosed principal, or to the particular principal. If the contract depends upon a trust or confidence reposed in the agent personally, the undisclosed principal cannot compel its performance by the other contracting party; but after complete performance by the agent, or performance by the principal which has been accepted by the other contracting party, the undisclosed principal may enforce the contract against the third party.

It is a general rule that one who contracts with the agent of an undisclosed principal may, when sued by the principal on the contract, set up any defenses and equities or setoffs which he could have set up against the agent if the latter had been suing on his own behalf.

V. RIGHTS, DUTIES, AND LIABILITIES AS BETWEEN AGENT AND THIRD PERSONS

§ 1:19. Agent's duties and liabilities.

Am Jur 2d References: Agency, §§ 188–193, 293–304; Brokers, §§ 101–112.

Although an agent of a disclosed principal may assume personal liability, a contract made by him for the principal is that of the principal alone and the agent cannot generally be held personally liable thereon. Where an agent in negotiating a contract employs terms which in legal effect charge himself personally, he may be held liable on the contract, but if the contract is made in the name of a principal, the intention to bind the agent personally must be manifest. If the agent signs a contract in his own name, he may or may not be liable thereon, depending upon whether or not there is an indication in the rest of the instrument that he signs only as agent.

An agent who contracts in the name of a nonexistent or fictitious principal, or a principal without legal status, is personally liable on the contract so made, even though he acted in good faith. However, the fact that the principal is incompetent or under some legal disability, so that the contract may not be enforced against him, does not generally make the agent personally liable on the contract, if he acted in good faith without knowledge of the principal's incapacity.

It is well settled that one who purports to act as agent in making a contract, upon which the purported principal is not bound because the agent acted without authority or in excess of his authority, is personally liable for the damage occasioned to the other contracting party. An agent to whom money is paid erroneously by a third party may be liable to the payer for the return of the money unless he has paid it over to his principal in good faith.

An agent is liable for torts committed by him in the pursuit of his agency, regardless of his relationship with his principal.

§ 1:20. Third person's duties and liabilities.

Am Jur 2d References: Agency, §§ 305, 306.

Where an agent, acting for a disclosed principal, contracts with a third person for and on account of his principal and in the latter's name, the contract is that of the principal and does not give rise to any contractual obligation running to the agent personally. However, if the agent, even though disclosing his principal, and though contracting for his principal, executes the contract in his own name or in such manner as to make it his personal contract, the other contracting party becomes liable to the agent on the contract.

§ 1:21. Undisclosed agency.

Am Jur 2d References: Agency, §§ 317–321, 328.

One who acts as agent for another in making a contract is personally liable thereon if, at the time of making the contract, he fails to disclose his agency and the identity of his principal, regardless of whether or not he was authorized as agent to execute the contract. In order to avoid personal liability, the agent must disclose not only that he is an agent, but also the identity of his principal.

Conversely, an agent who contracts in his own name for an undisclosed principal is a party to the contract despite his agency, and as he thus makes himself personally liable on the contract, he has the corresponding right to enforce it as against the other contracting party.

COMMERCIAL PAPER; BILLS AND NOTES

§ 2:1. Introductory; definitions; character of instrument.

Am Jur 2d References: Bills and Notes, §§ 1–51; Letters of Credit, etc., §§ 1–41.

The law governing commercial paper such as bills of exchange and promissory notes is based upon the "law merchant" (lex mercatoria), the custom of merchants. This law was international in scope and was administered by special courts in the several commercial nations of Europe. The English common-law courts were reluctant to accept the law merchant as a part of the law of the land, and for a long while required it to be proved as a fact, as in the case of any custom or foreign law. It was not until the time of Lord Mansfield in the 18th Century that the law merchant actually became a part of the common law of England and America. For a while it was limited to foreign bills of exchange, but soon its application was extended to inland bills and promissory notes.

Although bills and notes are contracts and are subject to the fundamental rules of contract law, they are designed to meet two special and distinct needs of commercial transactions: They are simple in form and require no expert draftsman; and, most importantly, they are endowed by the law merchant with the quality of negotiability, which permits easier transfer by simple indorsement. This kind of commercial paper permits the transfer of funds between remote places without an actual transportation of money, and it circulates as a substitute for money. This quality of negotiability, which permits a person to accept commercial paper with assurance that he is protected against defenses, is the most vital and distinctive feature of negotiable instruments. But nonnegotiable commercial paper, i.e., instruments otherwise in the form of a bill or note but not payable to order or bearer (the words essential to negotiability), is valid and transferable by simple indorsement, although the holder cannot be a "holder in due course" and is hence subject to defenses to the paper.

A bill of exchange, or draft, is a written order of one party upon another for the payment of a sum of money to a third person, or to his order or to

15

bearer, upon demand or at a specified or determinable future time. A check is an order drawn upon a bank, purportedly upon a deposit of funds, for the payment of a certain sum of money to a person or his order or to bearer upon demand. A check is thus a kind of draft. A negotiable promissory note is an unconditional promise in writing made by one person to another engaging to pay, on demand or at a fixed or determinable future time, a sum certain in money to order or to bearer. A promissory note is distinguishable from a draft or check in that the former is a promise or undertaking by the maker himself, while a draft or check is an order to another.

The need for greater uniformity in the law governing commercial paper in the different states led to the promulgation of the Uniform Negotiable Instruments Act (NIL) in 1896. This law, which was eventually adopted in all of the states, in effect codified the law merchant, as applied in a great body of judicial decisions and statutes. The NIL has, however, been superseded in practically all American jurisdictions by the Uniform Commercial Code, §§ 3–104—3–805, which was designed to modernize the NIL with a view to the actual usages of business and commerce and to the harmonizing of conflicts that had accumulated over the years in the interpretation of the former law.

In addition to bills and notes, a number of other types of instruments in common use possess some of the attributes of negotiability and are governed by the Uniform Commercial Code. Among such instruments are certificates of deposit issued by banks (UCC § 3–104); warehouse receipts and bills of lading (UCC §§ 7–101—7–603); "Documents of title," issued by warehousemen, carriers, and other bailees, and representing ownership by the holder of specific goods; and stocks, bonds, and debentures, termed "Investment Securities" by the Uniform Commercial Code (UCC §§ 8–101—8–406). Another useful device frequently used in commercial transactions is the letter of credit. These instruments are governed by the Uniform Commercial Code, §§ 5–101—5–117. A "letter of credit" or "credit" is defined by the Code (UCC § 5–103) as "an engagement by a bank or other person made at the request of a customer . . . that the issuer will honor drafts and other demands for payment upon compliance with the conditions specified in the credit. . . ."

§ 2:2. Form, contents, requisites, and interpretation.

Am Jur 2d References: Bills and Notes, §§ 52–308.

A negotiable instrument must be in writing, which includes handwriting with pen or pencil, printing, typewriting, or any other intentional reduction to tangible form. Although the forms of bills, notes, and checks have become standardized over the centuries, with minor variations, and are generally well known, no particular or precise form is necessary in such an instrument, so long as it embodies the essential characteristics of one of the particular instruments. In order to be a negotiable instrument under the Uniform Commercial Code (§ 3–104), however, a writing must be signed by the maker or drawer; contain an unconditional promise or order to pay a sum certain in money, and no other promise, order, obligation, or power, except as noted below; be payable on demand or at a definite time; and be payable to order or to bearer.

The requirement of the Code as to an unconditional promise or order may be met although the instrument is subject to implied or constructive conditions;

or states its consideration or the transaction which gave rise to the instrument; or refers to or states that it arises out of a separate agreement, or that it was drawn under a letter of credit; or states that it is secured; or indicates a particular account to be debited; or, in the case of an instrument issued by a government or governmental agency, is limited to payment out of a particular fund or the proceeds of a particular source. However, a promise or order is not unconditional if the instrument states that it is subject to or governed by any other agreement or that it is to be paid only out of a particular fund or source, except as stated above.

The amount payable is a "sum certain" under the Code (UCC § 3–106), even though it is to be paid with stated interest or in stated instalments, or with stated discount or addition if paid before or after the date fixed for payment, or with exchange or less exchange, or with costs of collection or an attorney's fee or both upon default (assuming that such a provision is legal in the particular state). The requirement that the instrument be payable in money is met if it is payable in currency or current funds, including foreign currency.

Instruments payable on demand include (UCC § 3–108) those payable at sight or on presentation, and those in which no time for payment is stated. An instrument is payable "at a definite time" under the Code (UCC § 3–109) if it is payable on or before a stated date or a fixed period after such date, or at a fixed period after sight, or at a definite time subject to any acceleration or subject to extension as provided in the instrument. If the terms of the instrument make it payable only upon an act or event uncertain as to time of occurrence it does not meet the requirement as to "definite time," even though the act or event has occurred.

An instrument is "payable to order" under the Code (UCC § 3–110) "when by its terms it is payable to the order or assigns of any person therein specified with reasonable certainty, or to him or his order, or when it is conspicuously designated on its face as 'exchange' or the like and names a payee." This requirement is met if the instrument is payable to the order of the maker or drawer or of the drawee, or of two or more payees together or in the alternative, or of an estate, trust, or fund, or of an office or officer by his title, or of a partnership or unincorporated association. An instrument made payable both to order and to bearer is payable to order unless the bearer words are handwritten or typewritten. An instrument is payable to bearer within the meaning of the Code (UCC § 3–111) when it is payable to bearer or the order of bearer, or to a specified person or bearer, or to "cash" or to the order of "cash," or when the language does not purport to designate a specific payee.

The negotiability of an instrument is not affected, under the Code (UCC § 3–112), by the omission of a statement of any consideration or of the place where the instrument is drawn or payable; by a statement that collateral has been given for the instrument and that it may be sold upon default, or by a promise or power to maintain, protect, or add to collateral; by terms purporting to waive the benefit of any law; by terms in a draft providing that the indorsement or cashing by the payee acknowledges satisfaction of an obligation of the drawer; or by a statement in a draft drawn in a set of parts to the effect that the order is effective only if no other part has been honored. These provisions do not validate any term (such as that relating to confession of judgment) which is illegal in a particular state. The negotiability of an instrument is not affected by the attachment of a seal (UCC § 3–113) or by the fact that it is undated, antedated, or postdated (UCC § 3–114).

The parties to a draft are the drawer (sometimes called a maker in the case of an ordinary check), the payee, the drawee (to whom the order is directed, usually a bank), and if it is a time instrument, the acceptor, who is usually but not necessarily the drawee. The parties to a promissory note are the maker and the payee. Either kind of instrument may have indorsers as additional parties.

As between the obligor and his immediate obligee or any transferee, the terms of an instrument may be modified or affected by another written instrument executed as a part of the same transaction; but such separate agreement does not affect the negotiability of the instrument nor the rights of a holder in due course without notice thereof (UCC § 3–119).

A paper that is incomplete in any necessary respect, because of blanks or otherwise, becomes effective when it is completed in accordance with authority given; and under the Uniform Commercial Code (§ 3–115), the burden of establishing that any completion is unauthorized is on the party so asserting. The holder has implied authority to fill blanks and to add matter essential to a complete instrument in the absence of proof of lack of authority.

The Uniform Commercial Code (§ 3–116) states the rule that an instrument payable to the order of two or more persons in the alternative, i.e., to "A or B," may be negotiated, discharged, or enforced by any of them who has possession of it. If it is payable to the order of two or more, not in the alternative, i.e., to "A and B," all must join in a negotiation, etc. The Code (§ 3–117) also provides for instruments payable to a named person as agent, officer, or fiduciary of another.

The rules of construction established by the general law of contracts are usually applicable in the interpretation of commercial paper. The paramount and specific principles governing the interpretation of such instruments, however, are those prescribed by the law merchant, the accepted usages of the business or trade, and the provisions of governing statutes, such as the Uniform Commercial Code. The Code (§ 3–118) prescribes rules for resolving certain specific ambiguities. It is provided that where there is doubt whether the instrument is a draft or note, the holder may treat it as either, and that a draft drawn on the drawer is effective as a note. Handwritten terms control typewritten and printed terms, and typewritten terms control printed ones. Words control figures except where the words are ambiguous, when figures control. Unless otherwise specified, a provision for interest means interest at the legal or judgment rate at the place of payment from the date of the instrument, or if it is undated, from the date of issue.

§ 2:3. Transfer and negotiation.

Am Jur 2d References: Bills and Notes, §§ 309–369.

One of the distinctive qualities of commercial paper under the law merchant is that it may be transferred by indorsement, i.e., by a mere signature on the back of the paper. Transfer of a negotiable instrument by indorsement is a "negotiation" thereof and gives rise to certain obligations on the part of the indorser and corresponding rights in subsequent holders. Even a nonnegotiable bill or note (that is, one not payable to order or to bearer) may be transferred by indorsement, but this is not properly termed a "negotiation," and there can be no holders in due course. A transfer of commercial paper, either negotiable or nonnegotiable, may also be effected by an assignment thereof, either by writing on the paper itself or by separate agreement; but this kind of transfer, though passing title to the instrument, does not involve the consequences of negotiation under the law merchant. A transferee for value may require the transferor to make an unqualified indorsement of the instrument (UCC § 3–201). The requisites of negotiation or transfer of an instrument payable to two or more persons are stated in § 2:1, supra.

The Uniform Commercial Code defines "negotiation" as "the transfer of an instrument in such form that the transferee becomes a holder. If the instrument is payable to order it is negotiated by delivery with any necessary indorsement; if payable to bearer it is negotiated by delivery." An instrument indorsed in blank may be negotiated by delivery alone if it bears the indorsements of all prior special indorsees. The same section of the Code requires that an indorsement be written on the instrument or on a paper so firmly affixed thereto as to become a part thereof. If an instrument is made payable to a person under a misspelled name or a name other than his own, he may indorse either that name or his own name or both, but signature in both names may be required by a person giving value for the instrument.

The Code (§ 3–204) defines a special indorsement as one that specifies the person to whom or to whose order the instrument is payable, and states that an instrument so indorsed may be further negotiated only by the indorsement of such person. An indorsement in blank is usually the mere signature of a holder without specification of any indorsee; and where an instrument payable to order is indorsed in blank it becomes payable to bearer, negotiable by delivery alone until specially indorsed. The Code (§§ 3–205, 3–206) defines and provides the effect of restrictive indorsements. Such an indorsement is one which either is conditional; purports to prohibit further transfer of the instrument; includes the words "for collection," "for deposit," "pay any bank," or similar terms; or which otherwise states that it is for the benefit or use of the indorser or of another person. Restrictive indorsements do not prevent further transfer or negotiation of the instrument.

A negotiation may be effective under the Code (§ 3–207) to transfer the instrument although it is made by an infant or other person or corporation in excess of its powers or capacity, although obtained by fraud, duress, or mistake, although made as a part of an illegal transaction, or made in breach of duty. However, except as against a subsequent holder in due course, such a negotiation may be subject to rescission or other appropriate remedy.

The Code (§ 3–208) reaffirms the existing rule as to reacquisition: "Where an instrument is returned to or reacquired by a prior party he may cancel an indorsement which is not necessary to his title and reissue or further negotiate the instrument, but any intervening party is discharged as against the reacquiring party and subsequent holders not in due course and if his indorsement has been canceled is discharged as against subsequent holders in due course as well."

§ 2:4. Status and rights of holder.

Am Jur 2d References: Bills and Notes, §§ 370–423, 481–499.

While the term "holder" is sometimes loosely used in relation to a non-negotiable instrument or to describe the possessor of an instrument who does not have the status or rights of a holder under the law governing negotiable instruments, "holder" is a technical term in the law merchant and under statutes governing the subject. The word is generally defined as meaning one in possession of a negotiable instrument and entitled to maintain an action thereon. As used in the Uniform Commercial Code (§ 1–201), the term "holder" generally means a person who is in possession of a document of title or an instrument or an investment security drawn, issued, or indorsed to him or to his order or to bearer or in blank. The status and rights of an assignee of a bill or note under a mere assignment, as distinguished from a negotiation of the instrument, are not those of a holder under the negotiable instrument laws, even though the instrument is negotiable and the transferee is the physical holder, but are those of an assignee of a chose in action generally, and such an assignee generally acquires only such rights as his transferor has therein. And the transferee of a nonnegotiable instrument is a mere assignee, acquiring only such rights as his assignor had, whether he holds by assignment or by indorsement. There cannot be a holder in due course of a nonnegotiable instrument, and the doctrine protecting a bona fide holder for value without notice and before maturity does not apply. The transferee of such an instrument generally takes it subject to all equities and defenses which would be available as between the original parties or which could be urged against the payee and his assignor.

A "holder in due course," as defined by the Uniform Commercial Code (§ 3–302), is "a holder who takes the instrument (a) for value; and (b) in good faith; and (c) without notice that it is overdue or has been dishonored or of any defense against or claim to it on the part of any person." The Code provides expressly that "a payee may be a holder in due course," thus settling a point on which the authorities have been in conflict. However, a holder does not become a holder in due course by purchase of an instrument at a judicial sale or by taking it under legal process; by acquiring it in taking over an estate; or by purchasing it as a part of a bulk transaction not in the regular course of the business of the transferor. A purchaser of a limited interest, such as a pledgee in a security transaction, can be a holder in due course only to the extent of the interest purchased.

A holder is deemed to take an instrument "for value" within the meaning of the Code (UCC § 3–303) "(a) to the extent that the agreed consideration has been performed or that he acquires a security interest in or lien on the instrument otherwise than by legal process; or (b) when he takes the instrument in payment of or as security for an antecedent claim against any person whether or not the claim is due; or (c) when he gives a negotiable instrument for it or makes an irrevocable commitment to a third person."

A holder in due course enjoys a special status and protection under the law merchant and under laws based thereon. This is a part of the policy of the law to further the needs of commerce by insuring the free circulation and credit of negotiable commercial paper. Under the Uniform Commercial

Code (§ 3–305) a holder in due course takes the instrument free from all claims thereto on the part of any person and all defenses of any party to the instrument with whom the holder has not dealt, subject to certain specified exceptions. These exceptions are infancy, to the extent that it is a defense to a simple contract; any other incapacity, or duress, or illegality of the transaction, such as renders the obligation of the party a nullity; "such misrepresentation as has induced the party to sign the instrument with neither knowledge nor reasonable opportunity to obtain knowledge of its character or its essential terms"; discharge in insolvency proceedings; or any other discharge of which the holder had notice. The defense of infancy usually renders the instrument voidable but not void. The effect of mental incompetence and other kinds of incapacity depends upon local law, and if the instrument is void for such reasons by local law, the defense may be asserted against a holder in due course, but if its effect is merely to render the obligation voidable, the defense is cut off. The effect of illegality also depends upon local law, and the same is true of the defense of duress: if the illegality or the duress renders the obligation void, the defense may be asserted against a holder in due course; otherwise, it is cut off.

Any person who is not a holder in due course takes commercial paper subject to all valid claims to it on the part of any person; subject to all defenses of any party which would be available in an action on a simple contract, including the defenses of want or failure of consideration, nonperformance of any condition precedent, nondelivery, or delivery for a special purpose; and subject to the defense that he or a person under whom he holds the instrument acquired it by theft, or that payment to such holder would be inconsistent with the terms of a restrictive indorsement. The claim of a third person to the instrument is not otherwise available as a defense to a party liable thereon unless the third party defends the action. By definition, a holder in due course must not have taken the instrument after maturity or with notice of dishonor.

§ 2:5. — Good faith and notice.

Am Jur 2d References: Bills and Notes, §§ 424–480.

The tests of one's qualification as a "holder in due course" include the requirements that he take the instrument "in good faith" and without notice that it is overdue or has been dishonored, and without notice of any defense against or adverse claim to the instrument. These two requirements are closely related but not always identical.

Good faith as a requisite of the status of holder in due course presupposes the absence of bad faith and of guilty knowledge or notice. It generally means that the transaction was honestly conceived and consummated without collusion, fraud, or intent to assist in the perpetration of a fraudulent or unlawful transaction. To be a purchaser in good faith means that at the time one takes an instrument he acts honestly and fairly under the facts and circumstances within his knowledge with respect to the rights of all prior parties, particularly those with whom he knows his transferor occupied a relationship of trust. It is generally held that the test of bad faith is not the objective one of prudence, due care, negligence, diligence, or failure to inquire, but knowledge of facts which render the taking dishonest. And in the Uniform Commercial Code (§ 1–201) "good faith" is defined as "honesty in fact in the conduct or transaction concerned."

On the question of what constitutes "notice" to one taking a negotiable instrument, the Uniform Commercial Code (§ 3–304) has these provisions: "(1) the purchaser has notice of a claim or defense if (a) the instrument is so incomplete, bears such visible evidence of forgery or alteration, or is otherwise so irregular as to call into question its validity, terms or ownership or to create an ambiguity as to the party to pay; or (b) the purchaser has notice that the obligation of any party is voidable in whole or in part, or that all parties have been discharged. (2) The purchaser has notice of a claim against the instrument when he has knowledge that a fiduciary has negotiated the instrument in payment or as security for his own debt or in any transaction for his own benefit or otherwise in breach of duty. (3) The purchaser has notice that an instrument is overdue if he has reason to know (a) that any part of the principal amount is overdue or that there is an uncured default in payment of another instrument of the same series; or (b) that acceleration of the instrument has been made; or (c) that he is taking a demand instrument after demand has been made or more than a reasonable length of time after its issue. A reasonable time for a check drawn and payable within the states and territories of the United States and the district of Columbia is presumed to be 30 days." The Code specifies certain facts the knowledge of which does not of itself charge the purchaser with notice of a defense or claim. Such facts are that the instrument is antedated or postdated, that it was issued or negotiated in return for an executory promise or accompanied by a separate agreement, unless the purchaser has notice of a defense or claim arising from the terms thereof; that any party has signed for accommodation; that the instrument was incomplete and has been completed, unless the purchaser knows that the completion was improper; that any person negotiating the instrument is or was a fiduciary; that there has been default in payment of interest on the instrument or in payment of any other instrument, except one of the same series. It is specifically provided in this section of the Code that notice, to be effective, must be received at such time and in such manner as to give a reasonable opportunity to act on it. And it is provided that "the filing or recording of a document does not of itself constitute notice . . . to a person who would otherwise be a holder in due course."

§ 2:6. Acceptance of draft.

Am Jur 2d References: Bills and Notes, §§ 500–520.

A distinctive feature of a draft or bill of exchange is the necessity and effect of "acceptance" by the person to whom the order is directed, i.e., the drawee. The drawee is not liable on a check or other draft until he accepts it, as such an instrument is not per se an assignment of any funds in the hand of the drawee, as stated in the Uniform Commercial Code (§ 3–409), although the drawee may incur liability under some other agreement or obligation, such as a letter of credit. "Acceptance" under the Code (UCC § 3–410) is the drawee's signed engagement to honor the draft as presented. It must be written on the draft, and may consist of his signature alone. It becomes operative when completed by delivery or notification. The fact that a draft has not been signed by the drawer or is otherwise incomplete or is overdue or has been dishonored does not preclude acceptance by the drawee. The certification of a check is an acceptance. Where a holder procures certification, the drawer and all prior indorsers are discharged; and the drawer is discharged also if a bank certifies a check without returning it for lack of proper indorsement. (UCC § 3–411.) The acceptor of a draft binds himself to pay the instrument according to its terms.

If the drawee's acceptance varies the draft as presented, the holder may refuse the acceptance and treat the draft as dishonored. If the holder assents to an acceptance varying the terms of the draft, any drawer or indorser who does not affirmatively assent is discharged. However, the terms of the draft are not deemed to be varied by an acceptance to pay at any particular bank or place in the continental United States, unless it is stated that payment is to be made only at such bank or place. (UCC § 3–412.)

§ 2:7. Liability of parties.

Am Jur 2d References: Bills and Notes, §§ 521–650.

The obligation and liability of every party to a negotiable instrument are determined by the rules of the law merchant as declared in the latest codification thereof, the Uniform Commercial Code. Liability depends upon the capacity in which a person signs an instrument; and, as stated in the Code (§ 3–401), no person is liable unless his signature appears on the instrument. The capacity in which a person signs such an instrument is determined primarily by the place where his signature appears, if there is nothing to indicate a different capacity. One who signs an instrument in its lower right-hand corner is the maker (if it is a note) or the drawer (if it is a check or other draft). One who signs on the back of the instrument is prima facie an indorser, even though he is not otherwise a party to the instrument and is what is termed an "irregular indorser."

It is frequently necessary to determine the order in which the several parties are liable upon an instrument. The legal relation of the parties to each other is presumed to be that indicated by the order in which their names stand on it. The maker of a note is liable to the payee, the payee to his indorsee, and so on down the line of indorsements. The last indorsee is presumed to be the holder and owner of the note and entitled to its proceeds. After a draft or check has passed by indorsement from the hands of the original parties and into the hands of others, the drawee, who is the acceptor unless the instrument has been dishonored by his refusal to accept, is the party primarily liable; the drawer is the second who is liable, and the payee, who is the first indorser, is the third. As respects one another, indorsers are liable prima facie in the order in which they indorse, but every indorser is liable directly to the holder of the instrument.

The nature of the contract or obligation of each party to commercial paper is stated in the Uniform Commercial Code. The maker or acceptor engages that he will pay the instrument according to its tenor. The drawer engages that upon dishonor of the draft and any necessary notice of dishonor or protest he will pay the amount thereof to the holder or to any indorser who takes it up, unless the drawer disclaims this liability by drawing "without recourse" (UCC § 3–413). The contract of an indorser is thus stated (UCC § 3–414): "(1) Unless the indorsement otherwise specifies (as by such words as 'without recourse') every indorser engages that upon dishonor and any necessary notice of dishonor and protest he will pay the instrument according to its tenor at the time of his indorsement to the holder or to any subsequent indorser who takes it up, even though the indorser who takes it up was not obligated to do so. (2) Unless they otherwise agree indorsers are liable to one another in the order in which they indorse, which is presumed to be the order in which their signatures appear on the instrument."

An accommodation party is defined in the Uniform Commercial Code (§ 3–415) as "one who signs the instrument in any capacity for the purpose of lending his name to another party to it." He is liable in the capacity in which he has signed to any person who has taken for value before the instrument is due, even though the taker knows of the accommodation. As against a holder in due course and without notice of the accommodation, oral proof of the accommodation is not admissible to give the accommodation party the benefit of discharges dependent on his character as such. If an indorsement shows that it is not in the chain of title, it is notice of its accommodation character. As against the party accommodated, an accommodation party incurs no liability, and if he pays the instrument he has a right of recourse against him.

The meaning and effect of words of guaranty added to a signature on commercial paper are defined in UCC § 3–416. The Code (§ 3–417) also states the obligations in the nature of warranties imposed upon a person who obtains payment or acceptance, and of any prior transferor, to a person who in good faith pays or accepts the instrument, and of any person who transfers an instrument, including transfer "without recourse." These warranties relate mainly to title to the instrument, authenticity of signatures, the integrity of the instrument as regards alteration, and the like.

There has been considerable disagreement as to the liability of an indorser of nonnegotiable commercial paper. Some courts have taken the view that a mere blank indorsement by the payee of a nonnegotiable note merely transfers the instrument and does not subject himself to any liability to an indorsee. However, many courts have held that the indorsement of a nonnegotiable bill or note by the payee or transferee renders him liable to his indorsee, although the authorities are in hopeless conflict as to the nature and extent of such liability. The Uniform Commercial Code (§ 3–805) places a bill or note which is in the general form of a negotiable instrument, but is nonnegotiable because not payable to order or to bearer, in the same class as negotiable instruments, except that there can be no holder in due course of the former. In other words, the indorser of such nonnegotiable commercial paper assumes the same obligation as the indorser of negotiable instruments.

A person signing an instrument as agent or in any other representative capacity is personally obligated, under the Uniform Commercial Code (§ 3–403), unless he names the principal and indicates his representative capacity. An unauthorized signature is inoperative under the Code (§ 3–404) as that of the person whose name is signed unless he ratifies it or is precluded from denying it; but it operates as the signature of the unauthorized signer in favor of one who pays the instrument in good faith or takes it for value.

§ 2:8. Defenses and grounds for relief.

Am Jur 2d References: Bills and Notes, §§ 651–729.

The question of what defenses are available with respect to commercial paper is correlative with the status and rights of the person against whom a defense is asserted. As noted above (supra, §§ 2:4, 2:5), a holder in due course takes the instrument free from most of the defenses available against other parties. Unless the holder qualifies as a holder in due course, however, he takes the instrument subject to any defense which might be asserted under general contract law against an ordinary contract. And the same is true as to nonnegotiable commercial paper, as to which there can be no holder in due course.

As between the original parties, and as against any transferee other than a holder in due course, absence or failure of consideration is a good defense, in toto, or pro tanto, against a negotiable instrument. Other defenses available against such parties are nondelivery; defect in title; payment or discharge; illegality or violation of public policy; fraud; duress; forgery or unauthorized signing (unless the party is precluded from asserting this defense because of his negligence, ratification, or other conduct); incapacity or incompetence of parties; and material alteration of the instrument.

The defenses which may be asserted against a holder in due course are usually those that go to the very existence of the contract or which render it absolutely null and void. A holder in due course takes the instrument free from any defect of title of prior parties and free of all claims to the instrument on the part of any person, and free from all defenses of any party to the instrument with whom the holder has not dealt, with the exception of certain defenses specified in the Uniform Commercial Code (§ 3–305). These excepted defenses, which may be asserted against even a holder in due course, are: "(a) infancy, to the extent that it is a defense to a simple contract; and (b) such other incapacity, or duress, or illegality of the transaction, as renders obligation of the party a nullity; and (c) such misrepresentation as has induced the party to sign the instrument with neither knowledge nor reasonable opportunity to obtain knowledge of its character or its essential terms; and (d) discharge in insolvency proceedings; and (e) any other discharge of which the holder has notice when he takes the instrument." (UCC § 3–305.) The misrepresentation or fraud referred to in this section of the Code is the kind referred to as fraud in the essence or fraud in the factum, as where the maker of a note is tricked into signing it in the belief that it is merely a receipt or some other document. The test of this defense is that of excusable ignorance of the contents of the writing signed. Although a fraudulent and material alteration of an instrument has the effect of discharging any party whose contract is thereby changed, as against any person other than a holder in due course, a subsequent holder in due course may enforce the instrument according to its original tenor, and when an incomplete instrument has been completed, he may enforce it as completed (UCC § 3–407). And a person who, by his negligence, substantially contributes to a material alteration of an instrument or to the making of an unauthorized signature, is precluded from asserting the alteration or lack of authority against a holder in due course (UCC § 3–406).

§ 2:9. Presentment, notice of dishonor, and protest.

Am Jur 2d References: Bills and Notes, §§ 730–900.

The rules developed under the law merchant and codified in the Uniform Negotiable Instruments Law governing presentment, notice of dishonor, and protest have been simplified and clarified by the Uniform Commercial Code, §§ 3–501 to 3–511.

"Presentment is a demand for acceptance or payment made upon the maker, acceptor, drawee or other payor by or on behalf of the holder" (UCC § 3–504); and presentment may be made by mail (its time being determined by the time of its receipt), through a clearing house, or at the place of acceptance or payment specified in the instrument, or, if there is none, at the place of business or residence of the party to accept or pay.   Presentment may be made to any one of two or more makers, acceptors, drawees, or other payors, or to any other person who has authority to make or refuse acceptance or payment.   A draft accepted or a note payable at a bank in the continental United States must be presented at such bank.

Unless it is "excused" or waived under the provisions of the Code, presentment for acceptance is necessary to charge the drawer and indorsers of a draft where the draft so provides or is payable elsewhere than at the residence or place of business of the drawee, or where its date of payment depends upon such presentment; and presentment for payment is necessary to charge any indorser.   As to any drawer, acceptor of a draft payable at a bank, or maker of a note payable at a bank, presentment for payment is necessary.   Notice of any dishonor is necessary (unless "excused") to charge any indorser or any drawer, acceptor of a draft payable at a bank, or the maker of a note payable at a bank.   The requirement of protest, necessary to charge the drawer and indorsers of a draft, is limited to drafts drawn or payable outside of the United States and its territories, although the holder may at his option make protest of any dishonor of any other instrument.   No presentment, notice of dishonor, or protest is necessary under these provisions of the Code (UCC § 3–501) to charge an indorser who has indorsed an instrument after maturity.

An unexcused delay in presentment or notice of dishonor or a necessary protest, beyond the time when it is due, has the effect of discharging any indorser.   The time when presentment must be made under the Code (UCC § 3–503), unless a different time is stated in the instrument, is as follows: Presentment for acceptance must be made on or before the date it is payable, and in the case of an instrument payable at sight, it must be presented for acceptance or negotiated within a reasonable time after date or issue, whichever is later.   Where an instrument shows the date on which it is payable, presentment for payment is due on that date.   In the case of acceleration of the time for payment, presentment for payment is due within a reasonable time after the acceleration period; with respect to the liability of any secondary party, presentment for acceptance or payment is due within a reasonable time after such party becomes liable.   What constitutes a "reasonable time" for presentment is determined by the nature of the instrument, any usage of banking or trade, and the facts of the particular case. In the case of an ordinary uncertified check, 30 days after date or issue is presumed to be a reasonable period as against the drawer, and 7 days after his indorsement as against an indorser. Any required presentment must be made at a reasonable hour, and if at a bank, during its banking day. If the day when presentment is due is not a full business day for either party, presentment is due on the next following full business day.

The party to whom presentment is made may require exhibition of the instrument and reasonable identification of the person making the presentment. He is also entitled to a signed receipt on the instrument for any payment, and its surrender upon full payment. Acceptance may be deferred until the close of the next business day following presentment. Payment of an instrument may generally be deferred pending reasonable examination to determine whether it is properly payable, but not longer than the close of business on the day of presentment.

An instrument is deemed to be "dishonored" (UCC § 3–507) when it is not accepted or not paid within the prescribed time upon or after presentment. However, return of an instrument for lack of proper indorsement is not dishonor. Upon dishonor, the holder has (subject to any necessary notice of dishonor and protest) an immediate right of recourse against the drawers and indorsers. Notice of dishonor may be given under the Code (UCC § 3–508) in any reasonable manner, and it may be oral or written and in any terms which identify the instrument and state that it has been dishonored. The notice may be given to any person who may be liable on the instrument, by or on behalf of the holder or any party who has received notice, or any other party who can be compelled to pay the instrument, as well as by the agent of a bank in whose hands the instrument is dishonored. The notice operates for the benefit of all parties who have rights on the instrument against the party notified. Any necessary notice of dishonor must be given by a bank before its "midnight deadline" (midnight on the bank's next banking day following the banking day on which the event occurs), and by any other person before midnight of the third business day after dishonor or receipt of notice of dishonor. The fact of dishonor and notice of dishonor may be established by a protest, a stamp or writing of the drawee, payor bank, or presenting bank on the instrument, or any book or record of the drawee or of such bank showing such dishonor. A protest is a certificate of dishonor made under the hand and seal of a United States consul or vice consul or a notary public or other authorized person. Protest is not necessary except on drafts drawn or payable outside of the United States.

Delay in presentment, protest, or notice of dishonor is "excused" under the Code (§ 3–511) "when the party is without notice that it is due or when the delay is caused by circumstances beyond his control and he exercises reasonable diligence after the cause of the delay ceases to operate." And such presentment, notice, or protest may be entirely excused when the party to be charged has waived it expressly or by implication, or where such party has himself dishonored the instrument or has countermanded payment, or where, by reasonable diligence, the presentment or protest cannot be made or the notice given. Presentment is excused also when the maker, acceptor, or drawee is dead or in insolvency proceedings, or where acceptance or payment is refused but not for want of proper presentment. A waiver of protest is also a waiver of presentment and of notice of dishonor, even though protest is not required.

§ 2:10. Discharge.

Am Jur 2d References: Bills and Notes, §§ 901–1018.

Matters relating to the discharge of any party from liability on commercial paper are itemized in the Uniform Commercial Code, § 3–601, as payment or satisfaction, or tender of payment; cancellation or renunciation; or impairment of right of recourse or of collateral. Other acts and circumstances which may result in a discharge of parties have been discussed above, viz., reacquisition of the instrument by a prior party; fraudulent and material alterations; certification of a check; acceptance varying a draft; or unexcused delay in presentment or notice of dishonor or protest. A party may also be discharged from that liability to another party by any act or agreement which would discharge his simple contract for the payment of money. And the liability of all parties is discharged when any party who has himself no right of action or recourse on the instrument reacquires the instrument in his right or is discharged, except as otherwise provided with respect to discharge for impairment of recourse or of collateral. No discharge under these provisions is effective against a subsequent holder in due course unless he has notice thereof when he takes the instrument (UCC § 3–602).

The liability of a party is discharged to the extent of his payment or satisfaction to the holder of an instrument, even though it is made with knowledge of a claim of another person to the instrument, unless the person making the claim has supplied indemnity deemed adequate by the party seeking the discharge or has enjoined payment or satisfaction by order of court. This provision of the Code (UCC § 3–603) does not, however, discharge the liability of a party who in bad faith pays or satisfies a holder who acquired the instrument by trust or who (unless he has the rights of a holder in due course) holds through one who so acquired it; nor of a party (other than an intermediary bank or a payor bank which is not a depository bank) who pays or satisfies the holder of an instrument contrary to a restrictive indorsement. Payment may be made, with the consent of the holder, by any person, including a stranger to the instrument, and surrender of the instrument to such person gives him the rights of a transferee. A tender of full payment to a holder when or after it is due discharges the party making the tender from all subsequent liability for interest, costs, and attorneys' fees. The holder's refusal of such tender wholly discharges any party who has a right of recourse against the party making the tender.

The holder of an instrument may, even without consideration, discharge any party by intentionally canceling the instrument or the party's signature by destruction or mutilation, or by striking out the signature or in other manner apparent on the face of the instrument, or by renouncing his rights by a writing signed and delivered, or by surrender of the instrument to the party to be discharged. (UCC § 3–605.)

The provisions of the Code (§ 3–606) as to impairment of recourse or of collateral are that "[t]he holder discharges any party to the instrument to the extent that without such party's consent the holder (a) without express reservation of rights releases or agrees not to sue any person against whom the party has to the knowledge of the holder a right of recourse or agrees to suspend the right to enforce against such person the instrument or collateral or otherwise discharges such person . . . ; or (b) unjustifiably impairs any collateral for the instrument given by or on behalf of the party or any person against whom he has a right of recourse." By express reservation of rights against a party with a right of recourse a holder may preserve all his rights against such party as of the time when the instrument was originally due, and the right of the party to pay the instrument as of that time, and all rights of such party to recourse against others.

*

CONFLICT OF LAWS,

§ 3:1. In general; fundamental principles.

Am Jur 2d References: Conflict of Laws, §§ 1–12, 76, 77; Limitation of Actions, §§ 66–75; Marriage, §§ 79–102.

Under the rules of comity the courts of a state or country in which an action is brought will frequently apply or give effect to the law of another state or sovereignty as governing the rights of the parties. In the determination of the question of what law is to be applied, courts follow the principles of conflict of laws, or as it is sometimes called, private international law. Depending upon the nature and circumstances of the case and the subject matter involved, the choice may be the law of the forum (lex fori), i.e., the law of the jurisdiction in which the litigation occurs; the law of the place where the contract was made (lex loci contractus) or the place of performance or payment (lex loci solutionis); the law of the place of the tort or wrong (lex loci delicti); or the law of the place where the property is located or the subject matter is situated (lex loci sitae rei, or lex loci rei sitae). The phrase "lex loci" is used in a general sense to designate the place in which the circumstances on which the action is based arose or occurred.

In determining which law will be applied, courts usually follow the rules of the forum as to conflict of laws, and do not consider how the other jurisdiction would determine the question of which law is applicable. However, under the so-called renvoi doctrine, some courts have considered the "whole law" of the other jurisdiction, including its rules as to conflict of laws, which may result in a circuity of reasoning which cancels out all problems of conflict of laws and applies the substantive law of the forum. A related question arises from the necessity of characterizing or classifying a cause of action as being based on contract, tort, property rights, etc. Such characterization, which may determine which law is applicable, is usually made in accordance with the law of the forum, although an exception is made in determining whether tangible property is to be classified as real or personal property, a matter depending upon the lex loci rei sitae.

Where the law of a sister state is relied upon, it must be proved as a fact, unless judicial notice is taken of it. In the absence of such proof, the foreign law is presumed to be the same as that of the forum.

The extent to which the law of one state or nation is allowed to operate within another depends upon what is called "the comity of nations." Comity is the recognition which one state or nation accords within its territory to the legislative, executive, or judicial acts of another state or nation, having due regard to both international or interstate duty and convenience and to the rights of its own citizens. In this connection, each state of the United States constitutes a distinct and independent sovereignty, and the laws of one state do not operate in any other state by their own force. Courts will not give effect to a foreign law where to do so would prejudice the state's own rights or the rights of its citizens, or where such laws are purely penal in nature or are contrary to the positive policy of the law of the forum. The power to deny effect to the laws of a sister state is limited by the provision of the Federal Constitution (Article 4, § 1) that "full faith and credit shall be given in each state to the public acts, records, and judicial proceedings of every other state." But even the full faith and credit clause gives a state some latitude to apply its own laws and policy as against foreign laws that are in conflict therewith. As the laws, treaties, and Constitution of the United States are supreme, any conflict between them and state laws or policies must be resolved in favor of the former.

The most basic principle of conflict of laws is that where there is a conflict between the law of the jurisdiction in which the litigation occurs and the law of the place in which the circumstances arose on which the litigation is based, the lex loci will govern as to all matters going to the basis of the right of action itself, while the lex fori controls all that is connected merely with the remedy. The status or condition of a person and the relation in which he stands to others are fixed by the law of his domicil, although the incidents of the status are determined by the law of the jurisdiction in which the transaction takes place. The validity of a marriage, for example, is determined by the law of the place where it is contracted, although a foreign marriage will not be recognized where it is contrary to such basic local laws as those prohibiting bigamy or incest.

On questions of procedure and remedial rights, it is well settled that every case must be governed by the law of the place where the remedy is sought, the lex fori. This rule applies in general to all matters relating to pleading, practice, evidence, and ancillary remedies, as well as to questions of venue. Statutes of limitation are generally deemed to affect the remedy only and not the substantive right, and therefore, in the absence of a statute of the forum changing the rule, the statutes of limitation of the place where the action is brought, and not the lex loci, control and will be applied in the event of a conflict of laws. In other words, the lex fori determines the time within which a cause of action may be enforced. However, where a liability or cause of action sought to be enforced was created by a statute of another state, a limitation period prescribed by that statute will be applied, although some courts observe an exception to this exception where the limitation period prescribed by the lex fori would bar the cause of action, although the action would not be barred by the terms of the lex loci, which allows a longer period.

Matters relating to defenses are generally regarded as substantive in nature, rather than procedural, and are therefore governed by the lex loci rather than the lex fori. But this rule would not apply to a defense based upon a mere technicality of practice or procedure.

§ 3:2. Property.

Am Jur 2d References: Conflict of Laws, §§ 13–35.

The law applicable in cases involving property usually depends upon the nature of the property as real or personal. The determination of this preliminary question is governed by the law of the place where the property is situated, the lex loci rei sitae. If the property is real estate, it is exclusively subject to the laws of the country or state in which it is located, and all matters concerning title and disposition thereof are determined by the law of that jurisdiction. This rule includes all questions relating to title and estates, descent, alienation, and the validity, effect, and construction of wills and conveyances affecting real property. A distinction is made, however, between contracts directly affecting title to real property, which are construed according to the law of the state where the property is situated, and contracts which, while relating to real property, do not affect the title to or an interest in the property itself, but are purely personal. Agreements of the latter nature are governed by the usual rules relating to contracts, discussed in the next following section, and not by the lex rei sitae.

Personal property is governed by different rules, as regards conflict of laws, from those applicable to real property. By an ancient legal fiction, personal property is supposed to adhere to the person of the owner and to have no situs other than his domicil. By force of this fiction, personal property, no matter how ponderous or unwieldy, in legal contemplation changes location with every change of the owner's domicil. On these principles, the rule was formerly well established that for most purposes personal property should be governed, no matter where it was physically located, by the law of the domicil of the owner.

The foregoing rule, based on the maxim "mobilia sequuntur personam," was developed in the days when personal property consisted mainly of gold and jewels easily carried by the owner from place to place, and the rule has in modern times yielded more and more to the lex rei sitae, the law of the place where the property is kept and used. In any event, the rule that the situs of personal property follows the domicil of the owner, when invoked as to property located in one state and owned by a resident of another, is one of comity in the former state and will be applied by the courts of such state only where they choose to apply laws other than their own. The law of the domicil of the property owner will not generally be applied in another state to the prejudice of the latter's citizens or when opposed to the policy of its laws; nor will it be applied where, for the purpose of justice and convenience, it is necessary that the law of the actual situs of the property should govern.

The prevailing modern rule is that the law of the situs governs the transfer of personal property. Under this rule, the effect of any transfer purporting to pass the title to personal property is governed by the law of the state in which the property was located at the time of the transaction, regardless of the owner's domicil. This rule applies to the essential or substantial validity, as well as to the formalities, of a transfer of property in chattels. The rule does not apply, however, to the passage of title to personal property by will or by the laws of descent and distribution, such matters being determined by the law of the decedent owner's domicil. The question of what law governs liens, encumbrances, and security transactions involving personal property may depend on whether the property is located in the place where the contract or lien is executed, and may be affected by the rights or claims of third persons.

As to intangible personal property, such as evidences of debt and other choses in action, the old general rule still applies and most questions relating thereto are determined by the law of the owner's domicil. However, exceptions have been engrafted on this rule; and the validity of a transfer of a chose in action is generally governed by the law of the state where the transfer is made, or the lex loci contractus.

§ 3.3. Contracts.

Am Jur 2d References: Conflict of Laws, §§ 36–53.

In cases involving a contract which possesses possible elements in two or more jurisdictions, the court is frequently called on to determine the preliminary question as to the place in which the contract is made, completed, or executed, before the ultimate question as to which law governs may be properly determined. It may be laid down as a broad general rule that where the parties to a prospective contract are in different jurisdictions, the place where the last act is done which is necessary to complete the contract and give it validity is regarded as the place in which the contract is made or completed. An informal contract consisting of an offer in one state and an acceptance in another is usually regarded as having been made in the latter state. If the offeror authorizes the mail or telegraph as a means of acceptance, the offer is deemed to be accepted when the acceptance is properly placed in the post or delivered to the telegraph company for transmission. Where an acceptance of an offer is made by telephone, it is generally held that the place of contracting is where the acceptor speaks his acceptance.

The field of contracts presents a highly complex and confused part of conflict of laws. There is much diversity of opinion among the different jurisdictions, and even in different decisions within the same state, as to the applicability of the various rules—the place of making the contract, place of performance, place intended by the parties, or the more recent rule of the place having the most significant contacts. And it is doubtful whether this area of the law has been clarified, or the law to be applied in any particular case has been more easily predictable, by recent attempts to rationalize the subject in abstract terms.

According to the traditional rule, which is still widely accepted, the validity and construction of a contract are governed by the law of the place where it is made. If the place where the contract is made is also a place where it is to be performed, the applicability of this rule is even clearer. Some courts hold that the contract is governed by the laws of the state where it is made, unless it is executed with a view to its performance in another state; and a number of courts have stated broadly that where a contract is to be performed in a place other than the place where it is made, the law of the place where the contract is to be performed will determine its validity, nature, obligation, and effect. Many courts have based this rule on the presumed intent of the parties. Some courts have taken the position that the true test for the determination of the proper law of a contract is the intent of the parties, express or implied.

The most recently formulated conflict of laws theory resorted to for determining the law applicable to matters bearing on the execution, interpretations, validity, and performance of a contract, is the so-called "center of gravity" or "grouping of contacts" theory, under which the courts, instead of regarding as conclusive the parties' intention or the place of making or performance, lay emphasis rather upon the law of the place which has the most significant contacts with the matter in dispute.

All these uncertainties have led to an increase in the practice of stipulating which law shall govern the validity, construction, and effect of the contract, and the modern trend is to give effect to such expressed agreements of the parties unless it contravenes the law or public policy.

The general rule that unless a contrary intention is expressed in the contract, matters connected with the performance of a contract are governed by the law of the place where, by its terms, the contract is to be performed, is generally applicable to questions as to whether a contract has been breached, rescinded, or otherwise terminated or repudiated.

Under any of the above theories as to the law applicable in determining the validity, construction, and effect of a contract, the laws of the jurisdiction where the action is brought play an important part in determining the outcome. It is well settled that matters relating to the remedies and procedure are governed entirely by the lex fori. And a court may decline to entertain jurisdiction of an action on a contract, although the contract was valid by the law of both the place where it was made and the place where it was to be performed, where the contract violates the statutes or public policy of the forum.

§ 3:4. Wills.

Am Jur 2d References: Conflict of Laws, §§ 54–70.

The basic general rules of conflict of laws relating to wills are that all questions arising under the will in regard to personal property are determined according to the law of the domicil of the testator at the time of his death, and that all questions arising under wills in regard to real property are governed by the place where the property is located, the lex rei sitae. Under these general rules, the validity and effect of a will with respect to the disposition of personal property, and the rights of legatees thereunder, are governed by the law of the testator's last domicil, regardless of where the property is physically located or where the legatees are domiciled or have their situs. And the validity and effect of a will with respect to the disposition of real property or an interest therein are governed by the law of the state where the land is located, regardless of the testator's domicil or the place where the will was executed; and this general rule is applied to questions involving both the formal and essential validity of wills. These rules apply to the capacity of the testator to make a will and to the capacity of a devisee to take under the will, although some courts hold, with respect to personal property, that the capacity of a legatee to take personal property depends upon the law of his domicil.

The same general rules, as regards personal and real property, respectively, apply to the revocation of wills, in the absence of statute to the contrary. And the same general rules apply, with some exceptions, to questions relating to the election or renunciation of rights under a will by a surviving spouse or heir. There is, however, some conflict of authority on the extraterritorial effect of an election to take under a will or of a renunciation of the will.

In connection with the application of conflict of laws rules in the construction of wills, it has been held that construction of a will involves first, an interpretation of the language used, and secondly, a determination of the legal effect of that language. As regards personal property such a distinction generally makes no difference in the result. As to real property, however, a distinction is sometimes made between these two aspects of construction. The legal effect of the language used in a will, including such questions as the estate or interest created thereby, is determined by the law of the place where the land is located. On the other hand, when the sole question is the ascertainment of the testator's intention from the language used in the will, or the sense in which certain words or phrases are used, and not their legal effect, they are generally construed according to the law of the testator's last domicil in the case of both real and personal property.

§ 3:5. Torts.

Am Jur 2d References: Conflict of Laws, §§ 71–75.

Where an action is brought in one jurisdiction for a tort committed in another, the general rule is that all matters going to the basis of the right of action or affecting the substantive rights of the parties are governed by the lex loci delicti or law of the place of the wrong. Where the issue is the choice between the law of the place where an allegedly wrongful act or omission took place and the law of the place where the injury or harm was sustained, the general rule is that the place of the tort, within the meaning of the foregoing general rule, is the place of the injury or harm. Thus, where a person standing in one state shoots a person standing in another state, the place of the wrong is the latter state, the law of which is therefore applicable. However, some courts under some circumstances have held that the place where the wrongful act or conduct was committed, rather than the place where injury resulted therefrom, is the place of the tort. Where the question relates to a choice between the law of the place in which a fatal injury was inflicted and the law of the place in which the resulting death took place, the general rule is that the place of the tort, the law of which is governing, is the place where the fatal injury was inflicted, and not the place where the resulting death occurred. A number of courts have held that the place of the tort is in the state where the last event necessary to make an actor liable for an alleged wrong takes place; i.e., tort liability is controlled by the law of the state where the tort is completed.

There has been a tendency among some courts in tort cases to depart from the traditional general rule that the law of the place of the wrong governs liability, and to adopt a theory analogous to the relatively new "grouping of contacts" or "center of gravity" theory discussed above in relation to contracts. Under this theory, the determination of the state having the greatest or most significant contact or relationship with the parties and the wrongs involved may be the one whose law is applied.

It is not by strict right, but comity, which enables one to bring an action in one state or country for a tort committed in another, and under the principles of comity, such action will not be entertained if it would violate the public policy of the forum. Thus, a state which considers certain kinds of causes of action, such as the right to recover for alienation of affections, to be against public policy, may refuse to take jurisdiction of such a cause arising in another state which recognizes the right to recover. And the law of the forum governs matters relating to the remedy and procedure, including statutes of limitation.

CONSTITUTIONAL LAW

I. INTRODUCTORY; ADOPTION, AMENDMENT, CONSTRUCTION, AND EFFECT OF CONSTITUTIONS

II. DISTRIBUTION OF GOVERNMENTAL POWERS

III. COMMERCE CLAUSE

IV. POLICE POWER

V. FUNDAMENTAL RIGHTS AND IMMUNITIES; BILL OF RIGHTS

VI. RETROSPECTIVE LEGISLATION; EX POST FACTO LAWS

VII. IMPAIRING OBLIGATION OF CONTRACTS

VIII. FULL FAITH AND CREDIT

IX. PRIVILEGES AND IMMUNITIES OF CITIZENSHIP

X. EQUAL PROTECTION OF THE LAWS

XI. DUE PROCESS OF LAW

§ 4:24. Generally
§ 4:25. Notice, hearing, and procedural requirements

I. INTRODUCTORY; ADOPTION, AMENDMENT, CONSTRUCTION, AND EFFECT OF CONSTITUTIONS

§ 4:1. Generally.

Am Jur 2d References: Constitutional Law, §§ 1–17, 45–57; Treaties (1st ed, §§ 1–24); Am Jur 2d Desk Book, Document No. 1.

A constitution is a system of fundamental laws or principles for the government of a nation or state. In the United States, a constitution is a written charter adopted by the people, creating a government and outlining the form and powers thereof, and defining the basic rights of the people. The constitution of England is of a different nature, consisting of an indefinite body of rules and principles in the form of customs, judicial decisions, and basic statutes, and not formalized in any written charter. In America a constitution is the supreme law, binding upon all branches of government, including the legislative department, whereas in England the supreme power is vested in Parliament. Under the American system the ultimate and supreme power resides in the people, including the power to make and change constitutions. "Constitutional law" consists of the principles and decisions governing the interpretation and operation of constitutions.

The Constitution of the United States, together with laws made in pursuance thereof and treaties made under the authority of the United States, is, by the express declaration of Article 6, § 2, the supreme law of the land. As a general rule, the adoption of a constitution does not affect the operation of laws not in conflict therewith, and some constitutions contain express provisions to that effect. No emergency justifies the violation or disregard of any provisions of a constitution. However, while an emergency cannot create a governmental power where none existed before, it may furnish a proper occasion for the exercise of an existing power.

Many of the specific applications of constitutional principles are discussed herein under the particular topic in connection with which the problems arose.

§ 4:2. Adoption and amendment.

Am Jur 2d References: Constitutional Law, §§ 18–47.

The inadequacy of the association of the states under the Articles of Confederation led to the calling of a convention in 1787, at which all of the 13 states were represented, for the purpose of creating a new constitution and a new nation. The deliberations of this convention produced our Federal Constitution, which was presented to the Congress for submission to conventions of the several states and was to become effective upon its approval by nine states. The Constitution went into effect March 3, 1789.

All of the states have adopted constitutions of their own. The only limitation upon the power of the people of a state in this respect is that expressly imposed by the Federal Constitution. All power not relinquished by the people through their constitutions inheres in the people. And with regard to the power of state legislatures, as the representatives of the people, a state constitution operates solely as a limitation of power, not as a grant of power.

The manner of amending a constitution under the American system of government is determined by the constitution itself. The Federal Constitution, Article 5, provides that amendments may be proposed by Congress by vote of two-thirds of both Houses thereof, or by a constitutional convention called by Congress on the application of the legislatures of two-thirds of the states. This Article further specifies that an amendment becomes effective as part of the Constitution when ratified by the legislatures of three-fourths of the states, or by conventions in three-fourths of the states, as one or the other mode of ratification may be proposed by Congress. In proposing an amendment to the Constitution, Congress does not act in a legislative capacity, and a congressional resolution proposing an amendment does not require the approval of the President. Any question as to whether the amendment procedure specified in Article 5 has been properly followed is a federal question which must ultimately be decided by the United States Supreme Court.

Changes in state constitutions are usually effected by amendments proposed by the legislatures and approved by vote of the people, or through constitutional conventions called according to the provisions of the constitutions. By either method, the proposed change in the constitution must be approved by the people.

§ 4:3. Construction.

Am Jur 2d References: Constitutional Law, §§ 58–100.

Every public officer, in whatever department of government, is frequently required in the discharge of his duties, to determine the meaning and effect of various constitutional provisions. This, in a sense, involves the interpretation of the constitution. However, where there is doubt or dispute as to the meaning or application of a constitutional provision, the ultimate power to determine the question and to construe the constitution lies in the courts. In performing this function, the courts apply various rules of construction which are to some extent peculiar to constitutions. Where the language of the constitution is plain and unambiguous, however, effect must be given to its clear meaning, and there is no occasion to consider any technical rule of construction.

The fundamental principle of constitutional construction is that the intent of its framers and of the people who adopted it must be given effect. Every constitutional provision should be construed so as to carry out the purpose intended to be accomplished thereby. A principle easily forgotten is that constitutions do not change with the varying tides of public opinion. The will of the people therein recorded remains the basic law until changed in the manner provided by the constitution. A constitution should not be held to mean one thing at one time and something else at another time, even though the circumstances or popular sentiment may have so changed as to make a different rule seem desirable. The stability of the constitutions in the face of continual pressure from various sources is a principal reason for the success of the American constitutional system. And it was deliberately planned that the constitutions are not to be changed by every passing whim of popular sentiment, but only by prescribed methods and after mature consideration by the people and their representatives.

Much has been said about the flexibility of our constitutions. This flexibility is due to the basic generality of the Federal Constitution and some of the state constitutions. Such constitutions adapt themselves without distortion to changes in society which inevitably occur in the course of history, and they will be construed so as to embrace new conditions. But this does not justify a court in attributing a different meaning to language of a constitution, because of actual or supposed changes in popular views or in the political climate, where there has been no substantial change in the circumstances or conditions to which the provision is to be applied. To do so is to change the meaning of the constitution, not to adapt it to new conditions.

It has been frequently stated that a constitution should be liberally construed. A liberal interpretation is especially appropriate with respect to provisions designed to safeguard the rights and liberty of citizens.

A well established rule of construction applicable to constitutions is that the court should consider all parts of the document in determining the meaning of any provision. If there is an apparent repugnancy between different provisions, the court should harmonize them if possible. Amendments should be harmonized with preexisting constitutional provisions where this is practicable; but if there is a real and irreconcilable conflict between the original provision and an amendment, the latter must govern.

As a constitution is a creature of the people, being approved by them, its language and terms are construed in the sense most obvious to the common understanding at the time of its adoption. Words used in a constitution are presumed to have their plain, natural, and usual import and meaning. As the common law of England was the governing law of the American states at the time of the adoption of the Federal Constitution, and as the framers of the Constitution were familiar with the principles and terminology of that system of jurisprudence, the Constitution is construed with references to the common law.

Certain extrinsic aids are used by the courts in construing constitutions. Thus, where a new constitution adopts provisions contained in a former constitution, the construction placed on the earlier provision will generally be applied to the new. And where a state adopts a provision of the Federal Constitution or of the constitution of another state, the construction applied to such other constitutions is usually also adopted. Resort may also be had to debates in constitutional conventions, and the history and literature contemporaneous with such conventions, including the Federalist. Although the spirit and principles of the Declaration of Independence are sometimes invoked in construing the Federal Constitution, the former document has no binding legal effect. A contemporaneous and long-continued construction placed on a constitutional provision by the public officials affected thereby, whether they be of the legislative or the executive branch, will be given considerable weight by the courts in construing the provision.

§ 4:4. Determination of constitutionality of legislation.

Am Jur 2d References: Constitutional Law, §§ 101–197.

Although the doctrine was not established without dispute, it is now a settled principle of the American system of constitutional government that the courts have inherent power to determine whether statutes enacted by the legislative transcend the limits imposed by the federal and state constitutions, and to make the authoritative and final decision as to whether or not such laws are constitutional. This principle was formulated in the opinion of Chief Justice Marshall in the landmark case of Marbury v Madison, 5 US 137, 2 L Ed 60, decided in 1803.

The power assumed by the courts to determine the constitutionality of legislation involves dual responsibilities. On the one hand, it is the duty of the court to strike down a statute that clearly violates the constitution, as it is the function of a court to determine what law is valid and applicable in the case before it. On the other hand, a proper respect for a co-ordinate branch of government requires that a court exercise self-restraint in exercising this power. Hence, a court will not declare a statute unconstitutional unless its invalidity is beyond reasonable doubt, nor will a court pass upon the constitutionality of a statute except in a proceeding in which the question is necessarily involved. The question of constitutionality will not be considered and determined by the courts as a hypothetical, abstract or academic matter. Except in some states in which provision is made for such procedure, courts will not render advisory opinions on the constitutionality of proposed or pending legislation. Questions of constitutionality which have become moot will also not be considered by the courts.

It is settled as a general principle that a court will not decide on the constitutionality of a statute if the merits of the actual case before the court may be fairly determined without doing so. If the litigation before the court can be effectively disposed of on other grounds, questions involving the constitutionality of statutes will not be considered. Similarly, the constitutionality of a part of a statute will not be considered where that part is severable from the rest, and the constitutionality of the remainder is sufficient to dispose of the case before the court.

The constitutionality of legislation is open to attack only by a person whose rights are affected thereby. Before a court will consider an attack on the law on the ground that it is unconstitutional, the person making the attack must show that he has an interest in the question, that the enforcement of the law would be an infringement of his rights. No one can obtain a decision as to the constitutionality of a law on the ground that it impairs the rights of others, as one attacking a law may not be the champion of any rights except his own. And a person has no standing to challenge the constitutionality of a statute on the ground that it discriminates against a class unless he belongs to that class.

When the constitutionality of a statute is challenged, the court will indulge every reasonable presumption in favor of its validity. And in construing statutes with relation to constitutional provisions, the statutes will be read in the light of the constitution and will be reconciled therewith if such is possible. If a statute is reasonably susceptible of two interpretations, one of which would render it unconstitutional and the other would make it valid, the latter construction will be applied. A proper respect for the legislative department as a co-ordinate branch of government impels the courts to adopt this principle.

Similar considerations have firmly established the rule that the wisdom, justice, propriety, necessity, utility, and expediency of legislation are matters solely for the determination of the legislature, and that the courts will not substitute their judgment for that of the legislature by declaring a statute invalid on these grounds, unless it violates some specific constitutional provision. The remedy for the correction of unwise legislation remains in the legislature and, ultimately, in the people by means of changes in the legislative body.

§ 4:5. Guaranty of republican form of government.

Am Jur 2d References: Constitutional Law, §§ 389–394.

The Constitution of the United States provides, in Article IV, § 4, that the United States "shall guarantee to every state in this union a republican form of government." This provision prohibits a state from adopting an anti-republican form of government for the state, but it does not limit the power of a state to prescribe the manner of government of municipalities and other subdivisions of the state. A republican form of government, within the meaning of this provision, is generally understood to be that form existing in the original thirteen states at the time of the adoption of the Constitution and the form provided by the Constitution for the federal government. This means, in general terms, a government of representatives chosen by the people.

II. DISTRIBUTION OF GOVERNMENTAL POWERS

§ 4:6. As between federal and state governments.

Am Jur 2d References: Constitutional Law, §§ 198–209; United States (1st ed, §§ 1–9).

The United States of America was created by the voluntary union of the several existing sovereign states by their adoption of the Constitution of the United States. The American system of government created by this instrument is dual in nature, certain powers being vested in the federal government and others being retained by the several states. These powers are distributed according to four classes: (1) those which belong exclusively to the national government; (2) those which belong exclusively to the state; (3) those which may be exercised concurrently and independently by both; and (4) those which may be exercised by the state, but only until Congress shall see fit to act upon the subject. The two governments—state and national—are each to exercise their powers so as not to interfere with the free and full exercise by the other of its powers.

The Federal Constitution contains an enumeration of powers granted by the people to the federal government; and it is axiomatic that the United States is a government of limited, enumerated and delegated powers, and that it cannot exercise any authority not granted by the Constitution, either expressly or by necessary implication. Indeed, the Tenth Amendment to the Constitution provides that the "powers not delegated to the United States by the Constitution . . . are reserved to the states . . . or to the people," except where the Constitution prohibits the exercise of particular powers by states.

The thirteen states existing prior to the adoption of the Federal Constitution possessed all the attributes of sovereignty; and all of these attributes and powers except, those surrendered by the adoption of the Constitution and the amendments thereto, have been retained. New states admitted to the Union are invested with equal powers and are subject to the same restrictions as are imposed upon the states already admitted. Under our dual form of government, each state has the right to order its own affairs and govern its own people except to the extent that the Federal Constitution has limited that power expressly or by fair implication.

Although the federal government is based upon the powers delegated and enumerated in the Constitution, the powers expressly granted carry with them implied powers necessary to the effective exercise of an express power. By Article I, § 8, clause 18, of the Federal Constitution, Congress is specifically empowered to enact all laws which may be necessary and proper to carry into effect the powers expressly granted to it; and Congress must, in its discretion, determine the manner in which it will exercise its powers and select the means which it deems best adapted to accomplish legitimate ends.

§ 4:7. Departmental separation of governmental powers and functions.

Am Jur 2d References: Constitutional Law, §§ 210–258; United States (1st ed, §§ 10–58).

A distinctive and fundamental feature of the American constitutional system is the division of governmental powers among three departments of government; the legislative, executive, and judicial; each of which performs its allotted functions separately from and independently of the others. This separation of powers is inherent in the federal government, not by any express declaration thereof in the Constitution, but because of the actual separate allocation of legislative, executive, and judicial powers to the Congress, the President, and the courts, respectively. In some states the doctrine is expressly stated in their constitutions. The departmental separation of governmental powers is not a mere philosophical abstraction; it has always been regarded as vital to the maintenance of a republican form of government and as a safeguard of the liberties of the people as against despotic rule.

Each of the departments of government derives its authority from the people through their constitutions; and each has the power and the duty to discharge its functions without interference or encroachment by other departments. The separation of powers, however, is not absolute or without exception. There are circumstances in which the practical administration of government requires some blending or interchange of the powers of the separate departments. Indeed, the constitutions themselves do not follow the departmental lines with absolute and literal preciseness. For example, the qualified power of veto vested in chief executives is actually of legislative and not executive character; and his pardoning power may practically annul judgments of the judiciary. The Senate of the United States participates in the executive function of appointing officers and of making treaties. The Senate exercises the judicial power of trying impeachments, and the House of Representatives of preferring articles of impeachment. The power of the judiciary to invalidate a legislative act does not involve a legislative function, but does limit the power of the legislative department. Exceptions of this kind are examples of the "checks and balances" built into the American system of government.

The separation of the powers of government not only prevents encroachment by one department upon another; it also requires each department to perform its designated duties and prohibits it from abdicating or delegating its lawful duties and functions to another department. Questions in this area most frequently involve the delegation of legislative power. The general rule is well settled that a legislature cannot delegate the power to make laws to any other authority or department. Any attempt to delegate its legislative power is unconstitutional and void, unless authorized by the constitution. This principle applies to the Congress as well as to state legislatures. It does not, however, prevent state legislatures from vesting the power of self-government as to local affairs in municipalities and other political subdivisions; nor does it affect the power of the Congress, in dealing with a territory which is not a state, to delegate legislative authority to such agencies as it may select.

A state may not delegate its legislative power to the Congress. This does not, however, prevent a state from adopting all or a part of a federal law already in effect, or from adopting the features of a similar federal law as a basis of determining taxable income. The Congress may provide for the application of state rules or procedures in certain cases, and may apply state laws to crimes or torts occurring in federal territory located within state boundaries. The legislature cannot delegate its legislative power to the executive, or even to the voters. But it may make a law to become effective on the happening of a specified contingency or future event, and that contingency or event may be the consent of the voters of a certain territory or part of the state, or it may be the proclamation or determination by the executive as to a fact, condition or exigency.

III. COMMERCE CLAUSE

§ 4:8. Generally; federal and state powers.

Am Jur 2d References: Commerce, §§ 1–24.

Article I, § 8, clause 3 of the Constitution of the United States provides that "the Congress shall have power . . . to regulate commerce with foreign nations, and among the several states, and with the Indian tribes." This provision is generally known as the "commerce clause," and its purposes were to eliminate the conflicts and confusion which plagued the states at the time of the adoption of the Constitution, to assure an area of free trade among the several states, to protect commercial intercourse against conflicting and harmful regulations, and to insure uniformity of regulation throughout the nation. This clause also conferred upon the nation the power to deal with foreign nations with respect to international commerce. The term "commerce" as used in this clause is held to include every kind of traffic, trade and intercourse, and every kind of communication and transportation, whether for commercial purposes or otherwise. It includes the purchase, sale, exchange and hiring of chattels, the transportation of persons or property by land, water or air, and all instrumentalities by which such intercourse is carried on.

The respective powers of Congress and the states under the commerce clause are divided into three categories: (1) that in which the authority is exclusive; (2) that in which the power of the state is exclusive; and (3) that in which the state may act in the absence of legislation by Congress. The power of Congress to regulate commerce among the states and with foreign nations is supreme, exclusive, and plenary, and it is subject to no limitations except those prescribed by the Federal Constitution. This power does not, however, extend to purely local and intrastate transactions not directly or materially affecting interstate or foreign commerce. These matters are left to regulation by the states. However, transactions which are otherwise purely local and intrastate may be subjected to the regulatory power of Congress if they directly or materially affect interstate or foreign commerce, or, because of interconnections with business across state lines, exert substantial economic effect on interstate commerce.

As stated above, there are areas in which the states may act until Congress pre-empts them, although interstate commerce is involved. In subjects of local interest and concern involving fields of commerce in which national uniformity is not essential, the state may act, even though its action unavoidably involves some regulation of interstate commerce, so long as the state's action serves local ends and does not discriminate against interstate commerce and is not calculated to place interstate commerce at a disadvantage. But the power of Congress in this field is supreme, and once it legislates therein the power of the states ends.

§ 4:9. Subjects of commerce and regulation.

Am Jur 2d References: Commerce, §§ 25–83.

The power of Congress to regulate commerce authorizes legislation with respect to all the subjects of interstate and foreign commerce, all the persons engaged therein, all the instrumentalities and means by which it is carried on, and all acts which burden or obstruct the free flow of such commerce. It has been frequently stated broadly that manufacture is not commerce, but there may be circumstances that would give Congress regulatory power with respect thereto. In any event, manufacturing is subject to local taxation and regulation, since it is not the purpose of the commerce clause to relieve even those engaged in interstate commerce from their share of the state tax burden. Building or construction work does not ordinarily constitute interstate commerce, even though the materials used are shipped in from other states. Whether or not the performance of services is considered interstate commerce depends on the factual situation presented in the particular case.

Generally, the sale of goods in one state and shipment into another state constitutes interstate commerce, not subject to regulation or taxation by the latter state. The rule also generally applies to the solicitation within a state of orders for goods by the agent of a foreign corporation or manufacturer. The shipment of goods pursuant to such orders from another state constitutes interstate commerce, especially where the orders are subject to acceptance or rejection in the other state. A mere incidental agreement to assemble or install property sold in interstate commerce does not change the interstate nature of the transaction or bring it within state control. Formerly much importance was attached to the circumstance that goods imported from a foreign country or from another state remained in the original or unbroken package because the protection afforded by the commerce clause against local taxation or regulation applied in such cases. However, the "original package doctrine" has little application today except as to goods imported from a foreign country.

Transportation of persons or property wholly within a state is ordinarily intrastate commerce, subject to the control of the state only. However, if such transportation is a link in interstate transportation by connecting carriers, it is a part of interstate commerce. And forwarding, switching and terminal services in connection with goods shipped between states constitute interstate commerce.

IV. POLICE POWER

§ 4:10. Generally; exercise of power.

Am Jur 2d References: Constitutional Law, §§ 259–276, 305–327; Zoning (1st ed, §§ 14–24).

In the sense in which the term is used in constitutional law, "police power" is the inherent power of a government to pass such laws and take such action as it deems necessary for the welfare of the state and its people. In its broadest sense, police power is practically identical with governmental power. It is an essential and inherent attribute of sovereignty possessed by every state. Police power is not derived from any grant contained in a written constitution, and it is unlimited except to the extent of constitutional limitations. The police power is flexible and adaptable to changing conditions and needs. It is an inalienable power which cannot be abdicated or bartered away by the legislature. It is distinct from the power of taxation, the two powers being coexistent powers of the state. It is also distinguishable from the power of eminent domain, in that many restrictions may be imposed under the police power without giving compensation, whereas under the power of eminent domain compensation is required; and when property is taken by eminent domain it is for a public use, while property is subjected to restrictions or is damaged or destroyed under the police power to protect the safety, health, and general welfare of the public.

As the federal government has only such powers as are granted to it by the Constitution of the United States, it has no general police powers such as belong to the states, which have all powers of sovereignty not surrendered by them through the Federal Constitution and their own constitutions. The federal government does, however, possess whatever police power is appropriate to the exercise of any attribute of sovereignty granted to it by the Constitution.

The scope of the police power is co-extensive with the power of the government. It extends to the protection of the lives, health, and property of the people; to the preservation of good order and the public morals; to the restraint and punishment of crime; and to the preservation of the general welfare of the community. The police power is not limited to guarding the physical or material interests of the citizen, but it extends to the promotion of moral, intellectual and spiritual needs of the people, including education. It includes the power to regulate trades, occupations, businesses, and professions for the protection of the public health, morals, and welfare, subject to the constitutional requirement of reasonable classification. Zoning laws and building restrictions are familiar examples of the exercise of the police power.

§ 4:11. Limitations on police power.

Am Jur 2d References: Constitutional Law, §§ 277–304.

The basic standard by which the validity of a state's exercise of the police power is tested is whether or not the particular act is reasonable. And in order for a police measure to be reasonable, the means adopted must be reasonably necessary for the accomplishment of the legitimate objects falling within the scope of the power. The act must have some reasonable relation to such objects. Not only must the end or object sought to be attained be within the scope of the police power, but the particular means or method adopted by the legislature must be reasonably adapted to the accomplishment of that end. The legislature has a broad discretion in determining both the need of measures to protect the public interests and the means best adapted to accomplish its object. Although the determination of these matters as constitutional questions is ultimately a matter for the courts, they are reluctant to overturn the legislative act if there is any reasonable basis on which to sustain it.

Although the boundaries of the rule are hazy and its application depends upon the circumstances of each particular case and is sometimes difficult, the general principle is well settled that the police power is exercisable only within the limits which, under the state and federal constitutions, are applicable to all governmental action. A constitutional right cannot be abridged by legislation under the guise of the exercise of the police power. Personal rights and liberties, and contract rights, may not be unreasonably invaded under the police power; but all such rights are subject to reasonable regulation in the interest of the general welfare. While property rights may not be invaded by the exercise of the police power, it is settled that all property is held subject to the right of the state reasonably to regulate its use under the police power in order to secure the safety, good order and general welfare of the community. Every title and right is subject to this condition.

The foregoing principles apply in resolving an alleged conflict between an attempted exercise of the police power and a right asserted under any constitutional guaranty. Clearly, the due process provisions are a limitation upon the police power; but such provisions do not invalidate reasonable laws necessary to secure the health, morals, and general welfare of the people. Indeed, regulation under the police power in such a case is a perfect example of due process of law. The constitutional provision against the impairment of the obligation of contracts does not prevent the states from declaring, in an emergency, a moratorium on the enforcement of mortgages. Other constitutional rights and immunities, such as the rights of freedom of speech and of the press, and freedom of religion, are subject to the same power of the state to impose reasonable restrictions necessary to the safety, health, and welfare of the general public.

V. FUNDAMENTAL RIGHTS AND IMMUNITIES; BILL OF RIGHTS

§ 4:12. Generally.

Am Jur 2d References: Constitutional Law, §§ 328–335, 353–360, 382–388.

Some of the fundamental rights and privileges guaranteed to the individual under the American constitutions were of ancient origin under the English common law. The prototype of the due process clauses is the provision of Magna Charta protecting every freeman against violation of the rights of life, liberty and property, "Except by lawful judgment of his peers or by the law of the land"—i.e., due process of law. Other guaranties, such as those relating to freedom of religion, of speech and of the press, reflect the political philosophy of the framers of the Federal Constitution and the difficulties experienced by the colonists and the original states with respect to these problems prior to the adoption of the Federal Constitution.

The first ten amendments to the Constitution of the United States were proposed at the first session of Congress after the adoption of the Constitution; and their proposal was, in effect, a condition of the approval of the Constitution by states where there was serious apprehension that the instrument as originally presented did not adequately protect the individual rights and liberties of the people. The Bill of Rights provides that Congress shall make no law respecting the establishment of religion or prohibiting the free exercise thereof, or abridging the freedom of speech or of the press, or the right of the people peaceably to assemble and petition the government. These amendments also provide that the right to bear arms shall not be infringed, and provide against the quartering of soldiers, unreasonable searches and seizures, excessive bail or fines, cruel and unusual punishments, double jeopardy, compelled self-incrimination, deprivation of life, liberty, or property without due process of law, and the taking of property for public use without just compensation. These amendments preserve the right to trial by jury, the right to a speedy and public trial, the right to presentment or indictment of a grand jury, the right to be informed of the nature and cause of an accusation, to be confronted with witnesses against an accused, to have compulsory process for obtaining witnesses, and to have the assistance of counsel.

The first ten amendments originally applied only to acts by the federal government. They were not intended to apply to acts of the states, as such matters were left to the control of the people of each state. However, it has been established by a series of decisions of the Supreme Court of the United States that the adoption of the Fourteenth Amendment in effect made the provisions of the first eight amendments applicable to the states. While technically the federal Bill of Rights, as such and by its own force, still limits only the power of the federal government, the provision of the Fourteenth Amendment prohibiting any state from depriving any person of life, liberty, or property without due process of law, forbids a denial of any of the fundamental principles of liberty and justice which are declared in the Bill of Rights. In other words, infringement of any of the fundamental principles declared in the Bill of Rights is a denial of due process of law under the Fourteenth Amendment. It may be noted also that the constitutions of many states contain limitations similar to those of the Bill of Rights.

The constitutions of many states contain provisions stating, in varying terms, that justice shall be administered to all without delay or denial, without sale or prejudice, and that the courts shall be open to all alike. Most of these constitutions also contain provisions generally prohibiting imprisonment for debt.

Occasional reference is made to "natural" rights. But this expression should be interpreted as meaning merely those fundamental rights actually guaranteed by the constitution, and not rights in addition to or beyond those specifically guaranteed. There would seem to be no basis under the American system for the conception of any transcendent personal rights founded on instinctive nature in addition to those guaranteed by a written constitution.

In considering constitutional rights and powers, it must always be borne in mind, as already stated, that none of the rights specified in a constitution is absolute in the sense that it may be asserted without regard for the rights of others. Every such right is subject to restriction or qualification necessary for the general welfare and for the preservation of orderly government. The guaranty of freedom of speech and of the press, for example, does not license libel and slander, the infringement of copyright or of the right of privacy. Freedom of religion does include human sacrifice or polygamy. And the right of assembly does not warrant riots, breaches of the peace, or action threatening the existence of the government.

§ 4:13. Religious freedom.

Am Jur 2d References: Constitutional Law, §§ 336–340; Schools, §§ 290–306; Sundays and Holidays (1st ed, § 10).

The First Amendment to the Constitution of the United States forbids Congress to make any law respecting the establishment of religion or prohibiting the free exercise thereof. This prohibition, like other provisions of the Bill of Rights, is held to apply to the states by virtue of the due process clause of the Fourteenth Amendment. The state constitutions also contain guaranties of the freedom of religion. These provisions protect all persons and all religious denominations and sects in the right to hold and follow their own beliefs and to practice and advocate the same; and they recognize the right of a person to disaffirm all religious belief and to decline to follow any religion. Neither the states nor the United States may support, contribute to or foster any religion in any way; nor may they pass laws or impose requirements which aid all religions as against nonbelievers or which aid those religions based on a belief in God as against those founded on different beliefs. The purpose and effect of these provisions is to secure the complete separation of church and state.

The freedom of religion which is guaranteed by the federal and state constitutions is not an absolute or unlimited freedom. While laws cannot interfere with religious beliefs and opinions, they may prohibit acts and practices

which are made criminal by the law of the land or which tend toward the sub-
version of the civil government. The police power of the states permits them
to adopt measures which inhibit particular acts deemed to be contrary to the
general welfare, so long as no attempt is made to interfere with the right
to maintain religious beliefs. Although the guaranty of the freedom to believe
is absolute, freedom to act cannot be absolute, and conduct remains subject
to regulation for the protection of society. Religious beliefs or conscientious
scruples do not relieve the individual from obedience of the general law not
aimed at the promotion or restriction of religion. The punitive power of the
government as to acts generally recognized as proper subjects of prohibitory
legislation, for example, polygamy, is not suspended to accommodate the
tenets of a religious sect.

A state law requiring the closing of businesses and public offices on Sunday
does not violate the constitutional inhibition of laws respecting the establishment of religion, as applied to the member of a religious faith whose sabbath
is Saturday, as such a measure is designed not to aid religion but to set aside
a day of rest and recreation.

The constitutional separation of church and state and the guaranty of
freedom of religion is frequently involved in connection with schools. This is
an area in which it is difficult to predict the ultimate decision in a particular
factual situation and which must be approached on a case-by-case basis.
Some general guidelines have, however, been laid down by the Supreme Court.
In a case involving public aid to sectarian schools, it was stated that in determining the validity of a statute attacked on the ground of the First Amendment, three tests are to be applied. First, the statute must have a secular
legislative purpose. Second, its principal or primary effect must be one that
neither advances nor inhibits religion; and finally, the statute must not foster
an excessive government entanglement with religion. It is settled that the
provisions of the First Amendment are violated by a statute or rule of a school
board requiring religious exercises, the reading or distribution of the Bible, or
prayers in public schools. The extent to which public aid may be provided
for private church-related schools depends upon the nature of the aid, as well
as upon the state constitutional provisions invoked. Many types of aid to
private schools generally have been sustained, although sectarian schools were
included. Bus service for children attending sectarian schools is generally
held not to be violative of the First Amendment, although some courts hold
such aid to be contrary to various provisions of state constitutions, such as a
provision forbidding financial aid to religious sects. It is held that the First
Amendment forbids the use of public funds to pay the tuition of students
attending a religious denominational school. The free public lending of
textbooks to all students, including those in private parochial schools has
been held not to violate the First Amendment; but the public reimbursement
of such schools themselves for the cost of textbooks violates the First Amendment; and the furnishing of textbooks and other school supplies to parochial
schools is held to be a forbidden use of public funds in some states. The
validity of "released time" programs to enable public school children to attend
religious instruction outside the schools depends upon the nature and details
of the program.

§ 4:14. Freedom of speech and press.

Am Jur 2d References: Constitutional Law, §§ 341–352.

The First Amendment to the Constitution of the United States (which is made applicable to the states by the Fourteenth Amendment) and the constitutions of many of the states prohibit the enactment of laws which abridge the freedom of speech or of the press. Although censorship, i.e., licensing and censorship of writings prior to and as a condition of publication, had been abolished in England for nearly a century, it still existed in other countries, and its evils were still familiar to the framers of the Constitution. These provisions include not only writings and printed publications, but also spoken words, and they are broad enough to protect any form or medium of communication; writing, speech, drama, motion picture, recording, and radio or television.

The constitutional right or privilege of free speech and publication has its limitations and is not an absolute right. Like other rights protected by the Bill of Rights, it is subject to regulation or restriction by the state for the protection of the superior interest of the public in peace and order. In determining the validity of a particular restriction the courts will weigh the interest of the public against the interest of the person asserting the right. No clear and definitive criteria have been formulated for the determination of such conflicts of interest. To say that the duty of the courts is to determine which of the two conflicting interests demands the greater protection under the particular circumstances presented, is of doubtful help as a general guide. The same is true of the "clear and present danger" doctrine, under which the issue in every case is said to be whether the words used are used in such circumstances and of such nature as to create a clear and present danger that they will bring about substantive evils which the legislature has the right to prevent; it is a question of proximity and degree.

It is clear that the courts will not consider the merits, validity or value of speech or publications for which protection of the First Amendment is invoked. A distinction has been made between words that advocate "concrete action" and those that advocate "principles divorced from action"; and it has been stated frequently that the privilege may not be limited so long as words seek to affect the beliefs of others, and not their conduct. But, as Judge Learned Hand has observed in 1958 ("The Bill of Rights," p. 57), "The trouble is that conduct is almost always based upon some belief, and that to change the hearer's belief will generally to some extent change his conduct, and may even evoke conduct that the law forbids. Everyone agrees that there may be so close a causal sequence between the belief engendered and the unlawful conduct as to toll the privilege; but what that sequence must be still remains obscure."

Certain types of utterances and publications are clearly beyond any constitutional protection or privilege. In this class are libel and slander and invasions of the right of privacy. No one would contend that the freedom of the press extends to the counterfeiting of currency or the use of the mails to defraud. Matter which is determined to be obscene according to the prevailing mores of the community or which constitutes "hard-core pornography" is subject to the control of the legislature. And other criminal offenses based on verbal acts, such as inciting to riot, solicitation of another to commit a crime, and aiding and abetting in the commission of an offense, cannot be defended as an exercise of freedom of speech.

§ 4:15. Civil rights.

Am Jur 2d References: Civil Rights, §§ 1–62; Covenants, Conditions, etc., § 184.

In the sense in which the term is used here, "civil rights" refers to the enjoyment of such guaranties as are contained in the Federal Constitution and in the constitutions of the states designed to prevent discrimination in the treatment of persons by reason of their race, color, religion, or place of origin. These constitutional guaranties are augmented by numerous statutes, federal and state, as well as by presidential executive orders, municipal ordinances and administrative regulations.

The Thirteenth Amendment to the Constitution of the United States abolished slavery and gave Congress enforcement powers. The Fifteenth Amendment provides that the right to vote shall not be denied or abridged on account of race, color, or previous condition of servitude. The Fourteenth Amendment, on which most civil rights are ultimately based, provides that no state shall make or enforce any law which shall abridge the privileges or immunities of citizens of the United States, and that no state shall deprive any person of life, liberty, or property, without due process of law, nor deny to any person within its jurisdiction the equal protection of the laws.

It is clear that the Fourteenth Amendment places restraints only on the action of the states, and does not affect the rights of one citizen as against another. State action, within the meaning of the Fourteenth Amendment, includes all state action infringing the rights secured thereby, whatever the state agency taking the action and whatever the guise in which it is manifested. It includes action by a state legislature, state courts, state executive or administrative officers, municipal ordinances, and the acts of a state's political subdivisions and administrative agencies. As seen below, the action of a court in enforcing a private covenant in a deed may constitute state action with respect to the substance of the covenant.

By the force of constitutional provisions and by federal and state statutes, discrimination because of race, color, etc., is now generally prohibited with respect to all public accommodations, such as hotels and restaurants, amusement parks, theaters and other places of recreation. If the facility is supported wholly or in part by public funds, discrimination violates the Fourteenth Amendment. And no form of racial discrimination or segregation is permissible in interstate transportation, and, where state action is involved, the same is true of local transportation. Although it was formerly held otherwise under the "separate but equal" doctrine, it is now settled that it is a denial of the equal protection of the laws guaranteed by the Fourteenth Amendment to deny Negro children admission to public schools attended by white children. Segregation based on race, or discrimination of any kind with respect to admission, accommodations, or treatment, is forbidden in any school, college or university supported by public funds. The extent to which the authorities must go to avoid inequalities and segregation is a matter that has occasioned much confusion. Privately owned and operated educational institutions are not subject to the constitutional inhibitions against discrimination.

While it was formerly held that such covenants were valid and enforceable, the Supreme Court has changed its view and now holds that a restrictive covenant in a deed or contract forbidding the sale or transfer of land to, or its occupancy by, persons of a certain race or religious faith cannot be enforced in the courts, either by injunctions or by action for damages. Lending the aid of the courts to enforce such covenants is held to constitute state action and to be inhibited by the equal protection provision of the Fourteenth Amendment. As the Fourteenth Amendment does not protect persons against merely private conduct, such covenants, standing alone and without state action, do not violate constitutional rights, and may be effectuated by voluntary adherence to their terms.

§4:16. Property rights.

Am Jur 2d References: Constitutional Law, §§ 361–381.

The right of property is a fundamental one. It existed in our country prior to the adoption of the Federal Constitution, and it is guaranteed by the Constitution. The Fifth Amendment prevents the federal government or its agencies from depriving any person of his property without due process of law; and the Fourteenth Amendment, as well as the state constitutions, prevent any action by a state which would accomplish such deprivation. These guaranties of due process of law apply to all kinds of property recognized by law. They protect all kinds of interest in property and all essential attributes of property, including the right to acquire, hold, and enjoy property and to devote it to any legitimate use. The right to sell or otherwise dispose of property is an important incident of the right of property. Contract rights are property within the meaning of the due process clause, as are a person's business, profession or trade and the right to earn a livelihood in a legitimate occupation.

Although the Constitution does not contain any definition of the word "deprive" as used in the Fourteenth Amendment, it may be stated generally that a law is a deprivation of property within the meaning of this constitutional inhibition if it deprives the owner of any of the essential attributes of property, destroys or materially diminishes its value, or restricts its common, necessary or profitable use, in a manner not warranted as a proper exercise of the police power of the state.

The constitutional right of property is not an absolute right. It is subject to the equal rights of others and of the general public. It is subject to reasonable restraints and regulations deemed necessary by the legislature in the exercise of the state's police power (supra, §4:10). Thus, in the interest of the general welfare, the state may impose or authorize zoning and building regulations on the use of property. And in a situation of great public emergency and extreme necessity, a state may, in the exercise of its police power (but not under the power of eminent domain), destroy property without compensation to the owner.

§ 4:17. Unlawful search and seizure.

Am Jur 2d References: Searches and Seizures, §§ 1–119.

The Fourth Amendment to the Constitution of the United States provides: "The right of the people to be secure in their persons, houses, papers, and effects, against unreasonable searches and seizures, shall not be violated, and no warrants shall issue, but upon probable cause, supported by oath or affirmation, and particularly describing the place to be searched, and the persons or things to be seized." This provision assures every person of the right of privacy and security with respect to his person, his home, and his effects, as against unwarranted intrusions by government officers or agents. It should be construed liberally, in favor of the individual. Although the Fourth Amendment, like other parts of the Bill of Rights, originally applied only to the federal government, it is now held to apply, by virtue of the Fourteenth Amendment, also to the states; and the state constitutions generally contain similar provisions against unreasonable searches and seizures.

In considering what constitutes a "search" or "seizure" within the scope of constitutional protection, care should be taken that there is not too much emphasis placed on the physical location of the alleged search or seizure. Generally, the Fourth Amendment protects people, not places; and accordingly, what a person knowingly exposes to the public, even in his own home or office, is not a subject of Fourth Amendment protection, but that which he seeks to preserve as private, even in a place accessible to the public, may be constitutionally protected. The Fourth Amendment protects against searches and seizures of the person. A person in a friend's apartment, or in a hotel or motel, in a taxicab or in a public telephone booth, may rely upon the immunity conferred by this Amendment. Private vehicles also come within the protection of these provisions, but the requirements as to warrantless searches and seizures with respect thereto are less stringent than in the case of residences and other buildings. The constitutional protection also extends to business and commercial property. The protection does not cover open fields and areas remote from any buildings, but it does apply to the "curtilage", the ground and buildings immediately adjacent to a dwelling and used in connection therewith.

Mere observation of what is in plain view, by an officer who has a right to be where he is, does not ordinarily constitute a search, even though he uses a flashlight or binoculars to aid in his observation. It has been established since 1967 that electronic surveillance or eavesdropping by means of electronic listening devices constitutes a search and seizure within the meaning of the Fourth Amendment. The constitutional inhibitions may be violated by guileful as well as by forcible intrusions, and a seizure may be prohibited although entry upon the premises was by subterfuge or fraud rather than force. But the Fourth Amendment does not inhibit the use of stratagem or deception in obtaining evidence, such as the utilization of informers or undercover agents.

The so-called "stop and frisk" practices of the police, consisting of an on-the-street interrogation and a "pat-down" for weapons is held to constitute a search and seizure of the person. The legality of a particular instance of this procedure depends upon the existence of sufficient cause therefor and upon whether the police officers kept within reasonable bounds and restricted their examination to what was reasonably necessary to discover whether the suspect was carrying weapons. Similar practices are permitted within reasonable limits, as regards airplane passengers as a precaution against hijacking.

Except in strictly defined cases, a search of private property is unreasonable under the Constitution unless it has been authorized by a valid search warrant. A search that is unlawful at its inception is not validated by what it turns up; it is good or bad when it starts, and does not change character from its success. The guilt or innocence of the person subjected to an unlawful search is irrelevant. Indeed, evidence obtained by an unlawful search is inadmissible (Evidence, § 8), no matter how incriminating it may be.

A warrant is not required under the Fourth Amendment for a search or seizure made incident to a valid arrest, although the courts have limited this rule somewhat in cases of arrests for traffic violations. Clearly a search voluntarily consented to by the owner of the premises dispenses with the requirement of a warrant. Another exception to the requirement of a search warrant is recognized in cases where officers have "probable cause" for the search and seizure, and "exigent circumstances" exist, making it impracticable to obtain a warrant. The requirement of probable cause is generally satisfied where the facts and circumstances within police officers' knowledge, and of which they have reasonably sufficient information, are sufficient in themselves to warrant a man of reasonable caution in the belief that an offense has been or is being committed. But the probabilities implied by the term "probable cause" are not technical; they are the factual and practical considerations of everyday life on which reasonable and prudent men, not legal technicans, act. Probable cause in this connection does not require proof sufficient to establish guilt, or even to make a prima facie case, in a criminal trial. Similar principles apply in determining probable cause for the issuance of a search warrant.

VI. RETROSPECTIVE LEGISLATION; EX POST FACTO LAWS

§ 4:18. Generally.

Am Jur 2d References: Constitutional Law, §§ 395–433.

The Constitution of the United States, Article I, §§ 9, 10, prohibits the enactment of ex post facto laws or bills of attainder by Congress or by any state. This prohibition applies not only to state legislatures, but also to the people of the states in adopting and amending their constitutions. These provisions have no application to crimes committed outside the jurisdiction of the United States in violation of the laws of a foreign country, nor to laws providing for the deportation of aliens. A definition of an ex post facto law which has received general approval is that it is a law which, in its operation, makes that criminal which was not so at the time the action was performed, or which increases the punishment, or which, in relation to the offense or its consequences, alters the situation of a party to his disadvantage.

By definition, an ex post facto law must be one relating to crimes or penalties. To be ex post facto, a law must provide for a punishment or penalty for an act which has already been done and which was not punishable when done, or it must increase the punishment or penalty for acts which were already criminally punishable. This constitutional inhibition does not apply to retrospective legislation not involving crimes or penalties. To be ex post facto, a law must alter the situation of the accused to his disadvantage. A retrospective law which does not deprive a party of some right to which he was entitled at the time the act or offense was committed, is not ex post facto. A law that mitigates or reduces the penalty for an act already done is not ex post facto. An act is not ex post facto as to prior crimes merely because it continues in force and keeps alive laws which existed when the crimes were committed. And it is settled that the prohibition of ex post facto laws is a restraint only on the legislative power. The provision has no application to judicial decisions.

Mere changes in procedure or in the form of remedies do not violate the prohibition against ex post facto laws, so long as they do not prejudicially change the position of a person or operate to deny him a defense available at the time of the commission of the alleged offense. Although changes in the mere formal rules of evidence may be permissible, a change in the degree of proof required to warrant a conviction may not be applied in the trial of an offense committed prior to the change.

As indicated above, the Federal Constitution does not prohibit retrospective laws, as such, unless they involve crimes or penalties and are therefore ex post facto laws. A retrospective law may, however, violate the constitutional provision against depriving one of property without due process of law, or the provision forbidding the impairment of the obligation of contracts. The constitutions of some of the states contain provisions prohibiting retrospective laws. The provisions vary in their terms; some of them applying to laws retrospectively, creating a right where none existed before, and covering all such laws as take away or impair any vested right acquired under a preexisting law, create a new obligation, or attach a new disability in respect of transactions already past.

VII. IMPAIRING OBLIGATION OF CONTRACTS

§ 4:19. Generally.

Am Jur 2d References: Constitutional Law, §§ 434–464.

The Constitution of the United States (Article I, § 10) provides that no state shall pass any law impairing the obligation of contracts; and some state constitutions contain similar provisions. By its terms, this provision of the Federal Constitution applies only to the states, and it does not affect the powers of the Congress of the United States, although the due process clause may be invoked in contract impairment cases in some situations.

For the purposes of this constitutional inhibition, the "obligation" of a contract is defined as the law or legal duty which binds the parties to perform their agreement. It is coeval with the undertaking to perform and consists in the means which, at the time of the creation of the contract, the law affords for its enforcement. In accordance with the principle that the laws which subsist at the time of making a contract enter into and form a part of it, it is held that the obligation of a contract is measured by the standard of the laws in force at the time it was entered into. The obligation of a contract protected against impairment includes the remedy for its enforcement. Without a legal remedy there is no legal obligation; and the withdrawal of a remedy available when a contract was made, without providing an adequate substitute remedy, clearly impairs the obligation of the contract.

The prohibition of laws impairing the obligation of contracts applies to all valid contracts and to contractual obligations of all kinds. It applies, however, only to contracts existing when the challenged law was enacted, not to contracts made thereafter. The obligation of a contract cannot properly be said to be impaired by a statute in force when the contract was made. Although ordinarily a state constitution or statute does not constitute a contract within the meaning of the prohibition against impairment, such a constitution or statute may contain provisions which, when accepted and acted upon according to its terms, may give rise to a contractual obligation which cannot be impaired by a change in the statute or constitution. It is well settled that this provision of the Federal Constitution applies to contracts entered into by states with individuals, and other governmental units, as well as to contracts between private persons. A legislative grant without reservation of the right to modify or repeal it, under which rights have vested, amounts to a contract, and a subsequent statute attempting to annul or impair such grant is unconstitutional, even though the grant was originally without consideration.

The obligation of a contract is impaired by any law that deprives a party of the benefits of his contract or changes the legal effect of the contract to the detriment of a party thereto. The repeal of a statute which constitutes a contract is an impairment of its obligation. And the obligation of a contract is impaired by a statute which alters its terms by imposing new conditions or dispensing with conditions, which diminishes the value of the contract, or which adds new duties, or releases or lessens any part of the contract obligation. Since the prohibition as to impairment of the obligation of contracts is absolute, the extent or degree of the impairment is immaterial. Although the constitutional provision against impairment of the obligation of contracts does not apply to the federal government and does not limit the power of Congress, it applies to all state laws and constitutions, and to municipal ordinances and to the acts of all state subdivisions and agencies. On the other hand, this provision of the Federal Constitution is directed only against impairment by legislation, and not by judgment of the courts. Hence, a change in judicial decisions after the making of a contract, having the effect of invalidating the contract or altering the construction or effect thereof, is not in violation of that inhibition.

As noted above, a remedy for the enforcement of a contract is an integral part of the obligation of the contract and cannot be impaired. However, a state may make changes in procedure and may alter form or details of the remedy, so long as it affords an adequate and complete remedy to protect rights under the contract. It is only necessary that the contract be left with the same force and effect, including the substantial means of enforcement, which existed when it was made. It is also a general rule that a legislature may pass a curative statute to correct errors or informalities in deeds, mortgages, and other instruments defectively executed or acknowledged, where the rights of third parties which have been acquired in good faith are saved. And a statute making valid a contract that was originally void does not impair the obligation of a contract.

Contracts entered into by states have a distinct status as regards remedies for their enforcement. Because of its sovereign immunity to suit, no action can be maintained against a state, without its consent, to enforce its contract. The only recourse is an appeal to the legislature. Moreover, even where a state, at the inception of the contract, consented as one of its conditions to subject itself to suit, it may subsequently withdraw that consent and resume its original immunity, or may subsequently prescribe additional conditions for bringing suit against it. In short, there is no remedy for the enforcement of contracts of a state that may not, under the Federal Constitution, be taken away by a law of the state.

VIII. FULL FAITH AND CREDIT

§ 4:20. Generally.

Am Jur 2d References: Constitutional Law, §§ 585–591; Judgments, §§ 1217–1223.

Article IV, § 1 of the Constitution of the United States, provides: "Full faith and credit shall be given in each state to the public acts, records, and judicial proceedings of every other state. And the Congress may by general laws prescribe the manner in which such acts, records and proceedings shall be proved, and the effect thereof." A similar provision, except for the provision for implementation by Congress, had been a part of the Articles of Confederation. Recognizing that each of the states is a separate sovereignty, except as its powers are limited by the Constitution, the full faith and credit clause was intended to replace and reinforce the loose concepts of "comity of nations" (see the topic, Conflict of Laws) in the relations between the states, and to promote a closer union of the states. Both statutes and constitutions of the states are "public acts" to which full faith and credit must be accorded. And by act of Congress the requirements of this constitutional provision have been extended to the territorial possessions of the United States.

The full faith and credit clause is not applied with absolute literalness in every situation. Its application may be affected by other constitutional provisions or by preponderant considerations of policy. At the outset it must be determined whether the law of a sister state, rather than that of the forum, is applicable to the case at hand under the established principles of conflict of laws. If by these rules the law of the forum governs, there is no need or occasion to give full faith and credit to a foreign law. Also, full faith and credit is required only for valid laws and judgments. If the law of a sister state is unconstitutional, or if a foreign judgment is invalid on constitutional grounds, such as a lack of due process of law with respect to notice and opportunity to be heard, then the law or the judgment is entitled to no recognition or credit.

Some room is left for the play of conflicting state policies under the full faith and credit clause. There is a limit to the extent to which a state will be required to enforce even a judgment of another state in contravention of its own statutes or policy. And in the case of statutes, where the policy of one state comes into conflict with that of another, the necessity of some accommodation of the conflicting interests of the two states is obvious. It has been observed that a literal application of the full faith and credit provision, without regard to the laws of the forum, would lead to the absurd result that whenever a conflict arises, the statute of each state must be enforced in the courts of another but cannot be given effect in its own courts.

Prima facie, every state is entitled to enforce its own valid statutes. The test and controlling principle to be applied, where there is a question of policy and a conflict of interests, is that the interest of the forum and the other state must be weighed and balanced, and the full faith and credit clause will be given effect except where the interest of the forum is strongly preponderant over the interest of the other state.

The full faith and credit clause limits the power of a state to determine the confines of the jurisdiction of its courts and the character of the controversies which may be heard therein. A state cannot escape its constitutional obligations under the clause by the simple device of denying jurisdiction to courts otherwise competent. Nor may a state, under the guise of merely affecting the remedy, deny the enforcement of claims or rights otherwise within the protection of the full faith and credit clause, where its courts have general jurisdiction of the subject matter and the parties.

IX. PRIVILEGES AND IMMUNITIES OF CITIZENSHIP

§ 4:21. Generally.

Am Jur 2d References: Constitutional Law, §§ 465–484.

Article IV, § 2 of the Constitution provides that "The citizens of each state shall be entitled to all privileges and immunities of citizens in the several states." And the Fourteenth Amendment declares that "All persons born or naturalized in the United States, and subject to the jurisdiction thereof, are citizens of the United States and of the state wherein they reside. No state shall make or enforce any law which shall abridge the privileges or immunities of citizens of the United States." The Articles of Confederation contained a similar provision. The purpose of these provisions was to help fuse into one nation a group of independent, sovereign states, and to promote mutual friendship and intercourse among the people of the different states of the Union by guaranteeing their fundamental rights as citizens everywhere in the nation.

The privileges and immunities protected by these constitutional provisions are those which are fundamental, which belong of right to the citizens of all free governments, and which have at all times been enjoyed by citizens of the several states of the Union. Among these privileges is the right to acquire and possess property, to engage in lawful occupations, to travel and move freely from state to state and from place to place within the United States, and to engage in lawful commerce. These provisions protect the right to access to the courts and judicial remedies for the protection of rights.

Neither Article IV, § 2, relating to citizens of the states, nor the provision of the Fourteenth Amendment, relating to citizens of the United States, prevents the states from enacting laws, in the exercise of the police power, for general welfare and protection of the people and for the maintenance of orderly government. Residence in or citizenship of a state is properly made a condition of the right to vote and to hold public office or to engage in the practice of law or medicine. The states may, and generally do, discriminate between its residents and nonresidents in the regulation and licensing of hunting and fishing. And the requirement that citizens of other states be afforded access to the courts does not preclude a state from requiring that nonresidents give security for court costs.

The privileges and immunities secured to citizens of each state by Article IV, § 2 of the Constitution are those fundamental privileges and immunities which are common to the citizens in those states under their laws and constitutions by virtue of their being citizens. The privileges and immunities of the United States, protected by the Fourteenth Amendment, are those which arise out of the nature and essential character of the national government and are granted or secured by the Constitution or by the laws and treaties made in pursuance thereof. These provisions do not apply to citizens of foreign countries, although they may be entitled to the protection of the equal protection and due process clauses of the Constitution.

X. EQUAL PROTECTION OF THE LAWS

§ 4:22. Generally.

Am Jur 2d References: Constitutional Law, §§ 485–493, 526–541.

One of the several provisions of the Fourteenth Amendment to the Constitution of the United States is that no state shall deny to any person within its jurisdiction the equal protection of the laws. One of the primary objects of this provision, at the time of its adoption, was to secure to the colored race, then recently emancipated, the full enjoyment of its freedom; but it extends its protection to all persons without regard to color or class, and prohibits any state act which has the effect of denying to any race, class, or individual the equal protection of the laws. The provision guarantees that all persons under like circumstances shall have equal protection and security in the enjoyment of personal, civil, and property rights.

By its terms, the equal protection of laws provision of the Fourteenth Amendment applies to action by the states only, and it does not restrict the power of the federal government, although a denial of equal protection by the latter may be such as to violate the due process clause of the Fifth Amendment. Nor does the Fourteenth Amendment provide a safeguard against the acts of individuals or persons, unless state action or aid is invoked or involved. The amendment does inhibit all kinds of acts by any department of a state, legislative, executive, or judicial, or by any officer, agency, or instrumentality of a state. The protection of the amendment extends to all "persons," and this includes corporations.

Although the precise meaning of "equal protection of the laws" has not been comprehensively delimited or defined by the courts, various broad and sweeping generalizations are frequently encountered as to the meaning and effect of this provision. Thus, it has been repeatedly stated that the guaranty of equal protection of the laws means that no person or class of persons shall be denied the same protection of the laws which is enjoyed by other persons or other classes in like circumstances, in their lives, liberty, and property, and in the pursuit of happiness. The guiding principle most often stated by the courts is that the constitutional guaranty of equal protection of the laws requires that all persons shall be treated alike under like circumstances, both in the privileges conferred and in the liabilities and duties imposed. Equality of right is the basic aim of this provision.

Many state constitutions contain provisions similar to the equal protection clause of the Fourteenth Amendment. Common also are state constitutional prohibitions of the granting of special privileges or the imposition of special burdens. And such special grants or impositions may also amount to a denial of the equal protection of the laws under the Federal Constitution. Most of the state constitutions contain provisions, varying in detail, forbidding local or special legislation, although the Federal Constitution does not prohibit local or special laws as such.

§ 4:23. Permissible classification.

Am Jur 2d References: Constitutional Law, §§ 494–525.

The prohibition of discrimination embodied in the equal protection of the laws provisions of the Fourteenth Amendment to the Federal Constitution does not prevent a state from classifying persons, things, and acts or conduct for the purpose of legislation. Indeed, all legislation must necessarily involve some classification with respect to its subject matter. Hence, the use of the popular term, "class legislation" in this connection should be avoided by courts and lawyers. The guaranty of equal protection of the laws does not deprive the states of the power to classify the subjects of legislation. It does not prevent classification of persons, things, and acts, provided the classification is reasonable for the purpose of legislation, is based on proper and justifiable distinctions in view of the purpose of the law, is not clearly arbitrary, and is not a subterfuge to shield one class or unduly burden another or to oppress unlawfully in its administration.

In enacting laws on a subject within its constitutional powers, a state legislature has a broad discretion in establishing classifications. The courts have the final word in determining the constitutionality of a legislative classification, but they will overrule the legislative discretion only where the classification is determined to be clearly arbitrary and unreasonable or capricious. The requisites of a valid classification under the Fourteenth Amendment is that it must rest upon material differences between the persons, activities, or things included in it and those excluded, and that it must be based upon real and substantial distinctions. The objects and purposes of a law are important considerations in determining the validity of a legislative classification, and a classification to be valid must be based on a difference which bears a fair, substantial, natural, reasonable, and just relation to that object and purpose.

Another principle governing the constitutional validity of legislative classifications is that the law must affect alike all persons in the same class and under similar conditions. And not only must all persons within a class be treated equally and uniformly, but a classification, to meet the requirements of equal protection of the laws, must include or embrace all persons who naturally belong to the class. A classification having a reasonable basis does not offend the Federal Constitution merely because it is not made with scientific precision or mathematical nicety, or because there cannot be an exact exclusion or inclusion of persons and things and in practice some inequality results.

As stated above, the basis of classification permitted under the equal protection of the laws provision rests largely in the discretion of the legislature, subject to the requirement that it have some reasonable relation to the object of the legislation. Differentiation may be based upon size, amount, or numbers, where these factors are significant. Classification may be based on locality. And although discrimination against women is unconstitutional, the courts have approved legislation intended to protect women by prohibiting their employment in certain occupations and by prescribing maximum hours of labor for them. Classifications of business, trades, and professions for the purpose of regulation under the police power are permissible if based on reasonable grounds and actual differences.

XI. DUE PROCESS OF LAW

§ 4:24. Generally.

Am Jur 2d References: Constitutional Law, §§ 542–559.

The Fifth Amendment of the Constitution of the United States (a part of the Bill of Rights) provides that no person shall "be deprived of life, liberty, or property without due process of law." The Fourteenth Amendment provides that no state shall "deprive any person of life, liberty, or property without due process of law." The Fifth Amendment is a limitation upon the powers of the federal government and of Congress, while the Fourteenth Amendment is a limitation upon the powers of the states. Similar provisions appear in the constitutions of the states. The same meaning and construction is usually given to all of these due process guaranties.

The principle that no person should be deprived of life, liberty, or property except by due process of law did not originate in the American system of constitutional law. It was a part of the ancient English liberties, reaffirmed in the provision of Magna Charta that "No freeman shall be taken, or imprisoned, or be disseised of his freehold, or liberties, or free customs, or be outlawed, or exiled, or any otherwise destroyed; nor will we pass upon him, nor condemn him, but by lawful judgment of his peers, or by the law of the land." This principle came to America as a part of the common law which was the heritage of the English Colonies and of the states formed from them. The phrase "law of the land" meant the common and statute law then existing in England; and as adopted in America it refers to the same common law, as previously modified, as far as it is suited to the wants and conditions of the people.

The Supreme Court of the United States has never attempted to pronounce a precise and comprehensive definition of due process of law. For the most part, the courts have contented themselves, in ascertaining the intent and application of this phrase, with the process of judicial inclusion and exclusion, according to the circumstances of each case, as the cases are presented for decision. However, the courts have defined the phrase in general terms as meaning law in the regular course of administration, through courts of justice, according to those rules and forms which have been established for the protection of private rights. Substantially the same idea is embodied in the statement that due process of law means law according to the settled course of judicial proceedings or in accordance with natural, inherent, and fundamental principles of justice. A famous definition is that of Daniel Webster in his argument in the Dartmouth College Case (4 Wheat 518, 4 L Ed 629) in the Supreme Court, in which he declared that due process of law meant "a law which hears before it condemns; which proceeds upon inquiry, and renders judgment only after trial." It is recognized that due process of law is equivalent to "law of the land" as that phrase is used in Magna Charta and in state constitutions; but "law of the land" means that body of principles guaranteeing the basic and traditional rights of men, and not the actual existing laws of the jurisdiction. If it were otherwise, the requirement of due process would never be a restraint upon legislative power.

The concept of due process of law has a dual aspect, substantive and procedural. Procedural due process, discussed in the next section, relates to the requirements as to notice, hearing, and procedure. Substantive due process reaches those situations where the deprivation of life, liberty, or property is accomplished by legislation, which can, even if given the fairest procedure, destroy the enjoyment of all three of these rights. Substantive due process may be roughly defined as the constitutional guaranty that no person shall be deprived of his life, liberty, or property for arbitrary reasons. It is a limitation upon arbitrary power and a guaranty against arbitrary legislation, demanding that a law shall not be unreasonable, arbitrary, or capricious, and that the means selected shall have a real and substantial relation to the object sought to be attained.

The right to due process of law must rest upon a basis more substantial than favor or discretion, and a law may be unconstitutional because it vests in the courts or in other officials arbitrary and uncontrolled power over matters protected by the Constitution. Merely giving reasonable discretion, however, does not necessarily invalidate a law. Another requirement of due process of law is that of definiteness. A statute which either forbids or requires the doing of an act in terms so vague and indefinite that men of common intelligence must necessarily guess at its meaning and differ as to its application, violates a main esesntial of due process of law. This requirement is especially important in its application to criminal and penal statutes.

The due process of law clauses are binding upon the federal and state governments and upon all branches, tribunals, officials, and agencies thereof. They do not, however, inhibit or affect the freedom of action of private persons, unless there is an interplay of governmental and private action or governmental action is invoked to give effect to the private action. This clause protects all persons within the territorial jurisdiction, and it is not limited to citizens of the United States or of the state in which the question arises. Private corporations are regarded as "persons" entitled to the protection of the due process clause.

§ 4:25. Notice, hearing, and procedural requirements.

Am Jur 2d References: Constitutional Law, §§ 548, 549, 560–584.

Procedural due process of law requires that, before a person may be deprived of life, liberty, or property, he must be given notice of the proceedings against him, he must be given a hearing and an opportunity to defend himself, and the matter must be resolved by a competent tribunal and in a manner consistent with essential fairness. These requirements are reflected in the old adage that no one may be personally bound until he has had his day in court. The due process clause requires no particular form of procedure; it does not control the forms of procedure in state courts or regulate practice therein. A state may regulate the procedure in its courts in accordance with its own conception of policy and fairness so long as it does not offend some principle of justice ranked as fundamental, such as the requirements of notice and hearing, and so long as it is not arbitrary or unreasonable.

The notice required by procedural due process of law must be reasonable and adequate for the purpose. It must give sufficient notice of the pendency of the action or proceeding, and a reasonable opportunity to the party to appear and assert his rights. Actual knowledge or a casual or extraofficial notice is not sufficient. Constructive notice or publication of notice is sufficient in some types of cases. The requirement of notice or summons may be waived by a party; and where he voluntarily appears in an action the question of notice does not arise.

An opportunity for a hearing is one of the essential elements of due process of law. The hearing or proceeding must be appropriate, fair, adequate, and such as is practicable and reasonable in the particular case. It must be an orderly proceeding, before an impartial tribunal, adapted to the nature of the case, and must afford the person to be affected an opportunity to defend and enforce his rights. Obviously, a hearing by a judge who has an interest in the outcome of the case, or a criminal trial dominated by a mob, does not afford due process of law. A party has a constitutional right to be present at any trial or hearing, as well as the right to be represented by counsel. The rights of the accused in a criminal prosecution are discussed in Criminal Law, §§ 7:23–7:31.

Generally speaking, the requirements of due process are satisfied by one hearing which provides a full and fair opportunity within the principles discussed above. The right to appeal or review is not essential to due process, provided due process has already been accorded in the tribunal of first instance.

CONTRACTS

I. NATURE, FORMATION, AND REQUISITES OF CONTRACTS
A. IN GENERAL

B. OFFER AND ACCEPTANCE

C. CONSIDERATION

D. STATUTE OF FRAUDS

II. LEGALITY

III. CONSTRUCTION AND EFFECT

IV. MODIFICATION AND EXTINGUISHMENT

V. PERFORMANCE OR BREACH

I. NATURE, FORMATION, AND REQUISITES OF CONTRACTS

A. In General

§ 5:1. Generally; definitions.

Am Jur 2d References: Contracts, §§ 1–10, 15–17; Assignments, §§ 9–22, 33; Building and Construction Contracts, §§ 1–7.

In modern law books designed for the practicing lawyer and for efficient research, the vast field of Contracts has been subdivided into many topics. Even in the present work, elementary as it is, it has been found desirable to treat some aspects of the law of contracts in separate topics (for example, SALES, BILLS AND NOTES, and INSURANCE) rather than in the present comprehensive topic. Though the same basic principles of contract law apply in all of these special areas, each is subject to its own distinctive applications and variations of rules.

A "contract" has been defined in brief as a promise or set of promises for the breach of which the law gives a remedy or the performance of which the law recognizes as a duty. But this is of little help in determining the real nature of a contract and indicates that nothing less than the whole body of applicable precedents will suffice to define the term "contract."

The requirement for the formation of a contract is that there must be mutual assent of two or more persons competent to contract founded on a sufficient consideration, to perform or to omit to do some act, the performance or omission of which is not contrary to law or public policy, nor obviously impossible. This is perhaps as good a definition as any of a "contract."

Contracts are said to be either express, implied, or constructive. Contracts are express when their terms are stated by the parties, and an implied contract is one inferred from the conduct of the parties, though not expressed in words. And contracts may be implied either in law or in fact. Contracts implied in fact are inferred from the facts and circumstances of the case and are not formally or explicitly stated in words. The source of the obligation of both express contracts and contracts implied in fact is the manifested intention of the parties, the only distinction being that the implied contract between two parties is raised only when the facts and circumstances are such that an intent may fairly be inferred on their part to make such a contract. For example, there is generally an implied promise to pay for valuable services rendered with the knowledge and approval of the recipient and under circumstances warranting an expectation of payment from the party benefited.

Another aspect of contracts classifies them as either "bilateral" or "unilateral." A bilateral contract consists of mutual promises on the part of both parties to do some future act in which the consideration of the promise of one party is a promise, express or implied, by the other party. A contract is unilateral when the party who makes a promise has received a consideration other than a promise to make the contract binding, or, as otherwise defined, where there is a promise on one side only, the consideration therefor being an act or being executed. Typical of unilateral contracts are promissory notes.

There is an important distinction between "void" and "voidable" contracts. A void contract is no contract at all; it is a mere nullity and no disaffirmance is required to avoid it, nor can it be validated by ratification. A voidable contract, on the other hand, is binding until it is avoided by the party entitled to avoid it, and the defect therein may be cured by ratification by the party who might have avoided it.

There must always be at least two parties to a contract. And the parties must be competent to make a contract and not incapacitated by mental incompetency, infancy, or the like.

A party to a contract may, as a general rule, assign all his beneficial rights therein. A contract which involves no personal confidential relation and no exceptional personal skill is generally assignable. A party to a contract may not, however, assign an obligation so as to avoid liability on the contract and shift liability to an assignee, unless the latter assumes the obligation with the consent of the other party to the contract and the latter releases the assignor from further liability, thus effecting a novation. A contract may, by its terms, make clear the right of assignment, or it may expressly or by implication prohibit an assignment. Generally, executory contracts for personal service or involving a relationship of confidence are not assignable by either party. A right of action arising out of a breach of contract is generally assignable. Even where the contract as a whole is not assignable, because involving personal skill or the like, the proceeds or money to become due under the contract may be assignable.

§ 5:2. Assent; meeting of minds.

Am Jur 2d References: Contracts, §§ 18–30.

It is a basic prerequisite to the formation of a binding contract that there must be mutual assent or a meeting of the minds of the parties on all essential elements and terms. There can be no contract unless all the parties involved intended to enter into one. An objective test is generally applied, however, in determining the question of assent and intention to contract. This means that the outward manifestation of a party's intention in the form of overt acts and words, and not inward or subjective or secret intention or understanding, is determinative. Different meaning attached by the parties to ambiguous language used by either of them may preclude the assent or meeting of the minds essential to the formation of a contract. Where an offerer, using language of latent ambiguity, reasonably means one thing and the offeree reasonably understands that he meant another thing, there is no contract.

If any material thing remains to be done by one party to a proposed contract before it is assented to by the other, there is not a complete contract. A contract is not made so long as, in the contemplation of the parties, something remains to be done to establish contract relations. The parties may impose a condition precedent, the performance of which is essential to the creation of the contract, as where they agree that a writing will not ripen into a contract until it has been approved by a party's attorney.

An agreement to make a future contract is not a contract, unless the agreement specifies all of the material and essential terms of the contract and leaves none of them to be agreed upon in future negotiations. Whether the parties to an oral or informal agreement become bound prior to the drafting and execution of a contemplated formal writing is a question which depends largely upon their intention as to whether the writing is viewed by the parties merely as a convenient memorial or record of their previous contract or is intended as a condition precedent to the final creation of a contract. The intention of the parties in this regard is to be determined by the surrounding facts and circumstances of each particular case.

§ 5:3. Definiteness and certainty.

Am Jur 2d References: Contracts, §§ 75–84; Vendor and Purchaser (1st ed, §§ 6–9).

A contract must be definite and certain as to its terms and requirements. Absolute certainty is not required; only reasonable certainty, such as will enable the courts, through the process of judicial construction, to determine the intention of the parties, is necessary. The maxim "id certum est quod certum reddi potest" (that is certain which can be made certain) applies, and a contract will not be invalidated for indefiniteness or uncertainty if its meaning and the intention of the parties can with reasonable certainty be ascertained by the consideration of admissible extrinsic evidence. The subsequent conduct or declarations of the parties may eliminate doubt or uncertainty. A contract should be reasonably definite as to the time of its operation and performance; but a provision for performance in a reasonable time is sufficiently definite, and a promise to perform in a reasonable time may be implied where the agreement contains no express stipulation as to the time of performance. There must be reasonable certainty as to the subject matter of a contract and as to the consideration.

A reservation to either party of an unlimited right to determine the nature and extent of his performance renders his obligation too indefinite for legal enforcement. While a contract is generally held to be too indefinite to be enforceable if the price or compensation is to be determined arbitrarily by one of the parties, a contract or option is not objectionable because the purchase price of property is to be determined by the amount offered by a third party.

§ 5:4. Mutuality.

Am Jur 2d References: Contracts, §§ 11–13.

It is frequently stated as a broad general rule that there must be mutuality of obligation in order to form an enforceable contract. Taken literally, however, this is too broad a statement. Where the consideration for the promise of one party is a promise by the other party, the invalidity of one of the promises renders the contract subject to attack for lack of consideration. The doctrine of mutuality of obligation, therefore, appears to be merely another aspect of the rule of consideration.

Where there is some consideration for a promise other than a promise on the part of the promisee, and each promise does not depend upon the other for consideration, mutuality of obligation is not essential. For example, mutuality of obligation is not required of unilateral contracts. If the promisor has received a sufficient consideration, as by the payment of money or the performance of an undertaking by the promisee, the contract is not subject to attack on the ground of lack of mutuality..

Mutuality of remedy, as distinguished from mutuality of obligation, is not always essential. Clearly, such mutuality is not required in a unilateral contract; and it is not always required for a bilateral contract, as is shown by the instance where one of the promises may be unenforceable because of the statute of frauds or because a promisor is an infant. Whether mutuality is a prerequisite of the equitable remedy of specific performance is discussed below in §§ 5:36, 5:37.

§ 5:5. Formal requirements.

Am Jur 2d References: Alteration of Instruments, §§ 12, 30; Contracts, §§ 67–74; Exchange of Property, §§ 8, 9; Seals, §§ 1–11.

A contract may be oral or written or partly written and partly oral. It need not be in writing unless a statute requires it. The principal statute making such a requirement is the statute of frauds (discussed below in §§ 5:13–5:20), requiring a writing for such contracts as those not to be performed within a year, promises to answer for the debt or default of another, contracts involving estates or interests in land, and contracts for the sale of goods, wares, and merchandise exceeding a certain value.

Except for contracts, such as insurance policies, the form of which is regulated by statute, the form in which a written contract is drawn is immaterial, so long as it is intelligible. A valid contract may consist of a series of letters, writings, and telegrams between the parties. Unless a statute requires the contract to be in writing, there may be a verbal acceptance of a written offer, and vice versa.

At common law, certain contracts were required to be under seal, and a seal on an instrument imported a good consideration therefor. In most jurisdictions now, however, private seals have been abolished by statute and are of no effect, although certain corporate and official instruments may require seals.

If a contract is in writing, any material alteration of the executed instrument, intentionally made by a party claiming thereunder without the consent of the other party, renders it void as against the latter.

In the absence of a statutory requirement to the contrary, parties may be bound by the terms of a contract even though they do not sign it, where their assent is otherwise indicated; and the form, manner, and place of a signature on a contract is unimportant. As a general rule, while delivery may be essential to the validity and operation of a contract, neither manual transfer nor any particular form of ceremony is necessary to constitute a good delivery, which may be by acts without words, words without acts, or both words and acts, delivery being largely a matter of the intention of the parties.

§ 5:6. Mistake, fraud, duress, and undue influence.

Am Jur 2d References: Contracts, §§ 143–154; Duress and Undue Influence, §§ 1–49; Fraud and Deceit, §§ 1 et seq.; Vendor and Purchaser (1st ed §§ 48–96).

A contract may be avoided on the ground of mistake of fact where the mistake is common to both parties and relates to an existing or past fact which is material and of the essence of the agreement, such as the subject matter, the price, or the terms of the contract. Such a mistake is commonly referred to as a "mutual mistake."

A unilateral mistake does not ordinarily avoid a contract unless accompanied by other factors affecting its validity. A party cannot avoid a contract on the ground that he made a mistake, where there has been no misrepresentation, there is no ambiguity in the terms of the contract, and the other party has no notice of the mistake and acts in good faith. Contracting parties are bound by the meaning of the words used in a contract as properly interpreted, even though one of the parties believed that the words meant something different, unless the other party knew of such mistake. Where a writing conveys a meaning not intended by either party, however, it may be reformed. There is a conflict of authority on the effect of a mistake in a telegram during contract negotiations resulting from the negligence of a telegraph company in the transmission of the message.

As a general rule, one who executes or accepts a written contract is conclusively presumed to know its contents and to assent to them, in the absence of fraud, misrepresentation, or other wrongful act by another contracting party. Ignorance of the contents of a written contract does not ordinarily affect the liability of one executing it, and failure to read a contract before signing it will not, as a general rule, affect its binding force. There may be circumstances, however, under which the failure to read a contract is excusable and the party is not precluded from attacking its validity.

A contract induced by material fraud perpetrated by one party upon the other may be avoided by the latter, although the right to assert the fraud may be waived. And the general rule that failure to read a contract before signing it precludes a party from complaining of its contents does not apply in the case of fraud or misrepresentation, as where he is prevented from reading it by some fraud or artifice of the other party or is fraudulently led to believe that the instrument is of a different character.

Duress, coercion, intimidation, threats, or undue influence may be such as to invalidate a contract. Where duress is exerted on one of the parties, of such a kind as to overcome his will and compel a formal assent to an agreement undertaken when he does not really agree to it, the agreement is not binding upon him. Agreements procured by duress may be ratified after the duress is removed. Influence exerted by a person occupying a fiduciary, confidential, or dominant relationship to the other party to the contract may, under certain circumstances, invalidate a contract although the conduct in question would not amount to duress as between persons dealing at arms' length.

B. Offer and Acceptance

§ 5:7. Offer.

Am Jur 2d References: Contracts, §§ 31–40; Exchange of Property, § 6; Rewards, §§ 5–12.

The formation of a contract contemplates an offer and an acceptance thereof. An offer must be definite and certain. A mere intention to do an act is not an offer to do it. It is necessary that the offer be communicated or published. A mere invitation to enter into negotiations does not amount to an offer. An offer need not be addressed to a particular individual in order to constitute a proposal which may be converted into a contract by acceptance. A binding obligation may even originate in advertisements addressed to the general public, such as offers of rewards.

In the absence of a specification of its duration or circumstances creating a limitation, an offer continues for a reasonable time. The person making an offer, not supported by consideration, may revoke it at any time before acceptance. In the absence of statutes to the contrary, an offer, unless made upon a sufficient consideration, can be withdrawn even though it provides that it cannot be withdrawn or purports to give the offeree a definite time to accept. On the other hand, a continuing offer supported by a good consideration, such as an option, cannot be withdrawn before the time agreed upon.

The death of a party after an offer is made and before the completion of the contract terminates the possibility of a contract. An offer is terminated by rejection and cannot thereafter be accepted so as to create a contract.

§ 5:8. Acceptance.

Am Jur 2d References: Contracts, §§ 41–66; Exchange of Property, § 6; Rewards, §§ 13–17; Vendor and Purchaser (1st ed, §§ 15–22).

To constitute a contract, there must be an acceptance of an offer. The acceptance of an offer gives rise to a binding contract and the offer cannot thereafter be withdrawn or varied. Nor can the acceptance be revoked after it is made. An offer may be accepted only by the person or persons to whom it is made.

As a general rule, the acceptance of an offer must be communicated to the offeror, unless the offer itself contemplates that acceptance may be by the performance of an act. Except for contracts required by statute to be in writing, the acceptance of an offer need not be in any particular form and may be by parol or implied from the circumstances. However, the conditions of the offer, such as those as to time, place, or manner of acceptance, must be complied with. Where the offer is published to the world and a person acts upon it and fulfils its conditions before it is withdrawn, the offeror is bound to perform his promise. Typical of such offers are offers of rewards and prospectuses of corporations.

As a general rule, silence or mere failure to reject an offer does not constitute an acceptance. Under exceptional circumstances, however, an inference of assent and acceptance may be warranted by silence or inaction.

An offer may ordinarily be accepted by mail. And where such an acceptance is authorized, the acceptance becomes effective, and a binding contract arises, at the time the acceptance, duly addressed and stamped, is deposited in the post office. The offer cannot be withdrawn unless the withdrawal reaches the party to whom it is addressed before his letter of acceptance has been mailed. The authorities are not in harmony as to the effect of the right of the party to withdraw his letter of acceptance from the mails. The party accepting must be alive when the letter of acceptance is mailed. But the contract completed by the mailing is not affected by his subsequent death. Acceptance of an offer may be manifested by telephone or telegraph. Acceptance by telegram is generally governed by the same rules as those governing correspondence through the post office.

An acceptance must comply with the terms of the offer without any substantial or material variance. The acceptance must be unequivocal and unconditional and may not introduce additional terms or conditions. By making a conditional acceptance, the offeree rejects the offer and he cannot thereafter revive it by tendering an unconditional acceptance of it. The offeror may, of course, by words or conduct, accept and be bound by qualifications or conditions tendered by the offeree in his acceptance.

§ 5:9. Options.

> Am Jur 2d References: Contracts, §§ 32, 60, 61; Vendor and Purchaser (1st ed, §§ 27–43).

A continuing offer which is to be kept open for a certain time and which is based upon a sufficient consideration is termed an option. An option may be defined as an agreement by which one binds himself to perform a certain act, usually the transfer of property, under stipulated terms, leaving it to the person to whom the option is given to accept upon the terms specified. In essence, an option is both a contract and a continuing offer. Considered as a contract, the distinguishing characteristic of an option is that it enforces no binding obligation upon the person holding the option. While an option, to be irrevocable, must be based upon a consideration, if the party to whom it is given accepts it or exercises it before it has been withdrawn, a valid contract results notwithstanding the lack of consideration for the option itself. There may be a valid option to purchase at a price offered to the optionor by a third person.

Upon acceptance by the optionee, an option becomes effective as a complete and mutual contract. But the option must be fully and completely accepted in all its parts within the time and in the manner provided in the option agreement before it can become an executory contract. The requisites attached to the acceptance of ordinary offers generally apply to the acceptance or exericse of options.

C. CONSIDERATION

§ 5:10. Necessity and sufficiency, generally.

Am Jur 2d References: Bonds, §§ 10, 11; Building and Construction Contracts, §§ 5–7; Contracts, §§ 85–118; Exchange of Property, § 7; Subscriptions (1st ed, §§ 10–15); Vendor and Purchaser (1st ed, §§ 23–26).

Consideration is defined as some right, interest, profit, or benefit accruing to one party, or some forbearance, detriment, loss, or responsibility given, suffered, or undertaken by the other. Consideration for a promise is commonly defined as any benefit to the promisor or any detriment to the promisee.

It is a well-settled general rule that consideration is an essential element of, and is necessary to, the enforceability or validity of a contract. In other words, a promise not supported by any consideration does not amount to an enforceable contract.

Nothing is consideration for a contract that is not accepted or regarded as such by both parties. The mere possibility of some fortuitous or incidental benefit or detriment, not considered by the parties as an inducement, is not a consideration. The motive which subjectively prompts one to enter into a contract is a different thing from the consideration for the contract. Love and affection or family relationships, although sufficient to support a deed or a contract completely executed, is not sufficient consideration to support an executory contract.

Generally, if consideration is otherwise sufficient, it does not matter from whom or to whom it moves. The consideration may move to the promisor or a third person, and it may be given by the promisee or a third person.

It is a general rule that the courts will not inquire into the adequacy of the consideration for a contract. Consideration is not insufficient merely because it is inadequate. Consideration sufficient to support one promise is sufficient to support any number of promises. However, if the consideration is so grossly inadequate as to shock the conscience, there may be a finding of fraud.

Mutual promises are sufficient considerations for each other. A promise by one party is a sufficient consideration for a promise by the other party, provided that the promises are binding. Equality of value or benefit is not essential. A conditional promise, and even a voidable promise, have been held to be sufficient consideration for a contract. The waiver or relinquishment of a legal right or privilege is sufficient consideration for a promise. In the absence of fraud or other invalidating circumstances, the surrender of a disputed or doubtful claim or right is a sufficient consideration for an agreement compromising or settling the claim or for an executory contract. The rule is otherwise, however, if the claim has no semblance of merit or foundation in law or equity.

The extension of time for the performance of a contract or the payment of a debt, if for a definite time, constitutes a sufficient consideration for a contract. Forbearance from exercising a right or doing an act which one has a right to do, or a promise to forbear or delay, is sufficient consideration, where the forbearance is requested and treated as consideration.

Subscription agreements are subject to quite liberal principles as regards consideration. For example, the fact that, upon the face of a subscription, moneys have been expended, liabilities incurred or acts performed may constitute a good consideration for a subscription; and the mutual promises of subscribers or the obligation assumed by the donee to apply the moneys subscribed in a certain way may be a sufficient consideration to support a subscription.

§ 5:11. Past consideration or existing obligation.

Am Jur 2d References: Contracts, §§ 119–129.

The general rule is that a promise to do that which the promisor is already legally bound to do, or the performance of an existing legal obligation, does not constitute a sufficient consideration for a contract. The payment of a debt which is due and undisputed will not constitute consideration for a promise, and a promise to pay a debt for which the promisor is already bound is not a consideration sufficient to support a new contract. The payment of all or part of a debt before it is due, however, may be a sufficient consideration for a promise by the creditor. In accordance with principles of accord and satisfaction, the part payment of an unliquidated or disputed claim may be a sufficient consideration or a promise to discharge the entire claim. The rule is otherwise in the case of a liquidated or undisputed debt, but the courts are inclined to seize upon any circumstance, such as a part payment made in a manner different from that required by the contract or before the maturity of the debt, or a part payment made by a third person, to uphold the agreement. And in some jurisdictions, by judicial decision or statute, the general rule as to part payment of undisputed claims has been abrogated.

The courts differ on the question whether there is a sufficient consideration for a promise by a third person made to induce a party to an existing contract to perform the contract.

It is a general rule that past consideration is insufficient to support a promise. Something given or done before a promise is made, and therefore without reference to it, does not constitute legal consideration. However, it is generally held that an express promise, made to a person entitled to the performance of an existing legal obligation, will be enforced. Thus, although a promise to do a thing which the promisor is legally bound to do is not sufficient consideration to support a reciprocal undertaking by the promisee, such promise may be enforced against the promisor.

Where the past act or service was performed by one person under circumstances implying a promise to pay therefor, an express promise to pay, made after the rendition of the service, has been held to be supported by a good consideration.

§ 5:12. Moral obligation.

Am Jur 2d References: Contracts, §§ 130–142.

"Moral obligation," per se, is not a sufficient consideration for an executory promise. Decisions sometimes attributed to a supposed exception to this rule are usually explainable upon conventional concepts of consideration, such as a benefit to the promisor or a detriment to the promisee. Other decisions attributed to "moral obligation" are actually founded upon equitable or imperfect legal duties, such as obligations that are voidable or are unenforceable because of some legal technicality. In this broad category are the decisions upholding the validity of a promise by an adult to pay an obligation incurred while he was an infant; a promise by a bankrupt to pay a debt barred by his bankruptcy; an undertaking by a surety to remain liable on an obligation from which he has been discharged by an extention of time to his principal; and a new promise based on an obligation barred by the statute of limitations or unenforceable under the statute of frauds.

D. Statute of Frauds

§ 5:13. Generally.

Am Jur 2d References: Statute of Frauds (1st ed, §§ 1–3, 532–580, 586–602).

The English statute of frauds, effective in 1677 and adopted with variations throughout the United States, provided that no action shall be brought on contracts specified therein unless the agreement or some memorandum or note thereof be in writing and signed by the party to be charged or some other person lawfully authorized. The inhibited contracts include agreements by an executor or administrator to answer in damages out of his own estate; agreements to answer for the debt, default, or miscarriage of another; agreements made upon consideration of marriage; agreements not to be performed within one year from the making thereof; contracts for the sale of lands, tenements, or hereditaments or any interest therein; and agreements for the sale of goods, wares, and merchandise in excess of a specified value. Most American statutes of frauds contain a provision, similar to that of Lord Tenterden's Act, to the effect that no action shall be brought to charge a person upon, or by reason of, any representation as to the character, credit, or dealings of another, unless it is made in writing.

In addition to the statute of frauds, there are numerous statutes in the several states requiring that particular classes of contracts and agreements be in writing.

In its original form, and as adopted in most American states, the statute of frauds did not render entirely void a contract not complying with its requirements. The effect of the statute is merely to render such contracts voidable and unenforceable at the option of the party sought to be charged. In some states, however, the statutes expressly provide that specified contracts shall be void if not in writing.

Where a part of a contract is within the statute of frauds and a portion of it is not, the enforceability of the latter portion depends upon the question whether the contract is an entire or severable one. If a parol contract is entire and indivisible, the whole contract is unenforceable although part of it is not covered by the statute of frauds. On the other hand, if the contract is a severable one, susceptible of division and apportionment, having two or more parts not necessarily dependent on each other, and if the several stipulations are not so interdependent but that a separate and distinct engagement as to one stipulation may reasonably be extracted from the whole, those which are not required by the statute of frauds to be in writing may be enforced.

As the statute of frauds applies only to executory contracts, it does not apply after a contract has been executed. Where so much of a divisible contract as would bring it within the statute has been executed, the remaining parts become enforceable, but not so where the portion of the contract which has been performed was not within the statute of frauds, and it is sought to enforce the portion which is within the statute.

A party who refuses to complete a contract unenforceable by reason of the statute of frauds, after having derived a benefit from a part performance by the other party, must pay for or return that which he received under the contract. The basis of recovery in such cases is not the contract itself, but the implied promise raised by the law to pay for the reasonable value of the benefits received. Thus, a party may recover back payments made under a contract unenforceable under the statute, where the other party refuses to perform.

The party to be charged upon a contract not meeting the requirements of the statute of frauds may waive the defense based on the statute, and generally he will be deemed to have done so unless he pleads the statute as a defense. Also, the defense of the statute is personal to the party himself and his privies, and it is not available to strangers.

§ 5:14. Contracts to which statute applies.

Am Jur 2d References: Statute of Frauds (1st ed, §§ 4–22, 301– 312).

The provision of the statute of frauds requiring that an agreement made in consideration of marriage be in writing does not apply to mutual promises to marry.

A written contract may be modified by a subsequent parol agreement, provided that the contract is not such as is required by statute to be in writing. In the latter case, it is generally held that any modification of the contract must also be in writing. There is a conflict of authority on the validity or enforceability of a parol rescission or abrogation of a contract required by the statute to be in writing.

The Uniform Commercial Code provides that the requirements of its statute of frauds section must be satisfied in the making of an agreement modifying a contract within the Code, if the contract as modified is within its provisions (UCC § 2–209).

§ 5:15. —Agreement not to be performed within a year.

Am Jur 2d References: Statute of Frauds (1st ed, §§ 23–59).

The negative form of the provision of the statute of frauds relating to contracts "not to be performed" within a year has led to the rule that the provision of the statute relates only to oral agreements which cannot possibly be performed within a year. If, by the terms of the agreement, there is a possibility of performance within a year, it is not within the statute. The mere eventuality or probability that more than a year may be required for performance does not bring the agreement within the statute. If performance is possible and permissible within a year, the fact that a longer maximum period is permitted or that no time for performance is fixed does not bring the contract within this provision of the statute.

There is conflict of authority on the question of the applicability of this provision of the statute where there is performance or possibility of performance on the part of one party within a year but not on the part of the other party. The view which seems to be favored by the majority is that this statute does not apply if the contract was to be performed and has been fully performed by the plaintiff within a year, although the defendant was not to perform his part of the contract within that time.

It is generally held that an agreement, the performance or duration of which is contingent on the duration of human life, is not within the statute, because a performance may be had within a year if death occurs within that time. It is generally held that a contract to refrain from doing a personal act, such as engaging in a particular business or calling, is not within this provision of the statute, because the death of the promisor may occur within a year. And the same reasoning removes from the operation of the statute an agreement to make a testamentary provision.

Contracts for personal services are subject to the general principal that if a contract is capable of full performance within a year, it is not within the statute. Where, however, the contract of employment is for a stated period longer than a year, the statute is generally held to be applicable, even though death may terminate the contract within the year. An employment contract terminable at the will of either party is not within this provision of the statute; nor are agreements to employ a person as long as he lives and proves competent, or the like.

§ 5:16. —Promise to answer for debt or default of another.

Am Jur 2d References: Statute of Frauds (1st ed, §§ 60–148).

A promise to answer for the debt, default, or miscarriage of another, within the meaning of this provision of the statute of frauds, has been defined as an undertaking by a person not before liable for the purpose of securing or performing the same duty for which the original obligor continues to be liable. The distinction between a promise to answer for the debt or default of another person, which is within the statute, and an independent obligation of the promisor, which is not within the statute, is the subject of much difficulty and confusion. No universal test of difference between an original undertaking and a collateral one has been established. It may be said generally, however, that an undertaking which renders the promisor a guarantor or surety upon a debt owing by a third person who is primarily liable is within the statute of frauds, whether made before, after, or contemporaneously with the inception of the third person's liability, if the promisee knows or should know of the guaranty or suretyship relation. If the original obligor remains liable, the undertaking of the new promisor usually falls within this provision of the statute.

The intention of the parties, ascertained from the words used and the attendant circumstances, usually controls in determining the person to whom credit is extended, and this fact usually determines whether a promise made before credit was furnished is collateral and within the statute or original and without the statute.

An obligation incurred jointly by two persons is not an undertaking by one to answer for the debt of the other. And a promise not made to the person entitled to enforce the liability assumed by the promisor is not within the statute. The terms "default or miscarriage" include a liability for a tort.

The mere fact that an oral promise to pay the debt of another is based upon adequate consideration does not take it out of the statute of frauds, at least if the consideration consists merely of harm to the creditor and is not beneficial to the promisor, unless the consideration is the discharge of the original debtor.

§ 5:17. —Estates and interests in land.

Am Jur 2d References: Statute of Frauds (1st ed, §§ 149–235).

Probably the most important provisions of the statute of frauds are those invalidating the transfer of real property by parol or livery of seisin only. The original English statute, and its counterparts adopted in the United States, require that any estate or interest in real estate (except leases extending for not more than a certain period, usually from 1 to 3 years) must be in writing. The statute also provides that no action shall be brought to charge any person upon any contract involving any real property or any interest therein unless the agreement or some memorandum or note thereof is in writing.

The terms "interest" or "estate" in land, as used in the statute of frauds, means some portion of the title or right of possession, and does not include agreements which may affect land but which do not contemplate the transfer of any title, ownership, or possession.

According to the great weight of authority, growing crops which are the product of annual cultivation, as distinguished from the natural product of the soil, are regarded as personal property and not an interest in land, under the statute. On the other hand, a contract for the sale of standing timber is generally regarded as one concerning an interest in land, as is a sale of mining or mineral rights. Generally, a contract relating to the disposition of the proceeds of land in case of its sale is not one for an interest in the land within the meaning of the statute.

An easement is clearly an interest in land within the meaning of the statute. And a profit a prendre, which is a right to take or use a part of the soil or produce of land, such as an exclusive right to hunt or fish in the lands or waters of another or to take coal therefrom, cannot be created by parol. On the other hand, a mere license in real property, which is a permission to enter the land to do certain acts, does not give an interest in the land and may be created by parol.

The English statute and some American statutes provide that an assignment of a leasehold must be in writing. However, where a written lease provides for its renewal or extension for an additional time at the opinion of the lessee, the exercise of the option is not affected by the statute.

A mortgage of real estate is clearly a conveyance of an estate or interest in land within the meaning of the statute. So is an exchange of lands or a contract therefor. And the better view is that the interest of the vendee under a land contract cannot be transferred or assigned by parol. It is settled that the statute of frauds requires an agreement to devise real estate to be in writing. A gift of real estate cannot be made by parol.

Many of the statutes except from their operation transfers by operation of law. While a sale of land by an officer under execution is held to be within the statute of frauds, and not effective until the execution of a deed, a judicial sale under order of a court is not within the statute.

§ 5:18. —Sale of personal property.

Am Jur 2d References: Statute of Frauds (1st ed, §§ 236–300).

Most of the states have adopted statutes, similar to the English statute of frauds, providing in effect that no contract for the sale of goods, wares, and merchandise for a price exceeding a specified sum shall be good except where the buyer accepts part of the goods or gives something in earnest to bind the bargain, or in part payment, unless some note or memorandum in writing of the bargain is made and signed by the parties or their agents.

The adoption of the Uniform Commercial Code has effected changes in the statute of frauds and in the Uniform Sales Act with respect to sales of various kinds of personal property. The Uniform Commercial Code (UCC § 2–201) provides that a contract for the sale of goods for the price of $500 or more is not enforceable by way of action or defense unless there is some writing sufficient to indicate that a contract for sale has been made between the parties and signed by the party against whom enforcement is sought, or by his authorized agent or broker. A writing is not insufficient because it omits or incorrectly states a term agreed upon, but the contract is not enforceable beyond the quantity of goods shown in such writing. As between merchants, a written confirmation is sufficient as against both parties unless there is a written objection thereto within 10 days after the confirmation is received. If it is otherwise valid, a contract not satisfying these requirements is enforceable if the goods are to be specially manufactured for the buyer and are not suitable for sale to others in the ordinary course of the seller's business, and the seller, before notice of repudiation, has made a substantial beginning of their manufacture or commitment for their procurement, or if the party against whom enforcement is sought admits the making of the contract in legal proceedings, or with respect to goods for which payment has been made and accepted or which have been received and accepted. Any "or return" provision is treated as a separate contract for sale and must satisfy the requirements of the statute of frauds provisions (UCC § 2–326(4)).

Separate but similar provisions are made (UCC § 8–319) governing the sale of securities. As regards such sales, no amount or value is fixed by the Code, and the provision relating to written confirmation is not limited to transactions between merchants.

A separate provision of the Uniform Commercial Code (UCC § 1–206) applies to sales of personal property of types, such as bilateral contracts, royalty rights, and other general intangibles, not otherwise provided for in the Code. This general provision is that, except in the cases described in other sections, a contract for the sale of personal property is not enforceable by way of action or defense beyond $5,000 in amount or value unless there is some writing which indicates that a contract for sale has been made between the parties at a defined or stated price, reasonably identifies the subject matter, and is signed by the party against whom enforcement is sought, or by his authorized agent. Under this provision a parol contract may be enforced up to the limit of $5,000.

§ 5:19. Memorandum.

Am Jur 2d References: Statute of Frauds (1st ed, §§ 313–418).

The original English statute of frauds provided that no action shall be brought on certain specified contracts "unless the agreement upon which such action shall be brought, or some memorandum or note thereof, shall be in writing and signed by the party to be charged therewith, or some other person thereonto by him lawfully authorized." Similar provisions, with some variations, have been enacted in the American jurisdictions. As regards contracts for the sale of goods and other personal property, these provisions have been largely superseded by the Uniform Commercial Code, discussed above, § 5:18.

The memorandum referred to in the statute is regarded as merely evidence of the contract and not as the contract itself. Hence, it is not necessary that it be made and signed at the time of the making of the contract. No particular form of language or instrument is required of the memorandum or note in writing under the statute. The memorandum may consist of letters or telegrams or of several different writings.

Generally speaking, a memorandum in writing meets the requirements of the statute of frauds if it contains the names of the parties, the terms and conditions of the contract, and a description of the property sufficient to render it capable of identification. The memorandum should show not only who is the person to be charged but also the other party. In the case of a contract to sell land, the memorandum must describe not only the land but also the interest therein which is to be conveyed. The memorandum must contain the essential terms of the contract so that they may be understood from the memorandum itself or some other writing to which it refers, although it need not state in detail all of the particulars of the contract so long as its essential terms and substance are stated.

Same statutes of frauds expressly require that the memorandum contain a statement of the consideration, while other statutes expressly provide that the memorandum need not state the consideration. In the absence of such a specific provision, there is a conflict of authority on the question whether the memorandum must state the consideration for the contract.

As the statute of frauds merely requires that the contract be signed by the party to be charged or his duly or lawfully authorized agent, it is generally held not to be necessary that the agent's authority be conferred by writing. This is sometimes required by statute, however, in regard to certain contracts.

§ 5:20. Part performance and estoppel.

Am Jur 2d References: Statute of Frauds (1st ed, §§ 419–531, 578–585).

Except in a few jurisdictions, it is settled that part performance of a parol contract for the sale of real estate has the effect, if the nature and extent of the acts of performance meet the requirements prescribed by the courts, of taking the contract from the operation of the statute of frauds, so that a court of equity may decree its specific performance or grant other equitable relief thereon. The basis of this doctrine is that it would be a fraud upon the plaintiff if the defendant were permitted to escape performance of the oral agreement after he has permitted the plaintiff to perform in reliance on the agreement: that courts of equity will not allow the statute of frauds to be used as an instrument of fraud. The basis of the doctrine of part performance lies in the same principles which invoke the doctrine of equitable estoppel.

The acts relied upon as a part performance of a parol contract for the sale of land must be such as bring about a change in the plaintiff's position and would result in fraud, injustice, or hardship upon him if the contract were not enforced. The situation must be such that the court cannot restore the performing party to his original position, except by enforcing the contract. The acts of part performance must be referable to and induced by the contract, and they must have been performed on the faith of the contract and in reliance upon the performance thereof by the defendant. The performance must have been done with the knowledge and consent or acquiescence of the defendant.

The sufficiency of particular acts relied upon to remove a parol contract from the statute of frauds depends upon many factors and upon the equities of the whole case. In some jurisdictions, but not in others, the delivery of possession to the vendee pursuant to the parol contract is itself a sufficient part performance. The making of valuable permanent improvements on the land by the purchaser, in pursuance of the parol agreement and with the knowledge of the vendor, is generally held to be a sufficient part performance. The view is followed in most jurisdictions that the mere payment of purchase money by the purchaser, without other acts, is not a sufficient part performance for this purpose. But where payment is accompanied by other acts of performance, or where otherwise fraud or irreparable injury would result to the vendee, it may be sufficient to invoke the doctrine of part performance.

The rendition of services by the vendee in consideration of the vendor's promise to convey is ordinarily not sufficient part performance to remove an oral contract from the operation of the statute of frauds, since the vendee can be adequately compensated for his services without enforcing the contract.

The doctrine of part performance is frequently applied to an oral agreement to devise land, and even to parol gifts of land, where the plaintiff has changed his position to his detriment in reliance upon or performance of the agreement.

As a general rule, the doctrine of part performance is not applicable to a parol contract not to be performed within a year. There is a conflict of authority as to whether and when the doctrine will be applied to an agreement made in consideration of marriage.

Apart from the doctrine of part performance as such, and on principles of equity similar to those supporting that doctrine, courts of equity frequently deny a defendant the right to assert the statute of frauds where to do so would operate as a fraud upon the plaintiff or where the elements of equitable estoppel operate against the defendant.

II. LEGALITY

§ 5:21. Generally.

Am Jur 2d References: Contracts, §§ 155–164, 181–192, 216–239; Damages, §§ 212–235.

Contracts which are contrary to law, morality, or public policy are illegal and void. An agreement to do an illegal act or to accomplish an unlawful purpose is itself illegal. If the effect of an agreement is to accomplish an unlawful purpose, the agreement is illegal regardless of the intention of the parties. Contracts resting upon an illegal consideration are invalid. Illegal consideration consists of any act or forebearance contrary to law or public policy. As a general rule, an illegal contract cannot be validated by a waiver of its illegality or by the application of the doctrine of estoppel.

Where an agreement is capable of performance in a legal manner, however, the mere fact that one of the parties intended to perform it in an illegal manner will not preclude its enforcement. And, according to the rule prevailing in most jurisdictions, mere knowledge by one party to a contract of the other party's intention to use the subject matter for an illegal or unlawful purpose does not make the contract illegal. But a party's participation in the unlawful intention or purpose of the other party renders the agreement illegal.

Included in the class of contracts held to be illegal are agreements tending to promote immoral, criminal, or tortious acts, fraud or deception, and breach of trust or breach of contract. An agreement to commit a tort is clearly illegal. So are agreements tending to promote or encourage illicit sexual relations. A provision of a contract purporting to exempt a party from liability for his own fraud is invalid because of public policy.

A stipulation for a penalty for nonperformance of a contract, as distinguished from liquidated damages therefor, is invalid and unenforceable. There is a conflict of authority on the legality of a stipulation for the payment of attorneys' fees, costs of collection, or legal expenses in a contract, note, or other instrument.

The general rule is that illegal agreements are void and the courts will not recognize rights as springing therefrom but will leave the parties where they find them. This rule is not absolute, however, or without exceptions. Relief may be granted to a party who is not in pari delicto or in equal fault with the other party or to one who has disaffirmed or repudiated the illegal part of an agreement while it was still wholly executory. And in determining whether illegality renders a contract absolutely void or merely voidable, the courts sometimes distinguish between acts and situations which are mala in se and those which are merely mala prohibita. And where a class of contracts is prohibited (for example, usurious contracts) for the protection of particular parties, the adverse parties cannot take advantage of the illegality of such contracts. The unenforceability of a stipulation because of its illegality does not affect the validity and enforceability of other provisions of the agreement, provided they are severable from the invalid portion.

§ 5:22. Contracts contrary to statute, ordinance, or public policy.

Am Jur 2d References: Contracts, §§ 165–180; Gambling, §§ 186–262; Indemnity, §§ 9–12; Sundays and Holidays (1st ed, §§ 43–71); Usury (1st ed, §§ 87–136).

It is a well-settled general rule that an agreement which violates a provision of the federal or a state constitution or of a valid statute or ordinance, or which cannot be performed without violating such a provision, is illegal and void.

The same is true of contracts contrary to public policy. Courts of justice will not uphold any transaction which, in its object, operation, or tendency, is calculated to be prejudicial to the public welfare, to sound morality, or to civic honesty. What the public policy is must be determined from a consideration of the federal and state constitutions, the laws, the decisions of the courts, and the course of administration. Obviously, public policy changes with changes in the laws or in the generally prevailing and accepted standards of human conduct. Whether or not a contract violates public policy is determined by the public policy existing at the time the contract was made.

The statutes of many states declare contracts based on gambling or wagering considerations to be invalid, and even in the absence of such statutes, the courts have generally refused to enforce wagering contracts. Whether or not they will be enforced where the wagering is legal under the laws of the state is a question on which the courts are not agreed. So long as an illegal gambling contract remains executory, however, it may be repudiated and rescinded, and the money paid or wagered thereunder may be recovered back. And in many jurisdictions there are statutes enabling the loser to recover back money or property lost or paid in a gambling contract.

Contracts made or to be performed on a Sunday are in some states prohibited by law and are declared to be invalid. The effect of a provision for usurious interest in a contract or instrument depends upon the terms of the local statute. Some statutes declare the entire contract void if it is tainted with usury. Other statutes bar recovery of any interest, while still others merely limit the recovery of interest to the lawful rate.

Although the majority view was to the contrary in the early days, the overwhelming trend of modern authority is to the effect that a contract to indemnify against the negligence of the indemnitee is valid and not contrary to law or public policy.

§ 5:23. Contracts affecting administration of justice or public service or officials.

Am Jur 2d References: Contracts, §§ 193–215.

Agreements which have a tendency to obstruct, control, or interfere with the administration of justice or to oust courts of their jurisdiction are contrary to public policy and invalid, even though they do not involve actual corruption.

An agreement to pay an ordinary witness amenable to process more than the regular fee, or to pay any witness compensation contingent on the result of the case, is void. On the other hand, an agreement employing a person to render services in gathering evidence to be used at a trial is valid, unless the agreement further requires the contracting party to furnish evidence to win the suit. Agreements to suppress testimony or conceal evidence are, of course, invalid.

Agreements tending to suppress legal investigations concerning crimes or to stifle criminal prosecutions are illegal. An agreement to compound a crime, that is, to accept compensation in return for an understanding that the offender will not be prosecuted, is illegal, and promises made in consideration thereof are unenforceable. The actual guilt or innocence of the person charged with crime does not affect the validity of an agreement to compound the crime or suppress a prosecution. However, there is no legal objection to an agreement between the injured party and a person committing a crime to compensate the former for civil injuries resulting from a criminal act, so long as there is no express or implied agreement or understanding that the criminal shall not be prosecuted.

Agreements to control the operations of government, the appointment of public officers, or the course of legislation, as well as contracts which tend to introduce personal influence to procure action by any department of the government, are generally illegal. But this does not invalidate agreements to render proper professional services intended to influence the action of public officers. The legality of agreements to influence administrative or executive officers or departments is determined in each case by weighing all of the elements involved.

III. CONSTRUCTION AND EFFECT

§ 5:24. Generally.

Am Jur 2d References: Contracts, §§ 240–301, 320–328; Customs and Usages, §§ 21–28.

The construction or interpretation of a contract is the determination of the meaning attached to the words, written or spoken, which make up the contract. If the terms of a writing are clear and unambiguous, there is no room for construction, and the meaning of the language should be determined without reference to extrinsic facts. On the other hand, agreements inartificially drafted or containing language which is obscure, imperfect, or ambiguous are always open to interpretation. But a court may not make a new contract for the parties or revise or rewrite their contract under the guise of construction.

The object of all rules of construction is to arrive at the intention of the parties as it is expressed in the contract. This intention is presumed to be that manifested by the terms of the contract, and if this is clear and unambiguous, the court will not inquire into any actual or secret intentions or motives of the parties. However, contracts are to be construed in the frame of reference of their subject matter, their nature, and their object.

Words used in a contract will be given their ordinary meaning where nothing appears to indicate that they were used in a different sense; and if the terms have a definite legal meaning, the parties will be presumed to have intended such terms to have their proper legal effect. Technical terms, words of art, or words connected with a particular trade will ordinarily be given the signification attached to them by experts in such art or trade.

Where the contract is ambiguous or uncertain, the surrounding circumstances at the time it was made will be considered for the purpose of ascertaining the intention of the parties. In such cases, the construction placed upon the contract by the parties themselves will be considered by the court.

Since the contracting parties are presumed to contract in reference to the existing law, all applicable statutes, ordinances, regulations, and other law of the land become a part of the contract and will be read into it. And parties will be deemed to have contracted with reference to customs and usages which are established and known to them, and such customs and usages may be considered in determining the meaning of an ambiguous contract.

Where the parties intend a writing to be the sole memorial or integration of the contract, the construction of the contract consists of the construction of the writing. All prior negotiations become embodied in the writing and it merges all prior correspondence, negotiations, and verbal agreements. If the contract, as written, is unambiguous, the preliminary negotiations and other extrinsic matters tending to vary or contradict its provisions cannot be considered in construing the contract. On the other hand, if the written contract is ambiguous, prior negotiations may be considered in determining the meaning of the contract. Other writings referred to in a written contract may be regarded as incorporated by reference as a part of the contract. Two or more written instruments executed by the parties at the same time for the same purpose and in the course of the same transaction will be construed together.

Where a part of a contract is written or typed and part is printed, the written or typed part will control in construing the contract where there is a doubt or inconsistency. Doubtful language in a contract will be interpreted most strongly against the party who drafted the contract or selected that language.

Courts attempt to arrive at the intention of the parties as expressed in the instrument as a whole and to give effect to all parts and provisions of the contract. As a general rule, contracts should be liberally construed so as to give them effect and carry out the intention of the parties. If a contract is open to two constructions, by one of which it would be lawful and by the other illegal, the former construction will be adopted.

Under the maxim "expressio unius est exclusio alterius," the express inclusion in a contract of one or more things of a class implies the exclusion of those not expressed. As a general rule, where a contract contains both general and special provisions relating to the same thing, the special provisions control. Under the doctrine of "ejusdem generis," where no intention to the contrary appears, general words used after specific terms will be confined to things of the same kind or class as those previously specified.

§ 5:25. Time and place.

Am Jur 2d References: Contracts, §§ 329–342; Vendor and Purchaser (1st ed, §§ 109–120).

Where there is no provision as to the time for performance, a reasonable time is implied. What constitutes a reasonable time depends on the subject matter of the contract, the situation of the parties, the intention of the parties when they made the contract, and the circumstances attending the performance. The determination of the question whether a contract must be performed at or within the exact time specified therein, that is, whether time is of the essence of the contract, was formerly governed by different rules, depending upon whether the case was at law or in equity. At law, in the absence of a manifestation of a contrary intention, time was of the essence of contracts, while in equity, time was not ordinarily regarded as of the essence. The trend of modern authority is toward the equitable rule, regarding the question as one of construction to be determined by the intent of the parties. The parties may stipulate that time shall be of the essence; and where time is of the essence of the contract, recovery thereon is conditioned upon performance within the time limited.

A provision in a contract or instrument as to the time of payment of money is effective according to its terms. A contract may provide that time for payment of money thereunder may be accelerated under specified conditions or circumstances, and such a provision is generally valid and enforceable. A stipulation for the payment of money upon the happening of a contingency or condition, such as death or ability to pay, is ordinarily enforceable only upon the happening or performance of the contingency or condition. A party entitled to payment may waive a requirement as to time of payment, as by accepting payment after the due date.

Where no time of payment is specified in a contract for the payment of money, it is payable immediately. This is the rule adopted by the Uniform Commercial Code (UCC § 2–310), to the effect that on a sale of goods payment is due, unless otherwise agreed, at the time and place at which the buyer is to receive the goods. Under a contract to render services, silent as to the time of payment, payment is due when the services are rendered.

The parties may, of course, stipulate the place of performance of a contract. In the absence of express terms, the place or performance may be determined by a fair construction of the contract as to the intention of the parties.

§ 5:26. Price or compensation.

Am Jur 2d References: Building and Construction Contracts, §§ 18–25; Contracts, §§ 343–354.

Compensation or price, like other obligations of a contract, is ordinarily determined by the terms of the contract. Where the contract does not specify the price, the law invokes the standard of reasonableness, and the fair value of the services or property is recoverable. Contract provisions as to price or compensation are to receive a reasonable construction to determine the intent of the parties.

The parties may stipulate for compensation on a "cost-plus" basis (that is, the cost of the materials and work plus a stipulated percentage thereof), or under an "escalator clause," where the contract fixes a base price but provides that in the event of specified cost increases or decreases the price will be raised or reduced by a fixed percentage. Such provisions are construed according to the general principles of construction applicable to contracts.

As a general rule, one who has agreed to do certain work for a stated sum will not be entitled to additional compensation because unforeseen difficulties are encountered. This is not true, however, where extra work is necessitated through the fault of the other party or by changes in specifications.

Building and construction contracts usually contain provisions requiring written orders for any alterations or extra work. Such provisions are frequently avoided, however, by the conduct or agreement of the parties, by modification, rescission, waiver, or estoppel. Waiver is frequently predicated on such acts as the owner's knowledge of, agreement to, or acquiescence in, the extra work, a course of dealing which repeatedly disregards the stipulation, or a promise to pay for the extra work. On the question whether a mere oral order of alterations or extra work by the owner or his agent amounts to an effective waiver of a stipulation requiring a written order for such work, there is a conflict of authority.

§5:27. Contracts for benefit of third persons.

Am Jur 2d References: Contractors' Bonds, §§ 14–23, 77–92; Contracts, §§ 302–319.

The rule prevails in nearly all American jurisdictions that a third person may, in his own right and name, enforce a promise made for his benefit, even though he is not a party to the contract and is a stranger to the consideration. Even in the few jurisdictions not recognizing this general doctrine, the contrary rule has been made the subject of many exceptions and the courts have on various theories found ways to enable third-party beneficiaries to attain effectual relief. Under the prevailing view, the test in determining the right of the third person to enforce the contract is whether the parties to the contract intended that it should be for his benefit. Generally, if the terms of the contract necessarily require the promisor to confer a benefit upon a third person, then the contract, and hence the parties thereto, are deemed to contemplate a benefit to the third person enforceable by him. A mere incidental, collateral, indirect, or consequential benefit which may accrue to a third person by reason of the performance of a contract is not sufficient to bring him within the third-party beneficiary doctrine.

The third-party beneficiary rule is applied to various types of contracts and undertakings. Thus, where two parties enter into a contract whereby one promises to pay the other's debt to a third person, the latter may recover from the promisor. And according to the prevailing view, a donee-beneficiary has a right of action to enforce a promise made for his benefit, the courts not requiring any privity of obligation as between the promisee and the third person.

An important area in which the third-party beneficiary doctrine is applied comprises contractors' bonds. The prevailing view is that persons furnishing materials or labor may recover on a bond given by a public or private contractor to the owner or governmental agency where the bond contains a condition for the benefit of laborers, materialmen, or subcontractors, and is intended for their protection, even though they are not named as obligees in the bond and there is no express provision that the bond shall inure to their benefit. Many statutes, state and federal, so provide.

The third-party beneficiary need not be named in the contract, if he is so described as to be ascertainable. Nor is it essential, in order for a third person to recover on a contract made and intended for his benefit, that he knew of the contract at the time it was made.

The beneficiary's rights depend upon, and are measured by, the terms of the contract between the promisor and the promisee. In order for a third person to enforce a contract made for his benefit, the agreement between the promisor and the promisee must possess the necessary elements to make it a binding obligation. The third person is affected with all of the infirmities of the contract as between the parties thereto, and is subject to all the equities and defenses that would be available against the promisee. According to the rule followed in most jurisdictions, the parties to a contract made for the benefit of a third person may rescind, vary, or abrogate the contract as they see fit, without the assent of the third person, at any time before the contract is accepted or acted upon by the latter.

IV. MODIFICATION AND EXTINGUISHMENT

§ 5:28. Modification, extension, or substitution.

Am Jur 2d References: Accord and Satisfaction, §§ 1–56; Accounts, etc., §§ 21–43; Compromise, etc., §§ 20, 21; Contracts, §§ 458–481; Novation, §§ 1–26; Release, §§ 1 et seq.

The parties to a contract may change it at any time. By later agreement having the requisites of contracts generally, they may alter or modify their contract in any respect, supplement it, rescind it in whole or in part, or substitute another contract for it.

One of the essential elements of a new agreement modifying a contract is that it be based upon a consideration. The sufficiency of this consideration is generally governed by the principles applicable to the formation of contracts. A promise of additional performance for the same consideration, or of additional compensation for doing what the party is already obligated by the original contract to perform, is generally held not to constitute a sufficient consideration for modifying or replacing a contract. But a promise to do something that the promisor is not already bound to do is a sufficient consideration for a modification.

Unless a writing is required by statute, the parties to a written contract may modify or replace it or any part of it by oral agreement. And, according to the weight of authority and in the absence of statute to the contrary, they may do this notwithstanding a stipulation in a written contract that it may not be varied except in writing.

Unless there are grounds for an equitable estoppel, a new consideration is necessary to support an agreement extending the time of performance of a contract, and this applies to the time of payment. The giving of additional security or an agreement to pay interest in advance or at an increased rate or for a time not required by the original contract, is generally held to be sufficient consideration for an extension of time.

Various forms or means of modifying or extinguishing contracts have given rise to several distinctive terms in the law. A contractual obligation or a cause of action based thereon may be disposed of by "accord and satisfaction" or by "compromise and settlement." The latter presupposes a disputed claim and must embody the elements of a valid contract, including consideration. A "novation" extinguishes one obligation or contract by the substitution of a new one, and frequently by the substitution of new parties. An "account stated" arrived at by the acceptance, express or implied, of a statement of an account, may have the effect of altering the original actual agreement of the parties.

§ 5:29. Rescission, termination, and discharge.

Am Jur 2d References: Contracts, §§ 482–520; Vendor and Purchaser (1st ed, §§ 585–648).

The parties to a subsisting contract may always rescind it by their agreement, and this requires no consideration other than their mutual assent.

Unless terminated by agreement or for cause, a contract continues in effect until the time of expiration fixed by the contract itself or by operation of law, or until complete performance. The death or disability of a party does not terminate a contract, except where it involves personal services or the contract itself provides for its termination by such event.

The law affords a number of grounds on which a party to a contract may, by unilateral act, rescind, avoid, or terminate a contract. Examples are contracts voidable because induced by fraud, obtained by duress or undue influence, executed under mistake, or made by an incompetent person. A total lack of consideration or a substantial failure of consideration for a contract will generally warrant its rescission. A material breach of a contract and failure to perform a substantial part thereof is a ground for rescission. An actual repudiation or renunciation of the contract by a party authorizes the other party to rescind it. And the impossibility of substantial performance may be a ground for rescission. The intention and decision to rescind a contract must be manifested and communicated to the other party to the contract. The right to rescind may be lost by waiver or by ratification.

A party who wishes to rescind a contract must generally place the other party in statu quo. There may be circumstances, however, under which impossibility of restoration or other strong equitable considerations will excuse compliance with this requirement.

It is a general rule that a lawful rescission of a contract puts an end to it for all purposes, not only to preclude the recovery of the contract price, but also to prevent the recovery of damages for breach of the contract. However, a party rescinding a contract, who has complied with, or is excused from complying with, the requirement that he restore the other party to the status quo, is generally entitled to receive back the consideration which he has furnished in pursuance of the contract. Money paid upon a contract which is subsequently rescinded is never forfeited unless there is an express or implied contract to that effect; and upon a rescission, the money so paid must be returned to him who advanced it.

V. PERFORMANCE OR BREACH

§ 5:30. Generally.

Am Jur 2d References: Contracts, §§ 355–365; Payment, §§ 2 et seq.

While a contract remains executory on both sides, the obligation of a party to perform frequently depends upon whether the mutual promises are dependent or independent. If the promises are independent of each other, a party must perform his part of the contract at the time specified although the other party has not performed his obligation. If, however, the promise of one party is dependent upon performance by the other, the former is not obliged to perform unless the other has done so.

Where performance of a contract is to be concurrent on both sides, neither party can recover without showing performance or tender of performance on his part. Such offer of performance is unnecessary, however, where it would be a vain and useless gesture, as would be the case where the other party has refused to perform or incapacitated himself to perform.

Unless required by the contract, notice or demand of performance is not necessary. Where a contract creates a condition precedent to a right of action, the condition must be substantially performed, or its requirements waived, before there may be a recovery on the contract. A party first guilty of a substantial or material breach of contract cannot complain if the other party thereafter refuses to perform.

§ 5:31. Sufficiency of performance.

Am Jur 2d References: Building and Construction Contracts, §§ 30–60; Contracts, §§ 366–389.

Even without an express requirement in the contract, every contract for work or services implies a duty to perform skillfully, carefully, diligently, and in a workmanlike manner. Absolute or literal perfection is not required of either party in the performance of a contract. A substantial performance, done in good faith, is sufficient to support a recovery on a contract. Substantial performance will support a recovery of the contract price less allowances for the defects or shortcomings.

A provision in a contract that performance by one party is to be rendered to the satisfaction of the other party will be given effect by the courts, so that recovery may not be had where the party having the right of approval expresses his actual and bona fide dissatisfaction, provided that he does not act arbitrarily or capriciously or merely feign dissatisfaction.

Contracts frequently require performance to the satisfaction of a third person. Construction contracts usually require approval of the work by an architect or engineer. Approval by such third person is generally essential to a recovery on the contract, in the absence of a showing of fraud or bad faith.

§ 5:32. Excuses for nonperformance.

Am Jur 2d References: Act of God, § 12; Building and Construction Contracts, §§ 61–71; Contracts, §§ 388, 390–399, 400–403, 413, 414, 425–440.

Of the excuses for nonperformance of a purported contract, the most obvious is that the contract is invalid because it lacks some requisite or involves some infirmity discussed above, or because performance would be illegal. The parties may, by a provision in their contract, excuse performance upon stated contingencies; and some situations arising after the contract is made will have the same effect by operation of law. Excuses for delay are usually governed by the same principles as apply to nonperformance generally.

Full performance of a contract or of a condition precedent may be waived by the party to whom performance is owed. Acceptance of a defective performance constitutes such a waiver. A party who is prevented by the conduct of the other party from performing a contract or a condition is not liable for the nonperformance. A repudiation of a contract by a party, or his definite refusal to perform, excuses the other party from his obligation to perform.

Changes in conditions or the occurrence of events which frustrate the objects contemplated by the parties when they made the contract will generally excuse performance. But the fact that it becomes difficult or even burdensome for a party to perform his promises is no excuse for nonperformance. Generally, the death or disability of a party occurring after the making of a contract does not excuse performance if the contract is not of a personal nature. Whether an Act of God will have this effect, in the absence of a provision therefor in the contract, is the subject of a conflict of authority. The mere existence of a state of war does not ordinarily excuse performance of a contract, though performance may be more difficult and expensive, in the absence of a contract provision governing the subject and if performance is not rendered impossible or illegal.

§ 5:33. —Impossibility of performance.

Am Jur 2d References: Act of God, § 12; Contracts, §§ 404–424, 433.

Generally, impossibility of performance may be classified as original impossibility or supervening impossibility. The former is impossibility of performance existing when the contract was entered into, and this may prevent the creation of a valid contract at the outset. A supervening impossibility is that which develops after the inception of the contract, and the effect thereof will vary according to the circumstances of the case and the jurisdiction in which the question is presented.

According to the strict general rule of the early common law, supervening impossibility of performance did not excuse the promisor from his duty to perform his contract, in the absence of a provision to that effect in the contract. This harsh rule has, however, been greatly eroded by the engraftment of exceptions and qualifications and by the outright repudiation of the general doctrine. The Restatement, with the support of many authorities, lays down the rule that where, after the formation of a contract, facts not anticipated, or contributed to, by a promisor render performance of a promise impossible, the duty of the promisor is discharged, unless a contrary intention has been manifested. Even this liberal view, representing the trend of modern authority, requires that the supervening impossibility of performance must be fortuitous and unavoidable on the part of the promisor.

If the act to be performed under the contract is necessarily dependent upon the continued existence of a specific thing or subject matter, the destruction or cessation of existence thereof before the time for performance, without default of the promisor, will excuse nonperformance of the contract.

Unless it is otherwise provided in the contract, the death or disability of a party does not terminate the contract if it is not of a personal nature. The test for determining this is whether the contract is of such character that it may be performed by the promisor's personal representative.

Subjective impossibility or personal inability to perform one's contractual promise, as distinguished from objective impossibility inhering in the nature of the act to be performed, does not excuse the promisor from performing. An example of subjective impossibility is the inability of the promisor to perform because he is unable to finance the contract. Strikes and other labor disputes do not excuse nonperformance, unless provision is made therefor in the contract. Impossibility of performance resulting from an Act of God is subject to the same principles as apply to impossibility for other causes.

A contract that is rendered impossible of performance by a change in the law need not be performed by either party. And where the existence of a state of war renders the performance of the contract impossible, there is no liability for failure to perform.

Except where the contract provides otherwise, most courts follow the rule that where one party has rendered performance under a contract, and the other party is excused by impossibility from performing his part of the bargain, the former may recover the value of what he has rendered, less the value of what he has received.

§ 5:34. Breach.

Am Jur 2d References:　Contracts, §§ 441–457.

A breach of a contract consists of a failure, without legal excuse, to perform any of the promises comprising the contract. A cause of action for damages arises upon any breach of contract. As a general rule, upon such breach the injured party may elect to rescind and recover the value of any performance or money paid by him, or to stand by the contract and recover damages for its breach. Of course, a default in performance may be waived.

The act of a party to a contract in preventing the other party from performing not only excuses the latter for nonperformance, but entitles him to damages as for a breach of the contract.

§ 5:35. Remedies for breach or nonperformance, generally.

Am Jur 2d References:　Arbitration and Award, §§ 11 et seq.; Contracts, §§ 521, 522.

A party defaulting in the performance of a contract is liable to the other party for the damages resulting from the breach. The measure and amount of such recovery are treated herein under the topic DAMAGES. Other remedies, such as unilateral rescission and refusal to continue performance of the contract have already been discussed herein.

In appropriate circumstances, contractual rights may be enforced by injunction or established by declaratory judgment (both of which matters are treated herein under the topic EXTRAORDINARY AND SPECIAL REMEDIES). And in a proper case an equitable suit for cancellation or reformation (discussed herein under the topic EQUITY) may be maintained. As pointed out in the next succeeding section, specific performance may be enforced of certain contractual undertakings and under appropriate circumstances.

The parties may submit their disputes concerning a contract to arbitration. When this is done, a valid award by the arbiters settles all claims and disputes arbitrated and precludes litigation thereon.

§ 5:36. Specific performance.

Am Jur 2d References:　Building and Construction Contracts, § 112; Specific Performance (1st ed, §§ 1–78).

In some cases, a party to a contract cannot be adequately compensated by a recovery of monetary damages for a breach. In such circumstances, if the requisite conditions are met, a court of equity will decree the specific performance of the contract, requiring the defaulting party to perform the specific act which he has agreed to do.

As it is an equitable remedy, a court will not grant such relief when it would be contrary to equity and justice to do so. In accordance with general principles of equity, the plaintiff must come into court with clean hands and must himself do equity. Specific performance will not be decreed unless it appears that the contract is a fair and equitable one. If there has been any fraud or misrepresentation or overreaching or oppression or unfair concealment on the part of plaintiff, specific performance may be denied.

The granting of a decree of specific performance is not a matter of absolute right, but rests in the sound discretion of the court. This discretion is not an arbitrary or capricious one, but is a judicial discretion to be exercised in accordance with settled rules of equity. As a practical matter, of course, the denial of specific performance where all of the requisites for such relief are established, is an abuse of discretion.

In accordance with general principles of equity, specific performance of a contract will not be granted unless it appears that the plaintiff has no adequate remedy at law and that an action at law for compensatory damages for breach of the contract would be inadequate, under the circumstances, to do complete justice between the parties. Adequacy of the remedy at law for this purpose means that it must be plain, adequate, complete, and efficient, and not circuitous or doubtful. Whether the insolvency of the defendant renders inadequate an action at law for damages is a question on which the courts do not agree.

The existence of a valid and legal contract is, of course, a prerequisite of the right to the specific enforcement of a contract. And the terms of the contract must be clear, definite, certain, and complete. The plaintiff must show that he has complied with the terms of the contract by performing or offering to perform, or that he is ready, willing, and able to perform.

A court may properly refuse to grant specific performance where the defendant entered into the contract under mistake, although, where such is fair and feasible, the court may order the mistake corrected and decree performance of the contract as corrected. Another ground for denial of specific performance is that the overall result of such a decree would be harsh, inequitable, or oppressive, or result in an unconscionable advantage to the plaintiff. A court will not decree specific performance where such performance is impossible. Laches, unreasonable delay, or the default on the part of the party seeking the specific enforcement of a contract is a sufficient ground for denial of the relief.

Mere inadequacy of consideration will not generally preclude relief by way of specific performance, unless there are elements of unfairness or overreaching or such gross inadequacy as to make the contract unfair and unreasonable and to shock the conscience of the court.

The element of mutuality in the contract is a prerequisite of the right to specific performance. Before equity will decree specific performance, it must be established that there is mutuality of obligation and of remedy. This does not mean that both parties must have the same remedy. For example, the mere fact that specific performance would not be available to one party will not, of itself, justify the refusal of a decree in favor of the other party. Mutuality need not exist at the inception of the contract if it is present at the time suit is filed.

§ 5:37. —Subject matter of contract.

Am Jur 2d, References: Building and Construction Contracts, § 112;
Specific Performance (1st ed, §§ 79–137).

The remedy of specific performance is not limited to any particular class of contracts or subject matter. Family settlements or family agreements, when fairly entered into and capable of performance, will be specifically enforced. A contract to adopt may be specifically enforced, at least to the extent of giving the child the rights of inheritance that an adopted child would have. An agreement to give security, such as a mortgage on realty, may in a proper case be specifically enforced.

The subject matter most commonly involved in actions for specific performance is that of contracts for the sale of land or which otherwise involve interests in real estate. The courts assume that no two parcels of land are identical and that money damages are not an adequate remedy for the breach of such a contract. The vendor in a contract for the sale of land may obtain a decree of specific performance against the vendee, although the actual relief granted is the recovery of the purchase price. To obtain this relief, however, the vendor must be able to convey a good and marketable title. On the other hand, although the vendor is not able to convey a perfect title or all of the property contracted for, the vendee may waive performance pro tanto and compel specific performance of the contract to the extent that the vendor is able to perform. And it is generally held that the vendee may compel the vendor to convey his defective title or deficient estate, and at the same time have an abatement of the purchase price to compensate for the deficiency of title or quantity.

The vendor himself, when unable to convey exactly what he contracted to convey, may compel the vendee to take the land with an abatement from the purchase price, if his partial inability to perform does not involve bad faith on his part, and if the deficiency in title or quantity is of small importance and the vendee will get substantially what he contracted for.

The general rule is that specific performance of contracts in relation to personal property will not be decreed, because ordinarily the recovery of damages affords an adequate remedy. There are, however, circumstances under which an action for damages is not an adequate remedy and specific performance may be decreed. Particular kinds of articles of personal property may fall within this exception because of special or peculiar qualities or associations which they possess. Personal property described by the phrase "cretium effectionis," embracing such classes of personalty as heirlooms, family pictures, and other articles possessing sentimental significance, works of art, portraits, and antiques, generally are within the exception to the general rule against specific enforcement of contracts relating to personal property. If the article contracted for is of unique character, or if it cannot be purchased in the market or can be supplied by no one except the defendant, the court will entertain a suit for specific performance if the other requirements for such relief are established.

An agreement to assign patents or copyrights may be specifically enforced. A contract for the sale of corporate stock is not ordinarily specifically enforceable, but where the value of the stock is not easily ascertainable, or it is not obtainable in the open market, or where the purpose of the purchase of the stock is to enable the purchaser to gain control of the corporation or to prevent control by antagonistic interests, the court may, if the equities of the case so indicate, specifically enforce the contract.

It is a familiar general rule that courts of equity will not decree the specific performance of a contract for personal services. For example, specific per-formance will not ordinarily be granted to enforce a building or construction contract. This rule is not without exceptions, however. Contracts for the performance of personal services or acts of a special, unique, or extraordinary character, or by persons eminent in their profession or calling and who possess special and extraordinary qualifications required for such services, may in a proper case be indirectly enforced by restraining the person employed from rendering services to another. The famous case of Lumley v Wagner (42 Eng Reprint 687) is an example of this kind of negative enforcement. In that case, a celebrated singer contracted to perform at the plaintiff's theater and not to sing elsewhere. The court did not specifically enforce the affirmative agreement to sing, but granted an injunction against singing elsewhere.

*

CORPORATIONS

I. GENERAL MATTERS; INCORPORATION, ORGANIZATION, AND NATURE

I. GENERAL MATTERS; INCORPORATION, ORGANIZATION, AND NATURE

§ 6:1. In general

Am Jur 2d References: Corporations, §§ 1–46, 63–80, 141–160.

As the term is used in the present topic, a corporation is a legal entity created by law, with an identity distinct and separate from that of its members or

97

organizers, and endowed with certain powers and franchises to be exercised in its designated corporate name. It is a fictitious person existing in contemplation of law. Among its distinctive attributes are its capacity of perpetual succession, or "immortality," unaffected by changes of membership or stockholders, and the powers to sue and be sued, to own property, and to carry on its authorized functions in its corporate name.

The earliest types of corporations in England were not business corporations and were not the kind of organizations with which we are presently concerned. They were "corporations sole," usually a bishop or some other ecclesiastic whose principal corporate characteristic was perpetual succession to church property, etc., by virtue of office; public or municipal corporations of various kinds; the numerous trade guilds, which did not carry on business as entities but merely governed the activities of its members; and peace guilds, formed for the mutual protection of members. The earliest chartered English trading or business companies were joint-stock companies, such as the East India Company and the Hudson's Bay Company.

Corporations are variously classified according to different bases. Under one basis of classification, corporations are either aggregate (the usual form) or sole. They are either public (municipal corporations and the like) or private. And private corporations are either profit (the ordinary business corporation) or nonprofit (the eleemosynary or charitable corporation). In addition to the foregoing classifications, the term "holding company" is frequently applied to a corporation whose sole or principal business is holding the stock of one or more other corporations.

By definition, a corporation is an entity distinct from its individual members or stockholders, and its property is vested in the corporation itself, and not in the stockholders; and neither is ordinarily charged with the debts or obligations of the other. And this is true although all or a majority of the stock of the corporation is owned by a single person.

The fiction of separate corporate entity may be disregarded by a court, however, where to recognize it would result in fraud or injustice. In an appropriate case and in furtherance of the ends of justice, a corporation and the individuals owning its stock may be treated as identical. Each case involving disregard of the corporate entity must rest upon its special facts. The usual ground for disregarding the corporate entity is its use as a cover for fraud or illegality, or to work an injustice, or where it is necessary to achieve equity. In some circumstances the theory of separate corporate existence of parent and subsidiary or affiliated corporations will not be recognized where one corporation is so organized and controlled and its business conducted in such manner as to make it merely an agency, instrumentality, or alter ego of another corporation. While the mere fact that a corporation is organized to take over a business formerly conducted by a firm or individual does not of itself render the corporation liable for a debt of the former firm or individual, it has been held that where the property of the former firm or individual is simply transferred to the corporation without consideration other than corporate stock, or where the corporation is in fact merely a continuation of the old business under a different name, it may be held liable for the debts of the pre-existing business.

The status of a corporation as a "person" or "citizen" depends upon the purposes for which this status is asserted. For most purposes, the term "person" applies to corporations as well as to natural persons. Thus, a corporation is a "person" within the meaning of the Fifth and Fourteenth Amendments to the Constitution of the United States that no person shall be deprived of life, liberty, or property without due process of law. The same is true as regards the equal protection of laws provisions of the Fourteenth Amendment. The due process clause, however, is held to apply to a corporation's property only, and not to liberty. And a corporation has been held not to be a "person" within the protection of the Fifth Amendment against self-incrimination. For most purposes, a corporation is held not to be a "citizen" within the meaning of statutory or constitutional provisions, including the provisions of the Federal Constitution regarding the "privileges and immunities of citizens." However, for some purposes corporations have been held to be "citizens."

A corporation must be organized according to the laws of the state creating it, or, as regards certain types of corporations, under the laws of the United States. Formerly, corporations were usually created by special grants of charters or special acts of the legislatures, but in modern times most corporations are organized and created under provisions of general laws authorizing the organization of corporations by compliance with prescribed conditions. The commencement and duration of corporate existence depend upon statute and the terms of the articles of incorporation. The lifetime of a corporation may be for a specified number of years, or it may be perpetual.

A name is essential to the very existence of a corporation. All of its acts must be in its corporate name. The name or type of name adopted for a corporation is subject to regulation by the state. Corporations usually adopt a corporate seal for use on instruments executed by them. Formerly, the use of the corporate seal was required in most corporate transactions, but this requirement has been relaxed in modern times, although a seal may be required for some purposes, and it is usually desirable to attest important corporate instruments with the seal, as it establishes, prima facie, that the instrument is the act of the corporation.

After the filing and approval of articles of incorporation, or the granting of a charter, there must be an "organization" of the corporation to enable it to function as such. Statutes usually provide the manner of organizing a corporation. This organization generally involves the election of officers, the subscription and payment of capital stock, the adoption of bylaws, and such other steps as are prescribed by statute or are necessary to enable the corporate creature to transact its business.

§ 6:2. Corporate charter; articles and certificate of incorporation.

Am Jur 2d References: Corporations, §§ 36–42, 81–105.

In earlier times corporate charters were usually granted by special acts of the legislature. Now, however, practically all corporations are created under general statutes, and the charters consist of the articles or certificates of incorporation. The form and contents of these documents are generally prescribed by statutes, which must be substantially complied with. Among other things, the statutes usually require that the articles or certificate state the name of the corporation, the purposes for which it is being organized, the place of business, the amount of authorized capital stock and a description of the classes of shares, the amount of paid-in capital, the number of directors for the first year and their names and addresses, and the names and addresses of the incorporators.

It is usually required that the articles or certificates of incorporation be signed by a specified number of incorporators, and some statutes require acknowledgments by them. The articles or certificate of incorporation must be filed in the public office specified by statute, usually with the Secretary of State and sometimes also in the office of the county clerk of the county designated as the principal place of business of the corporation.

Although the general rule is that corporate charters are strictly construed against the corporation, the construction of the charter must be reasonable and must give effect to the common usage of the language employed therein. All constitutional provisions and explicit statutory provisions are deemed to qualify or be incorporated in a corporate charter. It was established in the celebrated Dartmouth College Case (4 Wheat 518, 4 L Ed 629) that the charter of a private corporation is a contract entitled to protection under the provision of the Federal Constitution prohibiting the states from passing laws impairing the obligation of contract. This rule does not, however, deprive the state of the basic right to regulate corporate activities; and the right to amend a corporate charter may be reserved in the grant thereof or by general statute. The general statutes governing incorporation usually provide for amendment of the charter of a corporation by the corporation itself through a vote of its stockholders.

§ 6:3. Defective incorporations; de facto corporations.

Am Jur 2d References: Corporations, §§ 47–62.

If a corporation has been regularly created and organized in compliance with all legal requirements it is a de jure corporation, and its right to exercise a corporate franchise is invulnerable against attack, even a direct attack by the state itself. However, an association which may not be able to justify itself when called on by the state to show by what authority it assumes to be and act as a corporation may be so far a corporation that, for reasons of public policy, no one but the state will be permitted to challenge the lawfulness of its organization. Such an organization is termed a corporation de facto—that is, a corporation from the fact of its acting as such, though not in law or of right a corporation. It is an apparent corporate organization, exercising corporate rights and franchises under color of law without complying with all the prerequisites of the creation of a corporation.

As a general rule a corporation de facto exists when, from irregularity or defect in the organization or from an omission to comply with the conditions precedent, a corporation de jure is not created, but there has been a colorable compliance with the requirements of some law under which an association might be lawfully incorporated for the purposes and powers assumed, and a user of the rights claimed to be conferred by the law—that is, when there is an organization with color of law and the exercise of corporate franchises. According to the general rule, a de facto corporation possesses all the powers of a de jure corporation, except that it is open to direct attack by the state in quo warranto proceedings. As to all the world except the sovereign it occupies the same position as if its organization and creation were in all respects valid; and the same is true as against the state itself except in direct proceedings to arrest its usurpation of corporate power. If the alleged or pretending corporation has no color of right to claim that status, either de jure or de facto, its corporate existence may be challenged collaterally by anyone, and persons dealing with the members of the purported organization may proceed against them personally.

It is ordinarily essential to the existence of a de facto corporation that there be (1) a valid law under which a corporation with the powers assumed might be incorporated; (2) a bona fide attempt to organize a corporation under such law; and (3) an actual exercise of corporate powers. There cannot be even a de facto corporate existence if any of these elements is missing. No general or comprehensive rule may be laid down as to the nature or extent of the attempts to incorporate according to law or as to the steps or procedures which must be taken in order to give rise to a de facto corporate existence. The requirement of an attempt to incorporate according to law does not necessarily require a substantial compliance with the statute. The effect of any omission depends not only upon the materiality and seriousness thereof, but also upon the terms of the governing statutes. Clearly a de facto corporation can never be recognized in violation of a positive law expressly prohibiting the exercise of corporate powers until certain statutory steps have been taken. The lack of agreement among the courts as to whether a corporation de facto may be created notwithstanding a failure to file the articles of incorporation as required by statute may result in part from differences in the terms of the governing statutes.

§ 6:4. Promoters and promotion.

Am Jur 2d References: Corporations, §§ 106–140.

The modern business corporation does not come into being spontaneously, without the aid of a human agency. Someone must conceive and initiate the plan of its purposes and powers, bringing together persons interested in the enterprise, provide or raise capital by procuring subscriptions to stock or otherwise to enable it to function, and set in motion the procedures leading to the formation and creation of the corporation. Such a person is generally referred to as a "promoter." A promoter's work may begin long before the organization of the corporation, in seeking the opening for a venture, investigating opportunities, and projecting a plan for its development; and it may continue after the incorporation by attracting the investment of capital in its stock and other securities and providing it with commercial viability. If he continues after incorporation to perform the acts which characterize promoters, such as inducing persons to subscribe for capital stock, his relations and responsibilities as a promoter continue, especially if he remains in control of the affairs of the company.

There is some difference of opinion on the question of the liability of a corporation to compensate its promoters for services rendered or expenses incurred before its incorporation. Some courts take the view that, in the absence of a contrary charter or statutory provision, the corporation is not liable for such services or expenses unless, after its incorporation, it expressly agrees to make payment, or from other facts, the court can infer a new contract to reimburse them. These courts adopt the reasoning that there can be no implied promise by a corporation which is not in existence and that it cannot be said that the services were rendered or expenses incurred in behalf of a corporation prior to its creation. Other courts, however, take the view that when promoters perform necessary and reasonable services or incur necessary and reasonable expenses in obtaining a charter, in securing subscriptions to capital stock, and in otherwise perfecting the organization, with the understanding and expectation that they are to be repaid therefor, a promise of such payment by the corporation will be implied after its organization and acceptance of the benefits of such services or expenditures. After the organization of the corporation and with the consent of its stockholders, it may make reasonable compensation to its promoters, by the issuance of stock or otherwise, unless prohibited by statute.

Every person acting, by whatever name, in the forming and establishing of a corporation at any period prior to its complete incorporation occupies a fiduciary relation toward both the corporation and its stockholders, and as such he is bound to exercise the utmost good faith in his dealings with them. He must disclose fully all material facts touching his relation to them and must fully advise them of any interest that he has which may in any manner affect them. He may not benefit by any secret profit or advantage gained at the expense of the corporation or its members. He may not secure for himself any remuneration for his services without making a full disclosure thereof. A promoter who knowingly issues or sanctions the circulation of a false prospectus tending to mislead and to induce the public to purchase the stock of the corporation is responsible to those who are injured thereby.

While his fiduciary relationship does not deprive the promoter of the right of fairly and openly doing business with the corporation at a profit, his dealings must be fair in every respect, with a full disclosure of material facts. The obtaining of a secret profit by a promoter through the sale of property to a corporation is a fraud on the corporation and the stockholders, and the promoter may be required to account therefor. And a promoter is guilty of a breach of trust if he accepts a secret bonus or commission from a third person who sells property to the corporation.

Prior to its actual incorporation or creation, a corporation has no legal existence, and hence has no power to enter into contracts and can have no agents. Therefore, any contract which a promoter attempts to make for it prior to its authorization is not binding upon the corporation after it comes into being. However, the corporation may ratify or assume such contracts, either expressly or by the acceptance of the benefits thereof. The promoter himself is personally liable on such preincorporation contracts, in the absence of an agreement to the contrary with the other contracting party. The rights and liabilities of promoters as between themselves are governed by the terms of their contract.

§ 6:5. Bylaws and records.

Am Jur 2d References: Corporations, §§ 161–207.

The internal affairs and management of a corporation are governed by its bylaws. The bylaws supplement the charter or articles of incorporation in prescribing the details of corporate administration and government. The power to adopt bylaws for the regulation of its affairs is inherent in every corporation. In the absence of a statute or charter provision to the contrary, the power to make bylaws is vested in the members or stockholders of the corporation. However, this power may be delegated to the directors. The power to adopt bylaws includes the power to repeal or amend them. To be valid, a corporate bylaw must be reasonable and calculated to promote the objects of the corporation, must not be inconsistent with the corporation's charter or articles of incorporation, and must not be contrary to law or public policy.

Statutes generally require the keeping of records by corporations, and usually prescribe what records and books must be kept and where they must be kept. The records of the corporation include the transcript of its charter and bylaws, the minutes of its meetings, the books containing the accounts of its official actions, and the written evidence of its contract and business transactions. In addition to keeping records, corporations are required to make a great variety of reports to governmental departments and agencies.

It is well established at common law, and is so provided by statute in many jurisdictions, that a stockholder has a right to inspect the books and records of the corporation, at a proper and reasonable time and for proper purposes. This right is based upon the fact that the stockholders are the beneficial owners of the corporation and have the right to know how the affairs of the company are conducted and whether the capital contributed by them is being prudently and practically employed. A director also has this right of inspection. As a general rule, however, a corporation will not be compelled to submit its books and records to examination by a stockholder unless he seeks the inspection in good faith for a proper purpose—that is, for a lawful and reasonable purpose, germane to his status as a stockholder—and not for a purpose inimical or hostile to the corporation itself or other stockholders, or in aid of blackmail. It has been held that the right of inspection will not be enforced merely for the purpose of gratifying idle curiosity, to harass or annoy the corporation or its management, or to use the information obtained in speculation. It is generally held that a stockholder will not be aided in an attempt to inspect the corporate records for the purpose of aiding a competitor of the corporation by the discovery of trade secrets or otherwise.

Where the right of inspection is established, a stockholder has the right to the assistance of a skilled agent, such as an attorney, accountant, or stenographer; and he has the right to make copies or extracts from the records. Mandamus, or the statutory equivalent thereof, is the proper remedy for the enforcement of a stockholder's right to inspect the books and reords of a corporation.

§ 6:6. Consolidation, merger, reorganization, and dissolution.

Am Jur 2d References: Corporations, §§ 1490–1696.

Although the terms "consolidation" and "merger" are frequently used indiscriminately and interchangeably to describe the union of two or more corporations, the two processes and the legal consequences thereof are quite different. In the case of a consolidation of corporations, the constituent companies cease to exist, and a new corporation, the consolidated corporation, comes into being and generally inherits the property, powers, rights, duties, and obligations of the original corporations. A merger of corporations consists of a combination whereby one of the constituent companies remains in being and absorbs and merges into itself the other constitutent corporations.

A mere sale of its property by one corporation to another, or the acquisition by one corporation of all or the majority of the stock of another does not constitute a merger or consolidation of the corporations. Except as inhibited by their own charters or by laws relating to monopolies and restraints of trade, corporations may purchase the property or stock of other corporations without effecting a consolidation, merger, or other change in corporate status.

Corporations have the right and power to consolidate or merge only by the authority and consent of the legislature. The authority may be conferred by the charters of the corporations, by the general statutes authorizing their incorporation, or by statutes enacted after their incorporation. The consent of the stockholders is another condition limiting the power of corporations to merge or consolidate. Unless different conditions are prescribed by statute or in the charters of the corporations, all stockholders must consent to a consolidation or merger. However, in most jurisdictions, the statutes provide for consolidation or merger where it is approved by a specified percentage or majority of the stockholders, and provide for payment to dissenting stockholders of the appraised value of their shares.

Reorganization of corporations is provided for in many statutes. Such a reorganization is a means whereby those variously interested, as stockholders, creditors, etc., in a distressed business seek, through continuance of the business as a going concern, to solve the difficulties without the liquidation of the corporation. Elaborate provisions for such reorganizations are contained in the Federal Bankruptcy Act.

The dissolution and death of a corporation may occur in various ways. It is always dependent upon the statutes of the state which gave the corporation life. If the charter or articles of incorporation limit the lifetime of the corporation to a specified term of years, the expiration of that period ipso facto dissolves it and terminates its existence. Statutory provision is generally made for the dissolution of a corporation by the vote of its stockholders and by compliance with the statutory provisions.

A corporation may suffer extinction by forfeiture of its charter. For certain abuses of its corporate franchise, and depending upon the terms of the governing statutes, the state may terminate the charter of a corporation and dissolve it. Proceedings for the forfeiture of a corporate charter must usually be at the instance and in the name of the state. Such proceedings are ordinarily instituted by the Attorney General, although some statutes permit their institution by private individuals on behalf of the state. The administration of the affairs and the distribution of assets of the corporation upon its dissolution are governed by statutes. As a general rule, after the satisfaction of creditors of the corporation, its assets are distributed among its stockholders.

II. CAPITAL STOCK

§ 6:7. Generally.

Am Jur 2d References: Corporations, §§ 208–287.

The capital stock of a corporation is the amount of money, property, or other means authorized by its charter and contributed, or agreed to be contributed, by the shareholders as the financial basis for the prosecution of the business of the corporation. The term "capital," as distinguished from "capital stock," indicates the assets of the corporation or that portion of the assets, regardless of their source, which is utilized in the conduct of the corporate business. Shares of stock are units of interest in a corporation. These shares entitle their owners to a proportionate part of the distributed profits of the corporation and to aliquot parts of the property, or its proceeds, upon any distribution thereof.

The capital is the property of the corporate entity; all the shares of stock are the property of the shareholders.

Shares of stock are incorporeal personal property and are in the nature of choses in action, although they do not constitute an indebtedness of the corporation to the shareholders. A share of stock is the actual property of the shareholder, while the certificate of stock is merely evidence of the ownership of shares.

The amount and the different classes of stock which a corporation may sell or issue depend upon the terms of its charter and of the governing statutes. The basic class of corporate stock is common stock. This is the kind of stock ordinarily and usually issued, without extraordinary rights or privileges, and the class which, in the absence of other classes of stock having superior rights, represents the complete interest in the corporation. Preferred stock, as its name implies, is given certain preferences over common stock, and dividends on preferred stock are usually required to be paid before any distribution of profits to the common stock. Dividends on preferred stock are usually payable at a fixed rate per share, and they are sometimes made cumulative, so that dividends skipped in one or more years will be made up in succeeding years.

Convertible stock is that which may be changed from one class of stock to another. Preferred stock is frequently made convertible into common stock, under specified terms, at the option of the stockholder. Treasury stock, as distinguished from unissued stock, is corporate stock which has been subscribed and paid for, but has thereafter been reacquired by the corporation by purchase or otherwise. Treasury stock generally differs from retired stock in that the former may be sold whereas retired stock disappears altogther.

Corporate stock may have a designated "par value," stated on the certificate of stock, or it may be without par value. The par value, where stated, is usually an arbitrary amount, having little or no relation to the actual value or even the "book value" of the stock.

The amount of stock of any class which a corporation has the power to issue is usually limited by its charter or articles of incorporation. The amount of authorized capital stock may not be increased without an amendment of the charter according to law nor without the consent of the existing stockholders. The Uniform Commercial Code (§ 8–104) provides the remedy of the purchaser against the issuer of securities in case of overissue. A reduction of the nominal capitalization of a corporation also requires amendment of the charter and statutory authorization.

Where the capital stock of a corporation is increased and new shares of stock are offered, the original stockholders, in the absence of statutory or charter provisions to the contrary, have pre-emptive rights with respect to the new stock; that is, a holder of original stock is entitled to subscribe to the new issue in preference to nonholders, in proportion to the amount of stock held by him. This pre-emptive right may, of course, be waived by stockholders and it may be denied by provisions of the corporation's charter.

The statutory or charter authorization for the issuance of stock, and the express provisions of the certificates of stock themselves, sometimes provide for redemption and retirement of the stock by the corporation. This right of redemption is frequently reserved with respect to preferred stock.

§ 6:8. Subscriptions and purchase of shares from corporation.

Am Jur 2d References: Corporations, §§ 288–375; Securities Regulation—Federal; Securities Regulation—State.

A subscription to stock in a corporation is subject to the rules applicable to the formation of contracts generally: There must be an offer and an acceptance thereof, express or implied; there must be a meeting of the minds, a mutual assent of the parties; and there must be valid consideration. Such contracts are, of course, subject to such defenses as fraud, mutual mistake, and illegality. An offer of unissued stock by an existing corporation is accepted by a binding subscription therefor, resulting in a contract without further action on the part of the corporation. Where the original offer comes from a prospective subscriber, however, no binding contract comes into existence until the corporation in some way manifests its acceptance of the offer.

A subscription to stock in a corporation thereafter to be formed is, according to some cases, a mere offer by the subscriber to the proposed corporation, which does not become binding until the corporation comes into existence. However, other courts regard a subscription by a number of persons to stock in a corporation to be thereafter formed by them as having a double character: In addition to its being a continuing offer to the proposed corporation, such a subscription is held by these courts to constitute a contract between the subscribers to become stockholders without further act on their part immediately upon the formation of the corporation.

Corporations frequently adopt stock-option plans giving to selected officers or key employees an option to purchase shares from the corporation upon specified terms. Such a plan results in a binding subscription contract upon the acceptance thereof by the officer or employee. Corporations also issue to existing stockholders stock "rights" or "warrants" in the nature of options to purchase stock of the corporation upon specified terms.

Under the view that a subscription to stock in a corporation to be formed constitutes, in relation to the proposed corporation, merely a continuing offer until the organization of the corporation, it is held that, at least so far as the corporation is concerned, the subscriber may revoke or withdraw his subscription at any time before the formation of the corporation, with or without the consent of his cosubscribers. Other courts, however, take the view that a subscription to stock in a contemplated corporation is binding upon the subscriber from the time of subscription and cannot be withdrawn or revoked by him without the consent of the other subscribers. In any event, the subscription becomes a binding contract upon its acceptance by the corporation. Subscription agreements sometimes contain a provision requiring the corporation to repurchase the stock, at the option of the subscriber.

The sale and issuance of corporate stock and other securities is subject to strict and elaborate regulation by both state and federal statutes. Most states have statutes of the type generally known as "Blue Sky Laws," and Congress has enacted a number of acts, the most important of which are the Federal Securities Act of 1933, the Securities Exchange Act of 1934, the Trust Indenture Act of 1939, the Investment Company Act of 1940, and the Investment Advisers Act of 1940. The general purpose of these statutes is to require full disclosures concerning all stock or other securities offered for sale, and to protect the public against imposition and fraud resulting from the promotion of companies having no assets other than the "blue sky" or visionary oil wells or gold mines. These statutes are enforced by both civil consequences and criminal sanctions.

§ 6:9. Issuance and replacement of certificates.

Am Jur 2d References: Corporations, §§ 242–274.

A certificate of stock is evidence of the holder's interest in the corporation issuing it. It represents the holder's share in the capital stock of the company. The stock certificate also evidences the contract between the corporation and the stockholder and defines, to the extent of its provisions, the reciprocal rights and liabilities of the parties. Although the certificate is not essential to the complete ownership of the stock or to the creation of the relationship of stockholder, the purchaser of stock from a corporation is entitled to a certificate therefor, and he may compel the issuance of a certificate by a suit in equity or by mandamus proceedings.

Statutes of most states require the full payment of the consideration, whether in the form of money, property, or services, before a corporation may issue certificates of stock. The rights of a holder of stock that was improperly or irregularly issued, and the corresponding liabilities of the corporation, are stated in the Uniform Commercial Code, Article 8.

In most jurisdictions the remedies and procedures for the replacement of lost, destroyed, or stolen certificates of stock are provided by statutes, although the owner may compel such a replacement even in the absence of statute. Before he is entitled to the issuance of new certificates for those claimed to have been lost, destroyed, or stolen, the shareholder must, of course, establish the fact of their loss. Also he is generally required to give an indemnity bond or other security to protect the corporation against loss.

§ 6:10. Transfer of stock.

Am Jur 2d References: Corporations, §§ 376–459.

The transferability of corporate stock inheres in its character as personal property. The power to dispose of such stock is a right which is incident to ownership and which can be limited only by statute or valid charter or contract provisions. The transfer of stock is now provided for and regulated in all American jurisdictions by either the Uniform Commercial Code, Article 8 (Investment Securities) or the Uniform Stock Transfer Act. By express provision of the former (UCC § 8–105), certificates of stock are declared to be negotiable instruments.

Regulations may be made respecting the mode and formal requirements of a transfer; and restrictions on the power to transfer shares are sometimes imposed by provisions in the corporate charter or by the general law. However, such restrictions are strictly construed and those embodied in the corporate charter must be reasonable and not contrary to public policy.

The power of a corporation to make bylaws restricting the alienation or transfer of stock generally depends upon legislative authorization. Any corporate bylaw which unreasonably restrains the power of a stockholder to transfer corporate stock is against public policy and therefore invalid. In the absence of statutory authority, a corporation is generally held to have no power, by bylaws or other regulations, to prohibit the alienation or transfer of its stock without the consent or approval of the corporation or its directors, officers, or stock-holders. However, there are some decisions to the contrary. To be effective, any restriction on the transfer of stock must appear in the certificate of stock. The Uniform Commercial Code (§ 8–204) provides that, unless noted con-spicuously on the security, a restriction on its transfer is ineffective except against a person with actual knowledge of it.

Although there is some difference of opinion on the subject, most of the decisions sustain the validity of a provision in a bylaw, articles of incorporation, or stock certificate requiring a stockholder, before selling his stock, to afford the corporation or other stockholders an opportunity or option to purchase it. An agreement between the stockholders themselves or between them and the corporation that they would not sell or transfer their stock without giving the corporation or other stockholders the opportunity to purchase it is generally held to be valid and enforceable as against the stockholders and transferees with notice. Provisions requiring that the corporation or other stockholders be given an opportunity to purchase stock before it may be transferred to an-other generally apply only to voluntary sales, and not to judicial sales or other transfers by operation of law.

The mode of transfer generally authorized by statute is a delivery of the cer-tificate of stock, indorsed either in blank or to a specified person by the person appearing by the certificate to be the owner of the shares represented thereby, or by his attorney or personal representative, or by a delivery of the certificate accompanied by a separate document containing a written assignment of the certificate or a power of attorney to sell, assign, or transfer the same or the shares represented thereby. A person selling shares and delivering the certificate therefor may be compelled to make the necessary indorsement of the certificate.

The quality of negotiability given stock certificates by the Uniform Commer-cial Code carries a corresponding protection to a bona fide purchaser for value. Such a purchaser acquires the stock free from any adverse claims. Such a purchaser in good faith of certificates indorsed in blank by the owner is pro-tected even though the certificates may have been lost or stolen.

The purchaser of stock who has obtained the indorsement or assignment thereof, and has complied with the reasonable requirements as to transfer, is entitled, as a matter of right, to have the stock transferred to him on the books of the corporation, and this right is enforceable against the corporation and its transfer agents or registrars by the purchaser of the stock or his personal rep-resentatives, legatees, or heirs. The corporation may, of course, refuse to make a transfer on its books in order to protect itself from loss or against fraud, and it may require the surrender of the certificate of stock being transferred and the authentication or guaranty of the signature of the transferor. For a wrong-ful refusal to transfer stock on the books of the corporation, the transferee usually has a choice of remedies: he may either maintain an action at law for damages or a suit in equity to compel the transfer. In some jurisdictions mandamus will lie to compel the corporate officers to make the transfer.

Statutes and corporate charters or bylaws sometimes provide for a lien in favor of a corporation on the shares of its stockholders for debts owing by them to the corporation. Such a lien, however, is not effective as against a bona fide purchaser for value unless the right to the lien is noted on the certificate.

§ 6:11. Dividends.

Am Jur 2d References: Corporations, §§ 804–951.

A dividend of a business corporation is a division of profits among shareholders. It is the amount set apart by the governing body of a corporation from its net earnings and surplus funds to be paid in money or other medium to its shareholders according to their interests. The term "dividend" is sometimes loosely used, in an entirely different sense, to describe a division of capital assets or a distribution to stockholders or creditors upon the liquidation of a corporation. Although dividends are usually paid in money, they may also be paid in real or personal property, in stock, in bonds, or in scrip.

A stock dividend is one payable in the stock of the corporation, and involves the issuance of new stock to be distributed pro rata to the shareholders as evidence of the contemporaneous transfer of an equivalent amount of the surplus earnings or profits to the capital fund of the corporation. Such a dividend does not affect the proportionate interests of the stockholders, although transferring earnings to the capital fund instead of paying them as cash dividends may increase the aggregate value of the capital stock. Such a stock dividend differs from a "stock split" in that the latter adds nothing to the capital fund of the corporation but merely increases the total number of shares outstanding, reduces the unit value of each share, and may stimulate the trading of the shares on the stock market. Dividends payable by a corporation in stock held by it in another corporation, as well as dividends payable in other kinds of property, are usually classified as cash dividends.

It is a well-settled general rule that the net earnings or surplus of a going corporation constitute the proper fund for the payment of dividends, whether on its common or preferred stock, and that dividends cannot legally be declared and paid out of the capital of the corporation. The same general rule applies to stock dividends, properly so-called. This general rule does not, however, prevent a corporation engaged in a "wasting" business, such as mining, oil or gas production, or timber cutting, from declaring dividends payable from profits derived from the consumption or depletion of the capital assets.

Ordinarily, the directors, and they alone, have the power to declare cash dividends and to determine their amount. Stock dividends, however, may require the consent of the stockholders and other prerequisites. The fact that profits have accrued in the prosecution of the corporate business does not necessarily require the directors to distribute them as dividends to the stockholders. As a general rule, it rests in the sound discretion of the directors to determine the circumstances under which dividends will be declared out of net earnings or profits. So long as they act in good faith, they may either pay out profits as dividends or plow them back into the business to insure the health and growth of the corporation. However, this discretion is not unlimited, and the directors must act in good faith and not fraudulently, arbitrarily, or oppressively.

The preference accorded preferred stock entitles the holders thereof to priority of dividends over holders of common stock. This preference is entirely a matter of contract, which is generally set forth in the charter or bylaws of the corporation and on the certificate of stock. Dividends on preferred stock are, however, generally payable only out of net earnings, and in the absence of a statutory, charter, or contract provision to the contrary, the payment of dividends on preferred stock out of net earnings rests in the sound discretion of the directors of the corporation. And the same rules generally apply to interest-bearing stock or stock on which dividends are guaranteed by the corporation.

Where a dividend on stock is "passed" or omitted in any year because of deficiency in earnings, the holder of the stock loses any right to a share in the profits for that year unless the contract provides for the cumulation of dividends on the stock. The right of preferred stockholders to cumulative dividends depends upon a stipulation therefor in the agreement or upon a guaranty of dividends. Some courts take the view that the right of preferred stockholders to dividends is confined to the profits in a particular year and that, unless it is expressly so provided, the dividends do not accumulate and if they cannot be paid in any year they are not payable out of the profits of a subsequent year. However, other authorities take the position that in the absence of any specification to the contrary or of a limitation that dividends shall be paid only out of the net earnings for a certain period, the preferred stockholders are entitled to arrears of dividends to be paid out of profits of other and subsequent years. Determination of this question ultimately depends upon a construction of the charter and stock certificate.

The owner of stock at the time a dividend is declared is the person entitled to the dividend, in the absence of a statutory, charter, or contractual provision to the contrary. However, under modern corporate practice, corporations usually declare dividends payable to stockholders of record on a specified date; and where such date is subsequent to that of the declaration, the record holder of the stock on that date, and not the owner on the date of the declaration, is entitled to the dividend.

While courts will not ordinarily control the discretion of corporate officers and directors in the declaration and payment of dividends, judicial relief for this purpose may be had in a proper case. A court of equity may compel the declaration and payment of dividends, at the suit of stockholders, where the failure of corporate officers or directors to declare them is clearly due to fraud, bad faith, or in some cases, to arbitrary, oppressive, or wrongful conduct amounting to a breach of trust. And in a proper case a court of equity may enjoin a corporation or its directors from making a wrongful or unlawful distribution of dividends. The directors may be personally liable for the wrongful declaration and payment of dividends, at least where they act knowingly and not in good faith. Also, stockholders receiving wrongful or illegal dividends may, in some circumstances and under some statutes and decisions, be held liable to refund them to the corporation or its creditors.

III. STOCKHOLDERS

§ 6:12. Status, rights, and duties, generally.

Am Jur 2d References: Corporations, §§ 460–523.

The relationship between a corporation and its stockholders is contractual in nature, their rights and liabilities inter se being determined by the terms of their subscription agreements, the corporate charter and the governing statutes, and the provisions of the stock certificates. For many purposes, a corporation occupies a fiduciary relationship toward its stockholders. Some corporations, such as charitable and other nonprofit organizations, do not issue stock nor have stockholders, the incorporators and their successors being termed "members." Stockholders, as such, have no power to represent the corporation or act for it in the transaction of business. Title to the corporate property is vested in the corporation as a separate entity, and not in the stockholders.

The holders of the majority of the stock of a corporation have the power, by the election of directors and by the vote of their stock, to control and direct the action of the corporation and to determine the policies to be pursued by it, and the minority stockholders must submit to their decisions so long as the majority act in good faith and within the limitation of the law. This power vested in the majority stockholders imposes upon them a correlative duty of a fiduciary character to exercise good faith, care, and diligence in the control of corporate affairs and to protect the interests of the minority stockholders. These powers, rights, and corresponding duties are the same, whether the majority stockholder is an individual or another corporation. Clearly majority stockholders may not, as against a minority stockholder, dissipate or waste the corporate funds or property, and in their dealings with the corporation they must act in the interest of all stockholders. In the purchase or sale of property, in their contracts with the corporation, and in other dealings, the majority stockholders must act fairly and with due regard to the interests of the minority.

Although any fundamental change in a corporate charter normally requires the consent of all stockholders, statutes have been enacted in many states to prevent an arbitrary minority group of stockholders from obstructing changes and transactions which would be advantageous to the general corporate body. Under such statutes, a dissenting stockholder may not arbitrarily veto a majority decision to amend the charter, or to dispose of corporate property, or to merge or consolidate with another corporation, but he may have his stock appraised in the manner provided by the statute and receive payment for the fair value of his shares.

§ 6:13. Liability for corporation's debts.

Am Jur 2d References: Corporations, §§ 494, 495, 713–803.

It is a basic general rule of corporation law that stockholders are not liable as such for any of the obligations of the corporation, whatever their character and in whatever manner incurred. This rule is an aspect of the underlying principle that a corporation is a separate legal entity, distinct from its members and stockholders. In the absence of charter or constitutional or statutory provisions to the contrary, this rule applies to liability for torts as well as to obligations of a contractual nature. Except to the extent that stock subscriptions remain unpaid, creditors of the corporation generally have no recourse against its stockholders. Ownership of a controlling interest, a majority, or even all of the stock of a corporation by one person, does not in itself change this rule. Nor does the fact that the stockholder is itself a corporation render it liable as a stockholder. A parent or holding corporation is not generally liable on the contracts or for the torts of its subsidiary.

Under some circumstances, however, the courts may disregard the separate corporate entity and hold stockholders liable for its obligations. A dominant stockholder or a parent corporation may be held responsible for the obligations of a corporation where such stockholder treats the corporation as a mere agency, instrumentality, or adjunct of himself or itself or where the stockholder is guilty of fraud, actual or constructive, in the control of the property and business of the corporation.

It is well settled that stockholders are liable to creditors of the corporation for the amount which remains unpaid on their shares under their subscription contracts. A similar right exists against stockholders where stock has been issued wholly or partially without consideration, as where property accepted in exchange for stock has been grossly overvalued.

Where stock is issued in exchange for property or services at an overvaluation or at a discount, or in any manner other than for full value or agreement to pay full value therefor, the transaction is generally held to constitute a fraud upon creditors of the corporation, with the result that the subscriber or purchaser to whom such watered stock is issued, or his transferee with notice, is liable to creditors relying on such representations, to the extent of the difference between the par value of the shares and the amount actually paid therefor. The rule is the same where, after stock has been issued at par, the corporation votes to treat the stock as fully paid, if, in fact, the stockholders have not paid the full par value. In the case of overvaluation of property given to a corporation in exchange for its stock, some courts hold that a fraudulent intention to overvalue the property is necessary to establish liability on the part of a stockholder. Other courts, however, have adopted the "true value" rule, under which motive, intent, and good faith are disregarded.

§ 6:14. Stockholders' actions and intervention.

Am Jur 2d References: Corporations, §§ 524–598.

Actions by stockholders may be divided into three general categories: (1) derivative actions, (2) individual actions, and (3) representative actions. A derivative action is one brought by one or more stockholders, on behalf of the corporation, to remedy or prevent a wrong against the corporation. An individual action is one brought by one or more stockholders to protect their individual or personal rights as stockholders; and such actions may be brought against the corporation itself, against its directors, officers, or other persons, or against other stockholders. A representative action, in the strict and proper sense, is similar to an individual action, except that it is brought by one or more stockholders on behalf of all stockholders or all of a class of stockholders to protect their personal or individual rights as such. Such an action is in the nature of a class suit. Derivative actions by stockholders are sometimes referred to as representative actions.

Wrongs which affect the corporation itself give rise to causes of action which belong to the corporation and not to its stockholders. An action based on such a wrong may be brought only in the name of the corporation and on its behalf. However, where a corporation actually or virtually refuses to institute an action to enforce a corporate right or to prevent or remedy a wrong to the corporation, because it is controlled by the wrongdoers or for other reasons, one or more of its stockholders may bring a suit on behalf of the corporation and in its right. Such a derivative suit is equitable in nature and is governed by general principles of equity. The corporation in such a suit is the real party in interest, and the stockholder bringing the suit is only a nominal plaintiff. Any defense to an action by the corporation is also a defense to a derivative action by a stockholder. Stockholders may obtain relief in equity against officers or directors of a corporation who deal wrongfully with its property or who are otherwise guilty of fraud or breach of trust. And the court's jurisdiction extends to the prevention of ultra vires or illegal acts.

While the courts will protect minority stockholders against fraud or breach of trust by officers or directors of the corporation, the majority stockholders and their designated directors and officers have the right, in the absence of fraud, to manage the corporate affairs within the powers possessed by the corporation, and the courts will not usually exercise jurisdiction at the instance of the shareholders to control or interfere in the management of the corporate or internal affairs of the corporation. Mere errors of judgment on the part of officers or majority stockholders are not sufficient grounds for the interference of equity at the instance of minority stockholders. But a stockholder may resort to equity to protect his personal or individual rights, as distinguished from the rights or interests of the corporation itself.

The right to bring a stockholder's derivative action is subject to certain restrictions imposed by statutes and by judicial decisions. The courts will not ordinarily entertain a derivative suit by a stockholder unless it plainly appears that all remedies within the corporation itself have been resorted to in vain, including a demand upon the corporate officers and directors and, according to some decisions and court rules, a request upon the stockholders as a body to bring suit. The requirement of a demand upon officers or directors may be excused where such demand would obviously be futile; and the requirement of a demand of action by the stockholders as a body is not required where, under the facts, the stockholder cannot do so or it would be unreasonable or useless to require it. Under statutes in some states, where derivative actions are brought by a small minority of stockholders, the corporation may require the plaintiff or plaintiffs to give security for costs.

In some jurisdictions the plaintiff in a stockholder's derivative action is required to show that he was a stockholder at the time of the transaction of which he complains or that the stock thereafter devolved upon him by operation of law. And such an action cannot generally be maintained by one who has transferred or lost title to his stock.

Although the officers and directors have the right to control an action brought by the corporation, and may dismiss it if they act in good faith, stockholders may intervene in a corporate action where they show that those conducting the corporation's case were not doing so adequately or that their handling of the case or their dismissal thereof was collusive or fraudulent. And stockholders are permitted to intervene for the purpose of asserting a defense to an action against the corporation upon a showing of similar grounds.

§ 6:15. Meetings of stockholders; elections; voting.

Am Jur 2d References: Corporations, §§ 599–712.

The powers vested in stockholders are usually exercised through their votes at stockholders' meetings. Such meetings are held for the purpose of electing directors and transacting other business requiring the action or consent of the stockholders, such as amendment of the articles or certificate of incorporation, sale or encumbrance of corporate assets, consolidation or merger, and ratification of past acts of the directors and officers of the corporation. The times for the holding of stockholders' meetings are usually fixed by statute, and articles of incorporation, or bylaws, and meetings at least once a year are generally required. The power to determine the precise date of meetings within a limited period may be delegated to the directors or designated corporate officers. Unless the place of stockholders' meetings is specified by statute, the corporation may designate the place by charter, bylaws, or decision of the board of directors.

The power to call stockholders' meetings is usually vested in the board of directors, unless the corporation's charter or bylaws or an applicable statute provides otherwise. Sometimes a designated officer of the corporation is authorized to call a meeting of stockholders; and under certain circumstances the stockholders themselves may call a meeting. Notice of the time, place, and purpose of the meeting must be given in the manner provided by the corporate charter or bylaws or by statute to all stockholders eligible to vote at the meeting.

In the absence of express regulations by statute or bylaw, the conduct of corporate meetings, including the election of directors, is controlled largely by accepted usage and common practice, the fundamental rule being that all who are entitled to take part shall be treated with fairness and good faith. The selection of the presiding officer, the necessity and definition of a quorum, and matters relating to nominations and adjournments, are usually governed by the corporation's charter and bylaws. In the absence of statute or bylaw requiring more, a vote of a majority of the shares of stock represented at a legally constituted meeting of stockholders is generally sufficient to decide any question properly presented, a majority of all issued or outstanding stock not being required. Provision is usually made for the selection of inspectors or judges of elections at stockholders' meetings.

The right to vote stock at corporate meetings is an incident of stock ownership, although the right must be exercised in the manner and under the restrictions prescribed by statute or by the charter and bylaws. The right to vote stock follows the legal title thereto, and for this purpose those who appear on the corporate records as stockholders are considered to own the stock registered in their names. The voting right is usually limited to persons appearing as the owners of stock on the records of the corporation on a specified date. Cumulative voting of stock in the election of directors is sometimes provided for by statute, constitutional provisions, or charter, but there is no right to vote on this basis unless the method is so authorized. Cumulative voting is usually defined as a method of voting under which each shareholder is entitled to cast a number of votes equal to the number of his shares multiplied by the number of directors, or the number of directors to be elected, with the option of giving all his votes to a single candidate or of distributing them among two or more as he sees fit. The right of cumulative voting, where granted, is intended to enable minority stockholders to secure representation on the board of directors by electing one or more directors.

The right to vote corporate stock by proxy is generally an incident of ownership of the stock. A proxy to vote shares of stock is an authority given by the holder of the stock to another to exercise his voting rights. The term "proxy" is also used to designate the holder of the proxy. The duration of proxies may be limited by statute, charter provision, or by their own terms. A proxy may be revoked by the shareholder at any time, even though, by its terms, it is declared to be irrevocable, unless it is coupled with an interest or has been given as security.

Voting agreements among stockholders, by which they agree in effect to vote their stock in a certain manner, or in accordance with the decision of a majority of the parties, or the like, are generally upheld unless their purpose or consequences are contrary to law or public policy. A somewhat similar device is the voting trust, under which persons owning stock divorce the voting rights thereof from the ownership, retaining the ownership and transferring the voting rights to trustees in whom the voting rights are vested. Voting trusts, if created for a lawful purpose, are generally held to be valid.

IV. POWERS, FUNCTIONS, AND LIABILITIES OF CORPORATION

§ 6:16. Generally.

Am Jur 2d References: Corporations, §§ 952–962, 980–1068, 1427–1450.

A corporation has only such powers as are expressly granted in its charter or in statutes under which it is created, and such powers as are necessary to carry out its express powers and the object of its incorporation. The implied or incidental powers which a corporation has in order to make effectual use of the powers expressly granted and to enable it to accomplish the purposes of its creation are not limited to such as are indispensable for the purposes, but include all that are necessary, in the sense of being appropriate and suitable, including the right of reasonable choice of the means to be employed.

As a general rule, the grant of powers in a corporate charter is construed strictly, and any ambiguity in the terms of the charter will be construed against the corporation. Persons dealing with a corporation must take notice of any limitation of its powers by its charter and by the governing statutes.

Among the powers essential to the functioning of any corporation are the powers to enter into contracts and to acquire and hold property, real and personal. There is a conflict of authority on the question whether a corporation may purchase its own stock, in the absence of any statute or charter provision in that regard. The same conflict of authority exists with respect to the implied power to purchase stock of other corporations.

As a general rule, a corporation has power to alienate its property, both real and personal, unless restricted by its charter, statute, or considerations of public policy. The consent of stockholders is frequently required, however, to a sale or encumbrance of large amounts of corporate property otherwise than in the usual course of business of the corporation. The power of a business corporation to make a gift or contribution of its money or property is limited, according to many decisions, to donations which in some way tend to further the business or interests of the corporation. The modern trend, however, is to enlarge the incidental or implied powers of corporations to include the right to make charitable donations within reasonable limits.

A corporation does not have power to enter into contracts of guaranty or suretyship unless it is given express authority to do so or the contract is in the legitimate furtherance of its own purposes and business.

The power of a business corporation to incur indebtedness in the legitimate transaction of its proper business is necessarily implied. For proper corporate purposes a corporation may, except where limited or forbidden by statute or charter, borrow money whenever the necessity of its business so requires, and may issue evidences of indebtedness, such as notes, bonds, and mortgages therefor. However, the corporate charter or statutes may require the assent of stockholders as a condition of the right of a corporation to mortgage or otherwise encumber its property.

It is generally held that a corporation, in the absence of express statutory or charter authority to do so, has no power to enter into a partnership with an individual or other corporations. This rule does not, however, prevent a corporation from entering into joint ventures where the nature of the enterprise is within the scope of its legitimate powers.

From certain learned professions which can be practiced only by persons who have been licensed to do so, corporations are excluded. For example, a corporation cannot lawfully engage in the practice of law, nor in the practice of medicine, surgery, or dentistry. Some statutes, however, permit persons engaged in various professions to form corporations or associations for the practice of their professions.

It is well settled that an ordinary private corporation is liable for its torts. Under the doctrine of respondeat superior a corporation is liable for the torts and wrongful acts or omissions of its officers, agents, or employees acting within the scope of their authority or the course of their employment. This rule applies even though the wrongful character of the act is dependent upon motive or intent or upon malice or wantonness. Corporations may be held liable for the fraud and deceit of their officers and agents. And corporations are subject to criminal liability for many types of offenses.

§ 6:17. Ultra vires transactions.

Am Jur 2d References: Corporations, §§ 963–979.

An act of a corporation is properly said to be ultra vires where it is beyond the powers expressly or impliedly conferred upon the corporation by the state. Such acts are to be distinguished from acts of officers or agents of a corporation in excess of their authority in the course of transactions within the charter powers of the corporation. In actions between the corporation and strangers dealing with it, the question frequently arises as to whether the act is one which the corporation is not empowered to perform under any circumstances, or is one that it may perform for some purposes or under certain conditions. In the first case the act is strictly ultra vires; and as a general rule, in the absence of special circumstances, estoppel, or controlling statutes, there can be no recovery based on the contract or transaction. As applied to executory contracts, the effect of this rule is that a corporation may set up as a complete defense to an action on a contract the fact that it had no power to enter into the contract and that it was ultra vires in the strict sense. Also, where the corporation seeks to enforce an executory contract which is ultra vires on its part, the other party may avail himself of this fact as a defense.

The reasons underlying this general doctrine are: (1) the interest of the sovereign or the public that the corporation shall not transcend the powers granted; (2) the interest of stockholders that their capital shall not be subjected to the risk of enterprises not contemplated by the charter; and (3) the obligation of everyone dealing with the corporation to take notice of the limit of its powers.

The defense of ultra vires is looked upon by many courts with disfavor where it is presented for the purpose of avoiding an obligation which is merely in excess of corporate powers and is not in violation of an express prohibition of statute. The trend of modern decisions is to deny the plea of ultra vires, whether urged for or against the corporation, where it will not advance justice, but, on the contrary, would result in legal wrong or inequity. Statutes have been enacted in many jurisdictions expressing this modern trend and limiting the availability of ultra vires as a defense. However, even where the decisions or statutes limit the defense of ultra vires, the state may object to ultra vires transactions, by forfeiture of the corporate charter or otherwise; the limitation of power may be asserted in an action by or on behalf of the corporation against a director or officer; and a stockholder may enjoin threatened ultra vires acts. A corporation is liable for torts or criminal acts committed in the course of ultra vires undertakings; a title taken by a corporation in excess of its authority is nevertheless valid; and rights or benefits acquired under an ultra vires contract fully performed or executed are protected.

A corporation may generally assert a limitation of its power as against a person who had notice of the limitation at the time of the transaction in question.

In the absence of controlling statutes, some courts take the view that if a contract is ultra vires in the proper sense—that is, beyond the express and implied powers of the corporation—it is unenforceable under all circumstances and cannot be made valid subsequently by estoppel or by the receipt of benefits thereunder. Under this rule, the parties have no remedy upon the contract as such. According to other authorities, however, special circumstances may make it inequitable to allow the defense of ultra vires, as where benefits have been received or the contract has been performed by the party seeking the enforcement thereof. These courts seek to achieve equity by permitting a suit on the ultra vires contract and by estopping the corporation or party against whom enforcement of the contract is sought from asserting the ultra vires nature of the transaction. As indicated above, when an ultra vires contract has been fully executed by both parties, neither of them can assert its invalidity as a ground for relief against it.

Some courts deny a recovery directly upon an ultra vires contract even though there has been a performance by the party seeking to enforce it. However in many jurisdictions a recovery may be had on an ultra vires contract which has been performed by the party seeking its enforcement, on the ground that the corporation or party against whom the contract is sought to be enforced has received or caused such performance, and, having received money or other benefits by virtue of the contract, is estopped to deny liability thereon, unless the contract is illegal on other grounds. The receipt of benefits by the party against whom it is sought to enforce an ultra vires contract is determinative of the right to recover on the contract in some jurisdictions, but in others it does not permit recovery under the contract itself. However, it is agreed, both in jurisdictions which do and jurisdictions which do not recognize the doctrine of estoppel, that where benefits are received under an ultra vires contract, recovery may be had in a proper case under equitable principles, not on the contract itself, but under principles of unjust enrichment and restitution, or quasi-contract, for the reasonable value of the benefits—money, property, or services—received by the defendant. This amounts to a disaffirmance rather than an affirmance of the ultra vires agreement. To enforce this right of restitution, the claimant may maintain an action for money had and received or an equitable suit for an accounting.

§ 6:18. Actions by and against corporation.

Am Jur 2d References: Corporations, §§ 1451–1489.

The power of a corporation to sue and to prosecute actions to their conclusion is a necessary incident of its existence as a corporate entity, even without an express provision therefor in its charter. Similarly, a corporation may be sued although not expressly made subject to suit by the terms of its charter. Corporate existence implies amenability to legal process. The jurisdiction and venue of actions against corporations are usually fixed by statutes or rules of court, as is the manner of serving process on a corporation.

Provision is usually made for service of process on an officer, manager, or agent of the corporation or upon the person designated by the corporation pursuant to statute for that purpose. Provision is sometimes made for service upon designated state officers under certain circumstances. Under the Federal Rules of Civil Procedure, service of process may be made on a domestic corporation by delivering a copy of the summons and complaint to an officer, a managing or general agent, or to any other agent authorized by appointment or by law to receive service of process; and these rules also authorize service in the manner prescribed by the law of the state where the federal court is held. Provision is sometimes made for a mailing of a copy of the process to the defendant corporation.

V. DIRECTORS, OFFICERS, AND EMPLOYEES

§ 6:19. Generally; designation, tenure, functions, and powers.

Am Jur 2d References: Corporations, §§ 1079–1270.

Although a corporation is a distinct legal entity, it is not an automaton and it can function only through human agencies. At the base of the corporate structure are the stockholders, who elect directors who appoint officers who in turn employ agents and servants to perform the acts necessary to carry on the business of the corporation. Corporations have the power to appoint agents with authority to do the acts or enter into contracts within the powers of the corporation. The appointment or election of the administrative officers, such as the president, treasurer, secretary, etc., is usually entrusted to the board of directors.

Directors are usually elected by the stockholders at meetings held for that purpose in accordance with the provisions of statute and the articles of incorporation. The number of directors is determined by the provisions of the articles of incorporation or bylaws, as is the manner of filling vacancies, whether by the stockholders or by the board of directors. The eligibility and qualifications of directors and officers, as well as their time or tenure, are fixed by statute, articles of incorporation, or bylaws. The acts of de facto officers or directors may bind the corporation as regards a third person who deals with them in ignorance of their want of legal right to office. The power to remove officers of the corporation for cause is usually vested in the board of directors; and the power to remove directors belongs to the stockholders. An officer or director may, of course, resign.

The power and authority of directors are vested in them as a board, and the board of directors exercises these powers at meetings usually held at regular times fixed by the articles of incorporation or bylaws of the corporation, and provision is usually made for the calling of special meetings of the board. If the place of meeting is not fixed by the articles of incorporation or bylaws, the directors may determine the place of their meetings. Where a meeting is held at the time and place described by the articles or bylaws, notice thereof to the directors is not usually required. However, proper notice of special meetings must be given to the directors. The general rule is that at a directors' meeting the presence of a majority of the directors is required to constitute a quorum, which is necessary to enable them to exercise their powers. And a majority of those present at the meeting, if they constitute a quorum, make the decisions of the board, unless there is a provision to the contrary in the articles or bylaws. The minutes of the meetings of a board of directors, kept by the person appointed therefor, constitute the official record of the meetings.

The board of directors represents the corporate body and it is generally vested with all of the powers as regards corporate acts and management of corporate affairs. The directors have authority to transact all ordinary business of the corporation within the scope of its charter powers, and their acts are the acts of the corporation. The board of directors may delegate to a committee of their number the authority to act for the corporation in a particular matter. Executive committees are frequently appointed by the board of directors to act for the board in matters arising between meetings of the directors.

An officer or agent of a corporation has such authority as is expressly conferred upon him, and also the implied and ostensible authority arising under the general principles of agency. The implied authority includes all such incidental authority as is necessary, usual, and proper to effectuate the main authority expressly conferred. Ostensible or apparent authority binds the corporation by acts of an officer or agent, although not expressly authorized, where the officer or agent is held out by the corporation or permitted to act in such way as to justify third persons who deal with him in assuming that he is acting within the scope of authority. The general authority and power of each officer of the corporation is determined by its articles of incorporation and by-laws.

A corporation, like an individual, may ratify unauthorized acts on contracts of its officers and other agents. Such a ratification is equivalent to a prior authority and relates back and supplies the authority to do the act or make the contract. And a corporation may ratify unauthorized acts of officers or agents by acquiescing in or consenting to the acts or accepting the benefits thereof. An act or transaction cannot be ratified, however, unless it was such as could have been authorized by the officer or body charged with the ratification, and such as was within the charter powers of the corporation.

§ 6:20. Duties, liabilities, and rights.

Am Jur 2d References: Corporations, §§ 1271–1426.

The officers and directors of a private corporation are its agents through whom it functions and carries on its business. They occupy a fiduciary relation to the corporation and its stockholders, and they are required to act in the utmost good faith, to give to the enterprise the benefit of their care and best judgment, and to exercise their powers solely in the interest of the corporation or the stockholders and not for their own personal interests. It is their duty to act within the scope of their powers and authority and to manage the affairs of the corporation so that it keeps within its corporate powers. They are usually personally liable to the corporation for loss suffered by it resulting from their acts which are unauthorized and clearly beyond their power. In all personal or private dealings with the corporation, a director or officer must make full disclosure of material facts and must act with the utmost good faith and fairness and without any undue advantage from his position.

Officers and directors are, of course, liable to the corporation for the latter's losses resulting from their fraudulent acts or from their wasting, squandering, or misappropriation of corporate assets. They are bound to use due care and diligence in the management and administration of the affairs of the corporation and in the use and preservation of its property, and they are personally liable for losses or injuries resulting proximately to the corporation from a breach or neglect of this duty. Directors are not insurers, however, and are not held to any standard of absolute liability. The degree of care exacted of them is ordinary care and diligence. The standard of the care which a director is bound to exercise is generally held to be such care as a prudent man should exercise in like circumstances and charged with a like duty, which is usually, but not necessarily, the degree of care which a person would show in the conduct of his own affairs of a similar kind. Where they have exercised reasonable care, diligence, and good faith, directors and officers of the corporation are not liable for losses resulting from mere errors of judgment on their part.

A director or officer of a corporation is not permitted to make a private or secret profit out of his official position. He must give the corporation the benefit of any advantage which he has thereby obtained, and he is required to account for such secret profits even though the transaction in which they are made is advantageous or not harmful to the corporation, and even though he acted without intent to injure the corporation.

A corporation may maintain an action against its directors or officers for their mismanagement, waste or diversion of assets, or other wrongs; and in a proper case a derivative action may be maintained by stockholders in the name of and on behalf of the corporation.

Under statutes in some jurisdictions, directors or other officers of the corporation are liable for its debts where they are guilty of certain official delinquencies, such as failing to make the required financial reports of the corporation, or making false reports; allowing the corporate debts to exceed a certain proportion of the capital paid in; or transacting corporate business before certain steps have been taken to complete organization.

An officer or director of a corporation does not incur personal liability for its torts merely by reason of his official position; he is not liable for torts committed by or for the corporation unless he has participated in the wrong. But he is personally liable for injury to third persons from any tort which he commits or actually participates in. Thus, directors and other officers may be personally liable to outsiders for fraud perpetrated on the latter by false statements in reports, certificates, and the like.

Similar considerations govern the criminal liability of directors, officers, and agents of corporations. Such a person is not generally liable for an offense committed by the corporation, except where he has in some way participated in the criminal act as a principal or as an aider, abettor, or accessory. However, such a person cannot shield himself from criminal responsibility for his own act on the ground that it was done in his official capacity as an officer or director of a corporation. In some instances statutes have been enacted punishing corporate officers and agents for particular acts.

The rights of directors, officers, and employees as against the corporation consist mainly of the right to compensation for services. They also have the right generally to be reimbursed or indemnified for money properly advanced or expenses necessarily incurred for the corporation. The amount of such compensation generally depends upon contract; and the salaries of officers and directors are usually fixed by the board of directors, though the board may delegate this power to its committee set up for that purpose. The stockholders may have a remedy against directors or officers who have received grossly excessive salaries or other compensation.

VI. FOREIGN CORPORATIONS

§ 6:21. Status, powers, and functions.

Am Jur 2d References: Foreign Corporations, §§ 1–192, 316–606.

The term "foreign corporations" is used generally to denote, with reference to a particular state or country, any corporation created by or organized under the law of another state of country. No distinction is made in the use of this terminology between corporations of a sister state and those of a foreign country. However, in federal legislation the term "foreign" imports incorporation outside the territorial limits of the United States. Corporations organized under laws of the United States and known as "federal corporations" may be treated as foreign corporations for some purposes in any particular state, while they are domestic corporations for other purposes. A corporation created under the laws of one state has no legal or constitutional right to migrate to another state except with the consent of the latter state and subject to the terms and restrictions imposed by it. It has no constitutional right to engage in business in a state other than that of its creation, except interstate commerce and business of a federal nature.

The right of a foreign corporation to do business in a state depends solely upon the will of such state and exists only by virtue of the law of comity, and the grant of this privilege and the terms under which it will be granted are within the exclusive legislative control of the state. As a general rule, a corporation of one state permitted by comity to do business in another state may exercise within the latter state the general powers conferred by its own charter and permitted by the laws of the state of its origin, if such powers are not inconsistent with the laws and policy of the state where they are sought to be exercised. If it possesses such powers under the terms of its own charter, a foreign corporation may acquire, hold, sell, convey, or encumber real or personal property, subject to such restrictions as the local state may impose.

Except as limited by statute, a corporation of a sister state or friendly foreign nation may sue in the courts of the forum by reason of the doctrine of comity, and they may also defend actions brought against it. Whether it may be sued in a state other than that of its origin depends upon many factors, including the extent of its activities in and contact with the state of the forum and whether it is "doing business" there so as to subject it to the jurisdiction and processes of that state.

When a corporation enters a state other than that of its origin and engages in business or establishes a "commercial domicil" there, it is held to submit itself to the valid laws of such state and to the jurisdiction and processes of its courts to the extent required by such laws. And no matter where it attempts to exercise them, a corporation has no powers other than those granted it by its charter and the laws of the state of its origin.

The extent of a state's power and control over a corporation created by the United States is subject to the paramount power of the Federal Government, and state laws will not be permitted to operate in such manner as to impair the utility or effectiveness of such a corporation as an instrumentality or agency of the Federal Government.

A state may, by appropriate legislation, domesticate, adopt, or naturalize a corporation of another state so as to enable it to act within the state as a domestic corporation. Some states require such domestication as a condition of the right of a foreign corporation to do intrastate business therein. The manner of accomplishing such domestication and the consequences thereof are governed by the laws of the particular state.

The internal affairs of a corporation, such as the rights, powers, and relationships of stockholders and directors, and such matters as corporate meetings, the ownership and transfer of stock, and the like, are ordinarily the concern of the state where the corporation was created. The courts of another state, in which the corporation is doing business, will not ordinarily take jurisdiction of an action to determine the internal affairs of a foreign corporation, or in the exercise of visitorial powers, interfere with, supervise, or direct the management of such corporation. Exceptions are made to this rule, however, under some circumstances; and jurisdiction over the internal affairs of a foreign corporation may be exercised as an incident of the determination of other matters of which the court has jurisdiction.

While the courts of a state in which a foreign corporation is doing business may not dissolve or terminate the existence of the corporation, they may, under the provisions of the statutes of the state, oust the corporation from operating within the state and may terminate its license to do business there, and may take such steps as are necessary, as regards the property of the corporation, to protect the rights of local creditors.

§ 6:22. Regulation by state.

Am Jur 2d References: Foreign Corporations, §§ 193–372, 460–606

As seen in the foregoing section, the right of a corporation to carry on intrastate business in a state other than that of its origin depends upon the will and consent of the latter state. A state may exclude a foreign corporation entirely, or it may admit it upon such terms as it sees fit. Foreign corporations are subject to a great variety of statutory regulations in the several states, and these regulations are enforced by sanctions and penalties of various kinds.

As to certain types of foreign corporations, states sometimes require that certain standards as to capital structure, usually those applicable to similar domestic corporations, be met before admission to do business in the state. Many states require a foreign corporation to make application for permission to do business in the state and to obtain a license or permit therefor. As a condition of procuring such license or permit, it is not unusual to require the filing of an authenticated copy of the corporation's charter or articles of incorporation with a designated officer of the local state. Financial statements and descriptions of the corporate structure and management of the corporation are required in some states. And it is frequently required that as a condition of the right to do intrastate business in the state, a foreign corporation provide some kind of security for the performance of its contracts.

States may provide for service of process upon foreign corporations, within the limits of constitutional requirements. Substituted service upon such corporations, upon a person to be designated by either the corporation or the state, is frequently provided for. Many states, by statutes, designate the corporate agent or officer on whom process may be served in an action against a foreign corporation; and it is usual for a state to require a foreign corporation doing business therein to designate an agent or officer upon whom process may be served. It is a common regulatory practice for states to designate a state officer upon whom process may be served in an action against a foreign corporation doing business in the state.

There are, of course, constitutional limitations upon the powers of a state over a foreign corporation. Such a corporation is entitled to the protection of the due process and equal protection clauses of the Federal Constitution, as well as the provision prohibiting states from impairing the obligation of contracts. And obviously a state may not impose its regulations upon a foreign corporation which does not do business within the state and with which the state has no jurisdictional contact. It is also well settled that a state, under the commerce clause of the Federal Constitution, may not directly burden or interfere with interstate or foreign commerce by subjecting foreign corporations engaged exclusively in such commerce within the state to its statutory regulations or requirements. This rule does not, however, prevent a state from imposing reasonable terms on the right of a foreign corporation to carry on intrastate business within the state, even though the corporation is also engaged in interstate commerce.

The amenability of a foreign corporation to the jurisdiction and regulations of a state usually depends upon its activities in and contacts with that state, and this is frequently expressed in terms of its "doing business" in the state. The question whether such a corporation is "doing business" in a state or has a sufficient "minimum contact" with the state depends upon the circumstances of each case and upon the purposes for which the question is raised. The problem arises, and is governed by different criteria, in determining whether a foreign corporation may properly be treated as (1) within the terms of statutes excluding, or imposing conditions or regulations on, such corporations, (2) within the state's jurisdiction for purposes of taxation; (3)

amenable to the general jurisdiction and processes of the courts of the state; and various other types of legislation.

The act of a foreign corporation in qualifying to do business within a state in accordance with its statutes amounts to an assent on the part of the corporation to all the reasonable conditions imposed by the state. It thus subjects itself to taxation by the state and to the regulatory statutes affecting such corporations. If the foreign corporation transacts intrastate business within a state without complying with the requirements of its laws, it subjects itself to penalties and disabilities. Many states have statutes providing that a corporation thus defaulting may not maintain any action at law or in equity in the courts of the state, or that it may not maintain any suit on a contract made in the state.

CRIMINAL LAW

I. INTRODUCTORY

II. CAPACITY FOR CRIME OR PUNISHMENT

III. THE CRIMINAL STATE OF MIND: INTENT; MALICE; VOLITION

IV. PARTICIPATION IN CRIME; AIDING AND ABETTING; ACCESSORIES

V. DEFENSES

VI. RIGHTS OF ACCUSED; CONSTITUTIONAL PROTECTION

VII. JURISDICTION AND VENUE

VIII. PROCEDURE, PLEAS, AND REMEDIES

IX. JUDGMENT, SENTENCE, AND PUNISHMENT

X. PARTICULAR OFFENSES

I. INTRODUCTORY

§ 7:1. General matters.

Am Jur 2d References: Criminal Law, §§ 1–9, 18–25.

A crime is an act committed or omitted in violation of a public law. A crime of omission is the failure to perform a required act. Examples of this class of offenses are the failure of a motorist involved in an accident to stop and render aid and the failure to file income tax returns or a report required by law. By the common law of England, misprision of felony or treason was a crime of this nature, consisting of the failure of a person to make himself an informer as to any treason or felony of which he had knowledge. However, this common-law offense is not generally recognized in the United States. The similar offense created by federal statute requires some positive act in addition to failure to disclose, such as concealment, suppression of evidence, or harboring of a criminal.

At common law, if a misdemeanor was an ingredient of a felony, the misdemeanor was said to be merged in the felony and the prosecution could only be for the latter. The doctrine of merger has no application where both crimes are misdemeanors or both are felonies. The merger doctrine has been disfavored and confined within narrow limits in recent cases, and in some American jurisdictions it is not recognized at all.

The "degree" of a crime denotes a particular grade of crime more or less culpable than another grade of the same offense. The classification of an offense is ordinarily determined by the nature of the punishment provided therefor. At early common law, a felony was a crime for which the law provided a total forfeiture of the offender's land or goods or both. In the absence of statute, felonies were such serious offenses as were formerly punished by death or by forfeiture of lands or goods. The classification is now, however, generally governed by statute or constitution. A distinction commonly adopted, frequently by statute, is that offenses punishable by death or by imprisonment in the state prison are felonies, whereas all others, including those punishable by imprisonment in the county jail, are misdemeanors.

A distinction is made for various purposes and in different contexts between "infamous" crimes and other crimes. Thus, prosecution for an infamous crime must generally be on a presentment or indictment; and conviction of an infamous crime may affect the credibility of a witness or the eligibility of a person to vote or hold public office, and it is sometimes made a ground for divorce. Whether or not a crime is "infamous" usually turns on the nature of the punishment provided therefor. A crime punishable by imprisonment in a state prison is an infamous crime.

A crime involves "moral turpitude" if it is an act of baseness, vileness, or depravity in the private and social duties which a man owes to his fellow men or to society in general. The moral turpitude of a crime may affect the consequences of conviction in various connections, such as the disbarment of attorneys, the revocation of medical licenses, or the deportation of aliens.

For various purposes, the law has long divided crimes into acts wrong in themselves, called "acts mala in se," and acts which would not be wrong but for the fact that positive law forbids them, called "acts mala prohibita."

An act which is malum in se has been variously defined as one inherently wicked, one naturally evil, as adjudged by the sense of a civilized community, or one involving illegality from the very nature of the transaction, upon principles of natural, moral, or public law.

§ 7:2. Common law and statutory offenses.

Am Jur 2d References: Criminal Law, §§ 10–17.

In many jurisdictions there are no common-law offenses, and no act can be a crime unless made so by legislative enactment. There are, for example, no common-law crimes against the United States. In other jurisdictions, on the other hand, the common law prevails unless changed by statute, and an act which is not forbidden by statute may be indictable as a common-law offense. This is sometimes due to the fact that there has been a blanket legislative adoption of the common law as to crimes or of the common law generally. In jurisdictions where common-law offenses are still in force, a statute does not abrogate a common-law offense in the absence of an express or implied provision to that effect.

Common-law principles are frequently invoked in the interpretation of statutes creating or describing criminal offenses. Where such a statute uses a term that is not defined therein, the term will generally be given its common-law meaning; and the common-law definition of an offense will be applied where a statute creating the offense refers to it by its common-law name, without further definition.

Where the Legislature undertakes to create or define an offense, it must do so in terms of reasonable certainty and definiteness. A statute which either forbids or requires the doing of an act in terms so vague that men of common intelligence must guess as to its meaning does not comply with the constitutional requirement of due process of law.

§ 7:3. Attempts and solicitation.

Am Jur 2d References: Criminal Law, §§ 110–114.

An attempt to commit a crime was itself an indictable offense at common law. Criminal attempt may be defined as any overt act done with the intent to commit the crime, and which, except for the interference of some cause preventing the carrying out of the intent, would have resulted in the commission of the crime. An attempt has two elements: a specific intent to commit a particular crime and a direct ineffectual act toward its commission. Some authorities hold that a failure to consummate the ultimate crime intended is an element of the crime of attempt, so that no conviction for attempt may be had where the substantive offense is complete, but other authorities take a different view.

Mere intention to commit a particular crime does not amount to an attempt. It is essential that the defendant, with the intent of committing the crime, do some overt act adapted to and in the ordinary and likely course of things calculated to result in the commission of the crime. Many authorities hold that mere acts of preparation, not proximately leading to the consummation of the intended crime, are not sufficient to establish an attempt to commit it, as there must be some act moving directly toward the commission of the offense after the preparations are made. It is difficult or impossible to formulate general principles to distinguish between preparation for an attempt and the attempt itself. In a general way, it may be said that preparation consists in devising or arranging the means or measures necessary for the commission of the offense, and that the attempt is the direct movement toward the commission after the preparations are made. It is also difficult to formulate any precise rule as to how close the overt act must come to the accomplishment of the ultimate criminal result. If the accused expected his acts to accomplish that result without further effort on his part, this will usually be enough. Some cases state that while the act need not be the last proximate act to the consummation of the offense, it must approach sufficiently near to it to stand either as the first or some subsequent step in a direct movement toward the commission of the offense after the preparations are made.

If the other elements of a criminal attempt are present, it is no defense that, by reason of some fact unknown to the defendant at the time of his attempt, it could not be fully carried into effect. Thus, one who thrusts his hand into another's pocket, intending to steal what he finds there, may be guilty of attempted larceny, though the pocket was empty. And one who, believing a gun to be loaded, points it at another and pulls the trigger, may be convicted of attempted homicide, although the gun was not loaded. It is sometimes said that the thing attempted must not be an impossibility, but this refers only to inherent impossibility, not to impossibility due to outside interference, to miscalculation as to a supposed opportunity which failed to materialize, or to extraneous facts not within the control of the defendant. Of course, the act attempted must itself be a crime, and the defendant must have the capacity of committing the substantive offense.

Although solicitation may constitute an element in some attempts, it is the general, though not unanimous, view that soliciting another to commit a crime is not, by itself, sufficient to constitute an attempt to commit that crime. However, one who incites or solicits another to commit a crime which, either by common law or by statute, is a felony, is himself guilty of the substantive crime of solicitation. There is a conflict of authority as to whether solicitation to commit a misdemeanor is indictable. Solicitation is a substantive offense by statute in some states. The solicitor may be guilty even though his solicitation was of no effect and the crime counseled was not committed and even though no further steps were taken toward the consummation of the offense.

II. CAPACITY FOR CRIME OR PUNISHMENT

§ 7:4. In general; infants.

Am Jur 2d References: Associations and Clubs, § 49; Corporations, §§ 1434–1440; Criminal Law, §§ 26–30; Partnership, §§ 169–170.

Legal mental capacity to commit a crime is essential to criminal responsibility. The various factors which may affect such capacity are sometimes prescribed by statute. Physical handicaps, such as deafness or blindness, do not, per se, affect the legal capacity to commit crime. Subnormal mentality or mere weakness of intellect, ignorance, or deficiency in a mental function is not a defense to a criminal charge, unless the deficiency is such as to render the accused incapable of knowing the nature or quality of his act or to meet the tests for determining insanity discussed in the sections below. If a person is unconscious at the time he commits a criminal act, he cannot be held responsible.

The common-law rule was that infants under the age of 7 were conclusively presumed incapable of crime; those between 7 and 14 were rebuttably presumed incapable; and those 14 or over were presumptively capable. While legislatures have sometimes adopted the common-law rule, the age of irresponsibility has been changed by statute in many states. And much of the common-law rule has been rendered obsolete by statutes providing that offenders under a certain age shall be proceeded against as juvenile delinquents, rather than by criminal prosecution. Where a child is within the age span as to which incapacity to commit crime is rebuttably presumed, the burden is on the prosecution to show that he is capable of appreciating the nature of his acts. That he is so capable must generally be clearly established, although the strength of the presumption varies with the actual age of the child, decreasing as the upper limit is approached. Evidence as to intelligence, education, habits, general character, and moral or religious instruction may be considered by the jury on this issue. And opinion testimony of persons acquainted with the child has been held admissible.

A corporation may be criminally liable. They have been held subject to indictment for a wide variety of criminal violations. An unincorporated association or club, as such, cannot be held criminally liable, though its members, officers, or servants may be. Any prosecution for a criminal offense by a partnership must be against the individual partners.

§ 7:5. Insanity at the time of act.

Am Jur 2d References: Criminal Law, §§ 31, 32, 40–61.

An insane person is not capable of committing crime. Insanity at the time of the commission of an act is a complete defense in any criminal trial. What constitutes insanity for this purpose, however, is frequently a very difficult question, and the tests for determining it are the subject of much discussion and considerable conflict of authority.

The law does not require, as a condition of criminal responsibility, the possession of one's faculties in full vigor, or a mind unimpaired by disease or infirmity. One may be legally insane for one purpose, but not for another. Thus, a defendant may successfully plead insanity as a defense to a criminal charge, even though the evidence may not be such as would warrant his commitment; and conversely, insanity which justifies commitment will not necessarily exempt from responsibility for criminal acts. The cause of insanity does not generally determine its availability as a defense. While temporary insanity which arises from present voluntary intoxication is no defense, yet if the accused was suffering from a fixed insanity at the time of his act, even though it was caused by long-continued alcoholic indulgence or by the use of drugs, the rule is the same as in the case of insanity arising from any other cause.

Insanity at the time of the act goes to the guilt or innocence of the accused and is thus an issue which must be decided by the jury. Many jurisdictions have statutes providing for the examination of an accused by medical experts when a question arises as to his sanity.

A defendant is initially presumed to be sane, and where the evidence presented by the defense is insufficient to overcome this presumption, it is unnecessary for the prosecution to offer any affirmative proof of sanity. Insanity of a permanent or chronic nature is presumed to continue until the contrary is shown. Accordingly, when insanity of such a type is proved to have existed at some time prior to the offense, the general presumption of sanity is dispelled and a new presumption is raised that the proved insanity continued and that it existed at the time of the offense. Many jurisdictions place the burden of proof as to insanity upon the defendant. In other jurisdictions, the rule is that once some evidence of insanity has been introduced, the burden is on the prosecution to prove beyond a reasonable doubt that the defendant was legally sane at the time of the offense.

A defendant acquitted on the ground of insanity is not ordinarily entitled to his release, but may be committed to the care of a mental institution while his insanity continues.

§ 7:6. — Tests for determining insanity.

Am Jur 2d References: Criminal Law, §§ 33–39.

The "right-and-wrong" test for determining mental capacity for committing crime is followed in most jurisdictions. After some early experiments with other formulations, this test received its classic statement in 1843 in an advisory opinion of the English judges in M'Naghten's Case, 10 Clark & F 200, 8 Eng Reprint 718. As stated in this opinion and as generally applied, the test of mental responsibility is whether the accused was laboring under such a defect of reason, from disease of mind, as not to know the nature and quality of the act he was doing, or, if he did know it, that he did not know he was doing what was wrong. The courts following the M'Naghten or right-and-wrong test generally have engrafted several variations or qualifications thereon.

According to the prevailing rule, the "right and wrong" referred to in the M'Naghten test means moral right and wrong. Some courts, however, take the view that the word "wrong" in the test refers not to moral wrong, but to that which is prohibited by law, emphasizing the defendant's consciousness that the act is one which will subject him to punishment. In any event, the test under this rule is not the defendant's ability to distinguish between right and wrong in the abstract, but rather his ability to do so with respect to the particular act charged as a crime. Where the defendant understands that his act is wrong by society's standards, it does not constitute legal insanity or a legal defense that he may have moral views at variance with those of society, under which he conceives his act to be justified.

In some jurisdictions the "irresistible impulse" factor is attached to the test of legal responsibility for crime. According to this rule (which has been widely criticized and in many states expressly repudiated), it is held that notwithstanding the fact that one accused of committing a crime may have been able to comprehend the nature and consequences of his act, and to know that it was wrong, nevertheless, if he was forced to its execution by an impulse which he was powerless to control in consequence of a disease of the mind, he will be excused.

The American Law Institute, in its Model Penal Code, proposes the following rule: a person is not responsible for criminal conduct if at the time of such conduct, as a result of mental disease or defect, he lacked substantial capacity either to appreciate the criminality (wrongfulness) of his conduct or to conform his conduct to the requirements of law. This test has been adopted, either as proposed or in a modified form, in some jurisdictions.

The Currens Test (United States v Currens, 290 F2d 751), which is a modification of that proposed in the Model Penal Code, is that the jury must be satisfied that at the time of committing the prohibited act, the defendant, as a result of mental disease or defect, lacked substantial capacity to conform his conduct to the requirements of the law which he is alleged to have violated.

The District of Columbia Rule, enunciated in Durham v United States, 94 App DC 228, 214 F2d 862, 45 ALR2d 1430, is simply that an accused is not criminally responsible if his unlawful act was the product of mental disease or mental defect. The statement that the act must be the "product" of mental disease or defect means that the facts must reasonably justify the conclusion that but for the disease or defect the act would not have been committed. The Durham Rule does not exclude the other tests; it merely provides that they are no longer the exclusive criteria. This test is similar to that which has prevailed in New Hampshire for a century, that is, that the right-and-wrong, irresistible impulse, and other tests of legal insanity should all be considered as mere questions of fact for the jury, rather than as legal dogma.

§ 7:7. Capacity for trial and punishment.

Am Jur 2d References: Criminal Law, §§ 62–80.

An accused person, however guilty he may be, and even though he may have been sane at the time of the act charged, may not be tried, sentenced, or punished while presently insane. In determining the defendant's capacity to stand trial, the test is whether he has the capacity to comprehend his position, to understand the nature and object of the proceedings against him, to conduct his defense in a rational manner, and to cooperate with his counsel to the end that any available defense may be interposed. There is a clear distinction between the insanity which precludes responsibility for crime and insanity which precludes trial.

It is a firmly established tenet of our law, inherited from the common law, that an insane person ought not to be punished while he remains in that condition. This assumes that he was sane at the time of the act and has been legally convicted. Although theoretically this principle is probably applicable to any form of punishment, as a practical matter it has seldom been invoked for any other purpose than to prevent execution of the death penalty. The test of insanity which will preclude execution is not the same as those for determining responsibility for a criminal act. It is similar to the test employed to determine whether the defendant is competent to stand trial. The test is whether the prisoner has sufficient intelligence to understand the nature of the proceeding against him, the purpose of his punishment, the impending fate awaiting him, and sufficient understanding to know of, and communicate to his attorneys, any fact which might make his punishment unjust or unlawful.

III. THE CRIMINAL STATE OF MIND: INTENT; MALICE; VOLITION

§ 7:8. In general; intent; malice.

Am Jur 2d References: Criminal Law, §§ 81–91; Malice, §§ 1–5.

At common law, a crime required two elements: an act and an evil intention. This is expressed in the maxim, "actus non facit reum, nisi mens sit rea," meaning an act does not render one guilty unless the mind is guilty. This principle, that only conscious wrongdoing constitutes crime, is deeply rooted in our legal system, although there are some categories of modern statutory offenses to which it is not applied. Where the offense is one which requires a general criminal intent, but not a specific intent, a guilty intention may sometimes be inferred from the act. Though a guilty state of mind is part of the definition of most offenses, especially the more serious ones, there are instances where the law categorically forbids a certain act without regard to the state of mind which may accompany it. Where this is the case, the intent to do the act is the only element necessary to complete the offense. Where the offense, by its very definition, requires a specific intent, such an intent is as much an element of the offense as the act itself, and must be alleged and proved, although such proof must ordinarily be by circumstantial evidence.

Where the act which the defendant intended was a lawful one, free from negligence and not in itself of a dangerous tendency, he is not criminally responsible for its unintended result. But one who does an unlawful act is liable for the consequences even though they may not have been intended. Where, in the execution of an intent to do wrong, an unintended act resulting in a wrong ensues as a natural and probable consequence, the one acting with wrongful intent is responsible for the unintended wrong, even though the act producing that wrong was that of another.

Some offenses are defined in terms of negligence rather than intent. Negligence as an element of a criminal offense, however, must ordinarily be of a higher degree than is necessary to establish liability in a civil action. Criminal or culpable negligence is defined by such qualifying terms as wanton or flagrant, or in terms of disregard of consequences or indifference to the rights or safety of others.

In criminal law motive may be defined as that which leads or tempts the mind to indulge in a criminal act, or as the moving power which impels action for a definite result. It is different from intent. Although it occupies a prominent place in criminal fiction and folklore, motive is not an essential element of any crime. Proof of motive or absence of motive may be important, especially in cases depending on circumstantial evidence, but only as an evidentiary factor.

There are many statutory crimes which do not depend upon any mental element or mens rea, but consist only of forbidden acts or omissions. Where such an offense is created, criminal intent is not an element of the crime, although it is sometimes said that where a statute denounces the doing of an act as criminal, the law imputes criminal intend from the act. In such cases, the only question is whether the prohibited act was done or the required act omitted, and moral turpitude or knowledge of the criminal character of the act is immaterial.

As the term is used in the criminal law, "malice" does not necessarily have its popular connotation of ill will. Frequently it means merely that state of mind which prompts the intentional doing of a wrongful act. The word is sometimes given the other meaning, and the element of wickedness occurs in some of the legal definitions. Malice is frequently implied. Thus, the law implies malice where one deliberately injures another in an unlawful manner or intentionally uses a deadly weapon in a deadly manner. And the element of malice may be supplied by the presumption that one intends the natural and probable consequences of his deliberate acts.

§ 7:9. Mistake or belief.

Am Jur 2d References: Criminal Law, §§ 92–97.

As a general rule, religious beliefs cannot be accepted as a justification of an act made criminal by the law. For example, acts which would otherwise constitute bigamy cannot be justified on the ground that they were sanctioned or required by the defendant's religious beliefs, and the same is true regarding the failure to furnish medical attention where a statute makes such failure a criminal offense.

Ignorance or mistake of fact, at least if not unreasonable or due to negligence, is a defense if it negatives a mental state required as an element of the offense charged. Where criminal mind or intent is dependent on a knowledge of particular facts, ignorance or mistake as to those facts generally absolves one from criminal responsibility. However, ignorance or mistake of fact is of no consequence where a specified act is simply prohibited and made a criminal offense, without reference to intent. In some cases everyone is required to ascertain the facts at his peril.

It is axiomatic that ignorance or mistake of law will not excuse an act in violation of the criminal laws. Violation of a valid criminal statute cannot be excused on the ground that the defendant believed in good faith that the statute was unconstitutional. On the other hand, reliance on and obedience of a statute later held unconstitutional is frequently held to be a good defense. And where a criminal statute has been first held unconstitutional by the court of last resort and then later held constitutional, a person who committed the prohibited act during the interval between the two decisions is not liable to punishment. The same rule is applied where a decision holding a criminal statute inapplicable has been overruled.

As a general rule, it is no defense to a criminal prosecution that the defendant acted in good faith, relying on the advice of counsel. However, advice of counsel may be shown where it tends to disprove the intent requisite to the particular offense, as where the offense is one which requires a fraudulent intent, an evil motive or bad purpose, or malice. But advice of counsel is of no avail where the statute forbids an act regardless of intent.

§ 7:10. Coercion; volition.

Am Jur 2d References: Criminal Law, §§ 98–105.

Generally, an act does not constitute a crime unless some feasible and lawful alternative was open to the actor. Thus, nonperformance is not a crime where performance is impossible or would violate some other law or a court order. It is sometimes stated that an act done from compulsion or necessity is not a crime. But this necessity or compulsion must be clear and conclusive, not admitting of any other alternatives, and must arise without negligence on the part of the defendant.

Though coercion does not excuse taking the life of an innocent person, it is a defense against most other criminal charges. In order to constitute a defense, however, the coercion or duress must be present, eminent, and impending, and of such nature as to induce a well-grounded apprehension of death or serious bodily injury if the act is not done. Apprehension of loss of property or of slight personal injury is no excuse. The danger must be continuous throughout the time when the act is being committed and must be one from which the defendant cannot withdraw in safety. And a threat or fear of future injury is not sufficient.

At common law it was generally presumed, though not with relation to all offenses, that crimes committed by a married woman in her husband's presence were committed under his coercion. Since the basis of this presumption has to a large degree evaporated because of the changes in the legal status and rights of women, this presumption has little scope for application today, and it has been repudiated in some jurisdictions. Even where it is recognized, it does not apply to certain offenses, such as murder or treason and some other crimes of this grade. Even where applicable, this presumption is rebuttable.

Although there may be actual coercion of a child of tender years, unless the child has not yet reached the age of criminal responsibility, or is of such immature years or mind as to be entirely under the domination, direction, and control of the parent, a criminal act will not be excused on the ground that it was committed under parental command.

§ 7:11. Intoxication, narcosis, or mental deficiency.

Am Jur 2d References: Criminal Law, §§ 106–109.

Without questioning the general rule that a mental illness or defect not amounting to legal insanity is not a defense, some courts admit evidence of such mental condition where the crime charged requires a specific mental state, and because of mental abnormality, the defendant did not have that mental state. In other words, such evidence tends to disprove one of the facts which the prosecution must prove to establish the offense.

A similar rule is applied by many courts to intoxication. Although voluntary intoxication is not a defense, these authorities hold that where a mental state is a necessary element of the offense charged, or of a particular degree thereof, voluntary intoxication can be shown for its bearing on whether the accused had that state of mind at the time of the act. Where the offense is one requiring a specific intent, evidence of intoxication is held by these authorities to be admissible to be considered in determining whether such specific intent was actually present. And evidence of intoxication is sometimes admitted as bearing on such issues as malice or deliberation and premeditation where these are required elements of a particular offense. However, some jurisdictions do not permit intoxication to be considered, even on the issue of specific intent. Similar principles are applied in cases involving criminal responsibility for acts committed under the influence of drugs.

IV. PARTICIPATION IN CRIME; AIDING AND ABETTING; ACCESSORIES

§ 7:12. In general.

Am Jur 2d References: Criminal Law, §§ 115–119, 127–130.

A person may be criminally responsible for participating in a crime in any of several capacities. He may be a principal, an accessory, or an aider or abettor. "Accomplice" is a term applied to one who has participated in any of these capacities, when he is put on the witness stand and a question arises as to the necessity of corroborating his testimony.

An aider or abettor is one who advises, counsels, procures, or encourages another to commit a crime. Guilt in this capacity requires the commission of the crime by another. There are some crimes as to which a person may be criminally liable as aider or abettor or as accessory, which he does not have the capacity to commit as principal. For example, a woman may be punished for aiding or abetting the commission of rape, and a husband may be an accessory to the crime of rape upon his own wife.

A principal in a crime must be actually or constructively present, participating in some way in the commission of the offense. A person who encourages the commission of an unlawful act cannot escape responsibility by withdrawing from the scene, as the influence and effect of his encouragement continue until he renounces the common purpose and makes it clear to the others that he has done so and that he does not intend to participate further.

At common law, a principal in the first degree was one who did the act either in person or through an innocent agent. A principal in the second degree was present at the time the crime was committed, lending countenance, aid, or encouragement, or keeping watch while another person did the actual criminal act. The immediate presence of the party was not necessary to make him a principal in the second degree. It was sufficient if, pursuant to agreement, he was in a position to give any necessary aid in the perpetration of the offense. Under many statutes, the distinction between principals of the first and second degree is of little practical importance, and in some instances it has been entirely abolished. The statutes in varying terms make all persons who are present and concerned in the commission of a crime guilty as principals.

An aider and abettor before the fact is fully responsible for the acts of the actual perpetrator of an offense, and he may be indicted and tried separately or jointly with the principal. At common law, however, the aider and abettor could not, unless he consented, be tried before the principal, and conviction of the principal was necessary before the conviction of an aider or abettor could be sustained. Statutes may alter these rules. It is sometimes held that the acquittal of the principal is no impediment to the trial and conviction of a person charged with aiding and abetting the commission of the crime. But if, in fact, no crime has been committed, no one can be convicted as an aider and abettor.

§ 7:13. Principals and accessories.

Am Jur 2d References: Criminal Law, §§ 120–126.

An accessory before the fact is a person who contributes to a felony committed by another as principal, but who is too far away to aid in the felonious act. Some statutes abolish the common-law distinction between an accessory before the fact and a principal, and provide that such accessory may be convicted as a principal. There are no accessories at common law in the commission of misdemeanors, all who aid and abet, as well as those who perpetrate the acts, being principals.

At common law, an accessory after the fact is one who, knowing that a felony has been committed by another, receives, comforts, or assists the felon, or in some manner aids him to escape arrest or punishment. The accessory after the fact commits an offense separate and distinct from the crime of the principal.

§ 7:14. Responsibility for acts of another.

Am Jur 2d References: Criminal Law, §§ 131–134.

The criminal acts of one person cannot be charged to another without a showing that the other participated directly or constructively in the acts or that the acts were done in furtherance of a common design or common purpose for which the parties were combined. But an instigator may be responsible for acts done by an innocent or irresponsible person.

One who combines with others to accomplish an illegal purpose is liable criminally for everything that is done by his confederates incidental to the execution of the common design, as one of its probable and natural consequences, even though what was done was not intended as a part of the original design or common plan. This is true even though the defendant was not present when the act was committed. However, if one of the conspirators commits a fresh and independent act, wholly outside and foreign to the common design, the others are not held equally guilty of that act.

An employer or principal is criminally responsible for acts of his agent or employee where he participates in or requests or demands that the act be done. Unless he does so participate, aid, or command, however, an employer or principal is not, in the absence of statute, criminally liable for the acts of his employee or agent.

V. DEFENSES

§ 7:15. In general.

Am Jur 2d References: Criminal Law, §§ 135, 139–142.

The law permits the defendant in a criminal prosecution to assert and utilize any and all defenses that he believes to be available to him. An affirmative defense is one that admits the doing of the act charged, but seeks to justify, excuse, or mitigate it; or, as in the defense of former jeopardy, invokes a bar arising out of facts dehors the record. Some defenses, such as that of insanity, are based on the lack of mental capacity or on the absence of a criminal state of mind. The general denial simply denies that the defendant committed the crime with which he is charged. Good character or reputation of the accused is not a defense as a matter of law, but is a fact for consideration by the jury, its object being to show the improbability that a person of the defendant's good character would have committed the offense in question.

Contributory negligence is not available as a defense in the criminal prosecution. One who is guilty of criminal negligence is not relieved from criminal responsibility by the contributory negligence of the person injured or killed. And it is no defense that the victim of a crime may also be guilty of a criminal offense.

Whether or not the consent of the party injured by a crime constitutes a defense depends upon the character of the particular crime. If the doing of a particular act is a crime regardless of the consent of anyone, as in homicide or statutory rape, consent is no excuse.

On the other hand, if want of consent is an element of a crime, an act done with the consent of the person affected cannot be made the basis of a criminal charge. Where a person arranges for a crime to be committed against himself or his property, and aids, encourages, or solicits the commission thereof, such facts are a good defense to the person committing the acts. However, this is not true where the intended victim knows that a crime is contemplated against him and merely remains silent and permits matters to go on for the purpose of apprehending the criminal.

§ 7:16. Alibi or guilt of another.

Am Jur 2d References: Criminal Law, §§ 136–138.

The literal meaning of the word "alibi" is "elsewhere," and as used in criminal law, it indicates a line of proof by which the accused undertakes to show that he was not at the scene of the crime at the time of its commission, having been at another place at the time, and hence that he could not have committed the crime. Technically, an alibi is not an affirmative defense but is simply a denial that the accused committed the crime. Although the defense of alibi may ordinarily be presented under a general plea of not guilty, and an accused is not ordinarily required to give advance notice of the details of his claim of alibi, statutes in some jurisdictions require the accused to give notice to the prosecution of his intention to rely on alibi as a defense, or to give notice as to the place at which the defendant claims to have been when the crime was committed and of the witnesses on whose testimony he will rely in establishing this defense.

A defendant may, by proper evidence, prove that another person committed the crime with which he is charged, where the guilt of the other person is consistent with the defendant's innocence; but the fact that persons other than the accused have also violated or are violating the law is no defense. It is no defense that the accused committed the alleged crime merely as an agent, employee, or servant of another.

§ 7:17. Entrapment.

Am Jur 2d References: Criminal Law, §§ 143–145.

Entrapment is defined as the inducement of one to commit a crime not contemplated by him, for the purpose of instituting a criminal prosecution against him; it is the conception and planning of an offense by a person and the procurement of its commission by another person, who would not have perpetrated it except for the trickery, persuasion, or fraud of the other. There is a clear distinction between inducing a person to do an unlawful act and setting a trap to catch him in the execution of a criminal plan of his own conception. Entrapment is an affirmative defense, in the nature of a confession and avoidance, and one that the defendant must prove. It is held that the defense of entrapment is not available to one who denies commission of the offense, since the invocation of this defense assumes that the act charged was committed. This defense is not recognized, or is recognized only in prosecutions for certain crimes, in some jurisdictions.

The type of entrapment the law forbids is the inducing of another to violate the law. Generally, where the criminal intent originates in the mind of the entrapping person and the accused is lured into the commission of the offense in order that he may be prosecuted, no conviction may be had. But where the criminal intent originates in the mind of the accused and the criminal offense is completed, the fact that a person acting as a decoy for the state or public officials furnished the accused an opportunity for commission of the offense, or that the accused is aided in the commission of the crime in order to secure the evidence necessary to prosecute him, constitutes no defense. Merely affording an opportunity to one intending to violate the law is not entrapment. The mere fact that a police officer solicits and completes the purchase of a contraband article from one engaged in the sale thereof does not constitute entrapment.

§ 7:18. Compulsion to testify; agreement not to prosecute.

Am Jur 2d References: Criminal Law, §§ 146–153.

The practice of granting immunity to accomplices in return for their confessing their own offenses and testifying against their associates in crime has long been established as a means of detecting and convicting criminal offenders. In the absence of statutory or constitutional provision therefor, the mere fact that a participant or accomplice in the commission of a crime has given incriminating testimony does not entitle him to immunity from prosecution. Nor has any public officer the authority to make a binding promise or agreement to grant such immunity, unless there is statutory or constitutional provision therefor. Yet in actual practice such arrangements are frequently effectuated by entering a nolle prosequi or by merely refraining from prosecution.

Constitutional and statutory provisions, in varying terms, often grant immunity from prosecution to a witness who is compelled to testify in a manner likely to incriminate him. Generally, the provisions for immunity are as broad as, and coextensive with, the constitutional provisions granting the privilege against self-incrimination. In other words, the witness is immune only if he could have properly refused to testify because his answers would tend to incriminate him and his testimony was such as he was privileged to withhold.

The question whether a witness must first claim his privilege against self-incrimination in order to be entitled to immunity from subsequent prosecution where he does give testimony, has been given various answers by the courts, the answer depending largely upon the terms of the particular statute or constitutional provision.

§ 7:19. Statute of limitations.

Am Jur 2d References: Criminal Law, §§ 154–164.

Unless a period of limitation is fixed by statute, a prosecution for a criminal offense is not barred by lapse of time and may be instituted at any time, however long after the commission of the criminal act. However, statutes of limitation have been enacted to limit the time for the commencement of most criminal proceedings. Usually the limitations are made applicable to all or most misdemeanors and to some felonies, but not to murder.

Statutes of limitation in criminal cases create a bar to prosecution, and the defense goes to the merits of the case. A judgment for the defendant on a plea of the statute is an acquittal of the charge. Although a special plea of the statute of limitation is provided for in some jurisdictions, it is generally held that the statute need not be specially pleaded in criminal cases and may be raised under a plea of not guilty. Statutes of limitation are liberally construed in favor of the accused.

A statutory amendment extending the period of limitation applies to offenses not barred at the time of the passage of the act, so that a prosecution may be commenced at any time within the newly established period; but such a statute cannot operate to revive offenses which are barred at the time of its enactment.

It frequently happens that a charge of felony includes an offense of a lower grade with a different period of limitation, so that while the felony is not barred, the statute has run as to the lesser offense. In this situation, the general rule is that the bar cannot be evaded by indicting a defendant for the felony and convicting him of the lesser offense.

The statute of limitations begins to run from the time of the completed commission of the offense, not from the date the crime is discovered. And the statute runs until the prosecution is commenced, unless some intervening event interrupts it. If the finding of an indictment or the filing of an information is the first step in a criminal case, the prosecution is deemed to be commenced thereby and the running of the statute is thereby stopped. Where, however, there are preliminary proceedings, the prosecution is commenced and the statute is tolled at the time a complaint is laid before a magistrate and a warrant of arrest is issued.

Unless the statute contains an exception or condition that will toll its operation, the running of a criminal statute of limitations is not interrupted. However, some statutes contain provisions for the deduction from the period of limitation the time during which the accused is absent from the state, is fleeing from justice, conceals himself, or conceals the fact of the crime.

Generally, the return of an indictment or filing of an information on which no valid conviction or judgment can be had will not operate to stop the running of the statute of limitations pending the return or filing of another indictment or information. However, it has been held in some jurisdictions that a prosecution under an indictment returned or an information filed after the statutory limitation period has elapsed, will not be barred where a previous indictment or information charging the same offense had been returned or filed within the statutory period but was quashed, set aside, or dismissed, and the case directed to be resubmitted. And some jurisdictions have statutes to this effect.

§ 7:20. Former jeopardy; res judicata.

Am Jur 2d References: Criminal Law, §§ 165–178, 217.

The principle that no person shall be put in jeopardy of his life or limb more than once for the same offense is an ancient rule of the common law; and the principle is embodied in the Federal Constitution and the constitutions of the states. Former acquittal (autrefois acquit) and former conviction (autrefois convict) have long been recognized as defense pleas at common law. Both the common-law rule and the constitutional provisions against double jeopardy protect an accused not only against the peril of a second punishment, but also against being placed on trial or "put in jeopardy" for the same offense. The defense is available whether the accused was acquitted or convicted on the former trial. The plea is one which must be interposed by the accused.

It cannot be said that a person has been in jeopardy unless the court in which he was acquitted or convicted had jurisdiction to try him for the offense charged. The defense of former jeopardy cannot be based on a plea of guilty entered before a court not having jurisdiction of the matter. Neither a conviction nor an acquittal based on an accusatory pleading which fails to state any offense recognized by the law is a bar to a subsequent prosecution. Similarly, the granting of a motion to quash a bad accusatory pleading, or an acquittal secured under a decision of the court sustaining the defendant's objection to the accusation, or a ruling, in a postconviction proceeding, that the original indictment was invalid, will not bar a subsequent prosecution on a good pleading. But these principles do not apply where the accused was first prosecuted under an indictment that was merely defective but not void, so that a valid conviction could have been procured notwithstanding the defect. Where a defective indictment is amended during a trial to cure the defect, an uninterrupted continuation of the trial does not subject the defendant to double jeopardy.

A new trial granted because of errors in the first trial does not constitute double jeopardy. And a properly convicted defendant is not placed in double jeopardy when he is resentenced after a determination that the original sentence was illegal.

A plea of former jeopardy may not be based upon a sham or collusive proceeding under which the defendant pleads guilty to a minor offense in order to avoid an anticipated prosecution on a more serious charge based on the same facts.

A person is in jeopardy, within the meaning of the principles here discussed, when he is put on trial before a court of competent jurisdiction on an indictment or information which is sufficient in form and substance to sustain a conviction, and a jury has been impaneled and sworn or "charged with due deliverance." Jeopardy attaches in a nonjury case when the accused is brought to trial and the court begins to hear evidence. A defendant is not in jeopardy until the entire jury is selected and is sworn. Proceedings preliminary to a trial, such as those before a grand jury or a committing magistrate, do not constitute jeopardy. Whether a conviction from which an appeal is pending will support a plea of former conviction is the subject of a conflict of authorities.

The doctrine of res judicata, by which a fact or matter put in issue and determined by a court of competent jurisdiction cannot afterward be disputed between the same parties, is applicable to judgments in criminal prosecutions. The plea of res judicata may be available, to the extent of precluding the relitigation of facts and issues which have been determined in an earlier case, in cases where there is no such identity of offenses in the two prosecutions that a plea of former jeopardy, autrefois acquit, or autrefois convict could be sustained. There is a conflict of authority on the question whether a former acquittal or conviction of a criminal charge bars a civil action against the defendant to recover a statutory penalty for the same conduct.

§ 7:21. — Identity of offenses.

Am Jur 2d References: Criminal Law, §§ 182–193.

The common-law rule and the constitutional provisions against double jeopardy apply only to a second prosecution for the same act and crime, both in law and fact, on which the first prosecution was based. However, substantial identity of act and crime is all that is required. A defendant has been in jeopardy if, in the first prosecution, he could have been convicted of the offense charged in the second proceeding. A single identical offense cannot be divided into two offenses for which two separate punishments are imposed; and a prosecution for any part of a single crime bars any further prosecution based on the whole or a part of the same offense.

One test of identity of offenses is whether the same evidence is required to prove them. The fact that both charges relate to or grow out of one transaction does not necessarily make a single offense where two are defined by the statutes. If there is one act, one intent, and one volition, and the defendant has been tried on a charge based on that act, intent, and volition, no subsequent prosecution can be based thereon; but there is no identity of offenses if, on the trial of one offense, proof of some fact is required that is not required in the trial of the other, although some of the acts may necessarily be proved in the trial of each.

Where two distinct crimes are committed in one transaction, there may be separate prosecutions for both, although the separate acts were closely connected in point of time. Prosecutions for separate offenses based on the same transaction do not involve double jeopardy where there are distinct elements in one offense that are not included in the other. Where a single act constitutes two or more separate and distinct offenses, some jurisdictions permit the conviction and punishment of the offender for both. Where a single transaction constitutes two or more offenses, but the lesser offense is not necessarily involved in the greater and the facts necessary to convict on the second prosecution would not necessarily have convicted on the first, then the first prosecution is not a bar to the second.

A person tried for an offense cannot be tried thereafter for a lesser offense necessarily involved in and a part of the first charge, if, under the indictment for the first offense, the defendant could have been convicted of the lesser offense.

A conviction of a minor included offense will generally bar a subsequent prosecution for a higher crime embracing the minor offense, unless the first conviction was procured by fraud, connivance, or collusion of the defendant. It is generally held, however, that a conviction of a minor offense in an inferior court does not bar a prosecution for a higher crime of which the inferior court has no jurisdiction. And the first trial will not bar a subsequent prosecution where a new fact develops after the first trial, and the new fact plus those previously existing constitute a new crime not susceptible of adjudication in the first prosecution. Thus, an acquittal on a charge of assault will not bar a subsequent charge of murder where the victim of the assault dies after the first trial. Where a conviction of a lesser offense is set aside at the defendant's instance, he may not be retried for the greater offense charged against him.

Where the same act or transaction violates the laws of more than one jurisdiction, jeopardy in one jurisdiction will not generally free the party from trial in the other. Where the same act constitutes a violation of both federal and state laws, a conviction or acquittal in one jurisdiction will not prevent a subsequent prosecution in the other. Different results have been reached where the same act violates both a state statute and municipal ordinance.

§ 7:22. — Manner of termination or disposition of prior proceeding.

Am Jur 2d References: Criminal Law, §§ 179–181, 194–216.

The court may discharge a jury or declare a mistrial without working an acquittal of the defendant in any case where the ends of justice would otherwise be defeated. This requires the exercise of sound discretion on the part of the court, and the power may be exercised only where there is a cogent reason or a manifest necessity. In the absence of such necessity, the defendant may demand that a discharge of the jury be regarded as an acquittal of every offense on which the jury might have returned a verdict if they had not been discharged. The right of a defendant to have a trial proceed to a verdict may be waived by him, and if the jury is discharged at his instance or a mistrial declared on his motion, he cannot claim double jeopardy when arraigned before another jury. Events or circumstances which have been held to warrant the discharge of the jury without affording a basis for a claim of double jeopardy are the illness or disability of the trial judge or the accused; misconduct, disqualification, or incapacity of a juror; or the failure of the jury to agree on a verdict after deliberation for a reasonable time.

A nolle prosequi or dismissal before jeopardy attaches does not operate as an acquittal or prevent further prosecution for the same offense. And the same result follows a nolle prosequi entered after the evidence is in, if it was consented to or requested by the defendant; but it is otherwise where the dismissal at that stage was without the defendant's consent.

A defendant waives his constitutional protection against double jeopardy when a verdict or judgment against him is set aside at his own instance either on motion in the trial court or on a successful appeal. He may be tried anew on the same indictment for the same offense, or he may be prosecuted on a new information charging the offense. And he waives a future plea of former jeopardy when he successfully moves to quash an indictment, even though proceedings have reached the point of jeopardy.

A conviction of a lesser degree of the crime charged involves an acquittal of the higher degrees for all purposes, and a new trial granted on motion or appeal of the defendant is not a new trial of the greater offense of which he was acquitted, but must be confined to a retrial of the lesser offense of which he was convicted.

There is some difference of opinion among the state courts as to whether a statute giving the state a right of appeal after acquittal in a criminal case, and subjecting the defendant to another trial, is unconstitutional as putting the accused in jeopardy a second time.

VI. RIGHTS OF ACCUSED; CONSTITUTIONAL PROTECTION

§ 7:23. In general.

Am Jur 2d References: Criminal Law, §§ 218–233, 345–348, 370–
375.

Most of the safeguards provided for the protection of the rights of one accused of crime have their roots in the common law. Many of them have been formally declared in statutes and in the federal and state constitutions. Some of these rights are discussed separately in the sections which follow. The rights of a defendant in a criminal prosecution may be waived by him, even though the right is one guaranteed by the Constitution, unless some paramount public interest or policy is involved. However, it has been said that every reasonable presumption will be indulged against the waiver of fundamental constitutional rights by one charged with crime.

The due process clauses of the federal and state constitutions protect the more fundamental rights of the defendant in a criminal prosecution. Due process requires that a criminal prosecution shall be consistent with the fundamental principles of liberty and justice which lie at the base of our civil and political institutions, and it requires an observance of that fundamental fairness essential to the very concept of justice. The question whether a partticular right is essential to due process does not necessarily depend upon whether it existed at common law. Among the basic requirements of due process of law are reasonable notice of the charges and an adequate opportunity to defend against them, a legally and mentally competent tribunal which is impartial and which has jurisdiction of the case, and a fair hearing at which the accused has an adequate opportunity to present his case. Due process is denied if a criminal trial is mob-dominated, if a conviction is obtained by means of a coerced confession, or if the accused is denied the right to examine adverse witnesses, to offer testimony, or to be represented by counsel.

Due process requires that there be a regular course of judicial proceedings and that a criminal trial proceed according to the established procedure or rules of practice applicable to all such cases. However, due process does not require any particular form or mode of procedure, so long as fundamental rights are protected. Due process does not mean that state prosecutions must be without error or fault, or that the federal courts may substitute their judgment for that of the state courts or exercise any general review over their proceedings. An erroneous judgment of a court in a criminal case, based on a scrupulous and fair search for the truth, may yet be due process of law. Due process does not require that a defendant be accorded a right to appeal a criminal conviction; but where a defendant contends that his conviction was procured by means so fundamentally unfair as to deprive him of constitutional rights, due process does require that the state afford him some corrective process by which he can establish that contention and obtain a remedy.

Due process is denied by a conviction in a trial in which perjured testimony on a material point and prejudicial to the accused is knowingly used against him. And the suppression or withholding by the state of material evidence exculpatory to the accused is a violation of due process. So is a conviction without any evidence which would support a finding of guilt, or a conviction upon a charge which was not made or on which the defendant was not tried.

The constitutional guaranty of equal protection of the laws forbids arbitrary discrimination against persons or classes in criminal cases. There can be no equal justice where the kind of trial a man gets depends upon the amount of money he has. Indigent defendants must be afforded an equal opportunity to defend themselves. Although a state is not constitutionally required to grant appellate review, if it does grant such review, it must do so in a way that does not discriminate against some convicted defendants on account of their poverty. Indigent defendants must be accorded appellate review as full as that available to others, and such defendants must be furnished a free transcript where a transcript is necessary to an adequate review.

In most jurisdictions a defendant in a criminal case has a right to have the jury polled. This involves asking each juror individually the finding arrived at by him. The practice is intended to assure that a unanimous verdict has in fact been reached and that no juror has been coerced to agree to a verdict. In some jurisdictions, however, polling of the jury is regarded as unnecessary; and still other jurisdictions take the view that granting a request for a poll of the jury rests in the discretion of the trial court. It is well established everywhere that the right to have the jury polled may be waived; and in some jurisdictions the failure of the defendant to request a poll constitutes such a waiver.

Every person accused of crime is entitled to the benefit of the ancient and fundamental rule that he is presumed to be innocent until his guilt is proved beyond a reasonable doubt. And one of the rights guaranteed to the defendant in a criminal case is the right to have compulsory process to procure the attendance of witnesses.

§ 7:24. Fair and impartial trial.

Am Jur 2d References: Criminal Law, §§ 234–240.

Every person charged with crime has a fundamental right to a fair and impartial trial. A fair trial means one before an impartial judge and an honest jury, in an atmosphere of judicial calm. A fair trial may be precluded by the presence of a hostile crowd inside or outside the courtroom, improper pressures on a prosecution witness, or by anything likely to produce prejudice against the accused. Pretrial publicity adverse to the accused has in some cases been held sufficiently serious to amount to a denial of a fair trial, where there was a premature communication of the evidence by the prosecuting authorities and extensive comment thereon by the news media. Cases denying relief on this ground have frequently emphasized that no actual prejudicial effect on the jury was proved or that the defendant's possible remedies were not exhausted by moving for continuance or change of venue or by taking advantage of the opportunities available on voir dire or by peremptory challenges.

A person charged with crime should have a reasonable time to prepare his defense and produce his witnesses. He is entitled to be brought before the court with the appearance of a free and innocent man and not required to wear prison clothing, except where the necessary safety and decorum of the court otherwise require. The defendant is generally entitled to make his appearance in court free from all shackles or bonds, and to have his witnesses appear unmanacled. It is within the trial court's discretion, however, to have the prisoner or a witness shackled when it is manifest that such precaution is necessary to prevent violence or escape or to maintain order during the trial.

§ 7:25. Speedy trial.

Am Jur 2d References: Criminal Law, §§ 241–256.

From time immemorial at common law a prisoner accused of crime has had the right to a speedy trial. The right in federal criminal prosecutions is secured by the Sixth Amendment to the Federal Constitution and by similar provisions in most state constitutions; and the guaranty of the Sixth Amendment is held to protect such a fundamental right that it is made obligatory on the states by the Fourteenth Amendment. A speedy trial is one conducted according to fixed rules and procedures, free from vexatious, capricious, oppressive, and unreasonable delays. One arrested and accused of crime does not have the right to demand a trial immediately upon the accusation or arrest, as the prosecution must be given a reasonable time to prepare for trial.

Although the right to speedy trial is not ordinarily violated by delay between the offense and the indictment, it may be violated by an inordinate delay in the return of the indictment after the arrest has been made. An accused may be unconstitutionally deprived of his right to a speedy trial on a pending charge, notwithstanding the fact that he is a prisoner already serving a sentence in the same jurisdiction for a different offense. But this rule does not apply to a delay occasioned by the defendant's imprisonment in another jurisdiction.

The right to a speedy trial may be waived by the accused, and the right is not violated by a delay caused by his own condition or conduct. This is true of delays caused by the defendant's absence from the state or failure to appear for arraignment or trial, or by his filing of dilatory pleas or motions. In some jurisdictions, the right to speedy trial is waived unless the defendant demands trial, resists a postponement, or makes some effort to secure a speedier trial than the state accorded him.

§7:26. Public trial.

Am Jur 2d References: Criminal Law, §§ 257–270.

The right to public trial was recognized by the common law, and it is expressly protected, in federal criminal prosecutions, by the Sixth Amendment to the Federal Constitution, and similar guaranties are contained in most of the state constitutions and in many state statutes. A denial of public trial may, under some circumstances, violate the requirement of due process of law. The guaranty of public trial applies to the entire trial, from the impanelment of the jury to the return of the verdict. It does not apply to preliminary proceedings or conferences which are not a part of the trial. When a defendant's right to public trial has been violated over his timely objection, he is not required to show that he suffered actual prejudice as a result. However, the right to public trial may be waived.

According to some authorities, "public trial" means a trial at which the public is free to attend. Other authorities construe "public" as meaning merely "not secret." According to the latter view, the requirement is fairly observed if a reasonable proportion of the public is allowed to attend, without partiality or favoritism. Under either view, the right is not unlimited, but is subject to the inherent power of the court to preserve order and decorum in the courtroom, to protect the rights of the parties and witnesses, and generally to further the administration of justice. It is proper to limit the number of spectators according to the capacity of the courtroom so as to prevent overcrowding and disorder. Where the situation indicates that violence is threatened, the court may adopt and enforce precautions, and spectators who disturb the proceedings may be removed. In extreme cases the courtroom may be cleared to prevent interference with the due administration of justice. The extent to which spectators may be excluded from the trial of sex cases varies under the decisions and statutes of different jurisdictions.

§7:27. Presence of accused.

Am Jur 2d References: Criminal Law, §§ 271–308.

A principle pervading the entire law of criminal procedure is that after indictment is found, nothing shall be done in the absence of the accused. The right of the defendant to be present at his trial derives from the common law and is frequently guaranteed by constitution or statute. Where the right is denied, the accused is not required to show actual injury or prejudice. Denial of the right may violate the guaranty of due process of law, at least where a fair and just hearing would be thwarted by the defendant's absence.

The right of the defendant to be present at all stages of his trial applies in all felony cases. Whether and the extent to which the right applies in misdemeanor cases is the subject of much difference of opinion among the courts and is sometimes governed by statute. Some courts regard the defendant's presence at a felony trial as a jurisdictional requirement which cannot be waived. Many other courts, however, take a different view; and in some jurisdictions, the right may be waived even by one charged with a capital offense.

§ 7:28. Right to be heard in person and by counsel.

Am Jur 2d References: Criminal Law, §§ 309–323.

In accordance with the provisions contained in the Sixth Amendment to the Federal Constitution, which is held to be obligatory upon the states by virtue of the Fourteenth Amendment, a person accused of crime has the right to be heard and to be assisted by counsel in his defense. He is entitled to have an attorney appointed by the court to act in his behalf, or to be given a fair opportunity to employ counsel of his own choice. However, the right to counsel is permissive, and the accused may choose to rely on his own skill. If he is sui juris and mentally competent and if he understands the risks involved, an accused may elect to conduct his defense in person without the assistance of counsel.

The defendant in criminal proceedings is not entitled as a matter of right to be heard by himself and also by counsel, or to have the services of an attorney for purely advisory purposes. If he elects to be heard by counsel, an accused may not ordinarily participate in the conduct of his defense, although this is addressed to the discretion of the trial court.

The right to assistance of counsel includes the right to communicate and consult freely with the attorney at reasonable hours and intervals. The right to counsel extends to every stage of the prosecution. An accused is generally entitled to be assisted by counsel at preliminary hearings before a magistrate and during his arraignment and the acceptance of a plea. He has a right to the presence of his counsel at a police lineup. And the Supreme Court of the United States has established the rule that an individual who is taken into custody or otherwise deprived of his freedom by the authorities is entitled to counsel prior to any questioning, and that he must be advised of this right prior to questioning.

A judgment of conviction will not ordinarily be held invalid on the basis of inexperience or unskilfulness of an attorney of the defendant's own choice, or because of lack of preparation, improper advice, or errors on the part of such attorney. But where counsel's representation of the accused is so lacking in diligence or competence as to reduce the trial to a farce and a mockery of justice, a conviction will be declared invalid as an invasion of the defendant's right to the assistance of counsel.

The accused way waive his constitutional right to the assistance of counsel. To be effective, however, a waiver must be made intelligently, understandingly, and competently, without pressure or coercion, by a person having full knowledge of his rights. And the trial court is charged with a protective duty toward the defendant in this regard; a waiver may not ordinarily be accepted until the court has determined that the accused understands the nature of the charge, the pleas and defenses available, the elements of the offense, and the punishments that may be imposed. Mere failure to request counsel does not constitute a waiver.

Where an accused is financially unable to employ an attorney, the court must appoint one to act in his behalf, in the absence of an effective waiver thereof. The defendant is entitled to this protection at all stages of his interrogation and trial. Although the court is not obliged to appoint an attorney requested by the accused, the appointing judge must be satisfied that the attorney who is assigned has the ability and experience to represent the defendant fairly and to protect his rights. And the appointment of counsel must be made in time to allow adequate time for the preparation of the defense. Some jurisdictions provide for the appointment of a public defender to aid indigents accused of crime.

An indigent defendant is entitled on request to have counsel appointed to assist him in prosecuting an appeal which the state affords all convicted defendants as a matter of right. This does not apply, however, to habeas corpus proceedings to challenge the validity of a conviction or imprisonment.

§ 7:29. Right to information.

Am Jur 2d References: Criminal Law, §§ 324–332; Depositions and Discovery, §§ 307–324.

A person accused of crime is entitled to be informed of the nature of the accusation against him. In many jurisdictions, provision is made to furnish the defendant with a copy of the indictment or information against him. In some jurisdictions, statutes or constitutional provisions require that the defendant be furnished with a list of the witnesses to be produced against him, and in some states it is the practice, sometimes required by statute, to furnish the accused with a list of witnesses examined before the grand jury. The right to such lists does not exist, however, unless some statutory or constitutional provision is made therefor. It is a general rule that the prosecution is privileged to withhold from an accused the identity of an informer. In many jurisdictions an accused is entitled to a list of the jurors.

A person charged with crime ordinarily has the right to talk with persons having knowledge of matters bearing on the case, and to interview prospective witnesses. But the right to interview a witness in the custody of the state in jail or in a public institution generally lies in the discretion of the court.

In the absence of a statute or court rule providing therefor, an accused is not generally entitled to an inspection or disclosure, prior to trial, of the evidence in the possession of the prosecution. Nor is he entitled to an inspection of the grand jury minutes. However, these rules have been somewhat liberalized in some jurisdictions where the court will, in its discretion, grant the defendant leave to inspect the grand jury minutes where such is reasonably necessary for defense purposes. And the Federal Rules of Criminal Procedure provide for the inspection by the defendant of copies of certain books, papers, documents, or objects by the defendant, within the discretion of the trial court.

§ 7:30. Confrontation.

Am Jur 2d References: Criminal Law, §§ 333–344.

The right of the accused to be confronted by his accusers is a valuable and fundamental safeguard of the citizen and is guaranteed by the constitutions of most states and by the Federal Constitution, which is held to be applicable to trials in state courts as well as those in federal courts. The main purpose of this right is to secure the opportunity of cross-examination. Another advantage is that the judge and jury are enabled to observe the witness while testifying, and that the witness is subjected to some moral influence in facing the court, the jury, and the accused. The right of a defendant to be confronted by witnesses against him is a personal privilege which he may waive. The manner of protecting the rights of an accused person who is deaf or who does not understand the language in which witnesses testify rests largely in the discretion of the trial court.

The right to be confronted by the witnesses relates only to the actual trial for the commission of a criminal offense, and not to the preliminary examination to determine whether the accused should be bound over to the grand jury, nor to motions for continuance, nor to investigations before a grand jury.

Opposing counsel is ordinarily entitled, in a criminal case, to inspect a memorandum or writing which a witness is using on the witness stand to assist or refresh his memory in giving his testimony. The introduction, in a criminal case, of depositions regularly taken pursuant to statutory provision is usually held not to deny the defendant his right to confront witnesses, although there is some contrary opinion on this question. The proof of facts by a document or a duly authenticated copy thereof is not objectionable as violative of the right to be confronted by witnesses. Proof of public records, where they are relevant, does not violate this right. Although there is some authority to the contrary, it is generally held that the admission of the testimony of an absent witness given on the former trial or at a preliminary hearing in the presence of the accused does not violate the right of confrontation where the accused had the right of cross-examination at the former trial or hearing.

§ 7:31. Immunity against self-incrimination.

Am Jur 2d References: Criminal Law, §§ 349–369.

The Fifth Amendment to the Constitution of the United States provides that no person shall be compelled in any criminal case to be a witness against himself, and similar provisions appear in the constitutions of most of the states. The privilege against self-incrimination contained in the Fifth Amendment is extended, by virtue of the Fourteenth Amendment, to action by the states. And the doctrine that one accused of crime cannot be compelled to testify against himself is well settled at common law, independently of constitutional guaranties.

The privilege against self-incrimination is not restricted to criminal cases, but can be claimed by a witness in any proceeding, criminal or civil, administrative or judicial, and investigatory or adjudicatory, including legislative hearings; and it protects any disclosures which the witness may reasonably apprehend could be used in a criminal prosecution or which could lead to other evidence that might be so used. The privilege protects an individual not only from giving answers that are in themselves directly incriminating, but also from giving answers that may provide a link in the chain of evidence against him. This constitutional privilege, however, is a personal one, and does not permit a person to plead the fact that some third person, even his agent, might be incriminated by his testimony.

An accused cannot be compelled to produce private papers or documents that contain incriminating evidence. And it is held to be an invasion of his rights for the prosecuting attorney, or the court, in the presence of the jury, to call upon him or his counsel to produce a document as being in his possession. There is no such infringement, however, where the defendant has taken the witness stand and testified about a document, for the prosecution to make a request on cross-examination that the document be produced.

It is a violation of a defendant's privilege against self-incrimination to place him in a position by any means, such as an unwarranted comment by the court or prosecuting attorney, where he must testify in order to avoid an adverse inference that might arise from his failure to do so. The trial judge may not call attention to the fact that the defendant is entitled to testify, nor may the prosecution or the court comment on the failure of the accused to testify or on the fact that he claimed his privilege while on the stand.

The constitutional guaranty against compulsory self-incrimination may be waived by the accused. Where one charged with the crime has pleaded guilty or has been convicted, he cannot thereafter interpose his privilege against self-incrimination when called upon to testify as a witness against another or before another tribunal such as a grand jury.

The privilege against self-incrimination is not infringed by requiring the defendant to exhibit himself in any manner in which an ordinary person is commonly seen in public. The court, the jury, and the witnesses have the right to observe the appearance of the defendant, and the constitutional provision against self-incrimination is not violated by compelling the defendant to stand up for the purpose of identification or to assume certain postures. Although there is authority to the contrary, some courts hold that as a defendant waives his privilege against self-incrimination by taking the stand and testifying in his own behalf, he may be compelled to perform an act or demonstration in court, such as trying on clothing or producing a sample of his handwriting, which might have a bearing on his guilt or innocence.

It is generally held not to be a violation of the defendant's privilege against self-incrimination to permit a physician or other person to testify as to his findings on a physical examination of the defendant, even though made without the defendant's consent. Thus, it is not improper to require one who is accused of a crime to submit to such scientific tests as blood analysis, urinalysis, or breath tests. Some authorities, however, refuse to admit evidence of the result of such tests unless the defendant has consented thereto. Where the defense of insanity is interposed, the compulsory examination of an accused by experts to determine his mental condition and their testimony in regard thereto does not violate the constitutional privilege against self-incrimination.

It is not considered to be a violation of the privilege against self-incrimination to compel one accused or suspected of a crime to perform an act outside the court and not in the presence of the jury and to allow a witness to testify as to the act. Thus, a suspect or accused has been required to put on garments, appear in a police line-up, submit to a physical examination of his body, submit to having his fingerprints or footprints taken, assume certain poses, be photographed, speak for voice identification, and surrender his shoes for comparison with tracks found near the place where the crime was committed.

VII. JURISDICTION AND VENUE

§ 7:32. In general.

Am Jur 2d References: Criminal Law, §§ 376–382, 390; Juvenile Courts, etc., §§ 1–70.

Although the terms "jurisdiction" and "venue" are often used interchangeably in criminal cases, they are distinguishable. Jurisdiction refers to the power of a court to hear and determine a criminal prosecution, whereas venue relates to and defines the particular county or territorial area within a state or district in which the prosecution is to be brought or tried.

Jurisdiction of the subject matter is derived from the law, and it can neither be waived nor conferred by consent of the accused. Objection that the court does not have jurisdiction of the subject matter may be made at any stage of the proceedings, and the right to make such objection is never waived. But jurisdiction of the person of the defendant may be acquired by consent of the accused or by waiver of objections. If he fails to make his objection in time, he will be deemed to have waived it.

If a defendant is physically before the court on an accusatory pleading, either because he is in custody after an arrest or because he has appeared in person after giving bail, the invalidity of the original arrest does not affect the jurisdiction of the court to proceed with the case. And the fact that the accused is brought within the jurisdiction illegally does not affect the jurisdiction of the court to try him. If he is held under process legally issued, neither the jurisdiction of the court nor the right to put him on trial is impaired by the manner in which he is brought from another jurisdiction, whether by kidnapping, illegal arrest, abduction, or irregular extradition proceedings.

Jurisdiction in a criminal case must be initiated or invoked by an accusation, such as an indictment or information, charging the commission of a criminal offense. Such an accusation, in some form, is a basic essential of jurisdiction which cannot be waived.

Jurisdiction of many offenses committed by juveniles is vested by statute in most states in a special tribunal, frequently termed a juvenile court.

§ 7:33. Place where offense is committed.

Am Jur 2d References: Criminal Law, §§ 383–408; Homicide, §§ 197–203.

Jurisdiction in criminal matters rests solely in the courts of the state or country in which the crime is committed. The courts of one state or country will not execute the criminal laws of another state or country.

Where the requisite elements of a completed crime are committed in several different states, any state in which an essential part of the crime is committed may take jurisdiction. If a person sets in motion a force which operates in another state, as where a shot is fired at a person across a state line or an injurious substance is sent to a person in another state with intent to injure him, the offender is amenable to the laws of the state where the injury resulted although he was not physically present there. However, the state in which a fatal wound or blow is given has exclusive jurisdiction of a prosecution for homicide, although the victim died in another state.

On the high seas every vessel is, for jurisdictional purposes, regarded as a part of the territory of the nation of its owners, and an offense committed on board such a vessel is governed by the laws of that nation. Several statutes provide for the punishment of such crimes as well as offenses committed on aircraft while in flight. By virtue of the Federal Constitution, the United States has exclusive jurisdiction of cases involving offenses committed on lands acquired with the consent of a state for the purpose of public buildings or other facilities.

Venue, as applied to criminal cases, means the place in which prosecutions are to begin. It refers to the particular county or territorial area within a state or district in which the prosecution is to be brought or tried. The common-law rule that proper venue of an offense is the county where it was committed is generally followed in this country. To determine the proper venue under this rule necessarily requires a determination of where the crime was committed. The right of an accused as to the place of his trial is a personal privilege which may be waived by him.

In the absence of limitation by state constitutional provision, a state legislature has the power to fix the venue of criminal prosecutions in a county or district other than that in which the offense was committed. Many states have statutes providing for venue in either county, where an offense is committed partly in one county and partly in another.

§ 7:34. Change of venue; transfer of causes.

Am Jur 2d References: Criminal Law, §§ 409–439.

The statutes of the several states provide for changes of venue from the county in which a criminal prosecution is properly initiated to another county, where such change is necessary to promote the ends of justice by avoiding local prejudices that might operate to the detriment of the accused. A change of venue in a criminal case may be made by consent of the parties. Some statutes provide for the summoning of juries from another county when a local jury free from prejudice is not obtainable.

The right of the accused to a change of venue upon the ground of inability to obtain a fair trial in the county where the indictment is found or because of local prejudice and excitement, is universally recognized. The statutes of many states provide for a change of venue on the ground of the disqualification of the trial judge or because of his bias or prejudice. But this is not a ground for change of venue in the absence of statute.

It is a general rule that the grant or refusal of a change of venue in a criminal case rests in the sound discretion of the trial court and that the court's ruling thereon will not be disturbed by an appellate court unless an abuse of discretion appears from the record. And where a change of venue is granted, the selection of the county to which the cause is to be removed for trial rests in the sound discretion of the trial judge.

The Federal Rules of Criminal Procedure authorize the transfer of criminal cases from one district or division to another for trial, with the consent of the defendant or at his request, within the discretion of the trial court. The grounds for such transfer are outlined in the rules.

§ 7:35. Extradition.

Am Jur 2d References: Extradition, §§ 1–75.

"Extradition" may be defined as the surrender by one state or nation to another of any person accused or convicted of an offense committed within the territorial jurisdiction of the latter authority, which, being competent to try and punish the offender, demands his surrender. The surrender of fugitives from justice by one independent nation to another on request is based on international comity or on the provisions of a treaty between the two nations. The rights and duties of the several states of the United States with respect to interstate rendition of fugitives are governed by federal constitutional and statutory provisions and by state enactments ancillary to such provisions. The Federal Constitution provides that a person charged in any state with treason, felony, or other crime, who flees from justice and is found in another state, must, on demand of the state from which he fled, be delivered up to be removed to the state having jurisdiction of the crime; and the Congress has enacted a general extradition law prescribing the procedure to be followed. The federal law being dominant and controlling, the states may legislate on the subject only to the extent of aiding and effectuating the federal law by provisions consistent therewith. The Uniform Criminal Extradition Act has been adopted in most states.

A fugitive who has been surrendered in extradition proceedings may be tried in the demanding state for any offense committed there, although it is not one specified in the extradition papers. And he may be surrendered by the requisitioning state to a third state to answer for a different crime, without being given an opportunity to return to the asylum state. Once he is delivered to the demanding state, the regularity of the extradition proceedings does not affect the jurisdiction of the courts of that state.

VIII. PROCEDURE, PLEAS, AND REMEDIES

§ 7:36. In general.

Am Jur 2d References: Bail and Recognizance, §§ 9, 23, 29, 33, 34;
Evidence; Federal Practice and Procedure; Trial.

The procedure in criminal cases is governed by statutes and court rules in the several jurisdictions. In the federal courts it is governed by federal statutes and by the Federal Rules of Criminal Procedure. The basic form of procedure in most jurisdictions, including preliminary proceedings, accusation, trial, and rules of evidence, follow the general pattern of the common law in most jurisdictions.

Most states have constitutional or statutory provision making admission to bail mandatory except in certain cases. The most common exceptions to the provision guaranteeing bail are capital cases. In federal prosecutions the courts are still allowed considerable discretion, such as existed at common law, in granting and revoking bail. After conviction and pending appeal, a defendant is not entitled to be released on bail as a matter of right, the matter being generally left to the discretion of the court.

§ 7:37. Indictment and information.

Am Jur 2d References: Indictments and Informations, §§ 1–316.

The usual criminal accusation is by indictment or presentment or by information. An indictment is a written accusation or charge of crime presented by a grand jury and based on evidence introduced before that body. A presentment at common law is notice taken by a grand jury of any offense, from their own knowledge or observation and without any bill of indictment being laid before them by the state. As a form of criminal accusation of an individual, the presentment is practically obsolete in the United States. An information is a written accusation of crime preferred by a public prosecuting officer without the intervention of a grand jury.

At common law and from the earliest days of this country, it has been the settled rule that a formal accusation is an essential condition precedent to a valid prosecution for a criminal offense, and that no criminal proceeding can be instituted without a formal charge openly made against the accused by indictment or presentment by a grand jury, by an information preferred by a prosecuting attorney or some other officer authorized by law, or in some instances, usually in the case of minor offenses, by complaint or affidavit. The form of the accusation depends upon the constitutions and statutes of the several states. The Fifth Amendment to the Federal Constitution, providing that no person shall be held to answer for a capital or otherwise infamous crime unless upon a presentment or indictment of a grand jury, operates only on the federal courts and not on those of the state. And any state may provide for the prosecution of any crime by information rather than by indictment.

Every indictment must be found by a grand jury legally selected, organized, qualified, and competent to act. In most jurisdictions, an indictment must be found by the grand jury of the county or district in which the offense was committed. The requirement of the early common law, that, to be valid, an indictment or information must conform strictly to established formality and charge the offense with technical accuracy and nicety of language, has been relaxed in modern times as regards formal and technical matters not going to the essence of the charge. Many states have statutes prescribing short and relatively simple forms of indictment eliminating the technicalities and artificialities that characterized common-law indictments.

The constitutional right of the accused to be informed of the nature and cause of the accusation against him entitles him to a clear statement of the charge. An indictment must set forth the constituent elements of a criminal offense. Every material fact and ingredient and every essential element of the offense must be alleged with precision and certainty, and the accusation must include a characterization of the crime and such description of the particular act alleged to have been committed by the accused as will enable him properly to defend against the accusation. An indictment or information charging a statutory offense need not use the exact words of the statute; it is sufficient if it follows the language of the statute substantially or charges the offense in equivalent words, and if the defendant is thereby fully informed of the particular offense charged and the statute on which the charge is founded is apparent.

Where an indictment is substantially good but does not so exactly allege the nature and extent of the crime of which the defendant is accused as to enable him properly to prepare his defense, he may move in most jurisdictions for a bill of particulars for specification of the acts on which the prosecution intends to rely. However, except where it is otherwise provided by statute, the granting or refusal of such a motion rests in the sound discretion of the trial court.

In the federal courts and in state courts, in the absence of a statute to the contrary, a court has no authority to amend an indictment as to matters of substance, although some jurisdictions permit amendments as to matters of form where it is not prejudicial to the defendant's substantial rights. In most jurisdictions, however, it is permissible to amend informations, usually on leave of the court.

A joint indictment may be found against two or more persons where the same evidence as to the act constituting the crime applies to all persons indicted. And an indictment or information may consist of several counts charging the defendant with distinct offenses of a kindred nature and liable to punishment of the same general character.

It is the rule in most jurisdictions that the court is not permitted to go behind an indictment to inquire into the evidence considered by the grand jury to determine whether it was in whole or in part competent and legal. In some jurisdictions, however, an indictment may be quashed where the evidence before the grand jury is found to have been clearly illegal and incompetent as a whole. And in many jurisdictions an indictment will be quashed where it is based on testimony which the accused is compelled, over his objection, to give before the grand jury. Other courts, however, hold that this is merely a ground for the suppression of the evidence and does not affect the validity of the indictment. It is generally held that an indictment will be quashed, dismissed, or set aside by the court on motion where there is no evidence whatever before the grand jury tending to support the charges contained in the indictment, but this does not permit the quashing of an indictment on the ground of the mere insufficiency of the evidence, where there was some evidence tending to support the charge.

The proof in a criminal case must correspond with the allegations of the indictment which are essential and material to the charge. To be fatal, however, the variance between allegations and evidence must be material and prejudicial.

There are several forms of objections to indictments and informations. The attack may be in the form of a motion to quash, to dismiss, or to set aside, or it may be by demurrer. The matter is governed by statute in many jurisdictions. As a general rule, a motion to quash an indictment or information may be granted only for defects on the record, not for those dehors the record, the latter class of defects ordinarily being raised by a plea in abatement. A motion to quash is generally addressed to the sound discretion of the court, the guiding principle being whether prejudice may result to the accused from a denial of the motion. It should be granted where the indictment is fatally defective. Where an indictment itself discloses a fatal defect, the objection is properly taken by demurrer; and in some jurisdictions a defect apparent on the face of an indictment, which does not go to the substance thereof, must be raised by demurrer.

It is the general rule that defects or omissions in an indictment or in the mode of finding the indictment, which are of such fundamental character as to make the indictment wholly invalid, are not subject to waiver by the accused. But defects which go only to the form in which the various elements of an offense are stated or to the fact that the accusation is inartistically drawn, are waived if the accused does not raise seasonable objection thereto.

§ 7:38. Preliminary proceedings and arraignment.

Am Jur 2d References: Criminal Law, §§ 440–457.

The statutes or constitutions of many states provide for a preliminary examination of an accused. A preliminary examination before a magistrate is not a criminal prosecution or judicial trial. It is merely a judicial inquiry to determine whether there is "probable cause" for the accusation and to determine whether there is reasonable ground to believe that a crime has been committed and that the defendant committed it. Depending upon the statutes or rules in the particular jurisdiction, a preliminary examination in which the accused is held to answer or bound over is followed by the filing of an information by the prosecuting attorney, or it merely determines whether there is sufficient evidence against an accused to warrant his being held for action by the grand jury. The accused may waive his right to a preliminary examination.

One arrested without a warrant or on a warrant issued by a magistrate on the filing of a complaint or affidavit must be brought with reasonable promptness before the magistrate to be advised of his rights, including his right to preliminary examination and his right to have bail set if the offense is bailable. In some jurisdictions the complaint or affidavit filed for the obtaining of a warrant of arrest or after the defendant has been arrested without a warrant constitutes an accusatory pleading for minor offenses.

The purpose and necessity of an arraignment are to fix the identity of the accused, to inform him of the charge against him, and to give him an opportunity to plead. An arraignment is generally regarded as essential to a valid conviction of a felony; but the right thereto may be waived by the accused. The necessity of arraignment in misdemeanor cases is usually governed by statute. In modern procedure, there is a sufficient arraignment if the accused is called to the bar of the court, the accusatory pleading is read or explained to him, and his plea is demanded.

§ 7:39. Pleas.

Am Jur 2d References: Criminal Law, §§ 458–511.

A plea by the accused or the equivalent of one is generally a requisite for a proper criminal trial. The plea defines the issues to be tried. The plea should be entered after arraignment and before the impaneling and swearing of the jury, but this order of procedure is not inflexible. At common law the accused was required to plead in person, although some cases make a distinction between felony and misdemeanor cases, while other cases hold that a plea of guilty must be entered by the accused in person but that a plea of not guilty may be entered by his attorney. And many courts hold that even a plea of guilty may be made by the attorney where the accused is present and indicates acquiescence in the plea.

Generally, the accused has an absolute right to an opportunity to plead. Although there is authority to the effect that the accused may waive his right to plead, his attorney cannot do so. The record must affirmatively show that the accused did plead or that he was given an opportunity to do so. If the accused "stands mute" and neglects or refuses to plead, the court may enter a plea of not guilty and proceed to trial.

The accused may and should plead specially in bar any matter in confession and avoidance constituting a defense not admissible under a plea of not guilty. A plea in bar is appropriate to assert matters which, per se, destroy the right of action and bar its prosecution absolutely, such as a former acquittal or conviction, or pardon, or the bar of the statute of limitations, or a provision for immunity. Where a special plea not going to the merits is overruled, the accused may "plead over" by entering a plea of not guilty or guilty.

A plea of not guilty is a denial of every fact essential to constitute the crime charged or to establish the guilt of the accused, and places in issue every material allegation of the indictment or information and every essential element of the offense charged.

A plea in abatement is designed to challenge irregularities in procedure occurring before arraignment. It is appropriate generally to raise objections to irregularities in the organization or composition of the grand jury. Such pleas are strictly construed.

According to the prevailing rule, the defense of former jeopardy or of former acquittal or conviction must be presented at the proper time by a special plea in bar. In some jurisdictions, however, it may be proved under a plea of not guilty. In some states a plea of former jeopardy must be in writing, while in others it may be oral.

A plea of guilty must be voluntary and must be made intelligently and understandingly by one competent to know the consequences, and must not be induced by fear, persuasion, promises, inadvertence, ignorance, or fraud. Before receiving a plea of guilty, the court should determine that the accused understands the consequences of such a plea. A plea of guilty amounts to a confession of guilt and waives all defenses other than that the accusatory pleading charges no offense. Where the plea of guilty is to an offense involving several degrees and does not specify the degree confessed, it may be necessary for the court to hear evidence to determine the degree of the offense.

A plea of nolo contendere ("I do not wish to contend") is, for the purposes of the immediate prosecution, equivalent to a plea of guilty. The plea is not recognized in some jurisdictions, and where it is recognized, the acceptance of the plea is within the broad discretion of the court and is not a matter of right with the accused. The main difference between a plea of guilty and a plea of nolo contendere is that the latter plea does not bind the defendant in other proceedings and has no effect beyond the particular case. It cannot be used as an admission of guilt in any other action, civil or criminal. A judgment of conviction entered on a plea of nolo contendere may, however, be used by the accused as the basis of a plea of double jeopardy.

In the absence of statute or court rule to the contrary, the granting or refusing of leave to withdraw a plea in a criminal case rests in the sound discretion of the trial court. The accused is not generally entitled to withdraw a plea as a matter of right. This rule extends to a plea of guilty, nolo contendere, or not guilty.

§ 7:40. Dismissal, nolle prosequi, and arrest of judgment.

Am Jur 2d References: Criminal Law, §§ 512–524.

A nolle prosequi is a formal entry of record by the prosecuting attorney by which he declares that he will not prosecute the case further. It may apply to some counts of an indictment, a part of a divisible count, or to some of the defendants or all of them. In the absence of a controlling statute or rule of court, the power to enter a nolle prosequi lies in the sole discretion of the prosecuting attorney. The court has no jurisdiction to proceed further in the case after the entry of the nolle. An unqualified dismissal or nolle entered by the prosecuting attorney terminates the prosecution and frees the defendant. In some jurisdictions there are statutes or court rules requiring a consent of the trial court to the entry of a nolle prosequi or dismissal by the prosecutor, or authorizing the court itself to enter a dismissal.

A motion in arrest of judgment may be based on the ground that the court is without jurisdiction, that the accusatory pleading is not sufficient to charge a criminal offense or to support a conviction, or that the record is in some respect defective and insufficient to support a judgment. The granting of a motion in arrest of judgment does not operate as an acquittal but only places the defendant in the same situation in which he was before the prosecution was begun. He has not been in jeopardy, and the state may proceed against him upon a new and sufficient indictment.

§ 7:41. Appeal.

Am Jur 2d References: Appeal and Error, particularly §§ 1, 6, 159–167, 267–275, 345, 346, 574, 778–781, 798, 815, 821, 883, 952; Federal Practice and Procedure, particularly §§ 314–318, 345, 377–385, 396–400, 424–427.

Appellate jurisdiction is the authority of a superior tribunal to review, reverse, correct, or affirm the decisions of an inferior court. The review may be either by appeal or by writ of error, although the latter writ is becoming progressively less important and the term "appeal" is now commonly used generically to cover all forms of appellate review.

The right to appellate review in criminal cases depends entirely upon statutory and constitutional provisions therefor. The right to appeal is not essential to due process of law. The extent of the right to appellate review and the conditions and manner of its exercise are governed by statute or constitutional provisions in all American jurisdictions. Defenses based on constitutional grounds, to be available for review on appeal, must ordinarily be first asserted in the trial court. Although the right to appeal from certain kinds of orders in criminal cases is given to the prosecution in some jurisdictions, the right is generally limited to the accused and to orders and judgments by which he is aggrieved. And the order or judgment, to be appealable, must be final.

The guaranties of due process of law and equal protection of the law require that appellate review in criminal cases, if made generally available, may not be denied because of a defendant's inability to pay the expenses incident to the review. An indigent defendant in a criminal case is entitled to appeal in forma pauperis.

To warrant a reversal on appeal, the error complained of must have been prejudicial to the defendant. Mere technical errors, not impairing some substantial right of the defendant essential to a fair trial, will not warrant a reversal. In capital cases, however, the appellate court will scrutinize the record with extreme care for the possibility of prejudicial error. And in a criminal case, any material error is presumed to result in prejudice to the accused. Errors in the admission of evidence or in instructions which might be harmless in a civil action may be reversible in a criminal case.

§ 7:42. Habeas corpus and coram nobis.

Am Jur 2d References: Coram Nobis, §§ 1–40; Habeas Corpus,
§§ 1–85, 105–177.

The writ of habeas corpus (habeas corpus ad subjiciendum) is a high prerogative writ furnishing an extraordinary remedy to secure the release, by judicial decree, of persons who are restrained of their liberty illegally. The writ has long been an important bulwark guarding the liberties of individuals and protecting them against illegal imprisonment or detention. Habeas corpus proceedings are, for most purposes, treated as civil rather than criminal in nature, even though directed against the validity of a criminal prosecution. The inquiry on a writ of habeas corpus is addressed, not to errors committed by a court within its jurisdiction, but to the question whether the proceeding or judgment under which the petitioner is restrained are void. Such an inquiry ordinarily involves no questions other than those that pertain to jurisdiction. Statutes in some states provide a substitute for the common-law writ.

The writ of habeas corpus will not ordinarily be granted to determine a mere abstract or moot question. And generally the writ will not be granted where adequate relief may be had or could have been procured by resort to another remedy, such as appeal or writ of error, although this rule may yield to exceptional circumstances where the need for habeas corpus is apparent. To warrant interference by habeas corpus, there must ordinarily be actual or physical restraint, duress or restraint of the person whereby he is prevented from exercising the liberty of going when and where he pleases.

As indicated above, habeas corpus does not lie to review or correct mere errors in the proceedings leading up to a person's conviction or errors in sentencing. Its purpose is to free a person held without any legal right or under a judgment void because of lack of jurisdiction or violation of constitutional rights. The writ is available to challenge a conviction based on a violation of fundamental constitutional rights, as by coercing a confession, denying the right to counsel, or excluding from the jury members of the defendant's race. It will issue at the suit of one restrained under an unconstitutional law. And in some jurisdictions the writ is available to enforce a prisoner's right to be admitted to bail.

After the hearing on a writ of habeas corpus, the court should dispose of the petitioner in such manner as the justice of the case may require. If there is no legal ground for his detention, he should be discharged; but if it appears that he is subject to further criminal proceedings or to detention on other and legal grounds, the court may, instead of discharging him, remit him to the custody of the proper court or officers.

Coram nobis, although a writ of ancient origin, fell into disuse until relatively recent years, when it and its statutory equivalent or substitute have been considerably revived, especially in criminal cases. The writ of error coram nobis is employed in cases where there is no other remedy for the purpose of reviewing, correcting, or vacating a judgment in the same court in which it was rendered, on account of errors of fact which are extrinsic to, or do not appear in, the record, affecting the validity and regularity of the proceedings; which were not put in issue at the trial; which were unknown at the time of the trial to the party seeking relief without fault on his part; which were unknown to the trial court, and thus were not passed upon by it, and which, if known, would have prevented rendition of the judgment. Even when directed against a judgment in criminal proceedings, the writ of coram nobis is usually treated as civil rather than criminal in nature.

The right to relief under a writ of coram nobis is not absolute, but rests largely within the discretion of the trial court. It is generally limited to cases where no other remedy is provided by law; and the mistake of fact relied upon for relief must have been unknown to the applicant at the time of the trial and such that he could not, by the exercise of reasonable diligence, have discovered in time to have presented it to the court in the original proceeding. The writ is directed exclusively against mistakes of fact. Errors of law are excluded from the causes for which the writ may issue.

Coram nobis may be available as a postconviction remedy against a conviction based on a plea of guilty procured through mistake, ignorance, coercion, fraud, trickery, or deceit. It may be available to one wrongfully prevented from perfecting an appeal from a conviction where there is no other means of judicial relief. On the other hand, the writ is generally not available on the ground that the indictment or information was defective; or because of newly discovered evidence on issues litigated at the trial; or on the ground of illegal arrest, excessive bail, insufficiency of evidence at a preliminary hearing, denial of a speedy trial, or irregularities relating to the grand jury or petit jury which tried the defendant.

IX. JUDGMENT, SENTENCE, AND PUNISHMENT

§ 7:43. Generally.

Am Jur 2d References: Criminal Law, §§ 525–551, 575.

The defendant has the right to be present and to be represented by counsel at the time sentence or judgment is pronounced against him. Generally, the defendant also has the right of allocution, that is, the traditional inquiry of whether he has anything to say why sentence should not be pronounced against him.

The imposition of an unauthorized or merely erroneous sentence does not require vacation of the entire judgment or granting of a new trial, but is a ground for reversing the erroneous portion of the judgment or sentence, leaving the verdict to stand as the basis of a new and proper sentence. Of course, if the court has no jurisdiction, its sentence is deemed to be void and not merely erroneous. A sentence should be definite, certain, and not dependent on any contingency or condition. The judgment and sentence must conform strictly to the statute and may not include a punishment different from or in excess of that prescribed by the statute. Where the court imposes a sentence in excess of that permitted by law, the legal and authorized portion of the sentence is not void, but the excess portion of the sentence is open to attack. An indeterminate sentence is invalid where the controlling statute prescribes a sentence for a definite term; but a state may, by statute, provide for indeterminate sentences.

A defendant who is convicted under an indictment charging two or more distinct offenses, each requiring proof of some fact or element not required to establish the other offense, may be punished for both or all. On conviction of several offenses charged in separate indictments or in separate counts of the same indictment, the court may impose "concurrent sentences," meaning sentences operating simultaneously, or "consecutive sentences," meaning sentences succeeding one another. If the court fails to specify otherwise, the term of imprisonment on the second or subsequent sentence runs concurrently with the first, in the absence of statute to the contrary.

§ 7:44. Suspending, changing, or vacating sentence.

Am Jur 2d References: Criminal Law, §§ 552–574.

In some jurisdictions it is held that courts have inherent power to suspend imposition of sentences in criminal cases or to suspend or stay the execution of a sentence imposed. Other courts hold that there is no such power except as conferred by statute. Many jurisdictions have specific provisions for suspension of sentence or execution of sentence, on condition, such as during good behavior, or otherwise.

The power to grant probation is dependent upon statute and must be exercised before the execution or service of a sentence is begun. The objectives sought by probation are education and rehabilitation, and the conditions of probation should promote these objectives. The court may not impose banishment as a condition of probation. Upon violation of the conditions of probation, the court has the power to revoke probation. The procedure provided by statute must be followed in revoking probation, however; and the defendant is generally entitled to notice and hearing before such revocation.

In most jurisdictions, a court has discretionary power to revise, modify, or vacate a judgment in a criminal case during the term at which the judgment was entered, provided the court acts before the defendant begins service of the sentence. There is conflict of authority on the power of the court to set aside a sentence and grant a new trial after the defendant has been committed, where there was error which prevented him from having a fair trial. There is disagreement also on the power of the court, after the defendant has been committed under a sentence, to impose a different sentence reducing the punishment. It is agreed, however, that the punishment cannot be increased under these circumstances. Where the original sentence was illegal, the trial court may vacate it and substitute a legal sentence, even though the original sentence has been partially executed and the term of court at which it was imposed has expired. The court may at any time enter a nunc pro tunc order correcting mere formal or clerical errors, or omissions in entries concerning matters or procedure.

§ 7:45. Pardon and parole.

Am Jur 2d References: Pardon and Parole, §§ 1–102.

A pardon is a declaration on record by the chief magistrate or other designated official of a state or country, that a person named is relieved from the legal consequences of a specified crime. A pardon may be absolute or conditional. Amnesty is a kind of pardon or impunity usually granted by the sovereign to certain classes or groups of persons who are subject to trial for past offenses but who have not yet been convicted. A reprieve is a suspension or postponement of the execution of a sentence for a definite time. A commutation of sentence is the change of the punishment, usually by the chief magistrate of a state or country, to which a person is sentenced, to a less severe punishment, that is, the substitution of a less for a greater punishment.

The United States Constitution confers upon the President the power to grant pardons and reprieves for offenses against the United States. Most of the states vest this power in the governor, although it is sometimes vested in a board of which the governor is usually a member.

The legal effect of a full pardon is to relieve the punishment and blot out of existence the guilt of the offender to such an extent that, in the eye of the law, he is as innocent as if he had never committed the offense. As a general rule, a full pardon absolves one from all legal consequences of his crime. It removes the penalties and disabilities which ordinarily follow from conviction, and, generally speaking, restores the offender to all his civil rights. A pardon granted in a particular case, however, relates only to that case and will not cover other offenses not mentioned. A full pardon restores one to all citizenship rights, including the rights of suffrage, to serve on a jury, and to be a witness. It restores one to his eligibility for elective office which was forfeited by his conviction. It does not, however, restore one to property or interests which have vested in others by reason of his conviction. Nor does a pardon restore one to an office forfeited by reason of his conviction, nor to a license or other special privilege, such as the right to practice law, forfeited by reason of conviction of a crime. And a pardon has no effect on the offender's civil liability to an individual whom he has wronged.

A parole in criminal law is the release of a convict from imprisonment upon certain conditions to be observed by him. The law governing parole is generally statutory. Unlike a pardon, a parole does not vacate or set aside the sentence imposed or expiate or excuse the crime committed, but merely suspends the execution of the penalty and temporarily releases the convict from imprisonment upon the conditions stated in the parole.

§ 7:46. Punishment; disabilities attending conviction.

Am Jur 2d References: Criminal Law, §§ 567–629.

The power to prescribe the penalty to be imposed for the commission of a crime belongs to the legislature, and it is limited only by constitutional provisions.   With respect to the punishment for a particular crime, the legislature may allow the exercise of discretion, within prescribed limits, by the court or jury, or it may make mandatory a specified punishment on conviction. Where punishment is left to the discretion of the court or jury, evidence in aggravation or in mitigation may be heard.   In some jurisdictions, the punishment is fixed by the court, while in others the jury is authorized to fix the punishment or to make recommendations as to alternative penalties.

Some forms of punishment are beyond the power of the courts or legislatures. The Eighth Amendment of the Constitution of the United States, and most state constitutions, prohibit the infliction of cruel and unusual punishment. It is difficult to define with exactness the extent of these limitations.   The prohibition is generally aimed at inhuman and barbarous penalties.   Drawing and quartering, burning alive, or torturing are obviously cruel and unusual punishments by modern standards.   While ordinarily imprisonment, even imprisonment for life and at hard labor, is not cruel or unusual punishment, if the duration of the sentence is so disproportionate to the offense committed as to shock the moral sense of the community, the punishment is prohibited.   The imposition of the death penalty, whether by hanging, shooting, electrocution, or lethal gas was held until quite recently not to constitute cruel and unusual punishment within the constitutional prohibition.   The Supreme Court of the United States has changed its views on this matter, however, and has at least greatly restricted the power of the states to impose the death penalty.

Although the severity of the early common law, by which one convicted of a felony or treason was placed in a state of attainder and forfeited all property rights and other rights and suffered "civil death," has never prevailed in this country, there are some disabilities which attend conviction of serious crimes. The loss of civil rights incident to conviction may last only during the term of imprisonment, or it may be permanent, depending upon the provisions of the statute.   Conviction usually involves a loss of the right to practice law or to engage in other professions or to hold public office.

At common law, a person under death sentence or convicted of felony was said to be civilly dead, and could perform no legal function.   The existence, extent, and consequences of civil death in this country depend upon statute. Under modern law, the consequences of statutory civil death do not include forfeitures of property.   In some jurisdictions, when either spouse is sentenced to life imprisonment, the marriage is automatically dissolved, without divorce or other legal process.

§ 7:47. Habitual criminals and subsequent offenders.

Am Jur 2d References: Habitual Criminals and Subsequent Offenders, §§ 1–32.

A state legislature may provide more severe punishment for habitual criminals or successive offenders than for those convicted of crime for the first time. The enhanced punishment authorized under statutes of this kind is an incident of the subsequent offense, for which the accused is being tried, and he is subject to more severe punishment because of the incorrigible nature of his conduct demonstrated by the previous criminal record. The validity of statutes authorizing the imposition of heavier penalties on recidivists than on first offenders has been upheld as against attacks on the grounds that they invade the privileges and immunities of citizens, involve double jeopardy, are ex post facto laws, delegate legislative power to prosecutors, inflict cruel and unusual punishment, impair the right of trial by jury or of confrontation by adverse witnesses, or that they deny the accused due process of law or equal protection of the laws.

A person is generally deemed to have been previously convicted under habitual criminal statutes only when there has been an adjudication of guilt on the earlier charge and a pronouncement of sentence by the court thereon. The prior conviction must have been a final conviction, and the weight of authority is to the effect that it is not final for this purpose while an appeal is pending. Judgment that has been reversed, or one that is void, is not available to enhance subsequent punishment.

A person may not be charged under a habitual criminal statute unless he was previously convicted of an offense of the class or character specified in the statute. In some jurisdictions, enhanced punishment is prescribed for repeated commission of felonies or offenses involving turpitude; and under some statutes the recurrence of specific offenses or of the same or similar crimes warrants imposition of increased punishment. An offender's punishment may be increased by a showing of prior convictions against him in other jurisdictions.

A person accused of crime as a recidivist is entitled to be informed by indictment or information that he is being charged as such. The pleading must allege facts necessary to bring the case within the statute authorizing enhanced punishment, and must therefore allege the prior conviction or convictions relied on. The accused is entitled to a proper hearing on the issue of the prior convictions, although the court will not investigate or determine whether the accused was guilty or innocent of the former charges.

X. PARTICULAR OFFENSES

§ 7:48. Abortion.

Am Jur 2d References: Abortion, §§ 1–36.

Abortion is the expulsion of the fetus at so early a period of uterogestation that it has not acquired the power of sustaining an independent life. The crime of abortion is the wilful bringing about of an abortion without justification or excuse. At common law this was a misdemeanor. The gravamen of the charge of abortion under the usual statute is the intent with which the drugs, instruments, or the means of producing an abortion are used. While the statutes defining the crime of abortion vary, they generally apply to anyone who, with the intent to produce the miscarriage of any pregnant woman, or of "any woman," administers, or causes to be given to her, any drug or noxious substance, or uses any instrument or other means, with such intent. Under the usual statute prohibiting the administration or prescription of any medicine or drug with intent to procure an abortion, it is immaterial whether the medicine or drug used was capable of producing the result intended. Under such statutes, the crime is complete when the drug is prescribed or administered, or the instrument used, with intent to procure the miscarriage, regardless of whether or not a miscarriage actually resulted.

At common law, an essential element of the crime of abortion was that the woman was pregnant, and some authorities required proof that she was "quick with child." The statutes of the several states vary in their provisions concerning this element of the offense.

Many statutes prohibiting abortion contain an exception where a miscarriage or abortion is necessary to save the woman's life; and in some states there are statutes authorizing abortions by physicians for other and less imperative reasons.

In some jurisdictions the woman incurs no criminal liability by procuring or consenting to an abortion. However, some courts hold that the applicable statutes defining the crime of abortion, or other general statutes relating to principals and accessories in criminal cases, operate to render criminally liable a woman who solicits or consents to an abortion on herself.

§ 7:49. Adultery and fornication.

Am Jur 2d References: Adultery and Fornication, §§ 1–42.

The common-law definition of adultery is sexual intercourse by a man, married or single, with a married woman not his wife. Fornication is defined by the common law as the act of illicit intercourse by a man, married or single, with an unmarried woman. Adultery was formerly punished as a crime only in ecclesiastical courts. Fornication, as such, was not a punishable offense at common law.

It is essential to the commission of the offense of adultery that at least one of the persons alleged to have committed the act should have been married to a third person at the time of the commission of the act. Under most modern statutes, the offense is committed if either of the participants in the act is married. If both are married, both may be guilty. Under some statutes, an unmarried person, whether male or female, who has sexual intercourse with a married person of the opposite sex is guilty of adultery, equally with the married person; other authorities hold that the single person cannot be convicted of adultery.

§ 7:50. Arson.

Am Jur 2d References: Arson, etc., §§ 1–58.

At common law, arson was the malicious and wilful burning of another's house or dwelling house, or outhouse appurtenant to or a parcel of the dwelling house, or within the curtilage. The curtilage of the dwelling house is such space as is necessary and convenient, and habitually used, for family purposes and the carrying on of domestic employments, and includes a yard, a garden, or even a nearby field used in connection with the dwelling. Arson has always been deemed a felony of great enormity, because it not only involves the malicious destruction of property but also may endanger human life.

Statutes have generally enlarged the common-law definition of arson so as to include the burning of buildings and property other than dwelling houses and buildings within the curtilage. And while at common law an owner who burned his house while occupying it was not guilty of arson, statutes have been enacted making it a criminal offense to burn insured property with the intent to injure or defraud an insurer. The statutes frequently divide the crime of arson into degrees, providing more severe punishment for the burning of a dwelling house or burning in the nighttime or burning under such circumstances as might endanger human life, than in cases of other burnings prohibited by law. A person burning a dwelling house is guilty of arson even if the house is temporarily unoccupied. It is not necessary that the building be wholly or partially consumed or materially injured; it is sufficient if the fire is actually communicated to any part thereof, however small. Both at common law and under statutes, the burning must be wilful and malicious in order to constitute arson or its statutory equivalent.

§ 7:51. Assault and battery.

Am Jur 2d References: Assault and Battery, §§ 1–108.

Generally speaking, an assault is a demonstration of an unlawful intent by one person to inflict immediate injury on the person of another then present. Physical contact is not an essential element of this offense, but a threat or offer of violence is. The offense has been variously defined as an intentional attempt, by force or violence, to do injury to the person of another; and as any attempt to commit a battery or any threatening gesture showing in itself or by words accompanying it an immediate intention, coupled with a present ability, to commit a battery. Unless accompanied by some menacing act or gesture, mere words cannot amount to an assault constituting a crime.

A battery is the unlawful touching or striking of the person of another by the aggressor himself or by any substance put in motion by him, done with the intention of bringing about a harmful or offensive contact or apprehension thereof which is not consented to by the other and not legally justified. The slightest unlawful touching of the person of another may amount to a battery, although no physical harm resulted.

Generally, an intention to do harm, or an unlawful intent, is an essential element of the crime of assault or battery. And although this requirement has been relaxed in some jurisdictions to the extent of treating wantonness as a sufficient substitute for malice, ordinary negligence does not suffice.

On the question whether present ability to carry out a threatened or demonstrated intent to harm another is an essential element of criminal assault, and whether an apparent ability to do so is sufficient, there is a conflict of authority. For example, there are differing views on the question whether an assault may be committed with an unloaded firearm.

Criminal assault and battery may be committed by an act intended as a practical joke, or by sexual acts or indecent liberties with the person of a woman or man. Acts which would otherwise amount to assault and battery may not constitute a criminal offense where directed by one spouse against the other, by a parent or one in loco parentis, or by a teacher in imposing reasonable corporal punishment on a child as a disciplinary measure.

In many jurisdictions certain types of aggravated assault are distinguished from simple assault, and in some states the crime of assault is divided into several degrees and more severe penalties are provided for the aggravated types. The higher degrees of aggravated assault consist of such offenses as assault with intent to kill, assault with intent to rape, assault with intent to rob, or assault in a manner likely to inflict great bodily injury or disgrace upon the victim.

The defenses available in the criminal prosecutions generally may be raised in prosecutions for assault and battery. An act does not usually constitute criminal assault or battery where the person against whom it is committed consented thereto. However, in cases of mutual combat, or fights by mutual agreement, both participants may be guilty of assault and battery. Self-defense, or defense of a third person, may be asserted as a defense in a prosecution for assault and battery. The force used in defense must, however, bear a reasonable relation to the nature of the attack and the danger threatened thereby. Although there is some difference of opinion on the subject, it is now generally held that one who is assailed may meet force with force without retreating, so long as he uses only such force as is necessary. One who provokes an attack may be deprived of the right of self-defense, but there is a conflict of authority on the question whether provocation by offensive language alone has this effect.

An owner of property may justify an assault charged against him on the ground that he acted in defense of his property against an unlawful invasion or withholding thereof. A person has a right to defend his home against attack and to use any force necessary to eject a trespasser from his property.

§ 7:52. Automobiles: offenses relating to.

Am Jur 2d References: Automobiles and Highway Traffic, §§ 90–92, 125–128, 149–297, 303–346.

Numerous statutes and ordinances prohibit the operation of a motor vehicle which is not properly licensed or registered in accordance with statute, or the operation of an automobile without a driver's license required by law, and violation of such provisions is generally made a criminal offense. Most states have statutes regulating in detail the equipment of motor vehicles with respect to such things as steering mechanism, brakes, and lights; and many states require a periodic inspection of motor vehicles. The violation of such regulations is usually made a penal offense.

The states and municipalities have a vast number and variety of regulations governing traffic on highways and streets, with respect to such matters as speed, right of way, the direction of traffic, and the restriction or exclusion of motor vehicle traffic on certain ways. The failure to observe or obey traffic signs or lights is generally made a penal offense. Regulations governing the parking or standing of motor vehicles upon public ways are almost universal, especially in urban areas.

Statutes directed against the so-called "hit-and-run" drivers require that motorists involved in an accident, who know that property damage or personal injury has been sustained by another, stop and identify themselves, and in some states, motorists are also required to render such aid as is reasonable or necessary.

Driving a motor vehicle while intoxicated or under the influence of liquor is a criminal offense in all jurisdictions, and in some states driving under the influence of drugs is likewise an offense. Reckless driving, variously defined in the several jurisdictions, or driving in a careless manner or in any manner endangering the public, is frequently made a penal offense.

Depending upon the circumstances and the language of the particular statutes involved, causing the death of another by the reckless, unlawful, or negligent operation of a motor vehicle may constitute homicide. Under a variety of statutes and circumstances, such an act may constitute involuntary manslaughter or voluntary manslaughter or the statutory offense of homicide by operation of a motor vehicle. Where the essential elements are present, it may even constitute murder.

In addition to the general laws against larceny, the theft or unauthorized taking of motor vehicles is the subject of numerous statutes. For example, the taking, using, or operating of a motor vehicle without the consent of the owner is made a criminal offense by specific statute in many jurisdictions. And the National Motor Vehicle Theft Act makes it a federal offense to transport a motor vehicle in interstate or foreign commerce, knowing the same to have been stolen, or to receive, conceal, or sell such a vehicle; and "tampering" with a motor vehicle or removing parts or accessories therefrom is made a criminal offense in many states.

§ 7:53. Bigamy.

Am Jur 2d References: Bigamy, §§ 1–63.

Bigamy may be simply defined as the act of contracting a second marriage by one who has, at the time, a lawful spouse by a prior marriage. The crime of bigamy consists of the act of marrying by a person whose spouse by a former marriage is still alive and whose former marriage is still in force. The statutes denouncing bigamy usually relate to the marriage or attempted marriage of a person who is lawfully married to another, so that a single person who marries the spouse of another is not ordinarily guilty of bigamy as a principal, although in some jurisdictions he may be guilty of aiding and abetting the married person in committing the offense.

An essential element of the crime of bigamy is an existing marriage that is valid, or at least merely voidable. A prior void marriage cannot be the foundation of a prosecution for bigamy. In jurisdictions recognizing common-law marriages, a subsequent marriage of that kind may constitute bigamy. The crime of bigamy is complete when the second marriage is performed or contracted, and no cohabitation following it is generally necessary to fix the guilt of the defendant, although such cohabitation is made a separate crime in some jurisdictions.

Most of the defenses in prosecutions for bigamy are actually based on the absence of some essential element of the offense, such as the nonexistence of the prior marriage because of its invalidity, or its dissolution by divorce, or because of the death of the former spouse. Whether an honest mistaken belief that a prior marriage has been so terminated constitutes a defense to a prosecution for bigamy based on a subsequent marriage is the subject of some conflict of authority. The weight of authority seems to support the view that a mistake of law as to the validity or termination of a former marriage is not a defense to a charge of bigamy.

One cannot justify bigamy by proof that his plural marriage was a part of, or was sanctioned by, his religious beliefs. Some jurisdictions have statutes, so-called "Enoch Arden" laws, by which a second marriage is not bigamous where it is contracted after the first spouse has been absent for the prescribed statutory period and there are no circumstances indicating that he is still living.

§ 7:54. Breach of peace, disorderly conduct, affray, disturbing meetings, and malicious mischief.

Am Jur 2d References: Breach of Peace and Disorderly Conduct, §§ 1–51; Disturbing Meetings, §§ 1–11; Malicious Mischief, §§ 1–24.

The offense of breach of the peace is of common-law origin, but it is frequently defined and made an offense by statute or ordinance. The offense may be generally defined as such a violation of the public order as amounts to a disturbance of the public tranquility by act or conduct either directly having this effect or inciting or tending to incite such a disturbance of the public tranquility. Various types of acts or conduct have been held to constitute a breach of the peace, such as acts of violence or acts tending to produce or incite violence, disturbance of the public tranquility by yelling or uttering loud and vociferous language, making disturbing noises on a public street, or disturbance of a public assembly by improper conduct. Conduct "violating the public decorum" has been held to constitute a breach of the peace. Abusive, profane, indecent, or otherwise provocative language may constitute a breach of the peace under some circumstances.

An affray is generally defined as the fighting of two or more persons in a public place, to the terror of the people and the disturbance of public tranquility. While such conduct also constitutes a breach of the peace, affray is a distinct offense at common law and generally under statutes. Another offense closely related to breach of the peace is the statutory crime of disorderly conduct. It was not a distinct common-law offense. As it is defined in the various statutes and ordinances, it means an act which tends to breach the peace or to disturb those people who hear or see it, or to endanger the morals, safety, or health of the community or of a class of persons. A great variety of acts have been held to constitute disorderly conduct under various statutes and circumstances. Some of such acts are loud and boisterous language, especially if it is tainted by profanity, brawling or fighting, or the use of offensive or disorderly language. Prosecutions for this offense, as for that of breach of the peace, are frequently met with objections based on constitutional rights of freedom of speech, freedom of religion, and freedom of assembly.

Statutory enactments in most jurisdictions reflect the common-law principle that as a matter of preventive justice a person may, under certain circumstances, be required by a court to give bond or security against future breach of the peace by him. An offense threatened against the person or property of another is the usual basis for the initiation of a proceeding to require a peace bond.

To disturb persons gathered or assembled for the purpose of religious worship or for other lawful purposes was an offense at common law, and has been made so by statute in most states. What constitutes unlawful disturbance of a public meeting or assembly may depend upon the circumstances of each case. Generally, any conduct which is contrary to the usages of the particular sort of meeting and class of persons assembled, and which interferes with its due progress or annoys the assembly in whole or in part, is such a disturbance.

The offense commonly known as "malicious mischief" has no well-defined legal meaning, but is a name applied to acts denounced as crimes by a multitude of statutes varying widely in times and purpose. The offense has been variously defined as the wilful and unlawful injury or destruction of the property of another; or as any malicious physical injury to the rights of another, which impairs utility or materially diminishes value; or any malicious or mischievous physical injury, either to the rights of another or to those of the public in general.

§ 7:55. Burglary.

Am Jur 2d References: Burglary, §§ 1–77.

Common-law burglary is the breaking and entering of a dwelling or mansion house of another in the nighttime, with intent to commit a felony therein. To establish the crime, all of the five elements mentioned in this definition must appear. The dwelling specified by the definition of common-law burglary includes outhouses within the curtilage, as well as an apartment or hotel room where a person dwells. The temporary absence of the owner and his family from the building does not affect its status as a dwelling for the present purposes, but if the owner or occupant leaves the house with a settled purpose not to return, the house ceases to be a dwelling. Under the common law and by virtue of statutes in many jurisdictions, a criminal intent to steal or · to commit some felony at the time of breaking and entering is an essential element of the crime of burglary. Consummation or execution of the intent to steal or to commit a felony is not necessary to complete the crime of burglary. Statutes in some states have extended the concept of burglary to places other than dwelling houses. These statutes often embrace "any other building" or "any other house." Under some such statutes, burglary may be committed in a building used as a place of business or as a schoolhouse. Some statutes include motor vehicles.

Although breaking is not an element of burglary under some statutory provisions, where breaking must be shown to establish the offense, as at common law, there must be a breaking, moving, or putting aside of something material constituting a part of the dwelling house and relied on as security against intrusion. Any degree of force to effect an entrance through any usual place of ingress, whether open, partly open, or closed, constitutes a sufficient breaking.

The requirement of the common law that burglary must be committed in the nighttime did not contemplate the exact period between sunset and sunrise. The rule is thus laid down by Blackstone: "If there be daylight or crepusculum enough, begun or left, to discern a man's face withal, it is not burglary. But this does not extend to moonlight." This rule is substantially supported in the states where no statutory definition of nighttime is provided, and the rule has been extended to street lights as well as moonlight.

Statutes in many states make the possession of burglarious tools or implements a separate and distinct criminal offense. These statutes, in varying terms, base the crime on the possession of burglarious tools or implements, or the possession of such tools or implements with intent to use them for the purpose of effecting a burglarious breaking and entering.

§ 7:56. Conspiracy.

Am Jur 2d References: Conspiracy, §§ 1–42.

A conspiracy is an agreement between two or more persons to accomplish together a criminal or unlawful act or to achieve by criminal or unlawful means an act not in itself unlawful.   A conspiracy to commit a crime is an offense distinct from the crime that is the object of the conspiracy.   At common law, conspiracy was a misdemeanor only, though the purpose of the conspiracy was the commission of a felony.   It is the unlawful agreement itself, and not its accomplishment, that is the gist of the crime of conspiracy.   The guilt or innocence of the conspirators does not depend upon the success or failure of their enterprise.   An agreement, to amount to a conspiracy, need not be formal or express, but may be inferred from the circumstances.

A criminal intent is essential to the crime of conspiracy, and this intent must exist in the minds of at least two of the parties to the conspiracy.   And there must, of course, be knowledge of the conspiracy on the part of a person sought to be charged as a conspirator.   In the absence of a statutory provision to the contrary, a criminal conspiracy is completed when the agreement is made, and an overt act is not a necessary incident of the crime.   One who joins a conspiracy after its formation is equally culpable with the original members and is responsible for all that has previously been done pursuant to the conspiracy.

§ 7:57. Embezzlement.

Am Jur 2d References: Embezzlement, §§ 1–65.

Embezzlement is the fraudulent conversion of property by one who has rightfully come into possession thereof and who holds it in a fiduciary capacity. It is the fraudulent appropriation or conversion by an agent, employee, corporate officer, a trustee, a public officer, or other person acting in a fiduciary capacity, of money or other personal property, the possession of which has been entrusted to him by another.   Embezzlement by public officers or employees is the subject of special statutory provisions in many jurisdictions.   The main distinction between embezzlement and larceny is that the latter offense involves a trespass, and a wrongful taking or asportation, while embezzlement does not. The fact that a person rightfully in possession of property in a fiduciary capacity could not be convicted of larceny under the early common law when he wrongfully converted the property, was the reason for the creation of the statutory offense of embezzlement.

Although there is authority to the contrary, some courts hold that if an accused, at the time he received possession of property, harbored a fraudulent or felonious intent to convert the property to his own use, his subsequent conversion thereof is larceny rather than embezzlement.   In determining whether a conversion was larceny or embezzlement, some courts have distinguished between mere custody and legal possession, holding that one who has bare custody of property and feloniously appropriates it to his own use is guilty of larceny, whereas his offense is embezzlement if he had lawful possession of the property.   This distinction is difficult to apply in many cases, and its impracticability has led to its eradication by statute in some states.   Indeed, in some jurisdictions all distinctions between embezzlement and larceny have been eliminated by statute, under which any felonious theft is treated as a distinctive offense.

As a general rule, the fact that an agent who collects money for his principal is entitled to commissions out of the funds collected is no defense to a charge of embezzlement, if he wrongfully appropriates the proceeds. However, when the dealings between two persons create a relationship of debtor and creditor, rather than a fiduciary relationship, a failure to pay over money does not constitute embezzlement. The nature of the relationship of the parties depends upon the facts of the particular case.

In order to constitute the crime of embezzlement, there must be a criminal intent. However, when one wrongfully and intentionally misappropriates the property of another lawfully in his possession, the offense of embezzlement is complete, and the fact that he at the same time intends subsequently to return the property or to make restitution to its rightful owner is no defense.

The retention of property in good faith, without secrecy or concealment, under a bona fide claim of right based upon reasonable grounds, as where an employee collecting money retains it in the honest and reasonable belief that he has a right to keep it for his compensation, is not embezzlement. A general partner cannot be convicted of embezzling property which comes into his possession or under his control during the course of the partnership business and by reason of his being a partner. An attorney who appropriates to his own use money collected for his client may be guilty of embezzlement under some circumstances. And modern authorities hold that one spouse may be guilty of embezzlement with respect to the property of the other spouse.

§ 7:58. Extortion and blackmail.

Am Jur 2d References: Extortion, Blackmail, etc., §§ 1–28.

The common-law crime of extortion is defined as the unlawful taking by a public officer, by color of his office and under demand based on purported official authority, of any money or thing of value that is not owing to him. Some state statutes are substantially declaratory of this definition. Many statutes, however, have enlarged the scope of the offense to include any obtaining of property of another with his consent through a wrongful use of force or fear, under circumstances not amounting to robbery. Under such statutes the offense is not limited to public officials. The difference between extortion and robbery is that in order to constitute robbery, property must be taken against the will and without the consent of its possessor, whereas in extortion consent is obtained, though unwillingly and by wrongful means.

Historically, blackmail was the extortion of money or other property by freebooters as the price of protection or immunity. In modern terms, it is the price exacted for nondisclosure of discreditable secrets. This offense is generally defined in the statutes as the extortion of money from a person by threats of accusation or exposure, or threats of public prosecution; the extortion of hush money; a bribe to keep silent; or the obtaining of property from a person as a condition of refraining from making an accusation against him or disclosing some secret calculated to operate to his prejudice.

173

Under some circumstances, it is a criminal offense for a creditor to compel payment by a debtor by means of a threat to accuse the latter of a crime. Statutes in some states make it a criminal offense to compel, by malicious threats, a person to do or refrain from doing any act against his will. Federal statutes, including the "Anti-Racketeering Act" govern cases of extortion and similar offenses involving federal officials or affecting interstate or foreign commerce.

§ 7:59. False pretenses.

Am Jur 2d References: False Pretenses, §§ 1–89.

Obtaining money or property by false pretense or representation was not, as such, a crime at common law. By statutes of varying terms, however, such an act is now punishable as a crime. This statutory offense is based on the making of an intentionally false statement concerning a material matter of fact, in reliance on which the victim of the offense parts with the title and possession of property. Some statutes combine the elements of the common-law offense of cheating (effected by means of some token or device having the semblance of public authenticity, such as various money, false weights and measures, or false impersonation) and the offense of obtaining money or property by false pretenses.

The basis for a prosecution for obtaining money or property by false pretenses is the representation of a fact that is untrue, calculated to mislead, and adapted to induce the person to whom it is made to part with something of value. The misrepresentation must be a statement of a past event or an existing fact. A misrepresentation relating to a matter of law cannot be made the basis of a prosecution for obtaining money or property by false pretenses; but it is sometimes difficult to determine whether a particular representation is one of law or one of fact. A false pretense or a promissory statement as to future acts or events will not support a conviction of obtaining property under false pretenses. And this rule is generally applied even though the person making the promissory representation had no intention of performing, although the statutes and decisions in some jurisdictions do not go to this extent. The mere expression of an opinion does not render a person liable to a prosecution for obtaining money or property by false pretenses, unless he knows the opinion to be erroneous or false, so that the matter ceases to be an opinion and becomes a representation of a subsisting fact.

To be guilty of the offense of obtaining money or property by false pretenses, the accused must have had knowledge of the falsity of the representations or pretenses at the time he made them, unless they were made recklessly and without information justifying a belief that they were true. To sustain a charge of this offense, a felonious or fraudulent intent must be shown.

The offense of obtaining money or property by false pretenses is not committed until something of value has been actually obtained. Some courts hold that title to the money or property, and not merely possession or custody, must have been obtained by the accused. Some statutes make it a crime to obtain by false pretenses the signature of any person to a written instrument.

To establish the crime of obtaining money or property by false pretenses, it must be shown that a misrepresentation by the defendant was relied upon by the party defrauded and that he was actually deceived. The fraudulent pretense or representation must have induced a transfer of money or property or materially contributed to that end. It is generally held, however, that a misrepresentation under which property or money was obtained is punishable even though the victim's deception is due to his own credulity and the misrepresentation is not such as would deceive persons of ordinary prudence. Although the issuance of a worthless check, especially if a false representation extrinsic to the check is made at the time it is given, may be the basis of a prosecution for obtaining money or property by false pretenses under general statutes directed at that offense, special statutes have quite generally been enacted making it a crime to obtain money or property by means of checks or drafts issued without sufficient funds or credit. Another related statutory offense is obtaining money or property by means of a "confidence game." Generally under such statutes, where one leads another to repose confidence in him with a view of taking advantage of the other and does take advantage of the other's confidence and obtains the other's money or property, the offense is committed. Many statutes are specifically directed at the offense of obtaining money or property from the state or federal government or other public body by fraudulent representations or means. In some states the making of false or fraudulent statements in advertising is a criminal offense.

§ 7:60. Forgery.

Am Jur 2d References: Forgery, §§ 1–53.

Forgery may be defined as the fraudulent making or alteration of a writing to the prejudice of another's rights, or as the false making or material alteration, with intent to defraud, of any writing which, if genuine, might apparently be of legal efficacy or the foundation of a legal liability. Forgery was regarded as a misdemeanor under the early common law, but under most modern statutes it is a felony. Three essential elements are generally prescribed as necessary to constitute the offense of forgery: (1) there must be a false writing or alternation of an instrument; (2) the instrument as made must be apparently capable of defrauding; and (3) there must be an intent to defraud. The mode of "writing" is generally immaterial; there may be forgery by stamping, engraving, or typewriting, as well as by handwriting. A writing or instrument, in order to constitute a forgery, must possess some apparent legal efficacy, although it need not be a perfect representation of the instrument that it pretends to be, and it is sufficient if it bears such a resemblance to the document as may deceive a person of ordinary observation or business capacity. Fraudulent intent is of the essence of forgery, although it is not necessary that this intent be carried out to successful accomplishment.

The term "falsely," as applied to the making or altering of a writing in order to make it a forgery, does not refer to the contents or tenor of the writing or to the facts stated therein, but contemplates that the paper or writing is not genuine, that in itself it is false or counterfeit. Hence, a false statement of fact in the body of the instrument, such as a false assertion of authority to write another's name, is not forgery.

A person may be guilty of forgery in fraudulently signing his own name when it is identical with the name of the person who should have signed, if it is done with the intent to have the instrument received as that of the other person. And the crime of forgery may be committed by signing a fictitious or assumed name, provided the instrument is made with intent to defraud. Where authority is given to sign the name of another to a writing, there can be no forgery, and it is generally held that the signing of another's name as agent, though without authority and for fraudulent purposes, does not constitute forgery, although it may be some other crime.

If an instrument is fraudulently so altered that it is not the instrument signed by the maker, there is forgery. Any change fraudulently made in an instrument which alters its legal effect and materially or substantially increases, diminishes, or discharges the obligation of the original instrument, is a forgery. Altering of a check, or even of a receipt or of a cancelled check with intent to defraud, by changing the true amount to a larger one, constitutes forgery. While it is generally held that the filling of blanks in an instrument delivered as a completed instrument, without any authority, express or implied, is a forgery, there is a difference of opinion on the question whether filling in blanks by one authorized to fill in blank spaces, in a manner other than that authorized, constitutes forgery.

A concomitant of the act of forgery is the uttering of a forged instrument, which consists in offering to another the forged instrument with the knowledge of its falsity and with intent to defraud. Uttering is an offense at common law, distinct from the forgery itself. Sometimes, however, the two are held to constitute a single offense when committed by the same person in the course of the same transaction; and the distinction between the two offenses is sometimes obliterated by statute.

§ 7:61. Homicide.

Am Jur 2d References: Homicide, §§ 1–586.

As defined by statutes in most states, felonious homicide is either murder, in some one of the specified degrees, or manslaughter, depending upon the presence or absence of malice, express or implied, and of premeditation and deliberation, or upon the fact that the homicide was committed during the perpetration of another felony. The term "corpus delicti" means the body of the offense, or the substance of the crime. As applied in homicide cases in most jurisdictions, it has at least two component elements which must be established: (1) the fact of death, and (2) the criminal agency of another person as the cause thereof. In some jurisdictions, the identity of the slain person is a third element.

A person is not criminally responsible for a homicide unless his act was the cause of death. Although one may have feloniously assaulted, beaten, or wounded another, he is not deemed guilty of homicide where the death of the other person results proximately from a wound inflicted by a third person or from some other intervening cause. One cannot escape criminal responsibility for homicide, however, merely because factors other than his felonious acts contribute to the death, provided such other factors are not the proximate cause of death. One may be guilty of homicide even though his act merely accelerates the death of one who has been mortally wounded by another or who is suffering from some fatal malady.

Most jurisdictions follow the common-law rule that, in order to constitute punishable homicide, death must ensue within a year and a day from the infliction of a mortal wound. Some states, however, do not follow this rule. In the absence of a statute to the contrary, an accused who has inflicted an injury calculated to destroy or endanger life cannot exonerate himself by a showing that the victim's life might have been saved by more skilful medical treatment, unless the negligence of the physician or surgeon was the sole cause of death.

Murder at common law is the killing of one human being by another with malice aforethought, either express or implied. There were no degrees of the crime of murder at common law. Statutes have been enacted in most states, however, dividing the crime of murder into two or more degrees. Homicides, under such statutes, fall into three classes: (1) where death is accomplished with deliberation, as by means of poison or lying in wait; (2) where it results from the commission of a felony, there being no actual design to encompass death; and (3) where death results from a dangerous act, evidencing a depraved mind having no regard for human life. First degree murder is distinguished from other grades of homicide primarily by the mental element known as "malice aforethought" or "express" malice, and the unique characteristic of this degree of murder is deliberation or premeditation, a design to take life. Many statutes include as first degree murder, homicides committed in the perpetration of certain felonies. Actual or express malice, essential to first degree murder, contemplates the killing of another pursuant to a preconceived and deliberate design. The essential premeditation or deliberation need exist for only a very brief period, provided the formed intent to kill was consciously conceived in the mind of the slayer before the homicidal act was committed.

In many jurisdictions the statutes declare that when murder is not of the first degree it must be deemed to be of the second degree; and generally it may be said that where an unlawful killing is shown, and the evidence does not disclose express malice or a state of facts which would justify or excuse the homicide or reduce it to manslaughter, the slayer is guilty of murder in the second degree. Some statutes define second degree murder as a killing perpetrated by any act imminently dangerous to others and evincing a depraved mind regardless of human life, although without any premeditated design to effect the death of any particular individual.

If a homicide is neither a murder in the first nor in the second degree, and yet is neither justifiable nor excusable in law, it ordinarily constitutes manslaughter. This is the unlawful killing of a human being without malice, express or implied, either in a sudden quarrel or unintentionally while in the commission of an unlawful act. Under the common-law classification, manslaughter may be voluntary, as where the homicidal act is done under influence of passion produced or occasioned by some provocation, or it may be involuntary, as where it results from the commission of certain unlawful acts not accompanied by any intention to take life. Some states have created several degrees of manslaughter.

The basic rules governing criminal responsibility (supra, §§ 7:4–7:7) generally apply in determining criminal responsibility for homicide. Thus, insanity or infancy may excuse one from criminal liability for this offense. The defenses generally available in criminal prosecutions are applicable in homicide cases. Death resulting from an accident or misadventure not involving any criminal intent or negligence on the part of the accused, and not caused during the perpetration of another crime, does not generally constitute criminal homicide. The contributory negligence of the victim, or his consent, or the fact that the killing was done for a humanitarian purpose, as to relieve the victim from suffering, is no defense, nor is religious belief or duress or compulsion exerted by a third person.

A person is not punishable for taking the life of another when he has been put under the necessity or apparent necessity of doing so, without fault on his own part, in order to protect himself from the peril of death or serious bodily harm at the hands of the person whose life he took. Before one is justified in taking life in self-defense, however, it must appear reasonably certain that one is in immediate danger of death or great bodily injury. And to justify a homicide on the ground of self-defense, it is necessary to establish that the slayer was without fault in bringing on the difficulty, that is, that he was not the aggressor and did not provoke the conflict; that the accused believed at the time that he was in immediate danger of losing his own life, or of receiving serious bodily harm; that the circumstances were such as to give reasonable grounds for such belief in the mind of a man of ordinary reason and firmness; and that there was no reasonable way of escaping, retreating, or declining the combat. This defense is not generally available to one killing in voluntary mutual combat or in a duel.

It is the apparent, rather than the real or actual, necessity of taking another's life to protect one's self which determines whether a killing was justifiable or excusable as having been done in self-defense. Whether the belief that danger is apparently imminent is to be viewed from the standpoint of the defendant himself or that of a reasonable man is the subject of a conflict of authority. Some states follow what seems to have been the common-law rule, that when a person kills his assailant and asserts self-defense, the question to be determined is whether the slayer, under all the circumstances as they appeared to him, honestly believed that he was in imminent danger of losing his life or of suffering great bodily harm, and that it was necessary for him to act as he did in order to save himself from such apparent peril. This view involves the subjective difficulty of looking into the mind of the individual defendant and determining his actual thoughts. The rule followed by most of the courts is that the apprehension of danger and belief of necessity which will justify killing in self-defense must be a reasonable apprehension and belief, such as a reasonable man would have entertained under the circumstances.

In order to justify or excuse a homicide on the ground of self-defense, the slayer must have employed all means in his power, consistent with his own safety, to avoid danger and avert the necessity of taking another's life. Under the common-law rule, still followed in some jurisdictions, a person assailed, except in his own home, office, or place of business, or in the performance of the duty to make an arrest or prevent an escape, is bound to "retreat to the wall." Under this rule, the necessity for killing is not deemed to exist so long as there is any safe avenue of escape from the attack. In many jurisdictions, however, this rule has been repudiated or modified and supplanted by the doctrine that if a person is assailed without fault, and in a place where he has a right to be, and is put in reasonably apparent danger of losing his life or receiving great bodily harm, he need not retreat, but may stand his ground and repel force by force.

Circumstances which would warrant a person in taking life in his own defense may justify his doing so in defense of other persons. Where the requisite conditions exist, a person may kill another in defense of a member of his family, a relative, a friend, a master or servant, or even a stranger. Where the prerequisites of the right of self-defense exist, such as real or apparent necessity and peril, a person has the right to defend his home from attack and to kill another to prevent an attempted forcible entry made under such circumstances as to create a reasonable apprehension that it is the design of the assailant to commit a felony or to inflict on an inmate a personal injury which may result in loss of life or great bodily harm. In regard to the necessity for killing in defense of one's habitation, the rules are substantially the same as they are where the killing is done in defense of the person of the slayer. Except where it is necessary to prevent the commission of a felony or is in defense of his dwelling, one cannot defend his property to the extent of killing or inflicting serious bodily injury upon another for the purpose of preventing a trespass. While a person aggrieved by a trespass may repel the intruder by such force as may be reasonably necessary, he is not justified in taking human life for this purpose in the absence of imminent danger to the person of himself or of another person.

Killing a person to prevent the commission of a forcible and atrocious crime has been considered justifiable from the earliest days of the common law. However, the right to kill in these circumstances is limited to cases of absolute or apparent necessity, and the crimes in prevention of which life may be taken are only such as are committed by forcible means, violence, and surprise, such as murder, robbery, burglary, rape, or arson. A police officer in the performance of his duties to preserve the peace and apprehend criminals is given more latitude than is accorded private individuals as regards the use of force. He may use such force as is necessary to the proper performance of his duties, even though death results. If, however, he uses more force than is reasonably necessary under the circumstances, or if the attempted arrest or detention is unwarranted, or if he kills in a mere personal encounter and is not acting in self-defense, he may be guilty of culpable homicide.

§ 7:62. Incest.

Am Jur 2d References: Incest, §§ 1–27.

The crime of incest consists of sexual intercourse between persons too closely related in consanguinity or affinity to be entitled to intermarry. The offense may be committed with or without marraige of the persons concerned. Although punished by the ecclesiastical courts of England, incest was not an indictable offense at common law. The propinquity of kinship required to form the basis of the offense of incest is dependent upon the terms of the statutes of the particular jurisdiction. The statutes do not ordinarily differentiate between relationships of the half-blood and those of the whole blood. And the fact that one or both of the parties is illegitimate is immaterial. Some statutes extend to relatives by affinity, or marriage, the prohibition of incest. There is a division in authority as to whether one can be guilty of incest on the basis of relationship by affinity after the termination by death or divorce of the marriage on which the relationship is based. In some states, but not in all, it is an element of incest that the person charged with the crime have knowledge of the relationship between the parties.

§ 7:63. Kidnapping and abduction.

Am Jur 2d References: Abduction and Kidnapping, §§ 1–35.

Although abduction and kidnapping have some elements in common, they are distinct offenses in most jurisdictions.   Under the early common law, kidnapping was defined as the forcible abduction or stealing of a person from his own country and sending him into another country.   But while the statutes of the several jurisdictions vary in the terms of definition, the gravamen of kidnapping is the taking or detention of a person against his will and without lawful authority, whether by force, fraud, or duress, and usually involves taking the person away or detaining him with intent to do so.   Abduction is characteristically an unlawful interference with a family relationship, and at common law it was the taking or detention, by force, persuasion, or deception, of a person, such as a child or ward, from the custody or control of the person entitled thereto.

The Federal Kidnapping Act makes it a federal offense knowingly to transport in interstate or foreign commerce any person who has been unlawfully seized, confined, enveigled, decoyed, kidnapped, abducted, or carried away and held for ransom or reward, or otherwise, except in the case of a minor by its parent.   Receiving, possessing, or disposing of ransom or reward in connection with a violation of the Act is separately defined as a felony.

An unlawful taking or detention of the victim is essential to both abduction and kidnapping, though the use of force is not ordinarily required to establish guilt of either crime.   In the case of abduction, moral force, such as persuasion or enticement, usually suffices.   For kidnapping, it is generally sufficient that a threat is used, if it is of sufficient force to put an ordinarily prudent person in fear for his personal safety; and fraud may likewise be sufficient.   The victim's consent is ordinarily irrelevant insofar as the crime of abduction or child stealing is concerned, these offenses being deemed to be against the parent or person entitled to custody rather than against the victim himself.   In the case of kidnapping, however, a different rule prevails.   Both at common law and under modern statutes, the detention or taking or carrying away must be accompanied by some force or fraud and must be against the will of the victim, in order to constitute kidnapping.   This crime cannot be committed by an act to which the victim consents.   However, consent obtained by fraud or duress does not amount to legal consent.   And a child of tender years is regarded as incapable of consenting to its seizure or abduction.

At common law and under most modern statutes, the demand of ransom or reward is not a prerequisite of the offense of kidnapping.   Some statutes, however, make this either a general element of the offense or a ground for the imposition of more severe punishment.

§ 7:64. Larceny.

Am Jur 2d References: Larceny, §§ 1–180.

By its simplest definition, larceny is the wrongful taking and carrying away of the personal property of another with intent to steal it.   According to the common-law meaning of the term, larceny may be defined as the felonious taking, by a trespass and carrying away, of the personal property of another without his consent and with the felonious intent to permanently deprive the owner of his property and to convert to the taker's own use, or, as sometimes stated, to the use of some person other than the owner. Larceny is distinguished from embezzlement mainly by the manner in which the offender obtains possession of the property, embezzlement always involving a conversion by one who has been entrusted with possession by the owner. Robbery is a compound larceny composed of the crime of larceny from the person with the aggravation of force, actual or constructive, used in the taking.

The first element of larceny is a felonious or unlawful taking of property by the thief, amounting to a trespass, giving him actual custody and dominion of the property. The felonious taking must be followed by such an asportation or carrying away as to supersede the possession of the owner for an appreciable time. The slightest moving of the thing taken, or of a part thereof, with the intent to steal it, is a sufficient asportation to constitute larceny, even though the property is not quite carried off. The requirement of asportation does not mean that the goods must be removed from the owner's premises.

Larceny cannot be predicated upon a taking of property with the full knowledge and consent of the owner or his authorized servant or agent. But for consent to have this effect, the person giving consent must have legal capacity to do so. And where money or other property is delivered by mistake, as where a larger sum of money is parted with than is intended, and the receiver takes it with knowledge of the mistake and with the intent to keep it, the offense is larceny, since there is no consent on the part of the owner to part with the excessive amount or with the property delivered by mistake. The requirement of a felonious taking against the will of the owner may be met where a person intending to steal another's property obtains possession of it, although with the consent of the owner, by means of a fraudulent trick or device, and feloniously converts it pursuant to such intent.

To constitute larceny, the wrongful taking must be with felonious intent. There must be more than knowledge by the offender that he is doing an unlawful act; there must be "animus furandi," an intent to steal, which is an essential element of the crime of larceny at common law. A person who takes property in good faith, under claim of title and honestly believing that he is the owner and has the right to its possession, is not guilty of larceny, even though he is mistaken in such belief.

At common law, larceny may be either simple larceny, which is theft unaccompanied by any other atrocious circumstances, or compound or mixed larceny, which includes the aggravation of a taking from the house or person of another. The offense designated as simple larceny is further divided at common law and under the statutes of some jurisdictions into grades known as "grand" and "petit" (or "petty") larceny, on the basis of the value of the property stolen. The compound larcenies are frequently punishable more severely than the others. Statutes in some jurisdictions penalize as a crime the larceny of particular kinds of property, larceny from the person, or larceny from a dwelling house or other particular place.

The common-law rule that only goods or chattels can be subjects of larceny has yielded to the modern rule that, generally speaking, any money or personalty of value, corporeal in nature and recognized by law as property, may be the subject of larceny. Nor is it necessary that the owner be exercising actual dominion over it at the time of the taking. According to the modern rule, property may be the subject of larceny although it has been temporarily mislaid or casually lost, but not if it has been voluntarily abandoned.   Contraband or money or property illegally acquired or possessed may be the subject of larceny.   The common-law rule that written instruments, choses in action, and things constituting merely evidence or representation of property, including even bank notes, were not considered personal goods or chattels, and were therefore not the subjects of larceny, has been changed by modern statutes.

The rule that only personal property, as distinguished from real property, may be the subject of larceny was strictly followed under the common law. Thus, it was not larceny to take earth or minerals in place, or growing trees or fruits, or growing or matured crops in the field, not previously severed from the realty, where they were severed and instantly carried off.   The same was true of fixtures, or things annexed to the realty so as to partake of the character thereof.   These strict rules have been considerably modified in most jurisdictions through evolution of case law and by statutes.   However, even the strict common-law rule applies only to things severed by the thief as a part of the same transaction in which they are taken away, and does not extend to things which, by reason of their severance from the realty by a distinct and separate act of the owner, a third person, or the thief at a prior time, have become personal property before the thief carries them away.   Thus, cut timber or wood, crops previously harvested, and minerals extracted from the earth may be the subjects of larceny.   Even jurisdictions following the rule that where the severance and carrying away is one continuous act, the wrong amounts merely to a trespass and not criminal larceny, the courts recognize that where the severing and the carrying away constitute two transactions, the object severed may become a subject of larceny.   In some jurisdictions, the technical requirement of even a moment's lapse of time between severance and asportation has been superseded by the simpler and better doctrine that by the very act of severance, the wrongdoer converts the property into a chattel which is the subject of larceny.

§ 7:65. Mobs and riots.

Am Jur 2d References: Mobs and Riots, §§ 1–56.

Riot, rout, and unlawful assembly are closely related common-law offenses, all involving disturbances of the public peace.   Unlawful assembly is usually defined as a gathering of three or more persons with a common intent, formed before or at any time during the meeting, to attain a purpose, lawful or unlawful, which will interfere with the rights of others, by committing disorderly acts in such a manner as to cause reasonable, firm, and courageous persons in the neighborhood to apprehend a breach of the peace.   When the unlawful assembly moves forward toward the execution of its unlawful design, but fails, the offense is rout.   Actual execution of the illegal purpose gives rise to a riot. According to a definition frequently approved, a riot is a tumultuous disturbance of the peace by three or more persons assembling of their own authority, with an intent mutually to assist one another against anyone opposing them in the execution of their enterprise, and afterward actually executing the same in a violent and turbulent manner, to the terror of the people, whether the act intended was of itself lawful or unlawful.   The statutes of some states omit the elements of resisting opposition and of inspiring terror. Under some statutes, whenever three or more persons, having assembled for any purpose, disturb the public peace by using force or violence to any other person or to property, or threaten to attempt to commit such a disturbance or to do an unlawful act by the use of force or violence, accompanied with the power of immediate execution of such threat or attempt, they are guilty of riot.

Inciting a riot means such course of conduct, by use of words, signs, language, or any other means, by which one can be urged on into action, as would naturally lead or urge other men to engage in or enter upon conduct which, if completed, would constitute a riot.

§ 7:66. Perjury.

Am Jur 2d References: Perjury, §§ 2–74.

At common law, perjury is the crime of knowingly and wilfully giving false testimony, under oath or the legal equivalent of an oath, in a judicial proceeding in which the testimony is material to a question in issue. A distinct crime of false swearing consists of statements made under oath and knowingly false, but not in judicial proceedings. Under modern statutes, the offenses of perjury and false swearing are generally treated together, so that the crime is wilful false swearing in regard to any matter or thing respecting which an oath is required or authorized by law. To form the basis of a charge of perjury, a false statement must be made under oath, affirmation, or the legal equivalent, administered by a person authorized to do so. However, false statements in many official documents, such as tax returns, are made criminal offenses even though they are not made under oath.

In order to constitute perjury, a statement must be one of fact and not of opinion or belief. It cannot be based on opinions calling for the exercise of judgment or upon statements as to the legal effect of certain facts. However, a statement of belief or opinion, under oath, may constitute the offense when, as a matter of fact, the witness had no such belief or opinion. In other words, where the existence or nonexistence of the belief or opinion is in itself a material fact, a false statement in respect thereto may constitute perjury. To constitute perjury, it is necessary that the false testimony be material to an issue or point of inquiry. The relevance of the testimony, however, need not relate to the main issue, but is sufficient if it is material on a collateral matter.

The fact that a witness during the same trial or proceeding admits the falsity of earlier testimony and tells the truth, does not strictly or technically obviate the charge of perjury. But where he recants at an appropriate time and before he learns that the prosecution has knowledge of his perjury, some courts are disposed to excuse him, sometimes on the assumption that he made an innocent mistake.

Subornation of perjury is the crime of procuring another to commit perjury by inciting, instigating, or persuading the guilty party to do so. In order to complete this offense, it is necessary that the perjury be actually committed.

§ 7:67. Rape.

Am Jur 2d References, Rape, §§ 1–117.

Rape is the having of unlawful carnal knowledge by a man of a woman, forcibly and against her will or without her consent. Some degree of penetration of the female organ by the organ of the male is essential to complete the crime, but any penetration is generally held to be sufficient and full penetration is not necessary. Emission by the male is not essential to the crime.

Force is a necessary ingredient of the common-law crime of rape. The force contemplated by this requirement need not be actual physical force applied to the female, but may consist of threats or menacing acts sufficient to put the woman in fear of her life or of great bodily harm. The force exerted by the man must be met with resistance on the part of the woman. The degree or extent of her resistance necessary to establish rape is the subject of some difference of opinion, mostly semantic. It is settled, however, that resistance by mere words is not enough; that the resistance must be by acts reasonably proportionate to the strength and opportunities of the woman; and that it must continue from the beginning of the assault upon her until the consummation of the rape.

To constitute the crime of rape, the sexual act must be committed against the will of the woman and without her consent. Her assent at any time prior to penetration deprives the subsequent intercourse of its character as rape. However, unlawful intercourse with a woman in a state of unconsciousness is presumed to be without her consent, and is rape. This rule applies to cases of intercourse with a woman who is asleep, or unconscious from the effects of drugs or intoxication. And the consent of the woman cannot be available as a defense where she does not have the capacity to consent or to understand the nature or possible consequences of the act, as where she is mentally incompetent. The degree and nature of this incompetence varies in the different jurisdictions. Although there is some difference of opinion, it is generally held that the fact that consent to intercourse is obtained by fraud or stratagem, such as false impersonation or pretext of medical treatment or examination, is sufficient consent to negate guilt of the crime of rape.

The phrase "statutory rape" is unfortunately ambiguous and inexact, but its meaning is generally well understood. It designates the offense, created by statute, of having intercourse with a female under the age specified in the statute. To establish this offense, it is only necessary to show sexual connection with a female under the "age of consent," and it is not necessary to establish force or lack of consent.

Assault with intent to commit rape is a distinct crime. If an assault is made under such circumstances that the act of sexual intercourse, if it had been accomplished, would have been rape, the accused is guilty of assault with intent to commit rape. Attempt to rape is also a distinct offense, governed by the general principles applicable to criminal attempts.

§ 7:68. Robbery.

Am Jur 2d References: Robbery, §§ 1–85.

At common law and by statute in most jurisdictions, robbery is the felonious taking of money or goods of value from the person of another or in his presence, against his will, by force or by putting him in fear, with the intent to deprive the owner permanently of his property. Actual taking and asportation of the victim's personal property is an essential element of robbery. Severance of the goods from the possession of the owner and absolute control thereof by the taker, even for an instant, constitutes an asportation, without respect to subsequent retention of the property by the taker. It is an essential of the crime of robbery, as distinguished from ordinary larceny, that the property be taken from the person of another, or from his possession in his presence. It is not necessary, however, that the property be taken from the owner himself; it is sufficient if it is taken from the lawful possession of a bailee, agent, or other representative of the owner. To constitute robbery, the taking must be animo furandi, that is, with intent to steal. A person forcibly taking property from another under a bona fide belief that he is the owner of the property or is entitled to the possession thereof is not guilty of robbery, although his act may constitute some other offense.

The taking of the property, in order to constitute robbery, must be achieved by force or violence, or by putting the victim in fear. Any actual force or violence is sufficient to satisfy this requirement. But the required force may be constructive as well as actual, and may consist in the intimidation of the victim, or putting him in fear. Threats by the display of a dangerous weapon or a pretense of such a weapon, or by a threatening word or gesture likely to put the victim in fear for the safety of his person, may be sufficient to supply this element of the crime. However, the courts generally do not recognize a mere threat to accuse, arrest, or prosecute a person for an alleged crime (with the exception of sodomy and similar offenses) as the exercise of constructive force which, in the absence of actual force, is essential to constitute the crime of robbery, although such acts may constitute extortion or blackmail. Although there is some difference of opinion on the subject, it is generally held that the force or intimidation must precede or be contemporaneous with the taking in order to constitute robbery, so that a charge of robbery is not sustained by merely showing a retention of property, or an attempt to escape, by force or putting in fear after the culprit gets the property through stealth, fraud, or snatching.

Taking property from the person of another by stealth, as by picking his pocket without the use of more force than is necessary to remove the property, does not generally constitute robbery. The same rule is applied in many jurisdictions to the snatching or sudden taking of property from another without preceding intimidation or concomitant violence.

§7:69. Seduction.

Am Jur 2d References: Seduction, §§ 2–33.

The criminal offense of seduction has been created by statutes in most states. Although the terms of the statutes vary in the several jurisdictions, the following elements are requisite: (1) sexual intercourse with an unmarried female; (2) consent of the female; (3) a promise of marriage as an inducement to the consent of the female; (4) previous chastity of the female.

The statutes of most states, although not all, require that the sexual intercourse shall have been accomplished under a promise of marriage, in order to constitute the crime of seduction. It is generally agreed that seduction must be accomplished by means of an absolute or unconditional promise of marriage. Under this rule, a promise of marriage conditioned upon pregnancy resulting from the act of intercourse is not sufficient to form the basis of a prosecution for seduction. It must appear that the female granted her consent to the intercourse in consequence of the promise of marriage and not to gratify her own curiosity or passion. And illicit intercourse permitted by a woman as a mere barter and trade for a promise of marriage is not seduction. As a general rule, a promise of marriage by a man known by the female to be married cannot support a conviction of seduction. Seduction statutes generally require that the female be "of previous chaste character," or of good repute for chastity, in order to be the victim of criminal seduction. Pregnancy is not usually made an essential element of the crime of seduction, although some statutes do require it. Considerable variation exists in the statutory provisions in reference to the age of the woman seduced. Some states have no requirement whatever as to age, some require only that the female shall have attained the age of puberty, while others specify a maximum age for the victim.

The actual marriage of the man and woman will generally bar a prosecution for seduction. The statutes vary as to the effect of an offer of the man to perform his promise of marriage. In some jurisdictions, but not all, a bona fide offer of marriage is a defense to a prosecution for seduction.

§ 7:70. Treason.

Am Jur 2d References: Treason (1st ed, §§ 2–20).

Treason was divided into two classes by the early common law, petit treason and high treason. Petit treason was the violation of allegiance owing to a superior, as by the killing of a husband by a wife, the killing of a master by his servant, or the killing of a prelate by an ecclesiastic owing obedience to him. Petit treason is now obsolete as a distinct crime. High treason is now designated simply treason. Treason is regarded as the gravest of all crimes. It is neither a felony nor a misdemeanor, but is in a grade by itself. One distinctive feature of this offense is that there are no accessories before the fact and no aiders and abettors therein: all persons participating in treasonable acts to any extent, who are leagued in the treasonable conspiracy, are guilty of treason. Treason is fundamentally a breach of allegiance. In England many types of acts were declared at various times to constitute treason, such as compassing or imagining the death of the king, queen, or their heir apparent, evidenced by some overt act, levying war against the king, or adhering to the king's enemies by giving them aid and comfort, as by providing intelligence, provisions, or arms for them.

Treason is the only crime defined in the Constitution of the United States. That instrument declares that treason against the United States shall consist only in levying war against them, or in adhering to their enemies, giving them aid and comfort, and that no person shall be convicted of treason unless on the testimony of two witnesses to the same overt act, or on confession in open court. Congress is given the power to fix the punishment for treason, but no attainder of treason may work corruption of blood or forfeiture except during the life of the person attainted. By virtue of the common law and of constitutional and statutory provisions, there may be treason against a state as well as against the United States. However, since the period of the Revolution, such acts against states are usually prosecuted as offenses other than treason.

To constitute the specific crime of levying war against the United States within the meaning of the constitutional definition of treason, there must be more than a conspiracy to subvert or overthrow the government. There must be some actual assemblage of men for the purpose. It is not necessary, however, that the object be the complete overthrow of the government. Any insurrection by armed men to prevent, by force and intimidation, the execution of any act of Congress, is treason. And any assemblage of men for the purpose of revolutionizing by force the Government established by the United States in any of its territories amounts to levying war within the constitutional definition of treason. The phrase "adherence to enemies, giving them aid and comfort," means any overt act which, in its natural consequence, if successful, would encourage and advance the interests of the enemy. This may consist of taking an oath of allegiance to the enemy, joining their army, assisting others to do so, or furnishing materials to the enemy or to an armed combination known by him to be intending to overthrow the government.

§ 7:71. Miscellaneous offenses.

Am Jur 2d References: Animals, §§ 27–30; Blasphemy and Profanity, §§ 1–14; Bribery, §§ 1–30; Champerty and Maintenance, §§ 1–3, 18–20; Common Scold, §§ 1–3; Counterfeiting, §§ 1–9; Desertion and Nonsupport, §§ 1–161; Disorderly Houses, §§ 1–36; Drugs, Narcotics, and Poisons, §§ 1–48; Dueling, §§ 1–5; Eavesdropping, § 1; Embracery, §§ 1–7; Escape, Prison Breaking, and Rescue, §§ 1–26; False Personation, §§ 1–11; Fish and Game, §§ 29–54; Gambling, §§ 1–185; Harboring Criminals, §§ 1–6; Insurrection, §§ 1–3; Intoxicating Liquors, §§ 1–532; Lewdness, Indecency, and Obscenity, §§ 1–42; Libel and Slander, §§ 495–538; Mayhem, §§ 1–15; Marriage, § 78; Monopolies, Restraints of Trade, and Unfair Trade Practices; Obstructing Justice, §§ 1–29; Piracy, §§ 1–12; Prostitution, §§ 1–28; Sedition, Subversive Activities, and Treason, §§ 2–66; Sodomy, §§ 1–26; Vagrancy (1st ed, §§ 1–13); Weapons and Firearms (1st ed, §§ 2–21).

Animals, cruelty to.—During the last century, statutes and ordinances have been enacted in most jurisdictions for the protection of animals from the cruelty or mistreatment of man. While such legislation varies greatly in terms, it is generally directed against the infliction upon animals of unnecessary forms of cruelty, torture, and abuse, including neglect resulting in undue suffering. Cruelty includes, of course, excessive beating of an animal or subjecting it to cruel and painful pranks. Such legislation is not intended, however, to interfere with man's possession of reasonable use, enjoyment, or government of animals, and not every act which causes pain in a beast is prohibited. The usual practices of animal husbandry and the chastisement resorted to in good faith for the purpose of training or disciplining an animal does not constitute cruelty under such statutes. And experiments upon animals, conducted in good faith and without recklessly or unreasonably inflicting unnecessary pain or suffering, does not constitute cruelty.

Blasphemy as a common-law offense has been defined as speaking or publishing words reviling or ridiculing the Divine Being, the Bible, the church, or the Christian religion, with the intent to shock and insult or to pervert believers. Under modern standards of freedom of speech and freedom from established church or religion, it may be said that the criminal offense of blasphemy is obsolete, although statutes denouncing it still exist in some jurisdictions.

Profanity, as such, was not a common-law offense, and it was punishable only where it amounted to a public or common nuisance. Many statutes and ordinances, however, provide punishment for profanity or profane language used in public or other specified places. At common law and by ecclesiastical standards, profanity was either taking the name of God in vain or using words imprecating divine vengeance or divine condemnation. The tests for determining what language constitutes criminal profanity must vary with the times and with the standards and mores of the people.

Bribery is the voluntary giving or receiving of anything of value in corrupt payment for an official act done or to be done, or with the corrupt intent to influence the action of a public officer or employee. Some statutes cover bribery at an election, and the offense has been extended in some states so as to involve persons other than public officials or employees, such as representatives of labor organizations and participants in sports activities. And commercial bribery, that is, the giving or receiving of a gift for the purpose of influencing an agent of a private individual or corporation in the discharge of a duty entrusted to him, is a criminal offense in some states. An attempt to bribe constitutes bribery; but solicitation of a bribe, although a criminal offense, is not bribery.

Barratry or common barratry, a criminal offense at common law, is defined as the act of frequently exciting or stirring up suits and quarrels between others. Barratry does not consist of a single act, but of several acts, and it has been stated that at common law, at least three acts of barratrous nature were necessary to constitute the offense. The practice of solicitation of employment for attorneys constitutes barratry under some statutes. Barratry is related to common-law champerty and maintenance, discussed below.

Champerty and maintenance.—These doctrines were of some importance in the early days of the common law, but are practically obsolete today in most jurisdictions as regards both its civil and criminal aspects. At common law, maintenance signified an unlawful taking in hand or upholding of quarrels, to the disturbance or hindrance of common right. The word included champerty as well as embracery. Maintenance existed where a person assisted another with money to carry on his cause, and bore or shared the expense of the suit. It is an officious intermeddling in a suit which in no way belongs to the intermeddler, by maintaining or assisting either party to the action, with money or otherwise, to prosecute or defend it. Champerty is a species of maintenance and consists of a bargain by a champertor with a plaintiff or defendant for a portion of the matter involved in a suit in case of a successful termination of the action, which the champertor undertakes to maintain or carry on at his own expense. As indicated above, champerty and maintenance have disappeared from the list of common-law crimes prosecuted in the courts today.

A **common scold** has been defined as a troublesome and angry woman who, by brawling and wrangling among her neighbors, commits a breach of the peace, foments discord, and becomes a nuisance in the neighborhood. She was one who was habitually noisy, quarrelsome, and offensive as a scold. Being a common scold was an offense at common law, punishable by ducking the culprit a prescribed number of times in a cucking stool or ducking stool. Although it is possibly still punished as an offense in some jurisdictions, it has become, for practical purposes, merely a quaint phrase in our legal literature, and it is doubtful whether many cucking stools or branks are now available to carry out the traditional punishment.

Counterfeiting signifies the fabrication of a false image or representation. In its broadest sense, it means making a copy without authority or right and with a view to deceive or defraud by passing the copy as original or genuine. As a criminal offense today, counterfeiting usually consists of the violation of federal statutes against counterfeiting or copying currency, coins, stamps, securities, etc., of the United States or of a foreign government. These statutes also prohibit the passing, possessing, or uttering of such counterfeits.

Desertion and nonsupport of a wife or child is made a criminal offense by statute in all jurisdictions. In some of the statutes, the protection is extended to parent, grandparent, and grandchild. The Uniform Desertion and Nonsupport Act, which has been adopted in many states, makes the wrongful abandonment, desertion, or nonsupport of a wife or child a criminal offense. And the Uniform Reciprocal Enforcement of Support Act, which has been generally enacted by the states, assists in the criminal enforcement of the duties of support by providing for interstate extradition of persons against whom criminal charges of nonsupport have been brought.

A **disorderly house** has been variously defined in the several jurisdictions. By some definitions, it is a place where acts are performed that tend to corrupt the morals of the community or to promote breaches of the peace, or as a place kept for the purpose of public resort for thieves, drunkards, prostitutes, or other idle and vicious people. A disorderly house has also been defined so as to include any place where unlawful and illegal practices are habitually carried on, such as a house of ill fame or house of prostitution, a common gaming house, or a place where intoxicating liquor is illegally sold. According to a more restricted definition, a disorderly house is one so kept as to disturb, annoy, or scandalize the public generally, the inhabitants of any particular neighborhood, or passers-by on the street. It is the behavior of the inmates rather than the physical character of the place that makes it a disorderly "house." The term "house" in this connection has been defined so as to include a room or apartment, a place of business, a boat, a wagon, or a tent. To constitute the offense of maintaining a disorderly house, a single act or occurrence is not generally sufficient; it is generally required that there be recurrence of the disorderly or immoral acts on the premises. Maintaining a disorderly house is almost universally made a criminal offense by statutes and ordinances; and such places were classified as common nuisances at common law. It is an offense under some statutes and ordinances to resort to, frequent, or be an inmate of, a disorderly house.

Drugs, narcotics, and poisons are the subject of regulatory legislation in all of the states, as well as by the federal government. The Uniform Narcotic Drug Act, with various modifications, is in force in nearly all jurisdictions.

The penal sanctions supporting these regulations constitute a vast and varied body of criminal offenses.

Dueling is a criminal offense in all states, either as a specific crime or as some offense associated with the act, such as assault, breach of the peace, affray, or, depending on the consequences of the duel, murder. A duel is a combat with deadly weapons fought according to terms and rules agreed upon by the participants. The offense may be complete although no casualty ensues; but if death results from a duel, the offense of the killer is ordinarily murder, as pre-arrangement and premeditation are of the essence of the practice. The seconds and other persons actually participating in the duel are likewise guilty.

Eavesdropping is a common-law offense defined as waiting and listening at the walls, windows, or eaves of houses to listen to discourses and thereupon to proclaim slanderous or mischievous tales. The offense consisted of listening, and not of looking or peeping. Obviously related to this old common-law offense are the modern practices of wiretapping and "bugging" or secretly overhearing or recording private conversations by means of mechanical or electronic devices.

Embracery is a crime at common law and generally by statute. It is defined as attempting to corrupt, influence, or instruct a juror or jury or of inducing them in any way, as by promises, persuasions, entreaties, money, entertainment, etc., except by the strength of evidence and the arguments of counsel in open court, to be more favorable to one side of a case than to the other. The gravamen of the offense is an attempt to influence a jury or juror corruptly, and success of the attempt is not a necessary element. Embracery is closely related to, and may involve, maintenance, bribery, or obstruction of justice; and it usually involves contempt of court.

Escape is an offense at common law and generally by statutory provision, and consists of the act of unlawful departure of a legally confined prisoner from custody or the act of a prisoner in regaining his liberty before being released in due course of law. The term is also used to describe the offense committed by the custodian of a prisoner in permitting him unlawfully to depart from custody. As distinguished from escape, the offense of **prison breach** ("jail breaking") involves a breaking and escape from prison by means of the use of force. **Rescue** is the crime of a third person, other than the official custodian, who directly or indirectly unlawfully aids another person to escape from proper custody. And a related offense is harboring or concealing escaped prisoners.

False personation is the offense of pretending to be someone or something one is not in order to defraud. It is committed by falsely assuming the identity of a particular person or by falsely pretending to be a person with a certain status, with a certain occupation, or of a certain official status or position.

Firearms and other weapons are the subject of a great number and variety of regulatory statutes and ordinances, violations of which are criminal offenses. Such offenses may include the discharging of firearms in specified places, the carrying of deadly or dangerous weapons or concealed weapons, or even the sale or possession of such a weapon under certain circumstances.

Fish and game are the subject of a vast body of statutory and administrative regulations. Hunting and fishing are regulated by statutes in all states, and migratory birds are protected by federal statutes and regulations implementing treaties with other North American nations. These laws are enforced by means of a great variety of penal sanctions.

Gambling or gaming was not a criminal offense at common law, except where it was conducted by means of cheating or fraud or where it constituted a nuisance or became an incitement to a breach of the peace. By legislation in most jurisdictions, however, gaming or conducting or participating in games of chance has been made illegal. The terms of this proscription and the designation and definitions of the games, lotteries, and other acts prohibited, vary greatly in the different jurisdictions; and in some states certain forms of gambling are permitted under strict regulations, and a few states conduct their own lotteries, such as were common in former times, to raise revenue for public purposes.

Harboring criminals is made a specific criminal offense by some statutes. In the absence of such a statute and at common law, a person who, knowing that a felony has been committed by another, receives, comforts, or assists the felon, or in any manner aids him to escape arrest or punishment, is guilty as an accessory after the fact.

Insurrection is arising in open resistance to established civil or political authority. It is something more than a mob or riot, and it may amount to an incipient or limited rebellion. There are provisions in both federal and state statutes for the suppression and punishment of insurrection.

Intoxicating liquors and the problems associated therewith have given rise to a vast body of regulatory and penal statutes and ordinances, both federal and state. Every aspect of traffic in liquor is regulated by statutes, which vary greatly in the different jurisdictions and which are usually supported by penal sanctions.

Lewdness, indecency, and obscenity are punishable under statutes in most jurisdictions; and numerous particular acts contemplated by any of these terms were criminal offenses at common law. Lewdness has been defined as the unlawful indulgence of lust, and is generally used to indicate gross indecency with respect to sexual relations. At common law, the word "lewdness" means open and public indecency. Indecency generally includes anything which is lewd or lascivious, obscene or grossly vulgar, unfit to be seen or heard, or which violates the basic proprieties of language or behavior. Acts of gross and open obscenity, injurious to public morals, are indictable at common law; and statutes concerning obscenity are usually broadly worded so as to cover all methods of bringing the attention of decent persons to obscene papers, pictures, or articles. It is well settled that obscene matters are not protected by constitutional guaranties of freedom of speech and freedom of the press. However, it is very difficult to define obscene matters which are not so protected. As a matter of federal constitutional law, the test prescribed in the Roth Case (354 US 476, 1 L Ed 2d 1498, 77 S Ct 1304), is "whether to the average person, applying contemporary community standards, the dominant theme of the material taken as a whole appeals to prurient interest." To constitute obscenity under the rules laid down in the Roth Case, three elements must combine: (1) the dominant theme of the material taken as a whole must appeal to prurient interest in sex; (2) the material must be patently offensive because it affronts contemporary community standards relating to description or representation of sexual matters; and (3) the material must be utterly without redeeming social value.

Libel was recognized as a criminal offense at common law. In most jurisdictions, the offense is now governed by statute. The constitutional guaranties of freedom of speech and of the press do not license libel nor render invalid statutes penalizing criminal libel. The elements of the offense of criminal defamation are a defamatory imputation, publication thereof, and a malicious intent. Falsity is not an essential ingredient of criminal libel unless made so by statutory provision. Criminal libel is defined in various statutes and decisions as the publication of a statement which tends to expose a living person to hatred, contempt, disgrace, ridicule, or loss of confidence; to injure him in his business, occupation, or profession; to provoke him to wrath; or to blacken the memory of one who is dead. The criminality of defamatory publications has been said to be based on its tendency to provoke a breach of the peace, although many modern enactments disregard this element.

Mayhem is defined as the wilful and malicious maiming of another by severing or permanently depriving him of a limb or member of his body. Under the early common law, mere disfigurement, as by biting off an ear or nose, did not constitute the crime of mayhem because it did not render the victim unable to defend himself or to annoy his adversary, a military or combative basis of the offense at that time. This is no longer true, and definitions of mayhem now include, generally, all malicious injuries which disfigure or disable a person.

Miscegenation, the intermarriage of persons of different races, was formerly a criminal offense in a number of states. It is now settled, however, that statutes penalizing interracial marriages are invalid because they violate the equal protection and due process clauses of the Fourteenth Amendment to the Federal Constitution.

Monopolies, restraints of trade, unfair trade practices, and other similar conditions are the subject of extensive and elaborate regulation by both the federal government and the states. Criminal sanctions, as well as civil liability, are imposed for violation of the Federal Antitrust Laws and similar state statutes. And fair packaging and labeling laws and similar enactments for the protection of consumers are enforced through criminal sanctions.

Obstructing the administration of justice is an indictable offense under the common law and by statute in many jurisdictions. Acts falling within this category may also be punishable as contempt of court. Examples of this offense are publications or other acts calculated to intimidate or influence a judicial officer, or the influencing or attempting to influence a witness in regard to the testimony he will give, or inducing or attempting to induce a witness to absent himself from the trial. A related offense at common law and under statutes is the obstruction of, or resistance to, a public officer in the performance of his duties.

Piracy is essentially robbery or forcible deprivation on the high seas, committed without lawful authority and done animo furandi. It is primarily an offense against the law of nations, but the Congress of the United States, pursuant to specific authorization by the Constitution, has provided for the punishment of any person who commits the crime of piracy on the high seas.

Prostitution is the practice of a female offering her body to indiscriminate sexual intercourse with men. The offense involves a general practice or vocation, and a single act or illicit sexual intercourse with only one man does not constitute prostitution. The usual motive for indiscriminate sexual intercourse on the part of a woman is money or gain; and this is made an element of the offense by statutes in some jurisdictions. Pandering, or the act of deriving support and maintenance in part from the earnings of a known prostitute, and the act of procuring or inducing a female to enter, or become an inmate of, a house of prostitution, are criminal offenses under many statutes. The federal statute known as the White Slave Traffic Act penalizes as a felony the act of transporting or causing to be transported any female in interstate or foreign commerce for the purpose of prostitution or debauchery or other immoral purpose.

Sedition consists of acts directed against the government and tending toward treason, but without the overt act essential to treason. It may consist in the publishing or uttering of words tending to excite people to rebellion or breach of public order. As condemned by statutes generally, sedition is the wilful and knowing utterance or publication of disloyal, scurrilous, or abusive matter against the United States or a state, or the flag, military forces, or uniform of the nation, which matter is designed and calculated to bring them into contempt; matter which advocates, incites, fosters, or encourages antagonism, opposition, and hostility to organized government; or matter which obstructs or interferes with the national recruiting or enlistment services. Criminal anarchy, denounced by some statutes, is defined as the doctrine that organized government should be overthrown by force or violence, or by assassination or other unlawful means. Criminal syndicalism is defined as any doctrine or precept advocating, teaching, or aiding and abetting the commission of crime, sabotage, or unlawful acts of force and violence or unlawful methods of terrorism, as a means of accomplishing a change in industrial ownership or control, or effecting any political change.

Sodomy is generally and broadly defined as unnatural sexual relations between persons of the same sex. The definitions sometimes include sex relations between man and beast, but the latter offense is more precisely termed "bestiality." The acts which constitute the crime of sodomy, the nature of the sexual relations, and the other essential elements of the crime vary in the different jurisdictions.

Vagrancy at common law was the offense of wandering or going about from place to place by an idle person having no lawful, visible means of support, and not working for a living although able to do so. The offense is the subject of a great variety of definitions in the statutes and ordinances of the various jurisdictions. The validity of legislation in this field is, of course, circumscribed by the constitutional requirement of definiteness and the other limitations upon the powers of the state over the freedom of the individual.

*

DAMAGES

I. IN GENERAL; CLASSES OF DAMAGES

§ 8:1. Generally.

Am Jur 2d References: Damages, §§ 1–4, 269–412.

In legal contemplation, the term "damages" is the sum of money which the law awards or imposes as pecuniary compensation, recompense, or satisfaction for an injury done or a wrong sustained as a consequence of either a breach of a contractual obligation or a tortious act. Damages are the pecuniary consequences which the law imposes for the breach of some duty or the violation of some right. In the discussion of the subject below, damages are classified as compensatory damages, intended to compensate or indemnify the plaintiff for an injury sustained or a wrong suffered; punitive or exemplary damages, which are added to compensatory damages because of the wanton or malicious character of the wrong; liquidated damages, or the sum fixed by the parties in their contract as the sum recoverable upon a breach thereof; and nominal damages, given in vindication of a breach of duty which does not result in pecuniary loss.

Although the words, "damages," "damage," and "injury," are sometimes used synonymously, there is a material distinction between them. Injury is the illegal invasion of a legal right; damage is the loss, hurt, or harm which results from the injury; and damages are the recompense or compensation awarded for the damage suffered from the injury.

To warrant a recovery of damages, there must be both a right of action for a wrong inflicted by the defendant, and damage resulting to the plaintiff therefrom. Wrong without damage, or damage without wrong, does not give rise to a cause of action.

Where a prima facie case is established by a plaintiff, the right to recover damages and the amount thereof are determined by the jury or trier of facts, under instructions by the court on the governing law, including the measure of damages. Where there has been no prejudicial error in the trial or in the court's instructions on damages, a jury's award of damages will not be disturbed merely because the amount of the verdict was either more or less than the reviewing court would have awarded. Where, however, the amount of damages awarded either exceeds or falls below any rational appraisal or estimate of the damages under the evidence in the case, the verdict may be set aside as excessive or inadequate, and a new trial granted, either by the trial court or on appeal. To justify a court in upsetting a verdict on this ground, however, according to the test frequently stated by the courts, the amount must be so clearly unreasonable and outrageous as to shock the judicial conscience and to warrant an inference that the jury was actuated by passion, prejudice, or corruption.

§ 8:2. Nominal damages.

Am Jur 2d References: Damages, §§ 5–10.

Nominal damages are either those damages recoverable where a legal right is to be vindicated against an invasion that has produced no actual present loss of any kind, or where, from the nature of the case, some compensable injury has been shown but the amount of that injury has not been proved. The law infers some damage from the breach of an agreement or the violation of a right; and if no evidence is given of any particular amount of loss, it declares the right by awarding "nominal damages."

Nominal damages are generally recoverable whenever there has been a breach of legal duty or an invasion of a legal right, and no actual damage resulted or was proved. However, nominal damages are not recoverable in cases in which damages are an element of the cause of action and the plaintiff has failed to prove damages. Thus, nominal damages should not be awarded in an action for negligence, as damages are a part of the cause of action in such cases. However, this rule does not apply in actions based on a wilful wrong.

Nominal damages are recoverable in an action based on breach of a contract if no actual or substantial damage resulted from the breach or no damage has been proved. Nominal damages, and only nominal damages, may be recovered for a tort where there is no evidence that damage has been sustained or where there is no evidence from which damages can be calculated. As stated above, however, nominal damages are not recoverable in cases, such as actions for ordinary negligence, in which damages are an element of the cause of action itself and the plaintiff has failed to prove those damages. Nominal damages are recoverable for an illegal invasion of property rights, though no substantial damages result or are proved.

Where actual damage is shown to have resulted from a tort, and the wrong is committed under such circumstances as to entitle the injured party to actual damages, the fact that such actual damages are not susceptible of exact calculation does not limit the plaintiff to nominal damages.

§ 8:3. Liquidated damages.

Am Jur 2d References: Damages, §§ 212–235.

The phrase "liquidated damages" means a sum stipulated and agreed upon by the parties at the time of entering into a contract, as being payable as compensation for injuries in the event of a breach of the contract. It is settled that parties may stipulate, in advance, the amount to be paid as damages for loss or injury which may result in the event of a breach, and a stipulated sum which is determined to be liquidated damages rather than a penalty is enforceable. The purpose and justification of stipulations for liquidated damages are that it renders certain and definite that which appears to be uncertain and which might not be easily susceptible of proof.

As distinguished from liquidated damages, a penalty, in the sense in which the term is used here, is a sum inserted in a contract, not as the measure of compensation for its breach, but rather as a punishment for default, or by way of security for actual damages which may be sustained by reason of nonperformance; and, as such name implies, it involves the idea of punishment.

A penalty is an agreement to pay a stipulated sum on breach of a contract, irrespective of the damage sustained. A stipulated penalty operates in terrorem, while the essence of liquidated damages is a genuine covenanted pre-estimate of damages. The parties are bound by a stipulation for liquidated damages; but if the stipulated sum is held to be a penalty, it is not enforceable and the nondefaulting party is left to the recovery of such actual damages as he can prove.

In determining whether a stipulated sum is for a penalty or for liquidated damages, the courts usually apply one or more aspects of the following rule: A stipulated sum is deemed to be for liquidated damages only where (1) the damages which the parties might reasonably anticipate are difficult to ascertain because of their indefiniteness or uncertainty, and (2) the amount stipulated is either a reasonable estimate of the damages which would probably be caused by a breach or is reasonably proportionate to the damages which actually result from the breach. The fact that the contract characterizes the stipulated sum as "liquidated damages" is a circumstance to be considered in determining whether it is in fact liquidated damages or a penalty, but it is by no means conclusive. A stipulated sum will usually be regarded as a penalty where the defaulting party is rendered liable for the same amount whether the breach is total or partial. As indicated above, the certainty or uncertainty of the actual damages which a breach of contract will occasion and the ease or difficulty of ascertaining or proving damages is an important aspect of the test to be applied in determining whether the sum named is liquidated damages or a penalty. Another important consideration in determining this question is the reasonableness of the sum stipulated as liquidated damages. A stipulation for a sum as liquidated damages in an amount which is not disproportionate to the damages which might probably result from a breach of the contract will usually be regarded as one for liquidated damages, at least where the actual damages were not readily ascertainable. If the sum stipulated is so large as to be out of all proportion to the probable or presumptive loss or damage, and was therefore not a fair estimate of probable damages, it will generally be regarded as a penalty. If the stipulated sum proves to be grossly disproportionate to the damages actually resulting from a breach of the contract, the sum will be held to be a penalty; and this disproportion may result from the sum stipulated being either too high or too low.

§ 8:4. Exemplary or punitive damages.

Am Jur 2d References: Damages, §§ 236–268.

Punitive or exemplary damages are generally defined as damages which are given as an enhancement of compensatory damages because of the wanton, reckless, malicious, or oppressive character of the acts complained of. Such damages are sometimes called "smart money." In most jurisdictions exemplary damages are allowed as a punishment to the defendant and as a warning and example to deter him and others from committing similar wrongs in the future. Under this theory, such damages are allowed on grounds of public policy and in the interest of society, and not as compensatory damages. In a few states, however, exemplary damages are awarded, not by way of punishment of a defendant, but as additional compensation to the plaintiff because of the nature of the wrong.

Punitive or exemplary damages are allowed in proper cases in most of the states of this country. In a few states, such damages are not permitted except where authorized by statute; and statutes in some jurisdictions authorize or restrict the imposition of exemplary damages. Where such damages are permitted, their allowance, and the amount thereof, rest in the discretion of the jury.

The necessity of proving actual damages as a basis for the allowance of punitive or exemplary damages is the subject of some disagreement among courts. It is well settled that there is no cause of action for exemplary damages alone. The plaintiff must establish his cause of action independently of his claim for exemplary damages, and if he fails to plead or to prove his cause of action, he may not be allowed an award of exemplary damages. Furthermore, many causes of action to which a complainant might attach a claim for exemplary damages require, as an element of the cause of action, proof of compensatory damages. In such cases, where proof of actual damages is a part of the cause of action, the allegation and proof of compensatory damages is a prerequisite to a recovery of exemplary damages, or of any recovery at all.

Where, however, the allegation and proof of compensatory damages is not an essential element of the cause of action itself, the courts are divided as to whether an award of exemplary damages can be sustained in the absence of proof of compensatory damages. And in the jurisdictions following the rule that compensatory or actual damages are a prerequisite of the right to punitive damages, there is a disagreement among the courts on the question whether an award of nominal damages will support an award of exemplary damages. Some of this conflict is traceable to the lack of agreement as to the essential nature of nominal damages, discussed above, § 2.

As a general rule, punitive or exemplary damages are recoverable in all actions for damages based on tortious acts which involve circumstances or ingredients of malice, fraud, or insult, or a wanton and reckless disregard of the rights of the plaintiff. Stated in another way, the rule is that exemplary damages may be recovered only in cases where the wrongful act is characterized by circumstances of aggravation, such as wilfulness, wantonness, malice, gross negligence or recklessness, oppression, outrageous conduct, indignity, insult, contumely, or fraud.

Where such circumstances or ingredients are established as a predicate for the award of exemplary damages, such damages may be recoverable in actions for personal injuries received in consequence of tortious acts, in actions for injuries to, or for the wrongful taking or destruction of, property, and in actions to recover damages for the following: abuse of process; false arrest or imprisonment; fraud and deceit; criminal conversation or alienation of affections; interference with employment, contract, or business relations; libel and slander; malicious prosecution; nuisances; seduction; and wrongful acts in regard to the transmission or delivery of telegraphic messages. Such damages may also be allowed for interference with personal rights and privileges secured by the Federal Constitution. However, exemplary damages are not recoverable in actions for wrongful death unless the statutes authorizing such actions so provide; nor are such damages recoverable in actions for infringement of patents. Exemplary damages are not ordinarily recoverable in actions for breach of contract, although such recovery has been permitted in a few exceptional cases.

Where a master or principal is liable for the wrongful act of his servant or agent, it is generally held that liability for exemplary or punitive damages may be imposed upon the employer for such acts. This principle applies both to natural persons and to corporations in the capacities of master or principal. Some courts take the position that the master or principal is liable for exemplary damages in such cases only if he has authorized or ratified the act of the agent or servant, while other courts hold that he may be liable for such damages regardless of such authorization or ratification, so long as the servant or agent was acting within the scope of his employment or authority.

Statutes of many states and of the United States provide for the award of multiple (or double or treble) damages for certain specified wrongs. Such damages are closely related to punitive or exemplary damages awarded in the absence of statute, and some courts treat such statutes as penal laws and hold that they must be strictly construed, while other courts regard such statutes as remedial.

§ 8:5. Compensatory damages.

Am Jur 2d References: Damages, §§ 11–44.

Compensatory damages are damages in satisfaction of, or in recompense for, loss or injury sustained. The term covers all loss recoverable as a matter of right and includes all damages beyond nominal damages, other than punitive or exemplary damages. The phrase "actual damages" is sometimes used as synonymous with compensatory damages. Compensation is the stated goal of courts in awarding damages for tortious injury or for breach of a contractual promise. In the case of torts, compensation most often takes the form of putting the plaintiff in the same financial position he was in prior to the tort. For breach of contract, compensation is most often stated in terms of placing the plaintiff in the same financial position in which he would have been had the promise not been broken. Such statements are, of course, mere generalizations, and they disregard cases in which nominal damages or exemplary damages may be awarded, as well as recovery on the basis of restitution with the goal not of compensating the plaintiff but of taking from the defendant the benefit he has inequitably received.

The fundamental principle of the law of damages being compensation for injury sustained, the plaintiff in a civil action for damages cannot, except where punitive damages are recoverable, hold a defendant liable in damages for more than the actual loss which he has inflicted by his wrong. In other words, one injured by the breach of a contract or the commission of a tort is entitled only to fair compensation and indemnity for the injury which he has suffered, and the law will not put him in a better position than he would be in had the wrong not been done or the contract not been broken.

Compensatory damages are usually classified as either "general" or "special." General damages are those which are the natural and necessary result of the wrongful act or omission asserted as the foundation of liability, and include those which follow as a conclusion of law from the statement of the facts of the injury. In other words, general damages are those which are traceable to and presumably or necessarily the result of the injury. The term "special damages" denotes such damages as arise from the special circumstances of the case, which, if properly pleaded, may be added to the general damages which the law presumes or implies from the mere invasion of the plaintiff's rights. Special damages are the natural, but not the necessary, result of an injury. The main practical distinction between general and special damages lies in the manner of pleading damages. General damages may be recovered under a general allegation of damage, whereas special damages must be specially pleaded.

In some states what are called "temperate damages" are allowed in certain classes of cases, without proof of actual or special damage, where the wrong done is such that the court concludes that it must in fact have caused actual damage to the plaintiff, though, from the nature of the case, he cannot furnish actual and distinct proof thereof. Temperate damages are more than nominal damages, and in theory are such as would be a reasonable compensation for the injury sustained.

As a general rule, only those damages may be recovered which result proximately and naturally from the wrong complained of. No damages can be allowed for injuries which are the remote consequences of the wrongful act or which are too uncertain, speculative, or contingent. The damages must be proved with reasonable certainty to have been suffered by the plaintiff and to have been the result of the defendant's wrong. This does not mean, however, that where it is established that the plaintiff has been damaged, his recovery will be defeated by his inability to prove with certainty and exactness the amount of the damages.

Under the rule against splitting a cause of action, the owner of a single or entire cause of action may not divide or split it so as to make it the subject of several actions. He not only may, but he must, include all damages resulting from the injury, whether past or prospective, in his action to recover for the injury; and if suit is brought for only a part of the claim, the judgment obtained therein bars a second action for any remaining portion. Hence, in estimating the pecuniary loss which a plaintiff has sustained as a result of the defendant's tort or breach of contract, all the consequences of the injury, future as well as past, are taken into consideration, and the recovery, if any, must be for all damages resulting therefrom, whether past, present, or prospective.

Thus, in an action for personal injuries, recovery may be had for future pain and suffering and for future medical expenses and impaired earning capacity, to the extent that these damages are reasonably certain to accrue in the future as a result of the injury complained of.   In the case of a breach of an entire and indivisible contract, prospective damages to compensate for future losses reasonably certain to arise from the breach may be recovered. Where an injury to real property is permanent in character, all the damages caused thereby, whether past, present, or prospective, must be recovered in a single action.   Where, however, an injury to or trespass on real property is merely temporary, prospective damages are not recoverable, but only such damages as the plaintiff has already sustained.   Successive actions for damages may be maintained from time to time as they accrue, where the wrong in question consists of trespasses by the defendant or intermittent or recurring injuries from causes that are remediable, removable, or abatable.

Under the doctrine of avoidable consequences, a party cannot recover damages flowing from consequences which he could reasonably have avoided.   This principle is often expressed in terms of a duty on the part of the plaintiff to minimize his damage and to take reasonable action to avoid enhancing the damage caused by the defendant.   Some courts have suggested that the doctrine of avoidable consequences is an extension of the principle of proximate cause: if the plaintiff could reasonably have avoided the damage which resulted, then the wrongful acts of the defendant can no longer be considered the proximate cause of such damage.

That which is required of the plaintiff under this doctrine is that he use reasonable and ordinary diligence and care to minimize his damages, and he need not make extraordinary or unreasonable efforts to minimize or limit the liability of the defendant.   The efforts required of the injured party to prevent or lessen his damages may include a reasonable (or, as stated by some courts, a "trifling") expenditure of money, which he may recover as a part of his damages.   In the case of a breach of contract, the nondefaulting party may be required to make other contracts or other purchases or sales in order to mini-mize his damages.   In the case of injuries to property, if the owner fails to take reasonable precautions or to make reasonable expenditures to guard against or to minimize the injury, he cannot recover damages for any injuries which he could have avoided by the exercise of reasonable care.   In the case of personal injuries, the person injured is required to exercise reasonable care and diligence in securing medical aid and in making use of reasonable medical means to promote recovery and to prevent any aggravation of the injury.   If the injured plaintiff takes those measures which a reasonably prudent person would have taken under similar circumstances, the doctrine of avoidable consequences does not prevent the recovery of damages flowing from the injury. He need not take the best of all possible care of his injuries or employ the means best adapted to cure them.   Reasonable care may require the injured person to submit to a surgical operation or other drastic treatment, if a rea-sonably prudent man would have submitted to such an operation or treatment. However, if the operation proposed is serious, in that it is attended by risk of failure or death, damages will not be decreased because of the plaintiff's failure to submit to the operation.

II. MEASURE AND ELEMENTS OF COMPENSATORY DAMAGES

§ 8:6. Generally.

Am Jur 2d References: Damages, §§ 45, 157–170, 363–412.

In civil actions for damages, whether the action is one based on contract or on tort, the amount of damages allowed, in the absence of circumstances calling for exemplary or punitive damages, is compensation for whatever loss or injury directly or proximately results from the defendant's wrongful act. As noted in the preceding section, recovery may be had for any proximate consequences which can be established with the requisite certainty, including damages for future or prospective injuries that are reasonably certain to result, but not for any consequences which are remote and indirect or merely speculative. Necessary and reasonable expenses incurred by the plaintiff as a consequence of the defendant's wrong are a proper element of damages.

While, as stated above (supra, § 8:1), the amount of unliquidated damages to be awarded a plaintiff is left to the discretion of the jury, and the jury's verdict will not ordinarily be disturbed, yet in extreme cases, where the amount of the verdict is so grossly excessive or inadequate as to indicate passion, prejudice, or corruption on the part of the jury, the court may set aside the verdict.

§ 8:7. Breach of contract.

Am Jur 2d References: Damages, §§ 46–79, 158–161, 171–174, 183–188.

A party to a contract who is injured by its breach is entitled to compensation for the injury sustained and is entitled to be placed, insofar as this can be done by money, in the same financial position he would have occupied if the contract had been performed. His recovery is limited to the loss he has actually suffered by reason of the breach, and he is not entitled to be placed in a better position than he would have been in if the contract had not been broken. Otherwise stated, the measure of damages is the actual loss sustained by reason of the breach, which is the loss of what the promisee would have made if the contract had been performed, less the proper deductions.

Where the breach of a contract consists in repudiating it, without the fault or concurrence of the other party, the latter may recover the damages which he has sustained by reason of the breach. As to the portion of the promise not yet performed, the repudiation amounts to an anticipatory breach. Where there is such a breach by repudiation communicated to the other party, the latter may sue before the performance date and recover damages for future, as well as past, injuries caused by the breach. The nonrepudiating party also has the option of waiting until the time for the performance of the contract before he sues for an anticipatory breach. In the latter case, however, he runs the risk of going counter to the doctrine of avoidable consequences if he unreasonably increases his damages by proceeding with the contract and incurring expenses after the repudiation.

In the case of a defective performance, the measure of damages is generally the reasonable cost of making the work performed or the article furnished conform to the contract. However, where the cost of correction would be grossly out of proportion to the value which the correction would add to the property involved, the damages are measured, according to the weight of authority, by the diminution in value resulting from the breach, rather than by the cost of correction. The measure of damages for failure to perform a contract within the time agreed upon is the actual loss sustained by reason of the delay.

Under the rules stated above, by which the nondefaulting party is entitled to compensation for his injury or loss occasioned by a breach of contract, it is very seldom that he may recover the price agreed to be paid on full performance, although the contract price may be recovered in certain cases where the promisee has substantially performed his part of the contract prior to the breach thereof by the promisor.

A party who is injured by another's breach of a contract is entitled to recover from the latter damages for only such injuries as are the direct, natural, and proximate results of the breach. Those damages must also be within the contemplation of the defaulting party, as determined by the doctrine of foreseeability; that is, the damages must either have been actually within the contemplation of the defaulting party at the time he entered into the contract or be so likely to result from a breach that they can reasonably be said to have been foreseen, contemplated, or expected by him at the time the contract was made, as being a probable or natural result of a breach. The rule as to the contemplation of the parties had its classic statement in the English case of Hadley v Baxendale, 9 Exch 341, 156 Eng Reprint 145, decided in 1854. As stated in this case, the damages recoverable for breach of contract are such as may fairly and reasonably be considered as arising naturally and according to the usual course of things from the breach of the contract itself, or such as may reasonably be supposed to have been in the contemplation of both parties at the time they made the contract, as the probable result of its breach.

In addition to general damages, one injured by a breach of a contract to which he is a party is entitled to recover special damages which arise from circumstances peculiar to the particular case, where those circumstances were communicated to, or known by, the other party at the time the contract was made. Such damages are the reasonable and the natural consequences of the breach under such circumstances, and may reasonably be supposed to have been in the contemplation of both parties where they had notice thereof.

The existence of a collateral contract or transaction between the nondefaulting party and a third person may affect the amount of damages recoverable for a breach of the principal contract. For example, if one purchases materials for the purpose of incorporating them in a finished product at a profit, or if he buys land or other property for the purpose of reselling it at a profit, and the other party knows of such collateral purposes and contracts, he is liable upon his breach of the contract for the loss of profits or the special damages sustained by the nondefaulting party. Where the defaulting party had no notice of the possibility of such a collateral transaction, however, no recovery can be had for loss of profits on collateral contracts.

Upon the breach of a contract, the injured party is entitled to recover, as a part of his damages, reasonable expenses incurred and expenditures made, either in preparation for performance or in partial performance of the contract, or, after breach of the contract, in an attempt to lessen the damages resulting from the breach.

The right to recover interest on damages, as a part of damages for breach of contract, depends, according to many authorities, on the question whether the amount due the plaintiff under the contract can be considered as a liquidated claim or whether it is unliquidated. Interest is recoverable as damages for breach of a contract involving a certain and liquidated sum. Although there is a conflict of authority with respect to unliquidated claims, the modern trend is to allow interest as damages where the demand, although unliquidated, is of such nature that the amount is capable of ascertainment by mere computation, or can be established with reasonable certainty or determined by reference to well-established market values. Where recoverable, interest on damages for breach of contract ordinarily runs from the date of the breach or the time when payment was due under the contract.

§ 8:8. Torts.

Am Jur 2d References: Damages, §§ 80–130, 156, 162, 163, 175, 189–191, 195–198, 206–210.

The measure of damages in tort actions is found by determining the consequences of the defendant's breach of duty. A person injured by the commission of a tort is entitled to pecuniary compensation for the actual injuries sustained, and except where the circumstances are such as to warrant the allowance of punitive or exemplary damages, he is limited to such compensation. Only such damages are recoverable for a tort as can be shown with reasonable certainty to be the direct, natural, and proximate consequences of the defendant's wrongful act. Damages may be recovered against a tortfeasor for, and only for, the natural, direct, and proximate consequences of his wrongful act or omission. However, liability extends not only to injuries which are directly and immediately caused by the wrong, but also to such immediate consequential injuries as, according to the common experience of men, are likely to, and do in fact, result from such act. A more liberal rule of damages prevails in cases of torts involving elements of malice, wantonness, or wilfulness than in cases of mere negligence. In the former class of cases, the wrongdoer will be held responsible for injuries which he has directly caused, even though they lie beyond the limit of natural and apprehended results as established in cases where the injury is caused by mere negligence.

There is a difference of opinion among the courts as to the applicability in tort actions of the doctrine of foreseeability or contemplation of damages, which is discussed in the preceding section in relation to contracts. Many courts hold that this doctrine does not apply in negligence cases and that compensatory damages in tort actions include damages not only for consequences proceeding immediately from the cause which is the basis of the action, but also for unforeseen consequences, and that the liability of the defendant is for all consequences naturally resulting from the wrongful act or omission, whether or not anticipated or contemplated by the party at fault as a probable result of his act or omission. Other decisions state that damages can be recovered in a negligence action only for those injuries which could have been reasonably anticipated, or were reasonably foreseeable, at the time of the wrongdoing.

Where an intervening act of a third person is involved in a tort case, liability generally depends upon whether the intervening act or its results were either foreseeable or were the normal consequence of the defendant's negligence. If the intervening act was not foreseeable or a normal consequence of the defendant's act, the defendant's wrong is ordinarily regarded as the remote cause of the injury and there is no liability for damages. A plaintiff cannot hold a defendant liable for any additional or increased damages based upon an intervening act of the plaintiff or a third party which is independent of the defendant's act or omission and which results in damages distinct from the damages resulting from the defendant's wrong, if that intervening act was neither foreseeable nor the normal consequence of the defendant's negligence. On the other hand, where the intervening act, whether wrongful in itself or not, is made necessary or proper because of the act of the wrongdoer, he is liable for the additional or increased damages resulting therefrom, since such damages are the natural and probable consequences of his act. Thus, an injured person who received unskilful treatment by a physician or surgeon, increasing his injuries, may recover damages for such consequences where he has used reasonable care in selecting the doctor.

Physical pain and suffering constitute an important element of the plaintiff's damages in an action for physical injuries tortiously inflicted. The plaintiff's damages should include compensation for past pain and suffering and for future pain and suffering shown to be reasonably certain or probable as a consequence of the injury. And this includes mental pain and anguish, both past and future, resulting from a personal injury. Liability for fright, shock, or mental disturbance is discussed in the topic Torts.

Another important element of damages in a personal injury action is the value of medical services made reasonably necessary by the defendant's wrong. This item of damages includes medicine, medical services, nursing, hospital care, and the like, including such expenses as are reasonably certain to be necessarily incurred in the future. Other reasonable expenses necessarily incurred by the injured person in consequence of his injuries are also recoverable as a part of his damages.

In a personal injury action, the plaintiff is entitled to recover the value of the time which he has lost because of the injury, and for the impairment of his earning capacity during the expected remainder of his life.

In certain types of tort actions, the plaintiff is entitled to recover for injury to his reputation, credit, and financial or business standing. Among these actions are those for libel or slander, malicious prosecution, and abuse of process.

The question frequently arises as to whether benefits received by the plaintiff from a collateral source or from a third person in no way connected with the defendant must be deducted from his damages in an action for tort. The prevailing view is that such benefits, though in a broad sense they lessen the plaintiff's financial loss, will not diminish the damages otherwise recoverable from the wrongdoer. According to this rule, such benefits are intended for the injured person and not to relieve the tortfeasor, and the law has no interest in conferring a windfall upon the latter. Thus, the fact that the plaintiff has received or will receive gratuitous medical, hospital, or nursing care from his family, friends, government, or charity, that his salary or wage payments have been continued, or that he has received pension or welfare benefits or payments under insurance policies, is not to be taken into account in computing damages. However, some courts in such cases apply literally the general rule that the aim of the law is only to compensate an injured party for his loss, and they hold that certain benefits received by him from collateral sources should reduce the total damages assessed against the defendant. But even these courts generally recognize that benefits received by the plaintiff from insurance carried by himself, or from pension, welfare, or workmen's compensation, do not diminish the damages recoverable against the tortfeasor.

Where a tort claim is "unliquidated" in the sense that the defendant does not know the precise amount he is obligated to pay until judgment is entered, interest is not generally recoverable in an action based thereon. This rule generally applies in damage actions for personal injuries, assault and battery, libel or slander, seduction, and false imprisonment. However, where the claim is made reasonably certain in amount by reference to market values or by computation, the courts have sometimes allowed interest as a part of the damages.

There is no fixed rule or exact standard by which damages can be precisely measured in personal injury cases. The law does not assume that a particular injury calls for a certain amount of compensation; and for many injuries there is no real equivalence or correlation between dollars and the plaintiff's injury. Hence, within reasonable limits, the amount to be awarded is a question left largely to the discretion of the jury in the light of all of the circumstances of the case.

§ 8:9. —Injury to or taking of property.

Am Jur 2d References: Damages, §§ 131–153, 176, 192–193, 211.

The rule of damages applicable in actions for wrongful injuries to, or the wrongful taking, detention, or destruction of, property, is that which applies generally in tort cases: The injured party is entitled to such recovery as will compensate him fully for the losses which are the proximate result of the wrongdoer's negligent or wrongful act or omission. The plaintiff is entitled to such sum as damages as will restore him as nearly as possible to his former position. The amount to be awarded as damages depends upon the character of the property, the nature and extent of the injury, and upon all of the circumstances connected with the injury.

The property owner is generally entitled to recover compensation for discomfort, annoyance, and personal inconvenience, and for any other consequential damages which necessarily or naturally arise from the wrongful act complained of and which are the proximate result thereof. However, in accordance with the general principles of damages, remote, uncertain, conjectural, or speculative damages are not allowed.

One whose interest in real property has been injured by the tort of another is entitled to such damages as will compensate him for the injury sustained; and this principle is translated into two rules of damages: (1) The injured party is entitled to recover the difference between the value of the property immediately before and immediately after the injury, or (2) he is entitled to recover the cost of repairing the property by restoring it to its condition immediately prior to the injury. An alternative measure of recovery is often applied where the tortfeasor merely occupies land, without damaging it. In such cases, the plaintiff is generally allowed to recover the rental value of the property.

Where the injury to real property is of a permanent nature, the proper measure of damages is the diminution in the market value of the property by reason of that injury, i.e., the difference between the value of the property immediately before the injury and its value immediately after the injury. If real property is taken or the value thereof totally destroyed, the owner is entitled to recover the actual cash value of the property at the time of the taking or destruction, with legal interest thereon to the time of the trial.

Where the injury or damage to realty is temporary or reparable rather than permanent, several different rules of damages have been applied, the diversity resulting in part from differences in the character of the property and the nature and extent of the injury or damage. Most courts agree, however, that when the injuries to real estate are found to be temporary, the diminution of market value of the property will not be used as the measure of recovery. Some courts allow recovery of the diminution in rental or usable value of the realty when the injuries are temporary. In other jurisdictions, the measure of damages for injuries of temporary character is the reasonable cost of repairing the damage or restoring the property to its former condition. Additional damages are also allowed for incidental injuries, such as loss of crops, damage to improvements or to personalty, and usually, interest to the time of trial.

Some courts hold, in cases of temporary damage, that the cost of restoring the property to its former condition is the proper measure of damages, where this is less than the diminution in the market value of the whole property by reason of the injury, but that if the cost of the restoration is more than the diminution, the latter is the proper measure of damages. Other courts say that the measure of damages is the cost of restoration unless this exceeds the value of the land prior to the injury, in which case the measure of damages is its value. Still other authorities hold that the measure of damages is either the diminution in the rental value unless the land can be restored to its former condition for a lesser sum, or it is the rental value plus the cost of restoration, where this is less than the depreciation in the value of the property. Some courts have combined the principle of granting the plaintiff damages measured by the cost of repair (provided that this amount is not out of line with the diminution in the market value of the property) with the rule allowing damages for loss of use of the premises during the time the injury continued.

The ordinary and basic measure of damages for injury to personal property is the difference between its market value immediately before and immediately after the injury, or in the case of its destruction, its market value at the time of destruction. Where there is no demand or market value for the thing in question, the amount of recovery is generally its actual value or, in the case of such things as portraits, heirlooms, and the like, its value to the owner. Where personal property is merely damaged, partially destroyed, or impaired in value, some courts hold that the reasonable cost or value of repairs is the proper measure of damages. Generally, this measure is applied where the injury is susceptible of repair at reasonable expense, or where the property can be repaired at less expense than the difference in its market value before and after the injury. This rule has been held applicable where the article is one which cannot be procured in the market, or where only a portion of the article is damaged and repairs are necessary before it can be used. It is not applicable, however, where the property is totally destroyed or cannot be restored to its original condition.

In cases where the personal property injured or destroyed had no market value in the normal sense of the term, the courts have been confronted with considerable difficulty and have reached various results as to the measure of damages. Indeed, some courts have taken the easy course and have denied recovery altogether. Examples of such property are family photographs, letters, manuscripts, lecture notes, plans of an architect or draftsman, and a specially designed machine. The rule most frequently adopted for these cases is to award either the "actual" or "intrinsic" value of the item or the "value to the owner" of the property. In arriving at these values, courts frequently consider the original cost of the property, including the value of materials and labor going into the production thereof, and also the cost of reproduction or replacement of the property. If the property is merely injured and is capable of being repaired, damages are sometimes measured by the cost of repair.

Recovery for the value of the loss of use of a chattel is generally allowed as a separate item of damages where the chattel has been injured through the tortious conduct of the defendant and is reparable. And where personal property which has been used to produce profits has been injured, taken, or destroyed by the tortious conduct of the defendant, courts may allow a recovery for those profits which were lost during the time reasonably needed to repair or replace the item, where it appears that the defendant's tortious conduct was the legal cause of the lost profits.

The general rule is well settled in tort cases that the recovery of damages by the owner of property injured or destroyed by the fault of another is, as against the tortfeasor, unaffected by the fact that he has already received or is entitled to receive full or partial payment for his loss by insurance procured by him or by a person other than the tortfeasor, and the payment from the insurer to the insured neither precludes nor reduces the amount of damages recoverable against the tortfeasor. It may be noted that in the case of property insurance the insurer is usually subrogated to the rights of the insured as against tortfeasors, so that it might recover the amount of its loss as against the latter if the injured person does not prosecute his own cause of action.

DOMESTIC RELATIONS AND PERSONS

I. MARRIAGE

II. ANNULMENT OF MARRIAGE

III. DIVORCE AND SEPARATION

IV. HUSBAND AND WIFE

V. PARENT AND CHILD

I. MARRIAGE

§ 9:1. Generally; creation and nature of the status.

Am Jur 2d References: Marriage, §§ 1–13, 33–41, 116–126, 168–184.

The term "marriage" is applied both to the status or relation of a man and woman who have been united as husband and wife, and to the ceremony or other act by which that status or relation is created. Marriage is said to be contractual in nature; and this is true to the extent that the consent or agreement of the parties is required in order to create the relationship. However, marriage is more correctly defined as a status, and the terms and consequences of the marriage compact, including the duration of the relationship, are fixed by law and generally cannot be altered by the parties.

Marriage is subject to state regulation and control with respect to its inception, status, conditions, and termination. Thus, the right to marry is made to depend upon the existence of the requisite mental capacity to consent to the marriage agreement, and is subject to various restrictions as to age, physical capacity or condition, relationship between the parties, and freedom from existing marriage. The states also prescribe the duties and obligations incident to marriage and the effect of marriage on the property rights of the spouses.

Marriage is normally solemnized by a religious or civil official authorized by law to perform the marriage ceremony. Consummation through sexual intercourse or cohabitation is not a requirement of a valid ceremonial marriage. Statutes in all states prescribe certain forms and procedures to be followed in the celebration of marriages. A license to marry, issued under public authority, is one of such requirements. Most jurisdictions require, as a prerequisite to the issuance of a marriage license, that blood tests be taken by both parties to assure that neither has a venereal disease or other loathsome or hereditary disease. Some states require the posting of banns or publication of notice for a specified period before marriage, and others prescribe a waiting period between the blood test and the issuance of license, or between the issuance of license and the marriage ceremony. And statutes relating to the solemnization of marriages usually provide for the issuance of a marriage certificate and for the registration or recording of marriages. A proxy marriage, in which a contracting party is absent and is represented by an agent or proxy who acts on behalf of the principal in the marriage ceremony, is recognized as a valid ceremonial marriage in some jurisdictions, but not in others.

Statutory penalties are frequently prescribed for the violation of statutes relating to the solemnization of marriages or the issuance of marriage licenses, or the solicitation of marriages by persons authorized to perform the ceremony. Similarly, marriage brokerage contracts, by which, for a consideration, a person agrees to consent to or to promote or induce a certain marriage, are invalid and sometimes subject to criminal penalties. And the act of fraudulently inducing marriage may subject the guilty party to liability in damages to the victim.

Provisions in contracts, deeds, and wills that are in toto or general restraints of marriage are contrary to public policy and void. Restraint of marriage means the effect or tendency of provisions to induce or obligate a person not to marry. Partial restraints on marriage, that is, restraints designed not to bar marriage completely but to narrow the range of marriage possibilities, are valid unless unreasonable.

§ 9:2. Validity of marriage; impediments.

Am Jur 2d References: Marriage, §§ 14–41, 62–115.

Marriages attempted in violation of, or without compliance with, statutory restrictions or requirements are generally held to be not absolutely void but only voidable, subject to attack by annulment proceedings. Thus, marriage between persons under the statutory minimum age, but over the age of 7, is not void but only voidable. The common-law rule that marriage of one under the age of 7 is absolutely void is still applied. Where one of the parties was under the age for marriage without parental consent, lack of such consent is, at most, ground for annulling the marriage. A marriage of a person under the statutory minimum age may be ratified and become completely valid and binding when the underaged party reaches the age of consent.

One of the essential qualifications for marriage, both at common law and under statute, is the possession of sufficient mental capacity to agree or consent to the creation of the marital status. A test frequently applied is whether the party in question, at the time of the marriage, had sufficient mental capacity to understand the nature of the marriage contract and the duties and responsibilities that it creates. Intoxication or the effect of drugs may deprive a party of capacity to enter into a valid marriage. Physical defects or disabilities, consisting of certain specified diseases or impotency or sterility, or the pregnancy of the woman by a man other than the husband at the time of the marriage, are sometimes made grounds for voiding a marriage.

While at common law and under some statutes mental incapacity of a party to a marriage renders the marriage void and subject to attack in any proceeding in which the question of validity arises, including collateral actions during the lifetime of the parties and actions after the death of the incompetent party, many statutes provide that such incapacity merely renders the marriage voidable. Some statutes forbid or restrict posthumous attack on marriages on the ground of lack of mental capacity of one of the parties.

The free and understanding consent and agreement of the parties is essential to a valid ceremonial marriage. It is clear that an agreement by the parties to a marriage that their marriage is to be terminable at pleasure, by consent, or at some future time, is void, as contrary to public policy; but there is a difference of opinion as to whether a marriage entered into under such an agreement is itself invalid. Some courts hold that a marriage regularly solemnized is valid notwithstanding such an agreement, whether the purpose of attempting to create a limited or temporary marital status was to legitimatize a child or to achieve some other goal. Other courts hold that a marriage entered into with such reservations is void or at least voidable if the parties never intended to consummate the marriage or to live together afterward in a marital relationship. A mock marriage, one entered into in the spirit of jest, with no intention that it should be binding or that the parties should assume the duties and obligations or assert the rights pertaining to the marital status, and not followed by cohabitation, is ordinarily held to be void.

A marriage may be held invalid for lack of consent if it was procured or induced by fraud or duress. Such purported marriages are usually not absolutely void but only voidable. The fraud which renders a marriage invalid must be of such character as to go to the very essence of the marriage contract and to affect the free consent to such contract. To constitute duress invalidating a marriage, the force, restraint, or threat must be such as to overcome the will and bring about a marriage to which consent would not otherwise have been given. The most common situation in which duress is claimed to invalidate a marriage occurs where the relatives of the woman attempt to persuade or coerce the man to marry the woman because of premarital sexual relations or pregnancy. There is a conflict of authority on the question whether such "shotgun marriages" are valid or voidable because of duress. Even where duress is applied at some time before the marriage ceremony, the reluctant bridegroom may subsequently acquiesce and voluntarily participate in the ceremony, making the marriage valid.

Noncompliance with formal requirements of statutes with respect to licensing, solemnization, and registration or recording of marriages does not generally invalidate a marriage, although it may subject a party or official to a criminal penalty. This rule applies to the failure to observe statutory requirements as to blood test or other physical examination, publication of banns, or observance of required waiting periods. The rule is also usually applied in cases involving noncompliance with statutes requiring marriage licenses, but in a few states such statutes are so interpreted that noncompliance therewith results in a void marriage. The fact that a ceremonial marriage is performed by an unauthorized person does not generally render the marriage invalid, although the contrary is true under some statutes.

Marriage is prohibited in all jurisdictions between persons related to each other by blood or affinity within certain specified degrees. The degree of relationship by consanguinity or affinity within which marriage is prohibited varies in the several jurisdictions. Marriages between first cousins were not forbidden at common law, but are invalid in a number of states; and marriage between persons more closely related by blood than first cousins is incestuous everywhere. There is no distinction between the whole and the half blood in computing the degrees within which marriages are prohibited as incestuous; and illegitimacy has no effect on the question. Some incest statutes extend their prohibitions against marriage not only to persons related by blood, but also to persons related only by affinity, or by marriage or adoption, within certain specified degrees. Although at common law incestuous marriages were voidable only and not void, the question today depends upon local statutes and their construction, which vary considerably in the different jurisdictions.

Persons who are already married cannot marry again unless their existing marital relation is legally terminated by divorce or annulment, or by the death of the former spouse. An attempted marriage to any person having a living legal spouse is unlawful and bigamous and is generally held to be void from its inception. This rule does not apply, however, where the former marriage was void, as distinguished from one that was merely voidable. It is generally held that a bigamous marriage does not acquire validity when the prior subsisting marriage is legally terminated by divorce or by the death of the first spouse, or, according to some authorities, by annulment of the first marriage after the second marriage is contracted. Some statutes, however, validate marriages originally invalid because of a prior subsisting marriage where the parties continue to cohabit after this impediment to their marriage is removed.

If a purported divorce or annulment, either domestic or foreign, is void, a subsequent marriage by either spouse is void. The same is true where there is a second marriage following an interlocutory or conditional divorce decree prior to the effective date of the decree. Clearly a limited divorce, known as a divorce a mensa et thoro or divorce from bed and board, does not terminate a marriage so as to enable either party to marry another. In some states the statutes provide for a waiting period before remarriage after a divorce, and some statutes restrict in other ways the right to remarry. Whether or not a remarriage forbidden by such statutes is void or merely voidable depends upon the terms of the statute and the construction given it by the courts.

In determining the validity of a marriage entered into in a foreign country or in another state, the general rule is that the question is determined by the law of the place where it is contracted. A marriage which is valid under the law of the state or country in which its is contracted will generally be recognized as valid everywhere, although there are important exceptions to this rule. The converse of this rule has been said to be true also, that is, that a marriage invalid where contracted is invalid everywhere; but doubt has been expressed as to the validity of this principle, and it is limited by the policy of the law to sustain marriages wherever possible. The validity of marriages performed or contracted aboard ships in international waters is ordinarily determined by the law of the nation or state in which the shipowner is domiciled or in which the ship is registered. The general rule that marriages valid where contracted are valid everywhere applies to common-law marriages. The principal exception to the general rule that a marriage valid where contracted is valid everywhere is the universal rule that a marriage valid where contracted will nevertheless not be recognized as valid in another state if such recognition would be contrary to a strong public policy of that state. Such public policy is frequently evidenced by statutes declaring that certain types of marriage are void or subjecting them to criminal penalties, such as bigamous and incestuous marriages. Where an attack on the validity of a marriage involves the age or capacity of the parties or the formal or ceremonial requirements of marriage, the law of the jurisdiction where the marriage is contracted is held to govern.

Where divorced persons who are prohibited by statute or by the terms of the divorce decree from remarrying, nevertheless do remarry in another state, most courts hold that the prohibitions or restrictions against remarriage have no extraterritorial effect and do not invalidate the marriage in the other state. There is a conflict of authority, however, as to the validity of such a marriage, where the question is raised and the marriage is challenged in the divorcing state.

At common law a void marriage was an absolute nullity. No dower, curtesy, or other property rights could be based thereon; and the issue of such a marriage was illegitimate. In the case of a marriage that is merely voidable, the issue is generally held to be legitimate. And dower or curtesy may be based on a voidable marriage which is not attacked in annulment or other direct proceedings during the lifetime of the parties. Statutes in many jurisdictions ameliorate the drastic consequences of invalid marriages. These statutes may affect both the legitimacy of offspring and the property and other rights of the parties to the marriage.

§ 9:3. Common-law marriage.

Am Jur 2d References: Marriage, §§ 42–61.

The so-called common-law marriage is created by an agreement between the parties per verba de praesenti—that is, by words of the present tense or a present agreement—to be husband and wife, without any formal ceremony and ordinarily without compliance with such statutory formalities as those pertaining to marriage licenses. There is a sharp conflict of authority as to the validity of such a marriage. In a number of jurisdictions, the statutory requirements as to the manner and formalities of marriage are regarded as mandatory, so that common-law marriages alleged to have been contracted in such jurisdictions are invalid. However, even jurisdictions denying the validity of common-law marriages attempted to be contracted therein recognize the validity of such marriages contracted in another jurisdiction where they are valid.

Most jurisdictions recognizing the validity of common-law marriage require not only an agreement between competent parties to be presently and henceforth husband and wife, but also that such agreement be carried out or consummated by cohabitation or in such way that the public will recognize the marital status. A few courts hold, however, that a valid common-law marriage is created as soon as the parties agree to henceforth be husband and wife, and that no time need elapse, such as for cohabitation and reputation of marital status, before the marriage is completed.   A basic requirement of common-law marriage, as well as of ceremonial marriage, is that the parties be competent and have capacity to enter the marital state.   Another absolute requirement is that the parties agree to be husband and wife, without qualification or condition.   An agreement to cohabit for the present and marry later does not satisfy this requirement.   A number of jurisdictions require that the parties hold themselves out to the world as husband and wife, and in some states the parties relying on a common-law marriage must show that they have acquired a reputation as husband and wife.

A common-law marriage, where its validity is recognized, carries with it the same rights and incidents as a ceremonial marriage, and the laws of inheritance, descent and distribution, dower, and other property rights apply alike to common-law marriages and to ceremonial marriages.

§ 9:4. Breach of promise.

Am Jur 2d References: Breach of Promise, §§ 1–48.

An action lies at common law to recover damages for the breach of a promise of marriage.   However, breach of promise actions have been abolished in a number of states and restricted in others.   Where the state of the forum has such a statute, it has been held to represent a statement of the state's public policy, so that a breach of promise action may not be maintained therein, even though there was no such statute in the state where the contract to marry was made.   On the other hand, it has been held that where the contract to marry is made in a state having such a statute, a breach of promise action cannot be maintained in a state having no such statute, although the breach occurs in the latter state.

While an action for breach of promise or contract to marry may be in the form of an action on the contract, it actually has more of the features of an action in tort, especially when regarded from the aspect of the elements, nature, and measure of damages recoverable in such actions.

An action for breach of promise to marry must be predicated upon an existing valid contract to marry.   Such a contract must have all of the elements essential to contracts generally.   There must be a binding offer and acceptance and mutual promises by the parties, such promises providing the consideration for the contract.   The parties must have legal capacity to enter into contracts and to enter into a legal marriage.   If the parties are related by blood or affinity in a degree which makes their marriage unlawful, or if the promise of marriage is made by or to a person who, to the knowledge of the parties, has a husband or wife living, there can be no actionable promise or contract of marriage.   A contract to marry, like any other contract, is invalid and will not support an action for breach of promise to marry, if it was induced by fraud or duress.

In jurisdictions recognizing a right of action for breach of promise of marriage, an actionable breach consists of any act or omission which violates the terms of the marriage contract.   Where the time of performance is indefinite or left to future agreement, an action for breach will not lie until the complaining party demands performance or offers to perform.   No such demand or offer is necessary, however, where the other party has renounced the agreement, committed an anticipatory breach, or disabled himself from performing, as by marrying a third person.

Generally speaking, matters which are defenses to actions for breach of contract are available as defenses in actions for breach of promise to marry. In addition, the fact that either party, at the time of entering into the marriage contract, is affected with a serious and permanent disease which renders marriage improper or would endanger the life or health of the parties or the offspring if the marriage were consummated, is a defense to an action for breach of promise, unless the disease was known to both parties at the time the engagement was entered into. Insanity obviously is a good defense to the action. Unchastity or illicit intercourse of the woman, prior to the marriage promise and then unknown to the man, or subsequent to the promise, with a person other than the defendant, is a defense to an action for breach of promise.

II. ANNULMENT OF MARRIAGE

§ 9:5. Generally; grounds.

Am Jur 2d References: Annulment of Marriage, §§ 1–11, 71–79.

The principal distinction between an action for the annulment of a marriage and a suit for divorce is that the latter presupposes a valid marriage and seeks a dissolution thereof on grounds occurring usually after the creation of the marriage, whereas an annulment proceeding seeks a judicial declaration that no valid marriage ever took place between the parties and that the marital relation never existed between them. An annulment is necessary only where the marriage is merely voidable. If the purported marriage was absolutely void ab initio, it is generally a complete nullity for all purposes and will be so treated in all proceedings, direct or collateral. Annulment is frequently decreed where the marriage is absolutely void and not merely voidable, as where it is incestuous or where it was entered into in jest, with no intention of entering into the marital relationship. Annulment may also be granted on the ground that one or both of the parties to the marriage were under the legal marriageable age or were already bound by an existing undissolved marriage. Courts are generally less strict in their requirements for decreeing an annulment where the marriage has not been consummated or where no children have been born of the marriage, than in cases where either of these events has occurred.

The right to annul a void marriage is a personal right and the action for annulment of such a marriage can be maintained only by a party to the marriage contract or, if he or she is under legal disability, by someone in his or her behalf. Generally, if the ground for annulment is the nonage or other disability of one of the parties, the action must be brought by that party or someone in his or her behalf. Fraud or duress is a ground for annulment only at the suit of the injured party. However, if the marriage is void ab initio, and not merely voidable, either party is generally permitted to sue for its annulment. This rule permits the guilty party as well as the innocent party to maintain a suit to annul a marriage which is void because one of the parties had a spouse living at the time of the marriage.

§ 9:6. Fraud and duress.

Am Jur 2d References: Annulment of Marriage, §§ 12–25.

A marriage induced by fraud or deceit may be annulled where the fraud or deceit relates to some fact that affects in a vital way the very esssence of the marriage relation. Not every kind and degree of fraud that would vitiate an ordinary contract will suffice as a ground for annulling a marriage. Although there is a conflict of authority on the subject, the weight of authority is that concealment of a prior marriage which has been dissolved by death or divorce is not such fraud as to afford a ground for annulment of a second marriage. There is a difference of opinion as to whether a fraudulent promise, not intended to be kept, to participate in a religious ceremony of marriage in the future or to change one's religion constitutes a ground for annulment. A nondisclosed intent on the part of one of the parties at the time of marriage not to have children or not to consummate the marriage by sexual intercourse, if adhered to after marriage, is a ground for annulment.

Duress or coercion which is the inducing cause of a marriage and which is such as to overcome the will and eliminate the free consent and agreement essential to a valid marriage contract, is a ground for the annulment of the marriage. To have this effect, however, the influence of the duress must continue to the time of the marriage ceremony. There is some conflict of authority as to whether the duress must be sufficient to overcome the will of an ordinary person or whether it is sufficient that the will of the particular individual was in fact overcome. Courts are reluctant to grant annulments on the ground of pressure brought to bear on a seducer by relatives of the victim of seduction. It must clearly appear in such cases that the complaining party acted under compulsion and without the exercise of his free will at the time of the marriage ceremony. As a general rule, a marriage will not be annulled on the ground that it was entered into by the man to escape prosecution and imprisonment for bastardy or seduction. Marriages to avoid prosecution for seduction or other sexual offenses have been annulled, however, where an arrest or prosecution of the man was based upon the woman's false story or fraud.

§ 9:7. Mental or physical condition; unchastity

Am Jur 2d References: Annulment of Marriage, §§ 26–42.

Insanity or the lack of mental capacity to consent to or enter into the marital status is a ground for the annulment of a marriage. The test in such cases is whether, at the time of the marriage, there is a capacity to understand the nature of the contract and the duties and responsibilities incident to marriage. Intoxication to such degree as to render a party non compos mentis and incapable of knowing the nature of the contract and its consequences is a ground for annulment of a marriage. There is a difference of opinion as to whether or not the concealment by a party of his or her past mental derangement is a ground for annulment. Incurable physical defects and incapacities which render a party unable to consummate the marriage, existing at the time of the marriage, are generally held to be grounds for annulment. Impotency of one of the parties, permanent in nature and existing at the time of the marriage, is a ground for annulment in many jurisdictions. Sterility or barrenness, if not accompanied by impotency, is not generally a ground for annulment, although concealment of the fact of known sterility or barrenness may constitute such fraud as to warrant annulment.

Premarital unchastity of either party, or the fact that prior to the marriage one of the parties had an illegitimate child and concealed this fact from the other spouse, is not generally a ground for annulment. However, where the wife is pregnant at the time of marriage by one other than the husband, and the husband has not had premarital sexual relations with her, annulment will be granted in some jurisdictions. The courts have frequently denied annulment sought by a husband on the ground that he was induced to enter into marriage because of the wife's false representations of pregnancy. But it is generally held that the husband may secure the annulment of a marriage which he was induced to enter into because of fraudulent representations by the woman that the child with which she was pregnant at the time of the marriage was his, although some of the earlier decisions refused an annulment in such cases.

§ 9:8. Defenses.

Am Jur 2d References: Annulment of Marriage, §§ 43–58.

Even though grounds for annulment of a marriage may exist, the maintenance of such an action may be precluded by the postnuptial conduct or antenuptial knowledge of the party seeking the annulment. However, equitable defenses such as estoppel and the clean hands doctrine are frequently held not to be applicable in annulment cases, because marriage is a matter in which the state has an interest. Where a marriage is absolutely void, as where one of the parties has a spouse by a former undissolved marriage or where the marriage is incestuous, the marriage cannot be ratified, by a continued cohabitation or otherwise, so as to preclude an annulment. However, if the marriage is only voidable, such as one induced by fraud or duress or one voidable because of physical incapacity or defects, continued cohabitation with knowledge of the facts is usually a defense to an action for annulment. A marriage voidable because one of the parties is mentally incompetent at the time of the ceremony may be ratified by a continued cohabitation after the incompetent regains reason and competency. And a marriage entered into by a person under the age of consent may be ratified so as to preclude annulment, by cohabitation after the party in question arrives at the legal age.

III. DIVORCE AND SEPARATION

§ 9:9. Generally.

Am Jur 2d References: Divorce and Separation, §§ 1–19, 879–882, 925–946.

There are two types of divorce—absolute and limited. An absolute divorce or "divorce a vinculo matrimonii" is a judicial dissolution or termination of the bonds of matrimony. It terminates the marriage relation for all purposes. Statutes in some states authorize a limited divorce, also called a divorce a mensa et thoro or divorce from bed and board. A limited divorce varies in its consequences from state to state, but in general it may be defined as a judicial decree which terminates the right and obligation of cohabitation but does not affect the status of the parties as married persons, or dissolve the marriage. Divorce differs from annulment in that the former presupposes a valid marriage or marriage relationship which it is sought to terminate, whereas an annulment is based on the ground that no valid marriage ever took place between the parties.

It is the province of the legislatures of the several states to regulate the subject of divorce, and also the grounds, conditions, and effects thereof as applied to their citizens and persons domiciled within their jurisdiction. Under the early common law, the power to grant an absolute divorce was vested in Parliament and not in the courts. And divorces granted directly by the legislatures are not unknown in this country, although they are a rarity. A suit for divorce is esssentially a proceeding in rem or quasi in rem. The res upon which the judgment operates is the status of the parties. The proceeding is usually brought in equity and it is governed by the principles and practice of equity. The principles of ecclesiastical law applied by the courts of England prior to the Revolution relating to divorce are still influential guides for American courts in the interpretation and application of divorce statutes.

So great is the interest of the state in the integrity and stability of the marriage relation that the law will not permit the termination of the marriage by any kind of private contract, nor by any collusive or fraudulent divorce proceeding. And any agreement, whether between husband and wife or between either and a third person, and whether antenuptial or postnuptial, tending to facilitate or promote the procurement of a divorce, is contrary to public policy and void.

§ 9:10. Grounds.

Am Jur 2d References: Divorce and Separation, §§ 20–171.

A divorce will be granted only on grounds prescribed by statute and for causes arising prior to the commencement of the divorce proceeding. The grounds for divorce differ in the several jurisdictions. The law of the forum governs in determining the rights of the parties in a divorce proceeding, including the grounds for divorce.

The adultery of either party is a ground for divorce in this country. In many jurisdictions the conviction and imprisonment of one spouse for a felony or other specified crime, sometimes designated "infamous crime" or crime involving "moral turpitude," is a ground for divorce.

In most jurisdictions statutes authorize a divorce on the ground of cruelty, the grounds sometimes being designated as "extreme cruelty" or "cruel and inhuman treatment." It is impossible to give a precise definition of cruelty which is applicable in all cases and in all jurisdictions. The test of cruelty as a ground for divorce lies in its effect upon the victim rather than in the motives of the offender. The rule prevails in most jurisdictions that cruelty as a ground for divorce need not consist of physical violence or threats of violence, and that a divorce may be granted for mental cruelty. In determining whether particular acts constitute cruelty for divorce purposes, the question is not the effect of the conduct upon a person of average or normal sensibilities, but rather its effect upon the aggrieved spouse. Acts or treatment which would be expected and accepted by one person as a matter of course and without offense may be extreme cruelty to another person. The courts recognize that some friction must result from the close relationship of two human beings in marriage, and that sparks of temper, quarrels, and harsh language may ensue. Such ordinary ordeals the parties must endure. Ordinarily, cruelty as a ground for divorce consists of a course of conduct rather than a single act. As regards mental cruelty, the acts relied upon normally consist of an extended course of conduct. Even a single act of physical violence may not constitute cruelty warranting a divorce, unless there are circumstances of unusual atrocity or unless the facts warrant a reasonable apprehension of similar acts in the future.

Open or flagrant adultery by one's spouse, or outrageous or grossly offensive public conduct with a person of the opposite sex, may constitute such cruelty as will warrant a divorce on that ground. The excessive use of intoxicating liquors or drugs may be a circumstance to be considered with other conduct in determining whether there has been such cruelty as to afford a ground for divorce. Mere words, in the form of habitual or constant outbursts of rage or jealousy, insulting and humiliating language, false accusations of adultery or other crimes, or the use of offensive language and vile and opprobrius epithets, calculated to cause mental suffering or to impair health, may constitute cruelty as a ground for divorce. An attempt by one spouse to have the other committed to an institution for the insane may constitute cruelty, if the attempt is made in bad faith. A ground for divorce under the statutes of some states is "indignities" offered by one spouse to the other, or "such indignities as to render his or her condition intolerable." This ground is clearly related to, or an aspect of, the ground of cruelty.

Although fraud or duress inducing a marriage is primarily a ground for annulment, it is also a ground for divorce in some states. Although premarital unchastity, even though it results in the birth of an illegitimate child, is not a ground for divorce in the absence of statute so specifying, a wife's concealment of her pregnancy by another man at the time of marriage may constitute such fraud as warrants divorce under some statutes.

Impotency of either spouse, meaning the lack of capacity to engage in normal sexual intercourse, is not only a ground of annulment but is a ground for divorce by statute in many states. Mere sterility or barrenness, or inability to beget or bear children, is not a ground for divorce, unless it involves or is accompanied by impotency or lack of capacity to engage in normal sexual intercourse.

Statutes in some jurisdictions provide for divorce on the ground of insanity or mental incapacity, or on the ground of commitment to or confinement in a mental institution, usually for a specified period. And in some jurisdictions habitual drunkenness or excessive use of intoxicating liquors or narcotics is a ground for divorce. Neglect or abuse of the family is frequently a factor in establishing this ground for divorce.

Desertion or abandonment for a specified time is made a ground for divorce in most states. What constitutes desertion varies to some extent according to variations in the statutory provisions; but generally it is the voluntary or wilful separation of one of the married parties from the other, or refusal to renew suspended cohabitation, without justification either in the consent or the wrongful conduct of the other party. To constitute desertion as a ground for divorce, there must be a cessation of cohabitation, with intent to abandon, without cause therefor or consent thereto, persisted in for the statutory period.

A complete and unconditional resumption of cohabitation, even for a short period, puts an end to desertion or abandonment. There is a conflict of authority, however, as to whether the period necessary to establish desertion is interupted by single, isolated or sporadic acts of sexual intercourse. To constitute desertion, the act of separation and the continued intent to remain separate must be without reasonable excuse or justification. If one spouse has just cause for leaving or living apart from the other, he is not guilty of desertion; and most authorities hold that a spouse whose serious misconduct compels the other to leave the home or remain away is guilty of statutory desertion, sometimes referred to as "constructive desertion." As the husband is under duty to provide a home for the family, he has the right, within reason, to choose the place of residence; and the wife's refusal, without good reason, to accompany the husband to the home which he selects and provides may constitute desertion by her. The justification for the wife's refusal to follow the husband depends upon all of the circumstances of the case.

While the failure of the husband to support his wife is not generally a ground for divorce, statutes in some states make "nonsupport," "refusal to provide," or "gross neglect of duty" a ground for divorce under certain limited circumstances.

In many states statutes authorize a divorce on the ground that there has been a separation of the husband and wife and that they have lived apart for a specified length of time. Fault for the separation and living apart is not usually an element of this ground for divorce. The parties must, however, have lived separate and apart without cohabitation for the statutory period.

In some jurisdictions "incompatability" is made a ground for divorce. The meaning of this term is difficult to define and must necessarily depend upon the disposition of the court as well as the circumstances of the case.

§ 9:11. Defenses.

Am Jur 2d References: Divorce and Separation, §§ 172–239.

General principles of equity are frequently asserted in defense of divorce suits. Inequitable conduct, the doctrine of unclean hands, laches or unreasonable delay, or the running of a statute of limitations, may be a defense in such actions. In addition, there are several defenses which are distinctive to divorce proceedings and which, with variations, are universally recognized.

One of these defenses is collusion. As used in this connection, collusion is an agreement or understanding between a husband and wife to obtain or facilitate a divorce by having the accused spouse commit, or appear to commit, or be falsely represented in court as having committed, an act which constitutes a ground for divorce, or to suppress or refrain from presenting evidence tending to show a defense to the action for divorce. Collusion is a corrupt arrangement between husband and wife looking to the procurement of a divorce. There is collusion where the parties agree that the defendant shall not defend the action or that he shall suppress evidence of a defense. Mere failure to defend does not establish collusion.

Connivance, as a defense to an action for divorce on the ground of adultery, is broadly defined as a corrupt consent by one spouse that the other shall commit adultery. It is closely related to, but distinct from, the defense of collusion.   Consent is an essential element of connivance which will constitute a defense to an action for divorce on the ground of adultery.   If the plaintiff has promoted, arranged, or facilitated the defendant's commission of adultery, this constitutes connivance, even though the offending spouse was ignorant of the other's connivance.   Mere spying on a suspected spouse does not constitute connivance.

Condonation, the forgiveness by one spouse of a breach of marital duty by the other, is a defense to an action for divorce based on the act condoned.   The elements of condonation are (1) a forgiveness, express or implied, of conduct which would be a cause for divorce or separation, (2) with knowledge of the wrongdoing, and accompanied by (3) a continuance or resumption of the marital relation.   It is generally held that any misconduct constituting a ground for divorce may be condoned.   Condonation may result from a reconciliation of the parties pending a divorce suit.   However, condonation induced by fraud, or partial forgiveness or reconciliation not followed by a marital cohabitation, is not available as a defense to a divorce suit.   The forgiving spouse cannot revoke a condonation as long as the offender observes the conditions of the condonation.   However, condonation of a cause of action for divorce is conditional, the conditions being that the offender will not repeat the offense. Generally, condonation may be forfeited by a subsequent conduct of less grave nature than would warrant the granting of a divorce, and misconduct of one type may avoid the condonation of a ground of divorce of another type.

The defense of recrimination ordinarily contemplates that the party seeking the divorce is guilty of a matrimonial offense which would be a ground for divorce.   While recrimination is an absolute defense in many jurisdictions, it is the rule in other states that the fact that the plaintiff has committed a marital offense is not necessarily an absolute bar to a divorce, and that the trial court has discretion to grant a divorce notwithstanding the misconduct of the petitioner.   And in some states a divorce may be granted to both parties where both are guilty of misconduct warranting a divorce.   Several states have adopted the doctrine of comparative rectitude, which means that where both parties are guilty of misconduct for which a divorce might be granted, the court will grant a divorce to the one who is less at fault; but if the fault of the parties is found to be in equipoise, the court will refuse to grant relief to either party.   While there is some authority to the contrary, it is generally held, regardless of whether the defense of recrimination is absolute or discretionary, that the acts of the plaintiff constituting a defense need not be of the same character as the acts of the defendant for which a divorce is sought, or of the same gravity from a moral point of view, so long as the offense is such as constitutes a ground for divorce.

If a spouse is insane at the time he commits a matrimonial offense, his incompetency is a defense to an action for divorce based upon such misconduct.

§ 9:12. Alimony and other allowances.

Am Jur 2d References: Divorce and Separation, §§ 514–771.

Alimony is the allowance which a husband may be compelled to pay to his wife or former wife for her support and maintenance when she is living apart from him or has been divorced.   Alimony may be permanent, continuing indefinitely or for the lives of the parties, or it may be temporary or "pendente lite," an allowance made to the wife for her maintenance during the pendency of the action. As a general rule, a valid marriage must exist as a basis of awarding alimony or counsel fees and suit money in an action for divorce, although in jurisdictions where statutes authorize divorce, rather than annulment, where a marriage is void, alimony may be awarded in such cases. Although a provision for alimony and a settlement of property interests are frequently incorporated in a decree for divorce, an allowance of alimony does not constitute a winding up or settlement of all business dealings between the husband and wife and does not constitute a division or settlement of their property rights.

As alimony is allowed on the basis of the husband's duty to support his wife, and as there is no corresponding duty on the part of the wife, a husband is not entitled to alimony or suit money in a suit for divorce, in the absence of a statute providing therefor.

Alimony awarded a wife in a divorce suit cannot be subjected to the payment of debts contracted by her prior to the decree, but such alimony is subject to the claims of her creditors for debts contracted by her after the entry of the divorce decree. Nonaccrued instalments of alimony, or payments to become due in the future, may not be assigned by the wife.

The allowance of temporary alimony, or support money during the pendency of a divorce suit, and the amount thereof, are matters generally left to the discretion of the court. The preliminary showing which the wife must make to authorize such an allowance varies in the different jurisdictions. The primary considerations in determining the amount of temporary alimony are the economic circumstances of the husband and wife, their needs, station in life, and ability to pay. Provision is generally made for allowance of suit money to the wife in a divorce suit, to enable her to carry on or defend the action. This may include counsel fees, costs, and other expenses of maintaining her rights.

Whether permanent alimony shall be awarded in a divorce suit rests largely in the discretion of the court and depends upon all of the circumstances of the case. Among the factors to be considered by the court is the financial condition of the parties. The wife's separate income or estate and her actual needs, as well as the husband's financial ability, are to be considered, as is the wife's ability to earn a living. Generally, permanent alimony will not be awarded to a wife where the husband obtains a divorce on the ground of her marital misconduct. The amount of alimony to be awarded to a wife rests in the sound discretion of the court and depends upon all of the circumstances of the case. The financial condition of the parties, their station in life, and their respective earning capacities and future prospects are all matters to be taken into consideration.

Liability for payment of alimony awarded in a divorce decree ordinarily terminates upon the death of either the husband or the wife, or upon the remarriage of the wife. The court may limit the periodical payments of alimony to a specific period of time.

Many states have statutes authorizing the modification of a decree awarding permanent alimony, and such decrees frequently contain a reservation of jurisdiction to amend. In the absence of such a statute or reservation, the majority of courts hold that the court cannot modify the provisions of a decree of absolute divorce in respect of permanent alimony. The power to modify an allowance of alimony usually includes the power in proper cases to terminate finally the obligation to pay alimony. Where the award is in gross or for a lump sum, the court cannot generally modify the decree. It is generally held that the power of the court to modify a decree for alimony is not affected by the fact that the decree refers to or is based on an agreement between the parties to the action. Even where there are jurisdiction and grounds for a modification of an alimony decree as to future payments, there is a conflict of authority as to the court's power retrospectively to modify, cancel, or refuse to enforce instalments of alimony which have already accrued.

In order to warrant a modification of an award of alimony, it must be shown that there has been a change in the circumstances of the parties since the entry of the decree. The most frequent ground for modification is a material change in the financial circumstances of the parties. This may result from a change in the husband's or the wife's earnings, earning capacity, or assets. A general increase in the cost of living may be an important factor, although it may be offset by the husband's increased expenses. Remarriage of the husband is not ordinarily a ground for modification of an alimony decree. The remarriage of the wife, however, even where it does not automatically terminate her allowance of alimony, is frequently a ground for reducing the amount of the payments.

Although there are many remedies for the enforcement of decrees for the payment of alimony, the most common recourse is to have the husband committed for contempt of court. The ordinary writs, such as execution and attachment, are also available, and the circumstances may warrant a writ of ne exeat, an injunction, receivership, or a bond or other security. In contempt proceedings, the husband's inability to make the payments required by the decree is generally a defense, unless such inability is due to his own voluntary conduct.

§ 9:13. Property settlements, separation agreements, and support contracts.

Am Jur 2d References: Divorce and Separation, §§ 883–946.

Most jurisdictions recognize the validity of a separation agreement or contractual property settlement between a husband and wife, if the agreement conforms to the formal and other requisites of contracts generally. The parties may thus make a binding division of their property, determine their respective property rights, fix the amount which the husband is to pay for the support of the wife in lieu of alimony, and settle all claims between the spouses.

The validity of a separation agreement or property settlement depends upon the existence of a present separation of the parties or an actual cause or ground for separation or divorce. An agreement entered into to facilitate a divorce or as part of a scheme to obtain a divorce by collusion is void as contrary to public policy. For example, an agreement not to oppose or contest a divorce proceeding, pending or contemplated, cannot form a valid consideration for a contract between spouses. Property settlements and contracts for alimony are not invalidated by the fact that they are made in contemplation of a divorce and are not to be carried out unless and until a divorce is decreed, if there is no collusion in obtaining the divorce.

Where the parties to a divorce suit do not agree on the disposition of their property or the adjustment of their property rights, they may have a determination thereof in the divorce proceeding if they so request. In the absence of such a request, the jurisdiction of the divorce court to adjudicate the property rights of the parties depends upon the provisions of the statutes.

§9:14. Custody, support, and paternity of children.

Am Jur 2d References: Divorce and Separation, §§ 772–878.

The court in which divorce proceedings are pending has jurisdiction to determine who shall have custody of the children of the marriage and to make provision for their support. Difficult questions may arise, however, where the defendant is a nonresident or where the child is outside the state. Some courts hold that a child must have a domicil within the state in order to give a court jurisdiction to award its custody. In other states, the courts are deemed to have the power to award custody if they have jurisdiction in personam over both parents. If the court has jurisdiction to make an award of custody at the time the action is brought, it does not lose jurisdiction merely because the child is removed from the state before the decree is entered. There is a conflict of authority on the question whether the divorce court has jurisdiction to award the custody of children where neither party is granted a divorce.

In determining who shall have the custody of children, the court should take into consideration all the circumstances of the particular case and act in such manner as appears best calculated to secure for the children proper care and attention. The welfare of the child is the chief consideration. The wishes of a child who is sufficiently mature to form a rational preference as to its custody may be considered by the court, but in the absence of statutory provision to the contrary, the child's desire is not conclusive upon the court. Ordinarily the custody of an infant of tender years, or of a girl of more mature years, will be given to the mother if she is found to be fit to have custody and can supply a proper home. Immorality or misconduct of one of the parents may be an important factor in determining who shall have custody of children, especially where such conduct is reflected in the atmosphere of the home in which the child would be placed and would adversely affect its welfare. Where the circumstances warrant such action, custody of a minor child may be awarded to a stranger to the action, such as a grandparent or other relatives, the welfare of the child being the paramount consideration.

An agreement between parents as to the custody of their children is not controlling upon the court in awarding custody where the welfare of the children indicates a different disposition, although such an agreement may be considered by the court along with other factors.

Courts sometimes divide or alternate the custody of a child between divorced parents or other persons; and where custody of a child is awarded to one parent, it is the usual practice to insert in the decree a provision granting visitation rights to the other parent. Upon the death of the parent to whom custody of a child has been awarded, the right to its custody ordinarily reverts to the other parent without the necessity of a modification of the decree. It is the rule in most jurisdictions that divorce courts retain a continuing power to modify a custody order or to change custody of a child. An application for such modification is addressed to the sound discretion of the court and is usually based upon a change of circumstances after the decree affecting the welfare of the child.

The court in divorce proceedings generally has the power to provide for an allowance, in addition to alimony, for the support and maintenance of the minor children of the marriage. The amount to be allowed as child support rests within the sound discretion of the trial court. It depends largely upon the needs of the child and the financial condition and earning capacity of the father. The court should take into account the standard of living that the children would have enjoyed if the family had continued to live together. An agreement of the parties concerning the amount to be paid as child support is not binding upon the court, although the court may consider such agreement as one factor in reaching its determination. The court generally has the power to modify an allowance for the maintenance of children where there has been a change in the circumstances of the parties, such as a change in the needs of the children or the ability of the father, after the entry of the decree. Ordinarily an allowance for the maintenance of a child terminates when the child attains majority or marries. And the death of the parent ordered to make such payments usually terminates liability therefor, although the terms of decrees or statutes sometimes provide otherwise.

Whenever the issue is material to some other issue in a divorce suit, the divorce court has jurisdiction to determine whether the husband is the father of a child of the wife and whether the child is legitimate. For example, where the wife applies for an allowance for the support of the child and the husband asserts as a defense that he is not the father of the child, the court will determine the question of paternity.

§ 9:15. Foreign divorce.

Am Jur 2d References: Divorce and Separation, §§ 947–1001.

A divorce decree which is valid in the jurisdiction rendering it is generally valid in every other jurisdiction. This is true under the doctrine of comity with respect to decrees rendered in foreign countries as well as to those of sister states, and it is required with respect to the latter by the full faith and credit clause of the Federal Constitution. A decree of divorce granted within the United States by a court having jurisdiction to do so is entitled to full faith and credit in every other state. This is true even though the divorce was granted on a ground which would not be a ground for divorce in the state in which its recognition is sought, even though the ground of divorce occurred in another jurisdiction, and even though recognition of the divorce may offend the public policy of the state in which recognition is demanded.

The doctrine of res judicata as a bar and as a collateral estoppel applies to a valid final decree entered in a divorce proceeding in another jurisdiction. If such decree adjudicates a cause of action or an issue of fact, it operates as a bar, under the full faith and credit clause, to the relitigation of the same cause of action or the same issue between the same parties in another state. Even the issue of the jurisdiction of the divorce court may be res judicata where the parties were before the court and had an opportunity to litigate it.

In order that a court may gain jurisdiction to grant a divorce which will be entitled to full faith and credit in another state, there must be notice to the defendant, either by personal service of process or, if the defendant is a nonresident, by publication or other substituted or constructive service as required by the law of the divorce state and which meets the requirements of procedural due process. A divorce decree based on constructive service may be valid in other states with respect to the res of the action, that is, the termination of the marital status, and yet not be conclusive in other states on matters requiring jurisdiction in personam, such as alimony, property rights, and child custody.

If neither party had a domicile or residence in the divorce state, so that the court did not have jurisdiction of the subject matter, the decree is not entitled to full faith and credit and may be attacked in another jurisdiction, especially where the defendant was not served and did not appear in the action. However, an adjudication of jurisdiction of the res and parties in a divorce suit is binding in another state where the defendant appears or testifies in the divorce case and either admits the plaintiff's domicile within the state or fails to litigate the question of jurisdiction. An adjudication of jurisdiction is not binding, however, upon one who was not a party or privy to the foreign divorce suit.

The full faith and credit clause applies to a decree for alimony or child support or custody, if the court rendering the judgment had jurisdiction of the subject matter and of the parties. This is true whether the decree granted or denied alimony, custody, or support.

Although the full faith and credit clause of the Federal Constitution does not apply to divorce decrees rendered in foreign countries, the rule of comity requires that such a decree rendered by a court having jurisdiction will be given full force and effect in this country. The rule of comity, however, is subject to several qualifications. A decree of divorce obtained in a foreign country will not be recognized by comity where it was obtained by a procedure which denies due process of law in the real sense of the term, or was obtained by fraud, or where the divorce offends a public policy of the state in which recognition is sought.

IV. HUSBAND AND WIFE

§ 9:16. Status and relationship; disabilities of coverture, generally.

Am Jur 2d References: Husband and Wife, §§ 1–28, 418–426, 533–564.

Under the common law, husband and wife were one person, and that person was the husband. Upon marriage, the legal existence of the woman was for most purposes merged in that of the husband. This fundamental principle was the foundation of the common-law theory and rules as to the rights, duties, and disabilities attending marriage, until the enactment of the Married Women's Acts.

The relationship between husband and wife imposes on each of them certain legal marital duties and gives each of them certain legal marital rights. At common law, "consortium" was the term used to designate the rights of the husband arising from the marriage relationship, and "coverture" denoted the status and rights of the wife arising therefrom. However, consortium has come to mean the rights of both spouses resulting from the marriage. Consortium has been defined to include, in addition to material services, elements of companionship, felicity, and sexual intercourse, and the service, companionship, and comfort associated with the marriage relationship, to all of which both spouses have a right. It includes the wife's right to support and protection by the husband and the husband's right to the services of the wife, including the performance, without compensation, of household and domestic duties according to their station in life.

The husband, unless incapacitated, is the head of the family, not only at common law but also under the Married Women's Acts. This right is correlative with his duty to protect and provide for his wife and children. The authority of the husband as head of the family gives him the right, acting reasonably, to direct the family's affairs, to determine where and what the home of the family shall be, and to establish the matrimonial and family domicile. Under modern law the husband has no authority, apart from that as head of the family, over the person of the wife. Although the early common law gave the husband about the same powers of chastisement and restraint of the wife as he would have in the case of a child, it is now settled that the husband has no legal right to chastise his wife physically, or to restrain her person by confinement for the purpose of compelling her obedience to his wishes, or to compel her by a force to live with him, or to interfere with her social intercourse with her parents and relatives, or with her worship according to conscience.

At common law, a married woman was incapable of binding herself by contract, of acquiring or disposing of property without the husband's consent, and of suing or being sued alone. These disabilities and immunities have been removed, in part or entirely, in the American jurisdictions, by the so-called Married Women's Acts and other statutes, so that a married woman may contract, sue and be sued, and acquire, hold, and convey property in her own right free from interference by her husband. The courts differ on the question whether the Married Women's Acts are to be given a strict or a liberal construction with respect to the common-law consequences of coverture.

Under the common-law rule, the wife was under disability to engage in any trade or business on her separate account. The husband had an absolute right to all her earnings and the avails of any business carried on by her in her own name. This was not true, however, where the husband agreed that the earnings or profits should belong to the wife. The Married Women's Acts generally enable a married woman to carry on a separate trade or business or to perform services on her own separate account, and make the assets and profits of such business and earnings of such services her own property. Such statutes, however, do not entitle the wife to compensation for the performance of ordinary household duties. It is generally held that a husband can make a valid agreement with his wife to pay her for services rendered to him in his business and outside their home.

The common-law rule that a married woman cannot sue or be sued alone, without joining her husband, has been changed by the Married Women's Acts in the several jurisdictions. Some of these statutes provide that a married woman may sue and be sued as a feme sole or as any other person sui juris, while others merely enable a married woman to sue and be sued concerning her separate property.

§ 9:17. Property rights, generally.

Am Jur 2d References: Husband and Wife, §§ 29–54, 80–113.

Under the common law, the legal title to the wife's real property remained in her, but she could not convey it without the concurrence of the husband,

and the rents and profits of real estate owned by her at the time of marriage or acquired during marriage belonged to the husband. This right of the husband jure uxoris to the possession of the income from the wife's real estate continued until the death of either the husband or the wife, or an absolute divorce. The goods and chattels of the wife, owned at the time of marriage or acquired during marriage, became the absolute property of the husband under the common-law rule. And the wife's choses in action became the property of the husband if he reduced them to his possession by some act of ownership over them.

Today, under the Married Women's Acts, these rights of the husband in the property of the wife are generally abolished, as to both real and personal property. Under these statutes, a married woman owns and controls her property as any other person sui juris.

Estates and interests in property which are distinctive to the relationship of husband and wife, such as dower, curtesy, and estates by entireties, are treated herein under the topic Real Property.

§ 9:18. —Community property.

Am Jur 2d References: Community Property, §§ 1–107.

The community property system governing the property rights of husband and wife was not known to the common law, and in the United States it derives its existence from express legislation. Its background is the French or Spanish law, and it has been adopted in Arizona, California, Idaho, Louisiana, Nevada, New Mexico, Texas, and Washington. Under this system, property acquired by either spouse during marriage through his or her efforts belongs to the "community," to wit, the husband and wife equally. Community property usually includes all property acquired by either spouse during marriage, otherwise than by gift, devise, or inheritance. The community is in many respects analogous to a partnership in which the husband, as the head of the community, has the management and control of all community property.

Generally, all property owned by either spouse before marriage continues to be his or her separate property after marriage and does not become community property. Also, property acquired during marriage by either spouse by gift, bequest, devise, or descent is ordinarily that spouse's separate property. And the proceeds of the sale of separate property and property acquired therewith or with money which was separate property are usually classified as separate property. In some states, the fruits and profits of separate property accruing during marriage are community property, while in other states they are the separate property of the spouse who owns the source property. Generally, the earnings of either spouse are community property.

The succession to community property on the death of either spouse depends entirely on statutory provisions. Under some statutes, on the death of either the husband or wife, one-half of the community property remaining after the payment of the community debts belongs to the surviving spouse. Under others, the entire community property belongs to the husband on the death of the wife, but on the death of the husband, the surviving wife is entitled to only one-half of the community property.

§ 9:19. Contracts and conveyances by wife.

Am Jur 2d References:　Husband and Wife, §§ 132–229.

The general rule at common law is that a married woman is under disability to contract, and that a contract made by her while under such disability is void.　Being void, it cannot be ratified without a new consideration therefor. In most jurisdictions, however, the common-law disability of a married woman to enter into contracts has been generally removed by statutory or constitutional provisions, and she can contract as a feme sole or other person sui juris without the consent of her husband.　This removal of disability is still limited in some jurisdictions so that the wife can contract only in a particular mode, for particular purposes, or with respect to certain subjects or under particular circumstances.　The common-law disability of the wife to contract and the statutory removal of such disability wholly or in part apply to bills and notes executed by her, as well as to other forms of contracts.

The common law recognized exceptions to the disability of the wife to contract in cases where she was compelled by necessity to act as a feme sole, as where the husband was civilly dead, imprisoned for life, or permanently deserted her and departed from the state without providing support for her.

At common law a wife could not sell or otherwise dispose of personal property, because title thereto became vested in the husband by virtue of the marital relationship.　And a married woman could not make a conveyance of real estate at common law unless the husband joined therein, except that she could alienate or encumber her equitable separate estate where the instrument creating such estate gave her the power to do so.　Under the Married Women's Acts, however, a married woman can now transfer, encumber, or otherwise dispose of her personal property as any other person and as though she were a feme sole.　And the statutes generally empower a married woman to convey or encumber her real estate as any other person sui juris, without the joinder or consent of her husband, subject, of course, to his right of curtesy.

Some statutes limit the power of a wife to become a surety for anyone or from being a surety for her husband.

§ 9:20. Antenuptial and postnuptial property settlements.

Am Jur 2d References:　Husband and Wife, §§ 192–212, 276–319.

A property settlement or agreement between prospective spouses, commonly known as a "marriage settlement," was not enforceable at common law after the marriage of the parties.　Such agreements were enforceable in equity, however, and they are not only enforceable, but also favored, under the Married Women's Acts.　By an antenuptial agreement or settlement, the parties may define their property rights, including after-acquired property, and they may vary substantially the property rights that would otherwise arise on their marriage by operation of law.

A postnuptial property agreement or settlement between husband and wife, like other agreements between spouses, was not enforceable at common law. In equity, however, and under modern statutes, agreements of this kind are valid and enforceable.　The courts now recognize the validity of agreements whereby one spouse settles or agrees to settle certain property on the other, agrees to release his or her rights and interests, as surviving spouse or otherwise, in the estate of the other, agrees to leave certain property to the other by his or her will, or agrees to make a joint and mutual will.

A voluntary conveyance or transfer, by either party to a contract to marry, of his or her entire property or a large part of it, made without the knowledge of the other party and just prior to the marriage, is generally held to be a fraud on the marital rights of the other, at least where it is made with the intention of defeating such marital rights. Such conveyances are usually subject to attack under statutes relating to fraudulent conveyances.

§ 9:21. Transactions between spouses.

Am Jur 2d References: Husband and Wife, §§ 255–275, 320–322.

At common law, husband and wife could not enter into contractual transactions with each other, although equity, in certain cases, would enforce such agreements. Under the Married Women's Acts, husband and wife may contract with each other in any form. They may convey, transfer, sell, lease, or mortgage property to each other, and may either make a gift or incur an indebtedness to the other. However, as the relationship of husband and wife is a confidential one, transactions between the spouses will be strictly scrutinized to prevent fraud, overreaching, or undue influence by either party.

Contracts between husband and wife are subject to the usual requisites of contract law as regards the essential elements of a contract, including consideration. For example, a contract between husband and wife whereby one spouse agrees to perform specified obligations, already imposed by law as part of the spouse's marital duties to the other, such as an agreement by a husband to support the wife, a contract by the wife to render her husband the usual marital and domestic services of a wife, or a contract by the husband to pay his wife for services rendered as housekeeper, is without consideration and invalid.

§ 9:22. Agency of husband or wife.

Am Jur 2d References: Husband and Wife, §§ 230–247.

At common law, a married woman could not appoint her husband her agent, and he could not act as such. In equity, however, a husband could act as agent of his wife with respect to her equitable separate estate; and under modern statutes, by which a wife is rendered sui juris and capable of acting for herself, she may act through her husband as her agent. The general rules of agency govern the agency of a husband for his wife. The mere relationship of husband and wife does not create such an agency or any presumption thereof, although the agency may be implied from circumstances or he may be her ostensible agent, or she may be estopped to deny his agency for her, because of past transactions.

Under modern statutes and rules, a married woman may be authorized to act as agent for her husband, but authority in this connection will not be implied from the marital relation. Such an agency is generally governed by the principles applicable to other types of agency. As in other cases of agency, a course of conduct approved or acquiesced in by the husband may give rise to an ostensible agency. There is a rebuttable presumption that a wife has authority as the husband's agent to purchase necessaries for the family and in other matters relating to the care and management of the household.

§ 9:23. Partnership.

Am Jur 2d References: Husband and Wife, §§ 248–254.

At common law, there could be no partnership between a married woman and another, since she could not transact or engage in trade and since her husband was entitled to her personalty and to the usufruct of her realty. Under modern statutes, however, there may be a partnership between a married woman and a person other than her husband. Different conclusions have been reached as to whether a married woman, under the Married Women's Acts, may form a partnership in trade or business with her husband or may become a member of a partnership of which he also is a member. Some authorities recognize the validity of a partnership between spouses, while others hold that the wife may not enter into a partnership with the husband, even though she would have the power to do so with persons other than the husband.

§ 9:24. Duty of support; liability for debts of spouse.

Am Jur 2d References: Husband and Wife, §§ 323–386.

One of the most fundamental duties imposed by the law of domestic relations is that which requires a man to support his wife and family. This duty of the husband arises out of the marital relationship and continues during the existence of that relationship. This is a duty which generally the wife cannot waive and which survives even the husband's discharge in bankruptcy. The husband must provide the wife with those services and goods which the law calls necessaries and deems essential to her health, comfort, and peace of mind, including clothing, food, and medical, dental, and nursing attention, as well as a home, according to the means, ability, and circumstances of the parties and their station in life. The husband's duty to support his wife and family is not affected by the fact that the wife has a separate estate or independent means. The wife is under no duty to support the husband or their family. However, the wife is not generally entitled to reimbursement from the husband or his estate for her contributions to the support or maintenance of the family. And under modern statutes, a wife may, by contract, render herself liable for goods or services furnished for the support of the family, even though the husband continues under duty to support her.

The duty of a husband to support his wife terminates upon gross marital misconduct on her part and violation of her duties as a spouse, or upon divorce. And, as a general rule, there is no duty on the part of the husband to support his wife while they are living apart through her fault.

During cohabitation, a wife is presumed to have authority to bind the husband, as his agent, for necessaries for the support of the family and the maintenance of the household. Apart from any concept of agency, however, the husband is liable for necessaries furnished the wife or the family. He is liable for necessaries furnished the wife even after a separation of the parties, and notwithstanding a published notice that he will not be liable for goods purchased by the wife, where the separation was the result of the husband's fault and he has not made adequate provision for the wife's support.

The question of what constitutes "necessaries" for which the husband is liable under his duty to support the family depends upon the circumstances of the family. Such necessaries include food, board, lodging, clothing, and articles of utility and ornament suitable to the rank and condition of the parties. This may include domestic and household services in accordance with the means and social status of the family. Education of children suitable to rank and condition is a necessary. Medical services and care for the wife and family are obviously a necessary. And generally the husband is bound to provide his wife with legal services necessary for her protection.

The husband is liable for the general expenses of his wife, regardless of whether she leaves an estate or whether he contracts to pay for them. Generally, the common law imposes no liability on a wife for her husband's funeral expenses, although under modern statutes she may be liable therefor because of her contractual undertaking; and statutes in some jurisdictions render her liable therefor under certain circumstances.

Under modern statutes, the wife's separate estate is not liable for the debts of the husband, except where she has acquired the property from the husband in fraud of the rights of his creditors. At common law, the husband was liable for all the debts and obligations of the wife, including her antenuptial obligations. Under modern statutes, however, he is not liable for the wife's obligations.

The criminal responsibility of the husband for nonsupport or desertion is treated herein under the topic Criminal Law.

§ 9:25. Suit for alimony or maintenance without divorce.

Am Jur 2d References: Husband and Wife, §§ 387–417.

It is the rule in some jurisdictions that the courts have no original or inherent jurisdiction, in the absence of statutory authorization, to entertain an independent suit for separate maintenance or alimony, but can make such an allowance only as incidental to a suit for divorce or separation. In the majority of jurisdictions, however, the courts are held to have inherent jurisdiction to entertain, independently of any suit for divorce or separation, a suit by the wife for alimony, support, or maintenance out of the general estate of the husband. Such suits are authorized by express statutory provisions in some states.

Grounds for a suit for alimony, support, or maintenance, without divorce, have been held to exist where the husband fails, without just cause, to furnish suitable support for his wife; where he unjustifiably deserts or abandons his wife and neglects to maintain or provide for her; where the wife, by reason of the husband's misconduct, is justified in living separate and apart from him; or where the husband breaches a separation agreement. Generally, grounds that suffice for a divorce are sufficient to sustain an allowance of alimony or maintenance in an independent suit. There is a difference of opinion, however, on the question whether the existence of grounds for divorce are a prerequisite to such action.

Generally, any justification of the husband's neglect or refusal to support his wife is a defense to her suit for alimony or maintenance independent of a suit for divorce. His lack of income or estate, or the wife's separate income, is not generally a defense to such an action, although this factor may affect the amount of the allowance. Suits of this kind are of an equitable nature, and fault or misconduct of the wife, equal to or greater than that of the husband, which materially contributes to their separation, is a good defense. A wife cannot maintain such a suit where she voluntarily separates from her husband and leaves a proper home provided by him or refuses to accompany him to a new home, or where they separate by mutual consent or agreement. The wife's adultery or other serious misconduct or improprieties will constitute a defense to her independent suit for alimony or maintenance.

Generally, an independent suit for alimony or maintenance will not be entertained unless the parties are living apart, although some courts have awarded maintenance in such actions notwithstanding the fact that the spouses were still living under one roof, where they were not cohabiting as man and wife. Condonation of marital offenses is a defense to a suit for separate maintenance or alimony without divorce. Resumption of cohabitation terminates the wife's right to maintain such a suit on the ground of the misconduct condoned. A divorce decree terminating the marital relationship is generally a defense to any subsequent action for alimony without divorce, and a pending divorce suit usually has the same effect. Most courts regard a separation agreement between husband and wife, fairly entered into and making provision for the support or maintenance of the wife, a defense to the wife's action for separate maintenance.

A decree allowing alimony, support, or maintenance, without divorce, usually continues only for such time as the spouses are separated and during the lives of both of them. And as a general rule, such a decree is subject to be modified or terminated by future action of the court.

§ 9:26. Other actions by one spouse against other; torts.

Am Jur 2d References: Husband and Wife, §§ 515–532.

At common law neither husband nor wife could sue the other, this incapacity resulting from the legal unity of husband and wife. In equity, however, suits were maintainable between spouses for certain purposes, such as the protection of their respective property rights. The Married Women's Acts have generally extended the right of spouses to sue each other, although even under these statutes, the right is limited in many jurisdictions, and some courts limit such actions to suits with respect to property rights in the wife's separate property.

At common law, a tort committed by one spouse against the person or character of the other did not give rise to a cause of action in favor of the injured spouse. In some jurisdictions, statutes expressly provide for liability for such torts, while in other jurisdictions statutes expressly prohibit such actions. There is a difference of opinion on the question whether the Married Women's Acts make a spouse liable for a tort committed on the other. This conflict of authority results not only from differences in the wording of the statutes, but also from the diversity of views in the construction of such statutes. In jurisdictions recognizing the right of one spouse to sue the other in tort, actions for negligence between husband and wife have been sustained.

§ 9:27. Torts of spouses against others.

Am Jur 2d References: Husband and Wife, §§ 427–439.

The common-law rule is that both husband and wife are liable for the wife's separate torts that are not mixed with elements of contract.   For the separate torts of the husband, however, only he is liable.   The rule rendering both spouses liable for the wife's torts applied although the wrong was committed out of the husband's presence, without his knowledge or consent, or against his will.   The common-law rule holding the husband liable for the wife's torts committed without his participation has been abrogated in most jurisdictions.   Many statutes have abolished the liability of the husband for the torts of his wife by express provision.   Some statutes by their terms relieve the husband of liability for torts of his wife in which he does not participate, and others provide that neither spouse is answerable for the acts of the other.   In other jurisdictions, the husband's liability is held abrogated by statutes enabling a married woman to contract generally, to deal with property, and to sue and be sued as a feme sole.

§ 9:28. Torts of third persons; loss of consortium.

Am Jur 2d References: Husband and Wife, §§ 440–462.

At common law, the husband and wife had to join in an action for a tort on the person or character of the wife, and any recovery therein belonged to the husband.   The Married Women's Acts, however, have generally abrogated this rule, sometimes by express provision; and under such acts a married woman can sue alone in her own name for such torts.

At common law, a husband has a cause of action against one who wrongfully injures his wife and thereby causes him expense or loss of consortium. Whether the Married Women's Acts have abridged these common-law rights of the husband is a question on which the courts are not agreed.   One line of cases holds that this common-law right of the husband is not destroyed by the modern statutes, and that he may still recover for loss of consortium resulting from negligent injury to his wife, or at least for loss of her services. Another line of cases takes the view that under the Married Women's Acts a husband has no right of action for loss of consortium, with respect to either services or society, and that his right is restricted to recovery of expenses incurred by him by reason of the wife's injury.

At common law, the wife has no cause of action for loss of consortium of the husband.   Under the Married Women's Acts many jurisdictions permit a recovery by the wife for loss of consortium where the injury to her husband was wilful; and an increasing number of jurisdictions permit a recovery by the wife in such cases when the husband is injured by the negligent act of another, although many states still deny recovery where the injury to the husband was merely negligent.

§ 9:29. —Alienation of affections and criminal conversation.

Am Jur 2d References: Husband and Wife, §§ 463–514.

At common law there were two forms of actions available to the husband for offenses against the marital relation, one for enticing the wife away and the other for seduction. The former has evolved into what is commonly known as an "action for alienation of affections," and the latter into an "action for criminal conversation." Where such actions are recognized, they lie in favor of a wife as well as a husband, as a general rule, under the Married Women's Acts. Both of these actions are based on the loss of consortium. Injunction will lie in a proper case to prevent a third person from alienating the affections of the plaintiff's spouse. And an action lies for an executed conspiracy to alienate the affections of a spouse. Several states have, by statutes, abolished the right of action for alienation of affections or for criminal conversation, or both.

The gist of an action for alienation of affections is loss of consortium, which includes the loss of marital affections, society, companionship, and aid. Alienation by persuasion differs from alienation by adultery in that, in the former, loss of consortium must generally be proved, while in the latter it is presumed. The degree or depth of affection between the spouses before alienation by the defendant is generally material in an action for alienation of affections only as a factor affecting the amount of damages recoverable.

A parent may be liable for alienation of affections resulting from his malicious conduct, as where he wrongfully induces his child to leave his or her spouse. However, a stronger case of malicious and unjustified interference must be shown against a parent than against a stranger, to establish liability. A parent has the right, without liability, to advise his child in good faith with respect to the child's marital relations, to protect the child's welfare and happiness, even though the advice results in the separation of the spouses or the obtaining of a divorce or annulment; and where the parent acts without malice or recklessness, he is protected against liability even though his advice is ill-considered or based on misinformation. The courts differ as to whether and to what extent the protection afforded parents extends to relatives or kin in actions for alienation of affections.

A fundamental right flowing from the relation of marriage is that one spouse shall have exclusive marital intercourse with the other, and the act of a third person in committing adultery with either spouse is a tortious invasion of the rights of the other spouse, giving rise to a cause of action for criminal conversation. In an action for criminal conversation, it is no defense that the spouses were estranged or living apart, or that the defendant was led into the adulterous intercourse through the conduct of the plaintiff's spouse, instead of being himself the seducer, although these facts may be shown in mitigation of damages.

It is a defense to an action for alienation of affections or criminal conversation that the plaintiff connived at or consented to the adultery of the spouse and the defendant, whether the connivance was active or passive. Although there is some authority to the contrary, it is generally held that condonation and forgiveness by a husband, after knowledge that his wife has been guilty of criminal conversation, either expressly or by continuing to cohabit with her, do not preclude him from maintaining an action for criminal conversation against the seducer. And the same rule has been applied in actions for alienation of affections.

V. PARENT AND CHILD

§ 9:30. Nature and incidents of the relationship, generally.

Am Jur 2d References: Parent and Child, §§ 1–13, 46–49, 88–105, 139–147.

The relationship of parent and child gives the parent the right and duty to control, protect, support, and educate the child, and the child is under a corresponding duty to serve and obey the parents. By the common law, parental rights, like most rights pertaining to the family, were vested in the father alone. Upon the death of the father, the widowed mother succeeded to these rights and responsibilities. The modern tendency, however, is toward the equalization of the rights of the father and mother. The extent to which an adopting parent or one standing in loco parentis is subject to the rights and duties of a natural parent depends upon the statutes and policy of the particular jurisdiction.

The mere existence of the relation of parent and child does not establish any agency of the child for the parent or of the parent for the child. The parent, for example, cannot bind a minor child by contracts made in his behalf, nor can he dispose of property interests vested in the child. A parent, whether as natural guardian or otherwise, has no title to the property of his minor child, nor any custody or control over it. Where an infant is the owner of property, a guardian should be appointed to manage such property, and the extent of the father's right in this respect is to be preferred in the selection of the guardian. A parent has no authority to sell, pledge, or transfer his child's property, or to make contracts with respect to it. And a parent has no authority, unless he has been appointed guardian of the child, to compromise or release claims or causes of action belonging to the child.

A parent who is providing a home and support for his minor child is entitled to the child's reasonable and proper labor. He may avail himself of this by requiring the child to render services in the home or in the business of the parent, or by placing the child to work for others and recovering his wages. If a person employs a child without his parent's consent, he is liable to the parent for wages, unless the parent has waived this right. The right of parents to the services and earnings of their children continues during their minority and so long as the parents control and support them, unless the children have been emancipated. However, since this right is reciprocal to the duty of support, a parent who has abandoned his child cannot claim its earnings.

A parent may release his minor child from the bondage which the law imposes on it. Such release, which gives the child the right to labor for itself and to collect and control its own wages, is called "emancipation." A child is emancipated, of course, by operation of law on arriving at the age of majority. Emancipation by a parent may be in writing or by parol, and may be in express terms or implied from the parent's conduct and the surrounding circumstances, or it may arise from the conduct of the parent inconsistent with his claim for the further obedience or services of the child. An implied emancipation results where a parent impliedly consents by his acts and conduct for the child to contract for its own services. Emancipation may be either complete or partial, conditional or absolute. Thus, the parent may authorize his minor child to make its own contract of service and to collect and spend its wages, and still not emancipate it from parental custody and control. The marriage of a minor child results in its legal emancipation so far as parental rights and obligations are concerned. The emancipation of a child competent to support itself discharges the parent from obligation for its support, although the father's duty may revive if the child becomes unable to support itself.

An emancipation of a child is generally regarded as a mere license, gift, or indulgence on the part of the parent, which may be revoked, insofar as such revocation does not interfere with the rights of either the infant or third persons acquired during the period of emancipation. Such a revocation cannot affect the rights of either the child or a third person with respect to the child's earnings prior to the revocation.

A gift or conveyance from a parent to his child requires no other consideration than the natural parental affection. However, because of the relationship between the parties, transactions between parent and child are frequently attacked on the ground of undue influence or fraud, especially where there are other circumstances in addition to the parental relationship indicating a fiduciary relation; and such transactions are closely scrutinized by the courts.

§ 9:31. Custody, care, and support.

Am Jur 2d References: Parent and Child, §§ 25–87, 101–105.

At common law the father had the right, superior to that of everyone else, to the custody and control of the person of his child. The modern trend, however, sometimes as a result of statutes and sometimes because of judicial decisions, is to give the mother equal rights to the custody of the children of the marriage. And in the case of children of tender years, and especially of females, the mother is frequently given preference in contests over custody.

A parent has the right to exercise control and restraint over his child and to adopt such disciplinary measures for the child as will enable him to discharge his parental duty. This includes the right to chastise or otherwise discipline his child, provided he does not exceed the bounds of moderation. This right extends also to persons in loco parentis.

Since it is not an absolute right, but must yield to the best interests of the child, the natural right of a parent to the custody and control of his child is subject to the power of the state, and may be restricted and regulated by appropriate legislative or judicial action. In any court proceeding involving the custody of a minor child, the best interests and welfare of the child are the matters of paramount importance, and they will prevail over any other claim of legal right. This is true not only in controversies between the father and the mother, but also in controversies between either or both of the parents and strangers. The wishes of a child sufficiently mature to be able to formulate and express a rational opinion and desire as to its custody may be considered by the court in determining such custody, although the desire of the child is not conclusive on the court. A parent may be deprived of the custody and care of his child where it is shown that, from the viewpoint of the child's welfare, such parent is unfit to have custody.

A child cannot be bought and sold like a piece of property, and a parent is subject to obligations which he cannot transfer by his own act. Hence, a contract by which the parent, or one of them, has given the custody of a child to some other person will not ordinarily be enforced. This is especially true in the case of a parent who, having been compelled by poverty or unfavorable circumstances to surrender the custody of his child, wishes to reclaim it when his circumstances are improved. In some cases and under some circumstances, however, contracts for the custody of a child have been upheld as valid and enforceable. And it is generally held that the parents themselves, on separating, may make a valid contract for the care and custody of their children, unless the contract works to the detriment of the children. Some courts recognize the validity of a contract providing for the surrender by a parent of his child to another in consideration of the latter's promise to give or leave money or property to the child, where it appears that such contract promotes the welfare and best interests of the child, especially where the parent is not in a position to furnish proper care for the child. And even where such a contract is not binding when made, it becomes binding on the other party after the parent and child have fully executed their part.

Parents, and primarily the father, are under moral and legal duty to support and maintain their minor children. This legal duty of the parent is limited by his ability; and the extent of the duty is affected by many considerations, such as his health, his means, his station in life, and the special needs of the particular child. The parent's duty is to provide a minor child with necessaries. What constitutes necessaries depends upon all of the circumstances surrounding the family, their mode of life, social rank and condition, and the financial condition and capacity of the parents. Suitable shelter, food, clothing, medical attention, and education are universally regarded as necessaries. Modern authorities are inclined to extend the term beyond the bare essentials of physical existence, and to include the conveniences and amenities of refined life, according to the circumstances of the family.

The obligation of a parent who is able to support his child is not affected by the child's own income, property, or estate. Where the parents are not financially able to furnish adequate support, or where a trust instrument so authorizes, a court of equity may authorize the use of the child's separate estate for its support and education. The remedies available for the enforcement of the parent's duty of support depend largely upon the statutes in the particular jurisdiction. The decisions differ on the question whether an infant, suing by a next friend or guardian ad litem, may maintain an action to require a parent to make provision for the minor's support. Most states impose criminal penalties upon a parent for nonsupport of an infant. Where the parent has failed to perform such duty, he may be liable to others who perform it for him by furnishing the child with necessaries. However, as long as the child is under the direction and control of the father, it is in the father's discretion to determine what is necessary for it, and unless there is a manifest dereliction on his part, an outsider cannot substitute his judgment for the father's.

Funeral expenses incident to the burial of a minor child constitute a necessity for which the parents are liable.

Generally, when a child arrives at the age of majority, the parents are no longer under any legal obligation to support him; but when a child is of weak body or mind, unable to care for itself after coming of age, and remains unmarried and in the parents' home, it is generally held that the parents' duty to support the child continues as before. At common law an adult child is under no duty or obligation to contribute to the support of his parents. However, there are statutes in many jurisdictions requiring the support of indigent persons by their relatives, including their children.

§ 9:32. Tort actions affected by relationship.

Am Jur 2d References: Parent and Child, §§ 106–138.

In the absence of statute, the mere fact of paternity does not make a parent liable for the torts of his minor child. However, a parent may be liable for the act of his child if the parent himself has been negligent and his negligence was a proximate cause of the injury complained of. Such negligence on the part of the parent is shown, for example, where he entrusts a dangerous instrumentality to his child, or fails to control or restrain a child who he knows has dangerous tendencies. And the parent is liable also where he consents to or directs or sanctions the tortious act of his child. And a child may occupy the position of servant or agent of its parent, so as to render the latter liable for the child's torts under the general principles of master and servant or principal and agent.

A parent's right to the custody and companionship, and still more clearly, his right to the services and earnings, of his minor child are valuable rights, a wrongful injury to which by a third person will support an action by him. The simplest case of this kind is that where personal injuries are inflicted on a minor, rendering the child unable to serve the parent. In such case, in addition to the right of action which the child may have for the injury, the parent has a cause of action for his loss of the child's services. In such cases, the contributory negligence of the parent or the child may constitute a defense. The enticement or wrongful persuasion of a child to leave its parent is also a tort for which the latter may have redress at law. In the case of the seduction of a daughter, the same principles entitle the parent to an action, but this case is aggravated by the nature of the wrong and the injury to the feelings of the parents. In most jurisdictions the parent has a cause of action, enforceable either by him directly or by the personal representative for his benefit, for the death of the child caused by the wrongful act of another.

Although there seems to be a tendency to the contrary in some of the modern decisions, it is still the general rule that, with the possible exception of cases involving damage to property or property rights, tort actions are not maintainable between a parent and child. Under the prevailing rule, a child cannot sue its parent for a personal tort. This rule has been subjected to some criticism, and it does not apply where there is a master and servant relationship between the parent and child, or where the child has been emancipated. Upon principles and considerations of policy similar to those denying a child the right to sue its parent for a personal tort, it is held that such an action cannot be maintained by the parent against his child.

VI. ADOPTION

§ 9:33. Generally; contract to adopt.

Am Jur 2d References: Adoption, §§ 1–22.

Adoption signifies the means by which the legal relationship of parent and child is established between persons who are not so related by nature. By adoption, the child becomes the child of the adoptive parents to all intents and purposes. In this country the right or power to create, by legal proceedings, the relationship of parent and child between persons not so related by nature exists only by virtue of statutory provisions prescribing the conditions and procedure by which adoption may be effected.

The determination of the question of who may adopt another depends upon the terms of the statute authorizing adoption. Usually adoption statutes contemplate that adoption proceedings will be instituted by an adult who is a resident or inhabitant of the state in which the proceedings are instituted. If the governing statute designates procedure for adoption of a "minor child," there can be no adoption of an adult, and other forms of statutes have been construed to contemplate adoption of minors only. However, the use of the word "child" in an adoption statute does not necessarily preclude the adoption of an adult; and some adoption statutes clearly or expressly authorize the adoption of adults. In the absence of a statutory restriction to the contrary, a blood relationship between the parties is not a legal impediment to the adoption of one by the other. It has even been held that there may be a valid adoption where the relation of parent and child already exists by nature, and that a husband may adopt his wife as his child and heir at law. Such adoptions are frequently intended for the purpose of making the adopted person eligible to inherit property or to share in the distribution of a trust. An adoption decree, valid in the state where the proceedings are held, will be recognized for all purposes in other states.

Statutes in some states authorize adoption by contract, deed, or notarial act. In most states, however, a legal adoption can be effected only by a judicial proceeding in the method prescribed by law, although it is generally recognized that one who is legally competent to adopt another as his child may enter into a valid and binding contract to do so, and if such contract is not performed by the promisor during his lifetime, it may be enforced in equity in most jurisdictions against his estate at the instance of the intended adoptee. Such contract must, of course, be based upon a valid consideration. Courts which enforce such contracts against the promisor's estate will give the child the status of an adopted child entitled to the same right of inheritance to which it would have been entitled if the adoption proceedings had been legally consummated. Some authorities, however, take the view that the legal status resulting from adoption cannot be created except by compliance with the statutory proceedings, and that a contract to adopt not followed by the compliance with the statutory formalities, will not give the child any right of inheritance in the estate of the promisor. The failure of the child to perform substantially the duties of an adopted child, or to render services called for by the agreement to adopt him, may defeat his right in equity to enforce the contract in his favor against the estate of the promisor.

§ 9:34. Consent to and proceedings for adoption.

Am Jur 2d References: Adoption, §§ 23–82.

Consent of the natural parents to the adoption of their child is an essential requisite to the jurisdiction of a court to make an order of adoption under most statutes, unless the parents by their own misconduct, such as desertion or mistreatment of the child or failure to support it, have forfeited their rights as parents. At common law, it was generally recognized that the right to the custody of an illegitimate child was in the mother, and most adoption statutes recognize this right and require the consent of the mother to the adoption of her child. Where, however, the mother has abandoned or deserted her illegitimate child, her consent to the adoption is not required. Nor is the consent of the mother to the adoption of such a child necessary where she had voluntarily turned the child over to an agency and thereby relinquished control over it. In the absence of an acknowledgment of paternity by the father of an illegitimate child, and his marriage with the mother subsequent to its birth, the consent of the father to the adoption of such a child by another is not essential, and he is not generally entitled to notice of adoption proceedings. In some cases the consent of the father has been held unnecessary although he acknowledged the child as his and even where he married the mother after the birth of the child, although many courts hold that the father's consent is necessary in such cases.

In determining whether consent of both parents must be had to the adoption of their child after the parents have been divorced, the court must look not only to the statutes governing the requirement of consent of natural parents but also to the custody provisions of the divorce decree. Under the construction given some statutes, consent of both parents is not dispensed with merely because they are divorced or separated, even though custody of the child has been given to one parent who has consented. Many statutes, however, require only the consent of the parent to whom custody of the child was awarded by the divorce decree.

Under most adoption statutes, the consent of a natural parent to the adoption of his child by another is dispensed with where the parent has abandoned the child. Mere nonsupport of the child does not, however, constitute abandonment for this purpose, although the parent's wilful failure to provide support for his child is a factor to be considered.

Some statutes require the consent of a guardian who has been appointed for a child, as a prerequisite of the adoption of the child by another. And where a child has been placed in a foundling home, orphan asylum, or child care agency, consent of such institution has been held essential to the validity of a decree of adoption of the child. Most adoption statutes require the consent of a child who has reached a designated minimum age, as a prerequisite to the entry of a decree for its adoption.

On the question of the right of a parent to withdraw his consent to the proposed adoption of a child, duly given in compliance with a statute requiring such consent, there are differences of opinion, some of which result from variations in the provisions of the statutes.

A substantial compliance with the essentials of the provisions governing adoption proceedings is required to sustain the validity of the proceeding. To sustain a decree of adoption, jurisdiction must have been acquired by the court over the person seeking to adopt the child, over the child, and over the parents of the child, or, where the parents have forfeited their rights, over the guardian or agency having custody or control of the child.

In all proceedings involving the custody of a child or its adoption by another, the welfare of the child is the paramount consideration.

A decree of adoption, like other judgments of courts of general jurisdiction, is subject to collateral attack only for want of jurisdiction appearing on the face of the record of the adoption proceedings. Collateral attack on an adoption decree for alleged want or lack of jurisdiction over a necessary party to the proceedings is limited to the person or persons who were not served with notice actually or constructively and who did not consent to or appear in the proceedings. Those who participated in the proceedings, those claiming through them, or strangers to the proceedings, cannot attack the decree collaterally when the court rendering it had jurisdiction of the subject matter. Although it has been held that the failure of the court to obtain jurisdiction over the parent of the minor renders an adoption decree void and lays it open to collateral attack by any person interested, the trend of modern authority is that kindred of the adopting parent seeking to take by inheritance the property of that parent may not question the validity of the adoption decree under which the adopted child claims the right of inheritance, either by a direct or by a collateral proceeding.

§ 9:35. Effect of adoption upon rights and liabilities.

Am Jur 2d References: Adoption, §§ 83–116.

The legal consequences of an adoption are many and varied, depending upon the nature of the right involved and upon the terms of the governing statutes. For some purposes, the adoptive parents succeed to the rights and duties of the natural parents. Thus, they usually have the exclusive right to the custody and control of the adopted child and are charged with the corresponding duty of care and support. The relationship created by legal adoption is permanent and continues for life, and it is not affected by the death of the adoptive parent or parents. The natural parents' duty to support a child is terminated by its adoption by another.

In the determination of the right of an adopted child to succeed to interests in property which, by the terms of a deed, trust instrument, will, or other instrument, are limited to a "child," "children," "issue," or "heirs," provisions of adoption statutes fixing the rights of adopted children to inherit intestate property may be a factor, but they are considered only as aids in the construction of the instrument. The primary consideration is whether the person who executed the instrument intended, by the description used, to include an adopted child. In determining the right of an adopted child to take under a particular instrument, the question is not the right of such a child to inherit, but simply a question of the intention of the person who executed the instrument with respect to those who are to share under its provisions. It is generally held, in the absence of a controlling statute, that an adopted child is not entitled, on the death of the adoptive parent, to take property limited to the "children," "issue," or "heirs," of such parent unless the intention that the child shall so take sufficiently appears. And the determination of whether an adopted child is embraced within a class of persons described in a will or other instrument is generally determined by the law in force, and the attending circumstances existing, at the time the instrument was executed. And in construing the instrument in this respect, the court will look to the law of the state where the testator died, rather than to the law of the state where the adoption took place.

Rights of inheritance as defined by statutes of descent and distribution are generally modified by statutes regulating the effect of adoption. Statutes of adoption and those of succession, descent, or distribution are to be read and construed together in determining the right of adopted children to inherit from or through adopting parents or natural parents, as well as the rights of such parents to inherit from or through the adopted children. When an adopted child dies intestate without leaving a surviving spouse, children, or descendants, some courts hold that the right of inheritance from such child is in the natural parents, to the exclusion of the adoptive parents and their kindred. However, the modern trend is to construe adoption statutes as conferring upon the adoptive parents the right to inherit the estate of an adopted child to the exclusion of the child's natural parents. A similar difference of opinion exists as to the right of heirs or next of kin of adoptive parents to inherit from an adopted child.

An adopted child is, in a legal sense, the child of both its natural and its adopting parents, and it is not, because of the adoption, deprived of the right of inheritance from its natural parents, or from its natural grandparents or the natural kin, unless the statutes clearly so provide, as some modern statutes do. The right of an adopted child to inherit property of an adoptive parent who dies intestate is dependent upon the terms of the adoption statutes or statutes of the descent and distribution. This right is not a necessary incident of the relationship. In most jurisdictions, however, the statutes do give the adopted child the right to inherit intestate property of its adoptive parents. The statutes and decisions differ as to the right of an adopted child to inherit through its adoptive parents or from the kindred of such parents. According to the weight of authority, where an adopted child dies during the lifetime of the adopting parents, leaving children, such children are regarded as grandchildren of the adoptive parents and entitled to represent their parent and to receive from the estate of the adoptive parents what the adopted child would have been entitled to receive had he been living at the time of the parent's death.

VII. INFANTS

§ 9:36. Generally; capacities, disabilities, and liabilities.

Am Jur 2d References: Infants, §§ 1–57, 140–224.

While the word "infant" in its ordinary usage signifies a child of tender and helpless age, the words "infant" and "infancy" as used in law have a technical meaning different from their meaning in common speech. In the law, the word "infant" refers to a person who has not arrived at his majority as fixed by law, and the word "infancy" means minority or nonage. Majority is the age at which the disabilities of infancy are removed. Under the common law, infants attain their majority at the age of 21 years, and this rule remains in effect in this country except where changed by statute. Such statutes exist in several jurisdictions, and some of them empower courts to remove the general disabilities of minors on petition filed for that purpose. In the common-law states, an infant attains majority from the first moment of the day preceding its 21st birthday.

An infant is capable of taking title to real estate granted to him by deed and of receiving a gift and of acquiring contractual rights as a party to a contract or as a beneficiary. It is generally held that an infant is not capable, during infancy, of waiving his rights based on infancy.

The state has extensive power to provide for the protection of infants. This includes the custody of the infant, protection from neglect or ill treatment, provision for custody and support, and protection of the property and estate of the infant.

It is a general rule that an infant is liable for his own torts in the same manner and to the same extent as an adult if the tort does not arise out of, and is not connected with, a contract. Thus, an infant may be held liable for injuries caused by his negligence, and ordinarily infancy is not a defense in an action for fraud, assault and battery, trespass, conversion, or seduction. And the command or direction of the infant's parent or guardian is no defense to him, unless there has been actual duress. However, an infant is not liable for torts committed by his agent or servant under the doctrine of respondeat superior, since the appointment of an agent or servant by an infant is not binding upon him.

While ordinarily the age or mental capacity of an infant is immaterial in determining his tort liability, where a tort requires a particular state of mind, and an infant, because of his age or mental capacity, is incapable of forming such state of mind, he is not liable for the tort. And while an infant is liable for injuries caused by his own negligence, he is not generally held to the standard of the "ordinarily prudent man," but only to the standard of a child of similar age and experience. While it is frequently stated that an infant is not liable for his tort arising out of or connected with a contract, the mere fact that the infant's tort was connected with a contract does not always render him immune from liability for the tort. Tests for determining the infant's liability in such case is said to be not whether the tort in question arose out of, or was connected with, a contract, but whether the infant can be held liable for the tort without directly or indirectly enforcing his liability on the contract, or whether the cause of action is substantially or essentially tortious. It is the substance of the matter and not the form of the action as ex contractu or ex delicto which determines this question.

An infant may sue and be sued, provided he is properly represented by a legally authorized person. It is usually required that the infant be represented by a guardian, a guardian ad litem, or a next friend. When an infant is a party to an action, he becomes a ward of the court, and it is the court's duty to see that his interest is protected. If the infant is not represented by anyone who is fully charged with the power and duty of protecting his interests, it is the duty of the court to appoint a guardian ad litem for him. And any compromise of an infant's claim or right is usually subject to the approval of the court, whether the compromise was negotiated by the infant's next friend, guardian ad litem, or by his attorney.

§ 9:37. Contracts and conveyances of infants.

Am Jur 2d References:　Infants, §§ 58–83.

According to the earlier decisions under the common law, the agreements of infants were divisible into three classes: absolutely void, voidable, and valid. Agreements which were deemed clearly for the advantage of the infant were valid and binding, while those injurious to him were void. Agreements whose effect might be beneficial or might be injurious were held to be voidable at the election of the infant on arrival at majority. Similar rules were applied to deeds of infants. The prevailing modern rule, however, is that in the absence of statute to the contrary, an infant's contracts or conveyances are voidable, with the exception of certain limited classes of transactions. This modern rule is applicable to executed as well as executory contracts, and it applies where both parties to the contract are infants. And generally an infant's right to void his contract is not defeated by the fact that he is nearly of age or that he has been emancipated. Nor is such right affected by the fact that the contract was made by the infant and his father, or was made with the approval of his parent, guardian, or other adult relative.

An exception to the voidability of contracts and conveyances of infants is the case where an infant executes a deed or a contract which it is his legal duty to execute and which he can be compelled to execute by legal proceedings, as where he executes a bond pursuant to the requirement of a statute, or where he contracts to perform the obligation, imposed on him by law, to support his illegitimate child, or where he holds property in trust for another and conveys it to the beneficiary in execution of the trust.

It is well established that an infant is liable for the value of necessaries furnished him. His liability for necessaries is based not upon his actual contract to pay for them, but upon a contract implied by law, or a quasi contract. His liability in such case is generally limited to the reasonable value of the necessaries furnished to him, regardless of the agreed price.

Just what are necessaries within this rule cannot be precisely defined. The term "necessaries" is flexible and must vary according to the facts of each individual case. It depends on many things, including the particular circumstances of the minor, the actual need, and the use to which the purchased article is to be put. Aside from such things as are obviously necessary for the maintenance of existence, what are or what are not necessaries for an infant depends on what is reasonably necessary for his proper and suitable maintenance in view of his social position and situation in life, the customs of the social circle in which he moves or is likely to move, and the fortune possessed by him or by his parents. To be held liable under the theory of necessaries, an infant must be obliged to procure the things in question for himself, and articles are not necessaries for an infant if he has a parent or guardian who is able and willing to supply them, or if he already has a sufficient supply of such articles. The necessaries for which an infant is bound must be personal necessities, including the support of his wife and children, and do not ordinarily extend to articles needed for business purposes. Obviously, a proper education, medical and dental care, and legal services rendered the infant to protect his rights, are classed as necessaries under this principle.

§ 9:38. Avoidance or ratification of contracts.

Am Jur 2d References: Infants, §§ 60, 84–139.

The right to avoid a contract or transaction because of the infancy of one of the parties is a privilege which is personal to the infant. The other party to the contract or transaction is bound thereby so long as the infant adheres to it, and neither a coparty nor a stranger to the contract or transaction can question its validity because of the infancy of a party. If the infant dies before reaching majority, his legal representative (in transactions involving personal property) or his heirs (in transactions involving realty) may exercise his right of avoidance. The right to avoid a contract on the ground of infancy is not affected by the fact that the rights of third parties have supervened; and an infant's right to disaffirm a deed is not lost because his grantee has conveyed the property to an innocent purchaser.

It is generally held that an infant may avoid his contracts either during his minority or upon reaching his majority. Many courts hold, however, that the deed of an infant or other transactions by him relating to real estate, such as mortgages, leases, or contracts to purchase land, may not be disaffirmed by him during his minority.

Although it was stated in some early cases that the avoidance of an infant's contract must be evidenced by some act "of as high and solemn a nature" as the contract itself, the generally accepted rule is that any unequivocal act which indicates the present intention to avoid the former act is sufficient, and that there is no requirement that a disaffirmance of a contract by an infant shall be in any prescribed form. An infant's contract may be avoided by proper notice of an intention to disaffirm, by surrendering the thing received or demanding the return of the thing transferred by him, or by a plea of infancy when an action is brought against him on a contract. A release of a cause of action may be avoided by bringing an action upon such cause of action. A deed or mortgage of real estate may generally be disaffirmed in the same manner or by the execution of another deed to a third person. An infant cannot disaffirm a portion of a single contract or transaction and affirm the rest. Thus, where an infant buys property and, as a part of the same transaction, mortgages it for the purchase price, he cannot avoid the mortgage and ratify the purchase. And once an infant's contract or transaction is effectively disaffirmed, such disaffirmance cannot subsequently be repudiated. Such disaffirmance renders the contract or transaction void ab initio.

Upon avoidance of his contract or transaction, an infant is required to return the consideration received by him if he still has it in his possession or control. Thus, if an infant disaffirms a sales transaction, the purchaser may sue him for and recover so much of the purchase money as remains in his hands.

As to whether an infant's duty to return the consideration received by him, where he seeks to avoid a contract or transaction, is a condition precedent to an effectual disaffirmance, or is merely a consequence of an avoidance, not affecting its effectiveness, the decisions are in conflict. Under either view, however, it is generally held that an infant who disaffirms a contract or transaction cannot recover back what he has parted with under the contract or transaction unless he returns or offers to return the consideration received by him and remaining in his possession. As to whether an infant who disaffirms a transaction whereby he has obtained goods must account for the use or depreciation of the goods while in his possession prior to the disaffirmance, the decisions are not in agreement. Matters relating to the return of the consideration received by an infant where he disaffirms a contract are regulated by statutes in some states.

Upon avoidance of his contract, an infant is entitled to recover the consideration furnished by him, or any benefits paid under the contract.

The decisions are not in agreement as to whether an infant is estopped from avoiding his contract or transaction on the ground of infancy, where he made a false representation as to his age in order to induce the contract or transaction. Statutory provisions in some jurisdictions preclude an infant from disaffirming a contract where, on account of his own misrepresentations as to his age, the other party had good reason to believe him capable of contracting.

A voidable contract made by an infant may be affirmed or ratified, and such ratification may be made without a new consideration. If the infant's contract is void, however, any ratification must be based on a new consideration. Ratification, like avoidance, is a right personal to the infant, which can be exercised only by the infant himself or by his personal representatives at his death. Any effective ratification must come after the infant reaches majority. An infant cannot ratify his contract while his minority continues. The legal effect of a ratification is the same as though the agreement had been binding from the beginning. And a valid ratification cannot be withdrawn.

Generally speaking, ratification is a matter of intention. Ratification results where the former infant, after reaching majority, freely and without duress decides to let the contract stand, and definitely manifests that intention. The intent to ratify need not, however, be expressly declared, but may be inferred from words or acts. Any act which creates a clear implication of intention to ratify the contract constitutes a ratification. There is a conflict of authority on the question whether knowledge of the fact that one's contract or conveyance is voidable by reason of infancy is a necessary element of a ratification thereof after reaching majority. An express declaration affirming a contract or deed made during infancy is clearly a sufficient ratification. A promise to perform an executory contract made during infancy is held to be an explicit form of ratification. And it is generally held that the demanding or acceptance by the former infant of any part of the consideration, or the retention by him of the consideration for a substantial period of time after reaching majority without any expression of dissent, may be regarded as implying a ratification of a contract entered into during minority. And a ratification results where a former infant takes the benefit of a contract or transaction entered into during his infancy by selling, mortgaging, or converting to his own use property which he acquired under such contract or transaction, or where he otherwise exercises acts of ownership over such property.

As to whether the mere failure of a former infant to disaffirm a contract for some time after attaining majority operates as a ratification, the decisions are not in agreement with respect to the contracts executory on the part of the infant. It is generally held, however, that an executed contract, voidable on the ground of infancy, is deemed to be ratified by the failure of the former infant to disaffirm within a reasonable time after reaching majority. The reasonableness of the time for disaffirming a contract, whether executory or executed, must be determined under the circumstances of each particular case.

In the case of a deed executed by an infant, some authorities hold that the election to avoid the deed must be exercised within a reasonable time after the infant becomes sui juris. Other decisions take the view that the right to avoid a deed made by an infant, and to recover the land, continues until it is barred by the statute of limitations.

Statutes in some states require that the ratification of an infant's contract must be in writing. However, the conduct of the former infant after attaining majority may estop him from claiming the benefit of such a statute.

§ 9:39. Juvenile courts and delinquent and dependent children.

Am Jur 2d References: Juvenile Courts and Delinquent and Dependent Children, §§ 1–70.

All states have legislation providing for the disposition of delinquent, dependent, neglected, and abandoned children. Such legislation usually provides a complete scheme for the treatment of such children, and frequently includes the creation of special juvenile courts to deal with them. Some states have courts of domestic relations or family courts which have juvenile court jurisdiction. It is not the purpose of statutes creating juvenile courts to provide additional courts for the punishment of crime. The purpose is to establish special tribunals having jurisdiction of cases relating to the moral, physical, and mental well-being of children, to the end that they may be directed away from crime. Technicalities and formalities are largely eliminated from proceedings in juvenile courts.

The fundamental philosophy of juvenile court laws is that a delinquent child is to be considered and treated, not as a criminal to be punished, but as a person requiring care, education, and protection.

The jurisdiction of juvenile courts over proceedings arising out of the commission of certain proscribed acts by juveniles is frequently made exclusive by statute. However, some statutes creating juvenile courts do not take away the jurisdiction of the criminal courts to try juvenile offenders for crime.

Juvenile court legislation usually defines "delinquent" children. Generally, delinquent children within such statutes are those who have committed offenses against the law, or who are found to be falling into bad habits, or to be incorrigible, or who associate with vicious and immoral persons, or who are growing up in idleness and crime. And statutes dealing with "neglected" and "dependent" children usually include definitions of such children. Whether a particular child comes within the definition depends upon all of the circumstances of the case. The scope and operation of statutes relating to the custody and control of delinquent, dependent, and neglected children are limited to those within a specified age. Once the jurisdiction of the court attaches, it generally continues until the child attains majority. And so long as the juvenile remains within the age of which the juvenile courts have jurisdiction, such jurisdiction is not affected by the marriage of the juvenile.

Juvenile courts are generally empowered to determine the custody of infants found to be delinquent, dependent, or neglected. The statutes may authorize a court to order commitment to the care of probation officers, or to public or charitable institutions, or, in case of incorrigibility or actual criminal acts, to a reform school or reformatory.

Although proceedings in juvenile courts are generally held not to be criminal in nature, many of the constitutional guaranties protecting an accused apply also in such proceedings. Where delinquency proceedings may lead to commitment to a state institution, the following specific rights are recognized: written notice of the specific charge or factual allegations must be given to the child and his parents or guardian sufficiently in advance of the hearing to permit preparation; the child and his parents must be notified of the right to be represented by counsel retained by them, or, if they are unable to afford counsel, that counsel will be appointed to represent the child; and the constitutional privilege against self-incrimination. However, it is held that as juvenile court proceedings are noncriminal and do not involve any "jeopardy," they cannot give rise to any problem of former jeopardy. On the same ground, it is also held that the constitutional right to a "speedy trial" on a criminal charge does not apply to juvenile court proceedings. Also, it is generally held that constitutional guaranty of a jury trial and a public trial does not apply in such proceedings.

Statutes in many states make it a criminal offense to contribute to the neglect, or dependency, or delinquency of a minor. Generally, any act of commission or omission causing or tending to cause juvenile delinquency constitutes an offense under these statutes.

VIII. BASTARDS

§ 9:40. Generally; presumption of legitimacy.

Am Jur 2d References: Bastards, §§ 1–44, 60–73.

A bastard is defined as a person begotten and born out of lawful wedlock. The terms "bastard," "illegitimate child," and "natural child," are used interchangeably to connote a child born out of wedlock or born to a married woman under conditions where the presumption of legitimacy does not obtain. A child born to a married woman but conceived through her adulterous intercourse with a man other than her husband is an "adulterine bastard."

At common law the issue of a voidable marriage is considered legitimate, but the issue of an illegal or void marriage illegitimate. However, many statutes now declare legitimate the issue of certain or all void marriages. Such statutes do not apply, however, to the issue resulting from a meretricious cohabitation, where there has been no kind of marriage, either ceremonial, statutory, or common law. Nor do such statutes generally apply to children born before the invalid ceremony took place.

Many courts (but not all of them) hold that the relationship existing between the parties to a bigamous marriage is within the scope of statutes which legitimate the issue of void marriages. The dissolution of a marriage by a divorce decree does not affect the legitimacy of children born or begotten during the existence of the marriage relation. But since an annulment of a marriage has the effect of destroying the marriage relation ab initio, it may have the effect of making the issue of the purported marriage illegitimate, although many statutes change this rule.

At common law a bastard is said to be filius nullius, the child of nobody, or filius populi, the child of the people; and the status of such a child was extremely degraded and its rights severely restricted. The rigors of the common law in this respect have been substantially mitigated by modern statutes, however, and the general trend of legislation indicates increasing liberality toward the rights of illegitimates.

Children born in wedlock are presumed to be legitimate. This presumption is one of great antiquity, and under the early common law, if a wife had issue while her husband was within the four seas, that is, within the jurisdiction of the King of England, such issue was conclusively presumed to be legitimate, except upon proof of the husband's impotence; and even if the husband was beyond the four seas, he must have been away for so long a period before the birth of the child as to make it a natural impossibility that he could be the father. The rigidity of this rule has been tempered, however, and it is held in most jurisdictions that the presumption of legitimacy is rebuttable. This presumption remains a very strong one, however, and it can be rebutted only by very convincing evidence.

If a husband had access to his wife, so that by the laws of nature he could be the father of a child born in wedlock, it must be presumed to be his. Furthermore, access between husband and wife is presumed until the contrary is plainly proved. The presumption of legitimacy arising from birth in wedlock generally applies even where it is shown that conception occurred before the parties intermarried. In this case, however, the presumption of legitimacy is generally held to be rebuttable. The presumption of legitimacy extends to any child conceived in wedlock, notwithstanding it is born after the termination of the marriage by divorce or death of the husband. In such case, however, the birth of the child must have occurred within such period of time as to make it biologically possible that conception occurred in wedlock.

Proof of the husband's impotency is sufficient to overcome the presumption of the legitimacy of a child born to his wife; and undoubtedly clear proof that the husband was sterile at all times during which the conception could have taken place would have the same effect. In general, proof of access between husband and wife during the period within which a child must have been begotten is conclusive as to its legitimacy. However, the courts differ on the question whether proof of opportunity for sexual intercourse between the spouses renders conclusive the presumption of the legitimacy of a child born to the wife, or whether the presumption may be rebutted by showing that intercourse did not in fact take place.

Proof that the wife was guilty of adultery at or about the time when the child must have been begotten is not, of itself, sufficient to rebut the presumption of legitimacy of a child born in wedlock, although it may be sufficient if coupled with other evidence, such as proof that the husband was impotent or that he did not have access to the wife. The authorities are in conflict as to whether general reputation in the vicinage is admissible in evidence on the question of legitimacy. However, under the well-settled exception to the hearsay rule that evidence of family reputation, history, or tradition is admissible on questions of pedigree, the reputation in the families of the father and mother of a child is evidence as to its legitimacy. Serological blood tests are generally admissible on the issue of paternity, and such tests may be persuasive evidence to establish nonpaternity. Although not universally followed, and subject to some exceptions created by statutes and court decisions, the rule established in most jurisdictions where legitimacy or illegitimacy of a child born in wedlock is in issue is that neither the husband nor the wife may testify to nonaccess between them. A similar rule applies to declarations or admissions of either spouse tending to show illegitimacy of a child born or begotten in wedlock.

There is a difference of opinion among the courts as to the admissibility of evidence of the resemblance of a child to its putative father and on the question of the propriety of exhibiting the child to the jury for the purpose of showing resemblance. However, evidence that a child is of a different race or color than the mother's husband is admissible on the issue of its legitimacy or paternity.

The mother, if a suitable person, is the natural guardian of her bastard child, and, as such, has the right to its custody, care, and control, superior to the rights of the father or any other person. The principle that the welfare of a child should determine its custody is applicable to illegitimate as well as to legitimate children. And the duty to support and maintain an illegitimate child generally follows the right to its custody. Under the common law as applied in most states, the putative father owes no duty to support his illegitimate child. However, many statutes have modified the common law with respect to the duty to support bastards.

§ 9:41. Legitimation.

Am Jur 2d References: Bastards, §§ 45–59.

Legitimation is the act of giving the status of legitimate children to those who were not so born. The matter of legitimation of children is solely dependent upon statute, and the statutes of the several states differ widely in their terms. At common law, children born out of lawful wedlock could not be rendered legitimate by any subsequent act of their parents.

Statutes in some jurisdictions provide for the legitimation of a natural child in judicial proceedings. In most states statutes provide for legitimation of an illegitimate antenuptial child by the intermarriage of the parents, although some statutes impose the further requirement that the putative father must acknowledge the child as his own in order to effect legitimation.

In many jurisdictions statutes provide that the legitimation of a bastard may be effected by its recognition and acknowledgment by the putative father. Such statutes vary considerably in their language, some requiring that the recognition be in writing, and others providing for recognition in other ways. Some statutes merely require an acknowledgment of paternity by the father, while others specify that such acknowledgment must be general and notorious, or open and public. Some statutes provide that the father of an illegitimate child may adopt or legitimate it by publicly acknowledging it as his own, receiving it as such, with the consent of his wife if he is married, into his family, and otherwise treating it as if it were a legitimate child.

While the effect of the legitimation of a bastard depends largely upon the terms of the statute, generally speaking legitimation equalizes children born out of wedlock with legitimate children.

§ 9:42. Filiation or bastardy proceedings.

Am Jur 2d References: Bastards, §§ 74–132.

Statutes now exist in most, if not all, jurisdictions, providing for judicial proceedings, usually called filiation or bastardy proceedings, to establish the paternity of a bastard child and to compel the father to contribute to its support. Such statutes are generally considered to represent an exercise of the police power of the state for the primary purposes of securing the support and education of an illegitimate child and of protecting society by preventing the child from becoming a public charge. An incident of some such statutes is the imposition of criminal liability upon the father. In most jurisdictions filiation proceedings are held to be civil in nature, although in some states, where punishment of the father is an incident of the proceedings, they are held to be criminal or quasi criminal in nature.

The persons who may institute or maintain bastardy or filiation proceedings are usually designated by the statutes governing such actions. Such proceedings may generally be instituted by the mother of the bastard or by designated public officers. In some jurisdictions the illegitimate child, through its guardian or guardian ad litem, may maintain the proceedings.

Where bastardy proceedings are considered as being civil in nature or as partaking of more of the nature of civil than criminal proceedings, it is generally recognized that a settlement, compromise, or release of a bastardy claim entered into between the mother and putative father is a defense to subsequent proceedings by the mother under a bastardy statute. Some courts, however, hold that the parents cannot, by such a settlement, prejudice the rights of the illegitimate child.

§ 9:43. Rights under will, deed, or by inheritance.

Am Jur 2d References: Bastards, §§ 133–165.

Subject to some statutory restrictions, testamentary gifts to illegitimate children actually born or en ventre sa mere at the date of the will, if they are sufficiently designated, are valid and will be given effect whether the gift is to the testator's illegitimate children or to those of a third person.

Under the presumption that in disposing of property to his own "heirs" or the heirs of another, the testator means to designate those persons who would take in the absence of a will, such a gift is generally regarded as including illegitimates where by statute such persons are made heirs, but not otherwise unless the will further discloses an intent of the testator to include them. In the last analysis, the question whether illegitimate children are entitled to take under a will is one of true construction of the will and the intent of the testator, whatever may have been the rights of the illegitimate had the decedent died intestate. According to the rule generally recognized, a gift to "issue" imports, prima facie, legitimate children or issue; but where it appears from the terms of the will that the testator intended illegitimate children to be included, effect will be given to that intention.

The common-law rule is that the word "child" or "children," when used in a will, trust, deed, or other instrument, prima facie means a legitimate child or legitimate children unless the context of the instrument is such as to require a different construction, or the surrounding circumstances are such as to make the word import other than legitimate. The presumption that legitimate children are the objects of a testamentary gift to "children" yields to the testator's intention to benefit illegitimate children when such intention appears either by express designation or by necessary implication. The courts are not in complete agreement upon the effect of statutes permitting illegitimate children to take as heirs of their mother, although the trend of modern decisions under such statutes is to construe a testamentary gift in favor of the children of a woman as, prima facie, including her illegitimate children. An illegitimate child who has acquired the status of legitimacy by virtue of legitimation is generally held to come within the terms of a bequest, gift, or conveyance to a "child."

Under the English common law, a bastard could not be the heir of anyone, nor could he have heirs except the heirs of his own body. It is generally recognized that in the absence of statute conferring rights of inheritance upon them, illegitimate children are without capacity to inherit from or through either parent or to transmit inheritance except to the heirs of their own bodies. The common-law rule has been modified or abrogated in this country, so that now, in practically all states, an illegitimate child may at least inherit from its mother. There is a diversity of judicial opinion as to whether such statutes should be regarded as in derogation of the common law and strictly construed, or as remedial and hence liberally construed, although the trend of modern authority is toward the latter view. Statutes which provide generally for the distribution of intestate property of a deceased among certain classes of persons, such as "children," "brother," "sister," or "next of kin," without mentioning illegitimates, are generally construed to refer to the legitimates only, unless the language of the particular statute indicates a different intention on the part of the legislature. However, such terms as "children" and "issue," as used in a statute of descent, are not necessarily confined to children and issue born in lawful wedlock, but may include also such children and issue as are by law capable of inheriting. Statutes which make a child legitimate on performance of certain acts by one or both of the parents, as where they marry subsequently or where the father acknowledges the child to be his, have the implied effect of giving such child the rights of legitimate children, including the right to inherit from the parents.

The common-law rule that upon the death of an illegitimate intestate, his property will descend only to the heirs of his body, so that not even his mother or father could inherit from him, has been changed by statutes in most states. Such statutes frequently give the mother the right to inherit from her illegitimate child who dies intestate and without leaving surviving descendants; and the statutes frequently provide for inheritance by persons related to the illegitimate through his mother. Some statutes provide for inheritance from an illegitimate by its father, brothers, and sisters.

IX. INCOMPETENT PERSONS

§ 9:44. Generally; determination and restoration of status.

Am Jur 2d References: Incompetent Persons, §§ 1–30, 113–150.

The tests for determining insanity or mental incompetency vary with the laws of the several states and with the nature of the transaction or proceeding in which the issue of competency is presented. The criteria to be applied may depend upon whether the issue to be decided is the validity of a contract or of a conveyance, or a person's competence to care for himself or to manage his affairs, or his criminal responsibility.

Each of the states has its own statutes and rules governing lunacy proceedings and inquisitions into the sanity or competency of persons. These are special judicial proceedings, as distinguished from a criminal prosecution or an ordinary civil action. Such a proceeding does not determine any issue other than the status of the alleged lunatic, and it does not settle questions pertaining to property rights. Although a lunacy proceeding is governed by the laws of the state where it is held, the constitutional requirement of due process of law must be met, including proper notice to the person whose sanity is to be investigated, an adequate hearing at the inquisition, and observance of the person's right to counsel. In the absence of an affirmative statutory or constitutional provision to the contrary, however, there is generally held to be no constitutional right to a jury trial in proceedings of this nature. Most states have provision for judicial proceedings for the purpose of having a person who was once adjudicated insane declared competent and capable of managing his affairs.

Generally, an insane person has a legal capacity to sue and be sued, provided he has not been adjudicated incompetent and placed under guardianship. Actions by such incompetents are frequently maintained by a next friend or guardian ad litem. Where a person has been adjudged incompetent, however, and a conservator, guardian, or committee has been appointed for him, any action on his behalf must generally be commenced by such representative.

§ 9:45. Custody and protection.

Am Jur 2d References: Incompetent Persons, §§ 31–64.

The state is charged with the responsibility for the custody and care of insane and other incompetent persons. The state and its designated officers and agencies have the power to commit such persons to appropriate institutions for confinement and care, when this is reasonably necessary for the protection of the public or of the person so afflicted. The statutes of the several states contain provisions governing the proceedings for the commitment of insane or incompetent persons to institutions. Some states have statutes specifically relating to the confinement and treatment of sexual psychopaths and defective delinquents; and in some states provision is made for the sterilization of persons afflicted with certain serious forms of mental defects likely to be transmitted to offspring.

Discharge or release from confinement of one committed to an institution for the insane may be obtained on the ground of the recovery of sanity by such person, or because the original commitment was invalid.

In the absence of statutory provisions on the subject, the courts are not agreed on the right of the state to recover from an insane person or his relatives for his support while confined to an asylum or other state institution. Statutes in some states make the estate of an incompetent person liable for the cost of his treatment and maintenance in a public institution; and some statutes provide for liability on the part of the spouse or other designated relatives of such person.

§ 9:46. Contracts and conveyances.

Am Jur 2d References: Incompetent Persons, §§ 65–103.

Generally, the contracts and conveyances of an insane person made prior to an adjudication of his insanity are voidable only, and not absolutely void. The rule is different, however, as to contracts and conveyances made after an adjudication of incompetence. It is generally held that such contracts and conveyances made by an incompetent after the appointment of a guardian or committee for him are absolutely void. The validity of the contract depends upon the mental condition of the party at the time of making the contract, and not his condition before or after that event.

Not every substandard mentality or even every mental infirmity has the effect of rendering the afflicted person disabled for the purpose of entering into contracts and making conveyances. The law does not attempt to make a distinction between degrees of intellect; and neither average mental capacity nor reasonable prudence is required. A test frequently applied by the courts for this purpose is whether the person's mind has been so affected as to render him incapable of understanding the nature and consequences of his acts, or as otherwise stated, whether his mental powers have become so far affected as to make him unable to understand the character of the transaction in question.

It is generally held that a person who is so intoxicated as to have no knowledge of what he is doing or the effect thereof does not have the capacity to make a valid contract or deed, and that a contract or conveyance made by him while he is in such condition is voidable to the same extent as that of an insane person.

A deed or contract of an incompetent which is an absolute nullity cannot be ratified and need not be disaffirmed. However, where a deed or contract of a person is merely voidable because of his insanity when it was made may be disaffirmed or ratified by such person on his recovery of competency. It is not necessary that the ratification be made by expressed words; it may be evidenced by any intelligent act or conduct of the party, made with the full knowledge of the facts, which clearly shows an intention to be bound by the contract; and the acceptance of the benefits of an agreement after recovery of sanity may amount to a ratification.

A person who lacks capacity to contract or convey is equally incompetent to avoid or affirm his contract or conveyance. A party to a contract may not set up the insanity of the other party for the purpose of avoiding the contract; nor may a stranger or volunteer avoid contracts on the ground of the incompetency of a party. The right to avoid a contract or conveyance may be exercised in behalf of an incompetent by his guardian or committee or by his heirs, or executor or administrator, depending upon the nature of the interest to be furthered through avoidance.

An incompetent person is liable for necessaries furnished him in good faith and under circumstances which justify their sale to such person. It is generally held that liability for necessaries is quasi-contractual in character, based upon a contract implied by law for the payment of the reasonable value of the necessaries.

§9:47. Torts.

Am Jur 2d References: Incompetent Persons, §§ 104–112.

According to the prevailing rule, an insane person is liable for an injury caused by his tortious act, committed while he was insane, where malice or intent to injure is not a necessary element of the tort. This is the common-law rule and is contrary to the civil-law rule. Under this principle, an insane person may be held liable for assault and battery, for trespass or conversion, and for injury resulting from his negligence. As some intent to injure is an element of malicious prosecution, an insane person is not liable therefor. As to libel and slander, some authorities hold that insanity is a good defense to such an action, while other courts hold that insanity is not in itself a defense to an action for libel or slander, but that insanity will defeat a recovery in a case where malice is an essential element of the cause of action.

X. GUARDIANSHIP

§9:48. Generally; appointment and tenure.

Am Jur 2d References: Guardian and Ward, §§ 1–60.

A guardian is a person appointed to protect, manage, and control the person, property, and rights of a minor or incompetent person. One appointed by the court to control the property, but not the person, of a minor or incompetent is sometimes called a curator or conservator.

One may be treated as a constructive guardian, or guardian de son tort, and may be compelled to account for the property as if he were a guardian in fact, where, being a guardian by nature, he takes the possession and administration of his ward's property, or where, acting as a mere stranger or wrongdoer, he assumes to take possession and control of, and receives the rents, income, and profits from, the property of an infant or incompetent. The same result may follow as to one purporting to act as guardian under a void appointment.

Natural guardianship of children is vested in their parents and in the survivor of them. A natural guardianship confers only the right to the custody of the person of the ward, and such a guardian has no right of custody or control of the property of the ward, unless such right is conferred by statute. Testamentary guardians are those appointed by the deed or last will of the parent. Such guardianship is the creature of statute. Since the welfare of an infant ward is the primary consideration in the appointment of the guardian, it is generally held that the court, exercising its sound discretion, is not bound under all circumstances to appoint the person named in the will of the infant's parent as testamentary guardian, but such person will be given preference for the appointment if he is qualified and his appointment will not be detrimental to the child.

Provision for the appointment of guardians or committees for insane and other incompetent persons is made by statutes in the several states. The protection of the property of the ward is one of the main objects of such statutes, although they not infrequently authorize guardianship of both the person and the estate of the ward. The mental condition which will justify the appointment of a guardian or committee for an adult is discussed in § 44, supra. It may be said generally that, to warrant such appointment, it is not necessary to show complete lunacy or idiocy, and that it is sufficient to show that the person in question is incapable of managing his person, property, or affairs and that there is such mental impairment as renders him incapable of understanding and acting in the ordinary affairs of life. Mere lack of good business sense, impairment of memory, advanced age, or physical infirmity does not, alone, authorize the appointment of a guardian. Under the laws of some states, there must be a prior adjudication of incompetence as a basis for the appointment of a guardian or committee.

The jurisdiction to appoint guardians was originally exercised by courts of chancery, and courts exercising equity powers still possess general jurisdiction to appoint guardians of infants and incompetents where there is no statute designating other courts for that purpose. However, jurisdiction of matters relating to guardianships is now commonly conferred on probate courts, Orphans' Courts, Surrogates' Courts, and other designated courts.

Subject to statutory restrictions, the selection of the person to be appointed guardian is a matter which is committed largely to the discretion of the appointing court. The parents of a minor and close relatives of mental incompetents are generally given preference in selecting a guardian or committee. An infant over the age of 14, or of such other age as designated by statute, is usually given the right to choose his own guardian. However, the best interests of the child is always the paramount consideration in the selection of a guardian, to which the wishes of even parents must sometimes yield.

The guardianship for a minor terminates when the ward attains majority, and the guardianship of an incompetent person may be terminated when it is no longer necessary by reason of the ward's restoration to competency. The relationship of guardian and ward is necessarily terminated by the death of either the guardian or the ward. It is generally held that the marriage of an infant ward, whether male or female, terminates the guardianship as to his person. And marriage is generally held to terminate the guardianship of the estate of a female ward but not that of the male ward. The power to remove a guardian for cause, such as misbehavior or unfitness, is generally vested in the court making or approving the appointment.

§ 9:49. Powers, duties, and liability of guardian.

Am Jur 2d References: Guardian and Ward, §§ 61–159, 187–217.

The particular powers and duties of guardians are ordinarily outlined in the statutes and must be exercised and performed in accordance therewith.

The duties and trust of the guardian are administered under the control of the court.

Guardianship is a trust of the highest and most sacred character. The guardian is not permitted to gain any personal profit or advantage from dealings with the ward or with the latter's estate or affairs. As a trustee, the guardian is required to bear the loss if he has been guilty of negligence in keeping, caring for, or disposing of the ward's property, whereby the estate has incurred loss. And the guardian may be personally liable for damages or injuries resulting from a tort committed in the administration of the ward's estate.

Except under certain circumstances in which the controversy is between the parent and the guardian appointed by a court, the guardian of a minor is entitled to the custody of the ward and has such authority over him as is necessary to the proper execution of his duties. To the person of the ward, he stands in loco parentis. The guardian's duty in this respect requires that he look to the ward's health, education, and support. As a general rule, the guardian or committee of an insane or incompetent person has the right to the custody and control of the person of his ward. It is the duty of the guardian or committee to provide support and maintenance for the ward and the latter's family out of the ward's estate.

A guardian may use the interest and profits of his ward's estate for the support and education of the ward, except where the guardian is the parent of the ward or stands in loco parentis or is otherwise under obligation to support the ward from his own estate. In a proper case and where such is judicious and necessary, a guardian may expend the principal of the ward's estate for the support and maintenance of the latter.

Although it is not generally necessary for a guardian to obtain prior authorization by the court to expend the income from a ward's estate for his maintenance, it is a prudent practice to procure such authorization where there is any doubt as to the propriety of such expenditure. With respect to the use of the principal of a ward's estate for his maintenance or education, some courts hold that such expenditures are proper without prior authorization of the court, if the expenditures were judicious and proper and would have been authorized by the court had previous application been made. Other courts take the view that the principal of a ward's estate may not be invaded for his support without previous authorization by the court. Guardians usually have the power and duty to pay, from the funds in their hands, all just debts which are due from their wards. And the guardian may make charitable gifts from his ward's estate if he can show that the ward probably would have made the same gifts had he been competent to do so. And in proper cases noncharitable gifts may be made by a guardian from the principal or income of his ward's estate.

The rule which prohibits a guardian from risking his ward's funds in speculative investments applies most strongly against his engaging those funds in any kind of business. If it is necessary to continue temporarily a going business enterprise which the ward has inherited, the guardian should obtain authorization from the court before risking the ward's funds in such a venture.

It is the duty of a guardian to invest, in such a manner as to produce an income, funds of the ward which come into his possession and which are not needed for the ward's maintenance. Unless it is otherwise provided by statute, a guardian may make investments of his ward's funds without an order of court, provided the investment is made prudently, in good faith, and in something of a character proper for investment of trust funds. In some jurisdictions, however, the risk assumed by a guardian is such that it is advisable for him to obtain the court's approval before making such investments. In any event, the guardian must act in absolute good faith and with reasonable diligence to insure the safety of the investment. With respect to the retention or disposal of property coming into his hands as assets of the estate, the guardian must exercise reasonable care and diligence. The character of the investments which a guardian may make of his ward's estate is generally governed by statutes. The strict early rule that permitted no investment of such funds except in real-estate mortgages or government funds has generally been relaxed. Investment in the stock or bonds of private corporations is now frequently permitted if made in good faith and in the exercise of sound discretion.

Guardians are not bound to transact personally such business connected with the trust as prudent persons, acting for themselves, would ordinarily transact through agents. Thus, a guardian may employ an attorney for the collection and preservation of assets belonging to his ward's estate, a broker to procure securities for investment, or a real-estate agent to assist in the sale of the ward's property.

A guardian of an infant or incompetent is generally without power to bind the ward or his estate by any contract. Even if the contract is one which is proper or necessary for him to make in the execution of the trust, the liability thereunder rests upon the guardian personally, and not upon the ward or the estate of the ward. However, if the contract is a proper one, the guardian is protected by his right to be reimbursed from the assets of the ward's estate. In some jurisdictions the guardian may by contract bind the ward's estate where the agreement is made under the direction of the court, or where a statute so provides. Also, contracts for necessaries, such as care and support of the ward, are generally held to be binding upon the ward's estate.

It is the prevailing view that a guardian may not waive, surrender, or impair the legal rights of the ward or impose any legal burden thereon, by estoppel or otherwise, or exercise purely personal elective rights of the ward. Thus, a guardian or committee cannot make an election in behalf of the ward to take under or against the will of a deceased person, the approval of the court being required for such an election. As an incident of the duty of the guardian to enforce his ward's rights and collect claims due him, a guardian generally has the power to compromise claims on behalf of the ward.

In the management of the ward's personal estate, a guardian, if he exercises proper diligence and discretion, may sell the personal property of his ward or pledge such property for a debt properly incurred for the ward. The guardian does not have such powers, however, with respect to the real property of the ward. He has the right to take possession of such real estate, to manage the same, and, in proper circumstances, to execute a lease thereof. But he may not sell, exchange, or agree to a voluntary partition thereof in the absence of statute providing therefor. Nor, in the absence of statute, may he execute a mortgage or by his acts or agreement impose any lien or encumbrance on the realty of the ward.

§ 9:50. Accounting and compensation of guardian.

Am Jur 2d References: Guardian and Ward, §§ 162–186.

The law casts upon the guardian the duty of rendering a true and full accounting and requires the utmost good faith therein. The court having jurisdiction may compel such an accounting and when the account is rendered may allow or disallow the items therein. The usual practice requires an annual account at the end of every year and a final account when the guardianship is closed. The duty of the guardian with respect to accounting cannot be affected by any act or agreement of the ward during his minority or incompetence; but when a minor ward comes of age he is legally competent to adjust his affairs with the guardian, and if a settlement of the account is made between them without fraud or abuse of the guardian's possession of influence over the ward, it is binding upon both parties.

A guardian is chargeable in his accounts not only with all the estate of the ward, real and personal, and the proceeds thereof which actually came into his hands, but also with money or property lost by reason of his negligence or failure of duty, or which he might have recovered or received by the exercise of reasonable diligence. The guardian is always chargeable with interest actually received by him; and if he negligently permits money of the ward to remain uninvested, or invests it so negligently as to obtain no income, he is accountable for interest thereon. And the account of a guardian will be charged for losses resulting from his investment of the ward's funds in a negligent or improper manner.

A guardian is entitled to credit himself with all expenses reasonably and properly incurred in the performance of his trust. He is also entitled to credit on his account for losses of the ward's funds or property which have occurred without negligence or improper action on his part. Expenditures by the guardian for the maintenance and education of the ward are clearly a proper credit on the guardian's account.

A guardian who has faithfully and properly discharged the duties of his trust is usually entitled to compensation from the ward's estate for his services, generally in an amount based upon a regular percentage fixed by statute. Where a guardian dies before the complete administration of the trust estate, it has been held that his estate is, in the discretion of the court, entitled to reasonable compensation for services performed by him.

*

EQUITY

I. NATURE AND BASIS OF EQUITY JURISPRUDENCE

II. GROUNDS FOR AND PREREQUISITES OF RELIEF IN EQUITY; DEFENSES

III. NATURE AND FORMS OF RELIEF IN EQUITY

I. NATURE AND BASIS OF EQUITY JURISPRUDENCE

§ 10:1. Origin and development of equity.

Am Jur 2d References: Equity, §§ 1–18, 177, 178.

Equity is a system of jurisprudence developed by the English Chancery to mitigate the rigidity and limitations of the common law and to provide remedies where none existed at law or where the legal remedy was inadequate. From an early date in England the King's Council acted as a supreme supervisory court, granting relief in cases where no adequate remedy existed at common law and where injustice would otherwise result. As the chief law member of the Council, the chancellor gradually took over these special cases, and eventually Chancery became a separate court, with complete jurisdiction of such matters. From this point Chancery began the development of rules and principles of equity jurisprudence and jurisdiction of universal application, in contrast with the original practice of desultory and uncertain remedies in particular cases.

The American states inherited the English system of equity jurisprudence along with the English common law. In the beginning equity and law were generally administered by separate tribunals, courts of law and courts of chancery. Even where the same courts had jurisdiction of both law and equity causes, the two classes of proceedings were usually kept separate, one on the law side or law docket and the other on the equity side or equity docket. And this is still the practice in some states. The two systems have become so blended together, however, as to be one for most purposes. Courts universally apply equitable principles in actions at law. The trend to abolish the distinction between actions at law and suits in equity has steadily progressed to the point reached in Federal Rules of Civil Procedure, under which there is one form of action, known as a "civil action." However, equitable principles are still identified and characterized as such, and their application and effect are governed by the equity jurisprudence under which they were developed.

§ 10:2. Rights protected in equity; personal, contract, and property rights; forfeitures and penalties.

Am Jur 2d References: Equity, §§ 52–85.

The availability of equitable relief in a particular case depends more upon the need for such relief and the inadequacy of any legal remedies than upon the classification of the right sought to be protected or of the wrong to be prevented. Equity will not ordinarily afford relief against a tort or a crime, leaving such matters to be determined in ordinary actions at law or in criminal prosecutions. However, the fact that a tort or a crime is involved will not preclude relief in equity if the ordinary legal or criminal processes will not afford adequate protection or relief to the complainant.

The main concern of equity has always been with property rights. If there is no adequate remedy at law, equity will take jurisdiction of a suit which seeks the protection of property rights, whether the property is real estate or personalty. While ordinarily the remedy for an intrusion or trespass upon land is by an action at law in the form of ejectment or trespass, rather than a suit in equity, a court of equity will interpose for the purpose of securing to the landowner the enjoyment of his property free from injury or molestation, where this is necessary for the full protection of his rights. And while disputes concerning the title to the property are not ordinarily within the jurisdiction of equity, yet if a ground for equitable interposition is disclosed, the court in disposing of the case may determine the question of title.

Some courts have stated or suggested that equity is concerned only with rights of property and has no jurisdiction where merely personal rights are involved. However, even these courts, in the particular cases before them, have usually found a way to grant equitable relief on the basis of some fictitious property right. And it is generally recognized now that equity jurisdiction will be exercised in appropriate instances for the protection of personal rights. Equitable relief is frequently granted for the preservation of health and physical comfort and for the protection of reputation, civil rights and liberties, and the right of privacy.

While the remedy at law is generally adequate in case of a nonperformance of a contract, a court of equity, in the furtherance of justice, may compel a party to a contract to do that which ought to be done. Thus, a court of equity may decree that a party perform obligations of a contract, express or implied; and the jurisdiction of equity to grant specific performance of contracts, or to reform or cancel them in a proper case, is well settled.

Forfeitures and penalties are subject to the jurisdiction and scrutiny of courts of equity. The general principle that penalties and forfeitures are looked upon with disfavor by the law is especially applicable in equity. A court of equity is extremely reluctant to enforce any forfeiture or penalty, and it will grant affirmative relief against the same where equity and good conscience demand it. However, equity will not generally interpose to mitigate or grant relief from a forfeiture or penalty imposed by statute.

§ 10:3. Maxims and basic principles of equity.

Am Jur 2d References: Equitable Conversion, §§ 1–27; Equity, §§ 118–151.

A court of equity has no more right than has a court of law to act on its own motion of what is right in a particular case; it must be guided by the established rules and precedents of equity jurisprudence. Although equity will not deny relief simply because there is no precedent for it, it is its duty to follow those principles which have been established by precedent, except where the application thereof would compel an unjust or unreasonable result. It is the function of equity to provide adequate remedies for legal rights, and not to create new legal rights.

Many of the basic principles of equity jurisprudence have been epitomized in the form of maxims. In addition to the maxims individually discussed below, the courts frequently refer to these maxims: Equity delights in amicable adjustments; a court of equity ought to do justice completely and not by halves; a court of equity will not do or require the doing of a vain or useless thing.

"Equity will not suffer a wrong to be without a remedy" is one of the most important maxims of equity, underlying the very origin and foundation of equity jurisprudence. It was to supply the deficiencies of the remedies afforded by the common law that equity jurisdiction was originally instituted.

"Equity acts in personam, not in rem." As implied by this maxim, the remedies administered by courts of equity are generally made effectual by decrees operating in personam. Thus, by a decree restraining a party from prosecuting an action at law or from enforcing a judgment of a court of law, the court of equity does not assume to restrict the power of the court of law or to overthrow its judgment, but merely to control the conduct of the party.

"Equity follows the law" is a maxim susceptible of various applications. It sometimes means that equity adopts and follows the rules of law in all cases to which those rules may in terms be applicable; or it may mean that equity, in dealing with cases of an equitable nature, adopts and follows the analogies furnished by rules of law. The purpose of the maxim is to keep courts of equity within the course of established rules and precedents, and in applying equitable remedies, to avoid upsetting established rules of law.

"Equity is equality, and equality is equity." This maxim expresses the basic spirit of equity. Instances of its application are found in the law of contribution among persons jointly liable, the marshaling of assets, partition of real property, and the abatement of legacies.

"Equity regards as done that which ought to be done." This maxim means that in determining a dispute between litigants, a court of equity regards and treats as done that which, in fairness and good conscience, ought to be or should have been done. If, for instance, by means of fraud or misrepresentation, a litigant has prevented acts from being done, equity treats the case as though the acts had in fact been performed. The court considers as actually having been performed acts which have been directed or which have been agreed or intended to be done. The maxim is the basis of the doctrine of equitable conversion, under which money which has been covenanted or devised to be laid out in land is treated as real estate in equity and descends to the heir, and conversely, land which has been contracted or devised to be sold is considered and treated as money. A conveyance which ought to have been made may be treated as having been made.

"Equity regards substance and intent, rather than form," is a maxim expressing the direct and realistic approach of equity, and means that the rights of parties are not to be sacrified to the mere letter or by technicalities, but that the intent or spirit of a contract or transaction will be the paramount consideration in equity.

"Equity aids the vigilant and diligent" means that equity may refuse relief to one who has been dilatory or wanting in diligence in prosecuting his cause of action or who has slept on his rights. The maxim has been employed to deny relief to those who neglect to take care of themselves and who thereby suffer losses which ordinary care and diligence would have prevented. It is the basis of the doctrine of laches, discussed in a subsequent section of this topic.

"He who seeks equity must do equity" is one of the most frequently invoked maxims and is a sort of golden rule of equity. The principle is applicable in any kind of equitable proceeding. One who comes into a court of equity seeking equitable relief must offer to do equity and will be required by the court to do equity as a condition to the granting of the remedy or relief sought.

"He who comes into equity must come with clean hands" is an ancient and favorite precept of courts of equity and is given wide and frequent application in a great variety of situations. The principle underlying this maxim is that a litigant may be denied relief by a court of equity on the ground that his conduct has been inequitable, unfair, dishonest, or deceitful with respect to the matter in controversy. It means that the court will not grant the special favor of equitable relief to one whose conduct in relation to the matter in controversy has been offensive to equitable principles. Relief will be denied under this doctrine where it appears that the right upon which the complainant relies has arisen out of a wrong, a breach of duty, or a violation of law. A complainant will not be permitted to take advantage of his own wrong or fraud. And a court of equity will not adjust differences between wrongdoers, at least where the parties are in pari delicto, nor will it assist in the enforcement of an illegal or immoral contract or transaction, nor lend its aid to the division of profits or property which have been derived from an illegal agreement. However, where the parties are not in pari delicto with regard to the transaction in question, relief may be granted in some circumstances to the one whose wrong is less than that of the other. And relief will not be denied under the "clean hands" doctrine merely because the complainant has been guilty of improper or inequitable conduct. In order to invoke the maxim, it must be shown that the misconduct was related to the transaction giving rise to the cause of action.

Certain equitable principles govern the rights of litigants in equity where neither has been guilty of actual wrongdoing. As a general rule, the party who was in a better position to avert a loss or injury must bear the burden of the same. And where one of two parties, both guiltless of intentional wrong, must suffer a loss, the one whose conduct, act, or omission occasions the loss must stand the consequences. Where the prejudicial situation has resulted from the wrongful act of a third person, the decision must be against the party whose conduct or neglect made possible the wrongdoer's act, breach of trust, fraud, or other wrong.

It is a familiar principle of equity that as between equities otherwise equal, he who has the prior equity in point of time is entitled to priority in right. This rule is frequently applied in determining property rights. Another familiar maxim is that "where equities are equal, the law must prevail." In such a case, equity will follow the law. Thus, if two persons have equal equitable claims upon, or interests in, the same subject matter, so that each is equally entitled to the protection of equity with respect to his equitable interest, and one of them, in addition to his equity, has obtained some legal estate or right in the subject matter, the latter will prevail.

II. GROUNDS FOR AND PREREQUISITES OF RELIEF IN EQUITY; DEFENSES

§ 10:4. In general.

Am Jur 2d References: Equity, §§ 19–27.

Courts of equity act upon equitable causes by the administration of equitable remedies, and before such a court will assume jurisdiction of a case, it must appear that there are grounds for equitable relief. In order to merit a remedy in a court of equity, the complainant must present a case calling for relief under established equitable principles. However, equity jurisdiction does not necessarily depend upon an exact relation of the cause of action stated to some definite head of equitable relief. Nor does equity confine its relief to cases for which there is a precedent precisely in the situation presented to the court. Equity will not withhold relief merely because the question presented is a novel one, where the circumstances presented call for the exercise of equitable power. Equitable jurisdiction may be invoked by way of defense to an action, either in equity or at law.

One of the most important grounds for equitable intervention is fraud or fraudulent misrepresentation or concealment. While false representations, made with knowledge of their falsity and with a fraudulent intent, are clear grounds for relief in equity, such relief is also granted where statements are made recklessly and without regard to truth or falsity. Relief may be granted also in cases involving misstatements made as a result of misapprehension or mistake, without fraudulent intent, if such misrepresentations actually mislead the person to whom they are made, to his prejudice. A misrepresentation, to constitute a ground for equitable relief, must generally relate to something material or important to the transaction between the parties, and it must actually mislead the other party. And generally the misrepresentation, to warrant equitable relief, must not be a mere matter of opinion.

A suppression or concealment of the truth may constitute a ground of equitable relief no less than misrepresentations openly made. However, in the case of suppression of truth, it is generally necessary to prove that the person charged had knowledge of the fact which he is said to have suppressed, and the fact must be such that the party is under legal or equitable obligation to communicate it.

The prevention of irreparable injury is one of the chief functions of courts of equity. Where a continuation of wrongful acts or threatened danger therefrom is such as to cause reasonable apprehension of irreparable injury, it is not necessary to show actual damage or a completed violation of the plaintiff's rights in order to entitle him to the protection of equity. However, irreparable injury, like inadequacy of remedy at law (to which it is inseparably related), is only one factor determining the right to equitable relief; the wrongfulness of the defendant's conduct, actual or threatened, must be established before there can be relief based on an apprehended irreparable injury therefrom.

The modern doctrine of unjust enrichment (discussed herein under the topic Restitution, Quasi Contract, and Implied Contract) is an area of increasing importance in the application of equitable principles. Under this doctrine, referred to also as quasi contract or contract implied in law, a person is required to make restitution or compensation for payments, services, or property which he has received from another under circumstances which make it unjust and inequitable for him to retain such benefits without compensation.

§ 10:5. Inadequacy of remedy at law.

Am Jur 2d References: Equity, §§ 86–101.

The rigidity of the rights and remedies under the early common law and the lack of adequate legal remedies for new and unusual situations provided the original need and reason for the creation of equity as an auxiliary system of justice. The existence or absence of an adequate remedy at law is still probably the most important factor to be considered in determining equity jurisdiction.

This factor or principle has both a positive and a negative aspect. Stated in the negative form, it is a well-settled general rule that if the law affords an adequate remedy to enforce or protect the right in question, the cause may not be made the basis of a suit in equity. In other words, equity will not intervene if there is an adequate remedy at law. The converse of this rule, the positive aspect of the principle, is sometimes stated; that is, that equity will grant relief where there is no adequate remedy at law. However, this unqualified statement is not strictly and literally accurate. In order to invoke the jurisdiction of equity a party must show not only the lack of an adequate remedy at law, but also the existence of a right that is judicially cognizable. Notwithstanding the absence of an adequate remedy at law, equity may be prevented by its own principles, or by some other supervening rule, or by some infirmity in the obligation or right asserted, from exercising jurisdiction.

As a general rule, equity will not grant relief concerning a matter for which plaintiff can obtain a full remedy by asserting it as a defense in an action at law, assuming that the remedy by way of defense is adequate.

In order to preclude the granting of relief by a court of equity, an available remedy at law must be clear, prompt, sufficient, complete, practical, and efficient to the attainment of the ends of justice. The question to be determined is whether the remedy at law compares favorably with the remedy afforded by equity. If the equitable remedy is superior, the equity court will usually take jurisdiction.

On the principle that equity aids the vigilant and not one who sleeps on his rights, a court of equity may refuse to grant relief to one who, having had available a remedy at law, has intentionally or negligently failed to assert it.

Under some circumstances a court of equity will exercise jurisdiction and grant relief notwithstanding the existence of an adequate remedy at law. For example, the remedy at law does not preclude the granting of equitable relief where a party asserts an equitable cause of action. And where the jurisdiction of law and equity is concurrent, equity may administer relief irrespective of the existence of an adequate remedy at law.

§ 10:6. Mistake or accident.

Am Jur 2d References: Equity, §§ 28–45; Mistake, Accident, etc., §§ 1–27.

The granting of relief from the consequences of mistake is one of the most familiar grounds of equity jurisdiction. The right to equitable relief on the ground of mistake has already been discussed in this work under the topics Contracts, and Restitution, Quasi Contract, and Implied Contracts. Since equitable principles determine the right to relief on this ground, a court of equity is reluctant to grant the relief unless the parties can be put back in status quo, restored to the situation which they occupied prior to entering into the transaction in question.

A court of equity has unquestioned jurisdiction to relieve parties from the consequences of a mistake of fact. To entitle a party to relief on this ground, however, he must show that the particular fact, and his mistake with respect thereto, were such as were calculated to influence or control his conduct in entering into the transaction, and that his conduct was actually determined by the mistake. And as a general rule, in order to justify the granting of relief on the ground of mistake, the parties to the transaction must have been mutually mistaken, a mistake on the part of one party not being sufficient for this purpose in the absence of fraud or other inequitable conduct by the other party. According to many authorities, relief will not be granted on a mere showing that the complainant was ignorant of or mistaken as to some matter of fact, unless it appears that his mistake or ignorance was excusable. Hence, he is not entitled to relief on the ground of his mistake if he could have ascertained the facts by the exercise of reasonable care or diligence and where his means of knowledge were equal to those of the other party.   Other courts, however, have placed some qualifications on this principle.

There has been much discussion as to whether a court of equity should take jurisdiction and grant relief on the ground of a mistake of law, as distinguished from a mistake of fact.   Subject to certain departures and exceptions, it is the general rule that a court of equity will not grant relief from the consequences of a mistake of law, either by way of affirmative or defensive relief, in the absence of fraud, undue influence, or other inequitable conduct on the part of the opposing party.   However, some courts have rejected this rule, and other courts grant relief from mistakes of law in exceptional cases and where they conclude that the equities demand it.   The modern trend seems to be toward granting relief from mistakes of law as well as from mistakes of fact.   Where the general rule applies, a mutual mistake as to the construction or meaning of a contract or other instrument or transaction is one of law for which equity will not grant relief.   Nor will relief be granted, under this rule, on the ground that a party was misled by an erroneous court decision which was later reversed or overruled, or because he acted in reliance upon erroneous advice of counsel—although some courts have granted relief in the latter situation.

A mistake as to the law of a state or country other than that wherein the mistaken party resides is generally held to be a mistake of fact and not a mistake of law, so that equity may grant relief on the ground thereof.

A court will, in an appropriate case, grant equitable relief from the consequences of unavoidable accident.   Where a party seeks relief from an injurious or prejudicial situation in which he is placed as a result of accident, the granting of relief depends upon a showing that the complainant did not know and was not required to know or foresee the consequences.   And where it appears that injury or prejudice must be sustained by one of the parties because of an accident or unanticipated event, the failure of the complainant to use due diligence will deprive him of the right to equitable relief.

§ 10:7. Multiplicity of actions.

Am Jur 2d References: Equity, §§ 46–51.

It is well settled that a court will exercise equitable jurisdiction to prevent a multiplicity of actions.   Whether or not the court will grant relief on this ground depends upon all of the facts of the case, and a determination of the question involves an exercise of judicial discretion.   Among the factors which have been considered in determining the question of equity jurisdiction on the ground of avoiding a multiplicity of actions are: the right of trial by jury; the adequacy of the remedy at law; the expense of the litigation; the delay and hardship incidental to the multiplicity of actions; and the number of actions that may be avoided.   It has frequently been held that the court will not entertain a suit involving similar controversies where the object of coming into equity is merely to consolidate actions or avoid the expense of separate suits, especially if the several actions may be consolidated and tried together in a court of law.   Nor will the jurisdiction of equity be extended to a complainant who is in a position to avoid the litigation in question if he elects to do so, as where the multiplicity of actions consists in suits instituted by the complainant himself. And parties will not be compelled to try their causes in equity on the ground of avoiding a multiplicity of actions, where to do so would result in an inequitable advantage to the opposing party.

The prevention of circuity of action is a recognized ground of equitable jurisdiction. Thus, equity will settle in one suit the diverse rights and obligations of persons who are successively liable, and will impose liability on the one who is ultimately liable at law.

Equity will not generally take jurisdiction of distinct and separate claims of different persons, on the ground of preventing a multiplicity of actions, unless there is some community of right or interest between the parties. Equity will not generally intervene on this ground where there are numerous parties plaintiff or defendant, between whom and the adverse party the issues are not identical and are not to be determined by reference to the same facts or principles of law. The court will not act to prevent the bringing of numerous actions against the same party defendant by different plaintiffs where there is no common interest or common controverted question of law, although the actions may be of the same nature.

Equity jurisdiction is frequently exercised, on the ground of preventing a multiplicity of actions, to restrain repeated trespasses or continuing or recurring invasion of property rights, and in disputes concerning boundaries, nuisances, and waste.

The old equitable remedy known as a bill of peace has for its purpose the prevention of vexatious litigation and a multiplicity of actions. The bill of peace invoked equitable remedies where the dispute was between one person and many concerning a general right which could be adjudicated only by protracted litigation, or where further litigation was threatened after the disputed right had been determined by one or more trials at law. Under these principles, equity may take jurisdiction where it is necessary to protect the complainant from continued and oppressive or vexatious litigation.

§ 10:8. Estoppel.

Am Jur 2d References: Estoppel and Waiver, §§ 26–133.

Equitable estoppel, or estoppel in pais, is the principle which precludes a person from asserting a fact, claim, or defense where his conduct has been such as to make it inequitable for him to do so. Although it was originated by the chancery courts, this principle now pervades the whole system of Anglo-American jurisprudence, and is applied both at law and in equity. The doctrine is founded upon principles of morality and fair dealing and is intended to subserve the ends of justice. Its proper function is the prevention of fraud, actual or constructive, and it may not be successfully invoked where it would have a different result. The applicability of the doctrine depends upon the facts and circumstances of each individual case and the equities of each party in the light thereof.

Any comprehensive definition of equitable estoppel must consist of an enumeration of the essential elements and requisites of the doctrine. The essential elements, as related to the party to be estopped, are: conduct which amounts to a false representation or concealment of material facts, or which is calculated to convey the impression that the facts are different from those

271

which the party subsequently attempts to assert; the expectation or intention that such conduct shall be acted upon or shall influence the other party; and knowledge, actual, constructive, or imputed, of the real facts. As related to the party claiming the estoppel, the essential elements are lack of knowledge and of the means of knowledge of the truth as to the facts in question; reliance, in good faith and with justification, upon the conduct or statement of the party to be estopped; and action or inaction based thereon of such character as to change the position or status of the party claiming the estoppel, to his injury, detriment, or prejudice.

Actual fraud or misrepresentation, or wilful and intentional concealment or misleading, clearly provide the basis for an estoppel, if the other elements are present. However, it is not essential to the creation of an equitable estoppel that the party sought to be estopped should have had an actual intent to deceive, defraud, or mislead. All that is necessary to raise an estoppel is that the party sought to be charged therewith knew or ought to have known that his conduct or silence would probably cause the other party to act and change his position in reliance thereon.

Manifestly, where the other elements of an estoppel in pais are present, it may be based upon express representations or statements. As a general rule such representations or assurances must relate to some present or past fact, as distinguished from mere promises or statements as to the future. The bare statement of an honest estimate or opinion will not ordinarily form the basis of an estoppel. However, under the doctrine of "promissory estoppel," an estoppel may arise from the making of a promise as to the future, even though it is without consideration, if it is intended that the promise should be relied upon and it is in fact relied upon, and if a refusal to enforce it would sanction the perpetration of fraud or other injustice.

Estoppel by silence, inaction, acquiescence, or delay arises only where the party sought to be estopped is under duty, in equity and good conscience, to speak or to act, and where he knew, or should have known, that the other party would change his position in reliance upon his silence or inactivity. In order to give rise to an estoppel by silence or inaction, there must be not only a right and an opportunity to speak or act, but also an obligation or duty to do so. Equitable estoppel is frequently based upon acquiescence in a transaction or course of conduct or on the acceptance and retention of the benefits of a transaction with knowledge of the facts.

Since the doctrine of equitable estoppel is founded upon principles of morality and fair dealing and is available only for the protection of claims made in good faith, the party setting up an estoppel is himself bound to the exercise of good faith in the transaction and in his reliance upon the words or conduct of the other party. He cannot establish an estoppel if he had full knowledge of the true facts. Also, he may not claim that he was misled if his lack of knowledge was due to his own failure to use reasonable diligence in ascertaining the truth, or to obtain information reasonably at hand or to investigate suspicious circumstances. In the absence of exceptional circumstances, courts refuse to give effect to an estoppel where the parties are equally well informed as to the essential facts or where the means of knowledge are equally open to them.

Generally speaking, an estoppel operates only on the parties to the transaction out of which it arises, and their privies. On the question whether an estoppel may be invoked against a state or its governmental units, there is considerable diversity of opinion. Generally a state may not be estopped to exercise the ordinary functions of government, but estoppel has been applied against states and their political subdivisions in transactions involving purely proprietary functions. As against municipal corporations, the scope of the application of the doctrine of estoppel is less restricted than where the state is involved, but the courts are reluctant to apply the doctrine where a purely governmental function is involved.

The estoppels at common law were estoppel by deed or bond and estoppel by record, the latter including estoppel by judgment, or res judicata. These estoppels are quite different in concept and application from equitable estoppel or estoppel in pais.

Contractual rights and property rights of various kinds may be affected by equitable estoppel. Statutory provisions may be obviated by estoppel where they affect only private rights and not the public welfare. Thus, a party may, by his conduct, be estopped to plead a statute of limitations; and the doctrine of part performance (see § 5:20, supra), under which a contract may be enforced notwithstanding noncompliance with the statute of frauds, is based on equitable estoppel.

§ 10:9. Lapse of time or delay; laches.

Am Jur 2d References: Equity, §§ 152–176; Limitation of Actions, §§ 431–452.

Unreasonable delay may preclude a party from asserting a claim or right in a proceeding in equity, under the equitable doctrine of "laches," irrespective of any statute of limitations. The doctrine of laches is based on public policy, which requires, for the peace of society, the discouragement of stale demands. The doctrine is directly within the maxim, "equity aids the vigilant, not those who sleep on their rights," and it is also affected by the maxims, "he who seeks equity must do equity," and "he who comes into equity must come with clean hands."

It is held in some jurisdictions that statutes of limitation are not binding on a court of equity in an equitable proceeding involving only equitable rights and remedies. Even where a statute of limitations is binding upon a court of equity, the court may deny relief on the ground of laches, independently of the statute, where the conduct of the complainant and the equities of the case require the application of the doctrine. And it is well settled that a party may be estopped to plead a statute of limitations where his conduct has been such that it would be inequitable and prejudicial for him to do so. Even in jurisdictions in which the statute of limitations does not apply of its own force to demands which are purely equitable, courts of equity, in harmony with the maxim that equity follows the law, frequently act on the analogy of, rather an inobedience to, the statute of limitations. Under this practice, the equity court adopts the limitation period prescribed by the statute, for the purpose of applying the doctrine of laches, unless strong equitable considerations require a different course. In this latter contingency, the doctrine of laches may be applied although the statute of limitations has not run, and conversely, the circumstances of the case may be such that the doctrine of laches is not applicable even though an action at law would be barred by a limitation.

Time is only one factor or element to be considered in determining the applicability of the doctrine of laches. As a general rule, a suit is held to be barred on the ground of laches where and only where the following facts are disclosed: (1) conduct on the part of the defendant, or one under whom he claims, giving rise to the situation for which the complainant seeks a remedy; (2) delay in asserting the complainant's rights, after the complainant had knowledge or notice of the defendant's conduct and was afforded an opportunity to institute suit; (3) lack of knowledge or notice on the part of the defendant that the complainant would assert the right on which he bases his suit; and (4) injury or prejudice to the defendant or an innocent third person in the event relief is granted. Under these tests it must appear that the party to whom laches is imputed had knowledge of his rights, and an ample opportunity to establish them in the proper forum; that by reason of his delay the opposing party had good reason to believe that the alleged rights were worthless or had been abandoned, and that, because of a change in conditions, position, or relations during the period of delay, it would be inequitable to the latter to permit the other party to assert them. The propriety of applying the doctrine of laches depends upon the conduct and situation of all the parties, and upon all the other circumstances.

In order for laches to be a valid defense, the delay must not only have been unreasonable, but also unexplained and inexcusable. Whether or not a delay was excusable must be determined by the court, in its discretion, in the light of the circumstances of the case. Among the matters of explanation which may constitute such an excuse are hindrances or impediments to the institution of suit, such as a promise to satisfy the complainant's claim; an admission or recognition of the right or claim by the defendant or the latter's predecessor in interest; intimate or confidential relations between the complainant and the person whose conduct gave rise to the claim; or the latter's concealment or misrepresentation. Generally, where the delay was caused or contributed to by the conduct of the party claiming laches, it is held to be excusable.

One of the main elements or factors of laches involves knowledge on the part of the complainant as to the invasion of his rights by the defendant or one under whom he claims. If the complainant had no knowledge of the facts giving rise to the cause of action, he cannot generally be charged with laches. Knowledge may be imputed to him, however, where he had ample opportunity to acquire knowledge and his failure to do so amounts to a lack of reasonable diligence on his part. Another fundamental prerequisite of laches, as seen above, is injury, prejudice, or disadvantage to the defendant or an innocent third person in the event that relief is granted to the complainant. Laches is not, like statutory limitation, a mere matter of time, but is principally a question of the inequity of permitting a claim to be enforced; and the doctrine applies only where, because of lapse of time, it would be inequitable to allow a party to enforce his legal rights, because, for example, pending the complainant's delay there has been a change of conditions which cannot be disturbed without producing injustice, where rights or interest of third persons have come into existence, or where the defendant has justifiably placed himself in a position which will cause him injury or prejudice if the complainant is not held to be barred of relief. Such prejudice or injury is frequently held to exist where the defendant has expended money or incurred obligations in the reasonable belief that he had a clear or unencumbered right.

III. NATURE AND FORMS OF RELIEF IN EQUITY

§ 10:10. In general; retaining jurisdiction for complete relief.

Am Jur 2d References: Equity, §§ 102–117, 238–244.

Some areas of equity jurisdiction and various types of equitable relief are discussed in the sections which follow. Other matters over which equity exercises jurisdiction, such as trust estates, the foreclosure and redemption of mortgages, and the enforcement of liens, are discussed in other topics of this work.

A measure of discretion is exercised by a court of equity in determining whether it will take jurisdiction of a case, and what, if any, relief will be granted. In the administration of its remedies, a court of equity adapts its relief and molds its decrees to satisfy the requirements of the case and to protect and conserve the equities of the parties. It is fundamental that equitable relief must be practicable. Even if there is no adequate remedy at law, jurisdiction in equity may be declined because it would be impracticable to frame or enforce a decree suitable to the plaintiff's rights. However, courts of equity have been ingenious in devising remedies to meet new situations, and the fact that no precedent exists fitting the case before it will not deter a court of equity from granting relief in a proper case.

A court of equity which has taken jurisdiction of a cause for any purpose will ordinarily retain jurisdiction for all purposes, decide all issues involved in the subject matter of the dispute, and award relief which is complete and which finally disposes of the litigation so as to accomplish full justice between the parties and prevent future litigation. The court will do this even though it involves passing upon matters ordinarily cognizable at law and even though it requires the granting of legal relief and remedies, including a personal judgment for damages where that is appropriate.

The trial of a cause in a court of equity is usually before the court without the intervention of a jury. The judge or chancellor decides both the law and the facts. While the parties have no right to a trial by jury, in the absence of statutes, courts of equity do frequently submit issues of fact to a jury; and it was formerly the practice, sometimes still followed, to send an issue of fact into a court of law for trial before a jury according to legal forms.

§ 10:11. Cancellation of instruments.

Am Jur 2d References: Cancellation of Instruments, §§ 1–68.

A suit for judicial cancellation of an instrument is equitable in nature and is governed by the general principles of equity. The granting of this relief rests within the sound discretion of the court, and it may be granted or withheld according to the circumstances and the equities on both sides of the case. In accordance with general equitable principles, cancellation will be denied where there is an adequate remedy at law. And to justify judicial cancellation of an instrument there must be a particular equity warranting the relief, and no injustice or undue or disproportionate hardship inflicted thereby upon the other party.

The equitable jurisdiction to rescind, cancel, or set aside is exercised with respect to a great variety of instruments and documents, where proper grounds exist. This power extends to deeds, mortgages, contracts of all kinds, notes and other negotiable instruments, insurance policies, guaranties, releases, assignments, leases, options, stock subscriptions, and wrongful transfers of stock on corporate books. Jurisdiction to cancel a will, however, is generally reserved to courts exercising special probate jurisdiction. Where other grounds exist, equity has jurisdiction to cancel certificates, licenses, and records made or issued by governmental officials or boards.

Equity will ordinarily take jurisdiction of a suit to cancel an instrument absolutely void, at least where the instrument is not invalid on its face. With regard to instruments that are void on their face, some courts take the view that there is an adequate remedy at law and that equity will not intervene to cancel them. Other courts take jurisdiction to cancel such an instrument on the ground that the instrument may nevertheless create danger if it is left outstanding without an adjudication of its nullity, and may be a source of annoyance or embarrassment if not judicially canceled. Most courts hold that a forged instrument may be canceled in a suit in equity. Mental incompetency is a ground for cancellation in equity, and a deed or instrument executed by an infant and disaffirmed by him upon attaining majority may be canceled in equity. Fraud or fraudulent misrepresentation is a frequent ground for cancellation of instruments by courts of equity. The same is true of duress and undue influence. A mistake as to a material and substantial fact may be a ground for cancellation, but equity will not ordinarily cancel an instrument on the ground of a mistake of law. Lack, failure, or inadequacy of consideration is not ordinarily a ground for cancellation of a contract or other instrument, in the absence of extraordinary circumstances creating an independent ground for cancellation.

An equitable principle generally applied in a suit for judicial cancellation of an instrument is that the party seeking the cancellation must first restore or offer to restore the other party to the position he occupied before the transaction in question. The other party must be placed in statu quo. To do this, everything received from the other party must ordinarily be returned. Where restoration to the status quo is impossible, cancellation will generally be refused, unless the strongest equities demand it and a refusal of the relief would result in injustice or fraud. This rule applies to cancellation on the ground of infancy, except that the infant is generally required to return or surrender only that portion of the consideration which he still retains at the time of disaffirmance of the transaction.

The defenses generally available in proceedings in equity may be asserted in a suit for cancellation of an instrument. Thus, a party may be defeated on the ground that he has been guilty of laches, or that he has waived his right to cancellation or has ratified the transaction which he seeks to cancel. Thus, in cases of fraud, a person is deemed to have waived a right of cancellation if, after discovering the fraud, he deals with the property acquired in the transaction as his own or otherwise conducts himself in such manner as to recognize the contract as existing and binding. And the rule that equity will aid neither party to an illegal contract where the parties are in pari delicto applies in a suit for cancellation.

§ 10:12. Reformation of instruments.

Am Jur 2d References: Reformation of Instruments, §§ 1–130.

Reformation is the remedy afforded by courts of equity to the parties and privies of parties to written instruments which import a legal obligation, to reform or rectify such instruments whenever they fail, through fraud or mistake, to express the real agreement or intention of the parties. The remedy by way of reformation is available to correct not only contracts of all kinds, but deeds, leases, mortgages, etc.; but the remedy does not extend to wills. A suit for reformation presupposes that the parties came to an understanding or agreement, but in reducing it to writing, through mutual mistake or mistake and fraud, some provision or language was omitted, inserted, or incorrectly worded, and the relief sought is to change the instrument so as to conform it to the real agreement of the parties. This relief is never available unless there was actually an agreement and a meeting of the minds of the parties. Equity will not, under the guise of reformation, make a contract for the parties where there was no such agreement. The purpose and function of the remedy of reformation is not to make a new agreement for the parties, but to establish and perpetuate the true existing one by making the instrument express the real intent of the parties.

A court will not reform a void or illegal instrument, although this relief may be granted in a proper case where the instrument is defective merely because it was not effectively executed.

The existence of a remedy at law does not defeat the jurisdiction of equity to reform an instrument unless the remedy at law is as adequate and efficacious as the equitable remedy, and in actual practice the legal remedies are seldom adequate and complete as compared with the equitable relief. In some jurisdictions the court will afford the proper relief upon the basis of the contract intended by the parties and will permit the assertion of rights of action or defenses predicated on the true agreement, without the necessity of a formal reformation.

Upon the reformation of an instrument, it relates back to, and takes effect from, the time of its original execution, as between the parties thereto and as against all persons except bona fide purchasers without notice and those standing in similar relations.

A mistake, to constitute a ground for reformation, must have been a mutual mistake, one shared by both parties. And the mistake must have been material and must substantially affect the rights and obligations of the parties. It is sometimes stated that the mistake must be one of fact and that a mistake of law or an erroneous conclusion as to the legal effect of known facts is not a ground for reformation of an instrument. However, the distinction between mistakes of law and mistakes of fact is of diminishing importance in modern times, and some courts disregard the distinction entirely and others go to considerable lengths in characterizing a mistake as one of fact. It may be stated generally that relief by way of reformation will be granted on the ground of mutual mistake, whether of fact or of law, where to deny the relief would offend basic principles of equity and would work gross injustice. Where the instrument as executed fails to express the real intention or agreement of the parties because of a mutual mistake as to the real meaning of language used, reformation will be decreed even though there is no misunderstanding as to what words were actually employed therein. And courts may grant relief by reformation where the scrivener or draftsman of an instrument, through inadvertence, unskillfulness, lack of knowledge, or otherwise, fails to express the real intentions and agreement of the parties.

Fraud practiced in drawing or executing an instrument, so that it does not speak the real terms of the agreement of the parties, or unconscionable conduct amounting to fraud, constitutes a ground for reformation, if it was relied upon by the party seeking relief. And reformation may be granted where there is ignorance or mistake on one side and fraud or inequitable conduct on the other.

The general principles and prerequisites governing equitable relief apply in suits for reformation of instruments. The party seeking the relief must come into equity with clean hands, and he must offer to do equity. If a party acquiesces in an instrument or ratifies it after becoming aware of the mistake, he loses his right to reformation. According to the prevailing view, mere negligence of a party in executing or accepting a written instrument, as by his failure to read the instrument, does not preclude a reformation of the instrument on the ground of mistake, at least where other parties have not been prejudiced by the negligence. A person seeking a reformation of an instrument must act with reasonable diligence, and relief may be barred by the equitable doctrine of laches.

§ 10:13. Specific performance.

Am Jur 2d References: Specific Performance (1st ed, §§ 2–180).

Specific performance is an important equitable remedy of ancient origin. Its purpose and effect are to require a party to perform the acts provided for in his contract and necessary to accomplish its execution. This remedy has been discussed in §§ 5:36, 5:37, supra. The granting or withholding of relief of this type generally rests within the sound discretion of the court. The remedy is subject to all of the prerequisites and defenses generally applicable to proceedings in equity; and specific performance will not be decreed where the complainant does not come into equity with clean hands, where he has been guilty of laches, where he does not offer to do equity, where the granting of the relief would work inequitable and disproportionate hardship on the opposing party, or where there is an adequate remedy at law by recovery of damages or otherwise.

The most frequent occasion for the remedy of specific performance involves contracts relating to real property. For example, a party may be compelled to execute a deed in performance of his contracts for the sale of land. In a proper case specific performance of such a contract will be enforced although the contract does not comply with the statute of frauds, where the party seeking this remedy has partially performed the contract in good faith or where, for other reasons, it would amount to injustice or fraud if the opposing party were permitted to interpose the defense of the statute of frauds.

As a general rule, specific performance of contracts in relation to personal property will not be enforced in equity, for the reason that ordinarily an action at law for damages affords an adequate remedy. However, the relief may be granted under special circumstances where the remedy at law is not adequate, as where the property involved is of unique character or value and cannot be purchased in the market, or where the property has a peculiar sentimental value over and above its pecuniary or intrinsic value, as in the case of heirlooms. Thus, an agreement to assign patents or inventions may be the subject of specific performance.

The doctrine is well established that courts of equity will not decree the specific performance of a contract for personal services. Under exceptional circumstances, however, the court will sometimes attain a result similar to specific performance. For example, where the contract calls for the performance of services or acts of a special, unique, or extraordinary character, or by persons especially eminent in their profession or calling and possessing special and extraordinary qualifications, the court may restrain the person from rendering services to another.

§10:14. Removing cloud on title; bills quia timet.

Am Jur 2d References: Cancellation of Instruments, §7; Quieting Title, §§ 1–65.

A suit to quiet title or to remove a cloud on title is a remedy which originated in the chancery, and jurisdiction to grant this kind of relief is inherent in a court which exercises equity powers. The remedy is discussed in this work in the topic Real Property, §18:87. Such a proceeding has for its purpose an adjudication that a claim of title to or interest in property adverse to that of the complainant is invalid, with the result that the claimant and those claiming under him may be forever free from danger of the hostile claim. The suit to quiet title is associated with the old remedies by bill of peace and bill quia timet. The latter was intended to afford protective relief against instruments on the ground that they may be injuriously used against the petitioner after evidence to impeach them may be lost or his defenses may be circumvented.

The remedy is generally limited to real property, although there has been some tendency to extend it to personal property under exceptional circumstances. The conditions to the granting of this relief, the defenses available in such a suit, and the principles applicable in such a proceeding are those which govern other suits in equity. The petitioner must show that he has no adequate remedy at law, and he may be required to do equity by restoring any benefits that he may have received from the defendant. Generally speaking, in order to maintain a quiet-title suit, the complainant must have legal title to the property in question, or to some interest therein, and must be in possession of the property at the time of the institution of the action. Laches, or unreasonable delay in bringing suit, is a defense to a suit to remove a cloud on title, as it is in other cases in equity.

Where the court determines that the complainant is entitled to the relief, it will enter such a decree as is appropriate and necessary to afford complete relief, by the cancellation of instruments or otherwise. And the court may, in a proper case, not only remove a cloud on title and quiet title, but may make such orders as are necessary to prevent a threatened cloud on title.

§ 10:15. Remedies to prevent torts and other wrongs.

Am Jur 2d References: Injunctions, §§ 131–167.

Where there is no adequate remedy at law and where the other conditions of equitable relief are established, a court of equity will act, by injunction or other remedy, to prevent tortious acts which would cause irreparable injury to the complaining party.

This type of relief is most frequently granted to protect property rights by preventing repeated or continuing trespasses, nuisances, waste, or the pollution, obstruction, or diversion of waters, etc. Injunctive relief is also granted, however, to protect certain personal rights, such as the right of privacy. Equity has generally refused to restrain or enjoin assaults, batteries, insults, and molestations of the person; and generally injunction will not issue against the utterance or publication of libelous or slanderous statements, the constitutional guaranty of the freedom of speech and of the press precluding such relief, unless there is some independent ground for equitable relief. Equity will not generally restrain a purely criminal act; but the fact that a crime is involved does not preclude injunctive relief against tortious acts causing irreparable injury to the complainant.

§ 10:16. Remedies to aid or simplify legal proceedings; interpleader; discovery; perpetuation of testimony.

Am Jur 2d References: Depositions and Discovery, §§ 3–9, 140–142; Injunctions, §§ 201–237; Interpleader, §§ 2–20; Ne Exeat, §§ 1–20.

A court having equity jurisdiction may properly interpose to prevent vexatious or oppressive litigation. This relief may be obtained in a proper case either by a bill of peace or by a petition for injunction against such proceedings, regardless of whether the threatened litigation is legal or equitable. The vexatious litigation may be many suits by the same person or by different individuals. Injunction is resorted to also, in rare cases, to protect the jurisdiction of the court over the subject matter of a pending suit. This type of relief is closely related to the equitable remedy by bill of peace to prevent a multiplicity of actions, discussed above, § 10:7.

A bill of interpleader is an equitable remedy available in a proper case to one in possession of property, or liable for a debt or other obligation, where he does not claim the property and admits his obligation to someone, assuming the position of a mere stakeholder. The object of interpleader is to bring all claimants before the court for the determination of their claims in a single proceeding, and thus to prevent loss or embarrassment to the stakeholder from separate actions by rival claimants. This remedy is incorporated in the practice of many jurisdictions by statutes and rules.

The practice of introducing or securing evidence by depositions taken in advance of trial originated in the chancery courts and continues as a method of introducing evidence in equity proceedings. A related practice in equity, yet distinct from the ordinary deposition de bene esse, is the bill or petition to perpetuate testimony, or examination "in perpetual memory." This remedy, of ancient origin, was devised to enable a person to perpetuate the testimony of witnesses where no action was yet pending and he was unable at the time to bring his cause before a court for determination.

The bill of discovery in equity was designed to compel the opposing party to disclose information or evidence or to produce documents, books, etc., for use in a suit. Both discovery and depositions are in universal use today in both equity and law cases.

Ne exeat is a writ which issues from a court of equity, ancillary to proceedings in equity, to restrain a person from going beyond the limits of the court's jurisdiction until he has satisfied the plaintiff's claim or has given bond for his appearance or for the satisfaction of the decree of the court. This writ has been abolished or replaced in some states.

*

EVIDENCE

I. INTRODUCTORY; SUBSTITUTES FOR EVIDENCE

§ 11:1. Generally.

Am Jur 2d References: Evidence, §§ 1–13.

In legal usage, "evidence" is the means by which facts are established in legal proceedings; it is the means of ascertaining the truth as to a fact or point in issue. The word "proof," although sometimes used as a synonym of "evidence," properly signifies the effect of evidence or the ultimate establishment of a fact by evidence. "Testimony" is properly limited to evidence given orally. The classification of evidence may be on this basis, i.e., whether it is oral testimony or in the form of documents, such as public or private records, or other writings, or of objects or exhibits which themselves constitute evidence. Another classification of evidence characterizes it as "circumstantial" or "direct," the latter being evidence which, if believed, proves the existence of the fact in issue without inference or presumption, and the former being evidence relating to a series of facts other than the fact in issue, which series of facts are, by reason and experience, so associated with the fact in issue as to warrant an inference or conclusion as to the existence of that fact.

The law of evidence consists of a body of principles and rules developed by the courts and legislatures over the centuries, governing the mode or manner of proving facts in issue, and determining what shall be admitted or rejected in a legal proceeding and what weight is to be given to the evidence admitted. All rules of evidence are intended to aid in the establishment of the truth as to facts in issue, to minimize the chance of fraud or imposition upon the tribunal charged with the function of determining the facts, and to restrict the trial or proceedings to an orderly inquiry focused on the relevant facts. Some of the technical rules of evidence are dispensed with or relaxed in quasi-judicial proceedings and investigatory hearings before administrative tribunals and governmental commissions and boards. And in some jurisdictions these rules are liberalized or simplified in certain judicial proceedings in inferior courts.

There is a conflict of authority on the question of validity of a contractual provision changing the rules of evidence applicable in an action on the contract. On the general principle that the parties may not oust the jurisdiction of the courts, many cases hold that a stipulation requiring more positive and direct proof than the law generally requires, such as provisions requiring eyewitnesses to establish a fact, or eliminating the effect of a legal presumption which would otherwise be applicable, are not binding upon the parties nor upon the courts. In other jurisdictions, however, such stipulations are held to be valid.

§ 11:2. Judicial notice.

Am Jur 2d References: Evidence, §§ 14–122.

Although jurors were selected in the early days of the jury system for the very reason of their knowledge of the facts of the case to be tried, such knowledge usually disqualifies them as jurors today. In modern practice both the court and the jury are presumed to be uninformed concerning the facts involved in a case, and it is incumbent upon the parties to establish by evidence the facts upon which they rely. There are, however, many classes of facts which need not be proved by the introduction of evidence, since they are matters of common knowledge to all intelligent men, and will be judicially noticed by the court or jury. Judicial notice of such facts takes the place of proof and is of equal force; it dispenses with the necessity of introducing evidence to prove facts which do not admit of contradiction. Judicial notice is the cognizance of certain facts which a judge or jury may properly take and act upon without proof because knowledge of such facts is assumed or is imputed to the judge or jury. As has been observed, there is no reason why a judge should be assumed to be, or should pretend to be, ignorant of things known to the rest of mankind. The doctrine of judicial notice applies to appellate courts as well as to trial judges.

Judicial notice in any case is not determined or limited by the actual knowledge of the individual judge or court. It is not essential that matters of judicial cognizance be actually known to the judge; if they are proper subjects of judicial notice, the judge may inform himself in any way he pleases, and may refresh his memory or nourish his knowledge by reference to encyclopedias, textbooks, dictionaries, and other publications of established authenticity. Although courts may take judicial notice of matters of common knowledge without suggestion of counsel and without an allegation in a pleading, a court is not invariably bound to do so sua sponte; and it is usually advisable for counsel to bring such matters to the attention of the court and to provide supporting references and authorities.

Judicial notice covers a great variety of facts. To qualify for such notice, however, a "fact" must be a subject of common or general knowledge; and it must be well and authoritatively settled, without any substantial uncertainty or creditable dispute. Courts take judicial notice of the law prevailing within the state, and of the Federal Constitution, the public general acts of Congress, and the treaties of the United States. Laws of other states and foreign nations, municipal ordinances, and private acts of legislatures, are not judicially noticed in most states in the absence of statute providing therefor. However, municipal courts take judicial notice of ordinances of the same municipality, and statutes have been adopted in many states (generally in the form of the Uniform Judicial Notice of Foreign Law Act) providing that courts shall take judicial notice of the common law and statutes of every state, territory, and other jurisdictions of the United States, if the litigant invoking such law gives reasonable notice in his pleadings or otherwise of his intention to do so.

Courts generally take judicial notice of the names and terms of office of the principal or important public officials of the state and of the United States.

Judicial notice is taken of the record and proceedings in the same court and in the same case, but generally such notice does not extend to other proceedings in a different cause. Prominent geographical and natural features of the country, such as the large lakes and rivers, mountains, political subdivisions such as counties and cities, are proper subjects of judicial notice where they are matters of common knowledge. Matters of history, if sufficiently notorious to be subject to general knowledge, will be judicially noticed, as will important business, industrial, and economic matters. Judicial notice is taken of commonly known and well-established facts and principles relating to scientific and natural facts and phenomena, and of well-known and accepted statistical data, such as standard mortality and life expectancy tables and public health records. Customs and usages which are so generally known and accepted as to be, in effect, a part of the law of a jurisdiction, are a proper subject of judicial notice.

§ 11:3. Presumptions and inferences.

Am Jur 2d References: Evidence, §§ 159–248.

Presumptions play an important part in the proof of facts and in the law of evidence. A presumption may be defined as a principle of law that attaches definite probative value to specific facts or draws a particular inference as to the existence of one fact, not actually known, arising from its usual connection with other particular facts which are known or proved. Presumptions are intended to supply the place of facts, and, except for conclusive or irrebuttable presumptions of law, they may never be used to contradict or deny the existence of facts established by evidence. Where there is direct and positive proof of a fact, there is no need or room for a presumption relating to such fact.

Presumptions are divided into two general classes, presumptions of fact and presumptions of law. A presumption of fact is essentially an inference and may be defined as a logical and reasonable conclusion of the existence of a fact in a case, not presented by direct evidence as to the existence of the fact itself, but inferred from the establishment of other facts from which, by the process of logic and reason and on the basis of human experience, the existence of the assumed fact may be concluded by the trier of the fact. A presumption of this kind arises from the commonly accepted experiences of mankind and the inferences which reasonable men would draw from particular experiences and from the usual connection between the two facts. A presumption of fact must be based upon facts proved by evidence presented in the case, and there must be a rational connection between the facts proved and the ultimate fact presumed. And such a presumption ordinarily yields to the proof of the actual facts by evidence.

A presumption of law is an assumption made by the law itself, compelling the court to a resulting conclusion, which may or may not have a reasonable or logical foundation in basic fact. Such presumptions may be founded upon considerations of public policy and convenience, apart from or in addition to the probabilities arising from the facts proved by evidence. The law creates in some instances a conclusive or irrebuttable presumption upon the occurrence of specific facts. This is, in effect, a substantive rule of law, to be applied in the evaluation of the issues the same as any other fixed rule of law.

Presumptions of law must rest upon facts established by direct evidence, and as a general rule they cannot be based upon or inferred from other presumptions.

It is also sometimes stated that an inference cannot be based upon another inference; but this supposed principle is of doubtful validity and of little practical value, as all reasoning involving facts must proceed upon a series of inferences.

A rebuttable presumption of law is a rule of law declaring that for procedural purposes a certain prima facie probative force will be provisionally attached to a given state of facts until evidence sufficient to prove the contrary is introduced. Such a presumption imposes on the party against whom it is invoked the burden of "going forward with the evidence" and the duty to offer evidence as to the facts; and in the absence of such evidence, the trier of facts is compelled to reach a conclusion in accordance with the presumption. Most courts take the view that a presumption is not evidence, and that it disappears completely from the case upon the presentation of contravening evidence sufficient to meet the presumption, and that thereafter the assumed fact must be determined upon the evidence without any consideration of the presumption as such. However, some courts hold that a rebuttable presumption of law is itself evidence or has evidentiary value. Under this view, the presumption does not disappear when evidence contradicting it is received, but remains in the case to be considered by the jury as evidence. Whatever effect the introduction of contrary evidence has upon a presumption as such, however, it is generally agreed that the underlying facts upon which the presumption is based, and the inferences arising from such facts, remain in the case and retain their evidentiary value even though the presumption has vanished.

Where the same set of facts gives rise to two conflicting presumptions, their strength should be measured by the court, and the weaker presumption will yield to the stronger.

Among the numerous presumptions arising in particular factual situations, in the absence of proof to the contrary, may be mentioned the following:

— The presumption that persons act fairly, honestly, and in good faith and do not violate the law.

— The presumption that public officers, including judicial officers, have properly and faithfully discharged the duties of their office.

— Where a party fails to testify, or to produce available witnesses or evidence, or destroys or spoils evidence, without an adequate explanation, a presumption or inference arises that such evidence or testimony would have been unfavorable to him.

— The presumption that the law of a sister state is the same as that of the forum (which presumption applies in some jurisdictions, but not in others, with respect to the law of foreign countries, or to the law of countries whose jurisprudence is based upon the common law).

— The presumption that a letter duly mailed or a telegram regularly delivered to a telegraph company for transmission was received by the sendee.

— The presumption that every person is sane rather than incompetent.

— The presumption that every person understands and intends the natural and probable consequences of his voluntary acts.

— The presumption that a person exercised due care and was not guilty of negligence.

— The presumption against suicide where the cause of a death is not shown by the evidence.

— The presumption that everyone knows the law of the land, which presumption is ordinarily conclusive and is merely a different way of stating the substantive rule that ignorance of the law is not a defense or excuse.

— The presumption of innocence, which applies in both criminal and civil cases. This is a strong presumption of law, and in criminal cases it must be overcome by evidence establishing guilt beyond a reasonable doubt. That it is based upon the policy of the law to extend every possible precaution against the conviction of an innocent person, rather than on ordinary human experience or logical probability, is indicated by the fact that the presumption survives the indictment of an accused by a grand jury after due inquisition and consideration of the evidence.

— The presumption of identity of persons arising from identity of names.

— The presumption or inference that a condition or state of facts once established by proof continues to exist until the contrary is shown.

— The presumption that the possibility of issue is never extinct, regardless of the age of the woman or man involved.

§ 11:4. Burden of proof.

Am Jur 2d References:　Evidence, §§ 123–158.

The term "burden of proof" has two distinct meanings. In its strict and basic sense, the term denotes the burden of establishing the truth of a particular proposition or issue by such a quantum of evidence as the law requires in the case in which the issue arises. In its secondary sense, the term "burden of proof" is used to designate the obligation resting upon a party to meet with countervailing evidence a prima facie case created against him by evidence or presumption. The burden of proof in this secondary sense is frequently referred to as the necessity of going forward with the evidence and as the "burden of evidence."

The burden of proof in the primary sense of the term, i.e., the ultimate burden resting on a party to establish the truth of a given proposition or issue by the quantum of proof demanded by the law, never shifts during the course of the trial, but remains from the first to the last upon the party on whom the law cast it at the beginning of the trial. The burden of proof in the secondary sense, however, or the burden of going forward with evidence to meet the evidence produced or the prima facie case made by one's adversary, may shift or pass from side to side as the trial proceeds and evidence is introduced by the opposing parties. In short, the burden of proof, in the sense of the ultimate risk of non-persuasion, never shifts from the party who has the affirmative of an issue, but the burden of going forward with the evidence may shift from time to time during a trial.

As seen above, the burden of proof in the strict sense of the term rests upon the party who asserts the affirmative of the issue and who would be unsuccessful if no evidence at all were introduced. Thus, the burden is on the defendant to prove an affirmative defense. In criminal cases the burden is on the prosecution to prove, beyond a reasonable doubt, the essential elements of the offense with which the accused is charged. However, as to affirmative defenses, such as duress, entrapment, or insanity, the defendant has the burden of proving the matter by a preponderance of the evidence, although the ultimate and overall burden remains on the prosecution to prove the guilt of the defendant.

§ 11:5. Weight and sufficiency of evidence.

Am Jur 2d References: Evidence, §§ 1080–1178.

Although the comparative weight of different kinds of evidence is generally governed by rules of law, the weight to be given the testimony of witnesses depends in a large measure upon the credibility of the witnesses, and the determination of this matter is within the province of the jury. In weighing the evidence of witnesses, the jury may take into consideration their means of knowledge, their seeming honesty or lack of it, their opportunities for seeing and knowing about the things about which they testify, their demeanor on the witness stand, their manner of testifying, and their interest in the matter at issue or in the outcome of the case.

The testimony of a disinterested witness which is in no way discredited, or contradicted by other evidence, to a fact within his knowledge, which is not in itself improbable or in conflict with other evidence, must usually be accepted by the jury and may not be arbitrarily disregarded or rejected. It does not necessarily follow, however, that a verdict or finding must be made in favor of the party introducing such evidence, where the issue remains in dispute and doubt. Although the testimony of a disinterested witness is not directly contradicted by other witnesses, if there are circumstances which controvert it or explain it away, or if the testimony is clouded with uncertainty or improbability, or if it otherwise appears to be unworthy of belief, the trier of fact is not bound to accept it. Where testimony is on its face incredible, contrary to physical facts, settled scientific principles, or the laws of nature, or if it is opposed to common knowledge or to judicial notice, it may properly be disregarded, even though it is not controverted by other testimony. Upon the question of the weight to be given to the uncontradicted testimony of a party to an action or any person directly interested in the outcome of the trial, there is some difference of opinion. Many cases state the principle that such testimony does not conclusively establish the facts testified to, because the credibility of such a witness presents a question for the consideration of the jury.

In comparing the relative weight of different types of evidence, it is generally held that a writing or document made contemporaneously with a transaction is of greater probative force than oral testimony of a witness based upon memory of the transaction. Direct and positive testimony as to a fact is ordinarily accorded greater weight than circumstantial evidence relating to the same matter; but instances are not uncommon when circumstantial evidence is more convincing and reliable than direct testimony concerning the same facts. As a general rule, positive testimony is of greater weight than negative testimony. This means that as between two witnesses of equal credibility, the testimony of one that he saw or heard something will ordinarily outweigh the other's testimony that he did not see or hear the occurrence in question. In criminal prosecutions the testimony of accomplices is regarded with suspicion, and it is a common practice for the court to instruct the jury not to convict on the basis of such evidence without some corroborating evidence.

The degree of proof required depends upon the nature of the case. In a civil case the issues of fact are generally to be determined in accordance with the preponderance of the evidence, which means the greater weight of the credible evidence or the probability of truth. On some issues in civil cases a higher degree of proof is required, as noted in several places in the present work. In some instances "clear and convincing" proof is required. In a few cases proof "beyond a reasonable doubt" is required; but such a degree of proof is not ordinarily necessary, even as to an issue involving a crime. In a criminal prosecution, in order to warrant a conviction, the prosecution must present evidence proving the guilt of the accused beyond a reasonable doubt. A mere preponderance of the evidence will not support a conviction. "Reasonable doubt" in this connection means a real and substantial doubt of the defendant's guilt, based upon all of the evidence, and not a mere imaginary possibility of innocence. Where circumstantial evidence is relied upon in a criminal prosecution, it is generally required that the circumstances must not only concur to show that the defendant committed the crime and be consistent with the hypothesis of guilt, but also that they be inconsistent with or exclude every reasonable hypothesis or theory of innocence.

II. ADMISSIBILITY; RELEVANCY, MATERIALITY, AND COMPETENCY

§ 11:6. Generally.

Am Jur 2d References: Evidence, §§ 249–335, 352–407.

The admissibility of evidence in the trial of a civil action or criminal prosecution is governed by various rules of law, and in some instances by statutes and rules of court. Perhaps the most elementary and universal rule of evidence is that matters offered in evidence must be relevant to the issues of the case and must tend to establish or disprove them. To be admissible evidence offered must also be material, in that it must relate to the issues of the case. Evidence offered to prove a fact or proposition which is not in issue is "immaterial"; and evidence which does not logically tend to prove or disprove any material fact or proposition is "irrelevant." Even though proffered evidence is both relevant and material, it may be subject to objection under some other rule of law, such as the "best evidence" rule or the rule against hearsay evidence. Irrelevant and immaterial evidence is excluded not only bcause it may be unjustly inflammatory or prejudicial, but because its admission may cloud the issues and distract the jury's attention from the real issues to be resolved. The exclusion of evidence as not relevant or material is a matter largely within the discretion of the trial court, and a ruling thereon will not be disturbed on appeal unless an abuse of discretion clearly appears.

Evidence may be incompetent for one purpose but competent for another purpose; and where there are two or more defendants, evidence may be competent as against one of them but not against the other. In such cases the evidence should be admitted for the purpose, or as against the party, for which it is competent, with a proper instruction to the jury limiting the operation of the evidence.

As a general rule, the commission of an act cannot be proved by showing the commission of similar acts by the same person at other times, unless the acts are connected in some special way that indicates a relevancy beyond mere similarity of circumstances. Thus, in criminal cases evidence that the accused has committed another and separate offense is not admissible for the purpose of proving that he is guilty of the offense with which he stands charged. And in an action based on negligence, evidence of other acts of negligence on the part of the defendant on other occasions and not related to the present cause of action is not admissible to prove negligence. There are, however, several exceptions to this general rule. If the occurrence of other events or acts upon other like occasions has relevant and material bearing upon the fact in issue, evidence thereof may be admissible. The law permits proof of acts other than the one charged which are so related in character, time, and place of commission as to tend to support the conclusion that they were part of a single plan or system or as to tend to show the existence of such a plan or system. Evidence of other criminal acts is usually competent to prove the accused's identity, knowledge, intent, and motive, to show a common criminal scheme or plan, and to rebut a defense such as entrapment, accident, or mistake. And where evidence is relevant to the guilt of the accused of the offense with which he is presently charged, it will not be excluded merely because it tends to show the commission of other crimes by him.

In an action to recover for injury or damage resulting from the alleged dangerous condition of premises, appliances, or machinery, evidence of prior similar accidents or injuries to other persons at or near the same place or by the use of the same appliance or machinery is generally held to be admissible if the other accidents or injuries occurred under substantially the same conditions and are not too remote in point of time. Such evidence is admitted for the purpose of showing the existence of dangerous or defective premises or appliances, and notice or knowledge thereof on the part of the defendant, and generally not for the purpose of proving specific or independent acts of negligence or the cause of the accident or injury sued on. Under similar principles and on similar conditions, evidence of the absence of other accidents at the place in question or resulting from the use or operation of the same appliance is generally admissible.

Considerable latitude is allowed in the introduction of evidence for the purpose of identification of persons and things. Fingerprints may constitute strong evidence of identification where they are properly authenticated; and evidence of palmprints or of tracks or footprints is also competent in a proper case. Evidence of trailing by bloodhounds is admissible in many states, where the proper foundation is laid by showing the qualification of the dogs and the manner in which the trailing was conducted; but such evidence is rejected in some jurisdictions. Evidence of telephone conversations is admissible where it is relevant to the facts in issue and the parties to the conversation are properly identified; and the fact that a call was made may be a relevant matter in a case.

Where the value of real or personal property is in issue, the fact to be established is generally its market value. For this purpose, it is proper to receive direct opinion of experts as to such value, and market reports of prices for such property are admissible. Prices at which the particular property, or property of similar nature, has been sold in bona fide sales, are admissible as evidence of value; but mere offers to buy or sell are not generally admitted. Valuation for the purpose of taxation is not generally admissible.

As a broad general rule, evidence directly or indirectly showing that the defendant in a personal injury or death action carries liability insurance protecting him against liability to third persons on account of his negligence is not admissible. The fact that evidence, which is otherwise relevant and competent, incidentally or indirectly indicates that such insurance is carried does not render the evidence inadmissible.

§ 11:7. Character and reputation.

Am Jur 2d References: Evidence, §§ 336–351.

Except where it is directly in issue, the character or reputation of a party is regarded as irrelevant and inadmissible in most kinds of civil actions.   Where he testifies as a witness in his own behalf, however, his credibility may be impeached by evidence of his bad reputation for truth and veracity, and he may in turn introduce evidence of his good reputation in this regard where his reputation has been impeached.   In criminal cases, evidence of the good character and reputation of the accused is admissible in his behalf for the purpose of strengthening the presumption of innocence and of making it seem unlikely that he would have committed the offense charged against him.   Unless the defendant introduces evidence of his good character, however, the prosecution cannot introduce evidence of his bad character or reputation.

§ 11:8. Evidence illegally or improperly obtained.

Am Jur 2d References: Evidence, §§ 408–435.

At common law, the admissibility of evidence is not affected by the illegality of the means by which it was obtained.   Under this rule, if evidence offered in support of a fact in issue is relevant and otherwise competent, it is generally admissible although it may have been obtained wrongfully or unlawfully, unless its admission will violate some constitutional guaranty of the person against whom its admission is sought, or is in contravention of a statutory enactment of the jurisdiction.   Courts, in the administration of the criminal law, will not, as a general rule, inquire into or investigate the source from which evidence comes or the means by which it was obtained.

In 1914 the United States Supreme Court in the case of Weeks v United States, 232 US 383, 58 L Ed 652, 34 S Ct 341, laid down the rule that evidence obtained by an unlawful search and seizure by federal officers is not admissible against an accused in a prosecution in a federal court.   This rule was originally based upon the prohibition of unreasonable search and seizure in the Fourth Amendment to the Federal Constitution, but later decisions have predicated the rule upon the constitutional guaranty of the Fifth Amendment against self-incrimination and upon the theory that the rule is merely an exercise by the Supreme Court of its supervisory power over the administration of criminal justice in the federal courts.   Until 1960, this rule did not apply, under the so-called "silver platter" doctrine, to the use in federal courts of evidence obtained by illegal search and seizure by state officers, without federal participation; but the "silver platter" doctrine was overruled in that year by the Supreme Court in Elkins v United States, 364 US 206, 4 L Ed 2d 1669, 80 S Ct 1437.

In the state courts, some jurisdictions followed the doctrine laid down in the Weeks Case, while others applied the contrary common-law rule.   In 1961, however, the Supreme Court held in the case of Mapp v Ohio, 367 US 643, 6 L Ed 2d 1081, 81 S Ct 1684, 84 ALR2d 933, that as a matter of due process, evidence obtained by a search and seizure in violation of the Fourth Amendment is inadmissible in a state court, as it is in a federal court.   This new rule does not, however, require the states to follow the federal requirements as to reasonable and probable cause for arrest and search.

The rule of inadmissibility of evidence obtained by an unlawful search and seizure extends to and bars not only articles seized but also oral evidence of what was found, seen, or heard during the search, including statements made by the accused. And the rule proscribes the use of all evidence obtained as an indirect result of the unlawful search. The rule does not, however, prevent the admission of such evidence to discredit the voluntary testimony of the defendant.

An unlawful search made by a private individual on his own initiative is not within the rule barring evidence obtained by unlawful search and seizure. Thus, a trespasser may testify to pertinent acts observed by him or may put in evidence pertinent articles or papers found by him while trespassing, even though he may be civilly or criminally liable for the trespass.

In order to have a standing to complain of the use of evidence obtained by an unlawful search and seizure, an accused must show an interest in the premises searched or the property seized. A lessee or tenant is held to have such an interest in the premises which he rents; and the protection of the rule extends to guests and other persons legitimately on the premises unlawfully searched.

In the absence of a statute forbidding the use thereof, evidence is not inadmissible merely because it was obtained by intercepting letters or telephone or telegraph messages, or by eavesdropping or spying. It was ruled by the Supreme Court in 1928 in Olmstead v United States, 277 US 438, 72 L Ed 944, 48 S Ct 564, 66 ALR 376, that the Fourth Amendment prohibition of unreasonable searches and seizures is not violated by a tapping of telephone wires and that evidence is not rendered inadmissible by the fact that it was obtained by wiretapping. However, the Federal Communications Act (47 USC § 605) now provides that, with certain exceptions, no person not authorized by the sender shall intercept any communication and divulge or publish the contents or substance thereof. This statute is held to require the exclusion of evidence as to communications intercepted by the tapping of telephone or telegraph lines, in both federal and state courts, but not to affect the admissibility of evidence obtained by eavesdropping by means of electronic or mechanical devices not involving wiretapping. And the statute does not apply where either of the parties to a conversation or communication consented to its interception or permitted a third person to listen in.

§ 11:9. Privileged relations and communications

Am Jur 2d References: Witnesses (1st ed §§ 363–548).

Confidential communications between persons bearing certain relationships to each other are privileged against disclosure in evidence by either party without the consent of the other. Such privilege is based upon the policy of the law to encourage, and to protect the privacy of, full and frank disclosure of all matters as between persons occupying the particular relationships. The privilege of such communications is not related to the privilege against self-incrimination, discussed below, § 11:30.

The common-law privilege of confidential communications was originally limited to the relationships of husband and wife and attorney and client. Except for the privilege extended to communications between persons of these relationships, and the privileges declared by statute, the public interest in the disclosure of all facts relevant to a litigated issue is deemed to be paramount to any consideration of the inviolability of a communication made in reliance on personal confidence or on a fiduciary, contract, or business relationship. Even the most confidential communications between parent and child are not privileged. By statutes in many states, communications between physician and patient and confessions made to priests and clergymen in their professional capacity are now privileged. Unless so declared by statute, communications to nurses, or hospital or public health records, are not privileged; but statutes frequently regulate the disclosure of such communications and records, and under some circumstances they may be protected by the physician-patient privilege. Communications to newspaper reporters or journalists or to detectives are not privileged at common law, with respect to either the substance or the source of the information; but statutes in some states afford a limited privilege to such communications.

Communications to public officers and employees are not generally privileged in the absence of statute, unless they involve state secrets. The disclosure of such matters, however, including communications by informers to police or prosecuting officials, is frequently regulated by statute. Courts will not compel the disclosure of state or military secrets in ordinary judicial proceedings, but it is for the courts, rather than the executive branch of government, to determine whether particular documents or information qualify for such privilege and whether disclosure would be harmful to the public interest.

As a general rule, a privilege as to confidential communications may be invoked only by the person in whose favor it exists or someone in his behalf, and the privilege may be waived only by that person. A third person who overhears a confidential communication, by eavesdropping or otherwise, is not affected by the privilege and may testify as to the communication. However, some courts exclude even the testimony of third persons concerning confidential letters between husband and wife.

The privilege of communications between husband and wife exists independently of the rule that one spouse is incompetent to testify as a witness against the other; and the abrogation of the latter rule by statute does not affect the privilege of communications between spouses. Nor is this privilege, with respect to confidential communications made during marriage, affected by the subsequent divorce or death of the parties.

III. BEST AND SECONDARY EVIDENCE

§ 11:10. Generally.

Am Jur 2d References: Evidence, §§ 448–470.

It is an elementary principle of law that the best evidence of which the case or issue is susceptible and which is within the power of the party to produce must always be adduced in proof of every disputed fact. Evidence will not be received which indicates on its face that it is secondary—that is, merely substitutionary in its nature—and that the original source of information is in existence and accessible. This rule does not purport to include the substitution of weaker for stronger evidence, which any litigant has the right to decide for himself; it only comprehends a situation where the evidence offered is clearly substitutionary in its nature, although directed to the same issue as the original evidence which is withheld.

In modern practice the best evidence rule is usually invoked where proof is to be made of some fact of which there is a record in writing or where there is an attempt to substitute oral for documentary evidence. The rule as generally applied means merely that the contents of an available written document must be proved by introduction of the document itself. Where proof is to be made of some fact which is recorded in a writing, the best evidence of the contents of the writing consists in the actual production of the document itself, and the contents of the document may not ordinarily be proved by oral testimony, unless the failure to produce the document itself is properly accounted for.

The best evidence rule has no application to a case where a party seeks to prove a fact which has an existence independently of any writing; he may prove the independent fact by oral testimony, even though the fact has been reduced to, or is evidenced by, a writing. It is not contrary to the best evidence rule that oral testimony of a fact in issue may be primary evidence thereof, although there is written evidence of the same fact, where the essential fact to be proved is neither the existence nor the contents of the writing, but the existence of the independent fact itself to which the writing is merely collateral.

Secondary evidence of the contents of a writing may be submitted where a proper showing is made by the party offering it that the original writing cannot be produced by him within a reasonable time by the exercise of reasonable diligence. Circumstances which usually permit the introduction of secondary evidence include instances where the primary or best evidence is outside the jurisdiction of the court, where it has been lost or destroyed, and where it is in the possession of the adverse party, who fails to produce it after proper notice. Where a proper foundation has been laid for the introduction of secondary evidence, it is required in a majority of American jurisdictions that the party produce the best secondary evidence which is within his power to produce.

§ 11:11. Particular kinds of documents and writings.

Am Jur 2d References: Evidence, §§ 471–492.

The best evidence rule has been invoked with respect to a great many types of documents and writings, public and private. Thus, a witness will not be permitted to testify to the contents of a letter unless it is shown that the letter itself cannot be produced. And the same rule applies to telegrams. Insofar as books of account are admissible as evidence of the facts contained therein, the best evidence rule usually requires their production, or some excuse for nonproduction, before allowing proof of a secondary character. However, where no attempt is made to show the contents of such books, but to show certain facts independently thereof, a witness having knowledge of such facts may testify thereto without introducing books containing the same facts. The best evidence rule is frequently applied to the proof of instruments of title, such as deeds, leases, and mortgages. Where the acts of a corporation are recorded in the corporate books and records, those books and records are the best evidence of such acts, and if available, the rules of evidence require their production as proof of those acts.

The best evidence of a judicial record is the record itself or a duly authenticated copy thereof, and oral testimony will not generally be admitted as to the contents of such records or as to matters established by a judgment. Other public records and documents are subject to the same rule: the records or documents themselves, or certified copies thereof, should be produced where their contents are material to an inquiry.

The original of a writing, document, or record is the best or primary evidence of its contents. Copies are mere secondary evidence and will not ordinarily be admitted in evidence over objection, in the absence of statutory provision to the contrary, unless it is shown that the original cannot be produced. Where an instrument is executed in duplicate, both copies are regarded as originals. A carbon copy is a duplicate original for the purpose of the best evidence rule if it is duly executed by the parties. And unsigned carbon copies of letters and other writings, where duly authenticated, have been treated as duplicate originals in many cases, although other courts regard such unsigned carbon copies as secondary evidence. Photographic, photostatic, and other types of copies produced by modern copying machines are regarded as any other copy, in the absence of statute, and hence are secondary evidence under the best evidence rule. However, the increased use of the improved reproduction methods has led to the adoption in many jurisdictions of the Uniform Photographic Copies of Business and Public Records as Evidence Act, and similar statutes, under which copies so made are as admissible in evidence as the original writing or record itself.

IV. HEARSAY EVIDENCE

§ 11:12. Generally.

Am Jur 2d References: Evidence, §§ 493–507.

It is a general rule that hearsay evidence is not competent or admissible in judicial proceedings. "Hearsay" may be defined, for the purposes of this rule, as evidence which derives its value, not solely from the credit to be given the witness on the stand, but in part from the veracity and competency of some other person. The basis of the exclusion of hearsay evidence lies in the fact that such testimony is not subject to the tests which can ordinarily be applied for the ascertainment of the truth of testimony. The declarant or person quoted is not present and available for cross-examination, and the court and jury have no opportunity to test the credibility of hearsay statements by observing the demeanor of the person who made them. In addition, the hearsay statement is usually by one who is not under oath, although the hearsay rule may be applied to statements made under oath. Hearsay evidence is frequently admissible in certain types of proceedings, such as proceedings before administrative agencies, government commissions, and in some cases before inferior courts. And the incompetency of such evidence may be waived in any kind of proceeding by a failure to make timely objection the veto. Where it is admitted without objection, hearsay evidence will be considered along with the other evidence, although its weight is minimized by the same inherent weakness which affords grounds for its exclusion upon objection.

The hearsay rule is subject to several exceptions which are as firmly established as the rule itself. The reasons underlying these exceptions are a necessity for the exception and a circumstantial guaranty of the trustworthiness of the evidence offered. Among the exceptions to the general rule are those applied in cases of family history, relationship, and pedigree; matters involving prescription, custom, and usage, and boundaries, and matters of general and public history. Other important exceptions to the hearsay rule are applied in connection with admissions and declarations against interest, documents, business records, and statements and acts which are a part of the res gestae.

The clearest case of hearsay is that where a witness testifies as to the declarations of another for the purpose of proving the facts asserted by the declarant. But the hearsay rule has no application to evidence offered to prove that a statement was made or a conversation had, rather than the truth thereof. And where the sanity of a person is in issue, his declarations may be admissible as proof of his mental condition, not of what he said. The rule excluding hearsay as evidence is not limited to oral testimony, but applies to written statements as well. And statements made under oath may be objectionable as hearsay. The question whether the results of a survey or opinion poll are admissible or constitute hearsay is the subject of some difference of opinion.

§ 11:13. Family history, relationship, and pedigree.

Am Jur 2d References: Evidence, §§ 508–522.

A well-established exception to the rule excluding hearsay evidence exists in respect of proof of matters of family history, relationship, and pedigree, hearsay evidence being generally competent to prove such matters. This exception to the hearsay rule is commonly referred to as the "pedigree" exception, and it includes not only matters of ancestry and other relationship, but also certain facts which go to make up pedigree, such as birth, age, and race. Such evidence is held admissible not only because of the difficulty of producing better evidence, but also because of its general reliability.

In some instances it has been held that matters of pedigree may be proved by evidence of general reputation, but in other cases proof of pedigree is made by evidence of oral or written declarations. In order for declarations to be admissible for this purpose, it must be shown that it is impossible to produce the declarant himself as a witness because he has died or is otherwise unavailable. And the declarations must have been made prior to the filing of the action in which proof thereof is offered. Furthermore, it is held in many jurisdictions that such evidence will be received only if it emanates from a source within the family, from a person shown to be related by blood or affinity to the family in question. According to this view, declarations concerning pedigree by neighbors, friends or acquaintances, physicians, attorneys, or servants of the family, have been held not admissible in evidence. In other jurisdictions a broad view is taken on the admissibility of persons other than members of the family as to pedigree, these courts admitting evidence of the declarations of anyone who, because of his relations or association with the family, was in a position to know the facts. Although the testimony of a person as to his own parentage and age is obviously and necessarily based upon hearsay, this does not render such testimony inadmissible.

V. CONFESSIONS

§ 11:14. Generally.

Am Jur 2d References:　Evidence, §§ 523–542, 591–596.

A confession is an express acknowledgment by a defendant of his guilt of a crime with which he is charged. It is a voluntary admission or declaration made to another of one's commission of, or agency or participation in, a crime. A confession is an admission of guilt of a criminal act as distinguished from an admission of some fact or circumstance from which guilt may be inferred. Confessions are classified as either judicial or extrajudicial. A judicial confession is one made before a committing magistrate or in a court in the due course of legal proceedings; it is in effect a plea of guilty. Confessions on preliminary examinations before a magistrate, at a coroner's inquest, or before a grand jury are sometimes termed "quasi-judicial confessions."

The admissibility of confessions in evidence in a criminal prosecution is well settled. Extrajudicial confessions of an accused, if shown to have been made voluntarily, without improper inducements, and not in violation of his rights to counsel and to remain silent, are universally recognized as being admissible in evidence against him, subject to the requirement of corroboration and proof of the corpus delicti. A confession, to be admissible in evidence, need not be admissible as a whole, although, if introduced in part by the prosecution, the accused has the right to prove the whole statement. In some states statutes regulate the admission of confessions in evidence. In the absence of statutory provision to the contrary, a judicial confession voluntarily made is admissible in evidence, whether it takes the form of a plea of guilty or is found in other statements made by the accused in the course of legal proceedings in a court. There is a conflict of authority on the question of the admissibility of evidence of a plea of guilty which has been withdrawn by the accused by leave of court.

Voluntariness is the test of admissibility of any confession, judicial or extrajudicial. A confession is admissible against an accused, in either state or federal court, only if it was freely and voluntarily made, without duress, fear, or compulsion in its inducement, and with full knowledge of the nature and consequences of the confession. The exclusion of involuntary confessions is often based on the reason that such confessions cannot be relied upon as true, since persons influenced by hope of benefit or by fear induced by violence or threats may confess to alleged crimes which they did not commit. However, it need not be established that a confession is false to have it rejected because involuntarily made. Aside from other reasons for excluding involuntary confessions, it is well settled that a conviction obtained in a state court by means of a coerced confession deprives the defendant of liberty without due process of law, even though statements in the confession are independently established as true and there is ample evidence aside from the confession to support a conviction.

It is generally held that the admissibility of an extrajudicial confession is dependent upon its corroboration by other evidence, but the decisions differ as to the extent of such evidence required and the order of proof. In most cases, it has been required that the corroborative evidence relate to the corpus delicti, and that before the prosecution can use a confession of a defendant there must be submitted other evidence tending to prove the corpus delicti—that is, that the crime with which the defendant is charged and to which he confessed has actually been committed by someone. Other courts hold that the order of proof is unimportant, and that it is within the discretion of the trial court to permit the introduction of a confession before the production of the corroboration. In any event, however, independent corroborative evidence of the corpus delicti must be introduced at some stage of the trial in order to support a conviction.

If it meets the general requirements for admissibility, the form of a confession is immaterial: it may be in writing, oral, or embodied in a sound recording. A confession is not rendered inadmissible by the reference therein to the commission of unrelated and separate offenses. Where the relevant parts relating to the crime charged can be readily separated from the parts confessing to other crimes, it is usually required that this be done; but where such separation is impracticable, a cautionary instruction to the jury will generally suffice. A confession made by a codefendant or coconspirator after the commission of a crime or the termination of the conspiracy cannot be admitted against the other defendants, where such confession was not made in their presence and assented to by them. According to the general rule, if several defendants are tried together, the confession of one defendant may be admitted against him with instructions to the jury that it is only admitted against that one defendant and is not to be considered as evidence against his codefendants. Where it is feasible to do so, the part of the confession pertaining to the guilt of a codefendant may properly be omitted.

A difficult problem is presented where a defendant offers evidence of a confession by a third person that he committed the crime with which the defendant is charged. It is the general rule followed by most courts that evidence of such confession is not admissible as substantive evidence tending to exculpate the accused unless it constitutes part of the res gestae, even though it was made in expectation of imminent death or by a person jointly indicted with the accused. The reason given for excluding such evidence is that it is hearsay. The inaccessibility or death of the person making the confession is held not to affect the rule of inadmissibility. This general rule has been criticized, and some courts have declined to follow it.

§ 11:15. Voluntariness of confession; advising defendant of his rights.

Am Jur 2d References: Evidence, §§ 543–590.

As the term is used in the present discussion, a "voluntary" confession means a confession made of the free will and accord of the defendant without coercion induced by fear or threat of harm, and without inducement by promising or holding out hope of reward or immunity. A confession obtained under the influence of fear, especially fear induced by threats of bodily harm, torture, personal violence, or abuse, or by holding out a promise or hope of reward or immunity—in short, a confession which is forced or extorted in any manner by overpersuasion, promise, or threats—is an involuntary confession within the rule excluding such confessions as evidence. If the defendant's will is overborne or if his confession is not the product of a rational mind and a free will, his confession is inadmissible because coerced, and it is immaterial whether the coercion consists of physical intimidation or pyschological pressure.

The fact that a confession is made while the confesser is under arrest (even by an illegal arrest), or in the custody of a police officer, does not render it inadmissible in the absence of any force, threat, promise, or other conduct destroying the voluntariness of the confession. However, the circumstance of arrest or police custody may be taken into consideration, along with the other circumstances, in determining voluntariness. A mere delay in the arraignment of a defendant does not render involuntary his confession made during such delay, in prosecutions in state courts. In federal court prosecutions, however, such a delay may preclude the admission of a confession in evidence, under the provision of the Federal Rules of Criminal Procedure. And such a delay may be one of the factors to be taken into consideration in determining voluntariness even in a state court prosecution.

Spontaneity is not essential to the voluntariness of a confession, and the fact that a confession was elicited by inquiries and questions addressed to the accused does not render it inadmissible. Even prolonged questioning does not necessarily make involuntary a confession following the same. It is clear, however, that a confession secured by "third degree" methods is inadmissible. A process of interrogation can be so prolonged and unremitting, especially when accompanied by deprivation of rest, refreshment, or relief, or when conducted by relays of trained inquisitors for unreasonable periods of time under conditions calculated to overpower the will and resistance of the suspect, as to accomplish extortion of a confession, and such a confession is obviously inadmissible in evidence.

In a series of decisions culminating in Miranda v Arizona, the United States Supreme Court has in late years decreed certain procedural safeguards to secure the privilege against self-incrimination by means of interrogation of persons in the custody of law enforcement officers. The rule of the Miranda Case requires that, prior to any questioning of a person in custody, he must be warned that he has a right to remain silent, that any statement he makes may be used against him, and that he has a right to the presence of an attorney, either retained by him or appointed for him; and that the opportunity to exercise these rights must be afforded to him throughout the interrogation. After such warning has been given, and such opportunity given him, the individual may knowingly waive these rights and agree to answer questions or make a statement, but unless and until such warnings and waiver are shown by the prosecution at a trial, no evidence obtained as a result of interrogation can be used against him. However, the Miranda rule is concerned with the interrogation of suspects, and it does not affect the admissibility of a statement volunteered by a person or information furnished without questioning or request.

The fact that a confession is obtained by fraud, deception, or trickery practiced upon an accused does not render the confession inadmissible, provided the means employed are not calculated to procure an untrue statement and the confession is otherwise freely and voluntarily made. This rule has been applied to confessions obtained by representations to an accused that an accomplice has made statements incriminating him; to statements made to an informer or a fellow prisoner acting to entrap the accused; and to information obtained by eavesdropping.

Where objection is made to the introduction of evidence of a confession, on the ground that it was involuntary, it is the duty of the trial court to hear evidence and make a determination as to the voluntariness of the confession before admitting testimony before the jury concerning the confession. Although there was a contrariety of opinion as to the proper procedure prior to the decision in Jackson v Denno, 378 US 368, 12 L Ed 2d 908, 84 S Ct 1774, 1 ALR3d 1205, it appears to be settled now that the hearing by the court in the first instance to determine the admissibility of a pretrial confession must be had in the absence of the jury; in other words, the jury should be excluded from this preliminary hearing to determine voluntariness. If the court (or a special jury convened solely for that purpose) concludes that the confession was involuntary, it should not be submitted at all to the jury deciding the guilt or innocence of the accused. If it is decided on this preliminary hearing that the confession was voluntary and is admissible in evidence, the jury may, under the rule followed in some jurisdictions, still pass upon the voluntariness of the confession; in other jurisdictions, the jury is concerned only with the credibility of the confession and not its admissibility.

VI. DECLARATIONS AND ADMISSIONS

§ 11:16. Generally.

Am Jur 2d References: Evidence, §§ 597–622, 646–707.

In the law of evidence, a "declaration" may be defined as an unsworn statement made by a party to a transaction or by one having an interest in the existence of some fact in relation to the transaction. A "declaration" is the assertion or statement of a fact, whereas an "admission" is a voluntary acknowledgment made by a party of the existence or truth of certain facts which are inconsistent with his claim in an action and which amount therefore to proof against him. One principle applicable to both declarations and admissions is that if such a statement is admissible in evidence, it is admissible as an entirety, including parts that are unfavorable as well as those that are favorable to the party offering it in evidence. Where a statement admitted in evidence as a declaration or admission constitutes part of a conversation or correspondence, the opponent is entitled to have placed in evidence all that was said or written by or to the declarant in the course of such conversation or correspondence, provided the other statements have some bearing upon or connection with the admission or declaration in evidence. And these principles apply in criminal prosecutions as well as in civil actions.

The admissions of a party, made directly by him or through an authorized agent, or by a privy, relative to the subject matter of a suit, are admissible in evidence against such party where they are inconsistent with the claim he asserts in the action, whether he is the plaintiff or defendant, and whether or not he is available as a witness. Although referred to as an exception to the hearsay rule, this principle is as well established as the hearsay rule itself. On the other hand, declarations made out of court and without the sanction of an oath, by one not a party to the action, are merely hearsay, and as such are generally inadmissible in evidence, although exceptions have been engrafted on this rule in cases involving proof of family history, declarations against interest, certain dying declarations, and some other situations. In any event, to be admissible in evidence, an admission or declaration must be relevant to the issues of the case. The basic rules governing the admissibility of extrajudicial admissions and declarations are generally applicable in criminal prosecutions as well as in civil cases.

An important exception to the hearsay rule renders admissible in evidence relevant declarations against interest by one not a party nor in privity with a party to the action, where the declarant has since died or is otherwise unavailable as a witness. This is a departure from the general rule that, in the absence of statute, the death of the declarant is not a ground for admitting evidence of his declarations, and that even dying declarations are generally inadmissible in civil cases and are admitted in criminal cases only in prosecutions involving homicide. Self-serving declarations are not only hearsay but are obviously not trustworthy; and such declarations are not generally admissible in either a civil or criminal case.

Judicial admissions are competent evidence against the party who made them, and may constitute the basis of a verdict or judgment, whether made in writing, orally by counsel, or by the testimony of a party. Such admissions are substitutes for, and dispense with, the actual proof of facts. A party is bound and concluded by a statement made in his pleading in a case. It is an elementary rule of pleading, apart from the law of evidence, that a party is not required to prove allegations admitted by his adversary to be true. And by the rules of evidence, a statement of fact from a party in his pleading is an admission that the fact exists as stated, and as such is admissible against him in favor of his adversary. While a party is not bound by a statement inserted in a pleading filed in his behalf unless he authorized its insertion, allegations in his pleadings may fairly be deemed, prima facie, to have been approved by him. Admissions in a pleading may be admissible against the pleader in another action, on behalf of a stranger to the former action. In the absence of a statutory provision to the contrary, the record in a criminal case showing a plea of guilty by the accused is admissible against him in a subsequent civil action arising out of the same offense, as his deliberate declaration or admission against interest. This rule does not, however, apply to a plea of nolo contendere. According to the weight of authority, a pleading containing an admission against the pleader is admissible in evidence against him in the same or different proceedings, although the pleading was amended, superseded, abandoned, or withdrawn in the case in which it was filed.

§ 11:17. Admissions by acts, conduct, or silence.

Am Jur 2d References: Evidence, §§ 623–645.

The acts and conduct of a party are frequently as expressive as spoken or written statements, and they may be proved in some instances under the principles applicable to admissions. Thus, evidence to show that a party fled, concealed himself, assumed a false name, attempted to escape, or destroyed or concealed relevant evidence, is admissible as an admission of guilt or responsibility. The refusal of the accused in a criminal case to submit to a test to determine the amount of alcohol in his system has been held admissible in some cases, but has been rejected in others. Evidence of attempts to influence a witness of the opponent is generally held to be admissible. Evidence of repairs made or precautions taken subsequently to an accident is generally held not admissible as an admission of negligence in connection with the accident.

It is a general rule, based on the public policy favoring the settlement of disputed claims out of court, that an unaccepted offer of compromise does not constitute an admission on the part of the person making it. Such an offer is regarded as an effort to obtain peace rather than as an admission of liability or of the validity of the opponent's claim. However, an independent statement or admission may be admissible although it is contained in an offer of compromise or is made in the course of negotiations to effect a settlement, unless it is so closely connected with the offer of compromise as to be inseparable therefrom. And evidence of a valid agreement compromising a controversy is generally held to be admissible in an action involving the same controversy, where for some reason the agreement of settlement was not performed. A compromise settlement of claims of third persons arising out of the same accident or transaction as is involved in the instant action is not admissible as an admission of liability. And an offer to pay, or payment of, medical, hospital, or other expenses, is generally not admissible in a personal injury action, as such an offer or act may ordinarily be attributed to humane impulses rather than to an admission of liability.

The silence of a person under conditions and circumstances which call upon him to speak may be shown in evidence as indicating an admission by him. If a statement is made in the presence of a person in regard to facts affecting his rights, and he makes no reply, his silence may be construed as a tacit admission of the facts stated. Such evidence, however, is to be received and weighed with caution, since the assumption of assent based on silence is at best a flimsy one, and its validity and weight depend upon all of the circumstances attending the statement and the silence. Under the conditions that the courts have imposed upon the introduction of evidence of an admission by silence, it is generally held that the evidence must disclose that (1) the statement was made in the party's presence and hearing; (2) he was capable of understanding the meaning of the statement; (3) he had sufficient knowledge of the facts embraced in the statement to reply thereto; (4) he was at liberty and had the opportunity to deny it or reply thereto; and (5) the statement was made under such circumstances and by such persons as would naturally call for a reply. The doctrine of assent by silence does not ordinarily apply to statements made in the course of judicial proceedings.

A failure to reply to statements made in a letter is not ordinarily considered an implied admission by the addressee of the truth of the statements. However, where the letter is a part of a course of mutual correspondence that has been carried on by the parties concerning a particular subject, a failure to reply to a statement therein concerning such subject matter, which statement the addressee would naturally deny if not true, has been held in a number of cases to indicate an admission of the truth of the statement.

In criminal cases it is a general rule that when a statement tending to incriminate one accused of committing a crime is made in his presence, and the statement is not denied, contradicted, or objected to by him, both the statement and his failure to deny are admissible against him, as evidence of his acquiescence in its truth and of his tacit admission of the facts stated or as indicative of a consciousness of guilt. In order for the failure of the accused person to deny an incriminating statement to be admissible in evidence against him, however, the nature of the statement must be such as would, under the circumstances, naturally provoke a denial from an innocent person. Where the accusatory statement is made while the accused is under arrest and in police custodial interrogation, the fact that the accused stood mute and made no reply cannot be used in evidence against him, under the rule of the Miranda Case, supra §§ 11:14, 11:15. And silence on the advice of counsel may not be construed as an admission.

§ 11:18. Res gestae; spontaneous exclamations.

Am Jur 2d References: Evidence, §§ 708–737.

One of the exceptions to the hearsay rule is the "res gestae" or "spontaneous exclamations" exception. "Res gestae" may be broadly defined as matter incidental to the main or principal fact, and explanatory thereof. It may include acts and words which are so closely connected therewith as to constitute a part of the transaction or occurrence—that is, acts and words which are spontaneous and so related to the transaction or occurrence in question as reasonably to appear to be evoked and prompted by it. So far as statements are concerned, "res gestae" comprehends a situation which presents a startling or unusual occurrence sufficient to produce a spontaneous and instinctive reaction, during which interval certain statements are made under such circumstances as to show lack of forethought or deliberate design in the formulation of their content. Statements which conform to these requirements and which in some way elucidate, qualify, or characterize the act in question are admissible in evidence in both civil and criminal cases as a distinct exception to the hearsay rule.

The basis for the admission of declarations under the res gestae rule is the belief that statements made instinctively at the time of a transaction or event, without opportunity for formulation of statements favorable to one's own cause, are likely to be true and to cast important light upon the matter in issue. From the very nature of the res gestae or spontaneous statement rule, it is clear that spontaneity is the most important factor governing the admissibility of such utterances. Res gestae statements derive their sanction as evidence from the fact that the circumstances of their utterance so far eliminate intention or opportunity for fabrication as to provide a reasonable substitute for an oath. The factual situation in each case largely determines the extent to which the court will apply the rule.

Statements, written or oral, may themselves constitute facts which are a part of the transaction in question, and they are admissible in evidence under the rule of res gestae. Such statements are in the nature of verbal acts and are admissible to prove the nature of an act rather than to prove the truth of the statement. Evidence of statements may be received in order to establish the relevant fact that a particular conversation was had or that notice or warning was given.

It is frequently stated as a general rule that a declaration or utterance sought to be proved as res gestae or spontaneous exclamation must have been contemporaneous with the event established as the principal act; it must spring from this act at the time of its occurrence, without any interval or opportunity for deliberation in forming the statement. What is "contemporaneous," however, depends upon the circumstances of the case. Except for verbal acts, the declaration or utterance need not be simultaneous with the principal act; it may be subsequent to it, provided there has not been time for the influence of the act to be dissipated; and declarations made immediately preceding a specific occurrence which tend to illustrate and give character to the act are admissible as part of the res gestae. If the utterance springs from the principal fact, tends to explain it, and is made at a time so near it as to preclude the idea of deliberate design or fabrication, it may be regarded as "contemporaneous" and is admissible in evidence.

Declarations of a party himself may be admissible as evidence in his own behalf as part of the res gestae, when they accompany and explain his actions and otherwise meet the requirements of the res gestae rule. But the rule is not limited to statements of parties to the action. Thus, in both civil and criminal cases the view is followed by most of the courts that have considered the question, that declarations uttered under circumstances which would otherwise make them admissible as part of the res gestae are not to be excluded because they were uttered by a bystander who was not an actor or participant in the transaction, except as he was made such by the declarations themselves. In order that statements of bystanders may be admitted as part of the res gestae, however, it must appear that the bystander actually witnessed the principal act to which the statement relates. The fact that the declarant is incompetent to testify as a witness will not ordinarily affect the admissibility of his statements under the res gestae rule.

VII. EVIDENCE AT FORMER TRIAL OR PROCEEDING

§ 11:19. Generally.

Am Jur 2d References: Evidence, §§ 738–768.

Testimony given at a former trial or proceeding is not admissible in a subsequent action or proceeding between the parties, unless the proper foundation is laid, as pointed out below, to bring the testimony within an exception to the hearsay rule. The witness himself must be produced if he is available. The law recognizes, however, that it is sometimes impossible to produce a witness who has testified at a former trial, as where the witness dies, becomes insane, is out of the jurisdiction, or is kept away from the trial by the opposing party. In such cases, where the second action is between the same parties or their privies and involves the same issues, and where the party against whom the evidence is offered had an opportunity to cross-examine the witness who gave the testimony, such testimony given at the former hearing or trial is admissible in the later one. Because such testimony has been given under the sanction of an oath and subject to the right of cross-examination, it is not open to the objections ordinarily urged against hearsay evidence. It is admitted on the principle that it is the best of which the case admits. In many jurisdictions statutes have been enacted governing the reproduction of testimony given upon a former trial.

The foregoing principles are generally applicable to criminal prosecutions, and testimony given at a former trial, or on the preliminary examination of the accused, is admissible against him if the witness who gave it is dead, beyond the jurisdiction, or otherwise unavailable, subject, of course, to the local statutes or rules governing practice. The accused generally has a similar right to reproduce testimony of witnesses at former trials. The admissibility of testimony given in a criminal prosecution in a subsequent civil action, where the witness who testified is no longer available, is the subject of some difference of opinion among the courts. In the majority of the jurisdictions in which the matter has been adjudicated, the view is taken that such evidence is admissible, provided it appears that the party against whom the evidence is offered had the right of cross-examining the witness and that the parties and issues are substantially the same in both cases. Some courts, however, refuse to admit such evidence, on the ground that the parties and issues in the criminal and civil cases are not identical.

VIII. REAL AND DEMONSTRATIVE EVIDENCE

§ 11:20. Generally.

Am Jur 2d References: Evidence, §§ 769–817.

Proof which is addressed directly to the senses of the court or jury without the interposition of testimony of witnesses is generally characterized as real or demonstrative evidence and is admissible in both civil and criminal cases if it throws light on some issue in the case.   Evidence of this character is a most satisfactory and convincing form of proof where it is available.   It includes objects or articles brought into court and exhibited to the court and jury, as well as photographs, X-ray pictures, motion pictures, maps, diagrams, drawings, and models; comparisons of writing or typewriting; fingerprints, palmprints, and footprints; the exhibition of one's person or body; and experiments, demonstrations, and tests conducted either in or out of court.   Considerable discretion is vested in the trial court in the receipt of evidence of this kind, and the court should be alert to prevent any unnecessary dramatic, inflammatory, gruesome, or prejudicial effects of such evidence.

The comparison of fingerprints, as well as footprints and palmprints, to prove identity is a universal practice today, such proof usually being made by experts, frequently with the aid of photographic enlargements and projectoscopic display to the jury.   It is always proper, when a fact in issue may be explained by the production of an article or object to which testimony relates, to bring the article or object into court, and an object thus offered in evidence must be properly identified as the thing involved in the case, and it must be shown to be in substantially the same condition as at the time in issue.   This requirement as to identity and condition is particularly important when objects, such as bullets, specimens, or parts taken from a human body, are offered in evidence.

The exhibition of the person, or parts of the body, of a party is commonly permitted in personal injury actions.   Such an exhibition, or an active demonstration by physical acts and movements in the presence of the jury, is permitted to show the nature and effects of an injury.   Where the paternity of a child or other family relationship is in issue, it is usually held proper to exhibit such persons to the jury to determine family resemblance, racial characteristics, or hereditary peculiarities.   Some courts have declined to permit an exhibition to show relationship between an adult and a very young child whose features are immature and undergoing constant changes, in the absence of some marked corporal features.

A photograph, to be admissible in either a civil or criminal case, must be authenticated or verified by some other evidence to establish that the photograph is a substantially true, accurate, and faithful representation or portrayal of the place, person, or subject that it purports to represent or portray.   A photograph, of itself, can prove nothing without the testimony of a witness identifying its subject matter and contents.   The verification of a photograph may, of course, be by the testimony of the person who took it; but this is not ordinarily necessary, and any person having the required knowledge of the facts and of the subject matter of the photograph may verify it, even though he did not see the photographer take the picture.   The mere fact that there has been some change in conditions or in the things shown in a photograph between the time of the event or occurrence in question and the time when the photograph was made does not render it inadmissible in evidence, provided that it serves some purpose in identifying its subject matter and is not misleading, and provided that the person offering it in evidence must produce evidence fully explaining the change.

Posed photographs and those of a purported reproduction of the scene of a crime or accident are looked upon with disfavor by some courts, and the courts which admit such photographs require a showing that the objects and situations portrayed are faithfully represented. Photographs taken of the defendant at the scene of a crime in a re-enactment thereof are generally held to be admissible where the prosecution satisfactorily shows their relevancy and accuracy as well as the voluntariness of the defendant's participation in the re-enactment.

The admissibility of drawings, maps, charts, and models depends upon the relevance and materiality thereof and upon their adequate authentication. Medical and anatomical charts and models representing the human body or skeleton or parts thereof are frequently admitted in modern trials for the purpose of aiding the jury in an understanding of the facts. The admission of such evidence rests largely in the discretion of the trial court.

The proof of handwriting or signatures may, of course, be made by the testimony of the person whose writing or signature is in issue. Such proof may also be made by the testimony of a witness who has seen the party write or who has had access to and is familiar with the writing of such person, so that the witness has formed an opinion based on a comparison of his impression of the true handwriting of the person and that submitted for examination. It is said that under the earlier common-law rule, these were the only methods of proof that could be made. In modern practice, however, it is generally held that proof of the genuineness of a writing or signature may be made by a comparison thereof with other writings of the same person which are either admitted or proved to be genuine specimens, and which are submitted to the court and jury to enable them to determine the question by their own observation and judgment. It is also generally agreed that expert testimony may be received based on the conclusion of experts drawn from a comparison of the writings. It is essential, however, before any signature or writing is offered as a proper standard for comparison with a disputed signature or writing, to establish the authenticity and genuineness of the signature or writing offered as the standard of comparison.

§ 11:21. Experiments, demonstrations, and tests.

Am Jur 2d References: Evidence, §§ 818–833.

Although courts were formerly reluctant to admit such evidence, they now generally permit experiments, demonstrations, and tests to be made or performed in the presence of the jury (but not by the jury itself), or admit evidence of experiments, tests, or demonstrations performed out of court, when they are made under like circumstances and similar conditions to those existing in the case at issue, for the purpose of aiding the trier of facts in understanding and determining the issues of fact. The performance and regulation of experiments, tests, and demonstrations in the presence of the jury, or the admission of evidence thereof where performed out of court, rests in the sound discretion of the trial court, in both civil and criminal cases, and this discretion will not be interfered with on appeal unless it is clear that it has been abused.

Although one desiring to make an experiment, demonstration, or test in the presence of the jury, or to introduce evidence of one made out of court, must first show that the test, etc., is to be made or was conducted under conditions and circumstances similar to those prevailing at the time and place of the occurrence in question, it is not necessary that the conditions be identical. Substantial similarity usually suffices, and minor variations go to the weight, rather than to the admissibility, of the evidence. Speaking generally, the measure of permissible variation of the conditions of the experiment, demonstration, or test from those of the actual occurrence is determined by the likelihood that such variation may confuse or mislead the jury.

The scope of the subject matter of experiments, tests, and demonstrations which may be used as evidence is very wide. Under proper circumstances, a demonstration to show the operation of a mechanical device or appliance is admissible. Experiments and tests are admitted to determine such matters as the flammability or explosiveness of substances or materials, the quality or suitability of building materials, the effect of food, drinks, and drugs, including the adulteration thereof, the effect of gases and insecticides, and other experiments and tests to determine the chemical or physical qualities or character of materials or substances. Demonstrations and tests by ballistics experts are frequently admitted to identify bullets, by comparison or otherwise, to show the characteristic markings left by each gun upon ammunition fired therein and the ballistic data pertinent to particular ammunitions and firearms. Various tests to show the alcoholic content of the blood of an individual are frequently admitted, but evidence of such tests has been rejected by some courts. Lie detector tests are not admissible for the purpose of establishing the guilt or innocence of one accused of crime, because such devices and tests have not attained scientific acceptance as a reliable and accurate means of ascertaining truth or deception. And the so-called truth serum tests occupy much the same position as lie detector tests. There is some difference of judicial opinion on the admissibility of voice identification by voiceprints made by the use of a spectrograph.

IX. DOCUMENTARY EVIDENCE

§ 11:22. Generally; private writings and documents.

Am Jur 2d References: Evidence, §§ 834–913.

Legal evidence includes not only oral testimony given by witnesses under oath and tangible objects which tend to establish truth or untruth of matters at issue, but also all kinds of documents, records, and writings, generally classified as "documentary evidence." When offered, documentary evidence is subject to the same rules of evidence respecting relevancy, competency, or materiality as is oral testimony. Generally speaking, any relevant writing is admissible where, from its contents and other circumstances in evidence, it is reasonably inferable that the author is the person sought to be charged. Private writings which emanate from a source other than the party against whom they are sought to be introduced must be shown to have been authorized by him, or otherwise to be binding upon him. Generally speaking, the rights of an individual cannot be affected by written statements of persons who act in an unofficial capacity in respect of matters to which he is a stranger. As to him, such writings are inadmissible, being hearsay and res inter alios.

Private writings which contain material and competent evidence are not to be excluded merely because they also contain incompetent evidence, especially where the inadmissible parts can be so covered up or deleted as to prevent the jury from seeing them. If a party introduces only part of a writing or document, his opponent may prove the contents of the remainder of the instrument if such remaining parts bear upon, modify, or explain the part introduced, or if they are relevant to the issues and competent under rules of evidence.

As a preliminary to the introduction in evidence of private writings, other than those coming within the rule admitting "ancient documents," their execution must be proved and their authenticity established to the satisfaction of the court. The writing must be accompanied by competent proof from which it may be inferred that it is authentic and that it was executed or written by the party by whom it purports to be written or executed, unless such facts are admitted by the adversary. Statutes in many jurisdictions provide that an instrument purporting to have been signed by the defendant must be received in evidence unless its execution is denied under oath.

Under the common-law rule, which has been modified in some jurisdictions, when a written instrument attested by a subscribing witness is offered in evidence, its execution must be proved by the subscribing witness if he is available as a witness, unless the instrument is self-proving as an ancient document. Proof of execution by other means does not suffice under this rule. One of two attesting witnesses is sufficient to prove an attested instrument. The proof of wills, of course, is governed by laws directed specifically to wills. The rule requiring proof by the attesting witness does not apply if he is dead, insane, incompetent to testify, outside the jurisdiction of the court, or otherwise not available as a witness. Statutes in many states have either abrogated the common-law rule entirely, permitting the proof of attested instruments in the same manner as unattested writings, or have greatly modified that rule. And instruments which are acknowledged or recorded are generally excepted from the common-law rule as to the proof of attested documents.

"Ancient documents," as indicated above, are generally excepted from the requirements of authentication of writings offered in evidence. Documents and writings of all kinds, purporting to be 30 years or more old, if they are relevant to the inquiry, are produced from proper custody, and are on their face free from suspicion, are said to prove themselves, and are admissible in evidence without meeting the ordinary requirements as to proof of execution and authenticity. The rule relating to ancient documents is one of authentication, and not a rule of admissibility. The instrument must still comply with the general principles of evidence as regards relevance, etc.; and an instrument which is not valid on its face because of want of due execution will not be admitted under the ancient document rule. Where the original of an ancient document is no longer in existence, or has become illegible, a copy thereof, properly authenticated, may be admitted in evidence.

In addition to private instruments between parties, various other kinds of writings and documents may be admissible as documentary evidence. For example, recognized mortality or life expectancy tables are frequently admitted. And maps and plats of land are admissible to illustrate other evidence and to aid in locating the land in controversy and the boundaries thereof. Except in the case of ancient documents, a map or plat must, as a preliminary step to its admissibility in evidence, be authenticated by a showing that it is accurate and properly prepared by one qualified to make such a map or plat.

§ 11:23. — Business entries, records, and reports.

Am Jur 2d References: Evidence, §§ 914–961.

Under the English common law, the books of account of a party to a lawsuit were not admissible in evidence unless they were kept by a clerk or other disinterested person who was available to testify as to their accuracy. Where the entries were made personally by the party to the action, the books were inadmissible under the early common-law rule, since parties to lawsuits were disqualified as witnesses and hence could not prove the accuracy of their books. In view of the difficulties resulting from this rule, most of the American states at an early date adopted a different rule, sometimes referred to as the "shopbook" rule, under which a party to an action may, independently of any statute authorizing it, give in evidence, in support of his claim against his adversary, his books of account in which he himself has made the entries.

This shopbook rule has assumed two different forms, one of which may be designated as the New York rule and the other the New England rule. Under the former, books of account are not admitted in evidence unless a foundation is first laid by proving that the party had no clerk; that some of the articles charged have been delivered; that the books produced are the account books of the party; and that the party keeps fair and honest accounts. This rule has been modified and simplified in many states adopting the New York form, including the state of New York itself. Under the New England form of the shopbook rule, as applied by the courts in the absence of statutory modification, books of account kept by a party himself were received in evidence when supported by his suppletory oath administered in court, showing that the books were regularly and accurately made and that the entries are correct. The application of the New England rule was not affected by the fact that the party had a clerk who could be produced to testify; but cases following the New York form have required a party first to establish that he employed no clerk before he can introduce his books of account in evidence.

The old rules governing the admission of books of account and business records in evidence produced much inconvenience, expense, and waste of time as applied to modern conditions and business methods, and various statutes were enacted from time to time to liberalize these rules, culminating in the Model Act for Proof of Business Transactions and the Uniform Business Records as Evidence Act. The former Act has been adopted in several states and by Congress for federal courts, and the latter Act has been adopted in a majority of the states. The Model Act for Proof of Business Transactions provides in substance that any writing or record, whether in the form of an entry in a book or otherwise, made as a memorandum or record of any act, transaction, occurrence, or event, shall be admissible as evidence of such act, etc., if it was made in the regular course of business; if it was the regular course of business to make such record; and if it was made at or near the time of the act, transaction, or event. This statute permits the introduction of such writing or record without the necessity of calling as witnesses all persons who had any part in making it, provided the record was made as a part of the duty of the persons making it. The Uniform Business Records as Evidence Act provides that a record of an act, condition, or event shall, insofar as relevant, be competent evidence if the custodian or other qualified witness testifies to its identity and the mode of its preparation, and if it was made in the regular course of business, at or near the time of the act, condition, or event, and if, in the opinion of the court, the sources of information, method, and time of preparation were such as to justify its admission. The term business, as used in the Act, includes every kind of business, profession, occupation, or calling. These modern Acts apply to all intelligible forms and methods of keeping business records, including those kept or stored on electronic computing equipment.

It is still the general rule in some states that a book of accounts is admissible in evidence only if it is the book of original entries or the first permanent record of the transactions in question. However, the problem of original entry is diminishing in importance with the increasing adoption of the Uniform Business Records as Evidence Act, which makes no mention of originality of entries.

§ 11:24. Public or official records and reports.

Am Jur 2d References: Evidence, §§ 962–1015.

Documents of a public or governmental nature, such as public or official records and reports, including legislative records and acts, judicial records, and records and reports of executive and administrative officials, or any properly authenticated copy or transcript thereof, are admissible in the trial of an action, subject to the same requirements of relevancy and materiality as apply to private writings. Official documents and proclamations issued by the executive, and state papers published under authority of Congress, are admissible to prove their contents and the facts stated therein. Notwithstanding the general aura of trustworthiness accorded official or public documents and records, and though they need not be proved by the persons who actually made the entries therein, there must yet be an authentication thereof and some proof of the identity of the proffered records or documents.

The foregoing rules are not limited to documents and records of the state of the forum. Properly authenticated copies of public records kept by a public official of a sister state in the performance of his official duties are also admissible in evidence. The United States Constitution (Art. 4, § 1) requires that "full faith and credit" be given in each state to the public acts, records, and judicial proceedings of every other state, and empowers Congress to prescribe the manner in which such acts, records, and proceedings shall be proved; and Congress has enacted legislation in compliance with this provision. Copies of judicial and nonjudicial records of foreign nations are admissible in evidence in the courts of this country, provided they are properly authenticated, and in the case of nonjudicial records, provided there is proof that such records were made and kept according to the law of the foreign nation. Both the states and the Federal Government have adopted statutes and rules governing the anthentication and admissibility of foreign records.

With respect to all public records or reports it is a general prerequisite of admissibility in evidence that the record or report be shown to have been prepared or kept by a public official pursuant to a duty imposed by law, or that the record or report was required by the nature of his office. The manner of authenticating and proving public documents, records, and reports is regulated by statutes and court rules, state and federal.

X. PAROL OR EXTRINSIC EVIDENCE AFFECTING WRITINGS

§ 11:25. Generally.

Am Jur 2d References: Evidence, §§ 1016–1079.

The parol evidence rule forbids the introduction of parol or other extrinsic evidence for the purpose of changing, varying, adding to, or contradicting the terms of an instrument in writing. Where parties reduce their agreement to writing, and the written instrument is complete and free from ambiguity, the meaning and legal effect of the agreement is to be determined by the writing alone, without the aid of any outside evidence as to its construction or concerning the intention of the parties. The rule is said to be one of substantive law, and is based upon the policy of the law to enable parties to render their contracts certain and to avoid the risks of perjury, infirmity of memory, or death of witnesses, as well as to avoid the complication of trials with collateral issues.

Whatever the law implies from a contract in writing is as much a part of the contract as that which is therein expressed; and if the contract, with what the law implies, is clear, definite, and complete, it cannot be added to, varied, or contradicted by extrinsic evidence. In other words, parol evidence is inadmissible to vary or contradict either the express terms or the legal effect of a writing expressing the agreement of the parties.

All classes of contractual writings and instruments, by whatever name they are called, are within the scope of operation of the parol evidence rule. The rule applies not only to contracts which are required by law to be in writing, but to every written instrument containing the terms of a contract between the parties. The rule applies only where the parties to an agreement reduce it to writing and intend that the writing shall constitute their contract. The rule does not apply to writings which do not purport to be contractual agreements, such as letters, telegrams, book entries, and other writings of an informal nature constituting mere memoranda of the agreements. It is generally recognized that the rule excluding extrinsic evidence to vary or contradict a writing does not apply to a mere receipt which is not contractual in nature. However, if a receipt is contractual in nature and contains all of the elements necessary to constitute a complete contract between the parties, it is subject to the parol evidence rule.

Noncontractual written instruments are governed by rules similar to those applicable to contracts. The admissibility of extrinsic evidence in the interpretation of wills is considered in the topic Wills, Descent, and Decedents' Estates, § 17; and the application of the doctrine to deeds and other instruments relating to land is discussed in the topic Real Property. A principle tantamount to the parol evidence rule is applied to attempts to contradict or vary public records or documents by parol evidence.

The rule excluding parol evidence to vary, explain, or contradict a writing is primarily applicable to the parties to the writing and their privies. It is generally held that a stranger to a writing is not ordinarily precluded from introducing parol evidence to vary or contradict it. Where a writing comes into question collaterally between one of the parties to the writing and a stranger thereto, it is generally held that the parol evidence rule does not prevent either of them from introducing extrinsic evidence to vary, contradict, or explain the writings, although there are some decisions to the contrary.

The application of the parol evidence rule presupposes an action involving an existing valid contract or instrument. Parol evidence is always admissible to show the nonexistence of the contract because, for example, of the nonacceptance of an offer, the lack of an effective delivery of the instrument, or the absence of a proper execution thereof. And extrinsic evidence is admissible, where the validity of an instrument is in issue, to show that the contract was procured by fraud, that it resulted from mutual mistake, that it was based upon an illegal consideration, or that it was a mere sham and was never intended to be a binding contract. Such evidence is also admissible to show the nonperformance of a condition precedent, so that the contract never became an effective instrument.

Under the doctrine of "partial integration," where a written instrument is obviously not, or is shown not to be, the complete contract, parol evidence not inconsistent with the writing is admissible to show what the entire contract is, by supplementing, as distinguished from contradicting, the writing. In the application of this doctrine, it is frequently a difficult problem to determine whether the contract of the parties was actually embodied in the writing; and the manner of resolving this question is the subject of some conflict among the authorities. Another exception to the parol evidence rule, related to the doctrine of partial integration, is known as the "doctrine of collateral contract." Under this doctrine, a prior or contemporaneous oral contract which is independent of, collateral to, and not inconsistent with, the written contract, may be proved by parol evidence. In order for such evidence to be admissible, however, the collateral oral agreement must relate to a fact or matter which does not interfere with or contradict the terms of the written contract, or it must relate to a particular matter as to which the written instrument is silent, although it may relate to the same general subject matter.

In the absence of statute to the contrary, it is competent for the parties to a simple contract in writing to waive or abandon it, or to change, modify, add to, or vary its terms in any way, either orally or in writing, and thus in effect make a new contract. And where a written agreement is thus modified by an oral agreement, parol evidence of the oral agreement is admissible. Parol evidence of such a modification of a written contract is generally admitted even though the parties stipulate in the written contract that it may not be changed except by a writing.

The identity of the parties to a written instrument may be established by parol evidence where there is ambiguity or uncertainty with respect thereto. And the relationship of the parties, and the capacity in which each party signed an instrument, may be shown by extrinsic evidence. As a general rule parol evidence is admissible to show the true consideration for a contract and that the consideration was greater or less than, or different from, that stated in the writing, provided that the statement of consideration was not intended to be contractual but was in the nature of a mere receipt. The statement of a contractual consideration in a writing, which cannot be varied by parol evidence, involves something of a promissory nature, such as a promise to perform some future act or an executory undertaking, as distinguished from an acknowledgment of something received.

Extrinsic evidence is admissible to show that a conveyance or assignment, absolute on its face, was intended merely as security for the payment of a debt. Thus, it may be shown by parol evidence that a deed, absolute on its face, is in fact a mortgage, and that a bill of sale is in fact a security instrument.

Whenever the terms of a written instrument are susceptible of more than one reasonable interpretation, or an ambiguity exists as to the meaning of the instrument or the intention of the parties as expressed therein, parol or extrinsic evidence may be introduced to resolve the ambiguity and to show the intended meaning of the language of the instrument. Although frequently characterized as an exception to the parol evidence rule, this principle is a co-ordinate rule as universally recognized as the parol evidence rule itself and implicit in any complete statement of the latter rule. An ambiguity, calling for the admission of extrinsic evidence, may arise from an unusual use of otherwise plain and unambiguous words or phrases, or from words which are plain in themselves, but uncertain when applied to the subject matter of the instrument. In short, an ambiguity may arise for this purpose if either the meaning of words or their application is uncertain.

All relevant evidence is admissible to show the meaning of an ambiguous or uncertain instrument in writing, where its meaning or the intention of the parties cannot be determined from a mere inspection of the instrument. Evidence of the subject matter of the instrument, of the relations of the parties to each other, and of the facts and circumstances surrounding them and the execution of the instrument, may be received to aid in the proper construction of the instrument.

In determining the admissibility of extrinsic evidence, some courts make a distinction between latent and patent ambiguities. A patent ambiguity is one appearing on the face of the instrument, while a latent ambiguity arises only by a showing of matters outside the instrument which create a doubt or uncertainty as to its meaning. According to one view, still held by some courts, a patent ambiguity must be resolved, if at all, by the application of the legal rules of construction to the language used in the writing, and the construction may not be aided by the introduction of extrinsic evidence. The importance of the distinction between latent and patent ambiguities is diminishing, however, and the trend of modern authority is to admit extrinsic evidence—at least evidence showing the surrounding circumstances and conditions and the relations between the parties—to aid in resolving any kind of ambiguity, whether patent or latent. Of course, if a writing is so incomplete or defective as not to constitute a valid instrument, no evidence can give it legal effect. Extrinsic evidence is never admitted to create a new agreement for the parties nor to give legal life to an instrument invalid on its face. And under any view, such evidence is not admissible to vary or contradict the actual language of a written instrument.

XI. EXPERT AND OPINION EVIDENCE

§ 11:26. Generally; nonexpert or lay witness.

Am Jur 2d References: Expert and Opinion Evidence, §§ 1–7, 14, 15, 24, 25, 181–189.

It is a fundamental general rule of the law of evidence as administered by the courts in civil and criminal proceedings, that the testimony of witnesses upon matters within the scope of the common knowledge and experience of mankind must be confined to statements of concrete facts within their own observation, knowledge, and recollection, and perceived by the use of their own senses, as distinguished from their opinions, inferences, and conclusions drawn from such facts. Generally speaking, subject to important exceptions discussed below, a witness must confine his testimony to facts within his actual knowledge, and his opinion or conclusion upon facts in issue is incompetent as evidence. It is the function of the court or jury, as trier of facts, to draw its own inferences and conclusions from the facts properly presented in evidence, and it is not proper to permit a witness to invade the province of the court or jury by stating his opinion as to the conclusions to be drawn from concrete facts which he has observed.

The general rule excluding opinions of witnesses is not only subject to exceptions, but it is not always simple in application, for it is sometimes difficult to distinguish facts within the knowledge or perception of a witness from his opinions on facts. A witness may generally testify directly to a composite fact, although in a sense his testimony may be based upon his conclusion from other facts. Testimony must occasionally be necessarily compounded of fact and opinion. Actually, a person's sensory perception of any object or occurrence involves a series of subjective inferences or conclusions.

The exceptions to the rule that witnesses must testify to facts, and not opinions, have been found necessary; and the exceptions are not confined to testimony of experts upon subjects requiring special knowledge or skill, but extend to the opinions or conclusions of lay or nonexpert witness where the facts could not otherwise be adequately presented to the jury. When it is not practicable to place before the jury all of the primary facts in such a way as to enable the jury to form an intelligent conclusion, witnesses may state their opinions and conclusions formed from such facts and circumstances as have come under their observation. When the subject matter relates to complex facts perceived by the senses, or to a series or great variety of circumstances and a combination of appearances which cannot be adequately represented to the jury by means of the separate, isolated facts, a witness may state his impressions or opinions based upon such facts and circumstances. Under these principles, the opinions, conclusions, or impressions of nonexpert or lay witnesses of ordinary intelligence are generally admissible on such issues as the mental or physical condition of persons known by the witness, their character and reputation, the authenticity of handwriting, the speed of moving objects, and on a great variety of other ordinary unscientific questions concerning topics and matters of common occurrence and observation, where it is not practical to lay before the jury the precise individual facts on which the opinions or conclusions are based.

The weight and sufficiency of expert and opinion testimony are within the province of the jury to decide, considering the ability, character, and technical training and experience of the witness, his conduct on the witness stand, the process of reasoning by which he has supported his opinion, his possible bias, whether he is a paid witness, the opportunities for observation and study of the matters about which he testifies, and any other matters which serve to throw light on the weight and credibility of his opinions. There is no rule of law which requires that controlling effect be given to the opinions of witnesses, and the court and jury are not bound to accept opinion testimony in the place of their own judgments. Expert opinions are not conclusive, and the court or jury, as the trier of facts, may place whatever weight they choose upon such testimony, and may reject it if they find that it is inconsistent with the facts of the case or is otherwise unreasonable.

§ 11:27. Expert witnesses.

Am Jur 2d References: Expert and Opinion Evidence, §§ 8–13, 16–23, 26–32, 36–180.

Frequently, the jury, or the court trying a case without a jury, is confronted with issues which require scientific or specialized knowledge or experience in order to be properly understood, and which cannot be determined intelligently merely from the deductions made and inferences drawn on the basis of ordinary knowledge, common sense, and practical experience gained in the ordinary affairs of life. On such issues, testimony of one possessing special knowledge and skill is required, and witnesses possessing the requisite knowledge, training, and skill, denominated "experts," may testify, not only to the facts, but to their opinions respecting the facts, so far as necessary to enlighten the jury or court.

The opinions of expert witnesses are admissible on matters not of common knowledge, where the experience of the witnesses in some art, science, business, or profession can aid the trier of facts in the search for the truth. The opinion of an expert concerning a scientific or technical matter beyond the knowledge of laymen is admissible wherever an explanation of such a matter is relevant to an issue of fact. The facts on which an expert opinion is based must permit of reasonably certain deductions, as distinguished from mere conjectures; but an expert should not be barred from presenting his opinion merely because he is not willing to state his conclusion with absolute certainty. There is no need for the opinions of experts, and such testimony is not ordinarily admissible, on matters of common knowledge, as to which the facts can be intelligibly described to the jury and understood by them so that they can reach a reasonable conclusion for themselves. The necessity and propriety of admitting expert opinions is ordinarily a matter for the determination of the trial court.

The objection is often made that particular expert testimony invades the province of the jury. Indeed, some courts take the view that an expert should not be permitted to testify to his opinion the precise and ultimate fact in issue before the jury. This supposed principle is rejected by many courts, however, and it is contrary to the trend of modern authority. In many cases expert witnesses have been permitted to state facts known to them because of their expert knowledge, even though their statements may involve the ultimate fact to be determined by the jury. The matter of the invasion of the province of the jury by expert opinion testimony has resulted in some disagreement as to the form of the opinion which an expert may give. Some courts which show no hesitancy in allowing the expert witness to state his opinion as to whether certain facts could or would produce a particular result will not allow him to state his opinion as to whether such facts actually produced such a result in the case at bar. However, the modern tendency appears to reject this fine distinction.

Opinion testimony of an expert witness may be based upon facts within his own knowledge or upon hypothetical questions embracing facts supported by the evidence and relating to the matter upon which the expert opinion is sought, such facts being assumed to be true for the purposes of the opinion. The usual and approved procedure in such cases is for counsel to present the facts by hypothetical questions which assume a state of facts which have been testified to by other witnesses, and then to ask the expert to state his opinion based on those facts. An expert witness may state the reasons for his opinion, and he may be examined and cross-examined with respect thereto.

The qualification of a witness to testify as an expert is a matter for the determination of the trial court. Such a witness must at least possess some special knowledge or skill on the subject on which the jury is in need of technical guidance. The court has inherent power to appoint an impartial expert witness on its own motion, and such appointments are expressly provided for by statute in some jurisdictions.

XII. WITNESSES

§ 11:28. Generally; competency.

Am Jur 2d References: Witnesses (1st ed, §§ 1–35, 102–213).

Each party to a legal proceeding, civil or criminal, usually presents the evidence supporting his case through the testimony of witnesses called by him. A party has the right to choose his own witnesses, although the court may, under some circumstances, call additional witnesses to testify. Parties may compel the attendance of witnesses by subpoena, and obedience of a subpoena is enforced by attachment for contempt of court. A witness is under legal duty to testify to matters within his knowledge, unless he is excused by some specific statutory or constitutional provision, such as that granting immunity against self-incrimination. By means of a subpoena duces tecum, a witness may be compelled, in a proper case, to bring with him into court books, papers, documents, and articles which are relevant to the issues in the case.

While the foregoing principles apply primarily to judicial proceedings, most of them are made applicable, by statute or otherwise, to certain quasi-judicial proceedings, administrative proceedings, and hearings before legislative committees.

The competency of a witness to testify is determined by rules of the common law as modified by statute. Although the rule was different under the early common law, it is now well settled that deaf-mutes are competent witnesses, testifying through proper means of communication. It has been stated that insane persons are not competent witnesses. However, in more recent times, it is generally held that a lunatic or person mentally defective or affected with some form of insanity may be competent as a witness if, at the time he is offered as a witness, he has sufficient understanding to comprehend the obligation of an oath and is capable of giving a correct account of the matters which he has seen or heard in reference to the questions at issue.

A person must be sensible to the obligation of an oath in order to be competent to testify as a witness. However, an adult is presumed to meet this requirement. At common law, it was required that a witness believe in God and believe that He would punish false swearing. However, in most states the requirement of religious belief as a requisite of competency of a witness has been abolished.

Except as otherwise provided by statute, the intelligence, not the age, of a young child is the test of its competency as a witness. No precise minimum age can be fixed at which children are excluded from testifying. To be competent as a witness a child must be able to receive accurate impressions of the facts to which its testimony relates, and to state truly and intelligently the impressions received. It is generally required that a child offered as a witness must understand the obligation of an oath, but the extent of this requirement varies in the several jurisdictions. In any event, the fact that a child is too young to be convicted of perjury does not make it incompetent as a witness.

At common law, a person who has been convicted of an infamous crime and sentenced therefor is disqualified as a witness. Some courts have disapproved of this rule, and it has been changed by statute in some states. The rule of disqualification does not apply to convictions in other jurisdictions. A pardon has the effect of removing the disqualification of a witness based on his conviction of a crime.

At common law, interest in the outcome of a lawsuit rendered a person incompetent to testify as a witness therein; and this was true whether the person was a party to the action or was otherwise materially interested therein. It was deemed that the temptation to falsify was such that an interested person could not be relied upon to testify accurately and truly. However, this disqualification has been removed in this country, subject to certain exceptions. It is now generally agreed that while the interest or bias of a witness may properly be considered as affecting his credibility, it should not preclude him from testifying as a witness.

It is a common-law rule of great antiquity, still generally accepted, that neither spouse can be a witness in favor of or against the other, in an action to which the other is a party or in which he has a direct or immediate interest, except in a few cases where their testimony is admitted on grounds of necessity. Neither husband nor wife is a competent witness in a criminal prosecution against the other, except where the crime charged is against the person of the spouse testifying. This rule is based largely on considerations of public policy designed to prevent domestic discord, and its basis is related to that underlying the privilege of communications between spouses (supra, § 11:9).

Exceptions are made to the foregoing rule where, from the nature of the case, no remedy could be had for a wrong without the testimony of the spouse. One spouse may testify for or against the other in an action between the spouses; and where both spouses are parties to an action by or against a third party, either of them may testify.

§ 11:29. Transactions with deceased or incompetent persons.

Am Jur 2d References: Witnesses (1st ed, §§ 214–362).

In abrogating the common-law rule disqualifying as witnesses the parties to an action and other persons interested in the outcome thereof (supra, § 11:28), the legislatures of the various states retained some fragments of that broad rule. The most important of these exceptions is the provision precluding a party or other interested person from testifying as to certain matters where the opposing party is the representative of a deceased person or of a lunatic. Such statutes, commonly referred to as dead man statutes, differ greatly in the several states. The disability is absolute in some jurisdictions, so that the interested witness is incompetent to testify at all, while it is qualified or partial in others, arising only when the witness seeks to testify to some personal transaction had with the decedent or the lunatic; and in other states, instead of disqualifying the witness, the statutes merely provide that no judgment shall be rendered in his favor founded on his uncorroborated testimony. Some statutes limit the disqualification to proceedings upon claims or demands against the estate of a decedent. Although these statutes vary in terms and construction in the several jurisdictions, all of them are based on the basic unreliability of the testimony of interested witnesses, with the added factor of the unfairness of permitting such witness to testify when his adversary's version of the transaction has been silenced by death.

As indicated above, the dead man statutes of the several states vary substantially as to the actions or proceedings included in the disqualifying provisions. Some of these statutes are held to apply to actions ex delicto and even to actions for wrongful death; and such torts as negligent injury by automobiles are held in some, but not all, jurisdictions to involve "transactions" with the decedent. There is a difference of opinion, sometime reflecting a variation in the statutes, as to the applicability of these disqualifying laws to probate proceedings. The majority rule is that such statutes do not apply to proceedings to probate a will or to will contests. Books of account and the like may be admitted notwithstanding these statutes, but there is some conflict as to the extent to which such books or records may be authenticated by interested parties. Transactions between the decedent and third persons are generally held not to be within the disqualifying terms of these statutes.

Statutory provisions disqualifying a person to testify where his adversary is deceased or incompetent may be waived by the opposite party to a proceeding. Such a waiver may arise from a failure to make a proper objection to the competency of the witness; from the fact that the personal representative of the decedent calls the adverse party as a witness and examines him as to transactions with the deceased; or from the fact that a person protected by the statute has testified on his own behalf as to such matters. And the cross-examination of a witness as to transactions with a deceased person is generally held to amount to a waiver of the incompetency of the witness.

§ 11:30. Privilege against self-incrimination.

Am Jur 2d References: Witnesses (1st ed, §§ 36–101).

As expressed in the maxim, "nemo tenetur seipsum accusare," the common law, apart from any constitutional or statutory provision, affords to a witness the privilege of refusing to answer any question that will criminate himself. The provision of the Fifth Amendment to the Constitution of the United States, that "No person . . . shall be compelled in any criminal case to be a witness against himself," was originally held to limit only the federal power, and to have no application to proceedings under the authority of a state; but this ruling has been changed by the United States Supreme Court, and it is now held that this provision extends to the states also by virtue of the due process clause of the Fourteenth Amendment. The same result might reasonably have been attained by a recognition that the common-law privilege against self-incrimination was so basic and venerable as to be a matter of due process of law. The constitutions of most states contain similar guaranties. These provisions give the defendant in a criminal prosecution the right to decline to testify in his own behalf, and neither the court nor the prosecuting attorney may comment on the failure of the accused to take the stand.

While the constitutional privilege against compulsory examination of an accused is limited to criminal proceedings and those to enforce a penalty or forfeiture, the privilege against self-incrimination is not so limited, but applies alike to civil and criminal proceedings, as well as to proceedings before legislative or administrative bodies. The privilege against self-incrimination does not generally protect witnesses against disclosures of violations of the laws of foreign countries. Although there is authority for the proposition that this privilege does not extend to matters which might subject the witness to prosecution in another state, and that investigations for federal purposes may not be prevented because of liability to prosecution under state law, and vice versa, later decisions cast grave doubt upon the validity of such a doctrine.

In order to invoke the privilege against self-incrimination, it is not necessary that a witness show that the testimony which he declines to give is certain to subject him to prosecution, or that it will prove the whole crime, unaided by the testimony of others. It is enough that there is a reasonable possibility of prosecution, and that his testimony will tend to a conviction when combined with proof which others may supply: if his testimony would furnish one link in the chain of evidence which might convict, or would disclose sources of evidence against him, a witness may properly claim his privilege.

A witness who has been granted immunity from prosecution for an offense, pursuant to statutory authorization of such procedure, may be required to testify as to matters which would otherwise be self-incriminatory. Unless the immunity granted the witness is in fact coextensive with the protection against self-incrimination afforded by the Constitution and laws, however, incriminatory testimony cannot be compelled. But the fact that a grant of immunity by a federal statute from prosecution by the Federal Government does not protect the witness from prosecution in state courts for offenses against states constitutes no ground on which a witness in a federal court or appearing before a federal body may refuse to answer. Conversely, the inability of a state to provide immunity from federal prosecutions, arising out of testimony given in state proceedings, does not give the witness the right to refuse to testify. Compelling a witness to testify in such cases does not violate the Fifth Amendment. The Congress may grant, and in some instances has granted, immunity from prosecution in either federal or state courts, as a basis of compelling testimony which would otherwise be incriminating.

The privilege not to give self-incriminating evidence may be waived by anyone entitled to invoke it. This rule applies to witnesses in either civil or criminal cases. A defendant in a criminal prosecution who elects to testify in his own behalf is held to waive his immunity to the extent that he is subject to cross-examination on incriminatory matters. Any waiver of the privilege against self-incrimination must be made voluntarily and knowingly, with full understanding by the witness of the nature of his rights.

As shown elsewhere in this work (Criminal Law § 7:31), police and prosecuting authorities may require an accused to exhibit his person and to submit to various kinds of tests and demonstrations for the purpose of identification, without infringing upon his privilege against self-incrimination.

*

EXTRAORDINARY REMEDIES

I. DECLARATORY JUDGMENTS

§ 12:1. In general; nature and availability of remedy.

Am Jur 2d References: Declaratory Judgments, §§ 1–19, 99–103.

A declaratory judgment is one that declares the rights and duties or the status of the parties. An action for a declaratory judgment is the appropriate remedy for the determination of a justiciable controversy where the plaintiff is in doubt as to his legal rights and wishes to avoid the hazard of taking action in advance of the determination of such rights. The distinctive characteristic of a declaratory judgment is that the declaration stands by itself as a determination of rights and duties, and no executory process follows as of course and no executory or coercive relief is involved.

Declaratory relief, as an independent general remedy, was unknown at common law. Courts have long rendered advice to trustees, executors, and administrators, upon request by the latter, to guide in the administration of estates; and suits to quiet title and bills of interpleader brought by stakeholders resemble declaratory judgment actions in many respects. However, these remedies are of specific and limited application. Practically all American jurisdictions now provide declaratory relief. The Uniform Declaratory Judgments Act has been adopted by the great majority of states, in some instances with slight modifications; and in states not adopting the Uniform

Act there usually are statutes providing for declaratory judgments. The Federal Declaratory Judgment Act provides for declaratory relief in the federal courts. Statutes of this kind, being remedial in nature, are liberally construed to accomplish their broad purpose.

The granting of declaratory relief rests in the sound discretion of the trial court, and its decision will not be disturbed on appeal in the absence of a clear showing of abuse of that discretion. A proceeding for a declaratory judgment must be based upon an actual controversy. Courts will not entertain jurisdiction of a proceeding to obtain a judgment which is merely advisory, or which merely answers a moot or abstract question; and the courts generally have no jurisdiction to deal with theoretical problems, academic matters, or hypothetical and speculative questions. The "actual" controversy which will justify a court's entertaining a suit for declaratory judgment must be a controversy of a "justiciable" nature, and this means that there must be a substantial, direct, and legally protectable present interest in the relief sought, and that the interest must be such that the judgment or decree will operate as res judicata as to the parties and will effectively terminate the controversy.

The existence of another adequate remedy does not preclude a judgment for declaratory relief in cases where it is appropriate, although some courts take the view that declaratory relief may properly be refused in the exercise of judicial discretion where another established remedy is available. To justify a denial of declaratory relief on this ground, however, the other available remedies must be speedy and adequate or as well suited to the plaintiff's needs as declaratory relief. As a general rule a court will not take jurisdiction to render a declaratory judgment where another statutory remedy has been especially and specifically provided for the character of case presented; and the courts are loath to interfere prematurely with administrative proceedings or to assume jurisdiction of declaratory judgment proceedings until administrative remedies have been exhausted. The pendency of another action between the same parties in which the same issues may be adjudicated is generally a ground for the court to refuse to take jurisdiction of a declaratory judgment action. And matters that have already been adjudicated between the same parties are not a proper subject of a declaratory judgment action.

Since the courts will not take jurisdiction to deal with hypothetical and speculative questions, and since they may not render declaratory judgments where the parties merely fear or apprehend that a controversy may arise in the future, courts generally will not declare the rights of parties upon a state of facts which has not arisen and may never arise. A court will not render a declaratory judgment as to future rights, nor will it attempt to decide or declare the rights or status of parties upon a state of facts which is contingent or uncertain, unless the settlement of present rights entails the determination of such future or contingent rights, or unless a present determination of future or contingent rights serves a practical need of the parties for guidance in their future conduct. While most courts hold that a controversy is not withdrawn from the operation of declaratory judgment statutes merely because it involves disputed questions of fact, declaratory judgment proceedings are not available where the object of the proceedings is to try such fact as a determinative issue rather than to seek a construction of definite stated rights, status, and other relations.

A declaratory judgment may be either affirmative or negative in form, and it should finally dispose of the issues presented and settle the rights and duties of the parties. Although a declaratory judgment does not ordinarily involve executory or coercive relief, such relief may be granted along with a declaration of rights and duties, whenever this is necessary or proper. The court, in a proceeding for declaratory relief, may grant consequential or incidental relief and enter a judgment granting both declaratory and coercive relief, where the proper grounds therefor appear from the pleadings and proof. Such incidental relief may consist of injunction, specific performance, accounting, or even a money judgment or judgment for damages. The defendant in such an action may, by counterclaim or cross-petition, secure coercive relief in a proper case. Since a declaratory judgment is res judicata as to the matters at issue as between the parties and their privies, it is self-enforcing to the extent of precluding further litigation between the parties of the rights and matters determined.

§ 12:2. Particular matters as to which relief is available.

Am Jur 2d References: Declaratory Judgments, §§ 20–73.

The subject matter of declaratory relief is almost unlimited under modern practice. The Uniform Declaratory Judgments Act authorizes the declaration of "rights, status, and other legal relations," and provides that any person interested under a deed, will, written contract, or other writing constituting a contract, or whose rights, status, or other legal relations are affected by a statute, municipal ordinance, contract, or franchise, may have a determination of any question of construction or validity arising thereunder and obtain a declaration of rights, status, or other legal relations thereunder.

Declaratory judgments may be rendered determining the validity of contracts against any ground of attack, as well as to interpret or construe contracts and declare their effect, to determine whether there has been a performance or breach, to determine whether a contract is subsisting or has been terminated, or to determine whether a right to terminate a contract does or did exist. A construction of the contract may be adjudicated either before or after there has been a breach thereof. Although the Uniform Act specifies "written contracts," it is generally held that declaratory judgments may be available as to both oral and written contracts, although there is some authority to the contrary.

Declaratory relief will not ordinarily be granted to determine the question of negligence or damage in a personal injury case; nor will such relief be substituted for a criminal proceeding to determine criminal liability. However, threatened violation of civil or political rights of an individual may give him the right to declaratory relief. Zoning ordinances are a frequent subject of declaratory judgments.

Declaratory judgment proceedings are particularly appropriate for the determination of the rights and duties of individuals as against public authorities and administrative agencies. This procedure is available to determine the powers and duties of various governmental agencies and officers, as well as to determine the validity and the construction of administrative regulations. Although declaratory judgment proceedings are available to a limited extent to determine the constitutionality or validity of a tax statute, ordinance, or regulation, and to obtain a construction thereof, the availability of such relief in the tax field is somewhat limited. The courts are usually reluctant to grant relief in tax cases, and prefer to leave the parties to other remedies. The Federal Declaratory Judgment Act expressly excepts federal taxes from the scope of declaratory relief.

It is well settled, under both federal and state declaratory judgment acts, that declaratory relief is proper for the determination of questions relating to the construction and operation of insurance policies with regard to rights and liabilities of the parties thereunder, and to determine whether a particular policy is valid, void, or in force. Such relief is available, in a proper case, with respect to life, fire, accident, health, liability, or indemnity insurance. As in other cases involving declaratory judgments, an actual and justiciable controversy between the parties must exist, and the controversy may not be merely on a question of fact, although the court, in determining whether an insurer is liable under a policy, may determine questions of fact necessary or incidental to a declaration of legal rights or relations. A typical and important use of declaratory judgment procedure in insurance cases occurs where a liability insurance policy provides that the insurer shall defend the insured against all actions brought against him which are within the coverage of the policy, and it is necessary to determine the duty of the insurer to defend in the particular case.

Declaratory relief is available to determine the existence, construction, and validity of wills, and the rights of parties under trusts. The decisions are in conflict on the question whether declaratory judgments should be granted to determine future interests in property.

Declaratory judgments may be granted to determine the validity, construction, and effect of bonds, both public and private, where an actual controversy exists. This remedy is clearly available to determine rights under deeds, leases, and mortgages. A person showing a proper interest and an actual controversy may maintain an action for a declaratory judgment to determine questions relating to the validity, construction, and infringement of a patent, trademark, or copyright.

II. INJUNCTIONS

§ 12:3. In general; nature and effect of relief.

Am Jur 2d References:　　Contempt, § 35; Injunctions, §§ 1–22, 296–385.

An injunction is a judicial writ or order of a court commanding a person to do or to refrain from doing a particular act. Injunction is distinctly an equitable remedy and is governed by the broad principles of equity jurisprudence. Its primary function is to maintain the status quo and to restrain wrongful acts. Although injunctive relief is ordinarily preventive, operating upon unperformed or unexecuted acts, it may in a proper case be given mandatory effect, compelling positively the performance of acts essential to the accomplishment of complete justice between the parties. Being of equitable nature, jurisdiction in injunction cases is exercised in personam, and not in rem, the decree being enforceable against the individual defendant personally and not against property, although injunctive relief may incidentally operate in rem.

The general rule that injunction is available only against future acts actually threatened or apprehended with reasonable probability and to preserve conditions in statu quo, rather than to provide a remedy for wrongful acts already committed or accomplished, will be departed from only in cases of strong necessity. So, acts or practices will not generally furnish a basis for injunctive relief when they have been discontinued or abandoned before the institution of the suit to restrain them or even after such suit is commenced, if there is nothing to indicate a probability that they will be resumed. And generally speaking, it is the condition of things at the time of the hearing, rather than that existing at its commencement, which determines the basis of injunctive relief. However, a defendant who proceeds to do the things complained of after the commencement of a suit to enjoin them may not defeat the injunction on the ground that the acts sought to be restrained have already been done, for he acts at his peril in such circumstances and is subject to the power of the court to restore the status.

Courts frequently issue restraining orders, in the nature of injunctions, to preserve the status quo pending a hearing on the application for a temporary injunction. A court may, when it is necessary to protect or preserve the subject matter of litigation before it and to protect its jurisdiction, issue a temporary injunction or temporary restraining order in aid of or ancillary to the principal action; and the court may give this kind of ancillary aid to a proceeding pending in another court.

A temporary injunction or interlocutory injunction may be issued, prior to the determination of the merits of a suit for permanent injunction, to protect and preserve the property or rights involved from further injury until the issues are determined after a full examination and hearing. A temporary or interlocutory injunction is distinguished from a temporary restraining order in that the latter is generally granted without notice to the opposing parties and without a hearing, while a temporary injunction will usually be issued only after notice and some kind of hearing to establish the urgent necessity of such relief to protect the rights of the plaintiff pending the litigation.

Although it is regarded as a drastic remedy, not to be granted unless it is urgently necessary to protect the rights of the parties, a mandatory injunction may be granted by a court in a proper case to compel the undoing of an injury already consummated and to require the performance of some affirmative act essential to restore the status quo. Thus, a mandatory injunction may issue against a defendant who proceeds to complete the act sought to be enjoined pending the suit for injunction, to compel him to restore the status quo. And subject to the general principle that mandatory injunction is not regarded with judicial favor and is issued only with caution and in cases of great necessity, the courts do issue such injunctions for various purposes, of which the following examples are representative: to compel the removal or abatement of nuisances, the removal of encroachments, the removal of an obstruction to an easement, right of way, riparian right, or of obstructions or encroachments upon public streets or highways, to protect rights in party walls, or to compel the restoration of lateral support of land. A defendant who has violated a temporary prohibitory injunction may be compelled by mandatory injunction to restore the status quo.

Although there is generally no liability in tort in the absence of statute, for damages caused by the wrongful suing out of an injunction, unless the circumstances give rise to a cause of action for malicious prosecution, it is generally required, as a condition precedent to the issuance of a temporary or interlocutory injunction or of a temporary restraining order that the plaintiff furnish a bond or other security to hold the defendants harmless against damage resulting from a wrongful or improper issuance of such injunction or order.

A court may enforce compliance with its injunctions by any of the processes within its jurisdiction, including contempt proceedings against a party violating an injunction. The court issuing an injunction, temporary or permanent, may modify or dissolve the same where, because of changes in circumstances or for other reasons, equity and justice require such action.

§ 12:4. Principles governing issuance; grounds and prerequisites of right to relief.

Am Jur 2d References: Injunctions, §§ 23–68.

Injunction is an equitable remedy, and its grant or denial in a particular case is governed by the fundamental principles of equity jurisprudence, which are discussed in the topic Equity. Injunctive relief is not granted as a matter of course, but rests in the sound discretion of the court, to be exercised in accordance with the settled equitable principles and in the light of all the facts and circumstances of the case. This discretion is applicable to all types of injunctive relief, permanent or temporary, preventive or mandatory.

To establish his right to an injunction, the plaintiff must show a clear legal right or title of a kind which equity will protect, and he must also show that the act or acts complained of constitute an injurious invasion of that right, which will result in or threatens actual and substantial damage. It must appear that the apprehension of injury or damage is well grounded, and that there is reasonable probability that a real injury, for which there is no adequate remedy at law, will occur if the injunction is not granted. And a court will not grant an injunction to protect or enforce the rights of a person where the acts sought to be enjoined are a proper exercise of property rights or of constitutional rights, such as the rights of freedom of speech and liberty of the press.

Among other equitable doctrines, the "clean hands" doctrine and the maxim that "he who seeks equity must do equity" apply in suits for injunctive relief. The complainant's own wrongful conduct with respect to the matter in which he seeks an injunction may preclude him from obtaining such relief. And under the general principle that equity always considers the effectiveness of the relief requested, an injunction will not be granted which would require the defendant to do something that is impossible, nor will such relief be granted where it would be inefficient or of no benefit to the person seeking it. Laches or inexcusable delay is generally a ground for denying equitable relief; and the remedy of injunction will not generally be granted in favor of one who, with full knowledge of the facts or with means of acquiring such knowledge, acquiesces therein or delays in asserting his rights until the defendant has placed himself in a position from which he is unable to extricate himself without great injury or damage.

The basic rule that equity will exercise jurisdiction only where there is no adequate remedy at law is applicable in suits for injunctions. The rule is well settled, in the absence of some positive provision of law to the contrary, that an injunction will not be granted where there is a choice between the ordinary processes of law and the extraordinary remedy by injunction, and where the remedy at law is adequate to furnish the injured party the full relief to which he is entitled in the circumstances. No useful general rule has been devised which would be applicable in all cases to define "adequate remedy at law" for this purpose. A determination of the adequacy of a remedy at law involves a consideration of all of the circumstances of the case. Where substantial redress can be afforded by the payment of money, injunction will usually be denied; but the mere existence of an action at law for damages does not preclude injunctive relief where, for any reason, such action would not furnish the complainant with full, complete, and prompt relief, as where it would be extremely difficult to ascertain the amount of damages. As a general rule, where administrative remedies are provided by statute, such remedies must be pursued and exhaused before a court will grant injunctive relief. In determining the adequacy of the remedy at law by way of recovery of damages, the financial condition and responsibility of the defendant and his possession of property in the state from which damages might be collected are important factors to be considered.

Closely related to the rule as to inadequacy of remedy at law is the general principle that injunctive relief will be granted only where it is essential to protect property or other rights against irreparable injury. If a certain injury may be fully compensated and adequately remedied by recovery of damages in money, an injunction will not ordinarily be granted. Exceptions are made to this rule, however, in some cases, as where the injunction is sought to restrain a party from wrongfully taking real property or from continuing acts which might give rise to a prescriptive right or easement.

The expense, annoyance, and delay involved in numerous actions at law to enforce or protect the plaintiff's rights constitute a well-established ground for equitable relief. The remedy at law cannot be said to be adequate in such a situation, and equity will grant injunctive relief to avoid a multiplicity of actions.

In determining whether to grant injunctive relief or to relegate the plaintiff to his ordinary remedies at law, a court of equity will always consider the equities on both sides and will balance the conveniences. If the benefits to be obtained by granting injunctive relief are outweighed by the inconvenience or hardship resulting from such relief, the court will ordinarily decline to issue an injunction.

§ 12:5. Rights protected and matters controllable.

Am Jur 2d References: Injunctions, §§ 69–246.

The availability of injunctive relief is not limited to any particular class of rights or subject matter, so long as the usual prerequisites of such relief are present. The protection of property rights is a frequent occasion for the exercise of equitable jurisdiction by way of injunction. Indeed, there was formerly a disposition on the part of some courts and writers to regard property rights as the only proper subject of equity's protection. The prevailing modern view, however, extends the jurisdiction of equity to personal rights as well as property rights, so long as the rights are clearly established, and because of the inadequacy of remedies at law, equitable relief is necessary to protect the rights. Courts will not, however, grant injunctive relief to control political matters or to protect purely political rights, such as those arising out of elections or involving the right to public office.

It is well settled that, in a proper case, an injunction may issue to prevent a violation of a valid and fair contract; and this relief is sometimes granted although the nature of the contract is such that specific performance thereof could not be enforced. Injunction is available to prevent a violation of an express negative covenant in a contract. Injunction may also lie to restrain the enforcement of an illegal or void contract. And the remedy lies against a third person in a proper case to prevent him from interfering with contract relations or from attempting to procure the breach of a contract.

The remedy of injunction is available to prevent tortious acts causing irreparable injury to the complaining party for which the law furnishes no adequate or complete relief. The relative hardship likely to result to the defendant if an injunction is granted, or to the plaintiff if it is denied, is one of the factors to be considered in determining the appropriateness of an injunction against a tort. Injunctive relief is available to prevent torts against real property and also to protect personal rights of certain types. For example, the right of privacy may be protected by means of injunction. On the other hand, equity has generally refused to restrain and enjoin assaults and batteries; and such relief will not be granted to restrain the publication or utterance of a libel or slander. It is deemed better to leave the parties to their right of action for damages than to interfere with the constitutional guaranties of freedom of speech and of the press. An injunction may issue either to protect patent rights against infringement or to restrain a person from maliciously and in bad faith making false claims of patent infringement and threatening to prosecute the complainant or his customers therefor.

An injunction will not be issued to enforce a criminal law as such or to restrain the commission of a criminal offense, as such matters are left to the jurisdiction of the criminal courts. However, the fact that an act sought to be enjoined is punishable under the criminal laws will not preclude equitable relief by injunction, in order to protect rights of individual parties where the acts sought to be enjoined are in violation of such rights and the facts of the case afford a basis for the exercise of equitable jurisdiction on recognized grounds. In other words, where the acts complained of violate the property or personal rights of the complainant, it is no obstacle to injunctive relief that the acts may also be of a criminal character.

While injunction will not ordinarily issue to control the discretionary acts of public or municipal officers, boards, or commissions, such relief may be available to protect the rights of private individuals against illegal, unauthorized, or arbitrary ministerial acts of such officials or boards. The mere fact, however, that such acts are illegal or unconstitutional will not warrant the issuance of an injunction at the instance of private suitors, unless the acts complained of will occasion irreparable injury to the complainants or necessitate a multiplicity of actions.

The mere fact that a statute or ordinance is unconstitutional or otherwise invalid is not a sufficient ground to warrant an injunction against the enforcement thereof at the suit of a private individual. However, an injunction will lie to restrain the threatened enforcement of an invalid law where the complainant's property or rights would be injuriously affected by its enforcement and where the complainant has no other adequate remedy. The complainant in such cases must show that enforcement of the law will affect his personal or property rights, and not merely that he suffers in some indefinite way in common with the public generally.

From the earliest times courts of equity have exercised jurisdiction to restrain the institution of threatened actions and to prevent the prosecution of suits already pending, where the institution or prosecution of such action would be vexatious or oppressive, would involve a multiplicity of actions, or would result in making an unfair use of a court of law to deprive the other party of his rights, and would be inequitable and unjust. The court has jurisdiction in a proper case to issue injunctions against other actions in order to protect its own jurisdiction. And a party may be enjoined from setting up an inequitable, fraudulent, or unconscionable defense in a pending action. It is well settled that a court of equity in one state may, in a proper case, restrain persons of whom it has jurisdiction from prosecuting actions in other states or in foreign countries. As in other cases in which the jurisdiction of equity is invoked, however, the person asking an injunction against the institution or maintenance of judicial proceedings must establish that he has no other adequate remedy.

In the exercise of the power to restrain judicial proceedings in other courts or tribunals, a court of equity proceeds not upon any claim of right to interfere with or control those courts or tribunals, but upon the theory that, having jurisdiction of the persons, it may compel them to do or to refrain from doing whatever the equities of the case may require. In other words, equity acts against the individual parties, in personam, and not against the other courts.

III. MANDAMUS

§ 12:6. In general; nature, purpose, and effect of the writ.

Am Jur 2d References: Contempt, § 37; Mandamus, §§ 1–62, 470–484, 495–498.

Mandamus is a writ or command issuing from a court of competent jurisdiction in the name of the state or sovereign, directed to an inferior court or to a public body, officer, corporation, or person, requiring it or him to perform a particular duty which is specified in the writ and which results from the official station of the party to whom the writ is directed or from operation of law. As mandamus was originally a command of the sovereign, issued only at his pleasure and in his discretion, it was classed as a prerogative writ. It is still frequently referred to as a prerogative writ, although this terminology is of little significance except as a reminder that the writ is an extraordinary remedy and that its issuance still rests largely in the discretion of the court.

Some states have eliminated the traditional names of some remedies, such as mandamus, and designate them only by a description of the purpose and effect of the proceeding. However, the principles governing the granting of the statutory relief are generally the same as those which apply to the writ of mandamus.

Mandamus is a legal remedy, although its issuance is governed by principles applicable to equitable remedies. The writ is designed to compel action by the defendant so as to give effect to rights already established or clear, rather than to establish or declare the rights of the parties. Mandamus is an extraordinary remedy available only in cases in which the usual forms of procedure would not afford relief. The writ is either peremptory or alternative, according to whether it requires the defendant absolutely to obey its command or gives him an opportunity to show cause to the contrary. The writ operates in personam against the officer or person to whom it is directed, and compels him personally to perform a specified legal duty.

Courts of general jurisdiction, or courts of the highest general jurisdiction, usually have jurisdiction of mandamus cases, although statutes in many states designate and allocate such jurisdiction. Appellate courts usually have jurisdiction to issue writs of mandamus only as to matters of which they have original jurisdiction, or in aid of their appellate jurisdiction.

According to the prevailing view, mandamus is not a writ of right, even though there is a clear legal right in the petitioner, a corresponding duty in the defendant, and want of other adequate remedy; the issuance or denial of the writ is a matter within the sound discretion of the trial court. This contemplates a sound judicial discretion and not one that is absolute, arbitrary, or capricious. As indicated above, the issuance or denial of the writ of mandamus is largely controlled by equitable principles. The rights of the public and the effect of the issuance of the writ upon the general welfare are important considerations; and a court will seldom grant the writ where it would result in disproportionate hardship upon the opposing party or upon third persons. A court will not issue mandamus where, for any reason, it would be ineffective and useless and would not be of substantial or practical benefit to the petitioner.

A court will not ordinarily grant the writ of mandamus if the petitioner has any other clear, adequate, and complete method of obtaining the relief to which he is entitled. In other words, to be entitled to this relief, the petitioner must show that he has no other adequate relief. To bar mandamus, however, the other remedy must not only be adequate in the general sense, but also specific and appropriate to the circumstances of the particular case, and it must generally be equally as convenient, complete, and effective as would mandamus.

The scope and nature of the relief granted to the petitioner in mandamus proceedings depend upon the nature and circumstances of the case. Statutes in some states permit the recovery of damages in a mandamus action. The power of courts to enforce their own judgments enables them to take whatever legal steps may be necessary or expedient to render binding and effective their peremptory writs of mandamus. Disobedience of the command of such a writ may render the party liable to punishment for contempt.

§ 12:7. Rights and duties enforceable.

Am Jur 2d References: Mandamus, §§ 63–127.

To warrant the issuance of a writ of mandamus, the petitioner must show not only that he has a specific legal right, but also that the right is clear and certain, complete and matured. A court will not ordinarily indulge in a collateral investigation in a mandamus case to determine the validity of the petitioner's rights. Mandamus is not ordinarily the proper remedy for the determination of property rights or contract rights; nor may it be used to determine feigned, moot, or test cases or to determine mere technical or empty rights.

To warrant the issuance of a writ of mandamus, there must, in addition to a clear legal right in the petitioner, be a duty imposed upon the respondent by law to perform the act sought to be enforced, and the writ will issue only if there is a clear showing of the existence of such a duty and of a default in the performance of it. Mandamus may be resorted to only for the purpose of enforcing the performance of legal duties of a public nature which arise from an office, station, or trust, and which are ministerial in character. The duty must be one imposed by law, and it must be specific, clearly defined, and peremptory in nature. If it is discretionary with the public officer whether or not he will perform certain acts, or if the duty is merely permissive, mandamus will not lie to compel him to perform it. If, however, the duty is peremptory or absolute, the officer may be compelled to perform the duty, even though its performance involves the exercise of discretion. He may be compelled by mandamus to exercise the discretion in the performance of his duty, but the court will not, by mandamus, control the discretion or interfere with the manner in which it is exercised, unless there is such a clear abuse of discretion as to amount to a failure to act as the law requires.

The character of an official duty as ministerial and hence controllable by mandamus, or as discretionary and not subject to such control, is determined by the nature of the act or thing to be done rather than by the character of the office of the one against whom the writ is sought. A duty or act is ministerial in this sense when there is no room for the exercise of discretion, official or otherwise, the performance being required by direct and positive command of the law.

The proper function of mandamus is to compel public officers or persons exercising public authority to perform their duty, and the remedy is not available between individuals to enforce purely private rights and duties, unless the duty is of a public or quasi-public nature. Mandamus is sometimes issued, however, to compel the proper officers of a private corporation to call a stockholders' or directors' meeting. And it is well settled that the writ will lie against a public service corporation or its officers to compel the performance of duties imposed upon it by law.

§ 12:8. — Duties of public officers.

Am Jur 2d References: Mandamus, §§ 128–379.

Compelling public officers, bodies, and commissions to perform duties imposed upon them by virtue of their office is the ordinary and normal function of the writ of mandamus. The principles discussed above apply to the issuance of mandamus in such cases. A failure to perform an act which the law specifically orders as a duty arising out of the office must be shown, and the act sought to be compelled must be ministerial or nondiscretionary in nature. Since the writ is directed against individual public officers in their official capacities, it is not affected by sovereign immunity to suit, which prohibits an action against a state or the United States without its consent.

At common law the writ of mandamus did not run to Parliament; and in this country, in view of the separation of powers of government, the judicial and legislative departments are independent of each other, and mandamus will not issue to compel a state legislature or its officers, or a municipal legislative body, to exercise their legislative functions, or to control their action with respect to duties involving the exercise of discretion. However, this immunity does not extend to duties of a mere ministerial character, and courts frequently enforce by mandamus ministerial duties not involving the exercise of discretion, which are imposed by law on legislative officers and clerks.

The mere fact that an officer belongs to the executive department of the state or federal government does not exempt him from the process of mandamus to compel him to perform a plain ministerial duty not involving official discretion. With respect to the chief executive of a state, however, there is some difference of opinion. As to the purely executive or political functions devolving upon the governor of a state, and as to any other duties or powers involving the exercise of official judgment and discretion, the rule is settled everywhere that mandamus will not lie to control or compel his action. And some courts take the position that the governor is absolutely immune from the writ of mandamus with respect to all of his official acts, whether discretionary or ministerial. Other courts, however, restrict the rule of immunity to such matters as are entrusted to the judgment and discretion of the governor, and allow the remedy of mandamus to compel him to perform purely ministerial duties imperatively imposed upon him by law.

The President of the United States is clearly immune from control by the writ of mandamus in the exercise of the executive and administrative discretion incident to his office. Moreover, the celebrated case of Marbury v Madison, 1 Cranch 137, 2 L Ed 60, is generally considered as authority for the view that the courts have no jurisdiction to issue a writ of mandamus against the President to compel him to perform any act incidental to his office, whether purely ministerial in its character or not.

Officers of the state and federal governments, other than the chief executives, even the heads of departments of the executive branch of government, are generally subject to control by mandamus with respect to acts and duties which are purely ministerial in character and involve no element of official discretion. The same is generally true of officials of counties, towns, and municipal corporations, and of administrative bodies, boards, and commissions.

IV. PROHIBITION

§ 12:9. Generally.

Am Jur 2d References: Prohibition, §§ 1–52.

Prohibition is a common-law writ of ancient origin, and like mandamus, was classed as a prerogative writ. The broad purpose and function of the writ of prohibition is to prevent a court from exceeding its jurisdiction. The writ is commonly defined as one to prevent a tribunal possessing judicial or quasi-judicial powers from exercising jurisdiction over matters not properly within its cognizance, or exceeding its jurisdiction in matters of which it has cognizance. According to the definition of Blackstone, the writ is one "directed to the judge and parties of a suit in any inferior court, commanding them to cease from the prosecution thereof, upon suggestion that either the cause originally, or some collateral matter arising therein, does not belong to that jurisdiction, but to the cognizance of some other court." The principal purpose of the writ is to prevent an encroachment, excess, or usurpation of jurisdiction by an inferior court or tribunal. As indicated by its name, the writ is prohibitory rather than mandatory, and in this respect differs from mandamus.

The application for a writ of prohibition must generally be made by a party to the proceedings sought to be prohibited, although in a proper case the state may make the application. The writ will be issued only in cases of extreme necessity, and the applicant therefor or relator must show that some court, officer, or person is about to exercise judicial or quasi-judicial power, that the exercise of such power is unauthorized by law, and that it will result in an injury for which there is no other adequate remedy. It is generally held that the court has some discretion as to the granting of the writ, although this rule has been changed in some degree, by statute or otherwise, in some states.

In the absence of a statutory provision to the contrary, it is a general rule that prohibition, being an extraordinary writ, may not be resorted to when ordinary and usual remedies provided by law are adequate and available. If there is a complete remedy by appeal, writ of error, writ of review, certiorari, injunction, mandamus, motion, or in any other manner, the writ should be denied. This rule is held applicable to criminal prosecutions as well as to civil actions.

As a general rule, the writ of prohibition lies only to prevent or control judicial or quasi-judicial action, as distinguished from legislative, executive, or ministerial action; and the writ must generally be directed to some judicial tribunal or officer. However, it is generally held that the writ lies against ministerial or administrative officers or bodies which have some incidental judicial or quasi-judicial powers. Conversely, if the acts or conduct sought to be prohibited are ministerial rather than judicial in nature, the writ will not issue even though the defendant is a court or quasi-judicial body. The gist of a proceeding for a writ of prohibition is the lack or loss of jurisdiction by the tribunal assuming to exercise jurisdiction, and the applicant for the writ must always show such want of jurisdiction of the subject matter or of the parties. The existence of any other defense to the challenged proceeding does not suffice.

V. QUO WARRANTO

§ 12:10. Generally.

Am Jur 2d References: Quo Warranto, §§ 1–53, 112–131.

Quo warranto is an ancient prerogative writ originally used by the King against one who usurped, misused, or failed to exercise some office or franchise. It is the remedy or proceeding by which the sovereign or state determines the legality of a claim which a party asserts to an office or franchise and by which it ousts the holder from its enjoyment, if the claim is not well founded, or if the right to enjoy the privilege or office has been forfeited or lost. It is a demand made by the state upon an individual or corporation to show by what warrant or right they exercise some privilege or franchise appertaining to the state, which they cannot legally exercise except by virtue of grant or authority under the laws of the state. The writ still has extensive use in this country for its original purposes, and sometimes in additional situations. In states where statutory proceedings have been substituted for quo warranto, the principles governing the issuance of the writ generally still apply.

Since quo warranto is a somewhat drastic remedy, the courts proceed with some caution and deliberation in administering it. And the issuance of the writ lies, to a considerable degree, in the sound discretion of the court. As a general rule, the writ will not be issued if there are other adequate and complete remedies to afford relief or protection to the public and to the parties affected.

Quo warranto is generally regarded as an appropriate remedy to determine the right or title to a public office and to oust an incumbent who has unlawfully usurped or intruded into such office or is unlawfully holding the same. It is the proper proceeding for the trial of the direct issue of title to office. It is also an appropriate method of determining whether a person is eligible to the office to which he is appointed or elected, and whether he has become disqualified to continue to hold such office. Quo warranto is extensively used as a remedy by which to contest an election, although many states have special statutes governing election contests. In many jurisdictions quo warranto is a proper procedure to try title to an office in a private corporation.

Quo warranto is an appropriate proceeding by which to challenge the right to exercise a franchise or special privilege that can be granted only by the state or a municipality, such as a license to operate a ferry or a permit to occupy a part of a street. Quo warranto is also available against persons who practice, without the required license or authority, a profession such as law or medicine. And the writ is an appropriate remedy for the usurpation of corporate franchises without authorization and to challenge corporate existence and the legality of corporate organization. And quo warranto will lie at the instance of the state to challenge the corporate existence of a municipal or other public corporation which is in de facto exercise of corporate life.

The right to institute quo warranto proceedings resides in the state, unless it is delegated by statute to individuals. Ordinarily the proceeding is instituted by the Attorney General as the chief law officer of the state. A county attorney may be given authority to prosecute such a proceeding which is limited to the county in which he is an officer. Statutory authority is sometimes conferred upon individuals to institute such proceedings in the name of the state on relation of the individual. Leave of court is required in some states for the prosecution of such an action by a person other than the state or the Attorney General.

*

INSURANCE

I. IN GENERAL

I. IN GENERAL

§ 13:1. Nature and types of insurance.

Am Jur 2d References: Automobile Insurance, §§ 1–10; Insurance, §§ 1–16, 1857–1896, 2087–2125.

Insurance may be broadly defined as a contract by which one party (the insurer), for a consideration called the premium, assumes particular specified

339

risks of the other party (the insured), and promises to pay to him or his nominee a certain or ascertainable sum of money or other benefit upon a specified contingency. According to another definition, insurance is an agreement by which one person for a consideration promises to pay money or its equivalent, or to perform some act of value, to another on the destruction, death, loss, or injury of some person or thing by specified perils. An essential feature of most types of insurance (apart from life, health, and accident insurance) is that it provides indemnity to the insured by way of compensation for loss occasioned by the perils insured against.

The types of insurance policies available today are so numerous and varied that protection may be bought against almost any conceivable kind of risk or loss. Marine insurance (which was apparently the earliest form of insurance in the modern sense of the word) may cover all risks of loss to ship or cargo from the perils of the sea. Life insurance is essentially a contract to pay a specified sum, in a lump sum or in instalments, to a named beneficiary or to the estate of the insured, upon the death of the insured. But there is a great variety of life insurance, and many life policies include investment features in addition to the payment upon the death of the insured. One such feature is a guaranteed amount in the form of cash value or paid-up insurance, which increases with the payment of each premium and which is not defeated by the termination of the policy prior to the death of the insured. Endowment policies are payable to the named beneficiaries if the insured dies before the termination of the endowment period, otherwise to the surviving insured himself. In the case of limited-payment life insurance, such as 20-year payment, premiums are paid for only a specified number of years, and the amount of the policy is payable at the death of the insured to the named beneficiary or to the insured's estate. Term insurance continues only for a stated number of years, at the end of which the policy terminates.

Accident insurance covers accidental injury or death from specified perils and under stated conditions. Health, medical, and hospitalization insurance is designed to indemnify the insured, within specified limits and subject to stated conditions, against loss on account of sickness, disability, and for medical and hospital expenses.

Property insurance covers a great variety of risks, the most common of which is fire insurance, which is an agreement to indemnify the insured against loss by fire to the property insured. As a part of a fire insurance policy or as an independent contract, it is a frequent practice to insure against damage from wind, hail, and other forces of nature, and against damage from smoke, smudge, or soot or from the discharge or leakage of plumbing or sprinklers. Boiler insurance or plate-glass insurance may be a part of a broader policy, or it may be the subject of a separate or independent contract.

Burglary, theft, robbery, forgery, vandalism, and malicious mischief insurance is designed to indemnify the insured against loss by reason of those specified criminal offenses.

Title insurance covers the risk or loss because of a defect in the title to property. Credit insurance covers losses, in whole or in part, occasioned by the insolvency or default of those to whom the insured extends credit.

Business interruption insurance and strike or labor dispute insurance are designed to protect business enterprises against losses arising from the events specified.

Liability insurance is designed to indemnify the insured against liability, or against loss or damage resulting therefrom, on account of the acts, conduct, or conditions specified in the policy.

Several distinct classes of risks are frequently embraced in the same policy. For example, the so-called automobile insurance policy or aircraft insurance policy frequently covers not only indemnity against liability to third persons in connection with the property, but also insurance of the property itself against loss or damage. And the so-called "homeowner's policy," covering residential property, frequently includes insurance against fire, wind, water damage (except from floods), theft, vandalism, personal liability, and a sum to cover the cost of rental of another residence in case of loss.

Group life insurance is frequently provided as an employee benefit. Generally speaking, group insurance is the coverage of a number of individuals by means of a single or blanket policy whereby the employees' lives are insured by the employer in consideration of a flat premium based on the average age of the employees. The premiums may be paid, in whole or in part by the employer, and the beneficiary is usually named by the employee. Such policies usually limit the coverage of an employee to the time of his employment.

Various types of life insurance have been made available to servicemen and veterans of the Armed Forces of the United States. Such insurance, which includes United States Government Life Insurance and National Service Life Insurance, are governed by federal statutes and are administered by the Veterans' Administration.

Insurers frequently obtain reinsurance from other companies in order to lessen their exposure under a particular policy or in a particular area of risk. Reinsurance may be defined as a contract whereby one party, the reinsurer, agrees to indemnify another, the reinsured, either in whole or in part, against loss or liability which the latter may sustain or incur under a separate and original contract of insurance with a third party, the original insured.

§ 13:2. Insurance companies, agents and brokers; regulation.

Am Jur 2d References: Insurance, §§ 51–193.

As the business of insurance is one that is affected with a public interest, it is a proper subject of regulation and control by the state in the exercise of its police power. The states have adopted elaborate regulations governing insurance companies and all phases of their business. In most states there are insurance boards, superintendents, or commissioners whose general duty is to regulate and supervise the transaction of insurance business within the state so as to protect the interest of the public, to make uniform rates, and to see that violations of the insurance laws are properly dealt with. These bodies are frequently given the power to license insurance companies to do business, and to revoke such licenses.

As part of the power to regulate the insurance business, a state may prescribe the kind and character of insurance contracts that may be made. State legislatures frequently prescribe a standard form of insurance policy and permit or require insurers to use it, or provide that in the alternative to the use of such a policy, the policy issued must contain or exclude certain provisions. The state may delegate to an insurance commissioner or similar board or official the authority to see that the requirements prescribed by standard policy statutes are complied with, although it may not, under the constitutional inhibition against the delegation of legislative power, delegate to such board or official the power to draft such a policy and force insurers in the state to adopt it. The states generally require insurance companies to make periodical reports and statements concerning their business, reserves, and financial condition. Modern statutes usually require insurers to maintain reserves to assure the payment of losses covered by their policies and the return of unearned premiums. And some states require insurance companies to file or deposit security for the performance of their obligations. Also, the power to regulate the business of insurance includes the power to regulate insurance rates and to require the submission of reports to determine whether lawful rates are being charged. The states may also prohibit insurance companies from discriminating between insurants of the same class.

The power of a state with respect to the admission and regulation of foreign corporations to do business in the state, discussed in the topic Corporations, §§ 6:21, 6:22, apply generally to foreign insurance companies.

The state also has the power to regulate and license insurance agents and brokers and to revoke their licenses for cause. The general principles of agency apply in determining the power and authority of insurance agents and brokers, their relationship to insurance companies and to insured persons, and the effect of their acts upon the rights and liabilities of the parties.

§ 13:3. Premiums and assessments; loans.

Am Jur 2d References: Insurance, §§ 530–653.

The amount payable as premiums, and the kind and manner of payment thereof, are determined by the terms of the insurance contract or policy, subject to the power of the state to fix or regulate the rate or amount of premiums and to prohibit discrimination as between insurants. In the case of mutual insurance companies, in which the members are both insurers and insureds, their payments for coverage are frequently termed assessments. These assessments are sums levied upon a fixed and definite plan on the members of the company to cover its losses and liabilities. The amount and limit of such assessments are determined by the fundamental law under which the company is organized, the general nature of the organization, and the entire contract between the parties.

Where the amount of the premium and the time for payment thereof are stipulated in the policy, no notice or demand is generally necessary unless it is required by the policy or by statute. Such notice is usually required, however, with respect to life insurance and similar contracts.

The manner and medium of payment are governed by the terms of the policy. An insurer may accept drafts, personal checks, promissory notes, or money orders, or it may demand cash. Where a personal check or note is accepted as a final and absolute payment, a dishonor of the check or nonpayment of the note when due does not affect the validity of the payment or result in a forfeiture of the policy. However, in the absence of an agreement or practice to the contrary, a payment of an insurance premium by check is ordinarily conditional upon the payment of the check.

A valid contract of insurance is not invalidated or forfeited by a nonpayment of a premium, unless the policy contains a provision to that effect. Many insurance policies, particularly life insurance policies, do contain provisions for the termination or forfeiture of the contract upon default in the payment of a premium. However, under nonforfeiture provisions of statutes and insurance policies, a defaulting policyholder may be entitled to an extension of the term of the insurance, or to a payment of money, to the extent that the policy has acquired a reserve or cash surrender value. And in certain cases where the policy was void ab initio or is terminated for some reason, the party paying premiums is permitted to recover the same.

Statutes have been enacted in some states requiring life insurance policies to contain provisions for loans by the insurer on the security thereof, and even in the absence of statute, provisions giving the insured a right to borrow from the insurer on the policy after a specified number of premiums have been paid are commonly inserted in life insurance policies. The loan value of the policy, like the cash surrender value, is usually determined by the number of premiums that have been paid. Actually, a policy "loan" is not a loan in the ordinary sense of the word, such as creates a debtor and creditor relationship, but is more accurately described as an advance which merely reduces the amount which the insurer must ultimately pay.

§ 13:4. Insurable interest.

Am Jur 2d References:　Automobile Insurance, §§ 11–13; Insurance,
　　　　　　　　　　　　§§ 460–529.

The general rule is that an insurable interest is essential to the validity of an insurance contract, whatever the subject matter of the policy, whether upon property or life, and that if no insurable interest exists, the contract is void. This rule is in accord with the modern view that wager policies are invalid. If the insured has no interest in the insured subject and cannot sustain any loss by the happening of the peril or misfortune insured against, the policy is invalid as a wager policy. Although the necessity of an insurable interest applies to all types of insurance, the question of what amounts to an insurable interest must be determined with reference to the nature of the policy and the risks covered. So far as concerns the right to recover the proceeds of an insurance policy, it is generally held that the insurer is the only one who can take advantage of a want of insurable interest; and it is generally, though not universally, held that the insurer may waive the defense of lack of insurable interest or be estopped from asserting it.

As regards property insurance, the general rule is that anyone has an insurable interest in property who derives a benefit from its existence or would suffer loss from its destruction. It is not necessary that the event insured against would necessarily subject the insured to loss; it is sufficient that it might do so and that pecuniary injury or loss would be the natural consequence. Moreover, an insurable interest in property does not necessarily imply a property interest in or lien upon or possession of the subject matter of the insurance, and neither title nor beneficial interest is requisite to the existence of an insurable interest. It is sufficient that the insured is so situated with reference to the property that he would be subjected to loss should it be damaged or destroyed by the peril against which it is insured.

The validity of a life or health insurance policy depends upon an insurable interest in the person contracting for the insurance. The question of the insurable interest of one taking out a policy on the life of another is clearly distinguishable from the right of a person to take out a policy on his own life for the benefit of another. The general rule is that every person has an insurable interest in his own life and may insure it for the benefit of his estate, and may also, in the absence of statute to the contrary, insure it in good faith for the benefit of any person whom he sees fit to name as the beneficiary, regardless of whether such person has an insurable interest in his life.

The authorities are not entirely agreed upon the question of what constitutes the requisite interest of one person in the life of another. Although a few cases hold that such interest must be a pecuniary one and that close relationship is not per se sufficient, the prevailing view is that any reasonable expectation of benefit or advantage from the continued life of another creates an insurable interest in such life; and under this view the advantage or benefit need not be capable of pecuniary estimation, but may be predicated upon any relation which warrants the conclusion that the person claiming an insurable interest, whether pecuniary or arising from dependence or natural affection, has an interest in the life of the person insured. An insurable interest at the inception of a contract of life insurance is regarded by the majority of courts as sufficient, although such interest ceases prior to the death of the insured.

An insurable interest in the life of another arises from a close relationship by blood or affinity, such as that between husband and wife, persons engaged to be married, parent and child, and between persons bearing a more remote relationship where the circumstances show an actual dependence or interest. Partners usually have an insurable interest in the life of a corpartner; and a corporation has such an interest in the life of an officer, director, or manager. A creditor has an insurable interest in the life of his debtor, at least to the extent of the amount of the debt and the cost of carrying the insurance.

II. THE CONTRACT OR POLICY

§ 13:5. Generally; construction.

Am Jur 2d References: Insurance, §§ 194–352, 654–686.

An insurance policy is a contract, and the rights and liabilities of the parties thereunder are governed by the general principles of contract law. Like other contracts, an insurance policy must be based upon a legal consideration and assent of the parties to the terms of the contract. Although the substance of certain provisions is sometimes prescribed by statute, and standard clauses and standard policies are required in some states, the form of the policy is otherwise left to the parties. In the absence of a statutory or charter provision to the contrary, a parol contract of insurance may be valid and binding. And this applies to executory agreements to insure, oral binders or contracts for temporary insurance pending an investigation of the risk by the insurer, or until the issuance of a formal policy.

An insurance contract, like any other contract, is invalid if it violates a state statute or is contrary to public policy. Thus, public policy requires an insurable interest in the person procuring insurance; and it renders unenforceable a policy of life insurance taken out without the knowledge or consent of the insured person. Insurance upon property the possession of which is forbidden by law is invalid, but where possession of the property is not in itself unlawful, insurance thereof is not invalidated by the fact that the property is used or is capable of being used for or in connection with an unlawful act or business, provided that the insurance does not have the effect of promoting or encouraging such act or business.

The rules established for the construction and interpretation of written contracts generally are applicable to policies of insurance. Thus, if the language of the policy is unambiguous and clear, there is no occasion for construction. The cardinal principle governing the construction of insurance contracts is that the intention of the parties should control. The policy should be construed as a whole, if possible, so as to give effect to the entire instrument and to each of its various parts and provisions. Like other contracts, insurance policies should receive a practical, reasonable, and fair construction consonant with the apparent object and intent of the parties. In case of a conflict between the two, the written or typed portions of a policy will prevail over the printed portions thereof. And the provisions of a rider attached to a policy will generally control where there is a conflict between the rider and the main body of the policy.

The rule applicable to contracts generally, that a written agreement should, in case of doubt as to the meaning thereof, be interpreted against the party who has drawn it, is of great importance in the construction of insurance policies. It is a general rule that the terms of an insurance contract which are ambiguous, equivocal, or uncertain to the extent that the intention of the parties is not clear are to be construed strictly and most strongly against the insurer, and liberally in favor of the insured, so as to effect the dominant purpose of indemnity or payment to the insured. And the general principle that the law looks with disfavor upon forfeitures is applied to insurance contracts, and the courts are generally disposed to avoid forfeiture if they can do so by a reasonable interpretation of the policy. Also, exceptions, exclusions, and exemptions from, or limitations of, liability of an insurer are construed strictly against the insurer and liberally in favor of the insured, although this rule will not be carried to the extent of disregarding or distorting the clear purport of the language of the policy.

§ 13:6. Modification, cancellation, termination, and renewal.

Am Jur 2d References: Insurance, §§ 353–459.

An insurance policy, like any other contract, may be modified by agreement of the parties. A change in the terms or conditions of a policy must, however, be based upon a legal consideration. In the absence of a statute requiring a writing, a modification or amendment of an insurance policy may be by either parol agreement or writing.

Reformation of an insurance policy may be had where, by reason of fraud, inequitable conduct, or mutual mistake, the policy as written does not express the actual agreement of the parties. If by inadvertence, accident, or mistake, the terms of a contract of insurance are not fully or correctly set forth in the policy, it may be reformed in equity so as to express the actual contract intended by the parties. Generally, reformation will not lie for a unilateral mistake on the part of the insured, unless there has been some element of fraud, concealment, or overreaching on the part of the insurer.

The right to reformation of an insurance policy may be defeated by an equitable defense, such as laches or acquiescence. The mere failure of the insured to read his policy does not necessarily preclude reformation thereof. However, some courts have held that the receipt and retention of a policy by the insured and his failure to read and examine it preclude his right to a reformation, and in other cases it has been said that the failure to read the policy may or may not bar reformation, depending upon the circumstances. Where there are grounds for reformation of an insurance contract, suit therefor may be, and usually is, maintained after a loss which would fall within the policy as reformed. There is some difference of opinion as to whether it is necessary to secure a formal reformation of an insurance contract in order to enforce the instrument as it should have been written. In many jurisdictions recovery may be had upon the true contract as it should have been written, without the necessity of a previous formal reformation. Some courts hold, however, that no recovery can be had on a contract different from the written policy, on the ground that the policy does not express the real agreement of the parties without a prior reformation of the policy.

As a general rule, a renewal of insurance by the payment and acceptance of a new premium is a new contract on the same terms as the old one, in the absence of a provision in the policy for its renewal; but where the renewal is in pursuance of a provision in the policy therefor, it is an extension of the old policy and not a new contract. In any event, the right to a renewal, and the terms and conditions of any renewal or extension, depend upon the provisions of the policy or upon a new or supplemental agreement of the parties.

An insurance policy that has lapsed or become forfeited because of nonpayment of premiums, breach of warranty or condition, or other reason, may be revived and reinstated pursuant to a provision therefor contained in the policy and the performance of such conditions as are imposed by such provision, or pursuant to agreement of the parties.

The right of cancellation of an insurance policy, which is the right to rescind, abandon, or cancel the contract, may arise from any of the following sources: statutory provisions; the terms and stipulations of the policy itself, including provisions therein for cancellation upon notice or request; the mutual agreement, consent, or acquiescence of the parties; fraud or misrepresentation; mistake; or the insolvency or dissolution of the insurance company. A court of equity may decree the cancellation of an insurance policy where grounds therefor are established. Provision is frequently made in policies of insurance upon property for cancellation by the insurer upon a prescribed notice to the insured and upon the refund of the unearned portion of the premium.

Where a policy is wrongfully canceled by an insurer, it is generally held that the insured has a choice of three courses: (1) He may elect to consider the policy at an end and recover the just value of the policy or such measure of damages as a court in the particular jurisdiction approves; (2) he may institute proceedings of an equitable nature to have the policy declared to be in force; or (3) he may tender the premiums, and if acceptance is refused, wait until the policy by its terms becomes payable and test the forfeiture in a proper action on the policy.

§ 13:7. Assignment or transfer.

Am Jur 2d References: Insurance, §§ 687–724.

According to the prevailing view, a life insurance policy and disability benefits thereunder may be assigned by the insured. As to fire and other property insurance, however, a different rule prevails. As to the latter, it is generally held that there can be no assignment before loss without the consent of the insurer and without compliance with the terms of the policy with respect to assignment. But after a loss has been sustained within the coverage of such a policy, there is no question as to the right of the insured to assign the proceeds.

It is generally recognized that the pledge or assignment of an insurance policy as collateral security for the payment of a debt is not an assignment within the meaning of a general policy provision against assignment without the consent of the insurer. Where a life insurance policy reserves to the insured the right to change the beneficiary, and the insured also has the right to assign the policy, he may make such an assignment without complying with the provisions of the policy prescribing the manner of changing the beneficiary.

In accordance with the general principles governing the assignment of non-negotiable choses in action, an assignee of an insurance policy generally acquires no greater rights than the assignor had, and ordinarily the rights of an assignee may be lost by a violation of the terms of the policy by the insured.

III. CONCEALMENT, REPRESENTATIONS, WARRANTIES, AND CONDITIONS

§ 13:8. Generally.

Am Jur 2d References: Automobile Insurance, §§ 14–40; Insurance, §§ 725–1051.

Concealment, in the law of insurance, is the designed and intentional withholding of any fact material to the risk which the insured in honesty and good faith ought to communicate to the insurer. Concealment in this sense is correlative with a duty to disclose. In most types of insurance the general rule is that if the insurer makes no inquiry and the insured makes no representations as to the facts in question, concealment not amounting to actual fraud is not a ground of avoidance of the contract, since the insured may assume that the insurer has satisfied itself as to the risk. In the case of marine insurance, the law imposes upon the insured a stricter duty to disclose any fact which may increase the liability to loss or affect the risk or obligation assumed. In any case, however, concealment such as will avoid a policy must involve a matter material to the risk.

If the insurer propounds questions to the applicant and he makes full and true answers, the applicant is not answerable for an omission to mention the existence of facts about which no inquiry is made of him, although they may turn out to be material to the insurer's risk.   And in the absence of express stipulation to the contrary, and where no inquiry is made, it is the general rule applicable to all insurance policies that a failure to disclose facts known to the insurer or its authorized agent, or which it or such agent should have known, is not a concealment which will avoid the policy.

A "representation" in the law of insurance is an oral or written statement by the insured to the insurer, made prior to the completion of the contract, giving information as to some fact with respect to the subject of the insurance, which is intended or necessary for the purpose of enabling the insurer to determine whether it will accept the risk, and at what premium.   A "misrepresentation" is a statement as a fact of something which is untrue, and which the insured states with the knowledge that it is untrue or with an intent to deceive, or which he states positively as true without knowing it to be true, and which has a tendency to mislead, where such fact in either case is material to the risk. Such a misrepresentation, which is material to the risk, renders an insurance policy voidable at the option of the party to whom the misrepresentation is made.   To render an insurance contract voidable, a misrepresentation must relate to a matter material to the risk, and the insurer must have relied upon the misrepresentation.

A "warranty" in the law of insurance is a statement, description, or undertaking on the part of the insured, appearing in the policy of insurance or in another instrument properly incorporated in the policy, relating contractually to the risk insured against.   In the absence of statute to the contrary, a warranty binds the insured absolutely as to the matter or fact warranted, without regard to whether its breach proceeds from negligence, misinformation, or other cause.   And generally, a warranty is binding on the insured without regard to whether it is material to the risk.

The fundamental distinction between a warranty and a representation in an insurance contract is that a representation precedes, is collateral to, and is not necessarily or ordinarily a part of, the contract of insurance, whereas a warranty is a part of the contract and must be either contained in the policy itself or incorporated therein by reference.   The determination of the question whether a statement made by the insured is a warranty depends primarily upon the intention of the parties with regard thereto.   Courts do not favor warranties in relation to insurance, and in case of doubt they will construe a statement as a representation rather than as a warranty.

In the absence of statutory provisions to the contrary, insurers may impose whatever conditions they please upon their obligations, so long as they are not inconsistent with public policy, and if they are clearly expressed in the policy. Conditions in policies of insurance are part of the consideration for assuming the risk, and by accepting the policy the insured becomes bound by the conditions contained therein.   Such conditions are thus similar to warranties.

There is a conflict of authority on the question whether the violation of a provision or condition of a policy forbidding the doing of stipulated acts during the life of the policy, or declaring the policy void if stipulated things are done or permitted to exist, merely suspends the risk so that the subsequent removal or cessation of the cause of forfeiture prior to loss prevents the insurer from asserting the past breach as a defense, or whether the breach of the condition renders the policy void.

In many jurisdictions statutes have been enacted for the purpose of relieving against the rigorous consequences of the common-law rules as to warranties and misrepresentations concerning insurance. Many of these statutes place warranties and representations on the same basis, and prescribe the conditions under which a policy may be avoided therefor; and some such statutes provide that no misstatement or breach of warranty, if made in good faith and without fraud, will avoid a policy unless it relates to a matter material to the risk.

§ 13:9. Waiver and estoppel as to forfeitures and conditions; incontestability provisions.

Am Jur 2d References: Insurance, §§ 1052–1179.

The general principles of waiver and estoppel are applicable to insurance contracts. A provision for the forfeiture of an insurance policy for nonpayment of premiums or assessments, for misrepresentations, breach of a condition or warranty, or on other grounds, is inserted for the benefit of the insurer, which may waive the provision or be estopped to assert it. Moreover, since forfeitures of insurance policies are not favored, courts are inclined to seize upon any conduct or circumstances on which the insured has relied and acted, as constituting a waiver of or estoppel to assert a forfeiture. The doctrines of waiver and estoppel extend to practically every ground upon which an insurer may deny liability, including the nonpayment of premiums, assessments, or premium notes; provisions and statements as to the age, health, physical condition, medical history and treatment, residence, habits, and occupation of the insured; provisions and statements as to title or ownership of property or as to encumbrances thereon; and provisions against other or additional insurance. These doctrines are not usually available, however, to bring within the coverage of a policy risks not covered by its terms or risks expressly excluded.

In order to establish a waiver by, or estoppel of, an insurer, it must be shown to have acted or to have failed to act with full knowledge of the facts giving it the right to treat the policy as unenforceable. Under the general principles of agency, an insurance company is generally chargeable with the knowledge of or notice to its duly authorized agent.

The operation of the rules of waiver and estoppel which bind the insurer as a result of the acts or knowledge of its agents is frequently limited by provisions in insurance policies restricting the power of agents to waive the conditions therein, or specifying the manner in which waivers may be made. Such provisions are usually called "nonwaiver provisions." The courts generally do not favor provisions of this kind, and the effect thereof in individual cases is often minimized, qualified, or obviated.

In addition to the express waiver or consent by the insurer as to the performance or breach of warranties or policy provisions, there are many other ways in which an insurer may be deemed to waive, or to be estopped to assert, such breach or cause of forfeiture. In general, any act, declaration, or course of dealing by the insurer with knowledge of the facts constituting a cause of forfeiture or a breach of a condition in the policy, which recognizes and treats the policy as still in force and leads the insured to regard himself as still

349

protected thereby, will amount to a waiver of the forfeiture by reason of such breach, or will estop the insurer from insisting on the forfeiture or setting up the same as a defense in an action for a subsequent loss.

The insurance company is generally responsible for the fault or fraud of its agent in preparing an application or policy, and will not be permitted to assert the falsity of answers or statements inserted in an application by its agents without the participation of the insured. A waiver of or estoppel to assert a forfeiture may be based upon negotiations by the insurer with the insured after a loss, where such negotiations recognize the continued validity of the policy and lead the insured to incur expense or trouble under the belief that his loss will be paid.

Many life insurance policies contain provisions, commonly referred to as "incontestable clauses," providing that the policies shall be incontestable after a specified period. Statutes in some states make life insurance policies incontestable or require such policies to contain incontestability provisions. It has been held that an incontestability provision does not prevent the insurer from resisting payment on the ground that the loss for which a claim is made is not within the coverage of the policy or within the risk assumed by the insurer. And such a clause does not generally prevent the insurer from setting up the fact that the contract has been abandoned or that the premiums due thereunder have not been paid, or that the policy in question is invalid as being violative of statute or public policy.

IV. RISKS AND COVERAGE

§ 13:10. Generally.

Am Jur 2d References: Insurance, §§ 1180–1213, 1347–1453.

Generally speaking, all foreseeable losses or risks may be insured against except those for which insurance would be repugnant to public policy or statute. The parties may make such contracts as they choose, and may qualify or limit the liability assumed, either by specification of the amount of indemnity or by the enumeration of certain perils or the exclusion of specified perils, or by limitation of the trade or occupation in which the insured may engage, etc. To recover upon a policy of insurance, however, the insured or his beneficiary must show a loss or injury falling within the provisions of the policy, and the insurer may designate the terms upon which it will be liable, and may include in the insurance contract exceptions or exemptions from liability which narrow or restrict the coverage and which are fully binding upon the insured if they are stated clearly and without ambiguity. However, if an exception or restriction of liability is ambiguous or uncertain, it will be construed against the insurer and liberally in favor of the insured.

The risk covered by a policy of life insurance is obviously the death of the insured. However, such policies frequently limit the risks assumed by the insurer with respect to certain causes of death, and it is frequently provided that there shall be no liability if the insured dies while engaged or participating in aviation or aeronautics; while engaged in military or naval service, or in a certain occupation; while violating the law; or as a result of the intentional act of another or of the use of intoxicants or narcotics, and the like.

Like insurance policies frequently exclude coverage of death by suicide; and even in the absence of such an express exclusion, there can be no recovery on a life policy payable to the estate of the insured where his death is caused by suicide when he is of sound mind. However, according to the weight of authority, if the policy is made payable to a nominated beneficiary other than the insured or his estate, and contains no stipulation that it shall be void in case of the death of the insured by suicide, it may be enforced if it was not fraudulently procured with the intention of committing suicide, notwithstanding that the insured dies by his own hand. The suicide of the insured while insane is as much insured against as death resulting from any other cause, if the policy contains no provision in reference thereto. Statutes in some states preclude the defense of suicide in actions on insurance policies.

Health insurance is an undertaking to indemnify a person for losses caused by illness. Such insurance, and policies covering disability caused by disease, and losses and expenses of medical care and hospitalization, are usually quite specific in the risks excepted from the coverage. Pre-existing conditions or diseases, or those originating within a specified time after the date of the policy, are frequently excepted from the coverage. Even without an express exclusion, insurance against disability as a result of a "disease" does not generally cover disability caused by chronic alcoholism or drug addiction. In some policies exception is made as to diseases not common to both sexes, or as to diseases of organs not common to both sexes.

The risks and hazards covered or excepted in fire insurance policies are usually specified with considerable particularity in the contract. The same is true with respect to marine insurance and insurance against the forces of nature, such as windstorm, tornado, hurricane, lightning, hail, ice and snow, and rain, flood, or water damage.

Insurance against criminal acts such as burglary, robbery, theft, and forgery, and against "mysterious disappearance," frequently requires certain precautions on the part of the insured; and such policies may make their own binding definitions of the particular crimes covered.

"Liability insurance" is a general term used to designate contracts for indemnity against loss or liability to third parties on account of injury to person or property. Such insurance may cover liability resulting from any and all acts or omissions of the insured, with the exception of risks and acts specified in the policy, or it may be limited to liability in connection with certain kinds of property, business, occupation, or activity. Many liability insurance policies exclude from their coverage injuries intentionally caused by the insured. The question whether a policy insures against actual loss depends upon the terms of the contract. If the policy is construed to be one of insurance against liability, the coverage attaches when the liability arises, regardless of actual loss by the insured at that time; but if the policy is one of indemnity only, an action does not lie against the insurer until the insured has sustained an actual loss by the payment or discharge of his liability.

Among the risks covered by liability insurance are those related to the ownership and operation of aircraft, automobiles, and other motor vehicles (infra, § 13:12), and those incident to the ownership and use of real property ("premises liability"). Products liability insurance covers the liability of a manufacturer or seller of articles for injuries resulting from defects therein. Physicians, attorneys, and other professional persons commonly carry insurance to indemnify them against liability or loss on account of malpractice or negligence. And special policies are issued to cover employers' liability and contractors' liability.

§ 13:11. Accident insurance.

Am Jur 2d References: Insurance, §§ 1214–1346.

Policies insuring against injury or death by accident or accidental means sometimes limit their coverage to particular specified causes or types of accidents, and such contracts frequently exclude certain risks or conditions from their coverage. Such policies are usually limited to injury or death by "accidental means," and they frequently require that such means be "violent," and "external," and that there be "bodily injury" or "external and visible signs of injury"; and it is sometimes required that there be "visible contusions and wounds."

Ordinarily the insured's negligence does not defeat a recovery on an accident insurance policy, unless the contract expressly excepts from the risk accidents due to such negligence. However, if an injury or death results from a voluntary and intentional act of the insured it is not caused by accident or accidental means within the terms of an accident policy, where the injury or death is the natural result of the insured's voluntary act, unaccompanied by anything unforeseen except the death or injury. If the death or injury is not the natural or probable result of the insured's act, or something unforeseen occurs in the doing of the act, the death or injury is generally held to be within the coverage of an accident policy, although some courts, making a distinction between the terms "accident" and "accidental means," hold that where an unusual or unexpected result accompanies a voluntary act of the insured, with no mischance or slip occurring in doing the act itself, the ensuing injury or death is not caused by "accidental means." The act of the insured in voluntarily exposing himself to danger will not defeat recovery on an accident policy, in the absence of a provision therein to the contrary, unless the insured intended to produce the injury or death. However, such policies frequently except risks based on such voluntary exposure to danger. In many cases public policy has been held to preclude recovery on an accident insurance policy where the insured's injury or death was a direct result of his own criminal acts. Some courts take a different view. Under either view, this risk may be excluded by express provision of the policy.

In the absence of any policy provision on the subject, it is a settled rule that where an insured is intentionally injured or killed by another, and such injury or death was not the result of the insured's own acts and was unforeseen by him, the injury or death is deemed to be accidental within the meaning of an accident insurance policy. There may be instances, however, where provocation or aggression on the part of the insured will be considered the cause of his injury or death at the hands of another, so as to preclude recovery on such a policy. And some policies expressly exclude or limit liability in cases of homicide, burglary, robbery, combat, assault, etc. According to the weight of authority, death or injury resulting from war or military service is by accident or accidental means within the meaning of insurance contracts. Liability for such injury or death may be excluded or limited, however, by provisions of the policy. Intentional and deliberate suicide by an insured who is not insane is not an accident or accidental within the meaning of an accident insurance policy. However, statutes in some states limit the availability of the defense of suicide. And it is settled that self-destruction by the insured while insane is within the coverage of accident insurance.

Accident policies commonly exempt the insurer from liability in case the insured's death or disability arises from or is caused by disease or bodily infirmity. The mere existence of disease or bodily infirmity does not relieve the insurer from liability under such a provision, however, where the injury or death of the insured was proximately caused by accident rather than by the disease or infirmity. And if an accident results in disease or some other physical condition not directly within the coverage of a policy, and death or disability follows, the accident is considered to be the proximate cause of the death or disability, so that recovery may be had upon the policy.

§ 13:12. Automobile insurance.

Am Jur 2d References: Automobile Insurance, §§ 41–138.

Several distinct types of insurance are designed to cover the various kinds of risks incident to the ownership and operation of automobiles and other motor vehicles. "Automobile insurance" may cover the risk of loss by fire, theft, robbery, or pilferage. Other types of policies or provisions cover loss or damage from collision, upset, falling objects, missiles, vandalism, and malicious mischief. Injury to person or property by uninsured or unknown motorists is covered in many automobile insurance policies. And liability insurance, which is required by statute in some states, insures against liability to third persons for injuries to person or property resulting from the operation of a motor vehicle. Several or all of the foregoing risks or types of insurance may be, and usually are, embraced in a single policy of insurance.

Automobile theft insurance policies generally provide coverage against "theft," or in the "broad form," against "theft, larceny, robbery, or pilferage." This coverage is frequently provided in "comprehensive" insurance contracts. The general rule of construction requires that words used in connection with automobile theft insurance be given their plain and ordinary meaning; and in case of ambiguity or doubt with respect to the risks or losses insured against, the policy will be liberally construed in favor of the insured. Under any of these terms of theft insurance policies, the taking of the insured automobile must have constituted a crime, and the elements of the criminal offense must be proved by the insured.

The language used in "collision" policies varies somewhat, but in substance such policies provide for coverage in case of loss or damage to the insured vehicle by reason of its being in an accidental collision with any other automobile, vehicle, or other object. Such policies frequently contain additional coverage of loss or damage caused by the upset or overturning of the insured vehicle. The word "object" as used in collision insurance is usually given a broad interpretation so as to include almost any material substance forming part of, or on or near, a highway. Thus, contact with a ditch, embankment, excavation, hole, post, abutment, curb, stones, piles of earth or sand, or other physical object in or alongside a highway is generally held to constitute a "collision" within the meaning of such policies.

Policies insuring against liability to others for personal injuries or death or for property damage resulting from the operation of motor vehicles are governed by the same general principles as apply to other forms of liability insurance. In such a policy the insurer usually agrees to pay, on behalf of the insured and within specified limits, all sums which the insured shall become obligated to pay as damages because of personal injury to or death of any person not excepted by the policy, or because of injury to or destruction of property, caused by accident and arising out of the ownership, maintenance, or use of the vehicle insured. Most policies of this kind covering automobiles provide "liability" insurance and protect the insured against liability although he has not actually paid the injured person, as distinguished from an "indemnity" policy which binds the insurer to pay only after a final judgment against the insured has been paid. Automobile liability insurance is generally limited to such liability as is caused by "accident." This includes liability based on the insured's negligence, even gross or wanton negligence. It does not, however, include intentional acts of the insured, except in the case of compulsory liability insurance required by state law.

Automobile liability policies usually apply to certain specified vehicles, although they frequently extend their coverage to replacement or substituted vehicles. And some policies are written to cover "fleets" of cars owned by the insured. A clause frequently found in such policies is the "use of other automobiles" or "drive other cars" provision, which extends the driver's regular insurance to casual driving of automobiles other than his own. Such clauses generally do not apply to the driving of other and uninsured cars of the insured nor to cars belonging to members of his household or regularly furnished for his use. Many liability policies expressly provide coverage for "hired automobiles" driven by the insured.

Under the "omnibus" clause now contained in most automobile liability policies, the protection of a policy is extended, not only to the named insured, but to any person using the vehicle with the permission of the named insured. In legal effect such persons become additional insureds and are protected as such so long as they operate the vehicle with the permission of the named insured and do not substantially deviate from the terms and conditions of such permission. The permission may be either express or implied. The question whether permission granted to another to use an insured vehicle authorizes the latter to permit a third party to use the car has occasioned much litigation. It has frequently been stated as a general rule that the permittee does not have such authority and that he may not delegate the permission granted to him. The trend, however, has been to avoid the effect of this strict rule by finding implied authority in the original permittee to permit others to use the vehicle.

The persons whose injuries are covered by automobile liability insurance are a matter depending largely on the provisions of the policy. Under the usual form of policy, which undertakes to pay such sums as the insured shall become liable for or obligated to pay, the insured cannot recover for his own injuries caused by the negligent operation of the insured vehicle by himself or, according to some authorities, by one who was an additional insured under an omnibus clause. There is a conflict of authority on the question whether persons whose relationship to the insured is such as to preclude any liability of the insured to them may recover on a liability policy. Such policies frequently contain express exclusions of liability to such persons, to members of the insured's family or household, or to employees of the insured.

V. OBLIGATIONS AND RIGHTS AFTER LOSS

§ 13:13. Generally; notice and proof of loss.

Am Jur 2d References: Automobile Insurance, §§ 139–150; Insurance, §§ 1454–1522.

The obligations of the parties to contracts of insurance after a loss or accident are determined by the terms of their policies. Most policies contain provisions requiring the insured to furnish the insurer with notice or proof of loss, or, in the case of liability insurance, with notice of accident, and the furnishing of such proof or notice may be made a condition of the right to recover on a policy.

In the absence of a provision of the policy fixing the time for presenting proof of loss, the law requires that such proof be made within a reasonable time. Policy provisions making the furnishing of proofs of loss or the giving of notice within the prescribed time a condition precedent to liability on the part of the insurer, or providing for forfeiture for failure to file within that time, will ordinarily be given effect if a satisfactory excuse for the delay or noncompliance is not given. There is a conflict of opinion, however, on the question whether, in the absence of an express provision making the insured's failure to give timely notice a ground of forfeiture, a requirement in the usual form, that notice or proof be presented within a certain time, is a condition precedent to liability on a policy. Some courts hold that a failure to comply with the provision within the period specified defeats a recovery on a policy, while other courts hold that although the insured must present the proof of loss or give the notice before he may sue on the policy, failure to do so within the time specified in the policy does not avoid the policy or work a forfeiture in the absence of a stipulation in the policy to that effect. According to the latter view, the insured's delay merely postpones the day of payment.

The insurance contract may prescribe the form and contents of a notice or proof of loss, and it is sometimes required that such proof be made on printed forms furnished by the insurer. Substantial compliance with such requirements is generally sufficient; and no particular form of proof or notice is required, other than one adequate to enable the insurer to consider and determine its rights and liabilities, in the absence of specific requirements in the policy.

Extrinsic circumstances may be such as to excuse noncompliance or delay in compliance with provisions of a policy requiring notice or proof of loss. The prevailing rule is that where, because of circumstances and conditions surrounding the transaction and through no fault or negligence on the part of the insured or his beneficiary, the giving of notice or loss within the specified time becomes impossible, the failure to give such notice does not bar a recovery, and it is sufficient if notice is given within a reasonable time after the removal of the obstacle. The mental incapacity of the insured is generally held to excuse his failure to give such notice within the prescribed time. And the time for giving notice or making proof of loss does not begin to run until the insured has knowledge, or is charged with notice, of the loss or event on which his rights are based. Thus, where the beneficiary of a life or accident policy is ignorant of the existence of the policy, delay in giving notice or furnishing proof of loss is excused until a reasonable time after his discovery of the existence of the policy. And the insured may be excused for delay or failure to give notice where it appears that he believed, acting as a reasonably prudent person, that an accident or injury was not covered by the policy or that he was not liable for the accident in question.

Provisions of insurance policies concerning notice or proof of loss may be waived by the insurer, or it may be estopped by its conduct and the circumstances to assert a default on the part of the insured or his beneficiary. Such a waiver may be expressly made by an authorized agent of the insurer; and a waiver will be implied from conduct amounting to a recognition of liability, such as proceeding with an adjustment of a loss or settlement of a claim. The insurer's failure to object to an attempted notice or proof of loss amounts to a waiver of defects therein. A denial of liability by an insurer, made during the period prescribed by the policy for the presentation of proof of loss, on grounds not related to the proof, will ordinarily be considered as a waiver of a provision of the policy requiring proofs to be presented, or a waiver of the insufficiency of the proofs. A denial of liability is equivalent to a declaration by the insurer that it will not pay even though proofs are furnished, and the law will not require the doing of a vain or useless thing.

A provision of a policy requiring the insured to undergo a physical or medical examination at stated intervals, or at the request of the insurer, will be given effect by the courts, and compliance by the insured may be made a condition of his right to recover on the policy. And a provision of a life or accident insurance policy giving the insurer the right and opportunity to conduct an autopsy is valid and enforceable. However, a provision giving the insurer the right to "examine" the body of the insured does not include the right to make an autopsy or dissection.

§ 13:14. Under liability policy.

Am Jur 2d References: Automobile Insurance, §§ 151–188; Insurance, §§ 1523–1574.

Requirements as to notice of accident and proof of loss are discussed in the preceding section. Liability insurance contracts, including automobile liability policies, ordinarily require immediate notice to the insurer of the occurrence of an accident or of a claim for damages which might be within the coverage of the policy. The purpose of such notice is to enable the insurer to inform itself promptly concerning the accident, so that it may investigate the circumstances, prepare a defense, and be advised as to whether it is prudent to settle claims. The giving of such notice may be made a condition precedent to the liability of the insurer, and many decisions hold that a policy requirement as to notice is a condition precedent even though the policy does not expressly so provide.

Liability insurance policies usually contain a provision giving the insurer the right to make such investigation, negotiation, and settlement of any claim or suit as it deems expedient. Such policies usually also prohibit the insured from voluntarily assuming any liability, settling any claims, incurring any expense, or interfering in any legal proceedings or negotiations for settlement, unless with the consent of the insurer. Although the right of the insurer to make a settlement of a claim against the insured is clear under such provisions, such a settlement without the consent or participation of the insured or contrary to his protest, will not ordinarily bar an action by the insured against the person receiving the settlement, on a claim arising out of the same incident. If the insurer denies liability for a claim asserted against the insured and refuses to defend an action thereon, the insured is generally held to be released from a provision against settlement of claims without the insurer's consent, as well as from a provision making the liability of the insurer dependent on the rendition of a judgment against the insured, and under such circumstances the insured may make a reasonable compromise or settlement without losing his right to recover on the policy.

The right reserved to the insurer to make the decision on the acceptance of any offer of settlement of a claim against the insured is not an absolute right that may be exercised arbitrarily and without regard to the interests of the insured, where a conflict of interests exists between the insurer and the insured because the claim or action against the latter is for an amount exceeding the policy limit and an offer of compromise is for the policy limit or a sum slightly below such limit. The insurer is bound to give due consideration to the interests of the insured in such a situation. There is a conflict of authority, however, on the question whether the insurer's obligation in making or declining a settlement is only to act in good faith toward the insured, or whether it is required to exercise due care and is liable for a negligent rejection of a reasonable compromise offer.

The right of the insurer under a liability policy to exclusive control over litigation against the insured is accompanied by a correlative duty on the part of the insurer to defend the insured against all actions brought against him on allegations of facts and circumstances covered by the policy; and this is true under most policies even though the suits are groundless or fraudulent or the allegations false. But this obligation does not extend to the defense of actions based on claims not covered by the policy. The insurer must decide at its peril whether or not to assume the burden of defending an action against the insured if there is doubt as to the coverage of the claim sued on or as to the liability of the insurer under the policy, although declaratory judgment proceedings may be available to determine the question. Generally speaking, the obligation of a liability insurer under a policy provision requiring it to defend an action brought against the insured by a third party is to be determined by the allegations of the complaint or petition in such action. If the complaint in the action against the insured upon its face alleges facts which come within the coverage of the liability policy, the insurer is obligated to assume the defense of the action, even though such allegations are false. Under public liability policies the insurer may be obligated to defend actions against the insured even though the action against the insured is groundless or it is not liable to pay. If the insurer wrongfully refuses to defend an action against the insured it becomes liable to the insured for all damages resulting from its breach of duty, including, in a proper case, the amount of the judgment recovered against the insured.

Where a liability insurer undertakes the defense of an action against the insured, it must exercise reasonable care and the utmost good faith toward the insured in conducting the defense, and it is liable in damages for a breach of that duty.　As a general rule, the insurer's assumption of or participation in the defense of an action against the insured will not preclude it from setting up the defense that the insured's loss was not covered by the policy, if the insurer gives timely notice to the insured that it has not waived its defenses under the policy.　However, some courts require the consent of the insured to such an arrangement.

"Co-operation clauses" appear in most liability insurance policies, providing in substance that the insured shall co-operate with the insurer, and upon the latter's request, shall attend hearings and trials and shall assist in effecting settlements, securing and giving evidence, obtaining the attendance of witnesses, and conducting suits.　A breach of such a clause may relieve the insurer of its obligations under the policy if the lack of co-operation is substantial and material. Most liability policies contain also a provision requiring the insured, if claim is made or suit is brought against him, to forward to the insurer the suit papers and every demand, notice, summons, or other process received by him.

VI. LIABILITY FOR LOSS AND RIGHT TO PROCEEDS

§ 13:15. Generally; extent of loss and liability.

Am Jur 2d References:　Automobile Insurance, §§ 189–198; Insurance, §§ 1590–1700.

Assuming that a loss is covered by a policy of insurance, the amount for which the insurer is liable is determined by the terms of the policy.　In the case of life insurance there is ordinarily no difficulty in ascertaining the sum recoverable.　Health and accident insurance policies, and life insurance policies with disability provisions, usually provide for the payment of a certain sum in case of specified injuries, or for periodical payments in case of total, permanent, or partial disability.　"Total disability," within a sickness or accident policy or the disability clause of a life insurance policy, does not mean a state of absolute helplessness.　Whether it refers to disability which renders the insured unable to perform all the substantial and material acts necessary to the prosecution of his particular business or occupation in the customary and usual manner, or requires a disability to work in any occupation whatever, depends largely on the wording of the contract.　In the case of an "occupational disability" policy, inability to work at the insured's business or occupation is generally held to be sufficient to constitute total disability, even though the insured is able to perform other types of work.　In the case of a "general disability" policy, however, the courts are in conflict, some of them applying a rule similar to that applicable to occupational disability policies, and others denying recovery for total disability if the insured is able to engage in other kinds of work or occupations.

The amount payable under a fire insurance policy is the amount of the actual loss sustained by the insured not to exceed the amount of the policy.　Many such policies contain provisions limiting the insurance to the actual cash value of the property at the time of any loss or damage.　Some policies limit the liability of the insurer to the cost of repair or replacement of the insured building; but this is an option reserved to the insurer and not a measure of recovery which the insured can invoke. In the case of a "valued policy," the value of insured property is fixed in the policy and such valuation is conclusive in the case of total loss. Such provisions are required by statutes in some states.

The extent of the insurer's liability under a liability insurance policy is determined by the terms of the policy. The limit is usually fixed by the policy as regards injury or damage suffered by any one person in an accident, and another limit is specified for any one accident. The courts are not agreed on the proper construction of the "per accident" clauses. According to the prevailing view, such a clause is to be construed on the basis of the cause of the accident rather than its effect; under this rule, where one proximate, uninterrupted, and continuing cause results in injuries to more than one person or damage to more than one item of property, there is a single accident or occurrence within the meaning of a liability policy limiting the insurer's liability to a certain sum for each accident or occurrence. In some cases, however, it has been held that such a clause is to be construed as referring to the result or effect of the accident on the persons injured or damaged.

§ 13:16. Adjustment, compromise, arbitration, and payment.

Am Jur 2d References: Insurance, §§ 1701–1726, 1791–1806.

The adjustment and settlement of the amount due the insured, beneficiary, or other persons are conducted through agents of the insurer. Where there is disagreement as to the sum payable, a compromise and settlement may be agreed upon, and such a settlement is binding upon the parties in the absence of fraud or misrepresentation. Property insurance policies frequently contain provisions for the submission to appraisers or arbitrators of the issue of the amount of a loss under the policy, where the parties cannot agree thereon. Compliance with such a provision may be made a condition precedent to recovery on a policy by express stipulation to that effect. An award by appraisers or arbitrators selected and acting in accordance with the insurance contract will not be disturbed by the courts except on the ground of fraud, mistake, or misfeasance, or to prevent a manifest injustice. Where there is a failure to secure an award after submission to arbitration, without fault on the part of either party, the insured is not required to submit to the delay of another arbitration, but may proceed at once with an action in the courts.

Insurance policies often contain provisions known as "facility of payment" clauses, which specify certain persons or classes of persons to whom the insurer may make payment of the benefits or proceeds accruing under a policy. The insurer has an option as to whether it will make payment pursuant to this kind of clause, and a person who would be eligible for payment thereunder cannot ordinarily compel the insurer to make payment to him. If the insurer does exercise its option to make payment under the facility of payment clause, it is thereby discharged from further liability.

In a few exceptional circumstances an insured has been permitted to recover damages resulting from the refusal of the insurer to make payments required by an insurance contract. And in some jurisdictions statutes have been enacted making insurance companies liable for damages in case of failure or delay in bad faith in paying a claim, or for failure to pay claims within a specified period after they have accrued. Such statutes are held to be constitutional, even as applied to contracts made before their enactment; but, being penal in nature, these statutes are strictly construed. Liability is not incurred under statutes of this kind where a failure to pay is based upon a disagreement in good faith as to the insurer's liability or upon real doubt as to the amount payable. A demand for payment is a prerequisite to liability under statutes of this kind.

A payment of a supposed loss under an insurance policy may be recovered back by the insurer where it was procured by the fraud of the insured; and it has been held that payments made under a mistake on the part of the insurer may also be recovered back. This does not, however, permit a repudiation of a settlement made by way of compromise where doubt or disparity existed as to the insurer's liability.

§ 13:17. Right to proceeds.

Am Jur 2d References: Automobile Insurance, §§ 199, 210–230;
Insurance, §§ 1575–1589, 1727–1790.

The terms of the insurance contract determine the right to the proceeds thereof. In the case of insurance of property, the owner-insured is ordinarily entitled to recover for any loss or damage; but such policies frequently name mortgagees or others as being entitled to the proceeds "as their interest may appear."   The beneficiary named in a life insurance policy is entitled to the proceeds thereof if the insured has not changed the beneficiary prior to his death; and the right to change beneficiaries exists only where it is reserved in the policy.   Where a life insurance policy is payable to the "estate" of the insured or to his "legal representatives" or the like, the insured may dispose of the proceeds by his will.   A beneficiary of a life insurance policy who murders or feloniously causes the death of the insured forfeits rights under the policy, and the forfeiture is generally effective against those claiming through or under such beneficiary.   The insurer is not relieved of liability in such a case, however, but the proceeds are payable to the estate of the insured or to the alternative beneficiary named in the policy.

The effect of the death of the beneficiary during the lifetime of the insured upon the rights to the proceeds of a life insurance policy depends mainly upon the absolute or conditional nature of the beneficiary's interest, and upon the existence or nonexistence of statutory or policy provisions in relation to such a contingency.   If the policy does not provide for this contingency and does not reserve the right to change the beneficiary, the named beneficiary has a vested right which descends to his estate upon his death prior to that of the insured and which cannot be divested by an action of the insured short of permitting the policy to lapse.   If the policy permits a change of beneficiary by the insured but no other beneficiary is named by him, the proceeds of the policy are payable to the estate or legal representative of the insured where the named beneficiary predeceases the insured.   Various results are reached where one of several beneficiaries or one of a group of beneficiaries dies prior to the death of the insured, or where some of the alternate or substitute beneficiaries named by the insured predecease him.

In the case of liability insurance, the rights of a person who has been injured, against the insurer of a tortfeasor, depend upon the nature and provisions of the policy and upon the governing statutes. As a general rule, there is no privity between an injured person and the tortfeasor's liability insurer, and the injured person has no right of action against the insurer and therefore cannot join the insurer and the insured as parties defendant. Whether an injured person can, after recovering judgment against an insured, recover therefor from the insurer depends to a large extent, in the absence of a governing statute, upon whether the policy is one protecting the insured against liability or one indemnifying him against actual loss resulting from liability. If the policy is construed as one against liability, a person who has recovered a judgment against the insured for an injury covered by the policy may have garnishment against the insurer. But if the policy is treated as a contract of indemnity against loss actually sustained, the insurer is not ordinarily subject to garnishment, as no amount is due the insured until he has actually made payment to the injured person. Statutes have been enacted in many states enabling an injured party to reach the proceeds of liability insurance or to proceed against the liability insurer. In any proceeding under such statutes, however, defenses available to the insurer against the insured (except those based on releases after the accident causing the injury) are good as against the injured party.

Where the liability insurer conducts the defense of an action by an injured person against the insured, a judgment in the action is generally held to be binding and conclusive upon the insurer when it is later sued by the injured person, even though the insurer was not formally a party to the first action. However, the judgment is res judicata only as to facts and issues which were or might have been litigated in the prior action. Hence, such judgment is not conclusive as to whether the injury or accident involved was within the coverage of the policy, where the insurer defended the action against the insured under a nonwaiver agreement with the insured. A judgment in favor of the insured in an action by the injured person is generally conclusive in favor of the insurer as against the injured person as to issues decided in that action.

VII. APPORTIONMENT AND CONTRIBUTION BETWEEN INSURERS; SUBROGATION

§ 13:18. Generally.

Am Jur 2d References: Automobile Insurance, §§ 200–207; Insurance, §§ 1807–1856.

Where several policies of insurance exist on the same property and amount in the aggregate to more than its value, a recovery by the owner is generally limited to the actual loss. In the absence of any provision in the several policies for a proportionate recovery, the insured may recover the entire amount from any one of the insurers. However, most policies now issued contain a "pro rata clause" providing that the insurer shall not be liable for any greater proportion of any loss than the amount named in the policy shall bear to the entire amount of insurance on the property. Such a clause is valid and prevents a recovery against an insurer of more than the pro rata amount stipulated. Pro rata clauses apply only where the several policies cover the same interests, and can have no application to insurance obtained upon another distinct insurable interest in the property. And statutes in some states will not permit the application of pro rata provisions to "valued" policies. Apportionment or pro rata clauses are not employed in life insurance contracts, but they are frequently inserted in health and accident policies. Insurance policies sometimes provide that as to particular risks or coverages they shall be "excess" insurance only. Under such a policy or provision, the insurer is not liable for any part of the loss or damage which is covered by other insurance, but is liable only for the loss or damage in excess of the coverage provided by other policies.

Where several insurers bind themselves to pay the entire loss, and one insurer pays the whole loss, the one so paying has a right to contribution by the other insurers, and has a right of action against them for a ratable proportion of the amount paid by it.

It is a general rule that upon payment of a loss an insurer is entitled to be subrogated pro tanto to any right of action which the insured may have against a third person whose negligence or wrongful act caused the loss or injury. This right to be subrogated to the rights of the insured may be either the right of conventional subrogation—that is, subrogation by agreement between the insurer and the insured—or the right of equitable subrogation by operation of law, upon the payment of the loss. The insurer's right of subrogation as against a wrongdoer is based upon and limited to the rights of the insured and is subject to any defenses which the wrongdoer might assert against the insured. The right of subrogation exists under policies of liability insurance and fire insurance; but it does not exist with respect to life insurance so as to enable the insurer to recover from one who has caused the death of the insured; nor, in the absence of a stipulation in the policy, is an insurer who has paid under an accident policy subrogated to the rights of the insured against the person who caused the injury. Since the right of an insurer to subrogation against one responsible for a loss is derived from and limited by the right of the insured against such person, the insurer's right against the wrongdoer may be defeated by any act of the insured amounting to an effective release of the wrongdoer from liability. Such a release of the wrongdoer by the insured has the effect of discharging the insurer from liability to the insured to the extent that the latter has defeated the insurer's right of subrogation.

MORTGAGES

§ 14:1. Nature, form, and elements of mortgage.

Am Jur 2d References: Mortgages, §§ 1–177.

The present topic is limited to mortgages of real property, chattel mortgages being discussed in connection with other security transactions in the topic Personal Property.

A mortgage is a conveyance of real property as security for the payment of a debt or the performance of a legal obligation, on condition that the conveyance shall be void on the due performance thereof. The early common-law mortgage was in the form of a conveyance in fee upon condition that title should revert to the mortgagor if he paid the mortgage debt on the day it was due, the date of maturity being called the "law day." If payment was not made on that day, the mortgagee's title became absolute and the mortgagor lost his property. The hardships resulting from this rule led to the intervention of equity to give the mortgagor the right of redemption. In equity, the mortgagor was regarded as the legal owner and the mortgagee as holding the legal title only by way of security. Although a few states still nominally apply the legal-title theory of mortgages, the equitable or lien theory prevails in most jurisdictions. Under the latter theory, a mortgage does not convey the legal title to land, but merely creates a lien to secure payment of the mortgage debt. In any event, the equity of redemption reduces the difference between the two theories to one largely of procedures and terminology.

The prerequisites of a valid deed of conveyance generally apply to mortgages of real estate. Such a mortgage must be in writing, bear the signature of the mortgagor, and be based upon a legal and valid consideration. And it is subject to the defenses, such as fraud, duress, undue influence, and illegality, which would invalidate a deed of conveyance. The rules of construction are generally the same as those applied to a deed: the intention of the parties, as gathered from the terms of the mortgage instrument, in the light of the attendant circumstances, governs the interpretation of such instruments.

363

Any kind of real estate and any interest in real estate may be made the subject of a mortgage, so long as it is sufficiently described. A mortgage on land generally covers all of its appurtenances and the improvements thereon, including those made after the execution of the mortgage. Although the rule was otherwise at common law, it has been recognized in many cases that a mortgage may cover property to be acquired in the future, embraced within the description of the mortgage, to which the mortgagor acquires either the legal or equitable title. In the absence of a statute to the contrary, the prevailing rule is that a mortgage may be given to secure future advances to be made by the mortgagor, or other obligations to be assumed by him, or to indemnify against future liabilities to be incurred in his behalf. A mortgage to secure future advances is, at any particular time, a lien only for the amount for which the mortgagor is actually indebted to the mortgagee at that time. Mortgages may be executed to secure the obligations of third persons.

Under the modern view of mortgages, the debt secured by a mortgage is regarded as the primary obligation between the parties, and the mortgage is merely incidental to such indebtedness. Hence, the existence of a valid obligation is an essential element of a mortgage, and if the obligation purported to be secured is invalid, the mortgage is of no effect.

Another common form of security instrument is the deed of trust. Such an instrument has many of the aspects and consequences of an ordinary trust, and at the same time it affords security similar to that of mortgages. Deeds of trust are frequently used to secure corporate bond issues. The distinctive feature of this kind of instrument is that the property which is to stand as security is conveyed in trust to a trustee, whose powers and duties are fixed by the trust deed. The trustee occupies a fiduciary relationship to both the bondholders or creditors and the creator of the trust, the "mortgagor," and he is under duty to protect the interests of the bondholders. For most purposes, a deed of trust to secure an indebtedness is treated as equivalent to a mortgage.

If an instrument conveys land for the purpose of securing an indebtedness or obligation, it is generally treated as a mortgage, regardless of its form. A deed which is absolute on its face will be construed as a mortgage if it was given and intended to secure an obligation. Ordinarily parol or extrinsic evidence is admissible to show that a deed absolute in form was intended as a mortgage.

§ 14:2. Rights of parties; use and enjoyment of property.

Am Jur 2d References: Mortgages, §§ 178–322.

Under the modern rule prevailing in most jurisdictions a mortgage vests title in the mortgagee merely for the protection of his interest and to give him the full benefit of the security, but for no other purpose. Under this rule, the title is retained by the mortgagor until the foreclosure of the mortgage. Ordinarily, and unless it is provided in the mortgage to the contrary, the mortgagor is entitled to the possession and use of the mortgaged premises and to the rents and profits therefrom. The mortgage may provide for possession by the mortgagee where the mortgagor would otherwise be entitled to possession, or it may give the mortgagor the right to possession where this right would otherwise belong to the mortgagee. The right to rents and profits of mortgaged land depends upon the title, the right to possession, and the actual possession, of the premises. As the contract of the mortgagor is to pay interest, rather than rent, the general rule is that the mortgagor is not liable to the mortgagee for rent for the period of his occupancy. The contract may change this rule, however, and require certain portions of rents or profits to be applied on the mortgage debt. Where the mortgagee is in possession, he is entitled to rents and profits, not in his own right or for his own profit, but merely for application upon the mortgage debt; and he is required to account therefor on this basis.

As a general rule, a person who takes a mortgage on land thereby admits the title of the mortgagor and is estopped to contest the mortgagor's title. Also, a mortgagor may not set up an outstanding paramount title in a third person as against the mortgagee. Nor may the mortgagor set up as against the mortgagee an interest or title subsequently acquired by him, especially where the mortgage contains covenants of warranty. In the case of a purchase-money mortgage, however, a determination of the right of the mortgagor to set up an outstanding title raises considerations that are peculiar to the situation. The mortgagor in a purchase-money mortgage occupies the dual capacity of mortgagor and vendee, which gives rise to rights in him under the covenants in the deed of the mortgagee to him, as well as obligations under the covenants of the mortgage.

A mortgagee has a right to prevent the impairment of his security. He is entitled to have his security preserved against loss or diminution in value by reason of obligations owed by the mortgagor upon prior encumbrances, and he may protect his interest by paying off prior liens and encumbrances on the mortgaged property; and when he does so, he subrogates himself to the interests so discharged, and he may also generally add to the amount of the mortgage debt the amount of the obligations thus discharged by him. Both the mortgagor and the mortgagee have an insurable interest in the mortgaged property, and either may procure insurance thereon to protect himself or the other party or both. Mortgages frequently contain provisions requiring the mortgagor to maintain insurance on the property naming the mortgagee as beneficiary as his interest may appear. It is ordinarily the duty of the mortgagor to pay taxes and assessments levied on the mortgaged property; and if the mortgagee, to protect his interest, pays such taxes or assessments, he is generally entitled to be reimbursed for the amount so paid and to add it to the mortgage debt.

Where the mortgagor retains possession, he must refrain from acts that constitute waste (see the topic Real Property, §§ 18:12, 18:86), at least where such acts would substantially impair the mortgagee's security. If the mortgagee is in possession, he is bound to exercise the same degree of care and supervision over the mortgaged property that a prudent man would exercise over his own. A mortgagee may maintain an action against a third person who impairs his security by damaging the mortgaged property.

§ 14:3. Priorities.

Am Jur 2d References: Mortgages, §§ 323–361.

The general principle expressed in the maxim "prior in tempore, potior in jure" (first in time, superior in right) applies to mortgages, in the absence of an applicable statutory provision or agreement to the contrary. Under this rule, any encumbrance which attaches to the mortgaged property after the execution of a mortgage is subject to the mortgage, and it is beyond the power of the mortgagor to disturb this priority. Dealings of the mortgagor with a third person after the execution of the mortgage cannot prejudicially affect the rights of the mortgagee. Similarly, the interest and rights of a mortgagee are subject to any outstanding interest in the mortgaged property, acquired prior to the execution of the mortgage.

A mortgagee is for some purposes regarded as a purchaser, and he is entitled to the same protection as is accorded a bona fide purchaser. This is true in regard to the priority of a mortgage over an outstanding equity. Although there are authorities to the contrary, the prevailing view is that a mortgage for a pre-existing debt is not deemed to be given for value so as to entitle the mortgagee to protection as a bona fide purchaser for value; in any event, however, and under either view, if a mortgage is taken for a pre-existing debt and the creditor at the time agrees to extend the time of payment, this additional consideration will entitle the mortgagee to protection as a purchaser for value. Priority of a mortgage over an earlier interest in the mortgaged property may be precluded by notice of such interest. In determining the priority of several mortgages on the same property, the recording acts of the state may be determinative. Under such acts, priorities between mortgages on the same land are determined by the priority of filing or recording the mortgages rather than by the priority of their execution, in the absence of actual notice of the existence of the mortgage first executed.

The general rule is that a renewal or extension of an existing senior mortgage and note or other obligations secured thereby, without any increase of principal or interest payable on the secured indebtedness, will not result in any loss of priority of the senior mortgage over junior encumbrances.

Many decisions support the rule that there is no priority as between the holders of notes or bonds secured by the same mortgage or deed of trust. Some courts, however, apply the rule that the holders of obligations secured by the same mortgage or deed of trust are entitled to priority according to the respective dates of maturity of their notes or bonds, the earliest being first and the latest last. The parties may, by provision in the mortgage or deed of trust, fix this order of priority.

An exception to the general rule of priorities is applied to purchase-money mortgages, i.e., a mortgage executed to secure the purchase money by a purchaser of land contemporaneously with the acquisition of legal title thereto, or afterward but as a part of the same transaction. Such a mortgage is generally entitled to a preference over all other claims or liens arising through the mortgagor although they are prior in point of time. The reason frequently advanced for this rule is that the execution of the deed and the mortgage are regarded as simultaneous acts, so that no claim or lien arising through the mortgagor can attach before the mortgage.

On the question of the priority between a mortgage to secure future advances, and persons claiming intervening subsequent interests in or encumbrances on the mortgaged property, there is some diversity of opinion. According to the generally prevailing doctrine, advances made under a recorded mortgage given to secure future advances will not be denied priority in lien merely because the intervening encumbrancer could not have determined from the mortgage, without extraneous inquiry, the true amount of the indebtedness or of advances secured thereby. And it is generally agreed that if advances are made under such a mortgage without notice on the part of the mortgagee that the subsequent interest or lien exists, his mortgage interest is prior and superior to the interest of the subsequent or intervening encumbrancer.

§ 14:4. Payment and discharge; equity of redemption.

Am Jur 2d References: Mortgages, §§ 394–532.

Payment of the indebtedness secured by a mortgage on real estate must be made at the time and in the manner provided in the mortgage or trust deed. Unless there is a provision therefor in the mortgage, the mortgagor has no right to make the payment before the maturity of the mortgage. Such instruments sometimes authorize prepayment but provide a penalty therefor. A payment or tender of payment on the date of maturity has the effect of extinguishing the lien of the mortgage or deed of trust, as well as discharging the mortgage indebtedness. A legal tender generally has the same effect. A mortgage debt may be discharged and the mortgage lien extinguished by an agreement between the parties. And the running of a statute of limitations, the presumption of payment from the lapse of time, or a decree of court canceling the mortgage, may have the same effect.

The mortgagee customarily executes some kind of release or discharge upon the payment and satisfaction of the mortgage debt. Statutes in some states require the execution of such a discharge or the recording thereof on the public records. Where the satisfaction is not complete, there may be a partial release of the mortgage and a discharge thereof with respect to a designated portion of the mortgaged property.

Under the early common law the failure to pay a mortgage indebtedness on the exact date on which it matured—the "law day"—had the effect of extinguishing the mortgagor's right and title to the mortgaged property and of making the mortgagee's title absolute. This harsh rule not only became a theme of melodrama and fiction; it also received the early attention of Chancery, and the equitable theory of mortgages was developed to alleviate the situation. In equity the mortgagor was regarded as the real owner of the mortgaged property and the mortgagee held the legal title only by way of security. The "equity of redemption" was created to avoid the penalty of forfeiture of title by default in payment.

The equity of redemption gives a mortgagor who has failed to pay the mortgage debt at its maturity, and who is thus in default, the right to make such payment and satisfaction at any time prior to the actual foreclosure of the mortgage. This right of redemption is so jealously guarded by the policy of the law for the protection of the mortgagor, that he may not waive or relinquish the right by agreement. Any agreement made contemporaneously with or as a part of the mortgage transaction not to assert the right or equity of redemption is not binding upon the mortgagor, being contrary to public policy. And the same rule has been applied to an agreement made after the execution of the mortgage relinquishing or limiting the right to redeem. The right to redeem a mortgage after default or breach of condition is extended not only to the mortgagor, but to those in privity with him and to those having an interest in or lien upon the land, such as subsequent encumbrancers and judgment creditors.

An equity of redemption may be enforced by suit brought for that purpose after a breach of condition and a refusal of the mortgagee to accept a proper tender. In order to maintain such an action, the tender of payment of the mortgage debt must be kept good. The right to maintain such a suit may be barred by delay in instituting it, i.e., by laches of the complainant or by the running of a statute of limitations.

§ 14:5. Enforcement or foreclosure.

Am Jur 2d References: Mortgages, §§ 362–393, 533–863, 905–966.

Upon default by the mortgagor in the payment of the mortgage indebtedness when it is due, the mortgagee has the right to proceed to enforce or foreclose the mortgage and to recover judgment for the debt. Defaults by the mortgagor in matters other than the payment of the mortgage debt may be made a ground for foreclosure prior to the maturity of the debt. And where payments are to be made in instalments, acceleration provisions may cause the entire indebtedness to become immediately due upon a default in the payment of any instalment. A premature or improper foreclosure may render the mortgagee liable in an action for damages. The procedure for the foreclosure or enforcement of mortgages is usually provided by a statute or court rules, and it is generally governed by equitable principles.

The usual procedure upon the default of the mortgagor is for the mortgagee to institute a single action for the collection of the mortgage indebtedness and the foreclosure or enforcement of the mortgage. In the absence of statutory inhibition, however, separate proceedings may be maintained to accomplish the two purposes. A recovery in an action on the debt, or a judgment to foreclose or enforce the mortgage, does not generally bar an action for the other kind of relief. However, in some states statutes require a single action to recover the debt and foreclose a mortgage, and a separate action for either kind of relief is held to bar the other kind. And it is held in some states that where a judgment is recovered in a separate action on the mortgage indebtedness, no foreclosure suit can be maintained until an execution on such judgment is returned unsatisfied.

The sale of the mortgaged property in foreclosure proceedings is conducted by a commissioner or such other person as the court may designate, after proper notice of the time, purpose, place, and terms of the sale posted or published as required by statute or by order or decree of the court. Where there are several parcels of land involved in the foreclosure, the court may, in its discretion, order a sale of each parcel separately or a sale en masse. The court may confirm the sale, or on the grounds of irregularities therein or fraud, it may vacate the sale and order a resale.

The general rule, in the absence of mistake, fraud, or unfairness, is that mere inadequacy of price does not furnish a sufficient ground to invalidate a foreclosure sale, unless the price is so grossly inadequate and unconscionable as to shock the moral sense, or unless there are additional circumstances militating against the regularity of the sale.

Sale under a power contained in a trust deed or a mortgage, or created by separate instrument, is one of the established modes of mortgage foreclosure. In jurisdictions where such foreclosures are recognized, the sale is made without recourse to courts, although statutes generally prescribe the manner of advertising and conducting such sales. Such power of sale may be conferred upon the trustee or the mortgagee, and in such cases the power is held to be one coupled with an interest. A sale under such a power must be made strictly in accordance with the power conferred and with the terms of the mortgage or deed of trust.

As a general rule, the doctrine of caveat emptor applies to foreclosure sales, whether under decree of court or pursuant to a power contained in the mortgage or deed of trust. The purchaser at such a sale must generally determine for himself the validity of the title which he is acquiring. However, he may be entitled to relief where he is misled by fraud or mistake without negligence on his part. And if the foreclosure sale is invalid for any reason for which he is not responsible, he generally stands in the position of a mortgagee and may prosecute another foreclosure proceeding.

If the foreclosure, whether in judicial proceedings or under a power contained in the mortgage or deed of trust, does not produce an amount sufficient to satisfy the mortgage debt, the mortgagee has a right to a judgment for the balance of such debt, in the absence of a statute or agreement to the contrary. A deficiency decree may be rendered by the court enforcing the mortgage.

In the absence of any binding stipulation in the mortgage or deed of trust with respect to the distribution or application of the proceeds of a foreclosure sale, the court having jurisdiction of the proceeding may determine the order of priority of various liens on the property and give specific directions as to the distribution and application of the proceeds. Generally, the proceeds must be applied first to the mortgage debt. Any surplus remaining after the discharge of the mortgage indebtedness and other liens on the property must be paid to the mortgagor.

On several occasions in the history of our country, because of emergencies such as war or economic depression, moratoria have been imposed by federal and state statutes upon the foreclosure or enforcement of mortgages, with the result that such foreclosures have been prohibited, suspended, or restricted.

§ 14:6. Redemption from sale.

Am Jur 2d References: Mortgages, §§ 864–904.

Statutes in many states provide for redemption from a mortgage after a foreclosure sale. This right of redemption is quite distinct from the equity of redemption discussed in § 14:4, supra, which is entirely cut off by a foreclosure. The right to redeem after a foreclosure sale is purely statutory and may be exercised only in the manner prescribed by statute. Where the right of redemption is exercised in the manner and within the time limit prescribed by statute, it generally has the effect of defeating the inchoate right of the purchaser at the foreclosure sale and of restoring the title to the property to the same condition as if no sale had been attempted. The purchaser at a foreclosure sale buys the property subject to the statutory right of redemption.

The statutory right of redemption from a foreclosure sale usually exists in favor of the mortgagor and those claiming under him, including any person having an interest in or lien upon the land and in privity with the mortgagor. This right usually exists in favor of a junior mortgagee, encumbrancer, or lienor. A judgment creditor of the mortgagor generally has this right to redeem.

As indicated above, a redemption of property from a foreclosure sale may be had only by strict compliance with the provision of the statute conferring the right of redemption, and this requires the payment or tender of all sums due or required to be paid by the statute. And the right of redemption must be exercised within the time limited by the statute giving the right.

§ 14:7. Receivers.

Am Jur 2d References: Mortgages, §§ 967–1030.

Courts frequently appoint receivers for the protection of the rights of mortgagees or other persons with respect to the mortgaged property. Such receiverships are ancillary to suits based on the mortgage, most often foreclosure proceedings. A receiver may be appointed in a proper case at the instance of the mortgagee, a junior encumbrancer, or the holders of notes or bonds secured by a mortgage or deed of trust.

The granting of an application for the appointment of a receiver in mortgage cases rests largely in the discretion of the court. The mere inadequacy of the security for the mortgage debt is not a ground for the appointment of a receiver, in the absence of statute. In some jurisdictions the mortgagee can claim the rents, income, and profits of the mortgaged property after the mortgagor defaults, and the mortgagee is given a right to the appointment of a receiver to take charge thereof under these circumstances. In some jurisdictions the insolvency of the mortgagor, combined with the insufficiency of the security to pay the mortgage debt, may be a ground for the appointment of a receiver, at least where the mortgagor is in default. And where these factors are combined with the additional ground of danger of loss, waste, destruction, or serious impairment of the property, the appointment of a receiver is proper. The power of a court to appoint a receiver in foreclosure proceedings, for the purpose of continuing the business of the mortgagor or of managing his property, is frequently recognized; but the circumstances of each case determine the propriety of a receivership for this purpose.

§ 14:8. Transfer of mortgaged property or of mortgagor's interest.

Am Jur 2d References: Mortgages, §§ 1031–1267, 1388–1407.

Until it has been divested by foreclosure and sale, a mortgagor's interest and estate in the mortgaged property may be sold and conveyed by him. The mortgagor's interest is also devisable and descendible, subject to the mortgage.

The conveyance of mortgaged premises by the mortgagor does not in itself exonerate him from personal liability for the debt secured, even though the grantee personally assumes and agrees to pay the mortgage debt, unless the mortgagee expressly agrees to release the mortgagor and accept the grantee as the debtor. It is generally held that there is no personal liability on the part of the grantee of mortgaged property for the indebtedness secured by the mortgage, where there is no agreement by him for the payment thereof and no statutory provision imposing such liability. An agreement by the grantee to assume and pay the mortgage debt may, however, be implied by the language of the instrument or the surrounding circumstances. The mere statement in the deed that it is made "subject to" a mortgage does not alone make the grantee personally liable for the mortgage debt. Where the grantee of mortgaged property does actually assume and agree to pay the mortgage debt, he becomes liable therefor not only to the mortgagor but also to the mortgagee.

Ordinarily, a transfer of the interest of the mortgagor in mortgaged property to the mortgagee operates as a merger of the two estates, which effects a discharge of the mortgage and satisfaction of the debt, whether the interest transferred by the mortgagor is a legal title or an equity of redemption. This result does not follow, however, where the intention of the parties, express or implied, was to keep the mortgage alive.

§ 14:9. Transfer of mortgage or debt or of mortgagee's interest.

Am Jur 2d References: Mortgages, §§ 1268–1407.

It is well settled that a mortgage is assignable. However, under the general view that the mortgagee's interest is a mere lien and for security only, it is generally held that his conveyance or transfer of the mortgage only, and not of the mortgage debt, is ineffectual. When a valid assignment of the mortgage has been consummated, the assignee is vested with the rights and powers of the mortgagee as fully as if he had been named such in the mortgage; he may enforce or foreclose the mortgage upon default and exercise the other rights of a mortgagee. It is generally held that an assignment of the mortgage debt or obligation evidencing such debt operates as an assignment of the mortgage securing it. And this rule applies to a partial assignment of the mortgage debt, which carries with it a proportional interest in the mortgage. Upon the death of the mortgagee of real estate, his interest is generally held to pass as personal property to his personal representatives, and not as real property to his heirs.

The rule that there is no priority between the holders of notes or bonds secured by the same mortgage or deed of trust is generally applied, in the absence of an express stipulation or controlling equity to the contrary, in the case of an assignment of such notes or bonds to different persons; in such case there is no priority of any of the assignees over the others, regardless of the order of assignment. This rule has been applied where the obligations fall due at different dates, although there is some difference of opinion on this point. The priority in such cases may be affected by agreements between the mortgagor and mortgagee or between the mortgagee and his assignee.

*

PARTNERSHIP AND OTHER UNINCORPORATED ORGANIZATIONS

I. PARTNERSHIP

I. PARTNERSHIP

§ 15:1. Nature, formation, and existence.

Am Jur 2d References: Partnership, §§ 1–81, 322–326, 370–392.

The Uniform Partnership Act, which has been adopted in more than 40 American jurisdictions, was primarily intended to codify the existing statutory and common law relating to partnerships. In most areas it makes no substantial changes in the rules previously prevailing. The Act does, however, materially affect the rules governing the acquisition and conveyance of real property in the partnership name, the character of a partner's property as personal property, the nature of the liability of an incoming partner, the dissolution of partnerships, and the rights of creditors after the retirement or admission of a partner.

A partnership is defined by the Uniform Partnership Act as "an association of two or more persons to carry on as co-owners a business for profit." According to the comprehensive definition of Chancellor Kent, which has been widely approved by the courts, a partnership is a contract of two or more competent persons to place their money, effects, labor, and skill, or some or all of them, in lawful commerce or business, and to divide the profits and bear the losses in certain proportions. The formation of a partnership involves a contractual relationship, and the contract must meet the prerequisites for contracts generally, including the assent of the parties and a legal consideration.

At common law a partnership is not deemed to be a legal entity, separate and distinct from its members. Although the partners join together in a common enterprise, their separate identities are not merged and obliterated in the partnership organization. This is one of the features distinguishing a partnership from a corporation. In civil-law jurisdictions, such as Louisiana, and in a few common-law states, a partnership is treated as a separate legal entity. The Uniform Partnership Act as adopted in most states does not go to the full extent of declaring a partnership to be a legal entity; but it is given this effect in some jurisdictions, and some of the provisions of the Act clearly treat the partnership as a separate entity for particular purposes.

The Uniform Partnership Act permits a partnership or a corporation to be a member of a partnership, but the general corporation laws of many states preclude such membership by a corporation. Partnerships may be formed for almost any purpose not violative of some declared public policy or statutory inhibition. Although most partnerships are formed for commercial or trading purposes, a nontrading partnership may exist between attorneys, physicians, and others. It is customary for a partnership to adopt a name in which the joint business is conducted, and this name need not contain the name of any of the partners. However, statutes in most states require the filing of a statement or certificate in the latter case.

In determining whether a partnership exists, the courts consider numerous factors, and no single test or indicia is determinative of the question. A basic and essential element of a partnership is the intention of the parties to be partners. Without such intention there can be no partnership, as between the parties. There must be a community of interest between the parties for business purposes, although co-ownership of property is not essential. Although a sharing of profits is not of itself conclusive as to the existence of a partnership relation, it is well settled that an agreement to share both profits and losses is an essential element of the partnership relation.

Parties may be held liable under some circumstances as partners as against third persons, although, as between themselves, the partnership relationship does not exist. One who holds himself out or knowingly permits himself to be held out as a member of a partnership is estopped to deny the partnership relation as against a third person who has dealt with the alleged partnership or firm with knowledge of and reliance on the ostensible partnership and has been misled thereby to his injury. Such a party is a "partner by estoppel." And under the Uniform Partnership Act, one who has allowed or caused the general community to believe that he is a partner may be estopped to deny such relationship even as against a particular creditor who has not heard the representations.

At common law, a partnership could not sue or be sued in its firm name. It was necessary to join all the partners in an action by or against the partnership. The rule is otherwise, however, in jurisdictions recognizing a partnership as a legal entity, and actions in the partnership name are expressly authorized in some states by statutes or rules.

Limited partnerships are recognized by the civil law, but were unknown at common law. The Uniform Limited Partnership Act, which has been adopted in most of the states, provides for the formation of limited partnerships and defines such a partnership as one formed by two or more persons under the Act, by complying with the statutory requirements, having as members one or more general partners and one or more limited partners. A limited partner is liable to creditors, or for losses of the partnership, only to the extent of his investment in the assets of the business. However, he may become liable as a general partner if he participates in the control of the business.

§ 15:2. Partnership property.

Am Jur 2d References: Partnership, §§ 11, 82–107, 148–153.

Under the provisions of the Uniform Partnership Act, all property originally brought into the partnership stock or subsequently acquired by purchase or otherwise, on account of the partnership, is partnership property. Unless the contrary intention appears, property acquired with partnership funds is partnership property. It is everywhere recognized, even in jurisdictions which hold that a partnership as such cannot hold legal title to real property, that the personal property of a partnership is owned by the partnership itself and not by the partners individually. Prior to and apart from the Uniform Partnership Act, the doctrine of equitable conversion has been applied, so as to treat, for certain purposes, real estate belonging to a partnership, as personal property. Under this doctrine, the real estate was regarded as personal property for the purpose of the payment of debts of the partnership and the adjustment of the equities of the partners. Under the English rule, followed in some American states, partnership real estate was treated as being converted into personalty for all purposes. The Uniform Partnership Act seems to have adopted the English "out and out" conversion rule, so that all partnership real estate is treated as personalty.

Since a partnership was not recognized as a legal entity at common law, it did not have the power to take title to real property in its firm name, although in equity the ownership of real estate by a partnership was recognized, regardless of the state of the legal title. Under the common-law rule, a conveyance of real property to partners normally vested them with the legal title as joint tenants or tenants in common. Under the Uniform Partnership Act real estate may be acquired in the partnership name, and title so acquired can be conveyed only in the partnership name. The Act created a "tenancy in partnership" in which partnership real estate is held. Real property purchased for partnership purposes, with partnership funds, becomes partnership property, held by the partners in tenancy in partnership, although title is taken in the names of the partners or of one of the partners.

Under the Uniform Partnership Act, a partner cannot sell or transfer his interest in any specific partnership property, but he may, on withdrawing from the partnership, transfer his interest in the partnership to another. If the transfer is to an outsider, the latter acquires only a right to the transferor's share in the profits and surplus and does not become a partner without the consent of the other partners. A sale of his interest to the other partners includes his interest in all partnership property, including good will.

Title to real property held by tenancy in partnership under the Uniform Partnership Act can be conveyed only in the partnership name. Any partner may convey title to such property by a conveyance executed in the partnership name, provided he acts within the scope of his authority. At common law, as real property was held in the name of the partners, it could be conveyed only by all of the partners. Under the Uniform Act, leases and mortgages are subject to the same rules as other conveyances of realty.

In contrast to its regulation of sales of real property, the Uniform Partnership Act does not specifically deal with sales of personal property, such transactions being encompassed within the general powers of partners to enter into contracts with third persons.

§ 15:3. Powers of partners; agency.

Am Jur 2d References: Partnership, §§ 129–157.

The general rules of law applicable to agents likewise apply to partners, and the liability of one partner for the acts of his copartners is founded on principles of agency. Thus, every partner, apart from any special powers conferred on him by the articles of copartnership, is not only a principal, but is also, for all purposes within the scope and objects of the partnership, a general and authorized agent of the firm and of all of the partners. With respect to the business of the partnership, a partner virtually acts as principal for himself and as agent for his partners. Each partner is deemed to be authorized to transact the whole business of the firm, his acts being treated as the acts of all partners. If he has the requisite authority, he binds the partnership whether he acts in its name or in his own name. Notice to one partner is notice to all, and knowledge by one partner is imputed to the other members of the firm. The authority of a partner to act as agent is limited to transactions within the scope of the partnership business, or within the apparent scope of the partner's authority. A partner has no authority to do any act which would make it impossible to carry on the ordinary business of the partnership, unless authorized by the other partners or unless they have abandoned the business.

Neither the partnership nor the other partners are bound by the unauthorized acts of a copartner in a matter not within the apparent scope of the business of the partnership. By a provision inserted in the articles of copartnership, or by special agreement between themselves, partners may restrict their authority as agents of the firm. Such agreements and restrictions are binding not only as between the partners themselves, but also as to those who have notice thereof when entering into dealings with the partnership or who have knowledge of such facts or circumstances as to lead a man of common prudence to make inquiry. Secret limitations on the authority of a partner do not apply, however, as against third persons dealing with the firm without knowledge of such limitations. Under general principles of agency, acts performed by a partner beyond the scope of his authority may be ratified by the other partners and become binding upon them.

It is within the scope of the powers of a partner to pay the debts of the firm and to use the assets of the firm for that purpose. He has authority to enter into contracts in the name of and on behalf of the partnership and to bind the firm by such contracts. He has authority to execute bills and notes and other instruments on behalf of the firm, and to collect, release, and compromise claims or debts due the firm, and to pay or compromise claims against the partnership. A partner who undertakes to bind his copartners by a contract or other transaction without authority is himself personally liable on such contract.

The powers of partners with respect to the sale and conveyance of partnership property is discussed in § 15:2, supra.

§ 15:4. Rights and duties of partners inter se.

Am Jur 2d References: Partnership, §§ 108–128, 264–288.

The relationship existing between partners is one of trust and imposes upon them the obligation of the utmost good faith and integrity in their dealings with one another with respect to partnership affairs. This fiduciary relationship requires a partner to share with the partnership all business opportunities clearly related to the subject of its operations, and to refrain from reaping any personal profit or advantage not shared by his partners, in his dealings with the partnership property and affairs.

The rights and duties of partners inter se are specified in considerable detail by the Uniform Partnership Act. Among the rights ordinarily included in the partnership relationship is the right of each partner (1) to share equally in the profits of the firm, (2) to receive repayment of his contribution, (3) to receive indemnification for payments made on behalf of the firm, (4) to receive interest on advances and, under some circumstances, on capital contributions, (5) to share in the management and conduct of the business, (6) to have access to the firm books, and (7) to have a formal account of partnership affairs. The corresponding duties generally imposed upon partners include the duty (1) to contribute toward losses sustained by the partnership, (2) to work for the partnership without remuneration other than a share of profits, (3) to submit to a majority vote when differences arise among partners as to the conduct of the firm's business, (4) to share with other partners any information regarding partnership matters, and (5) to account to the firm for any profit derived by a partner from any partnership transaction or from the use of partnership property.

These rights and duties of partners may be changed by agreement between them. Thus, the partnership agreement may provide for the exclusion of a partner from the management of the firm, or may vest the management in one or more of the partners. They may by agreement modify the general principle of majority rule, and require unanimous decision of the partners on certain matters, or provide for arbitration of differences of opinion regarding partnership affairs. And the partnership agreement may change the general rules as to the distribution of profits or the sharing of losses as between the partners. Although there is no common-law or statutory right to expel or dismiss a partner from the firm, the partnership agreement may provide for expulsion.

Each partner is ordinarily obligated to render services to the firm and give it all of his time, skill, and ability; and he is not entitled to compensation therefor, other than his share of the profits of the firm. However, the partners may agree as to the rendition or apportionment of services, and may provide for extra compensation to a particular partner or for particular services.

One of the ordinary duties of partners is to keep true and correct books showing the firm accounts and to make such books at all times open to the inspection of all members of the firm. Any partner has a right to a formal accounting as to partnership affairs if he is wrongfully excluded from the partnership business or its property by the other partners, or if the partnership agreement provides for an accounting, and whenever other circumstances render it just and reasonable. This right to an accounting may be enforced by action, or they may agree to the statement of an account as between themselves. However, an action cannot generally be maintained to compel an accounting where the business is illegal, although some courts have departed from the rule under particular circumstances.

§ 15:5. Liability to third parties.

Am Jur 2d References: Partnership, §§ 158–170.

A partnership is, of course, liable on contracts made by it, or by an authorized partner on behalf of the partnership. The Uniform Partnership Act provides that for all debts and obligations of a partnership, other than those arising from a tort or breach of trust, the partners are jointly liable. This is a codification of the general common-law rule that partnership contracts are joint only, and not joint and several, making partnership debts joint, and not several, obligations. It is specifically provided in the Act, however, that any partner may enter into a separate obligation to perform a partnership contract, as by indorsing a partnership note. In some jurisdictions, prior to the adoption of the Uniform Partnership Act or where the Act has not been adopted, the liability of partners has been said to be joint and several, the promise of the partnership being joint as to all members and several as to each. Under this rule, a debt contracted by a partnership is not only a debt of the firm, but a debt of each individual member of the firm.

The liability of members of a partnership for a tort committed in the course of its business, whether by a partner or by an employee or agent acting within the scope of his duties or authority, is joint and several. Since partners are liable as joint tortfeasors, the party aggrieved has the election to sue the firm or to sue one or more of its members, and may even single out for action a partner who was not personally involved in the commission of the tort.

Some courts hold that a partnership, as such, may be held liable to certain types of criminal penalties. In other jurisdictions, however, on the ground that a partnership is not a legal entity, it is held that a partnership as such cannot commit a crime. Individual partners are criminally liable only where they participated in the criminal offense.

§ 15:6. Dissolution and winding up.

Am Jur 2d References: Partnership, §§ 171–233, 270–321.

The dissolution of a partnership may occur in various ways. Dissolution is not in itself a termination of the partnership or of the rights and powers of the partners, for many of these continue during the winding-up process which follows dissolution. Dissolution designates that point in time when the partners cease to carry on the business of the partnership together; winding up or liquidation is the process of settling partnership affairs after dissolution; and termination is the point in time when all of the partnership affairs are wound up and ended.

The dissolution of a partnership is caused by any event which makes it unlawful for the business of the partnership to be carried on or for the members to carry it on in partnership. Dissolution results also from the death of any partner or from the bankruptcy of any partner or of the partnership. Dissolution results from the expiration or termination of the definite period fixed by the agreement of the partners for the existence of the partnership or upon the completion or consummation of the particular transaction or enterprise for which the partnership was formed. A dissolution may be effected by the mutual agreement of the partners, or it may be brought about by the will of any partner at any time by a notice of dissolution communicated to the other partners. There is some uncertainty as to whether, under the Uniform Partnership Act, the admission of a new partner or the withdrawal or retirement of a partner necessarily effects a dissolution of the partnership. The expulsion of a partner under the terms of the partnership agreement causes a dissolution of the firm. The assignment by a partner of his interest in the partnership does not of itself dissolve the partnership, but such an assignment to a stranger transfers to him only limited rights and does not constitute him a full partner. The dissolution of a commercial partnership results from a sale of all or practically all of the property and effects of the firm used in carrying on its business.

A court may decree the dissolution of a partnership upon various grounds, such as the insanity or incapacity of a partner or misconduct or breach of agreement by him. A court may also dissolve a partnership where it is shown to be impossible to carry on the partnership business on a profitable basis, or where dissension or lack of confidence between partners make it impracticable for them to function as a partnership.

After dissolution a partnership continues only for the purpose of winding up the partnership affairs. The Uniform Partnership Act provides that when dissolution is caused in contravention of the partnership agreement, the partners who had not caused the dissolution may continue the business in the same name if they pay or secure to the partner who caused the dissolution the value of his interest in the partnership. The dissolution of the partnership does not of itself discharge the existing liability of any partner. And where the business of a dissolved partnership is continued by some of the former partners, creditors of the old firm are creditors of the partnership and partners continuing the business.

In order to protect themselves against liability to innocent third persons dealing with partners after dissolution of a partnership, such partners must give notice of their dissolution of the partnership. The sufficiency of the notice, and the persons to whom notice must be given, may depend upon the circumstances of the case; but generally actual notice must be given to all persons who have previously dealt with the partnership.

After dissolution, the partners themselves usually have the right and duty to wind up the affairs of the partnership, adjust or pay the claims of its creditors, and distribute the remaining assets of the partnership to the partners according to their interests.

§ 15:7. Death of partner.

Am Jur 2d References: Partnership, §§ 234–263.

The death of a partner has the effect of dissolving any partnership, whether organized to continue at will or for a fixed time, in the absence of an express agreement to the contrary. As in the case of dissolution by other causes (supra, § 6), the death of a partner does not terminate the partnership until the winding up of its affairs is completed by the surviving partners. The parties may by their agreement provide that the partnership shall not be dissolved by the death of a partner, and may provide the terms upon which the partnership will be continued by the surviving partners after such death. And it is competent for the partners to agree that their surviving partners shall have the right or option to purchase a deceased partner's interests in the firm on stated terms and conditions.

A surviving partner succeeds to the rights of a deceased partner in the partnership assets for the purpose of winding up the partnership business under the Uniform Partnership Act, and title to partnership real estate remains in the partnership and the deceased partner's rights in it pass to the surviving partner, in whose hands it is deemed to be converted into personalty. Hence, the deceased partner's interest in the firm and in its assets, as distinguished from any interest in specific property, passes to his personal representatives, and his rights in specific partnership property are not subject to dower, curtesy, or allowances to widows, heirs, or next of kin. The surviving partner can sell and convey the decedent's rights which are vested in him, in the course of the liquidation of the partnership, without joinder of the decedent's heirs or representatives. The common-law rule regarding these matters is different from that of the Act. At common law, on the death of a partner and the consequent dissolution of the firm, the surviving partner and the decedent's heirs become cotenants, with a superior lien in the surviving partner for the payment of the firm debts.

II. JOINT VENTURES

§ 15:8. Nature, formation, and incidents.

Am Jur 2d References: Joint Ventures, §§ 1–35, 57–60.

A joint venture, or adventure, is an association of persons with intent, by way of contract, express or implied, to engage in and carry out a single business venture for joint profit, for which purpose they combine their efforts, property, money, skill, and knowledge, without creating a partnership or a corporation. It is of the essence of a joint venture that there shall be a community of interests among the parties, and that each joint venturer shall stand in the relation of principal, as well as agent, as to each of the other coventurers. It is frequently difficult to distinguish joint ventures from other forms of business organizations, particularly partnerships. Despite the similarities, however, there are important distinctions between partnerships and joint ventures, the most significant being the single-transaction or ad hoc nature of a joint venture; the fact that loss-sharing is not essential; and the eligibility of corporations for membership in joint ventures.

As between the parties thereto, the creation of a joint venture depends upon the agreement and the intent of the parties, express or implied. Although joint ventures are usually limited to a single transaction or a single undertaking or to some particular ad hoc enterprise, it cannot be said that a joint venture must always and necessarily be limited to a single transaction. A contribution or combination of the property, money, efforts, skill, or knowledge in a common undertaking is essential to a joint venture; but the contributions of the respective parties need not be equal or of the same character. Community of interest and a right to joint control are generally held to be essential to a joint venture. An agreement, express or implied, for the sharing of profits is essential, although the manner of participation in the fruits of the undering may be left to the agreement of the parties. Whether or not there must be an agreement for the sharing of losses is the subject of considerable conflict of authority.

The duration of a joint venture may be fixed by the terms of the contract between the participants, and where this is done the venture is terminated when the specified time has expired, except for the purpose of winding up its affairs and accounting. If no date is fixed by the contract for its termination, the agreement generally remains in force until its purpose is accomplished or until such accomplishment has become impracticable. In general, the law relating to dissolution and termination of partnerships (supra, § 15:6) is applicable to joint ventures.

The death of one coventurer does not necessarily terminate the enterprise, although it will have that effect, in the absence of an agreement to the contrary, where the venture calls for the participation of such member in the conduct of its affairs and the agreement prescribes no definite term for its duration. The parties may agree to a continuation of the venture by the survivors upon the death of a member.

The rights and liabilities of coventurers as against third parties are governed, in general, by rules which are similar or analogous to those applicable to partnerships (supra, § 15:5) at common law. Joint venturers are generally jointly and severally liable to third parties on the contracts and for the debts of the venture. And the participants in a joint venture may each be liable for the torts of the others or for the torts of servants of the joint undertaking. The rule that the negligence of one participant in a joint enterprise may be imputed to another participant may be applicable to a joint venture.

§ 15:9. Rights and liabilities of members inter se.

Am Jur 2d References: Joint Ventures, §§ 36–56.

The rights and liabilities of members of a joint venture as between themselves are largely governed by the general common-law principles applicable to partnership (supra, § 15:4). The mutual rights of the parties may, of course, be fixed by the terms of their contract. The agreement may determine the amount and nature of the contribution of each party to the venture and the responsibility and power of each in the management and control of the enterprise. The rights of joint venturers in property acquired or used in connection with the venture also depend primarily upon agreement. Unless otherwise agreed, property purchased with the funds of the joint venture or with profits derived therefrom belongs to all of the coventurers for the purpose of the enterprise so long as it exists. If title to property is taken in the name of one of the coventurers, he ordinarily holds it as trustee for all. The coventurers occupy a fiduciary relationship as regards each other in their dealings with matters affecting the joint venture. In the absence of an agreement providing therefor, no participant in a joint venture is entitled to any compensation, aside from his share of the profits, for services in promoting or carrying on the enterprise.

All the benefits and profits arising out of a joint venture belong to the parties to the venture as a whole, and in the absence of an agreement to the contrary, the law implies that the profits are to be equally divided among the coventurers. As indicated above, the authorities are not in complete harmony as to whether a sharing of losses, as well as profits, is essential to the existence of a joint venture. In the absence of an agreement excusing one or more members from bearing the losses of the venture, however, an agreement will be implied that losses will be shared equally by the coventurers. However, a party may be charged for losses caused by his own negligence or misconduct.

The right of a party to a joint venture to withdraw therefrom, and the effect of such withdrawal, may depend upon the terms of the agreement and upon the circumstances. Generally, where the purposes of the enterprise have not been fulfilled, no party has the right to withdraw from or abandon it without the consent of his coventurers. A breach of their contract by the parties, or other circumstances, may, however, afford a coventurer a ground to withdraw or to invoke the jurisdiction of a court of equity to terminate the joint venture.

III. BUSINESS TRUSTS

§ 15:10. Generally; nature and formation.

Am Jur 2d References: Business Trusts, §§ 1–29, 74–97.

A business trust is an unincorporated business organization created by an instrument by which property is to be held and managed by trustees for the benefit and profit of such persons as may be or may become the holders of transferable certificates evidencing the beneficial interests in the trust estate. This form of business organization received extensive development and use in Massachusetts, and it is commonly referred to as a "Massachusetts trust."

The distinctive features of the business trust are indicated in the definition thereof. It is unincorporated; it is created by the voluntary act of the parties and is based on contract; it is intended for the purpose of carrying on some kind of business or commercial activity for profit; the title to the capital of the organization is vested in trustees, who usually manage the affairs of the trust; the beneficial interests in the trust estate and in the profits are evidenced by transferable certificates, similar to corporate shares; and the existence or life of the organization is not affected by the death or disability of a member or shareholder or by the sale or transfer of his interest. There is a difference of opinion as to whether a business trust is a distinct legal entity.

The advantages of this form of organization are obvious. It has flexibility and adaptability because of its contractual basis and because of the background of the great body of equity jurisprudence relating to trusts. It enjoys perpetuity of existence and, in most jurisdictions, immunity of the beneficial members from personal liability for the acts or obligations of the trust or of the trustees. Formerly a business trust was able to obtain most of the advantages of corporations without being subject to the restrictions, regulations, and taxation imposed by law upon corporations. These latter advantages, however, have been greatly diminished in recent years by the tendency to subject business trusts to regulations and taxes similar to those imposed upon corporations.

In the absence of statute or of a provision to the contrary in the contract or trust instrument, the property of a business trust cannot be subjected directly to the claims of persons dealing with the trustees, by the ordinary writs and processes in an action at law. The liability rests upon the trustees personally, and not upon the trust estate. However, a creditor who cannot get satisfaction from a trustee may be subrogated in equity to the trustee's right of reimbursement or indemnity from the trust.

Broadly speaking, business trusts are regarded as legal and valid, at least in the sense that such organizations are not, by reason of their nature, illegal or contrary to public policy. In some states, however, the efficacy of such trusts is greatly limited by the view that such an organization is in effect a partnership or a corporation, or that the members or cestuis que trustent are personally liable for the debts and obligations of the trust.

The trust instrument should embody all the elements necessary to constitute a business trust. It should contain an unequivocal declaration of trust, a vesting of title in named trustees, a description of the character of the business to be carried on, an outline of the powers and duties of the trustees, provisions for the tenure and election of trustees, provisions for the issuance of certificates evidencing the beneficial interests of the cestuis que trustent and the manner of transferring such certificates, and a statement of the rights of shareholders with respect to profits and dividends. If desired, there may be provisions fixing the time and duration of the trust, limiting or negativing the liability of shareholders and trustees to third persons, specifying the manner in which the trust instrument may be amended, and providing for a firm name and seal, and for the adoption of bylaws governing the details of the administration of the trust.

§ 15:11. Trustees, officers, and agents.

Am Jur 2d References: Business Trusts, §§ 43–73.

The trust instrument usually states the manner of the election, tenure, removal, and replacement of the trustees of a business trust. It is the normal function of the trustees to hold title to the property of the trust and to manage and administer the business and affairs of the trust for the benefit of the shareholders. In making contracts for the trust estate, in conducting its business, and in holding and managing its property, the trustees act as principals and not as agents or representatives of the shareholders. Instruments creating business trusts usually make provision for the compensation of the trustees. The general principle of trusts, that a trustee is entitled to reimbursement from the trust estate for all necessary and reasonable expenditures made in the execution of the trust, is applicable to business trusts. Where the trustee has acted in good faith for the benefit of the trust, he is entitled to indemnify himself for his engagements and liabilities out of the trust estate in his hands.

Where there are cotrustees of a business trust, they all form but one collective trustee or board and must act as a unit and in their joint capacity, in the absence of a provision to the contrary in the trust instrument. However, this instrument may provide for action by a majority of trustees or in some other manner. And in some such trusts provision is made for the appointment of a president, general manager, or other officers with power to manage certain aspects of the business. Where the trustees are charged with the duty to manage and control the trust business, they cannot divest themselves of that duty or delegate their discretionary powers to others. The trustees do, however, have the power to employ agents and servants for the performance of ministerial and nondiscretionary duties.

The trustees of a business trust, unless the trust instrument provides the contrary, have the power to acquire and hold title to property on behalf of the trust, to manage such property, and to lease, encumber, or convey the same. In the course of the business of the trust, they may execute bills and notes and other instruments, enter into contracts, and compromise claims or demands of or against the trust estate.

The fiduciary relationship existing between the trustees and the beneficiaries of a business trust imposes upon the trustees the duty to act for the beneficiaries, and not for themselves in antagonism to the interests of the beneficiaries. A trustee may not profit by any transactions in relation to the trust estate at the expense of the beneficiaries, nor is he entitled to derive any profit out of the trust, except his lawful compensation. The trustees are required to exercise such care and diligence in the management of the trust as would be exercised by a man of ordinary prudence and skill in the management of his own estate, and they are liable for losses resulting from their breach of trust or wrongful diversion of trust funds. However, trustees are not insurers.

The principle applicable to trusts generally, that a trustee is personally liable on obligations incurred by him as trustee, applies to business trusts in the absence of a provision to the contrary in the trust instrument or in the agreement. The trustees are personally liable for debts incurred and on contracts made by them on behalf of the trust; and they are personally liable for torts committed in the conduct of the business of the trust, either by them-

selves or by their agents and servants acting within the scope of their employment and authority. In contracting with third parties, trustees may stipulate
for their personal immunity from liability on the contracts; and a provision
in the trust instrument exempting the trustees from personal liability is binding
upon persons dealing with the trustees with notice thereof, actual or constructive.

§ 15:12. Status, rights, and liabilities of members, shareholders, or cestuis que trustent.

Am Jur 2d References: Business Trusts, §§ 30–42.

A shareholder of a valid and effective business trust occupies the status of
cestui que trust, although his position and rights are similar to those of a
stockholder of a corporation. His rights are governed largely by the provisions
of the declaration of trust. Where legal title to trust property is vested in the
trustees, the shareholders have only an equitable interest in the property, although this rule may be changed by the trust instrument. In the few jurisdictions which do not recognize business trusts as such and treat them as
partnerships, the shareholders are held to be partners.

According to the generally accepted view, the status of a purported business
trust for the purpose of determining the liability of the shareholders depends
upon who has the power of control over the business and property of the trust.
If the ultimate power of control is vested in the trustees, who also hold the
legal title to the trust property, the organization is treated as a true trust,
rather than as a partnership, and the shareholders are therefore not liable for
the debts or contractual obligations incurred by the trustees. But if the shareholders have the power of effectual control over the trustees or over the affairs
of the trust, the concern is regarded as a partnership and the shareholders are
consequently liable. In a few jurisdictions the shareholders of the business
trust are held liable, as partners, for the debts of the trust, irrespective of the
question of their control over the affairs of the trust. And in a jurisdiction
which regards business trusts as imperfect corporations, the trust shareholders
are held to occupy the position of persons who begin but never complete the
organization of a corporation, and as such, they are liable for the debts of
the trust.

While the beneficiary of an ordinary trust is not personally liable to third
persons for torts committed by the trustee, in determining the liability of
shareholders of a business trust in tort the courts seem to be inclined to apply
the "control test" in the same manner as in cases involving liability on contract.
It is held that the shareholders are personally liable for the torts of the trust
where they are vested with the ultimate and effectual control over the business
and property of the trust.

Under the control test, the character of an organization as a true trust or
a partnership, for the purposes of determining the personal liability of shareholders, depends generally upon the powers vested in the shareholders by the
trust instrument, rather than upon the powers actually exercised by them.
The determination of the question whether shareholders have such effectual
control of the organization as will render them personally liable generally
depends upon no single element of control, but upon a combination of factors
and circumstances. As a general rule, the reservation to the shareholders of

a business trust of the power to elect, remove, or replace trustees does not alone transform the organization into a partnership, under the control test, so as to render shareholders personally liable. The same is true of the mere reservation to the shareholders of the power to amend or to terminate the trust, although these powers, in combination with others, may render the shareholders liable as partners for debts of the trust. Where the shareholders of a business trust are personally liable for the debts of the trust, one of them who has been required to pay such a debt may enforce contribution from the other shareholders.

In a few jurisdictions, even a provision in the trust instrument exempting shareholders from personal liability is not effective to relieve them of such liability. In other jurisdictions the effectiveness of such a provision depends upon whether the person seeking to charge the shareholders had notice of the provision. However, everywhere and regardless of the views held of the nature of business trusts, it is competent for the trustees and persons dealing with them to stipulate for the exemption of shareholders from liability, and where the creditor agrees that the shareholders shall not be personally liable, no recovery can be had against them.

IV. OTHER FORMS OF ORGANIZATION

§ 15:13. Generally.

Am Jur 2d References: Associations and Clubs, §§ 1–60; Cooperative Associations, §§ 1–40; Joint-Stock Companies, §§ 1–21.

A joint-stock company may be defined as an unincorporated association of individuals for the purpose of carrying on business and making profits, having a capital stock contributed by the members, which is commonly divided into shares which are transferable by the owner, and governed by articles of association which, subject to statutory and other limitations, prescribe its objects, organization, and the rights and liabilities of its members, and usually provide that its business shall be under the control of managers or directors. The title to the property of such organizations is usually held by trustees.

Joint-stock companies or associations were a recognized form of business organization at common law, and provision is made for them by statutes in some states. They form a distinct class of association of individuals, having some of the features of partnerships, of private corporations, and of business trusts, but distinguishable in some important respects from each of those other forms of organization. As in the case of corporations and business trusts, the interests of the members are usually evidenced by certificates or shares which are transferable. As in the case of a partnership, the members of a joint-stock company are generally liable for the debts of the company. Unlike ordinary partnerships, the nature of a joint-stock company permits the transfer of the shares, and the members thus do not have the right to choose their associates.

Voluntary unincorporated associations are formed by groups of individuals for a great variety of purposes. Such associations are sometimes provided for and regulated by statutes. At common law, an unincorporated association is not a legal entity and has no status distinct from the persons composing it, but is rather a body of individuals acting together for the prosecution of a common enterprise. By statutes in some jurisdictions, however, such associations have the status of legal entities and are empowered to contract, to acquire, hold, and transfer property, and to sue and be sued. Many social clubs are organized in the form of unincorporated associations. Membership in a voluntary unincorporated association or club is a privilege which may be accorded or withheld, and is not a right which can be gained independently and then enforced. The grant or refusal of membership is within the complete control of the association.

In the absence of statute to the contrary, an unincorporated association or club does not have the capacity or power to own property or to enter into contracts. Property ostensibly held by such bodies is deemed to belong to the members jointly or as tenants in common. In the absence of statute to the contrary, the officers or members are generally held individually liable on contracts made in the name of an association. And the individual members of an unincorporated association, as well as the officers thereof, are personally liable for torts which they individually commit or participate in, or which they authorize, assent to, or ratify.

Cooperative associations are authorized by statutes in many states. Such cooperative associations may or may not be incorporated. Where organized under a statute, such an association is usually a legal entity. Cooperating marketing associations are organized to secure for their members the advantages of cooperative bargaining in selling their products and to secure economies not attainable by the individuals acting alone. Consumers' cooperative associations are organized to provide a purchasing agent which can deal on more advantageous terms than could the individual members.

*

PERSONAL PROPERTY

I. IN GENERAL; NATURE AND CLASSES OF PERSONAL PROPERTY

§ 16:1. Generally.

> Am Jur 2d References: Property, §§ 1–3, 8, 9, 22–27. For treatments of copyright and literary property, patents, and trademarks, see the Am Jur and Am Jur 2d articles on those topics.

In its strict legal sense, the term "property" signifies an abstract legal right rather than a corporeal object. It is that dominion or right of user, control, and disposition which one may lawfully exercise over particular things or objects. As so used, the word signifies the sum of all the rights and powers incident to ownership. The term "property" is more frequently used, however, in its more popular sense as signifying or describing the subject of property, such as a chattel or land.

Property is divided into several major and minor classes which are recognized by the law. The division of property into real and personal constitutes the most important classification. Having regard to its material and palpable nature, properties are also classified as corporeal and incorporeal. Intangibles, consisting of rights not related to physical things, are mere relationships between persons which the law recognizes by attaching to them certain sanctions enforceable in the courts. Such rights are incorporeal property. Corporeal property which is a compound of both real and personal property is classified as mixed property.

The distinction between real and personal property becomes important in many connections. It may determine the situs of the property for taxation or other purposes, and it may be decisive, under the principles of conflict of laws, of the rule of law to be applied in a case. The distinction is also observed in applying the rule that real property descends directly to the heir, while personal property passes to the personal representative of the decedent.

Personal property was defined by Blackstone as consisting of money, goods, and movable chattels. In its general and ordinary sense, the term "personal property" embraces all objects and rights which are capable of ownership except freehold estates in land and incorporeal hereditaments connected therewith. The term includes goods, chattels, things in action, evidences of debt, and money. The term "chattels" is used to describe visible, tangible, movable personal property. Included also in the classification of "personal property" are chattels real, choses in action, and, to a degree, so-called "mixed" property, which are discussed below. Important examples of personal property consisting of incorporeal rights are literary property and copyrights, patents, and trademarks.

§ 16:2. Choses in action.

> Am Jur 2d References: Property, §§ 26, 27.

A chose in action is a personal right not reduced into possession, but recoverable by an action at law, or, a thing of which one has not the possession or actual enjoyment, but only a right to or a right to demand by an action at law. Choses in action are personal property. The term is sometimes used in the broad sense of all rights of action, whether ex contractu or ex delicto, although it is sometimes limited to assignable rights of action ex contractu, and perhaps ex delicto for injuries to property, or for torts connected with a contract, to the exclusion of a right of action ex delicto for personal injuries. The term "chose in action" includes money due on a bond, note, or other contract, damages due for breach of contract, open or unliquidated accounts, and a policy of insurance. Shares of corporate stock, although they lack some essential characteristics of choses in action, are personal property in the nature of choses in action.

§ 16:3. Chattels real and mixed property; severance.

Am Jur 2d References: Crops, §§ 3, 5; Logs and Timber, §§ 9, 10, 16; Property, §§ 16–19, 24.

Chattels real are interests in real estate less than freehold, and are personal property. They are to be distinguished, on the one hand, from things which have no concern with the land, such as movables and the rights connected with them, which are chattels personal, and, on the other hand, from a freehold, which is realty. Where a person erects buildings on leased premises under an agreement that he remove them, or places his machinery in buildings under similar agreement, the buildings and the machinery partake of the character of a chattel real. A term for years is denominated a chattel real and is personal property regardless of the duration in years. Rent to accrue is a chattel real.

Common-law writers referred to a class of property, designated mixed property, which was neither real nor personal property. Examples of this class of property are heirlooms, tombstones, title deeds, keys to a house, and fixtures. In modern jurisprudence, however, this does not seem to be a valid distinct classification of property.

Property which is essentially real property may be changed into personal property by severance thereof from the land. Thus, gas, oil, coal, and other minerals may lose their status as realty when removed from the soil. And while standing timber is a part of the real estate, the severance of trees from the land on which they stand operates to change their character from realty to personalty. And although there are some fine distinctions and uncertainty as to the status of certain growing crops as real or personal property, it is settled that when crops are actually severed from the land by their proprietor, they become personal property.

II. ACQUISITION AND OWNERSHIP

§ 16:4. Generally.

Am Jur 2d References: Adverse Possession, § 202; Property, §§ 28–30, 37, 39, 46.

An essential incident of property is the right to acquire and dispose of it by any lawful means. The two principal ways of acquiring property are by descent and by purchase. The latter includes acquisition by sale, gift or bequest. Personal property may also be acquired by adverse possession for the time and in the manner contemplated by the statute of limitations. Title to personal property may be transferred by will, deed, gift, contract, or, in many instances, by simple manual delivery. The formalities required are generally less stringent than those applicable to real estate. However, certain types of property, such as motor vehicles, are subject to statutory requirements in transferring ownership. Some statutes require bills of sale in certain instances. And commercial paper is usually transferred by written indorsement or assignment. Possession of personal property, as of real property, may be either actual or constructive. Constructive possession is that possession which the law annexes to the title. The right of general property in a chattel draws with it the right of possession. The owner of personal property is not divested of his rights therein by the theft of the property by another. As a general rule, he may follow and reclaim the stolen goods wherever he may find them, even in the hands of an innocent purchaser.

§ 16:5. Estates and interests in personal property.

Am Jur 2d References: Estates, §§ 58, 114, 205, 351; Cotenancy, etc., §§ 6, 25; Husband and Wife, §§ 58, 65; Perpetuities, etc., §§ 39, 40, 49, 114.

Under modern law, personal property may be the subject of most of the same interests and estates which are recognized in the case of real estate. By gradual modification of the ancient common-law rule to the contrary, it is now generally settled that a life estate may be created in personal property, for the life of the holder thereof or for the life of another person, with remainder to another. And such estates are governed in the main by the same principles as apply to such estates in real property. And it is now generally established that personal property, in the same manner as real estate, is a proper subject of executory interests and limitations. There may be a joint tenancy, with the resulting right of survivorship, in personal property, whether corporeal or incorporeal. And tenancy in common may exist in personal property. According to the weight of authority, an estate by the entireties in husband and wife may exist in personal property. Where this rule prevails, an estate by the entireties is created by the acquisition of personal property in the names of both husband and wife. The incidents of such an estate is that both spouses hold the property jointly during their joint lives, and the survivor takes the whole.

The rule against perpetuities normally operates in like manner in regard to future interests in personal property as it does in reference to gifts of future estates in real property. Suspension of the power of alienation of personal property is thus limited. The principle which prevents restraints on alienation inconsistent with the nature of the estate given applies equally to personal and real property, in the absence of statute changing this rule.

16:6. Lost, abandoned, and unclaimed property.

Am Jur 2d References: Abandoned, Lost, etc. Property, §§ 1–6, 18–31.

Property which is abandoned by the owner with the intention of terminating his interest in it and without intending to vest ownership in another is said to go back into a state of nature or to return to the common mass of things in a state of nature. Such property is subject to appropriation by the first taker or finder who reduces it to possession. Such person acquires an absolute property therein as against both the former owner and the person upon whose land it happens to have been left.

The finder of a lost article does not acquire absolute ownership thereof, but he does acquire a property interest or right which will enable him to keep it against all the world except the rightful owner. This rule is not affected by the place of finding. The finder of lost property has a right to possession of the article superior to that of the owner or occupant of the premises where it is found. A servant is, as against his master, entitled to property which he finds on the latter's premises. If lost property is found by several persons under such circumstances that the finding is the joint act of all, they have equal rights in the thing found.

Treasure trove is an old name given to gold, silver, money, plate, or bullion which has been hidden in the earth or in other private places by an unknown owner, and which has been found by another. It is not essential to its character as treasure trove that the thing shall have been hidden in the ground; it is sufficient if it is found concealed in other articles, such as bureaus, safes, and the like. Under the early English law, treasure trove belonged to the King. In this country, in the absence of legislation, treasure trove belongs to the finder against all the world except the true owner. He has a right thereto superior to that of the owner or occupant of the premises where it is found, and this is true even though the finder is an employee of the owner of the premises. The rule relating to treasure trove is generally limited to gold, silver, and money. Other objects found "imbedded in the soil" under circumstances indicating that some person had placed it where it was found, are not regarded as "treasure," and the finder acquires no title thereto, the possession of such articles being in the owner of the land.

A person who finds property which has been casually mislaid acquires no special rights in it, where it is found upon another's premises. This is true whether the finder is an employee of the owner or occupier of the premises on which the mislaid article is found, or a customer of the owner or occupant. The right of possession of such articles as against all except the true owner is in the owner or occupant of the premises where it is found.

All the rules stated above are subject to modification by statute. Legislation in many states defines the rights and duties of the parties in respect of abandoned, lost, and mislaid property and of treasure trove and the like.

§ 16:7. Animals.

Am Jur 2d References: Animals, §§ 5–19, 46; Fish and Game, §§ 1–5.

In determining property rights therein, the law makes an important distinction between domestic animals and wild animals. In domestic animals, such as horses, cattle, poultry, and the like, a person may have as absolute a property as in any other useful and valuable chattel. On the other hand, with respect to wild animals, or animals ferae naturae, property rights may be acquired only by actually taking possession of the animal. The ancient common-law rule that dogs were considered an inferior sort of property, for certain purposes entitled to less regard and protection than property in other animals, has undergone a change. Under modern law, both dogs and cats are classed as domestic animals, subject to the same property rights as cattle, horses, and poultry.

The ownership of wild animals not reduced to actual possession by private persons is in the state. An individual generally has no property rights in such animals until he has subjected them to his own possession and dominion. Fish and game, as well as bees, are classified as ferae naturae, so that they become the absolute property of a person only when he reduces them to possession. Strictly speaking, this rule applies even to the owner of land on which ferae naturae exists in a wild state; but the owner of land, subject to regulation by the state, has the exclusive right to hunt and fish thereon and to take swarms of bees and honey found thereon. And fish propagated and confined in a private pond by the owner of land, and animals captured and confined or propagated by him, are his personal property so long as they do not escape.

The general rule, in the absence of an agreement to the contrary, is that the offspring or increase of domestic animals or of tamed or reclaimed wild animals belongs to the owner of the dam or mother. And where there is a life estate in animals, the life tenant, rather than the remainderman, is entitled to the increase.

The rights of the owner of domestic animals which become estrays, as well as the rights of persons taking up such estrays, are generally governed by statutes.

§ 16:8. Accession and confusion.

Am Jur 2d References: Accession and Confusion, §§ 1–31.

Accession, as a means of acquiring title to personal property, signifies the right of the owner of such property to the personal property of another which has been incorporated into or united with his property. This right includes accession of other materials as well as skill and labor. Rights by "specification" are acquired when, without the accession of other material, property of one person is innocently used and converted by another into something specifically different in the inherent and characteristic qualities which identify it, as for example, the conversion of corn into meal, or grapes into wine. A "confusion" of goods takes place when there has been such an intermingling or intermixture of goods owned by different persons that the property of each can no longer be distinguished.

Where materials belonging to one person are combined or united with the materials of another, forming a single, joint product, the owner of the principal materials making up the whole acquires by accession the right to the property in the whole, regardless of who performed the labor, unless the materials of each owner can be identified and severed without injury to the original property.

When accessories and other materials are added to or incorporated in property belonging to another, the right of the owner of the original property to claim title to such additions or accessories depends upon whether they become an integral part of the original article, or whether they are identifiable and capable of detachment without harm to the principal article or the thing attached. With respect to automobile parts, equipment, and accessories, which are usually removable and interchangeable, courts are less apt to apply the doctrine of accession. Ordinary repairs upon a chattel by the addition of materials furnished by the person making the repairs or by a third person become accessions to and merge in the article repaired, which, if it remains substantially the same thing, belongs, together with the additional materials, to the owner of the original article.

One delivering raw materials to a manufacturer under an agreement to manufacture such materials into finished products or articles retains title to the property during the manufacturing process, and to the finished product, even though the labor performed is equal or exceeds the value of the property received by the manufacturer; and this rule applies even where the manufacturer adds materials of his own in producing the finished article.

According to the prevailing view, when accession is produced by the labor of one who is technically or actually a trespasser, and the identity of the property is thereby changed or its value increased, the right to the property in its changed condition depends upon whether the person converting it acted in good faith, or acted intentionally or willfully. A wilful trespasser may not acquire any right or title by accession to the property or goods of another by reason of any change wrought in property or goods by his labor or skill, however great or small the change in the article may be or however much or little the enhancement of value may be. The new product, in its improved state, continues to belong to the owner of the original materials, and the trespasser loses his labor.

Under the doctrine of confusion of goods, an owner of goods who willfully and tortiously mixes and confuses his goods with those of another so that they are indistinguishable and not susceptible of division, must bear the loss, and the innocent party will take the whole property. It has been held, however, that if the mass formed by such confusion of goods is composed of parts of equal quality and value and if the proportion of the whole which each party originally owned is known, the parties will be deemed tenants in common and each will be entitled to his proportion. Where the intermingling of goods is the result of mere negligence without actual fraud or wrongful intent, there is a difference of opinion as to whether the wrongdoer forfeits his rights in the property. Forfeiture of one's rights in property which he intermingles with property of others does not result, if there was no fault or negligence on the part of the intermingler. In such case, both owners are entitled to share in the resulting mass. And this rule is generally applied where the goods of different owners are innocently confused as the result of mistake on the part of one owner, or by accident or by the act of a third party.

When goods of the same kind owned by different persons are, with the mutual consent of the owners, mixed and intermingled so that the portions of the various owners are indistinguishable, the several owners become tenants in common of the mixture, each having an interest in common in proportion to his respective share. This rule is frequently applied in cases where owners of fungible goods, such as grain or oil, delivers them for storage in a common bin or tank.

§ 16:9. Gifts.

Am Jur 2d References: Gifts, §§ 1–11, 16–38.

A "gift" is defined as a voluntary transfer of property without any consideration or compensation therefor.   Gifts are generally classified as gifts inter vivos
and gifts causa mortis.   A gift inter vivos is a gift between living persons,
perfected and becoming absolute during the lifetime of the parties.   A gift
causa mortis is a gift of personal property made in contemplation of the donor's
death from a present sickness or an impending peril.   A gift causa mortis
differs from a gift inter vivos in that in the latter the change in title is irrevocable once the gift is perfected, whereas a gift causa mortis must be made in
apprehension of death from a present sickness, and the gift is revocable and is
not perfected unless the donor dies as anticipated, without having revoked the
gift, and leaves the donee surviving him.

There must be an unequivocal intention on the part of the donor to make
a gift of his property in order to constitute a valid gift inter vivos or causa
mortis.   The donor must intend to relinquish his dominion and to confer it
upon the donee, and this intention must be a present one, an intention to give
in the future not sufficing.   Gifts inter vivos and causa mortis must be fully
and completely executed, that is, there must be a donative intent to transfer
title to the property, a delivery by the donor, and an acceptance by the donee.
To have the effect of a valid gift inter vivos, the transfer of possession and title
must be absolute and go into immediate effect, so far as the donor can make it
so by intent and delivery.   However, a gift causa mortis is subject to be divested
upon the happening of conditions subsequent, such as the actual revocation by
the donor, his survival of the apprehended peril, or his survival of the donee.

While there must be an actual or constructive delivery of property to the donee
in order to constitute a valid gift inter vivos or causa mortis, such delivery need
not be made to the donee personally, but may be made to a third person acting
as agent, trustee, or guardian.   Actual delivery is necessary for the consummation of a gift inter vivos or causa mortis when the subject of the gift is capable
of manual delivery; otherwise, there must be such a delivery as the nature of
the subject matter reasonably permits, and this delivery must clearly manifest
the donor's intention to divest himself of title and possession.   Where actual
manual delivery is not feasible, delivery to the donee may be by symbolical or
constructive acts, as by delivery of the key to a safe deposit box or other
receptacle, if such delivery places the property beyond the dominion of the
donor.   If property is already in the possession of the donee, and intention to
surrender all right to the property is clearly manifested by the donor, a
redelivery to the donee is not necessary to effectuate the gift.

An acceptance by the donee is generally held to be an essential element of a
gift inter vivos or causa mortis.   The exercise by the donee of dominion over
the subject of a gift, or an assertion of the right thereto by him, will generally
establish his acceptance; and where a gift is beneficial to the donee and imposes
no burdens upon him, acceptance is presumed.

Gifts, like other transactions, are subject to attack on the grounds of fraud,
duress, or undue influence.   A gift attacked on these grounds will be closely
scrutinized by the court where it is between persons occupying confidential
relations toward each other.

III. BAILMENTS

§ 16:10. Generally; nature and incidents.

Am Jur 2d, References: Bailment, §§ 1–119, 276–280; Garages, etc., §§ 27–80; Warehouses (1st ed, § 21).

A "bailment," in its ordinary legal signification, imports the delivery of personal property by a "bailor" to a "bailee" in trust for a specific purpose, with a contract, express or implied, that the trust shall be faithfully executed and the property returned or duly accounted for when the special purpose is accomplished, or kept until the bailor reclaims it. Any kind of personal property may be the subject of bailment, including money or a chose in action, as well as chattels. A bailment includes any delivery of personal property for a specific object or lawful purpose. As examples of particular transactions to which the law of bailments applies, may be mentioned the lending or hiring of personalty to another to be used for his own pleasure or in his own business, the delivery of property to another under agreement to clean, repair, remodel, or perform services thereon, the delivery of goods to a factor or commission merchant for purposes of sale, the delivery and acceptance of the custody of personal property for care, safekeeping, or storage, and the pledge or pawn of personal property with another as security for a debt. A typical example of a bailment arises when goods are stored in a warehouse. And the owner or operator of a garage or parking lot, who receives an automobile for storage or repairs, ordinarily has the status of a bailee.

Bailments are generally classified under three heads: (1) those for the sole benefit of the bailor; (2) those for the sole benefit of the bailee; and (3) those for the mutual benefit of both parties. A broader classification frequently observed in terminology describes a bailment as a gratuitous bailment or one for compensation or hire. Bailments sometimes arise without any agreement between the parties, as where a person holds possession of a chattel under such circumstances that the law imposes on him the obligation to deliver it to another. This is called a constructive bailment.

As the rights and liabilities of the parties depend upon the nature or class of the bailment, the determination of this question is always important. In general it may be said that there is a bailment for compensation, or bailment for mutual benefit of the parties, when the bailment relationship is one in which the parties contemplate some price or compensation in return for benefits flowing from the fact of bailment. It is clear that one who, for compensation, takes another's property into his care and custody, with or without an agreement for labor or services upon it, is a bailee for hire, and that one who lets the use of a chattel for a reward is a bailor for hire. But if no consideration moves to the recipient of the property as special bailee for safekeeping, the bailment is one for the benefit of the bailor and is a gratuitous bailment. And a loan for use is a bailment for the benefit of the bailee. In determining whether a bailment is one for the sole benefit of the bailor, without compensation or benefit to the bailee, or one for mutual benefit, from which the bailee is to derive benefit or profit, the inquiry is not directed to the character or certainty of the benefit or profit, but to whether the bailment was accepted for the purpose of deriving the one or the other. It is generally held that, to constitute a bailment for hire or for the mutual benefit of the parties, it is not essential that the hirer actually receive compensation in money or tangible property so long as the bailment is an incident of a business in which the bailee intends to make a profit, or was accepted because of benefits expected to accrue. When a bailment is at the instance of the bailee or at his invitation because of benefits, direct or contingent, which he expects to accrue, the bailee is not a gratuitous bailee. The typical case is the situation where the bailee assumes the custody and care of the bailor's property as an incident of transacting business with the bailor. In such cases, the bailee receives his compensation in the profits of the business to which the bailment is an incident. Examples of such bailments occur where the proprietor of a business assumes the custody of a customer's wearing apparel or other property while the latter is transacting business.

A constructive bailee, or bailee by operation of law, who comes into possession of personal property of another and who ordinarily receives nothing from the owner of the property, such as one who finds lost property or who assumes custody of personal property by virtue of ownership of the premises upon which it is mislaid, becomes a gratuitous bailee until the property is claimed by the owner.

In receiving property by virtue of a bailment, the bailee admits the right of the bailor to make the contract of bailment, and he cannot set up a want of title in the bailor as an excuse for his refusal to redeliver the property to the bailor. · He is estopped to deny that the bailor had title to the property at the time of the bailment, and he is not permitted to set up an adverse title in himself or in a third person. This estoppel does not apply, however, to conclude the rights of third persons who are strangers to the bailment contract. If a person other than the bailor is the true owner of the property, the bailee cannot hold the property as against the rights of such person.

§ 16:11. Rights and liabilities as between bailor and bailee.

Am Jur 2d References: Automobiles, etc., §§ 662–666; Bailments, §§ 120–226; Garages, etc., §§ 27–80.

The rights, duties, and liabilities of bailor and bailee as between each other are fixed by law, unless they are varied by the terms of a valid contract between the parties. As a general rule, the terms, express or implied, of the contract of bailment determine the rights and duties of the parties; and the parties may by express contract enlarge, abridge, qualify, or supersede the obligations which otherwise would arise from the bailment by implication of law, so long as the contract does not violate the law or contravene public policy. In the case of an ordinary, as distinguished from a professional, bailee, the parties may agree to relieve the bailee from all liability, other than for losses resulting from his own fraud, want of good faith, or gross negligence. However, the courts exhibit a strong tendency to hold contracts of this character, when entered into by bailees in the course of general dealing with the public, to be violative of public policy. These bailees, who are termed "professional," as distinguished from "ordinary," bailees, are those who make it their principle business to act as bailees and who deal with the public on a uniform and not an individual basis, such as proprietors of parcel checkrooms, garages, parking stations and lots, carriers, innkeepers, and warehousemen. Some courts, though not all, are more liberal in sustaining contractual provisions limiting the amount of liability or stipulating an agreed valuation, than in the case of contracts exempting the bailee from all liability.

Special provisions, to be effective as a modification of the contract implied by law from the bailment relation, must be either a part of the original contract of bailment or contained in a valid amendatory contract; and the assent of both parties is necessary to effectuate this result. When such a modification of the bailment obligations is attempted by notice, such notice is not effective unless its terms are assented to by the other party. Many courts hold that merely posting a notice on the bailee's premises, purporting to limit liability for loss of personal property bailed for hire, is not sufficient to constitute a contract for such limitation unless the bailor assents thereto. The trend of modern decisions is to the view that the receipt from the bailee, at the time of bailment, of what is ostensibly a ticket or receipt for later identification of the bailed property does not bind the bailor as to provisions printed on the ticket which purport to limit the bailee's liability, where the bailor's attention is not called to such provisions and he has no actual knowledge thereof at the time of the bailment.

The very nature of the bailment relation requires the bailee to return the subject matter of the bailment to the bailor upon determination of the bailment. And all bailees are under duty to exercise some degree of care to preserve the bailed property and to protect it against loss or injury. The degree of care required of the several classes of bailees is the subject of a great diversity of language, and some difference of opinion, on the parts of the courts and commentators. It is generally agreed, however, that the degree of care required of the bailee always depends upon the circumstances of the particular case, including the nature of the property and the objects and purposes of the bailment. And while the care required of the bailee varies in accordance with the class of the bailment, no bailee is an insurer of the safety of goods delivered into his keeping, in the absence of statute or express contract. There are, however, a few special types of bailees, such as common carriers and innkeepers, upon whom the law, on grounds of public policy, imposes a strict rule of liability. It is also generally agreed that in order to hold a bailee liable on account of loss or damage to bailment property on the ground of his failure to exercise due care for its protection, it must appear not only that he was negligent, but that his negligence was a proximate cause of the loss or damage complained of.

The bailee is not liable, in the absence of negligence on his part, for loss or injury of the thing bailed resulting from the inherent nature of the property itself, from disaster or accidental casualty, from robbery, burglary, or theft, or the negligence or contributory negligence of the bailor or his servants or agents or of another third person not the agent or servant of the bailee. This principle does not, however, excuse a bailee from the duty of care to anticipate and guard against the occurrence of loss or injury from theft, fire, and similar contingencies.

The standard or degree of care required of the bailee depends upon the class or type of the bailment. According to many authorities, when the bailment is for the sole benefit of the bailor, without any compensation to the bailee, the law makes the bailee answerable only for gross neglect; when the bailment is reciprocally beneficial to both parties, the bailee is held responsible for ordinary neglect; and when it is for the sole benefit of the bailee, as in the case of a simple loan of property without compensation, the bailee must exercise the highest degree of care and will be held liable for even slight negligence resulting in loss or damage of the property. Other authorities lay down the rule that it is the duty of any bailee to exercise reasonable care, and that what constitutes reasonable care will depend upon the nature, value, and quality of the subject of the bailment, circumstances under which it is deposited, and sometimes upon the character and confidence and particular dealings of the parties and the terms of the implied undertaking of the bailee. Even under this approach, however, where the factors are equal, what is reasonable care varies according to the factor of compensation, so that a compensated bailee is held to a higher degree of care than is a gratuitous bailee.

The "ordinary care" required of the bailee under a bailment for the benefit of both parties, has been defined as such care as ordinarily prudent men, as a class, would exercise in caring for their own property under similar circumstances; or that degree of care and diligence which may reasonably be expected of ordinarily prudent persons under similar circumstances; or that which capable and reasonably prudent persons engaged in the same business are accustomed to exercise in the discharge of their duties. An increasing number of authorities take the view that even a gratuitous bailee is required to exercise ordinary care and diligence, or that care and diligence which a prudent man would bestow upon his own property of similar character under like circumstances.

A bailor may be liable for injury resulting from the nature or condition of the property bailed. In every bailment a minimum obligation rests upon the bailor to refrain from knowingly delivering to the bailee any chattel of a nature or in a condition of which the bailee is ignorant, which is likely to imperil the life, limb, or property of one exercising the degree of care required of a bailee in a bailment of that class, without first disclosing the condition of the property. The extent of a bailor's obligation in this regard depends primarily upon the class to which the particular bailment belongs. Generally, the bailor of a chattel to be used by the bailee for a particular purpose known to the bailor impliedly warrants the reasonable suitability of the chattel for its intended use, unless the bailee, by inspection of the chattel or otherwise, depends upon his own judgment to determine suitability and fitness.

Where a bailment is purely gratuitous and for the exclusive benefit of the bailee, as where articles are loaned without compensation, the bailor's only duty in respect to defects is to inform the bailee of any of which he is aware; and the lender is not liable for failure to communicate anything which he did not in fact know, whether he ought to have known it or not. In a bailment for hire or for the mutual benefit of both parties, the bailor is held to a higher degree of responsibility. While such a bailor is not ordinarily an insurer against injuries to his bailee for defects in their article bailed, he is held to a high degree of care to make an examination of the chattel before letting it, and is frequently regarded as impliedly warranting that it is fit for the purpose for which it is hired, so that he is liable for injuries resulting from a breach of such warranty. The bailor is liable for injuries due to the defective condition of the chattel bailed if he knew of the defect or if it was discoverable by him through the exercise of due care.

§ 16:12. Rights and liabilities as regards third persons.

Am Jur 2d References: Bailments, §§ 243–275.

Either the bailee or the bailor may maintain an action against a third person for injury or conversion of property held under bailment, or, in a proper case, to recover possession of the property. A recovery of full damages by either the bailee or the bailor for injury to or conversion of the bailed property is a bar to a similar action by the other party to the bailment. Although there is some conflict of authority on the subject, most authorities support the rule that the bailee's contributory negligence is not imputable to the bailor in the latter's action against a third person for injury to or destruction of the subject of the bailment.

Since the relationship of bailor and bailee is not, as such, within the doctrine of respondeat superior, it is the general rule that the bailor cannot be held responsible to a third person for injuries resulting from the bailee's negligent use of the bailed property, in the absence of any control exercised by the bailor at the time, or of negligence of his own which proximately contributed to the injuries. This rule does not apply, however, where the bailor has himself been negligent in entrusting a dangerous article to one whom he knows to be unfamiliar with its dangerous character or incompetent to operate it safely. Where the subject of the bailment is a machine or other instrumentality, such as an automobile, which is likely to cause injury to third persons unless operated with care and skill, the bailor may be liable in damages for injuries inflicted by his bailee, to whom he entrusted the property with knowledge of his incompetence or recklessness.

While generally a bailor is not liable to a third person who is injured by reason of a defect in the article or property bailed, a bailor who negligently furnishes his bailee with a chattel which is not reasonably fit and proper for the known intended use may be answerable in tort to a third person who is injured from the use of the thing bailed. In such case, however, the third person cannot stand in a better position with respect to the liability of the bailor for defects than does the bailee. For example, if the third person was guilty of contributory negligence, or if the injuries resulted from patent defects in the bailed article, or if the defects were unknown to the bailor, or if the injury resulted from the improper or negligent use by the bailee, rather than from any defect in the thing bailed, the bailor is not liable.

The bailor may owe a special duty with respect to certain types of property. He may be held liable to third persons where the thing bailed is a dangerous article or substance and its character as such has not been disclosed to the bailee, where it is an animal with vicious propensities of which the bailor has knowledge or is charged with notice, or where the thing bailed is an instrumentality, such as an automobile, which, though not inherently dangerous, is known by the bailor to be in such defective condition as in the judgment of an ordinarily prudent person would constitute it a source of eminent danger to third persons if used for the purpose contemplated by the bailment.

While it has been held that a bailee who undertakes to repair an article, but fails to make the repairs as agreed, cannot be held liable to third persons for breach of the contract to repair, under the prevailing rule today a bailee is bound to exercise reasonable care in making repairs so as not to cause bodily harm or property damage to one whose person or property may reasonably be expected to be endangered by the probable use of the chattel, and may be held liable in tort for injury or damage caused by his negligence in making such repairs.

IV. LIENS AND SECURED TRANSACTIONS

A. UNIFORM COMMERCIAL CODE

§ 16:13. Generally; scope.

Am Jur 2d References: Commercial Code, §§ 49–60.

Most secured transactions involving personal property and fixtures are now governed by the Uniform Commercial Code, which has been generally adopted by the American states.   The Code sets out a comprehensive scheme for the regulation of "security interests" in personal property and fixtures, and its purpose is to provide a simple and unified structure within which the great variety of secured financing transactions can go forward with less complexity and cost than formerly.   "Security interest" is defined as an interest in personal property or fixtures which secures payment or performance of an obligation.

Except as to transactions expressly excluded, the Code applies to any transaction, regardless of its form, which is intended to create a security interest in personal property or fixtures including goods, documents, instruments, general intangibles, chattel paper, accounts, or contract rights, and also to any sale of accounts, contract rights, or chattel paper.   It applies to security interests created by contract, including pledge, assignment, chattel mortgage, conditional sale, chattel trust, trust deed, factors' lien, equipment trust, trust receipt, other lien or title retention contract, and lease or consignment intended as security. And it is intended to supersede existing legislation dealing with such security devices as chattel mortgages, conditional sales, trust receipts, factors' liens, and assignments of accounts receivable.   The Code does not purport to prescribe regulations and controls which may be necessary to curb abuses arising in the small-loan business or in the financing of consumer purchases on credit.

By its own provisions, the Code does not apply to a security interest created under and governed by a federal statute; to a landlord's lien; to a lien for services or materials, except that such liens are given general priority over other liens; to a transfer of a claim for wages or the compensation of an employee; to an equipment trust covering railway rolling stock; to a sale of accounts, contract rights, or chattel paper as part of a sale of the business out of which they arose, or an assignment of such accounts, etc., for the purpose of collection only, or a transfer of a contract right to an assignee who is also to do the performance under the contract; to a transfer of an interest or claim in or under a policy of insurance; to a right represented by a judgment; to any right of setoff; or to the creation or transfer of an interest in or lien on real estate, including a lease or rents thereunder, except to the extent of the provision made as to fixtures. Also excluded from the operation of the Code are any claims arising out of tort, any deposit, savings, passbook or like account maintained with a bank, savings and loan association, credit union, or like organization.

The old forms of security transactions, such as conditional sales, chattel mortgages, etc., may still be used, but all such forms are treated alike as secured transactions under the Code. As respects this broad treatment of all personal property security devices, it is immaterial under the Code who holds the title to the personal property which is the subject of the security transaction. As between debtor and creditor, and even as against third parties, the legal title to property may depend upon a determination of whether a transaction amounted to a chattel mortgage or a conditional sale, but this question is immaterial under the Code in determining the security interest of the creditor, so long as he has taken the proper steps to perfect such interest.

The formal requirements of the instruments creating a security interest have been simplified by the Code. Technical requirements such as acknowledgment or accompanying affidavits have been eliminated. Unless the collateral is in the possession of the secured party, the requirement of the Code is that the debtor must have signed a security agreement which contains a description of the collateral.

§ 16:14. Financing, continuation, and termination statements; filing; rights and priorities.

Am Jur 2d References: Commerical Code, §§ 7, 61–81.

It is generally necessary to file a financing statement in order to perfect security interests under the Uniform Commercial Code. An unperfected security interest is subordinate to the rights of a person who becomes a lien creditor without knowledge of the security interest and before it is perfected, and it is subordinate also to the rights of various classes of persons accorded priority under the terms of the Code. However, if the secured party files with respect to a purchase money security interest before or within 10 days after the collateral comes into the possession of the debtor, he takes priority over the rights of a transferee in bulk or of a lien creditor which arise between the time the security interest attaches and the time of filing.

The Code enumerates several types of transactions or security interests with respect to which financing statements need not be filed, such as a security interest in collateral in possession of the secured party, a purchase money security interest in consumer goods or in farm equipment having a purchase price not in excess of $2,500; but these exceptions do not apply to motor vehicles required to be licensed. While a security interest in accounts, contract rights, and general intangibles can generally only be perfected by filing, a security interest in letters of credit and advices of credit, bids, instruments, negotiable documents, or chattel paper may be perfected by the secured party's taking possession of the collateral.

A buyer in ordinary course of business, other than a person buying farm products from a person engaged in farming operations, takes free of a security interest created by the seller, even though the security interest is perfected and even though the buyer knows of its existence. A "buyer in ordinary course of business" is defined as a person who in good faith and without knowledge that the sale to him is in violation of the ownership rights or security interest of a third party in the goods, buys in ordinary course from a person in the business of selling goods of that kind; but it does not include a pawnbroker.

The Code sets forth rules governing priorities among conflicting security interests in the collateral. A person having a lien because of services or materials furnished by him with respect to goods in his possession has priority over a perfected security interest of another person unless the statute creating the lien provides otherwise. Subject to certain exceptions, a security interest which attaches to goods before they become fixtures takes priority as to goods over the claims of persons having an interest in the real estate. A security interest in goods which attaches before they are installed in or affixed to other goods generally takes priority, as to the goods installed or affixed, over the claims of all persons to the whole. And where goods as to which a security interest has been perfected have become part of a product or mass, the security interest continues in the product or mass if the goods are so manufactured, processed, assembled, or commingled that their identity is lost in the product or mass; and where more than one person has a security interest in the product or mass, they share equally according to the ratio which the goods of each bears to the cost of the total product or mass.

A financing statement is sufficient if it is signed by the debtor and the secured party, gives an address of the secured party from which information concerning the security interest may be obtained, gives a mailing address of the debtor, and contains a statement indicating the types, or describing the items, of collateral. A filed financing statement which states a maturity date of the obligation secured of 5 years or less is effective until such maturity date and thereafter for a period of 60 days. Any other filed financing statement is effective for a period of 5 years from the date of filing. If the obligation secured is payable on demand, the financing statement is effective for 5 years from the date of filing. Upon the lapse of the statutory period, the security interest becomes unperfected, unless a continuation statement is filed by the secured party within the time specified in the Code.

The Code specifies the places and offices where financing and other statements are to be filed and specifies the duties of the recording officials with respect to filing, indexing, etc.

Whenever there is no outstanding secured obligation and the security interest is terminated, the secured party must on written demand by the debtor send the latter a statement that he no longer claims a security interest under the financing statement. A failure to do so subjects the secured party to a penalty. On presentation to the filing officer of such a termination statement, he must note it in the index and remove the financing statement from the file. A secured party of record may by his signed statement release all or a part of any collateral described in a filed financing statement, and the filing officer is required to note the same in his records.

§ 16:15. Default and enforcement.

Am Jur 2d References: Commercial Code, §§ 82–87.

Where a debtor is in default under a security agreement, a secured party generally has the rights and remedies provided in the security agreement, and he may also reduce his claim to judgment, foreclose, or otherwise enforce the security interest by any available judicial procedure. Unless it is otherwise agreed, a secured party has on default the right to take possession of the collateral. In taking possession, a secured party may proceed without judicial process, if this can be done without breach of the peace, or he may proceed by action. After such default, a secured party may sell, lease, or otherwise dispose of any or all of the collateral, subject to the provisions of the Code. Disposition of the collateral may be by public or private sale. Unless the collateral is perishable or threatens to decline speedily in value or is of a type customarily sold on a recognized market, a simple notification of the time and place of any public sale or reasonable notification of the time after which any private sale or other intended disposition is to be made must be sent by the secured party to the debtor and, except in the case of consumer goods, to any other person having a perfected security interest in the collateral. The secured party may buy at any public sale and in any private sale of collateral of the type customarily sold in the recognized market or the subject of widely distributed standard price quotations.

The proceeds of the disposition of the collateral are to be applied, in the following order, to (a) the reasonable and legal expenses of retaking, holding, preparing for sale, and selling; (b) the satisfaction of indebtedness secured by the security interest under which the disposition is made; (c) the satisfaction of indebtedness secured by any subordinate security interest in the collateral if written notification thereof is received before distribution. If the security interest secures an indebtedness, the secured party must account to the debtor for any surplus; and, unless otherwise agreed, the debtor is liable for any deficiency. But if the underlying transaction was a sale of accounts, contract rights, or chattel paper, the debtor is entitled to any surplus or is liable for a deficiency only if the security agreement so provides.

Where the debtor has paid 60 percent of the secured obligation and the secured party has taken possession of the collateral, the latter is required to dispose of the collateral within 90 days after he takes possession. With the consent of the parties interested, or after written notice as provided in the Code and without objection by the debtor or other parties having a security interest, the secured party may retain the collateral in satisfaction of the obligation.

At any time before the secured party has disposed of collateral or entered into a contract for its disposition, or before the obligation has been discharged by retention of the collateral by the secured party, the debtor or any other secured party may, unless otherwise agreed in writing after default, redeem the collateral by tendering fulfilment of all obligations secured by the collateral as well as expenses reasonably incurred by the secured party in retaking the collateral and preparing for its disposition.

B. LIENS

§ 16:16. Generally; nature, creation, and incidents.

Am Jur 2d References: Liens, §§ 1–76.

In its broadest and most general signification, a lien is a charge upon property for the payment or discharge of a particular debt or duty in priority to the general debts or duties of the owner of the property. It is an encumberance, hold, or claim on another's property as security for the payment or performance of a debt or obligation. The right to a common-law lien is based on possession. Such a lien arises only when possession is obtained, and it ceases when possession is lost. And at common law the holder of a lien had no way to enforce it except to hold the property until he was paid. He had no right to use or dispose of the property. Courts of equity did, however, afford relief in some cases, and statutes today usually provide enforcement procedures.

Although in a technical sense the term "lien" signifies a right by which a person in possession of property of another holds and detains it against the owner in satisfaction of a demand, and common-law liens are dependent upon possession, the term has now acquired a much broader connotation. In common parlance the term "lien" is used to designate a great variety of charges upon property, not dependent upon possession, which are created by statute or recognized in equity or maritime law. Thus, there is the lien of a judgment, of an execution, of a partner, of a legal or equitable mortgage, or of a vendor. The term is frequently applied in connection with a chattel mortgage or a pledge. There is the landlord's lien to secure the payment of rent or discharge of other obligations of the tenant. And there are tax liens created by statute to secure the discharge of obligations to the state or federal government. As commonly employed, the term "lien" is similar in comprehensiveness to the term "security interest" as used in the Uniform Commercial Code. An equitable lien is a right to have a fund or specific property, or its proceeds, subjected and applied, in a court of equity, to the payment of a claim.

Particular liens have always been recognized by the common law in favor of those persons, such as innkeepers, carriers, and warehousemen, who are bound by law to serve the public in their trades and occupations. A similar common-law lien exists in favor of artisans, tradesmen, mechanics, and laborers who receive property for the purpose of repairing or improving it for compensation.

The priority of different lien claims, the necessity and effect of recordation of liens, and the procedure for the protection and enforcement of liens are the subjects of statutory regulation in all jurisdictions. It may be said generally that the priority of liens depends upon the time when they attach to the property involved.

§ 16:17. Lien for improvement or repair of chattel or other services.

Am Jur 2d References: Agriculture, §§ 10–14; Animals, § 74; Bailments, §§ 227–242, 270–275; Banks, §§ 660–665; Factors, §§ 20–24; Garages, etc., §§ 138–144, 152; Liens, §§ 20, 21, 64; Logs and Timber, §§ 105–112.

Artisans tradesmen, mechanics, and laborers who receive property for the purpose of repairing or improving it have, by the common law, a lien on such property until the reasonable charges for their labor, materials, and expenses thereon are paid. The basis of this type of lien is that the claimant is entitled to be secured in payment for labor and materials which have enhanced the value of the property. The lien depends upon possession by the claimant and continues only so long as such possession is retained. And this type of lien is generally given priority over any other type of lien or claim to the property.

A miller engaged to grind grain is entitled to a common-law lien on the flour or meal. The owner of a stallion is entitled to a lien on a mare delivered to him for the purpose of being served by the stallion. A garageman or service station operator has a common-law lien for labor and materials or parts used in repairing a motor vehicle. A person sawing logs into lumber or other products is entitled to a common-law lien on such products. There are many statutes declaring and amplifying the lien rights of loggers and millmen. While an agricultural laborer has no common-law lien on crops worked by him, statutes in some states give him a lien to secure payment for his labor. It may be noted that while a mere bailee, even one for hire, does not ordinarily have a lien on goods bailed, unless he is entitled to an artisan's lien for repairs or improvements, statutes in a number of states give such a lien.

A bank has a lien upon all the securities of a customer or depositor which may be in the bank's possession to secure the latter's indebtedness to the bank. And a factor has a general lien upon the goods of his principal in his possession (and upon the proceeds of the sale of such goods) for all commissions, advances, expenditures, or liabilities incurred in behalf of the principal.

§ 16:18. Liens of attorneys.

Am Jur 2d References: Attorneys at Law, §§ 272–308.

At common law and by statutes in some jurisdictions attorneys are entitled to two kinds of liens. One is a general or retaining lien, and the other is a special or charging lien. The general or retaining lien attaches to all papers, books, documents, securities, moneys, and property of the client coming into the possession of the attorney in the course of and with reference to his professional employment. This lien extends to moneys collected by the attorney for his client, whether on a judgment or not, and it covers all sums due from the client to the attorney for costs, charges, and disbursements, and it extends to the general balance due for professional services rendered to the client. The lien may be defeated or lost when the attorney unjustifiably terminates his relationship with the client or the latter justifiably discharges the attorney, or when the attorney voluntarily parts with possession of the items to which the lien may have attached. This lien, like other common-law liens, may not ordinarily be actively enforced, either at law or in equity. In the absence of statute to the contrary, it amounts to a mere right to retain property or funds of the client until the attorney is paid.

The special or charging lien of an attorney for his services, securing his right to compensation for obtaining a judgment or award for his client, is not dependent on possession, as in the case of a general or retaining lien. This lien, as recognized by the common law and frequently declared by statutes, gives an attorney the right to recover his fees, taxable costs, and money expended on behalf of his client from a fund recovered by his aid, and the right to have the court interfere to prevent payment by the judgment debtor to the client in fraud of the attorney's rights. It enables the attorney to have the proceeds of the enforcement of a judgment disbursed so as to protect the attorney's rights. As distinguished from a retaining lien, a charging lien does not extend beyond the charges and fees in the action in which the judgment was recovered; it does not cover general balances due the attorney from the client for professional services rendered in other causes or transactions.

§ 16:19. Carrier's, innkeeper's, warehouseman's, and wharfage liens.

Am Jur 2d References: Carriers, §§ 497–506; Garages, etc., §§ 144–151; Hotels, etc., §§ 187–196; Warehouses (1st ed, §§ 105–114); Wharves (1st ed, § 38).

At common law a common carrier has a lien on goods delivered to it for carriage, and the lien attaches as soon as its liability as carrier begins and continues as long as the goods remain in its possession, until the freight charges, including storage charges, are paid. Under the common law, this lien was given only to public or common carriers, who are required by law to accept goods for carriage, and was not available to a private carrier who specially undertakes to carry a particular load for hire, unless the agreement of carriage reserves a lien. Ordinarily, a carrier's lien is dependent upon its possession of the goods, so that a delivery of the goods to the consignee or a third person terminates or waives the lien. The Uniform Commercial Code (UCC § 7–307) makes provision for this lien in favor of a carrier, and extends it, with certain limitations, to all carriers, common or private. The Code (UCC § 7–308) also makes provision for the enforcement of a carrier's lien.

Under the Uniform Commercial Code as well as under statutes superseded by it, a warehouseman has a lien against the bailor on the goods covered by a warehouse receipt or on the proceeds thereof in his possession for charges for storage or transportation, insurance, labor, or charges present or future in relation to the goods, and for expenses necessary for the preservation of the goods or reasonably incurred in their sale pursuant to law. A warehouseman loses his lien on any goods which he voluntarily delivers or which he unjustifiably refuses to deliver. A warehouseman's lien may be enforced by public or private sale of the goods in bloc or in parcels, at any time or place and on any terms which are commercially reasonable, after notifying all persons known to claim an interest in the goods.

The general maritime law imposes a lien on vessels and their cargoes to secure payment for wharfage.

Although most authorities have held that a garagekeeper or parking lot operator has no common-law lien for charges for storage of a motor vehicle, statutes have been enacted in many states providing for liens in favor of such persons. Such a lien covers the reasonable value of the storage service rendered, in the absence of statute or agreement fixing the charges. The statutes generally provide the procedure for enforcing the lien.

In return for the extraordinary duties and liabilities imposed upon innkeepers, the law gives them a lien on the property of their guests for the amount of reasonable charges for their keeping and entertainment. This lien exists by common law and is not dependent on statute, although statutes have been generally enacted granting and regulating such liens. It is essential to the innkeeper's lien that the property upon which it is claimed had been brought into the inn by a person having the legal status of a guest, and that the establishment operated by the proprietor be an inn or hotel in legal contemplation. At common law, the proprietor of a boarding, lodging, or rooming house had no such lien, although many statutes now protect such proprietors. The lien of an innkeeper generally extends to all property brought by the guest to the inn and received by the innkeeper on the faith of their relationship. Although the common-law innkeeper's lien only gave him the right to hold the property till his charge was paid, with no right to sell the property, modern statutes usually provide procedure for the enforcement of the liens.

C. Other Secured Transactions Involving Personal Property

§ 16:20. Chattel mortgages.

Am Jur 2d References: Chattel Mortgages, §§ 1–241.

A chattel mortgage may be defined as an instrument whereby an owner transfers title to, or creates a lien upon, personal property as security for the payment of a debt or the performance of an act, with the title or lien subject to defeasance upon performance. Such transactions are now governed by the provisions of the Uniform Commercial Code. Although the Code does not retain the traditional distinctions between security devices, it permits the use of any such forms, including chattel mortgages. The particular form of a transaction may still be important as between the parties and with regard to the non-security aspects of the transaction. As a general rule, any personal property that is capable of being sold may be mortgaged.

The mere form of an instrument, or the name or characterization given it by the parties is not always controlling on the question whether it is a chattel mortgage. For example, a bill of sale absolute on its face will, under some circumstances, be regarded as a chattel mortgage and as passing only a security interest, where the intention of the parties was that the instrument should stand as security.

Under the original common-law rule, which still prevails in some states, a chattel mortgage gives the mortgagee a defeasible title to the property mortgaged which becomes absolute upon default in payment, the mortgagor retaining only an equity of redemption. However, in many states the legal title to mortgaged chattels remains in the mortgagor until divested by a fore-closure proceeding, and until the legal title of the mortgagor is thus divested the mortgagee has merely a lien on the mortgaged property. Under the Uniform Commercial Code the location of the title is immaterial.

Although the authorities have been divided upon the question of the validity of a chattel mortgage upon after-acquired property, such mortgages are now permitted by the Uniform Commercial Code. The Code also recognizes the validity of a floating lien or lien on a shifting stock of goods, under which the debtor-owner is permitted to dispose of and replace the collateral and to use the proceeds as he sees fit. The Code also provides that the obligations covered by a security agreement may include future advances, whether or not they are given pursuant to commitment. The Code rule permitting the coverage of after-acquired property in a chattel mortgage is subject to a number of quali-fications and limitations.

§ 16:21. Conditional sales.

Am Jur 2d References: Secured Transactions, §§ 99–107.

A conditional sale is a sale in which the vendee receives the possession and right of use of goods sold, but in which the transfer of the title to the vendee is made dependent upon the performance of some condition or the happening of some contingency, usually the full payment of the purchase price. The essential elements of a conditional sale of personalty are a reservation of title in the vendor, an obligation on the part of the vendee to accept and pay for the property in accordance with the terms of the contract, and the automatic passing of title on the performance of that condition. In some jurisdictions a conditional sale of personal property, as that term is generally understood, has never been recognized, and contracts which might in other jurisdictions be treated as conditional sales are held to be chattel mortgages or liens.

Conditional sales are now governed by the provisions of the Uniform Commercial Code and are subject to the same rules as apply to other secured contractions. The parties may still use the form of a conditional sale, but the consequences and the rights of the parties and of third parties as regard security interests are the same as those resulting from a chattel mortgage or other security device.

§ 16:22. Pledges.

Am Jur 2d References: Pledges, §§ 49–85.

A pledge or pawn is a bailment of personal property as security for some debt or engagement, the property being redeemable on specified terms and subject to sale in the event of default. Pledged property may be a corporeal chattel, or it may be incorporeal or in the form of an instrument or thing representing a property right or value, such as a contract, a bill of lading, a warehouse receipt, a policy of insurance, money, a negotiable instrument, a bond, a stock certificate, or a mortgage.

As in the case of contracts generally, the general rule is that a pledge must be supported by a consideration. The debt or obligation secured by a pledge must be a valid and effectual one. However, a pledge may be made to secure not only an existing or contemporaneously created debt, but also future advances to be made by the pledgee and other obligations not yet in existence. And property may be pledged as security for the obligation of one other than the owner. Although an agreement to pledge property may be binding on the parties as a contract without actual delivery of the property, it is essential to a consummated pledge that there shall have been a delivery of the pledged property, either actual or constructive, to the pledgee.

By pledging property, the pledgor does not part with his general right of property in the collateral. Only a special property, in the nature of a lien, vests in the pledgee, with the right to resort to the collateral for the satisfaction of the debt. Any increase in or income from pledge property is subject to the lien of the pledge, in the absence of an agreement to the contrary. Thus, a pledgee has the right and duty to collect the dividends on corporate stock pledged as collateral, but he must apply such amounts to the debt for which the stock is pledged or hold them as trustee for the pledgor. A pledgee is bound to use ordinary care in relation to the property pledged, and he is liable for injury to the pledged property or for its loss due to his negligence. Upon payment of the obligation secured by pledge, the pledgor is entitled to a return of the property pledged.

Pledges, as well as other forms of secured transactions, are now governed by the Uniform Commercial Code. The Code has provisions governing the creation and enforcement of all secured transactions, the security interests of the parties, and the rights of third persons in the security property.

§ 16:23. Trust receipts.

Am Jur 2d References: Trust Receipts (1st ed, §§ 1–13).

The trust receipt as a security transaction is an invention of modern origin. It is designed to finance importers and dealers in the importation or purchase of merchandise through the utilization of that merchandise as collateral. Originally designed as a convenient method of financing importations, the trust receipt is now used extensively in internal domestic transactions, such as financing sales of automobiles to dealers for resale to consumers and in financing retail dealers in other kinds of durable consumer goods. The usual trust receipt involves three parties: (1) a dealer in goods for resale who receives possession of the goods either directly from a manufacturer or distributor or on a bill of lading consigned to a bank or finance company; (2) a manufacturer or distributor who sells goods to a bank or finance company which does not intend to use them but to turn them over to the dealer; and (3) a bank or finance company which advances money or credit for the purchase of the goods, receiving title from a manufacturer or distributor and taking from the dealer a statement that he holds the goods in trust for the bank or finance company. The security interest afforded by a trust receipt is somewhat similar to many other forms of chattel security, such as chattel mortgages, pledges, or conditional sales, but is usually distinguishable from such transactions.

The Uniform Commercial Code now governs all secured transactions involving personal property, including trust receipts.

V. REMEDIES TO PROTECT PROPERTY RIGHTS

§ 16:24. Trespass.

Am Jur 2d References: Trespass (1st ed, §§ 2, 4, 10, 22–24, 48).

While the word "trespass" generally involves the idea of force, in its broadest sense in the law it comprehends any misfeasance, transgression, or offense which damages another's person, health, reputation, or property. At common law, trespass designated a form of action which lay for the recovery of damages inflicted by a direct application of force, the remedy often being called "trespass vi et armis." Where the injury consisted of taking chattel property, the action was known as "trespass de bonis asportatis," or "trespass de bonis." As regards personal property, the gist of the action of trespass is injury to such property. In trover, the action is based primarily on the wrongful conversion of the plaintiff's personal property; and in replevin the action is based on the wrongful taking or detention of such property. However, there is much overlapping in these forms of action, and in many cases the plaintiff may maintain either kind of action.

Any unlawful interference, however slight, with the enjoyment by another of his personal property is a trespass. Clearly, the unlawful taking away of another's personal property, the seizure of property under a wrongful execution, or the appropriation of another's property to one's own use, even for a temporary purpose, constitutes a trespass. Forcible dispossession is not necessary to support the action, any interference or exercise of dominion with respect to property by which the owner is damnified being sufficient. However, in order to support an action of trespass de bonis asportatis, there must be some infringement of the actual or constructive possession of the plaintiff. Trespass for injury to personal property may lie where the act causing the injury is the result of mere negligence, no element of wrongful intent or wilfulness being necessary.

As the gist of an action for trespass to personal property is the injury done to the plaintiff's possession, in order to maintain the action the plaintiff must have been in actual or constructive possession at the time of the injury. Although there has been some indication that the plaintiff in a trespass action must have title to the property, the prevailing rule is that one in peaceable possession of personalty under claim of ownership may maintain trespass against one who has seized or directly injured the property. In other words, as against a mere stranger or wrongdoer who shows no better right, possession without title is sufficient to maintain the action. If the plaintiff in an action of trespass did not have actual possession of the chattels when the wrong was committed, he must establish that he had constructive possession. The term "constructive possession," as used in this connection, means the right of a general owner of a chattel in the possession of another to reclaim possession of the property at any time, the person having the custody thereof not being entitled to retain it against the will of the owner, as, for example, where the chattel is in the custody of a servant or agent of the owner or where the property has been gratuitously loaned to another.

Where the plaintiff in a trespass action has been entirely deprived of his property, he is entitled to recover the value of the property at the time of the trespass plus compensation for incidental damages which are the natural and proximate result of the wrong. Where the property is merely damaged, the measure of damages is usually the actual loss sustained.

§ 16:25. Conversion.

Am Jur 2d References: Conversion, §§ 1–134.

Conversion is a tort consisting of a distinct act of dominion wrongfully exerted over another's personal property in denial of or inconsistent with his title or rights therein, or in derogation, exclusion, or defiance of such title or rights. There is a conversion where a person does such acts in reference to the personal property of another as amount to the appropriation of the property to himself and a denial or violation of the plaintiff's dominion over or rights in the property. Trover is the name of the action which lay, at common law, for the recovery of damages for the conversion of personal property. Although old forms of action have been abolished, the common-law action for conversion still exists in fact, if not in form.

Some affirmative act on the part of the defendant is usually regarded as necessary to constitute a conversion. Neither a mere intention to do a particular act, a wrongful assertion of ownership, nor a mere nonfeasance is ordinarily sufficient to support an action for conversion. There is some conflict in the decisions as to whether and when mere negligence with respect to the personal property of another will or may constitute conversion. The motive with which the defendant acts is generally immaterial in an action for conversion. Liability in such an action does not depend upon the defendant's knowledge or intent, and it is generally immaterial that he acted without malice and in good faith or in ignorance of the plaintiff's interest in the property.

Although in an action for wrongful conversion of personal property, the plaintiff may recover the full value of the property, and the satisfaction of the judgment ordinarily transfers the title in the property to the defendant, the title of the owner of the property is not affected by the mere conversion itself.

An action lies for the conversion of any kind of tangible personal property. Although the action will not lie for a conversion of a mere debt or chose in action or other intangible right, it may be maintained for the conversion of a written instrument evidencing such right; that is, written contracts, bonds, certificates of stock or certificates of membership, insurance policies, promissory notes and other commercial paper, and title papers, may be the subject of actionable conversion.

§ 16:26. Recovery of possession; replevin.

Am Jur 2d References: Actions, § 21; Replevin, §§ 1–53, 131.

The ancient writ of replevin was the common-law remedy for the recovery of possession of personal property wrongfully taken or detained. The object of the action was the recovery of a specific chattel, and not damages for its conversion or detention. The action of detinue was for the recovery of specific personal property detained by the defendant, or its value, and for damages for the wrongful detention. Originally, detinue was founded on the delivery of goods by the owner to another, who afterward refused to redeliver them to the owner. Hence, detinue would not lie where the property came into the defendant's possession through trespass or conversion. Under modern procedure, however, the form of action is of little importance, and both replevin and detinue are now generally surplanted by statutory remedies. Under the statutory remedies, such as that termed claim and delivery, the primary object is the recovery of specific property when possible, as in a replevin action, or the recovery of the value of the property and damages for its detention, as in trover or detinue, where the delivery of the specific property is not possible. Replevin can be maintained only by one entitled to the immediate possession of personal property and against one who wrongfully detains and is in actual or constructive possession of the property at the time of the commencement of the action.

In replevin proceedings, the plaintiff is usually required to execute a bond to indemnify the defendant against damage, and the property is immediately delivered to the plaintiff. Under some statutes, the defendant may retain possession by executing a bond. Under modern procedure, the change of possession may await the outcome of the action on the merits.

*

PRODUCTS LIABILITY

I. IN GENERAL; ELEMENTS NECESSARY TO ESTABLISH LIABILITY

II. THEORY OR BASIS OF LIABILITY

I. IN GENERAL; ELEMENTS NECESSARY TO ESTABLISH LIABILITY

§ 17:1. Generally.

Am Jur 2d References: Products Liability, §§ 1–8.

Products liability is a phrase that has come into common use in recent years to indicate the liability of the manufacturer, processor, or seller of an article for injury to person or property caused by a defect in or condition of the article or product. Although there is nothing new or unique in the basic legal problems presented by products liability cases, and liability is most frequently predicated upon old legal principles of warranty or negligence, these principles have been adapted or adjusted to fit the complex requirements of modern conditions, and in some instances new bases of liability, such as strict liability in tort, have been applied.

Where it is sought to hold the manufacturer or seller of an article liable for defects therein, the defendant must, of course, be identified as the manufacturer or seller. However, if a person other than the actual manufacturer holds himself out as the manufacturer, packer, or processor, he is subject to the same liability as though he were the manufacturer. Although most products liability cases involve a sale of the product causing the injury, there may be liability on the part of a bailor or lessor of a defective or dangerous article; and even a donor has been held liable under some circumstances. There may be liability, even on the theory of warranty, where the transaction consisted of the performance of services which included the use, application, or installation of a product. For example, a beauty parlor or the manufacturer of products used therein may be liable to a customer injured through the use

415

of a defective product.   And the same is true, under the Uniform Commercial Code (§ 2–314), of the service of food or drink to be consumed either on the premises or elsewhere.   Products liability concepts have also been applied in cases involving sales of real property, where recovery has been permitted for injury caused by defective house construction, as well as in cases involving house components, equipment, or appliances.

§ 17:2. Necessity that defect in product proximately caused injury.

Am Jur 2d References: Products Liability, §§ 9–24.

The first prerequisite of liability in any products liability case is proof that the article in question was defective or dangerous in some way.   The necessity of proving defectiveness of the product applies regardless of the theory invoked in the particular action, whether negligence, breach of express or implied warranty, strict liability, or any other theory.   And in order to hold a manufacturer or seller liable for a product-caused injury, it must be shown that the product was defective or dangerous at the time when the defendant had possession or control of it or when the product left the defendant's possession or control.   Proof of such matters may be aided by certain inferences or presumptions, especially where the product is purchased in sealed containers, bottles, or cans.

Regardless of the ground on which it is sought to recover for injury by a product sold, success requires proof that the injury was proximately caused by the product.   In other words, whether the cause of action is based on negligence, breach of warranty, strict liability in tort, or other theory, the defectiveness or the dangerousness of the product must be shown to have been the proximate cause of the injury complained of.   The causal connection need not be proved, of course, with absolute certainty or to the exclusion of every other possible cause.   It is a fact to be established, like any other, by a preponderance of the evidence, including circumstantial evidence.

II. THEORY OR BASIS OF LIABILITY

§ 17:3. Generally.

Am Jur 2d References: Products Liability, §§ 2–4, 207.

There are various theories, not necessarily mutually exclusive, upon which may be based an action against a manufacturer or seller to recover for product-caused harm.   In former years almost all of the cases involved allegations of negligence or breach of warranty, or both.   A smaller number of cases have involved claims of fraud or misrepresentation, the defendant's violation of a statute or ordinance, or the defendant's wilful acts.   In recent years, a new basis of liability, the principle of strict liability in tort, has gained in importance and effectiveness.

Each of the several theories of liability has its own distinct factors and requisites which may affect its availability or choice in a particular case. If the action is based on negligence, the plaintiff has the burden, sometimes very difficult, of proving negligence on the part of the defendant; but the requirements as to privity are less stringent.   In an action based on breach of warranty, the plaintiff is not required to show negligence on the defendant's part; but the absence of privity of contract between plaintiff and defendant may be fatal. If the injured party can bring his case within the modern doctrine of strict liability in tort, he is relieved of the necessity of proving either negligence or privity of contract; but he must still establish that a defect in the defendant's product was the proximate cause of his injury or damage. A joinder of causes of action based on two or more of these theories, as permitted under modern rules, may be of advantage in some situations to obviate or defer the necessity of a choice of remedies.

§ 17:4. Negligence.

Am Jur 2d References: Products Liability, §§ 25–41, 62–90, 197, 203, 204.

In products liability cases predicated on negligence, the definition of negligence, and the standard of care required, are the same as in other cases based on negligence. These general principles are discussed in this work under the topic Torts. A manufacturer, processor, or seller is held to a duty of ordinary or reasonable care. He must use that care, skill, and diligence regarding the product which a reasonably skillful, careful, and prudent person would use in the same or similar circumstances. Neither a manufacturer nor a seller is an insurer of the safety of their products. Absolute perfection and perfect safety are not required. This principle, and the requirement that a defect in the product must be the proximate cause of the plaintiff's injury, lead to the rule that neither a manufacturer nor a seller is liable for an injury traceable to an unavoidable accident. However, the reasonable care exacted of a manufacturer or seller must be commensurate with the risk of harm involved. This means that greater care is required with respect to certain types of products than would be necessary in the case of less dangerous things.

Liability for injury by a product may be based on negligence in the design of the thing. The duty of reasonable care extends not only to the process of manufacturing and fabricating an article, but also to the original planning and designing thereof. Also, in a proper case, advertising of a product may constitute actionable negligence if it leads to injury of one relying upon the advertisement. The reasonable care required of a manufacturer includes the duty to inspect and test the product as well as its container, in such a manner and at such times as may be reasonably necessary to detect defects therein. On the other hand, a seller of products manufactured by another is generally under no duty to inspect or test the articles that he sells to discover latent defects, unless he has some reason to suspect a defect. But he has been held to be under the duty to make a reasonable inspection of containers.

As a general rule, in a negligence action by the user of a product against the manufacturer or seller, there is no liability where the product is harmless to normal persons, and the plaintiff's injury from the use of the product is attributable to his hypersensitiveness or allergy, unless the defendant had knowledge of the dangerous character of the product. Where such knowledge is chargeable to the manufacturer or seller, he is under a duty to warn the user (§ 17:5, infra).

The general principles of contributory negligence and assumption of risk are applicable in products liability cases based on negligence. In spite of his negligence, a manufacturer or seller is not ordinarily liable therefor to one who has, by his own negligent conduct, contributed to his injury. And one who voluntarily chooses to use a product with full knowledge of the risks and dangers involved is held to assume the risks. Nor is there ordinarily any liability where the injury results from a misuse of the product or from its use in an abnormal manner or for a purpose different from that for which it was made.

The admissibility and weight of evidence to prove the defectiveness of an article alleged to have caused an injury, or to establish or disprove negligence in connection therewith, are governed by the general principles of evidence. Expert testimony is frequently of great importance in these cases. The plaintiff's burden of proving negligence on the part of the defendant is sometimes aided by application of the doctrine of res ipsa loquitur. Under this doctrine, proof that the product which caused injury was under the control and management of the defendant, and that the occurrence was such as, in the ordinary course of things, would not happen if those who had its control and management used proper care, is evidence that the injury was caused by the defendant's want of care. Such proof permits an inference that the defendant was guilty of negligence. Of course, the application of this doctrine does not relieve the plaintiff of the further necessity of showing that the product was actually defective and was the proximate cause of his injury.

§ 17:5. — Duty to warn of danger.

Am Jur 2d References: Products Liability, §§ 42–61, 204.

Where a product sold is dangerous when put to its normal and foreseeable use, and this fact is or should be known to the manufacturer or seller, and the danger is not one that is obvious or known to, or readily discoverable by, the user, the manufacturer or seller has a duty to warn of the danger. This duty to warn exists only where the manufacturer or seller has knowledge, actual or constructive, of a danger connected with the product, and the basis of the duty is his superior knowledge of the dangerous characteristics of the article, as where the seller has knowledge of a latent defect not discoverable upon an ordinary examination or by an ordinary user of the article.

There is ordinarily no duty to give a warning of a danger of which the manufacturer or seller has no actual or constructive knowledge, nor as to a product which, as a matter of fact, is not dangerous. And there is no duty to warn of a product-connected danger which is obvious and generally known, or known to the person who claims to be entitled to a warning. The fact that a simple instrumentality, such, for example, as an ax, may produce injury under some circumstances, does not impose any duty to warn of the danger of such injuries. And there is generally no duty to warn against a danger which does not inhere in the normal or expected use of the product, but arises only in its use in an unlikely, unexpected, and unforeseeable manner or from an unanticipated misuse of the product. The duty of a manufacturer or seller of a product which is safe for use by a normal person, to give warning of the danger involved in its use by certain unusually susceptible or allergic persons, depends upon knowledge by the manufacturer or seller of the dangerous character of the product.

§ 17:6. — Privity.

Am Jur 2d References: Products Liability, §§ 173–188.

It has traditionally been stated as a general rule that a manufacturer or seller of a product alleged to have caused injury cannot be held liable therefor, on the ground of negligence, to one with whom he is not in privity of contract. In other words, the negligence of the manufacturer or seller did not make him liable for injuries to an ultimate consumer or user who had no contractual relations with the former. This rule has been limited by the engraftment of exceptions, and the strong trend of modern authority is to repudiate it altogether.

One exception recognized even by courts giving lip service to the general rule requiring privity is that such privity is not required where the injury-causing product was inherently dangerous, that is, dangerous by its nature and not from any defect in the product. This exception to the privity requirement is applicable in actions for injury to property as well as to personal injuries. If the product is inherently dangerous, the manufacturer is generally charged with notice thereof.

Another exception to the rule requiring privity is applied to "imminently dangerous products." Under this exception, the manufacturer of an article which, although not inherently dangerous, may become so when put to its intended use, owes a duty to the public to employ reasonable care and skill in its manufacture. A product is "imminently dangerous" within this exception to the privity rule if, although it is not dangerous by its nature and is safe when properly constructed, it contains a defect which renders it dangerous when applied to its intended use in the usual and customary manner. In other words, a product is imminently dangerous under this exception if it is reasonably certain to place life and limb in peril when negligently made. Food products, drugs, and the like, come within the "imminently dangerous" exception to the rule requiring privity, if, indeed, the product does not come within the "inherently dangerous" exception.

As indicated above, the trend of the modern authorities is to repudiate entirely the old view requiring privity of contract in products liability actions based on negligence. If there was ever any sound legal basis for the requirement of privity in such cases, it is very obscure. A contractual relationship is not a prerequisite to the existence of a duty to exercise due care. Although the duty of care may be affected by special relationships and by contract, it does not depend upon contractual privity. Where the action is based on negligence, all that should be required is a showing that the defendant's product was defective because of the lack of reasonable care on his part, that the plaintiff was injured as a proximate result of the defect, and that the defendant should have foreseen the likelihood that someone would be exposed to the risk of injury by the product. Putting an article on the market and into the stream of commerce obviously contemplates contact with the article by persons remote from the original sale or transaction. The confusion as to the requirement of privity may have had its origin in the old forms of actions. An action for breach of warranty might be either ex contractu or ex delicto, on the contract or in tort; and either form of action generally required a showing of privity of contract. But there is no reason to extend this requirement to an action based on negligence, and not on warranty.

§ 17:7. Breach of warranty.

Am Jur 2d References: Products Liability, §§ 91–122, 193–196, 201, 202.

A person who has sustained personal injury or property damage as a result of the use, storage, or consumption of a product sold may, in a proper case, maintain an action to recover damages therefor against the seller or manufacturer on the ground of breach of express or implied warranty. Negligence is not essential to liability for breach of warranty. If the product is not as it was warranted, and injury results, liability follows regardless of the care exercised by the seller or manufacturer. However, to establish liability for injury or damage from a defective article on the basis of breach of warranty, the plaintiff must, of course, show that there was a warranty, express or implied, and that the article was not as it was warranted. The plaintiff in such an action must show not only that the product was defective in such a way as to constitute a breach of warranty, but also that the defectiveness was the proximate cause of his injury or loss.

Advertisements addressed to the general public and relied upon by the plaintiff may give rise to an express or implied warranty so as to form the basis of a products liability action. The creation and effect of warranties are discussed in this work under the title Sales; and the subject is now generally governed by the Uniform Commercial Code.

Much products liability litigation arises from claims based on breach of an implied warranty of merchantability or an implied warranty of fitness for ordinary purposes or for a particular purpose. The Uniform Commercial Code clearly affirms the existence of such implied warranties on the part of merchants and manufacturers. The Code also contains provisions for notice to the seller of any breach of warranty, and provides the exclusive and precise manner in which an implied warranty of merchantability or fitness may be excluded as between the parties to a sale.

Since negligence is not an element of an action based on breach of warranty, it would seem that contributory negligence, as such, would not be a defense in such an action. However, some courts have held that contributory negligence or assumption of risk is available as a defense in such actions. And, without characterizing the conduct of the plaintiff as contributory negligence or assumption of risk, courts have frequently reached the same result on the ground that there was no reliance on the warranty; that breach of warranty was not the proximate cause of the injury; that the plaintiff should have foreseen the harm and could have avoided it by reasonable effort; or that the injury resulted from a misuse of the product or by a use other than its normal, intended use, or that he continued to use the product with knowledge that the warranty had been breached, and suffered injury from such continued use.

It is generally held that there can be no recovery, on the ground of breach of warranty, for an injury alleged to have been caused by the use or consumption of a product, if the injury resulted from the unusual susceptibility or allergy of the user or consumer and if the product was safe for use by a normal person. However, an express warranty may render a manufacturer or seller liable even to an allergic or unusually susceptible person.

§ 17:8. — Privity.

Am Jur 2d References: Products Liability, §§ 159–172, 193–196.

Prior to the adoption of the Uniform Commercial Code, the prevailing view was that there could be no recovery on the theory of breach of warranty, against a manufacturer or seller of a product alleged to have caused injury, where there was no privity of contract between the injured person and the defendant manufacturer or seller. Since a warranty arises from contract, there is more justification for the requirement of privity in products liability cases based on breach of warranty than in actions based on negligence (supra, § 17:6). However, even before the adoption of the Uniform Commercial Code, the trend was toward the rejection of the rule requiring privity of contract between the injured person and the manufacturer or seller of a product causing the injury. And in jurisdictions not rejecting the privity requirement outright, the courts have created so many exceptions to the requirement as to obviate its effect to a great extent. Thus, the requirement of privity was held not to extend to cases involving products intended for human consumption, such as food, beverages, and drugs, nor to cases involving food or medicines intended for animals. And even in jurisdictions applying the general rule requiring privity, the courts have drawn an exception where it appeared that the injured person, in using or consuming the product, acted in reliance on statements by the manufacturer or seller in labels or advertising. Some courts have made exceptions on the basis of public policy.

The Uniform Commercial Code drastically curtails the requirement of privity between the person injured by a defective product and the manufacturer or seller thereof, in actions based on breach of warranty. It provides (UCC § 2–318) three alternative provisions, the choice among which is left to each adopting state. According to the first alternative, a seller's warranty, express or implied, extends to any natural person who is in the family or household of the buyer or who is a guest in his home, if it is reasonable to expect that such person may use, consume, or be affected by the goods, and who is injured in person by breach of the warranty; and a seller may not exclude or limit the operation of this provision. Under the second alternative, a seller's warranty, express or implied, extends to any natural person who may reasonably be expected to use, consume, or be affected by the goods and who is injured in person by breach of the warranty; and this alternative also provides that a seller may not exclude or limit its operation. The third alternative extends the warranty to any person who may reasonably be expected to use, consume, or be affected by the goods and who is injured by breach of the warranty; and it provides that the seller may not exclude or limit its operation with respect to injury to the person.

§ 17:9. Strict liability in tort.

Am Jur 2d References: Products Liability, §§ 123–150, 189, 205.

Another theory or basis of liability for injury by a defective product is referred to as "strict liability in tort." It is a recent extension to this area, of the concept of strict liability or liability without "fault" long applied (see Torts, § 21:9) in other situations involving extraordinary peril. Although relatively new in its application in products liability cases, the doctrine has been favorably received and there is a strong trend toward its acceptance. This doctrine is thus stated in Second Restatement of Torts, § 402A: "(1) One who sells any product in a defective condition unreasonably dangerous to the user or consumer or to his property is subject to liability for physical harm thereby caused to the ultimate user or consumer, or to his property, if (a) the seller is engaged in the business of selling such a product, and (b) it is expected to and does reach the user or consumer without substantial change in the condition in which it is sold. (2) The rule used in Subsection (1) applies although (a) the seller has exercised all possible care in the preparation and sale of his product, and (b) the user or consumer has not bought the product from or entered into any contractual relation with the seller."

This doctrine does not require a showing of any negligence on the part of the defendant, any knowledge on his part of the defective or dangerous character of the product, or any privity of contract between the injured party and the defendant. However, in order to invoke this doctrine, the plaintiff must show that the defendant was connected with the product as, for example, the manufacturer or seller of the product or the person who placed it in the stream of commerce; and he must show that the product was defective and unreasonably dangerous. Where a manufacturer or a seller has reason to anticipate that danger may result from a particular use of his product (as where a drug is sold which is safe for use only in limited doses), he may be required to give adequate warning of the danger and may be liable under the strict liability doctrine if he sells the product without such warning and the person injured does not have knowledge of the danger.

In order to recover under the doctrine of strict liability in tort, the plaintiff must establish that the defective or dangerous condition of the product in question was the proximate cause of his injury. If the injury was the result of his misuse of the product or of a use for which it was not intended, the doctrine does not afford relief. There is some conflict of authority on the question whether ordinary contributory negligence is a defense to an action based on the doctrine of strict liability in tort; but there is general agreement to the proposition that recovery under this doctrine is barred by proof establishing assumption of risk. If the user or consumer discovers the defect and is aware of the danger, but nevertheless proceeds unreasonably to make use of the product, he is barred from recovery.

As regards an allergic or unusually susceptible person, the same principles applicable in negligence and breach of warranty cases (supra, §§ 17:4, 17:7) should apply in an action based on strict liability in tort. In other words, there is no strict tort liability on the part of a manufacturer or seller to an allergic or unusually susceptible person who suffers injury for that reason while using a product, unless there is knowledge on the part of the manufacturer or the seller that the product may adversely affect some persons, and a failure to warn.

§ 17:10. Liability predicated on other grounds.

Am Jur 2d References: Products Liability, §§ 151–156, 190–192, 198, 199.

A manufacturer or seller may be held liable for injury or damage caused by a defective product, on the ground of fraud and deceit, independently of the major grounds on which products liability is based—negligence, breach of warranty, and strict liability in tort.   One who sells an article and represents it to be safe for the purposes or uses which it is designed to serve, knowing it to be dangerous because of concealed defects therein, commits a wrong, independently of his contract, and he may be held liable by a third person using the article without knowledge of its defective character, for any injury sustained by him by reason of the seller's deceit and concealment which may be reasonably contemplated as likely to result and which does in fact result therefrom, regardless of lack of privity of contract between the seller and such third person.   Such fraudulent representations are frequently in the form of advertisements or labels. The liability of the manufacturer or seller is the more obvious where he takes active steps to conceal dangerous defects in the article sold.   This liability for fraud is not limited to personal injuries, but extends to property damage.   However, to recover on the ground of fraud, the consumer must establish that the manufacturer or seller knew that its representations were false.

Even where the positive elements of fraud and deceit are lacking, a manufacturer or seller may be liable for injury caused by a defective product, on the ground of misrepresentation.   The Restatement of Torts 2d, § 402B, states that one engaged in the business of selling chattels who, by advertising, labels, or otherwise, makes a public misrepresentation of a material fact concerning the character or quality of a thing sold by him, is subject to liability for physical harm to a consumer of the chattel caused by his justifiable reliance upon the misrepresentation, even though it is not made fraudulently or negligently, and even though the consumer had no contractual relation with the defendant.

In addition to the grounds and theories of liability already discussed, a manufacturer or seller may be held liable on the ground of his wilful or wanton conduct, for injuries caused by his defective product.   One who deliberately places in the stream of commerce a product which he knows to be defective or harmful is liable for resultant injuries on the ground of committing an intentional wrong.

*

423

REAL PROPERTY

I. DEFINITION AND NATURE

II. ESTATES AND INTERESTS IN LAND

III. PERPETUITIES AND RESTRAINTS ON ALIENATION

IV. LANDLORD AND TENANT

X. DEDICATION

XI. RECORDING OF TITLE INSTRUMENTS; REGISTRATION OF TITLE

XII. ADVERSE POSSESSION

XIII. LIENS

XIV. REMEDIES TO PROTECT PROPERTY RIGHTS

I. DEFINITION AND NATURE

§ 18:1. Generally.

Am Jur 2d References: Aviation, §§ 3–8; Crops, §§ 3–5; Fences, § 3; Gas and Oil, §§ 1–9, 14; Logs and Timber, §§ 9–11; Mines and Minerals, §§ 1, 3, 102; Property, §§ 11–18, 25, 35; Waters (1st ed, § 2).

There are two basic classes of property in modern law, real property and personal property. Real property consists of fixed, immovable things, such as lands. The terms "land," "real estate," and "real property" are generally used synonymously. The old phrase, "lands, tenements and hereditaments," covered all kinds of real property and all interests therein. Included in the definition of real property are such incorporeal rights as easements and rights of profit a prendre.

Buildings, fixtures, fences, and other improvements affixed to land are generally a part of the real estate. Standing timber is a part of the land and is real property until it is severed from the land. Whether a growing crop is real property or personalty depends upon the nature of the crop, the relationship of the parties raising the question, and upon other circumstances.

One primary distinction in determining this question classifies crops as either fructus naturales or fructus industriales. The latter class consists of products of the earth which are annual and owe their existence to yearly planting and cultivation by man. For most purposes such crops are treated as personal chattels, even while still annexed to the soil. On the other hand, fructus naturales, such as grasses growing from perennial roots, and according to some courts, the fruit and other products of trees, bushes, vines, and plants growing from perennial roots, are regarded as realty while they are unsevered from the soil. However, courts now tend to regard as fructus industriales growing fruit and other products of trees, etc., which depend largely upon the care and cultivation of man.

Minerals in place are a part of the real estate, and in the absence of a contrary provision in a grant, belong to the owner of the land. Oil and gas underlying land are classified as minerals and are a part of the land, subject to "capture" and to loss by escape. Water also, in its natural state and before appropriation, is regarded as a part of the land in or upon which it is found.

An ancient maxim of the common law states, "cujus est solum, ejus est usque ad coelum et ad inferos," meaning that the owner of the soil owns to the heavens and to the lowest depths. Applied literally, this would give the landowner exclusive dominion over the air space above his land to an infinite vertical distance, as well as ownership of minerals and other things beneath the surface. The modern development of air navigation, however, has required a qualification of these rights with respect to the upper space. The landowner's ownership of such space is no longer regarded as exclusive and unlimited. It is now settled that the flight of aircraft over land does not constitute trespass or nuisance so long as such flights are at a proper height and do not unreasonably interfere with the landowner's use and enjoyment of his property. The owner's rights extend upward only so far as is necessary for the full use and enjoyment of the land, and the space beyond is regarded as open and navigable air space. The owner has a superior right to erect structures extending upward to any distance necessary for the full enjoyment of his property, however. And any flight over his land at such low altitude or in such manner as to interfere unreasonably with his enjoyment of his property, as by endangering his structures, frightening his domestic animals, or impairing the health and tranquillity of his family, will generally constitute a trespass or nuisance.

§ 18:2. Fixtures.

Am Jur 2d References: Fixtures, §§ 1–33, 75–127.

Fixtures have been variously defined as objects which were originally personal property but which, by reason of their annexation to or use in association with real property, have become a part of the realty; as chattels so attached to realty that, for the time being, they become a part thereof; and as chattels annexed to realty in such manner that they cannot be removed without injury to the freehold. However, there is no single statement defining such use which is capable of application in all situations. The principal significance of a determination that an object is a fixture is that it is thereafter treated as part and parcel of the land and may not generally be removed therefrom except by the owner of the realty.

The general tests for determining whether a particular object has become a fixture are usually said to comprise annexation to the realty, adaptation to the use to which the realty is devoted, and intention that the object become a permanent accession to the freehold. There is some disagreement, however, on the relative importance to be assigned to each of these several factors.

Annexation in this connection refers to the act of attaching or affixing personal property to real property. Although annexation or affixation to the soil was the primary or main test under the early common law in determining whether an object had assumed the character of a fixture, it is no longer the controlling factor in many situations. While the exact manner in which an object is annexed to the realty is a matter of diminishing relevance in the modern decisions, it may still be important under some circumstances. Slight attachment to the realty may be sufficient to constitute an article a fixture if other tests are met. There may be an annexation even though the object is held in place only by gravity, as a building upon its foundation or heavy machinery in a factory. The relative ease with which an object annexed to realty may be removed is often considered in determining whether the object has become a fixture. Thus, where an object which is physically attached to realty may be easily removed, it may be held to have retained its character as personalty notwithstanding the annexation. Conversely, if the object cannot be removed without injury to itself or to the realty, the object is usually deemed to be a fixture and a part of the realty.

Adaptation to the use of the realty, the second of the three factors generally held to comprise the test in determining whether an object has become a fixture, refers to the relationship between a chattel and the use which is made of the realty where it is located. According to the adaptation principle, an object introduced onto realty may become a fixture if it is a necessary adjunct to the realty, considering the purposes to which the latter is devoted. This principle, sometimes called the "institution doctrine," is often given great weight in determining whether a particular object has assumed the status of a fixture. The adaptation principle is often applied where a factory, plant, mill, or similar industrial establishment is involved. In such cases, it is frequently held that chattels placed in such an industrial establishment for permanent use and necessary to the operation of the plant become fixtures and hence a part of the real estate, regardless of whether they are physically attached thereto. As early as the sixteenth century it was held that millstones passed on a conveyance of the mill though temporarily detached at the time.

Intention, the third of the three factors comprising the general test, refers to the intent of the parties that the object being introduced onto realty become a permanent accession thereto. This is an important criterion in determining the character of property as fixtures, and it is frequently given controlling weight, at least where the other criteria leave the matter in doubt. It has been said that the mode of annexation is of little consequence except as it bears on the question of intent.

The parties may by contract determine the status of an object as a fixture or personalty. They may by agreement provide that, as between themselves, an object which would normally become a fixture shall remain personalty, or that an object which would normally retain its character as personalty shall become a fixture. As a general proposition, such special agreements are binding only on the contracting parties and their privies, and are not binding on third parties, such as a subsequent purchaser or mortgagee of the land without notice of the agreement.

An object may lose its status as a fixture by severance from the land and, provided the rights of third parties are not involved, may reacquire the character of personal property. An effective severance can be made only by the owner of the realty and must be effected under such circumstances that an intention to separate the object permanently from the realty may be presumed.

§ 18:3. — Rights as between particular persons.

Am Jur 2d References: Fixtures, §§ 34–74.

The relationship of the parties contesting the status of an object as a fixture or as personalty may be an important factor in determining the question. Such dispute may involve the landowner, on the one hand, and the asserted owner of the fixture, on the other; or it may be between either or both of the former and some third person, such as a conditional seller or chattel mortgagee. This approach to the problem does not derogate from the validity of the general tests for determining whether an object is a fixture, but merely furnishes a guideline for their application. For example, while an intention to make a permanent accession to the freehold may legitimately be presumed where the annexer is, for example, the owner of the fee, no such presumption necessarily arises where he is a lessee or life tenant. So, a given object may be a fixture as between vendor and vendee but a chattel as between lessor and lessee.

In disputes between landlord and tenant, there is a general presumption that the tenant, by annexing objects to the realty, did so for his own benefit and not to enrich the freehold; and the law accordingly is liberal in determining the tenant's right to remove his annexations, at least where removal may be effected without material injury to the freehold. The intention of the parties is ordinarily the controlling test in determining the tenant's rights in this regard. A fixture substituted by a tenant for another fixture which was upon the premises at the time of the making of the lease cannot ordinarily be removed by him. A tenant of residence property may remove fixtures which he has attached for his own domestic comfort and convenience or for ornamental purposes, if this may be done without unreasonable injury to the freehold.

A tenant is favored by the special principles of law governing "trade fixtures." Such fixtures consist of personal property brought upon land by a tenant, which is necessary to carry on the trade or business to which the land will be devoted. Trade fixtures remain the personal property of the tenant and are generally removable by him at the expiration of his term of occupancy, in the absence of an agreement to the contrary. Except where determined by the terms of a contract or lease, the question whether a given object is removable as a trade fixture depends on the circumstances of the case. The right of a tenant to remove trade fixtures is subject to the requirement that he must not substantially injure the freehold.

As between the mortgagor and mortgagee of realty, a liberal rule in favor of the mortgagee is applied, and it is generally held that objects which are attached to the realty at the time the mortgage is executed and which are, from all outward manifestations, intended for permanent use and enjoyment in connection therewith, are a part of the realty and are covered by the mortgage. And this rule generally applies whether the annexation took place before or after the granting of the mortgage.

Between vendor and vendee, the rules for determining the character of property as fixtures are construed most strongly against the vendor. As between a vendor and purchaser of land, the primary consideration is that of intention, and generally whatever is essential for the purposes for which the realty is used, and has been annexed, is a fixture and passes to the grantee, unless it is excepted from the operation of the deed. As between a vendor and vendee under an executory contract for the sale of land, fixtures attached by the vendee in possession become a part of the realty and may not be removed by him if he fails to acquire title by reason of his own default. It is the general rule that property annexed by a decedent to his realty may be presumed to have been intended by him as a permanent part of the realty, so as to pass to the heir as a fixture.

The strict rule of common law that whatever is affixed to the freehold becomes a part of it and passes with it is somewhat relaxed in favor of a life tenant as between him and a remainderman. The law indulges an inference that a life tenant does not intend to make a permanent addition to the freehold.

The rights of parties under a conditional sale, chattel mortgage, or other instrument creating a security interest in chattels, are now governed by the Uniform Commercial Code. The Code is controlling as to the priority of security interests in goods which are converted into fixtures and the rights of parties with respect to such security interests. The Code does not apply, however, to building materials such as lumber, brick, cement, and the like, incorporated into a structure.

II. ESTATES AND INTERESTS IN LAND

§ 18:4. Generally.

Am Jur 2d References: Estates, §§ 1–8, 130, 131, 374–382.

The common law governing property interests in land was developed after the Norman Conquest upon the base of the feudal system, with some degree of accommodation to the Anglo-Saxon system prevailing in most of England at the time of the conquest. The feudal aspects of tenures and the burden and limitations inherent in that system were eliminated over the centuries by a series of English statutes and through the ingenuity of the great English conveyancers and judges. Under the ancient system, estates in land were held under several kinds of "tenures," such as tenure by military service or knight's service, tenure in socage, each requiring services or payments by the tenant, as well as tenures by copyhold, in Burgage, Gavelkind, Frankalmoigne, and Serjeanty. The nature of the tenure determined the extent of the holder's rights and obligations, and also the alienability and descent or inheritance of the estate.

The term "estate" as used here means the nature, quantity, and extent of interest which a person has in real property. According to the classification adopted by Blackstone, estates may be considered from three different points of view: (1) with regard to their duration and extent, (2) with regard to the time when the beneficial enjoyment of the property is to commence, and (3) with regard to the number and connection of the tenants or possessors. Obviously, there is some overlapping in this classification, the first classification including most or all of the second and third. With respect to the time of their enjoyment, estates may be either in possession or in expectancy. Estates in possession are generally deemed to mean interests that may be immediately enjoyed, including the different types of estates in fee, such as fee simple, fee simple conditional, fee simple defeasible; determinable, base, or qualified fee; and such estates as fee tail, life estates, and estates for years, at will, by sufferance, and upon condition. Estates in expectancy are of two sorts, those created by act of the parties, called "remainders," and those created by operation of law, called "reversions." With respect to the number and connection of their tenants or owners, estates may be held in various ways; in severalty, in joint tenancy, in coparcenary, in common, and by the entireties. The same rules generally apply to both legal and equitable estates.

An estate of freehold is an estate of indeterminate duration other than an estate at will or by sufferance. A freehold is also defined as any estate of inheritance or for life, in either a corporeal or incorporeal hereditament, existing in, or arising from, real property of free tenure. An estate of inheritance is a freehold estate in land, called a "fee," under which the tenant enjoys the land for his own life, and after his death, it is cast by the law upon the persons who succeed him in right of blood according to a certain established order of descent. Freehold estates of inheritance include estates in fee simple absolute, fee simple conditional, fee simple determinable or defeasible, and estates in fee tail. Freehold estates not of inheritance consist of life estates.

Estates and interests in land less than a freehold are of three kinds: estates for years, estates at will, and estates at sufferance. Within this category, and also closely related to estates at will, are estates from period to period, such as tenancies from year to year or from month to month. The relationship of the parties under such tenancies are those of landlord and tenant. An estate at will is a tenancy for such time as both parties shall please; it can be determined at any time by either party. An estate by sufferance arises where one who has rightfully entered upon land continues in possession after his right has ceased, as, for example, where a person holding a lease from a life tenant continues in possession after the termination of the life estate.

It is a general rule of law that when a greater and a lesser estate meet in the same person, the lesser is merged in the greater. To constitute a merger, it is necessary that the two estates be in one and the same person, at one and the same time, and in one and the same right. A merger of estates will not occur where there is an intermediate estate or where a person holds one of the estates for himself and the other for another person. Modern courts, applying equitable principles, will not permit a merger of estates where a merger would be contrary to the intention of the parties, either actually proved or implied from the fact that merger would be against the interest of the party in whom the several estates or interests have united; and the doctrine of merger will not be applied where the rights of innocent third parties would be prejudiced by merger.

§ 18:5. Fee simple.

Am Jur 2d References: Estates, §§ 9–21.

The term "fee simple" defines the largest estate in land known to the law. It is frequently used interchangeably with the term "fee simple absolute"; and these terms are used in contradistinction to such terms as "fee tail," and "determinable," "qualified," "base," or "conditional" fee. A fee simple implies absolute ownership of the land. It is an estate of inheritance unlimited in duration, descendible to the heirs of the owner to the remotest generations, and carries an unlimited power of alienation. A fee simple estate may be either legal or equitable in nature.

Since the right to enjoy the benefits of property is the gist of ownership, a grant or gift of such right generally confers a corresponding estate in the property itself. Thus, it is the prevailing general rule, where there is no manifestation of intention to the contrary, that a direct grant or devise of income, interest, use, or profits of property, without limit of time or remainder over, is treated as a grant or devise of the fee simple or absolute title in the property itself.

It was an inflexible rule at common law that words of inheritance, such as the word "heirs" or its equivalent, were necessary in a deed in order to convey an estate in fee simple. At common law a deed without words of inheritance conveyed a life estate to the grantee and left a reversion in the grantor, which, if not otherwise disposed of, descended to his heirs. This strict rule exists today in only a very few American jurisdictions, having been altered in most states by statutes and judicial decisions. The common-law rule requiring words of inheritance to pass a fee simple title was never applied in this country to grants to a corporation or to a trustee. Under the present rule prevailing in most states, no particular verbal formula is required to pass a fee simple. Such an estate may be created without the word "heirs," unless the intention is manifested by the terms of the conveyance that the grantor intended to create a lesser estate. If words of inheritance are not used in a conveyance, the entire context of the instrument will be considered in determining the estate granted. Such words as "forever" and "absolutely" usually indicate a fee simple. In construing deeds, courts apply the principle that any doubt should be resolved in favor of the passing of the fee simple.

In the case of wills also, the earlier common law applied the rule that a devise of lands, without words of limitation or inheritance, conferred on the devisee an estate for life only. But this rule is not followed in this country, not only because it has been changed by statute, but also because, even in the absence of statute, the primary consideration controlling the quantum of a devise is the intention of the testator; and where the terms of a devise, considered with reference to its context, show that it was the intent of the testator to give an estate in fee simple, the devise will be construed to pass such an estate, although words of inheritance are not used. Thus, a devise of "all my property," "all of my real estate," or "the residue of my property," will give an estate in fee simple.

§ 18:6. Determinable, qualified, base, or conditional fee; fee tail.

Am Jur 2d References: Estates, §§ 22–55.

A "determinable," "qualified," or "base" fee is an estate limited to a person and his heirs, with a qualification providing that such estate must determine whenever that qualification is at an end. Because the estate may last forever, it is a fee; and because it may end on the happening of an event, it is called a "determinable or qualified fee." Determination of a determinable fee upon the happening of the event upon which its existence is conditioned, without any action by the creator of the estate or his successors in interest, is a characteristic of a determinable fee which distinguishes it from an estate held on condition subsequent; in the latter, the interest of the grantee or his successors in interest does not terminate automatically upon breach of the condition, but continues until the creator of the estate or his successors exercise the power of termination or the right of re-entry for condition broken. A determinable or qualified fee has all the attributes of a fee simple, except that it is subject to be defeated by the happening of the condition which is to terminate the estate. The owner of such an estate may convey or devise it, and it descends to his heirs, always subject to the qualification annexed to it.

An estate in fee simple determinable is created by any limitation which, in an otherwise effective conveyance or devise of land, (1) creates an estate in fee simple and (2) provides that the estate shall automatically expire upon the occurrence of the stated event. The technical words used to create a determinable fee are "until," "so long as," or "during."

A conditional fee or fee simple conditional under the early common law resulted from a conveyance or devise to a person and his or her bodily heirs, lawful heirs of his body, his or her heirs by the present wife or husband, or the like. In the descent of estates in fee simple conditional, only the lineal descendants were admitted, to the exclusion of collateral heirs. If the donee or grantee had no heirs of his body, the whole estate reverted to the grantor or donor. Upon the fulfilment of the condition by the birth of issue, the grantee or donee could convey a fee simple estate unaffected by the condition.

The enactment of the Statute de Donis in the year 1285 had the effect of converting the conditional fee into the estate in fee tail. In a few American jurisdictions, the existence of a fee simple conditional estate is recognized. In other states, such estates do not exist, because the Statute de Donis is in effect or because all estates of similar nature, including estates tail, have been abolished.

The estate tail or fee tail is still recognized in a few American jurisdictions. This estate resulted from the effect of the Statute de Donis in eliminating the estate of fee simple conditional. An estate tail or fee tail is one in which lands and tenements are given to one and the heirs of his body begotten. It is usually created by a grant or devise to one and his or her bodily heirs, or to one and the heirs male of his body, or to one and the heirs male of the body on his then wife to be begotten. To create this estate, words of inheritance as well as words of procreation are necessary. It is an estate of inheritance which is to pass by lineal descent only. One of the main incidents of an estate tail—and the incident from which the estate receives its name—is that if there are no heirs of the class to whom the estate is limited, the property reverts to the donor. The Statute de Donis was soon circumvented in England by means of fictitious proceedings, by common recovery or by fine, invented to give a tenant in tail an absolute power to dispose of the property in fee simple. As indicated above, the fee tail estate has been eliminated in most of the American jurisdictions.

§18:7. Life estates.

Am Jur 2d References: Estates, §§ 56–101; Life Tenants, etc., §§ 32–103.

A life estate is an estate of freehold but not of inheritance. A life estate, created by deed or will, is an estate to be held by the grantee or devisee for the term of his own life, or for that of another person, or for more lives than one. Such an estate may be either legal or equitable (in trust), and the same incidents, rights, and liabilities generally attend both kinds.

An estate to be held during the life of a third person is known as an estate per autre vie. This estate is terminated by the death of the third person and not by the death of the life tenant. Where the life tenant dies prior to the death of the person whose life limits the estate, the life estate descends to the persons designated by statute. The same is true where income is payable to a person during the life of another. A devise or conveyance of the use and enjoyment of the rents, profits, and income of property for life creates a life estate in the property itself. In a conveyance of a fee, the grantor may reserve to himself a life estate, if the instrument is not testamentary in character.

No particular form of words is necessary to create a life estate. In determining whether an instrument creates a life estate or some other interest, in cases of ambiguity, the fundamental principles governing the construction of deeds and wills are applied. The intention of the creator of the estate, as disclosed by the instrument as a whole, is the governing factor.

The question whether a fee simple or a life estate is created by a gift or grant coupled with a power of disposition presents one of the most troublesome subjects in the entire field of estates. The fact that a great diversity of result appears in the decisions is not because of disagreement on the underlying rules, but is the consequence of the application of the overriding principle that the intention of the creator of the estate, as disclosed by all of the provisions of the will or deed and the circumstances of the case, is the governing factor. It is a general rule that a life estate expressly created by an instrument will not be converted into a fee or other greater estate merely by reason of there being coupled with it a power of disposition, however general or extensive. In other words, where an estate for life, with remainder over, is given, with a power of disposition in fee of the remainder annexed, the limitation for the life of the first taker will control, and the life estate will not be enlarged by the power of the life tenant to dispose of the fee. The power conferred upon the life tenant is not an estate and does not enlarge his estate. This rule applies a fortiori where the power of disposal is qualified or limited.

A source of much litigation results from wills and deeds that do not state the character or duration of the estate given, and contain provisions purporting to dispose of what remains at the death of the grantee or devisee. There is no general rule of law determining whether the estate conferred is a life estate or a fee. The court seeks to ascertain the intention of the testator or grantor as evidenced by all of the provisions of the instrument creating the estate. If, in connection with a grant or devise in general terms, expressing neither fee nor life estate, there is a subsequent limitation over of what remains at the first taker's death, and there is also given to the first taker an un-limited power of disposal, most authorities hold that a fee passes to the first taker, the attempted limitation after a gift in fee being void. The result is usually different where the power of disposal is limited or qualified.

A life estate normally terminates upon the death of the life tenant or of the person on whose life the estate depends. By the terms of the grant or devise, however, the estate may be terminated by the happening of some event, such as marriage or removal from the property. Statutes in some states provide for termination or forfeiture of life estates for waste, failure to pay taxes, or neglect. And the instrument creating the estate may provide for a termination or forfeiture thereof on these or other grounds.

§ 18:8. Rule in Shelley's Case.

Am Jur 2d References: Estates, §§ 102–129.

The rule in Shelley's Case, which remains in effect in a few jurisdictions, is thus stated in the case from which it derived its name: "When the ancestor by any gift or conveyance takes an estate of freehold, and in the same gift or conveyance an estate is limited, either mediately or immediately, to his heirs in fee or in tail . . . 'the heirs' are words of limitation of the estate, and not words of purchase." This means that where there is a devise or conveyance to a person for life, with a remainder over mediately or immediately to his heirs or the heirs of his body, the heirs do not take remainders at all, the word "heirs" being regarded as limiting or defining the estate of the first taker, and his heirs take by descent and not by purchase. The effect of the operation of the rule in Shelley's Case is to vest the remainder in the first taker or ancestor so as to give him the fee. The heirs take as heirs and not by purchase or in remainder. The rule applies alike to equitable and legal estates.

Where this rule is recognized, it is generally (but not universally) held to be a rule of property and not of construction. In other words, where the right words are used, the rule is invoked regardless of the real intention of the testator or donor. Under this principle, even the addition of provisions expressly stating that the ancestor shall take no more than a life estate will not prevent the application of the rule in Shelley's Case.

The prerequisites to the application of the rule in Shelley's Case are that there must be (1) an estate in freehold in the ancestor or first taker; (2) the ancestor must acquire his prior estate by or through the same instrument which contains the limitation to his heirs; (3) the words "heirs" or "heirs of the body" must be used in their technical sense, as importing a class of persons to take indefinitely in succession in the course prescribed by the rules of descent; (4) the interest acquired by the ancestor and that limited to his heirs must both be either equitable or legal; and (5) the limitation to the heirs must be of an inheritance, in fee or in tail, and this must be made by way of remainder.

In most American jurisdictions the rule in Shelley's Case is not applied. It has been abolished by statute in many states and repudiated by judicial decision in others.

§ 18:9. Reversions; possibility of reverter; right of re-entry.

Am Jur 2d References: Estates, §§ 171–193; Life Tenants and Remaindermen, §§ 21–24.

A reversion is a future estate created by operation of law to take effect in possession in favor of a lessor or grantor or his heirs, or the heirs of a testator, after the termination of a prior particular estate leased, granted, or devised. The fee simple must exist in some person, and if the owner of such an estate grants a smaller estate, whatever is not granted remains in him. In the case of a grant, an estate in reversion is the residue of an estate left in the grantor, to commence in possession after the determination of some particular estate granted by him. Reversions are actual estates in praesenti, and are vested in the sense of a present fixed right of enjoyment in futuro. A reversioner has neither actual nor constructive possession nor the right to either, but only an estate in expectancy. However, this estate has all the attributes of transmissibility, and reversions are descendible, devisable, and alienable or assignable by deed, conveyance, and grant, and are subject to execution for debts of the reversioner.

In the case of an inter vivos conveyance for life, with remainder to the heirs or next of kin of the grantor, the question arises whether the latter words are terms of purchase, descriptive of persons to take under the instrument itself, or are merely words of limitation, descriptive of an estate they will take, if at all, by operation of law from their ancestor, the conveyer. In other words, does such a grant create a remainder in the heirs of the grantor, or does it leave a reversion in the grantor which will pass by operation of law upon his death, unless he otherwise disposes of it? Under the rule at common law and in many American jurisdictions, such a conveyance for life, with attempted remainder to the heirs or next of kin of the conveyer, is ineffective to create a remainder, but leaves a reversion in the conveyer. Some American decisions have reached a different result, holding that remainders were created under the terms of deeds granting a life estate with ultimate gift to the heirs of the grantor. In some of these decisions the doctrine of reversion has been rejected as inapplicable under the circumstances because of the facts and the apparent intention of the grantor, while in others no reference has been made to the doctrine. Although there is some authority to the contrary, the trend of American decisions is that the doctrine of reversion is one of construction, so that the result depends upon the intention of the grantor, rather than a rule of law or of property which overrules the intention of the grantor.

The doctrine of reversion is not to be confused with the rule in Shelley's Case. The latter rule involves only grants or devises for life with remainder to the heirs of the body of the grantee or devisee, whereas the reversion rule designates a remainder in the heirs of the grantor or testator. In the case of a conveyance to a trustee for the benefit of the settlor himself for life, with remainder to his heirs, the application of either the rule in Shelley's Case or the reversion rule would effect a similar result.

The reversion rule has been abrogated or modified by statute in some states.

A possibility of reverter is a future interest which remains in a grantor by deed or his successor in interest, or in a testator's heirs or devisees, where, by grant or devise, there has been created an estate in fee simple determinable or an estate in fee simple conditional, as discussed in § 18:6, supra. The possibility of reverter is not an estate, but is only the possibility of having an estate at a future time. The most important practical distinction between the right of entry for breach of a condition subsequent and a possibility of reverter on a determinable fee is that, in the former, the estate in fee does not terminate until entry by the person having the right, while in the latter, the estate reverts at once by operation of law on the occurrence of the event by which it is limited.

The possibility of reverter, accompanying either a determinable fee or a fee simple conditional, is inheritable by the heirs of the creator of the estate. There is conflict of authority on the question whether a possibility of reverter is alienable. Statutes in many states expressly permit the alienation of such interest or right. The same situation exists with respect to the question of the devisability of a possibility of reverter after a determinable fee. The authorities are agreed, however, that such a possibility of reverter is capable of being released to the tenant in fee simple determinable, such release having the effect of turning the determinable or qualified fee into a fee simple absolute.

The "right of re-entry for condition broken" is the interest which remains in the grantor or his successors, or the successors of a testator, where an estate on condition subsequent has been created. On proper analysis, the "right of re-entry" appears to be really a power, sometimes termed a "power of termination." Such right is not a reversion, a possibility of reverter, or any estate in land. It is a mere right, and if it is enforced the grantor succeeds by the failure of the condition and not by reverter. It is optional with the grantor whether he exercises a right of re-entry for condition broken, and it is necessary for him to take the proper steps to enforce his right if he decides to exercise it. A breach of condition subsequent can be taken advantage of only by the grantor and his heirs, and, some authorities add, his devisees. At common law, the right of re-entry is not alienable, assignable, or devisable. This rule has been changed, however, in some states. It seems to have been the rule in common law that an attempt to convey the right of re-entry was not only ineffective to transfer the right to the grantee, but also had the effect of destroying the right in the grantor, although this rule has been criticized.

§18:10. Remainders.

Am Jur 2d References: Estates, §§ 194–214, 304–332; Life Tenants and Remaindermen, §§ 1–20.

A remainder is defined by Coke as "a remnant of an estate in lands or tenements, expectant on a particular estate," created together with the same at one time. It is an estate limited to take effect in possession immediately after the expiration of a prior estate created at the same time and by the same instrument. The essence of a remainder is that it is to arise immediately on the determination of the particular estate by lapse of time or other determinant event, and not in abridgment of it. A devise to A for life (or for a designated term of years), remainder to B in fee, is the simplest illustration of a particular estate and a remainder. Whenever a grant is of a fee, there cannot be a remainder, although a fee may be a qualified or determinable one, because the fee is the whole estate and there is nothing left out of which a remainder may be carved. In the case of a grant or devise of a life estate with remainder to another, the remainderman succeeds to the possession of the life tenant upon the latter's death, but he does not succeed to his title. The remainderman gets title as a purchaser from the deed or will creating the estate, not by descent from the life tenant.

A remainder is essentially different from a reversion. A remainder is the remnant of the whole estate disposed of after a preceding part of the same has been given away, while a reversion is a remnant of the estate continuing in the grantor undisposed of, after a grant of part of his interest.

Whether an estate in remainder, or some other estate, is created by a particular deed or will, is generally determined today by ascertaining the kind of estate which the grantor or testator intended to create, under the rule that the intention of the maker of the instrument, as gathered from all its parts, must prevail. It is not necessary to use the term "remainder" in order to create such an estate, any form of expression indicating the intention of the grantor or testator to do so being sufficient.

The general rule, rigidly adhered to at common law, though relaxed in some states by statute or otherwise, is that a remainder must be supported by a particular preceding estate. The particular estate may be an estate for life or for years, but it cannot be a fee simple estate or a base, determinable, or conditional fee, since such a fee exhausts the entire estate and leaves no room for a remainder. Whether or not there may be a remainder after a life estate given with the power to dispose of the fee during the life of the life tenant depends upon whether the particular estate is the equivalent of a fee simple or is actually only a life estate. Under the prevailing modern rule, a valid remainder may be limited after such a life estate with a power of disposal, even though such power is absolute.

A vested remainder is an actual estate and is susceptible of transfer of title. Title to such an estate will pass by a conveyance, devise, or inheritance. A different rule applied at common law to contingent remainders, which were not considered to be actual estates, but mere possibilities. By force of statutes or otherwise, however, the prevailing modern rule is that contingent remainders also are alienable and devisable.

A remainder in interest may be accelerated when the precedent estate given by will fails to come into existence upon the death of the testator, or, having come into existence, terminates prematurely or in a manner not contemplated by the will in providing for the remainder over. Under the doctrine of acceleration, the general rule is that vested remainders take effect immediately upon the death of the testator where the life estate has failed prior to the testator's death, or immediately after the determination of the life estate subsequently to the death of the testator, whether the failure or determination of the life estate is by reason of death, revocation, incapacity of the devisee to take, or any other circumstance. The doctrine of acceleration of remainders rarely applies in the case of grants by deed. In any event, the doctrine of acceleration is a rule of construction and will not be applied so as to defeat the testator's intention.

There is some conflict in the authorities on the question whether a contingent remainder is subject to the doctrine of acceleration by the premature termination of the precedent estate. The prevailing view of the later decisions is that acceleration may occur notwithstanding the remainder interests were contingent.

A vested remainder is not subject to termination or destruction by the happening of any event prior to the falling of the particular estate. Contingent remainders, however, were subject to a different rule at common law. At common law a contingent remainder is destroyed by the destruction or determination of the particular estate before the vesting of the remainder. This result occurred at common law by the determination of the particular estate by surrender, merger, alienation, forfeiture, or otherwise, prior to the happening of the contingency upon which the remaindermen could take. Statutes have been enacted in many jurisdictions, however, abrogating or modifying the common-law rule as to the destructibility of contingent remainders.

A vested remainder may disappear by merger into a larger estate. Thus, the merger of a life estate and a vested remainder in the same person gives him a fee. The merger doctrine has little scope for application, however, to contingent remainders, as a contingent remainderman cannot, by the acquisition of the life estate, cut off others whose rights may be dependent on the same contingency.

§ 18:11. — Classes of remainders; vested and contingent remainders.

Am Jur 2d References: Estates, §§ 215–303.

The primary classification of estates in remainder divides them into vested remainders and contingent remainders. The consequences which flow from the nature of an estate in remainder as vested or contingent are of great practical importance. In the determination of the question whether a remainder is vested or contingent, the intention of the creator of the estate is an important factor.

A remainder is vested when it is limited to an ascertained person or persons with no further condition imposed upon the taking effect in possession than the determination of the precedent estate. A widely quoted definition is that where "a remainder is limited to take effect in possession, if ever, immediately upon the determination of a particular estate, which estate is to determine by an event that must unavoidably happen by the efflux of time, the remainder vests in interest as soon as the remainderman is in esse and ascertained, provided nothing but his own death before a determination of the particular estate will prevent such remainder from vesting in possession." The vesting of a remainder refers to the vesting of the title or estate, and not to the vesting of the right to possession, use, and enjoyment of the property. A remainderman whose interest is vested does not have an actual or constructive possession of the property, but simply an estate to vest in possession in the future.

A remainder is contingent if the taking effect in possession is subject to a condition precedent either as to the persons who are to take or as to the event upon which the preceding particular estate is to terminate. If there is uncertainty either as to the person who is to receive or in the gift itself to the remainderman, the remainder is contingent. When a remainder is limited to a person not in esse or not ascertained, or whenever it is limited so as to require the occurrence of some uncertain event, independent of the determination of the preceding estate and the duration of the estate limited in remainder, to give it a capacity of taking effect, the remainder is contingent. Fearne's definition, often quoted by the courts and reflected in statutes, is: "A contingent remainder is a remainder limited so as to depend on an event or condition which may never happen or be performed, or which may not happen or be performed till after the determination of the preceding estate." The contingency on which a valid remainder is limited must be such that there is a possibility of the contingent event occurring, even though it is not probable.

A contingent remainder may become a vested remainder during the continuance of the preceding particular estate, by the lapse or removal of all conditions precedent except the determination of the preceding particular estate. A remainder to a person not in existence is contingent, but if the only contingency is the existence of such person, the remainder becomes vested when a person answering the description of the limitation comes into existence or is en ventre sa mere.

The question sometimes arises as to the location of the fee or inheritance during the period intervening between the creation and determination or vesting of a contingent remainder. According to one view, the inheritance or fee remains in the person creating the remainder; the other view is that the remainder passes from its creator but remains in abeyance. The first view is generally applied where the remainder is created by will, and it seems to be the better rule for application to deeds.

Contingent remainders may be divided into two main classes (although some authorities further subdivide them): (1) those in which the contingency relates to the event on which the remainder is to take effect, and (2) those in which the uncertainty relates to the person who is to take the estate in remainder. An estate is contingent and not vested whenever the persons who are to enjoy the remainder are not ascertained at the time the preceding estate and the remainder estate are created, but are to be ascertained at the time the preceding estate ends. In other words, where the person or persons who will take the remainder can only be ascertained upon the determination of the particular estate, the remainder, until then, is contingent. A remainder to an unborn person or persons, being necessarily limited to an event which may happen before or after determination of the particular estate, or not at all, is contingent, at least until the birth of a person capable of taking; and if no such person is born during the continuance of the particular estate, the remainder necessarily fails. If such a person is born during the continuance of the particular estate, the remainder is no longer contingent, but vests in such person. A remainder may be contingent, although the person to whom it is limited is certain, if the event upon which it is to take effect is uncertain and contingent. So long as it remains uncertain whether the contingency will happen before or simultaneously with the expiration of the prior estate, it is uncertain whether the right of remainder will ever become fixed, and it is therefore a contingent remainder. Such a remainder exists where it is conditioned upon the remainderman attaining a certain age or surviving the life tenant or a third person.

The character of a remainder as vested is not affected by an uncertainty of the quantum of interest which will be received by the remainderman when he becomes entitled to possession. The remainder may be vested in interest although contingent as to amount. A remainder to a class of persons may be vested, although it is subject to be opened to let in members of the class as they come into being before the remaindermen are entitled to possession, so that, until then, there is an uncertainty as to the quantum of the interests of the remaindermen.

The character of a remainder as vested or contingent does not depend upon the defeasibility or indefeasibility of the right of possession. If there is a present right to a future possession, though that right may be defeated by some future event, there is a vested estate. A vested remainder may be determinable upon the happening of a contingency, or subject to be divested on the happening of a contingency subsequent. For example, a remainder is not made contingent by the fact that the interest of the remainderman may be divested by his death before the death of the life tenant or before reaching majority. The fact that the life tenant is given the power to dispose of the property, so that there is a possibility, undetermined until the termination of the life estate, that the property will not in fact be available to the remainderman, does not make the remainder contingent, but leaves it vested, subject to defeasance by the exercise of the power. The same rule applies where a power of appointment is given to the life tenant or another.

In construing a will or deed to determine whether a remainder is vested or contingent, the courts will attempt to follow the intention of the testator or grantor. As the law favors the vesting of estates generally, remainders are held to be vested rather than contingent unless the intent of the testator or grantor is made to appear to the contrary. And if there is uncertainty as to the time of the vesting of an estate in remainder, the courts will favor the vesting of the estate at the earliest moment consistent with the terms of the instrument creating it. Thus, the estate will vest at the death of the testator unless a later time for vesting is clearly indicated by the will.

More than one estate in remainder may be limited after a single particular estate if the limitation is in the alternative so that one may take effect if the other does not. Such alternative remainders are always contingent.

Another class of remainder is the cross remainder. This is defined as a remainder limited after particular estates to two or more persons in several parcels of land, or in several individual shares in the same parcel of land, in such a way that upon the determination of the particular estates in any of the parcels or undivided shares they remain over to the other grantees, and the reversioner or ultimate remainderman is not let in until the determination of all the particular estates. The ulterior estates are called cross remainders because each of the grantees has reciprocally a remainder in the share of the other.

§18:12. Relationship and rights between life tenants and owners of future interests.

Am Jur 2d References: Life Tenants and Remaindermen, §§ 25–31, 104–280; Waste (1st ed, §§ 1–36).

A tenant for life is entitled to the full use and enjoyment of the property in which he has a life estate, the only restriction upon this use being that the estate of those who are to follow him in possession shall not be permanently diminished in value by his neglecting to do that which an ordinarily prudent person would do in the preservation of his own property, or by his doing things which are not necessary to the full enjoyment of the particular estate and which have the effect of diminishing the value of the future estate. The life tenant is entitled to the exclusive possession and enjoyment of the property during his lifetime, and to all the rents, profits, and income therefrom during the period of the life estate.

The timber rights of a life tenant are founded on principles of prudent and proper husbandry with due regard for the rights of the life tenant to make reasonable use of premises. The basic rule is that a life tenant is entitled to take reasonable estovers—that is, wood from the land for fuel, fences, repairs, and other such uses essential for the proper enjoyment of the property. Any unreasonable taking or destruction of timber, however, to the injury of the inheritance, amounts to waste. A life tenant may take a reasonable amount of firewood, prudently selected, for use as fuel on the premises. He may take timber for necessary repairs of buildings and fences on the premises, although his right to use such timber for the construction of new buildings or improvements has been questioned. He may not generally cut timber to sell for profit, except where this is the custom of the particular estate, at least where such cutting impairs the value of the inheritance. This rule is subject to an exception applicable to estates which are held and cultivated merely for the produce of salable timber and in which the timber is cut periodically. In this case, the timber is regarded as the periodic fruits of the land and as the annual profits of the estate to which the life tenant is entitled. A life tenant is permitted to cut timber for the purpose of clearing the land for cultivation, provided that he does not exceed the proportion of cleared to wooded land usually maintained in good husbandry, and provided further that he does not materially lessen the value of the inheritance.

Unless given the right to do so by the instrument creating the estate, a life tenant does not have the right to open and work new mines or wells for the purpose of extracting the mineral contents of the land. This rule applies not only to metals, metallic ores, and coal, but also to oil and gas, salt, stone from quarries, clay from clay pits, and sand and gravel. However, under the principle that a life tenant is entitled to the issues and profits of the real estate in which he has been granted a life estate, he has the right to continue to work and operate mines or mineral deposits that were open when the life estate commenced. This rule applies also to oil and gas, stone from quarries, etc., as well as to solid minerals and metallic ores.

The rights of the life tenant with respect to timber and minerals are, of course, broader where the instrument creating the life estate gives him the power to encroach upon the corpus for his support and comfort, or to dispose of the property. The same is true where the life tenant holds "without impeachment of waste."

It is the duty of a life tenant to keep the property in repair; that is, he must make all ordinary, reasonable, and necessary repairs required to preserve the property. He is generally under no duty, however, to make new permanent improvements on the property or to replace buildings destroyed without his fault. And a life tenant is generally not entitled to compensation for improvements which he does make, although the courts, applying equitable principles, have allowed compensation to the life tenant in some cases.

It is the duty of the life tenant to pay the taxes levied on the real estate. As to special assessments for public improvements, the prevailing view is that the burden should be apportioned between the life tenant and the remainderman, although in some jurisdictions the entire cost of such permanent improvements is placed on the remainder interest.

A life tenant's liability to the owner of a future estate for damage to or misuse of property is usually based on the tort called "waste." This wrong was actionable under the early common law, and is so today. Waste may be defined as any wrongful or unauthorized act or omission by a life tenant or tenant for years which results in lasting injury to the freehold or destroys or lessens the value of the inheritance. To constitute waste, the act or omission must be wrongful and must be prejudicial to those entitled to the remainder or reversion. Waste may be either voluntary or actual, as by wrongfully cutting timber or destroying buildings, or permissive or negligent, as by permitting improvements to fall into ruin. The owner of a vested future estate, such as a remainderman or reversioner, may maintain an action to recover damages for waste. They may also be entitled to an injunction to prevent future waste. And while a contingent remainderman may not be able to maintain an action at law to recover damages for waste, he is entitled to equitable relief in many jurisdictions.

§ 18:13. Estates on condition.

Am Jur 2d References: Estates, §§ 132–170.

An estate on condition is one with a qualification annexed by which it may, on the happening of a particular event, be created, enlarged, or destroyed. Any condition annexed to an estate is either precedent or subsequent. Conditions precedent are those which must take place before an estate can vest or be enlarged; if land is conveyed or devised on a condition precedent, the title does not pass until the condition is performed.   Conditions subsequent are those in which the terms operate on an estate already vested and render it subject to be defeated by a breach or nonperformance of the condition.   Any particular estate, a fee, a life estate, or a term of years, may be granted subject to a condition.

A condition requiring an illegal act or compelling conduct which is contrary to public policy is void.   If a condition is thus void, the estate will be absolute and free of the condition.   Another restriction on the right to annex conditions to an estate granted or devised is that the condition will not be sustained if it is repugnant to the estate granted or devised.   A condition subsequent forfeiting the title to the creator in case of breach is not of itself repugnant to the granting clause of the instrument creating the estate; but where an estate is given, either by deed or by will, a restriction destructive of that estate, or a condition repugnant to the very nature thereof, such a restriction or condition is void.   Such a repugnant condition will not operate to limit the estate granted, although it may, if not illegal or contrary to public policy, be enforceable between the parties as a personal covenant.

As stated above, a fee simple subject to a condition subsequent is a fee simple estate which is subject to divestment by the failure or nonperformance of a condition subsequent.   The title passes to the grantee or devisee subject to divestiture on failure to perform the condition.   In general, conditions subsequent can only be reserved for the benefit of the creator of the estate and his heirs.

In accordance with the general principle that conditions tending to destroy estates are not favored in law, provisions creating such conditions are strictly construed and a grant or devise is construed strictly against conditions subsequent.   No provision will be interpreted to create such a condition if the language will bear any other reasonable interpretation.   As between a condition precedent and a condition subsequent, however, the law generally favors the latter, as it favors the vesting of estates.   In any event, the determination of the question whether an instrument creates a condition, and if so, whether the condition is precedent or subsequent, depends upon the construction of the language of the instrument as a whole and the intent of the parties as disclosed thereby.

It is sometimes difficult to distinguish between an estate subject to a condition subsequent and one involving a conditional limitation, as discussed in the next section.   In the case of a conditional limitation, the estate automatically ceases and terminates upon the happening of the condition on which it is limited, while in the case of a condition subsequent the creator of the estate must have expressly or by implication reserved to himself or his heirs a right of entry on breach of the condition, and re-entry is necessary to revest the estate.

Although no form of words is necessary to create any condition subsequent, it must be created by express terms or by clear implication.   Although it is not absolutely indispensable to the creation of an estate on condition subsequent that the grant or devise in express terms reserve a right of re-entry for breach of condition to the creator of the estate and his heirs, a provision for forfeiture or re-entry, or something from which it can fairly be inferred that the continuance of the estate is to depend upon the condition, is usually essential.

445

On the one hand, the inclusion of a provision for forfeiture or re-entry in connection with a condition usually indicates a condition subsequent; and on the other hand, in case of doubt, the absence of such a clause may be significant of an intention to create a covenant or a trust rather than a condition.

Where a grant or devise for a particular purpose is accompanied by a clear provision for forfeiture or reverter and discloses a clear intent that the use for the particular purpose is a condition of the continuation of the estate, a condition is created. However, generally a devise or conveyance of land for a stated purpose, without the use of language usually employed to create a fee on condition subsequent, and without a reverter clause or provision for re-entry, does not create a fee subject to a condition subsequent. In other words, such a condition is not raised by implication from a mere declaration that the grant is made for a special or particular purpose, without being coupled with words appropriate to create such a condition. Such recitals are usually construed as giving rise, at most, to an implied covenant that the grantee will use the property for the specified purpose only.

It is a general rule that a condition precedent must be literally performed, while substantial performance is sufficient with respect to a condition subsequent. If a condition precedent is or becomes impossible of performance, no estate vests, according to the weight of authority. With regard to a condition subsequent, however, it is a general principle that performance of the condition is excused where it is impossible to comply with it at the time of its creation or if it becomes so afterward without fault of the grantee or devisee. This results, in the latter instance, in a vesting of the estate freed of the condition.

A condition subsequent may be waived or released by the person entitled to enforce it, and a breach of the condition subsequent, together with the attendant right of re-entry for breach, may be waived by the creator of the estate or his successors in interest. The result in either case is to convert the estate into a fee simple absolute.

§ 18:14. Executory interests.

Am Jur 2d References: Estates, §§ 333–373.

Executory interests are estates created in third persons to arise upon the defeasance of prior estates in the same property. They are a class of future interests which may be created in some person other than the transferor; and, except for remainders, they are the only future interests which may be so created. Executory interests are distinguishable from remainders in that a remainder must be limited to take effect immediately upon the termination of a prior estate of freehold created at the same time and in the same instrument, it cannot take effect by way of cutting off a prior estate, and the prior estate must be less than a fee simple. These restrictions do not apply to executory interests, by which a freehold may be made to commence in futuro by an executory limitation; and such estates arise, when their time comes, of their own inherent strength, and do not depend for their existence or protection on any prior estate. It is a general rule of construction that a limitation which may operate as a valid remainder will not be construed as an executory limitation.

A conditional limitation partakes of the nature of a condition and of a limitation. It is like a condition because it defeats the estate previously limited, and it is a limitation because, on the happening of the contingency, the estate passes to the person having the next expectant interest, without entry or claim or other act by the person entitled to take thereunder. A conditional limitation limits an estate granted or devised upon a specified condition or contingency, and automatically vests such estate in another upon the same condition or contingency.

An executory interest is distinguishable from a determinable fee in that, in the latter, there is a possibility of reverter in the creator of the estate or his successors in interest, while in the case of an executory limitation, the succeeding interest must always go over to a third person and never goes to the grantor. An executory interest is distinguishable from an estate upon condition subsequent, in that the latter estate continues to exist, even after breach of the condition, until there is an affirmative act by the creator of the estate or his successors in interest which terminates the estate, as by re-entry, whereas an executory limitation or conditional limitation vests title automatically in a third person, not in the creator of the estate, upon the happening of the stated event terminating the preceding interest.

Under the rule generally prevailing in this country, executory estates and limitations, like other future interests, may be created not only by will but by a deed of bargain and sale or by covenant to stand seised to the use of the grantee.

An executory limitation or conditional limitation may be effective to accomplish some results which would be impossible in the case of a condition subsequent. For example, it is generally held that a conditional limitation or provision for cesser in a will or deed, to the effect that a sale of the property for the debts of the devisee or grantee, or an attempt by his creditors to subject the property to their claims, or the event of the bankruptcy or insolvency of the grantee or devisee, shall have the effect of immediately determining the estate of the devisee or grantee, and that the property shall thereupon go to another person, is valid. Another common contingency on which an estate in fee is to be defeasible and on which the estate is to go to another is the failure of issue of the first taker, and an executory limitation of this nature is valid where it contemplates the failure of issue during the life of the first taker, and not an indefinite failure of issue, which would offend the rule against perpetuities.

Executory interests are generally considered as actual estates, and as such to be assignable, devisable, and transmissible to the representatives of the devisee.

§ 18:15. Cotenancy: joint tenancy and tenancy in common.

Am Jur 2d References: Cotenancy and Joint Ownership, §§ 1–31, 90–103.

The term "cotenancy" refers to the ownership of property by two or more persons in such manner that they have an undivided possession or right to possession, but several freeholds, and the term includes joint tenancies, tenancies in common, and estates by the entireties. Also classifiable as a cotenancy is the common-law estate in coparcenary, which joint heirs formerly acquired; but such heirs generally hold as tenants in common under modern law.

In a true cotenancy the interest of each cotenant is coextensive with the common property and extends to every part thereof. The right of each cotenant to possession is the primary essential element of all cotenancies. Thus, where several persons own distinct parts of the same house, or where several persons purchase a tract of land but each takes a deed to a distinct part thereof, or where one person owns the land and another the timber thereon, such persons are not cotenants.

A joint tenancy is an estate held by two or more persons jointly, with equal rights to share in its enjoyment during their lives, and having as its distinguishing feature the right of survivorship, by virtue of which the entire estate, upon the death of a joint tenant, goes to the survivor or survivors. This right of survivorship distinguishes a joint tenancy from a tenancy in common. Because of the survivorship factor, a joint tenant cannot devise his interest in the land and his interest cannot descend to his heirs or be seized by his creditors after his death. The creation and existence of a joint tenancy depends upon the coexistence of four requisites: the tenants must have one and the same interest (unity of interest); the interests must accrue by one and the same conveyance (unity of title); they must commence at one and the same time (unity of time); and the property must be held by one and the same undivided possession (unity of possession). If any of these elements is lacking, the estate will not be a joint tenancy.

A distinguishing characteristic of the estate in joint tenancy, in either real or personal property, is that it arises only by way of grant or devise and never by way of descent or inheritance. The joint tenancy, with the entire property going to the survivor, is not favored in this country, and statutes have been enacted in most states limiting or circumscribing the creation of such estates.

Under modern law, a grant or devise of property to two or more persons will be construed to create estates in common, and not in joint tenancy, unless the instrument expressly declares the estates to be in joint tenancy or the instrument clearly discloses an intent to create a joint tenancy. In order to insure a construction of the instrument as creating a joint tenancy rather than a tenancy in common, no doubt should be left as to the intention of the creator of the estates. A grant or devise to two or more persons, "and the survivor of them, as joint tenants," would generally be adequate to accomplish this purpose; and the addition of the words "as joint tenants and not as tenants in common" would usually be conclusive.

Any act of a joint tenant which destroys one or more of its necessarily coexistent unities operates as a severance of the joint tenancy and extinguishes the right of survivorship. Thus, if one joint tenant severs his interest in the property by conveying the same to a third person, the joint tenancy is terminated if there are only two tenants or where all but one of several joint tenants convey their interests to a stranger. However, if there are three or more joint tenants, a conveyance by one to a stranger will sever the joint tenancy only as to the share conveyed, which will be held by the grantee as a tenancy in common. A severance usually results from a contract by one joint tenant to sell his interest to a stranger. A mere lease by one or more of the joint tenants does not have this effect, however. A joint tenancy may be terminated by contract or agreement of the joint tenants between themselves, or by a partition.

A tenancy in common is a tenancy whereby two or more persons are entitled to the land in such manner that they have an undivided possession, but several freeholds or interests. A tenancy in common, as distinguished from a joint tenancy, does not involve the right of survivorship. Unlike a joint tenancy, tenancy in common is characterized by a single essential unity—that of possession, or of the right to possession, of the common property. If such unity exists, there is a tenancy in common, irrespective of the concurrence of any other unities, and if it does not exist, the estate is not a tenancy in common. As noted above, any conveyance or devise of undivided interests to two or more persons will generally be treated as creating tenancies in common, rather than joint tenancies, unless an intention to the contrary is clearly evident.

A cotenant may deal with strangers as he pleases insofar as his own undivided interest is concerned. He can sell and convey, lease, or encumber it the same as any other property he may own. However, he cannot bind his cotenants by any unauthorized attempt to alienate or encumber the entire estate or any specific part or portion thereof, or an undivided interest in any such portion. Any such attempt by a cotenant affects only his own interest. An undivided interest under a tenancy in common, as distinguished from a joint tenancy, may be devised or bequeathed by the owner thereof.

§ 18:16. — Rights and duties as between cotenants.

Am Jur 2d References: Cotenancy and Joint Ownership, §§ 32–89.

As a general rule, any cotenant of real property has a right to enter upon the common estate and take possession of the whole thereof, subject only to use and occupancy of common premises or some part thereof is not liable to not interfere. Subject to the rights of his cotenants, a cotenant may use and enjoy the common estate as though he were the sole proprietor, and he may occupy and use every portion of the property at all times, although he has no right, without the consent of his co-owners, to exclude them from the common property or to appropriate to his sole use any particular portion thereof. In some states there is an apportionment of the time of occupancy among the several cotenants. The same general rules apply to mines and minerals. A tenant in common of a mine has a right to work it and does not become a trespasser in so doing. But this right is not exclusive, and the other co-owners have the right to enter upon the premises at any time and commence development on their own account. Similar rules apply to the exploitation of oil and gas property owned by several cotenants. While a co-owner of land has a right to cut and use timber from the common property in the usual and legitimate mode of enjoying his estate, many courts hold him liable for waste if he clears the woodland to an extent beyond his interests in the fee. It is the general rule now, contrary to the early common-law doctrine, that a cotenant may be liable to the other cotenants for waste.

A cotenant who receives rents under a letting of the common property is generally accountable to his cotenants for their shares of the rents. This rule does not apply, however, where the rents received from a third person are for the cotenant's undivided interest only in the common property.

The rule prevails in many jurisdictions that a cotenant who has enjoyed the use and occupancy of common premises or some part thereof is not liable to the other cotenants for rent and is not accountable to them for the reasonable value of his occupancy, where he has not ousted or excluded them and has not denied their equal rights. Some courts, however, take a different view, holding that the occupying cotenant must account to his fellows for the occupancy value. Regardless of the view taken on this question, however, the courts generally agree that a cotenant in occupancy of common premises who has ousted or excluded his cotenants therefrom is accountable to them in respect of the rental value of their interests for the period of exclusion. What amounts to an ouster or exclusion for this purpose depends upon the circumstances of the particular case.

Where there is no ouster or exclusion of other cotenants, a tenant in possession is not ordinarily accountable to his cotenants for profits derived from his own occupation of and labor on the common premises. However, a cotenant operating a mine and taking ore from the premises is generally held accountable to his cotenants for their share of the profits.

The burden of defraying necessary expenses incident to the common estate, such as repairs, taxes, etc., devolves equally upon all the cotenants in proportion to their respective interests. If one cotenant has paid a debt or obligation for the benefit of the common property, or has discharged a lien or assessment thereon, he is entitled to contribution or reimbursement from his cotenants for their proportionate shares of the amounts paid.

Because of the close and confidential relationship between cotenants, the courts agree that it would ordinarily be inequitable to permit one, without the consent of the others, to buy an outstanding adversary title or claim and assert it for his exclusive benefit; and the courts will usually regard the purchasing cotenant as holding the title or claim so acquired for the benefit of his cotenants upon contribution by them of their respective proportions of the necessary expenditure. Some courts, however, have imposed some limitations upon this rule. The general rule applies, however, to the purchase by one cotenant at a judicial or execution sale or at a tax sale.

§ 18:17. — Partition.

Am Jur 2d References: Partition, §§ 1–197.

Partition is the act or proceeding by which co-owners of property cause it to be either divided into as many shares as there are owners, according to their interests therein, or if that cannot be done equitably, to be sold and the proceeds distributed. Partition proceedings enable those who own property as joint tenants, coparceners, or tenants in common to put an end to the tenancy so as to vest in each a sole estate in specific property or an allotment of the property. They contemplate an absolute severance of the individual interests of each cotenant, and after partition each of them has the sole right to and enjoyment of the property allotted to him. A partition may be either compulsory, by judicial proceedings, or voluntary, by mutual consent of the cotenants.

As a general rule, only property held in joint tenancy, tenancy in common, or coparcenary may be the subject of a partition action. There can be no partition where different parts of the property are owned in severalty by different persons. It is a general rule that to enable a person to maintain proceedings for a partition he must have an estate in possession, one by which he is entitled to enjoy the present rents or the possession of the property as one of the cotenants thereof.

As equitable principles are applied in partition proceedings, where one cotenant has expended money in making permanent improvements on the common property, the court, in decreeing partition, will make a suitable allowance therefor. Where a partition in kind results in unequal proportions, the payment of a sum called "owelty" may be awarded to the cotenant receiving the lesser portion, so as to equalize the shares of the respective parties.

Where the common-law rule is still in effect, a true estate by the entireties may not be the subject of a judicial partition.

The procedure in partition cases varies in the several states, but it applies equitable principles. Commissioners are usually appointed by the court to examine the premises and all of the facts and make a report to the court of their preliminary partition of the property. The court may accept the report of the commissioners, or reject or modify it. And a court of equity may appoint a receiver in partition proceedings where the circumstances indicate the necessity thereof.

At common law cotenants were entitled to a partition in kind, regardless of the difficulty or inconvenience thereof. Under modern statutes, however, a person entitled to a partition may have the property sold and the proceeds apportioned to the cotenants where, because of the nature of the property, the interests of the cotenants, or other circumstances, the property cannot be equitably partitioned in kind without manifest prejudice to the parties. One test of such prejudice is whether the value of the share of each cotenant in case of partition would be materially less than his share of the money equivalent that could be obtained by a sale of the whole. Partition by sale is usually the proper method of partition of property in minerals, oil and gas, considered separately from the soil.

§ 18:18. Estate by the entireties.

Am Jur 2d References: Husband and Wife, §§ 55–76.

An estate by the entireties can be held only by husband and wife. It resembles a joint tenancy, in that there is a right of survivorship in both husband and wife. It is distinguishable from a joint tenancy, however, in that the latter may be vested in any number of natural persons, each of whom is seised of an undivided share of the whole, whereas a tenancy by entirety is vested in two persons only, who are regarded at law as only one and who are seised of the estate as a whole. Another distinguishing feature is that, without express statutory authorizations, tenants by the entireties cannot have their estate partitioned.

Estates by the entireties exist today in many American jurisdictions, other than community property states, despite the adoption of Married Women's Acts or Property Acts, which are construed as providing for separate estates of married women without abolishing estates by entireties. In some jurisdictions these statutes are construed to change some of the features of estates by the entireties. In some jurisdictions estates by the entireties, as such, do not exist.

As a general rule, in jurisdictions that recognize estates by the entireties, such an estate will arise from a conveyance or devise to husband and wife, even where the deed or will does not express how they are to take. The grantor or testator is presumed to intend to create such an estate in the absence of an expression of a contrary intention. An estate by the entireties involves the unities of time, title, interest, and possession characteristic of all joint tenancies, as well as the husband and wife unity of ownership.

An estate by the entireties continues only during coverture, and may be terminated by a conveyance thereof by the spouses to third persons. Upon the death of a spouse, the whole of an estate by the entireties remains in the surviving spouse, not because he or she is vested with any new or increased interest therein, but because each took the entirety to remain to the survivor.

§ 18:19. Dower and curtesy.

Am Jur 2d References: Dower and Curtesy, §§ 1–111, 171–193.

Dower is the legal right or interest the wife acquires by marriage in the estate of her husband. At common law it consists in the use, during her natural life after the death of her husband, of one-third of all the real estate of which the husband was seised, at any time during the marriage, by a title such as might pass by inheritance to the children of the marriage. During the lifetime of the husband, the wife's right or interest is called an "inchoate right of dower." If the husband dies leaving her surviving, her right of dower becomes consummate. The wife's common-law dower is limited to the specific one-third of the deceased husband's lands set off or assigned to her after the husband's death. Upon the death of the widow her dower right terminates and disappears in the fee.

The husband's common-law interest in his wife's land, corresponding to her dower right, is the estate by the curtesy. This estate gave the husband a life estate in the real property of which his wife is seised of an estate of inheritance during the marriage. In addition to the conditions prerequisite to the wife's dower rights, it is necessary to the common-law estate by the curtesy that there be birth of issue alive and capable of inheriting. If such issue is born alive, it is not essential to the creation of the husband's curtesy that the issue survive. At common law, the husband had what was called curtesy initiate during the lifetime of the wife, and it became curtesy consummate upon the wife's death during his lifetime. During the marriage the husband was entitled to the rents and profits of the wife's lands. Upon her death he was entitled to a life estate in all of such lands.

Both dower and curtesy, as they existed at common law, have been modified by statute in all jurisdictions. In many states dower and curtesy have been replaced by the right to inherit a specified share of the spouse's estate upon his or her death. Some statutes give the surviving spouse a life estate in one-third of the lands of the deceased spouse. The right of curtesy initiate, i.e., the husband's right to the use and profits of the wife's lands during her lifetime, has been generally abolished by statute. In some states, but not in all, the birth of living issue has been dispensed with as a prerequisite of the creation of the estate by the curtesy.

The widow's right of "quarantine" is closely related to her dower rights. At common law, she is entitled to have her dower assigned within 40 days from the death of her husband. During that 40-day period she is entitled to remain in and use the mansion house of the husband. This is the right of quarantine. The right has been modified by statute in many jurisdictions, and in some states the surviving husband is given a similar right.

§18:20. — Bar or release of dower or curtesy.

Am Jur 2d References: Dower and Curtesy, §§ 112–170.

A spouse cannot be deprived of dower or curtesy rights except by voluntary consent, by his or her own act, or by statute. There is a wide variety of statutes relating to the barring, forfeiture, or otherwise limiting of dower and curtesy.

It may be stated generally that a wife's dower cannot be defeated or impaired by any act of the husband or by any title emanating from him. Although he can convey the property to which dower has attached, the conveyance is subject to the encumbrance of the dower unless the wife joins therein. The same is generally true of the husband's curtesy, although some statutes modify this rule. And a different rule applies where, by statute, dower or curtesy exists only in land owned by the husband or wife at the time of his or her death.

In the absence of a statute to the contrary, a husband or wife cannot dispose of his or her property by will so as to deprive the other spouse of dower or curtesy. However, in many jurisdictions a testator may, by appropriate language in testamentary provisions for a surviving spouse, put the survivor to an election between such provisions and the right to dower or curtesy. The general rule, except where altered by statute, is that a testamentary provision for a widow of the testator is presumed to be in addition to dower, and not in lieu thereof, and that she may take both unless an intention to exclude her from dower appears clearly from the terms of the will. Under some statutes, however, the acceptance by the widow of the provision made for her in her husband's will bars her claim of dower unless it plainly appears from the will to have been the intention of the testator that she should have both. A widow or widower is put to an election where the provisions of the will for his or her benefit and a claim of curtesy or dower are so inconsistent that to enforce one would destroy the other.

In some states a jointure is a bar to dower. The term "jointure" means the settlement on the wife before marriage of a competent livelihood by way of a freehold in the husband's property, to take effect in possession upon his death and to continue at least for the life of the wife. Such a settlement must be made in satisfaction of the dower and this must appear in the deed. Dower and curtesy may be released also by due execution of a formal release as a part of the spouse's deed of conveyance or encumbrance, or by a joint conveyance of husband and wife, duly executed and acknowledged. In some states a wife's dower is released if she joins in and acknowledges a conveyance by her husband, while under statutes in other states, to have this effect the deed must contain apt words releasing the wife's dower interest.

In most jurisdictions a wife's dower rights may be barred by a fair and just antenuptial agreement releasing the right of dower in consideration of marriage or supported by other valuable consideration; but in some states a release of dower by the wife to the husband before coverture is void. At common law a husband could waive or forfeit his right of curtesy by antenuptial agreement in consideration of marriage. Any antenuptial contract barring the wife's dower will be carefully scrutinized by the courts to see that the agreement was freely and voluntarily entered into by the wife with full knowledge of her rights.

At common law husband and wife were incompetent to contract with each other because the law regarded them as a unity. Hence, any postnuptial agreement between husband and wife purporting to release dower or curtesy was void. Although this is still the rule in some jurisdictions, statutes in many states recognize the validity of a fair and equitable postnuptial agreement between husband and wife releasing dower or curtesy.

Some types of grave marital misconduct had the effect of barring dower at common law. Thus, adultery and abandonment by the wife terminated her dower rights. This rule still applies in some states, but not in others. Many states (but not all) have statutes which bar dower and curtesy where the surviving spouse feloniously kills his or her spouse.

The general rule as to both dower and curtesy is that in the absence of statute to the contrary, an annulment of marriage or an absolute divorce terminates and bars both rights and is a defense to any claim by the surviving spouse for dower or curtesy. This rule does not apply, however, to a mere judicial separation or divorce a mensa et thoro. And even in the case of an absolute divorce, some authorities hold that a wife's inchoate right of dower or a husband's curtesy initiate, which is already vested, is not affected by the divorce. In some states dower or curtesy is forfeited by the guilty spouse but not by the other.

The remarriage of a widow does not bar or forfeit her dower rights.

§ 18:21. Power of appointment.

Am Jur 2d References: Powers of Appointment, etc., §§ 1–23, 104–116.

A power of appointment is authority vested in a person to transfer property to someone selected or appointed by him. The Restatement (Property, § 318) defines a power of appointment as a power created or reserved by a person having property subject to his disposition, enabling the donee of the power to designate, within such limits as the donor may prescribe, the transferees of the property or the shares in which it shall be received. A typical example of a power of appointment is created by a conveyance or devise of land to a donee for life, with power to designate the person to whom the remainder shall go upon the donee's death. Both real and personal property may be the subjects of a power of appointment. A power of appointment does not vest in the donee of the power any title or estate on the property, but is only a personal privilege. A power of appointment may be created by any instrument sufficient to transfer an interest in land, such as a will, deed, or contract. An instrument creating a power of appointment is to be interpreted so as to give effect to the intention of the donor.

A power of appointment may be either general or special or limited. A general power of appointment is one authorizing the donee of the power to appoint anyone, including himself or his estate. Special or limited powers of appointment are those in which the donee of the power is restricted to passing the property on to certain specified individuals, or to a specified class of individuals, or to any beneficiaries except those specifically excluded, or in which the donee can exercise a power only for certain named purposes or under certain conditions.

One to whom property is appointed in the exercise of a power has the right to renounce the appointment. The renunciation must be of the whole appointed property, however; and an appointee cannot renounce the appointment as to part of the property and claim the other part directly under the donor's will.

As a power of appointment does not give the donee of the power any title or estate in the property, it would seem to follow that the property is not liable for the debts of the donee; and this is the general rule applicable to an unexercised general power of appointment. However, where the power has been exercised by the donee by appointing the property to volunteers or to particular creditors, the numerical weight of authority holds that the property constitutes in equity assets of the donee's estate for the payment of his creditors. The reasoning for this view is that where the power is general, so that the donee may appoint whomever he chooses, it is his duty to appoint his creditors.

§ 18:22. — Exercise of the power.

Am Jur 2d References: Powers of Appointment, etc., §§ 24–103.

In exercising a power of appointment, the donee is confined to the mode of execution provided for or designated by the donor of the power. Thus, a power to appoint by will cannot be exercised by a deed or other nontestamentary instrument; and the power to appoint by deed cannot be exercised through any other type of instrument. Where a general power to dispose of property is given without specifying the manner of execution, the power may be executed either by deed or by will.

In the absence of a statute providing otherwise, it is the general rule that if the donee of a power executes an instrument not expressly referring to the power, such instrument or provision by itself does not constitute an exercise of the donee's power. According to this rule, a general devise of the donee's property or a general residuary clause not expressly referring to a power of appointment will not be deemed an execution of the power. This, however, is a mere rule of construction rather than a rule of law, and it may be overcome by evidence of surrounding circumstances. The question whether an instrument is an execution of the power depends ultimately upon the intent of the donee. Statutes have been enacted in a number of jurisdictions creating a presumption in favor of the exercise of a power of appointment, generally providing that a general devise of property described in a general manner will operate as an execution of a general power to appoint, unless a contrary intention appears in the will.

A general power of appointment, by definition, authorizes the donee to appoint anyone, including himself. In the case of a special or limited power, the appointment must be to a person or class designated by the donor of the power.

The question of what estates or interests may be created under the power of appointment must depend upon the terms of the power and the intention disclosed thereby. A general power of appointment enables the donee to appoint a fee, unless a contrary intention appears. But under a power to appoint a fee, lesser estates or interests may be created, if such are within the apparent intent of the donor. The question whether a power of appointment may be exercised in part, with respect either to the entire property involved or the estate or interests therein, depends upon the true construction of the instrument creating the power.

Upon the exercise of a power of appointment, the appointee takes from the donor, since the donee, in exercising the power, is disposing of the donor's property.

An attempted execution of a power of appointment will usually be given effect as to the valid parts, although some provisions or parts thereof are invalid. Where an attempted appointment under a general power fails completely, or where the power is not exercised at all, the power becomes inoperative and the property which was the subject thereof devolves as the estate of the donor, unless the latter has made a gift in default of appointment.

§ 18:23. Easements.

Am Jur 2d References: Easements, §§ 1–16, 64–114.

An easement may be defined as a right which one person has to use the land of another for a specified purpose not inconsistent with the general property of the owner; it is in the nature of a servitude imposed upon land; it is a liberty, privilege, or advantage in land, existing distinct from the ownership of the soil. An easement has also been defined as a privilege which the owner of one tenement has to enjoy another tenement; a privilege without profit, which the owner of one tenement has to enjoy in respect of that tenement, in or over the tenement of another person, by reason of which the latter is obliged to suffer or refrain from doing something on his tenement for the advantage of the former; it is a charge or burden on one estate, the servient, for the benefit of another, the dominant. However, these latter definitions are applicable only to easements appurtenant and not to easements in gross, discussed below. An easement is not land or an estate in land, but it is property and an interest in land; it is an incorporeal hereditament.

Easements are generally divided into two broad classes, easements appurtenant and easements in gross. On other bases of classification, easements are said to be affirmative or negative, apparent or nonapparent, and continuous or noncontinuous.

An appurtenant easement is an incorporeal right which is attached to, and belongs with, some greater or superior right; something annexed to another thing more worthy and which passes as an incident to it. It inheres in the land, and pertains to its enjoyment. It is incapable of existence separate and apart from the particular land to which it is annexed. Two distinct tenements are involved in the case of an easement appurtenant—the dominant, to which the right belongs, and the servient, upon which the obligation rests.

An easement in gross is a mere personal interest or right to use the land of another. It is not supported by or attached to a dominant estate, but is vested in the person to whom it is granted. It is a right in favor of a person and not for the benefit of another tract of land. Although doubt has been expressed as to whether there is such a thing as an easement in gross, the courts generally recognize their existence and validity. Whether an easement in a given case is appurtenant or in gross depends mainly on the nature of the right and the intention of the parties creating it. If the easement is in its nature an appropriate and useful adjunct of the land conveyed, having in view the intention of the parties as to its use, and there is nothing to show that the parties intended it to be a mere personal right, it is an easement appurtenant and not an easement in gross. Easements in gross are not favored by the courts, and an easement will never be treated as personal when it may fairly be construed as appurtenant to some other estate.

It is frequently stated that an easement in gross, as a right personal to the one to whom it is granted, cannot be assigned or otherwise transmitted by him to another. However, there is authority to the contrary; and the question of assignability is frequently held to depend upon the terms of the instrument creating the easement and the intention of the parties as evidenced thereby.

An appurtenant easement cannot be separated from, or transferred independently of, the land to which it is appurtenant. Unless expressly excepted, a transfer of real property passes all easements appurtenant thereto although not referred to in the instrument of transfer and even without the use of the usual term "appurtenances." As a general rule, if the dominant tenement is transferred in separate parcels to different persons, each grantee acquires a right to use the easements, provided the easements can be enjoyed as to the separate parcels without an additional burden on the servient estate.

A purchaser of land with knowledge or with actual or constructive notice that it is burdened with an easement ordinarily takes the estate subject to the easement.

If the instrument creating an easement does not definitely fix its location, or, in the case of an implied way, such as a way of necessity, a reasonable and convenient way for all parties is implied. However, the way must have a particular definite line, and the grantee does not have the right to go at random over any and all parts of the servient estate. Moreover, as a general rule, a person having a way of necessity across the land of another is entitled to only one route, and the way must be the shortest reasonably convenient passage to the nearest public highway. If there is an existing visible way across land at the time of the creation of an easement of way, this way will be held to be the location of the way newly acquired, unless it is not a reasonable and convenient way for both parties. Where the parties are unable to agree on the location of a way, the court will fix its location upon equitable principles.

The use and enjoyment of an easement must be reasonable in manner and extent and must be related to the purpose for which the easement was created. In the case of an easement of way, "reasonable use" includes not only the use required at the time of the creation of the easement, but also the right to use the way for any purposes connected with the use to which the dominant tenement may naturally and reasonably be devoted. Where the width of the way is not specified in the grant or reservation, the right of way will be of such width as is reasonably convenient and necessary for the purposes for which the way was created. In the case of a prescriptive easement, its character and extent are fixed and determined by the user under which it was acquired, and no different or greater use can be made of the easement.

The owner of an easement has the right to keep it in repair and to enter upon the servient estate at all reasonable times and in a reasonable manner for the purpose of necessary repairs and maintenance; but he is under no duty to maintain or repair the easement. In maintaining an easement of way for proper use, the easement owner may grade and pave the same. The essential character of the easement cannot be changed, however, so as to impose an additional servitude.

The owner of the servient estate may use his property in any manner which does not interfere with the reasonable use of the easement. Where the grant of an easement of way is not by terms exclusive, the servient owner has the right of user in common with the owner of the easement, if it can be reasonably enjoyed by both. The servient owner may not, however, obstruct or in any way interfere with the proper enjoyment of an easement.

An easement may be terminated by unequivocal acts inconsistent with further assertion of rights thereunder and clearly indicating an abandonment of the easement. The acts relied on to constitute the abandonment, however, must be of a character so decisive and conclusive as to indicate a clear intention to abandon the easement. Generally, an easement acquired by grant or reservation is not lost by mere nonuser for any length of time, unless the nonuser is accompanied by an express or implied intention to abandon. An easement may also terminate through merger of titles, where title to both the dominant and servient estates becomes vested in the same person.

§ 18:24. — Manner of creating easements.

Am Jur 2d References: Easements and Licenses, §§ 17–63.

Since an easement is an interest in land, it may be created only by grant, will, or contract, express or implied, or by prescription, and it cannot be created by parol. An easement appurtenant to the grantor's remaining land may be created by a reservation in a conveyance by him.

An easement may be created by implication in favor of either a grantor or a grantee, although implied easements are not favored by the law. For example, it is generally held that where a street or other way is called for as a boundary in a conveyance of land, and the grantor owns the fee in the land represented as the way or street, he is estopped, as against the grantee, to deny that the street or other way exists, and an easement in such way passes to the grantee by implication of law. Similarly, where property sold is described in the conveyance with reference to a plat or map on which streets, alleys, parks, or the like, are shown, an easement therein is created in favor of the grantee. Also, where, during the unity of title, an apparently permanent and obvious servitude is imposed on one part of an estate in favor of another part, which servitude is in use at the time of severance and is necessary for the reasonable enjoyment of the other part, a grant of the right to continue such use arises by implication of law upon a severance of the ownership. This rule is based on the presumed intention of the parties to the conveyance and on the assumption that the parties contracted with a view to the condition of the property as it actually was at the time of the transaction.

A way of necessity is an easement founded on an implied grant or implied reservation. It arises when there is a conveyance of a part of a tract of land of such nature and extent that either the part conveyed or the part retained is shut off from access to a road to the outer world by the land from which it is severed or by this land and the land of strangers. In such a situation there is an implied grant of a way across the grantor's remaining land to the part conveyed, or conversely, an implied reservation of a way to the grantor's remaining land across the portion of the land conveyed. A way of necessity is based on the presumption that whenever a person conveys property he conveys whatever is necessary for the beneficial use and enjoyment of that property and retains whatever is necessary for the beneficial use of the land he still possesses. A way of necessity is dependent on unity of ownership of the dominant and servient estates, followed by a severance thereof, and it obviously cannot exist over the land of a third person.

An easement may be created by prescription. By adverse user under the required conditions and for the required period of time, a person may acquire by prescription a right of way over another's land, a right to the flowage of water and the disposal of waste in pipes or drains through, or the right to cast waters upon, another's land, the right to dam or obstruct the water of a stream so as to flood the land of another, and other types of easement. It is generally held to be essential to the acquisition of an easement by prescription that there be a continuous and uninterrupted, open and notorious, use of a definite right in the land of another which is identical to that claimed as an easement and which has a relation to the use of, and a direct and apparent connection with, the dominant tenement, under an adverse user and claim of right for the required prescriptive period. The further condition that the user must be exclusive is sometimes added in stating the essentials of prescription. There is a conflict of authority on the question whether the adverse user must be under color of title. Under the early common law, when prescription was based on the fiction of a "lost grant," the prescriptive period was held to begin at a period "beyond the time whereof the memory of man runneth not to the contrary." Now, however, the period necessary to acquire an easement by prescription corresponds by analogy to that required for the acquisition of title to land by adverse possession.

§ 18:25. Licenses.

Am Jur 2d References: Easements and Licenses, §§ 123–133.

As the term is used with reference to real property, a license is defined as a personal, revocable, and unassignable privilege, conferred either by writing or parol, to do certain acts on land without possessing any interest therein. It is not essential that a license be based on a consideration. A license confers authority to do certain acts which would be unlawful without the license. Being a mere personal privilege, a license is not generally assignable or inheritable.

Unless the time or duration of the license is fixed by agreement, it continues for a reasonable time, or in the absence of revocation, for the time necessary to accomplish the specific purpose for which the privilege was granted. Generally, a mere license is revocable at any time at the pleasure of the licensor.

This rule, however, is subject to exception under some circumstances. For example, the right to revoke a license is ordinarily denied where the license is coupled with a grant or interest. It is frequently held also that a license is irrevocable where it has become executed, or where a licensee has expended money or labor in the execution of the license. And some courts have held that the payment of a valuable consideration for a license may prevent its revocation.

§ 18:26. Profit a prendre.

Am Jur 2d References: Easements and Licenses, § 4.

A profit a prendre (sometimes called "right of common") is a right exercised by one person in the soil of another, accompanied with participation in the profits of the soil, or a right to take a part of the soil or produce of the land. It is distinguishable from an easement because of its feature of sharing in the profits; but it is similar to an easement in that it is an interest in the land which cannot be created by parol, and which may be either appurtenant to other land or in gross. If it belongs to an individual distinct from any ownership of other lands, it has the character of an estate in the land itself and is assignable and inheritable. Examples of rights of profit a prendre are the right to take timber, gravel, coal, minerals, firewood, or ice from the land of another. The right to fish or hunt on the land of another is also a profit a prendre. As flowing water is not considered a product of the soil, a right to take such water is not a right of profit a prendre, but rather is an easement.

§ 18:27. Covenants relating to use and enjoyment of land.

Am Jur 2d References: Covenants, Conditions, and Restrictions, §§ 29–42, 165–332.

Covenants relating to real property are divisible into two broad classes: (1) Real covenants which run with the land, binding not only the covenantor and his heirs and personal representatives, but also his assigns, and (2) personal covenants which pass no such rights to the vendee or assignee of the property sold, and bind only the covenantor personally, or, in certain cases, those who take lands which are subject to restrictive covenants, with notice thereof. The primary test for determining whether a covenant runs with the land or is merely personal in whether it concerns the thing granted and the occupation or enjoyment thereof, or is a collateral or personal covenant not immediately concerning the thing granted. In order that a covenant may run with the land, it must have relation to the land or the interest or estate conveyed, and the thing required to be done must be something which touches such land, interest, or estate and the occupation, use, or enjoyment thereof. There must also be privity of estate between the parties to the covenant, and the covenant must be consistent with the estate to which it adheres and of such character that the estate will not be defeated or changed by the performance thereof. A covenant does not run with the land unless it is contained in a grant thereof or of some estate therein.

Examples of covenants that run with the land are covenants by the grantor to furnish water, gas, electricity, or other power for the benefit of the land conveyed; a covenant by a grantor to provide and dedicate a street adjoining the land conveyed; a covenant by a grantee restricting the kinds of structures to be erected on the land conveyed or the uses to be made thereof; and covenants for the making of improvements on the land conveyed or the payment of taxes or assessments thereon. Party wall agreements are frequently held to constitute covenants running with the land, as are covenants to build or maintain a fence between the lands of the parties. Covenants pertaining to waters and ditches generally run with the land.

Restrictive covenants relating to the use of land or the location or character of structures thereon are frequently characterized as easements or servitudes; and when negative in character, as most of them are, such covenants are said to create equitable easements or servitudes, or as sometimes stated, negative easements or reciprocal negative easements. Such covenants are generally viewed as creating property rights, although there is some authority to the contrary.

In the absence of a permanent building scheme or general plan of development and improvement of a tract, the mere fact that a grantor imposes restrictions on part of a tract which he sells does not obligate him to restrict the remainder of the property; nor does it create implied restrictions upon the remaining lots in the tract. And a conveyance of lots by reference to a recorded map or plat does not in itself raise an implied covenant that the lots shall remain as shown on the map or plat, or that they may not later be changed in size or further subdivided.

Building restrictions and other restrictions on the use of land are frequently imposed by the establishment of a general building plan or scheme of improvement or development covering a tract divided into a number of lots. Such a plan may be established in various ways, such as by express covenant, by implication from a filed map or plat, or by representations made in brochures, maps, advertising, and the like, on which the purchaser relied in making his purchase. The clearest way in which such a scheme may be established is by a reciprocal covenant in a deed whereby the grantor covenants to insert like covenants in all deeds out of the common development.

Where such a general plan or scheme is established for the benefit of purchasers of lots in a tract, the parts of the tract remaining in the hands of the vendor or subsequently sold are subject to the restrictive covenants. All purchasers of lots within the subdivision are bound by the covenants contemplated by the general plan of development; and the omission of the covenant from a particular conveyance does not prevent the enforcement of the restriction against the grantee of such lot or his successor in title, if either took with notice of the restriction or with knowledge of the general plan.

Covenants restricting the use of property are not, per se, violative of the public good or public policy. The courts will enforce such restrictions where reasonable, not contrary to public policy or to law, and not in restraint of trade or tending to create a monopoly. The courts recognize the validity of restrictions limiting buildings to residences, and restrictions as to their minimum cost; restrictions as to the character or location of buildings or structures to be erected on land; and front line and side line restrictions. While a contrary rule was formerly followed by the courts, it is now established that judicial enforcement of covenants in deeds or real-estate contracts, forbidding the sale or transfer of the property to, or occupancy thereof by, persons of a certain race or religious faith, constitutes state action in violation of the equal protection provision of the Fourteenth Amendment to the Federal Constitution.

The construction of covenants imposing restrictions on the use of land is generally subject to the rules applicable to any contract or covenant, including the rule that the intention of the parties as shown by the instrument containing the covenant, in the light of the surrounding circumstances in case of ambiguity, will govern. Such covenants are strictly construed against any limitation upon the use of property, and doubts will be resolved in favor of unrestricted use.

Where the duration of a restrictive covenant is not specified, the rule followed generally is that the covenant will be limited to such time as seems reasonable from the nature of the case. A change in the character of the neighborhood which was intended to be created by restrictions will generally prevent their enforcement in equity, where the change is such that it is no longer possible to accomplish the original purpose intended by the restriction, or where enforcement would be inequitable, unreasonable, or oppressive, or would impose hardship rather than a benefit upon those who were parties to the restrictions. For example, where a tract of land developed as a residential area has so changed in character, owing to the general growth of a municipality, that the original purpose can no longer be accomplished, equity will not enforce the restrictions. To warrant the application of this principle, however, the change of conditions must be so great or so fundamental as to defeat the purpose of the covenant or to destroy the usefulness or benefit thereof.

A restrictive covenant is generally enforceable by the parties thereto. The right of a person not a party to the covenant to enforce it depends upon the intention of the parties in imposing it. A covenant imposed for the benefit of land retained by the grantor is generally enforceable by any person who obtains title of such land. Where a restriction is imposed in accordance with or as a part of a general plan or scheme for the development of a tract of land, any grantee of land within such tract may enforce the restriction against any other grantee.

III. PERPETUITIES AND RESTRAINTS ON ALIENATION

§ 18:28. Rule against perpetuities.

Am Jur 2d References: Perpetuities and Restraints on Alienation, §§ 1–92.

The rule against perpetuities prohibits the creation of future interests or estates which by a possibility may not become vested within a life or lives in being at the time of the testator's death or the effective date of the instrument creating the future interest, and 21 years thereafter, together with the gestation period when the inclusion of the latter is necessary to cover cases of posthumous birth. The rule against perpetuities allows the postponement of the vesting of an estate or interest for the period of lives in being and 21 years and the period of gestation, and no longer. Any limitation of a future interest which violates this rule is void. The rule applies to attempts to create by limitation any future estate, whether executory or by way of remainder, where such estate does not become vested within the prescribed period. The rule is based on considerations of policy and is intended to promote the free alienability and transferability of property. It is designed to prevent impediments to the marketability of property over long periods of time. The common-law rule against perpetuities has been modified or restated by statutes in some states.

While the rule against perpetuities is not a rule of construction but a positive mandate of law applicable irrespective of the question of intention, a document will be interpreted if feasible to avoid the conclusion that it violates the rule.

Where the vesting of an estate is not limited upon the life of any person, the period cannot be longer than 21 years, continued from the time of the creation of the future interest or estate. "Lives in being," within the meaning of the rule against perpetuities, has reference to those living at the date of the testator's death, and not at the time of the execution of the will. It is not necessary that the persons whose lives are selected be expressly designated by name, it being sufficient if a plain implication arises that a certain class or number of lives are selected for a limitation of the gift or trust. Furthermore, the lives selected need not be of persons taking any share or interest in the estate, and they need not be holders of previous estates nor connected in any way with the property or the persons designated to take it. And under the common-law rule against perpetuities, there is generally no restriction on the number of lives in being which may be selected as the measure of the period of time permitted by the rule.

The addition of the usual gestation period to the time allowed for the vesting of an estate under the rule against perpetuities is based on the theory that a child in ventre sa mere at the time of the creation of the estate and who is subsequently born alive is to be regarded as having been alive at the time of the creation of the estate, and hence the child is a "life in being" for the purposes of the rule.

Under the "certainty-of-vesting" principle, a limitation of a future interest must necessarily vest within the period of the rule, and if at the effective date of the instrument creating the future estate there is a possibility that the interest will not vest within the period of the rule against perpetuities, the interest is void. A mere possibility or even probability that the interest or estate may vest within the required time is not enough; it must appear that at the time the future interest is created the condition precedent to vesting must necessarily happen, if it happens at all, within the period prescribed by the rule against perpetuities. And under the prevailing view, the rule against perpetuities is not to be tested by actualities, but by possibilities; so that the fact that the event actually does happen within the period does not render the limitation valid where the possibility existed of its happening beyond the limits of the rule. Some states, by statutes or otherwise, have adopted a rule modifying the traditional "certainty-of-vesting" requirements by substituting a so-called "wait and see" or "second look" doctrine, under which the interest is held to be valid if the contingency upon which it is limited actually occurs within the period of the rule against perpetuities.

Since a vested interest does not necessarily include a right to immediate possession or enjoyment, the rule against perpetuities is not concerned with the postponement of the enjoyment of the estate. An estate which is vested is not affected by the rule, however remote may be the time when it may come into possession or enjoyment.

By definition, the rule against perpetuities is concerned only with the postponement of the vesting of estates. The rule applies only to future contingent estates and is inapplicable to estates already vested. Hence, the rule does not affect vested remainders or reversions.

The rule against perpetuities applies to powers of appointment and to options to purchase property. It applies equally in the same manner to equitable as to legal estates.

Where the limitation over is to a class the number of members of which is undeterminable at the time the interest is created, it is the general rule that the class must be such that all the members of it must necessarily be ascertained and take absolutely vested interests within the period permissible under the rule against perpetuities. If, because the class is subject to be open to let in afterborn members or members afterward fulfilling a condition, full vesting may, by possibility, be delayed until a time beyond the period of the perpetuities rule, the gift will be void as to all members of the class, including those in being at the time of the gift.

§ 18:29. Restraints on alienation.

Am Jur 2d References: Perpetuities and Restraints on Alienation, §§ 93–119.

One of the incidents of the ownership of property is the right to transfer it. And any general restraint on alienation, whether imposed by deed or will, is ordinarily void. The rule against restraints on alienation is to be distinguished from the rule against the suspension of the power of alienation or the rule against perpetuities, the latter relating only to the remoteness of the vesting of the estate, while the restraints on alienation relate to unreasonable restraints after the vesting of the estate.

The rule prohibiting restraints on alienation applies to involuntary as well as voluntary alienation. Hence, a provision that property conveyed or devised shall be not be subject to the debts of the grantee or devisee violates the general rule and is invalid. This rule does not apply, however, to the so-called "spendthrift trust."

It is generally held that a conditional limitation or provision for cesser in a deed or will may prevent subjection of the property conveyed or devised to the debts of the grantee or devisee. Thus, a provision that a sale of the property for the debts of the devisee or grantee, or an attempt by creditors to subject the property to payment of their claims, shall have the effect of immediately terminating the estate of the devisee or grantee and of passing the property to another person, will be upheld. This principle applies to a devise of a life interest on condition that it shall cease upon the recovery of judgment subjecting the property to the claim of a creditor or upon the occurrence of bankruptcy or insolvency of the grantee or devisee. In order for this rule to be applicable, however, the occurrence of the condition limiting the estate must have the effect of automatically vesting the estate in another person.

As a general rule, an adjudication of the invalidity of a restraint on alienation does not affect the validity of the estate conveyed or devised, but merely nullifies the condition or limitation attempted to be imposed.

Some courts take the view that a partial restraint on alienation is valid if it is reasonable. Thus, although most courts hold that a restraint on alienation is void as being repugnant to the nature of an estate in fee, even though the restraint is limited as to time, however short the period, the rule prevailing in some jurisdictions permits restraints from aliening for a reasonable time. And, although the majority view is to the contrary, some courts sustain the validity of provisions limiting the class of persons to whom the property may be aliened or prohibiting its alienation to certain persons or classes of persons.

The general rule against restraints on alienation applies to all estates in fee. The courts are more inclined, however, to permit reasonable restraints where a life estate is involved, especially in the case of equitable life estates. And the owner of real property may restrict the alienation thereof in a lease for a term of years.

IV. LANDLORD AND TENANT

§ 18:30. Nature and creation of the relation.

Am Jur 2d References: Landlord and Tenant, §§ 6–8, 11–190.

The relationship of landlord and tenant is always based upon contract, express or implied; and their reciprocal rights and duties are determined by such contract, which is usually in the form of a lease. The tenant has possession and use of the premises during the term of the lease, and he has to that extent an interest in the land. However, a leasehold for a term of years is usually deemed to be personal property of the tenant, a chattel real, regardless of the duration of the tenancy.

As in the case of contracts and conveyances generally, the cardinal principle followed in the construction of leases is to give effect to the intention of the parties as manifested by the words used in the instrument. Where the lease is ambiguous, extrinsic evidence may be considered in determining such intention.

Whether an occupant or user of real property is a tenant or a licensee depends upon the intent of the parties, which is sometimes difficult to determine, although the distinction involves important consequences. A licensee, as distinguished from a tenant, has a mere revocable and nonassignable privilege to do some act on the land, and he does not have any estate in the land itself nor any right of possession. Guests, such as occupants of rooms in a hotel, boarders in a boardinghouse, or roomers or lodgers in a rooming or lodging house, are usually held to be mere licensees and not tenants, and they generally have no interest in the realty.

Leases are generally governed by the same principles as apply to other contracts. Executory provisions therein must be supported by a good consideration; the lease must comply with the statute of frauds or other statute requiring a writing signed by the lessor where the term of the lease exceeds a certain period; and some statutes require that the lease be acknowledged.

The leased premises must be described with sufficient certainty to identify them; there must be a delivery and an acceptance of the lease; and fraud or mutual mistake, or the illegality of the purpose for which the lease is made, may invalidate the instrument.

An entry and occupation and payment of rent under an invalid or unenforceable lease, such as one invalid under the statute of frauds, may result in a legal relation of landlord and tenant. The tenancy in such case is not created by the invalid lease, but is implied by the law. Whether such a tenancy is one at will, from year to year, or from month to month, depends upon the circumstances of the case, including the periods for which rent is paid, and upon the statutes of the particular jurisdiction.

In the absence of a statute limiting the duration of leases, a leasehold estate may be created for any period of time, no matter how long or how short. In the case of a lease for a term of years, the term must be certain as to both the commencement and the duration of the time. Upon the expiration of the term of such a lease, the lease terminates of its own force and the landlord is then entitled to possession without giving notice. In the case of a periodic tenancy, such as one from year to year or from month to month, however, notice of termination is frequently required.

A tenancy at will simply confers a right to possession of the premises for such indefinite period as both parties shall determine. Such a tenancy may be created either by lease or by implication of law. A tenancy at will is ordinarily terminable at any time by either party by giving notice to the other party.

A tenancy at sufferance arises where a person who came rightfully into possession continues possession after his right thereto has terminated. Such tenancies arise where a tenant for a term of years holds over after the expiration of the time or where a person holding under a lease from a life tenant continues in possession after the termination of the life estate. The landlord can terminate such a tenancy whenever he wishes.

A landlord may convey or transfer his reversion, and upon such a transfer the transferee is substituted for the original landlord as regards both the rights and duties under the lease, without the necessity of an attornment as required under the early common law.

It is a well-settled general rule that during the existence of the relation of landlord and tenant the tenant is estopped to deny his landlord's title. The tenant may not assert that a better title than the landlord's is outstanding in some third person or in himself. Some authorities hold that a tenant cannot, during the term of the leasehold, acquire a title which is adverse to his landlord's title, but other courts hold that the relation of landlord and tenant does not prevent the latter from acquiring a title to be asserted after the termination of the tenancy. The estoppel of the tenant generally extends only to a denial of the title which the landlord had at the time of the lease, and the tenant is not estopped from showing that the landlord's title has expired or has been transferred during the tenancy. It is generally held that a tenant may show that, subsequent to the lease, he has acquired his landlord's title by purchase at an execution or judicial sale.

Leases may contain provisions conferring on the lessee the option to purchase the demised premises. Such an option, where definite and certain and otherwise valid, is enforceable and is subject to the principles governing options generally, discussed in the topic Contracts.

§ 18:31. Use and enjoyment of leased premises.

Am Jur 2d References: Landlord and Tenant, §§ 191–390.

A tenant has the right to the use and occupancy of the premises described in the lease and of any personal property included therein, the rights and liabilities as regards personal property, where included in the lease, being governed by the general principles of bailments.

A lease includes all appurtenances that are essential or reasonably necessary to the full beneficial use and enjoyment of the property. Thus, if the use of a part of the building not included in a lease is necessary to the enjoyment of the part of the building demised, then the easement or privilege therein passes by implication to the tenant; and a right of way or means of ingress, egress, and access, including the right to use steps, halls, stairways, and elevators, will ordinarily be implied. The duty of the landlord to furnish water, lights, heat, gas, etc., depends upon the terms of the lease.

During the term of a lease, the tenant is the owner of the demised premises for all practical purposes, and the landlord's rights are confined to his reversionary interest. In the absence of a contrary provision in the lease, the lessee generally has the sole and exclusive right to the occupation and control of the premises during the term, and the landlord has no right to enter or otherwise disturb the tenant in his occupancy and control.

In the absence of a restriction in the lease, the tenant has the right to occupy and use the land demised in the same manner that the owner might have done and for any lawful purpose or business which does not injure the reversion, so long as his use does not constitute waste or a nuisance. The parties to a lease may, however, by express provisions therein, restrict the uses to which the lessee may put the leased premises, so long as such restrictions are not for the purpose of creating a monopoly or restraining trade and are not otherwise contrary to law or public policy. A tenant generally has no right to remove, destroy, or even alter buildings or other improvements on the leased premises without the consent of the lessor.

A tenant of farm land, whether for life or for years (see § 18:7, supra), has the right to reasonable estovers, that is, the right to take from the demised premises such amount of wood or timber, of a kind appropriate for the purpose, as is necessary and proper for fuel, the repair of buildings, implements of husbandry, the repair of fences, and other agricultural needs. The lessee of farming land is under the implied duty to cultivate it according to the course of good husbandry and to avoid any practice that would constitute waste or injury to the reversion.

An eviction of a tenant consists in any act of the landlord which deprives the tenant of possession of the demised premises, expels him from the premises, or deprives him of the enjoyment thereof. An eviction must be distinguished from a voluntary abandonment of the premises by the tenant. Eviction may be either actual or constructive. Any disturbance of the tenant's possession by the landlord, or by someone acting under his authority, which renders the premises unfit for occupancy for the purposes for which they were demised, or which deprives the tenant of the beneficial enjoyment of the premises, causing the tenant to abandon the premises within a reasonable time, amounts to a constructive eviction. Thus, the failure of the landlord to perform his obligation to furnish heat, light, water, elevator service, or means of ingress and egress, which have the effect of depriving the tenant of the beneficial enjoyment of the premises in the manner contemplated by the lease, may amount to a constructive eviction.

The wrongful eviction of a tenant by the landlord not only terminates the tenant's obligations under the lease but also entitles him to recover damages, measured by the actual or rental value of the unexpired term less the rent reserved. An eviction of a tenant may also constitute a breach of a covenant of title or quiet enjoyment. This is true whether the eviction is by an act of the landlord or under a paramount title in a third person. Express covenants of quiet enjoyment are frequently inserted in leases; and it is generally held that a lease of realty raises an implied covenant that the lessee shall have quiet and peaceable possession and enjoyment of the premises.

§ 18:32. Assignment and subletting.

Am Jur 2d References: Landlord and Tenant, §§ 391–512.

An assignment of a leasehold is a transaction whereby a lessee transfers his entire interest in the demised premises, or a part thereof, for the entire unexpired term of the original lease, thereby parting with all of the reversionary estate in the property; and it is distinguishable from a sublease which contemplates the retention of a reversion by the lessee. In the absence of a statutory provision to the contrary or a restriction on the right of assignment fixed by the parties themselves, a tenant under a lease for a definite term has, as an incident of his estate, the right to assign his leasehold interest in the demised premises without the consent of the lessor. The right of assignment does not exist, however, in the case of a tenancy at will; and it has been held that agricultural leases, especially leases of land on shares, are not assignable unless made so by the lease.

The rule against restraints on alienation of estates in fee does not apply to tenancies for a term of years or for lesser periods. It is settled that the owner of real property, when leasing it to a tenant for such a period, may validly impose a restriction against the assignment of the term or any part thereof by the tenant. And in some jurisdictions the right of a tenant to assign is restricted by statutory provisions.

The assignee of a lease takes the whole estate of the lessee subject to the performance on his part of the covenants running with the land, and the law implies a promise on his part to perform the duties thus imposed. If, through the neglect or refusal of the assignee to perform them, the lessee is obliged to pay rent, taxes, or other sums of money to the original lessor under the covenants of his lease, he may recover such sums from his assignee. The duties of the assignee in this regard terminate, however, in the absence of an agreement to the contrary, where the assignee reassigns the lease to a third party.

The obligation and liabilities of the lessee to the lessor, arising from express covenants in the lease, are not affected by the lessee's assignment of the lease to a third person, in the absence of an agreement by the lessor to that effect, or of a waiver or estoppel. In this regard, a distinction is made between express and implied covenants in a lease. The liability of the lessee in respect of the latter is discharged by a valid assignment, as the privity of estate upon which such liability depends is thereby destroyed. Thus, the lessee remains liable after assignment upon his express covenant to pay taxes, to repair, or to pay rent, but not upon his implied covenant to pay rent.

The assignee of a leasehold estate succeeds to all the interests of the lessee and to the benefit of all the covenants and agreements of the lessor which are annexed to and run with the estate. And the assignee, apart from any express agreement to assume or perform, is in privity of estate with the lessor, and is liable to him personally for the breach of the lessee's covenants which are annexed to and run with the leasehold and which are broken while he holds the leasehold estate. Thus, the assignee becomes liable for the payment of rents provided for in the original lease. A re-assignment of the term by the assignee, however, generally terminates his liability to the original lessor, in the absence of a pre-existing contract to the contrary.

It is well settled that in the absence of restrictions thereon by the parties, or of statutory prohibitions, a tenant under a lease for a definite period has the right to sublet the premises in whole or in part. The only limitation on this right to sublet is that the premises may not be sublet for use in a manner inconsistent with the terms of the original lease or injurious to the premises. Also, a tenancy at will cannot be sublet by the tenant to another without the consent of the landlord; and agricultural leases on shares, being personal contracts, are held not to be subject to subletting.

A lessee's right to sublet may be expressly restricted by covenant or stipulation against subletting, although such restrictions are not looked upon with favor by the courts, and are strictly construed. A subletting does not in any manner affect the liability of the lessee to his lessor for the payment of rent or the performance of the covenants of the original lease. The lessee is liable to the original lessor for damage to the leased premises by the negligence or the wrongful act of the sublessee. Generally, the relation between the sublessee and sublessor is that of landlord and tenant, and their rights are governed by the terms of the sublease. As against the original lessor, however, the sublessee can acquire no greater rights in the use and enjoyment of the premises than the original lessee had. As between a sublessee and the original lessor, there is no privity either of contract or of estate. Consequently, the sublessee incurs no liability directly to the lessor, merely because of the subletting, either for the payment of rent reserved in the original lease or for the performance of other covenants on the part of the lessee, in the absence of an assumption of liability therefor.

§ 18:33. Rent.

Am Jur 2d References: Landlord and Tenant, §§ 513–760.

Rent is the usual price or consideration paid by a tenant to his landlord for the use and occupation of real estate under a leasehold. If the lease or the contract between the parties fixes the amount and terms of payment of rent, such provisions will govern. Where the relation of landlord and tenant is established without any express agreement as to rent, the law implies the promise by the tenant or the occupant to pay the reasonable value of his use and occupation. Where the landlord transfers his reversion, his grantee is entitled to the rents reserved in a lease from the grantor, but not to rents accrued prior to the conveyance.

Unless the lease provides otherwise, rent is payable at the end of the period by which the rent is measured. That is, the gross amount of rent specified for a term of years is due at the end of the term; and rent payable yearly, monthly, or weekly is payable at the end of the specified period.

An eviction of the tenant by the landlord, actual or constructive, relieves the tenant of the duty to pay rent during the time he has abandoned the premises. And the taking of leased premises under the power of eminent domain terminates liability for future rents. In the absence of agreement or statute to the contrary, the prevailing rule is that the accidental destruction of a leased building by fire or other casualty does not affect the liability of a tenant for future rents under an agreement to pay rent for a definite period. Some courts have refused to follow this rule, however. And where the lease is of a building only or of a part thereof, as a room or apartment therein, the complete destruction of the building is generally held to relieve the tenant from liability for future rentals. The tenant's rights and liabilities upon the destruction of the leased premises may, of course, be determined by the terms of the lease. And statutes have been enacted in several states for the relief of the tenant where the leased premises are destroyed by fire or other casualty.

At common law a landlord has no lien on the tenant's property to secure the payment of rent. However, statutes in many states give the landlord a lien on the personal property of tenants, or on crops in the case of agricultural leases, to secure the payment of rent. And the parties may provide for such a lien by contract. Apart from statutory remedies, the common law gives the landlord the remedy of distress for rent in arrears. Under this ancient procedure, the landlord may go upon the demised premises and seize anything he finds there and hold it until the rent is paid. As in the case of other common-law liens, however, the right to distrain does not permit the landlord to sell the tenant's property, but only to retain it. Statutes in some states have substituted other remedies for the common-law distress.

§ 18:34. Duties of landlord as to condition and repair of premises.

Am Jur 2d References: Landlord and Tenant, §§ 761–921.

In considering the duties and liabilities of the landlord as to the condition, use, repair, and improvement of premises, it is important to distinguish between his responsibility to the tenant and persons on the premises in the right of the tenant and his responsibility to third persons such as trespassers, persons on the premises with the consent of the landlord, or persons on adjoining or nearby premises or on a highway or street. The landlord's obligations may also be affected by express agreement.

Although the landlord is not generally liable for the acts of his tenant where injuries result to others from the tenant's negligent use of the premises, the landlord may be liable to persons outside the demised premises for injury or damage resulting from his own negligent maintenance of the premises or from a nuisance existing thereon at the time of the lease. This liability may extend to owners or occupants of adjoining or neighboring premises or to users of adjacent public ways.

As between the landlord and the tenant, in the absence of a contractual or statutory provision to the contrary, the demise of real property does not carry any covenant or warranty implying that the premises shall be tenantable, fit for the use for which the lessee requires them, or safe for use or occupancy. In the absence of express warranty, statute, or of fraud or misrepresentation or concealment by the landlord, the lessee must take the property as he finds it, with all existing defects of which he knows or can ascertain by reasonable inspection, and take the risk of apparent defects. The logical conclusion from this principle is that the landlord is not responsible to the tenant for injuries to person or property caused by defects in the demised premises where the landlord has not made any warranty or contract as to the condition of the premises or as to the repair of defects therein, and is guilty of no wilful wrong or fraud. Statutes in some states, however, have modified this rule. Nor is the landlord under duty to make repairs upon the demised premises during the term, even to put the premises in repair or to keep them in such condition, in the absence of a contractual or statutory provision to the contrary.

The duties and the liabilities of a landlord to persons on the leased premises by consent of the tenant are the same as those owed to the tenant himself, and this rule applies to members of the tenant's family as well as invitees and subtenants. There is an important exception to this rule, however, frequently termed the "public purpose" rule. Under this doctrine, where there is a lease for a purpose involving the use of the premises by the public, the rights of business patrons to recover from injuries from defects in the demised premises are not necessarily limited to the rights of the tenant, and there are many cases holding that where the property leased for such purposes is not safe for the purpose intended, and the owner knew, or by the exercise of reasonable diligence would have known, of such conditions, he is liable to patrons on the premises for injury resulting from such conditions.

Where the owner of premises leases parts thereof to different tenants, and expressly or impliedly reserves other parts thereof, such as entrances, halls, stairways, porches, walks, etc., for the common use of the different tenants, it is his duty to exercise reasonable care to keep such places safe, and he is liable to a tenant or a person on the premises in the right of a tenant for injuries resulting from negligence in this regard.

As to a trespasser upon the leased premises without right, the owner is not liable for injuries received through his failure to exercise reasonable care to keep the premises in a safe condition, but he is liable if he wilfully or wantonly injures a trespasser or licensee.

Where it is sought to hold a landlord liable for injury to person or property because of his negligence, the general principles of negligence apply, as discussed in the topic Torts, including the principles governing contributory negligence, assumption of risk, and proximate cause. Where it is sought to hold the landlord liable on the basis of his covenant or agreement concerning the

471

condition or fitness of the premises or the repair or upkeep thereof, the case will be governed by the general principles of contract law.

§ 18:35. Duties of tenant as to condition, use, and repair of premises.

Am Jur 2d References: Landlord and Tenant, §§ 922–989.

The relation of landlord and tenant imposes upon the tenant the duty to treat the demised premises in such manner that no injury is done to them through his negligence or wilful misconduct. He is liable to the landlord for any injuries resulting to the premises from such acts or from his commission of voluntary waste or of a nuisance. There is authority to the effect that a tenant for years is liable in tort for permissive waste and, even in the absence of an agreement therefor, he must make such fair and tenantable repairs as are necessary to prevent the premises from falling into ruin or dilapidation. Beyond this, however, the tenant is not obliged to make repairs, in the absence of an agreement therefor; and he is not bound to make substantial and lasting repairs or improvements such as putting on a new roof or reconstructing buildings. And the tenant is not liable for injury or damage to the premises caused by an act of God or by accident without fault on his part.

At common law, when property is demised in good condition and state of repair, suitable for the ordinary and contemplated use thereof by the lessee, the tenant, and not the owner or landlord, is liable for injuries to a third person on or off the premises caused by the condition or use of the premises under the tenant's control. Thus, the lessee of a place of business is liable for injuries to customers and other invitees resulting from the defective or unsafe condition of the premises.

§ 18:36. Termination and forfeiture.

Am Jur 2d References: Landlord and Tenant, §§ 990–1114, 1205–1218.

The termination of a leasehold estate may result from any of several types of events. A lease terminates with the passage of the time constituting the term; upon the happening of a condition subsequent and re-entry, or of a conditional limitation; by operation of law, as in the case of the merger of the tenancy in the reversion in the same person; by cancellation by the act and agreement of the lessor and the lessee, or by a rescission by the lessee in a proper case; by the exercise of an option to terminate; by the enforcement of a forfeiture; or by the acceptance by the landlord of a surrender by the tenant. Under some circumstances, a lease is terminated when the premises are destroyed or rendered uninhabitable. Ordinarily the death of the lessee or lessor or the conveyance of the premises by the latter to a third person does not terminate a lease.

Whether or not the breach of a covenant in a lease will operate to terminate the lease or to give a party the right to a rescission or cancellation, depends upon the terms of the lease and upon how vital and essential the provision was. Ordinarily a mere default in the payment of rent is not a ground for the termination of a lease unless it is made so by the agreement of the parties.

As pointed out in the discussion of liability for rent (supra, § 18:33), the destruction of or damage to buildings upon the leased premises does not ordinarily terminate a lease, although it may have this effect by agreement of the parties, by virtue of statutory provision, or where the lease is of rooms or an apartment in a building which is destroyed.

A forfeiture of a leasehold may result by virtue of the common law, as in the case of forfeiture for disclaimer of title, by virtue of a statutory provision, or by virtue of some clause in the lease providing for forfeiture in case of breach of a covenant or condition. In the absence, however, of an express stipulation to that effect, the general rule is that the breach by the lessee of the covenants of a lease does not work a forfeiture of the term, and that the lessor's remedy is by way of an action for damages. Thus, in the absence of a stipulation for forfeiture, a lessee does not forfeit his term by the nonpayment of rent or of taxes which he has convenanted to pay. Nor will a forfeiture be decreed because of a violation of a covenant against subletting or assignment. However, the commission of waste is generally regarded as a ground of forfeiture. Forfeiture provisions in a lease are looked upon with disfavor by the courts and are strictly construed. A landlord may waive his right to a forfeiture or may be estopped from asserting it by his conduct after the occurrence of the grounds for a forfeiture and with full knowledge thereof, as by the acceptance of rent from his tenant.

A surrender of a tenancy for years or a lesser tenancy is a yielding of the tenancy to the owner of the reversion or remainder, wherein the tenancy is submerged and extinguished by agreement or by operation of law. A surrender extinguishes all interest of the tenant. Generally a surrender occurs only through the consent and agreement of the parties.

A notice to quit is generally necessary to terminate periodic tenancies, such as those from year to year or month to month, where the term of the tenancy is not definitely fixed. And the same rule is frequently applied to tenancies at will. Where, however, the lease or agreement fixes the time for the termination of the lease, notice to quit is not necessary.

§ 18:37. Renewal, extension, and holding over.

Am Jur 2d References: Landlord and Tenant, §§ 1115–1204.

The parties to a lease may, either in the original lease or by subsequent agreement, covenant to renew or extend the lease after the expiration of the original time. Such provisions for renewal or extension are frequently in the form of an option extended to the lessee. Where a general covenant to renew or extend a lease makes no provision as to the terms of renewal or extension, it will be construed as meaning a renewal or extension upon the same terms as provided in the original lease, including the amount and terms of payment of the rental and the duration of the lease. Under such a general covenant to renew, however, the lessee is not entitled to have inserted in the renewal lease a covenant for further renewal. However, it is competent for the parties to provide for a number of renewals of a lease. Indeed, in the absence of statute to the contrary, it is generally held that a provision in a lease clearly giving the lessee and his assigns the right to perpetual renewals is valid.

A lessee, in order to avail himself of a right or option to renew or extend a lease, must give the lessor proper notice of his demand for renewal or extension.

A tenant has no right to hold over or remain in possession of the leased premises after the termination of his lease, without the agreement of the landlord. It is optional with a landlord to treat a tenant wrongfully holding over as a trespasser or to waive the wrong of holding over and to treat him as a tenant. If the landlord exercises his election to refuse to allow the tenant to remain, the latter from that moment is a trespasser and can be ejected. If the landlord elects to allow the tenant to remain, he may be a tenant at sufferance, at will, from year to year, month to month, or for a definite term, depending on circumstances and statutes. Some courts hold that where a tenant for a year or other definite term holds over after his term and the landlord elects to hold him for another term, the tenant is bound thereby, although this result may be changed by the agreement of the parties, express or implied. In the absence of an agreement or a statute to the contrary, the tenancy arising from a tenant's holding over with the consent of the landlord is presumed to be upon the same covenants and terms as the original lease, including the amount of the rent.

Where the landlord does not assent to the tenant's holding over, nor agree to an extended or renewed term, the tenant is liable to the landlord for his unlawful occupancy of the premises. The measure of such damages is generally the rental value of the property for the time that the tenant retains the possession, although some statutes provide for multiple damages or penalties in such cases.

§ 18:38. Landlord's possessory remedies.

Am Jur 2d References: Forcible Entry and Detainer, § 7; Landlord and Tenant, §§ 1219–1247.

The possessory remedies of the landlord, when he becomes entitled to the possession of leased premises, because of the termination of the lease by efflux of time, forfeiture, condition subsequent, conditional limitation, or other reason, include the following: peaceable re-entry, such as re-entry in the absence of the tenant; a writ of entry or action of ejectment, which were at common law his usual possessory remedies; an action for forcible detainer; and the various dispossessory proceedings, usually summary in character, provided by statutes. At common law, the landlord had the right of re-entry by means of any reasonably necessary force, but this remedy has generally been replaced by statutory proceedings such as forcible entry and detainer. The statutory remedies provided in most jurisdictions, under a variety of names and provisions, are usually summary in character, designed to simplify and expedite the proceeding by which the landlord may recover possession of his property and to avoid the violence involved in the old remedy of re-entry by force.

V. WATERS

A. IN GENERAL

§ 18:39. Introductory; definitions; water rights generally.

Am Jur 2d References: Waters (1st ed, §§ 2, 3, 6, 65, 108, 111, 132, 138, 240–268, 273, 291–339).

In its natural state, water is ordinarily regarded as constituting a part of the land in or upon which it is found, and is therefore in the nature of real rather than personal property. Waters are classified, in respect of their location, form, and physical characteristics, as tide or inland, surface or subterranean, watercourses, lakes, or ponds; in respect of their origin or existence as natural or artificial; and in respect of their use, ownership, and control as navigable or nonnavigable, and as public or private.

A "watercourse" is a stream of water flowing in a definite direction or course in a bed with banks. The term is applied to streams regardless of size, whether rivers, rivulets, brooks, or creeks. "Surface water" is that which is derived from falling rain or melting snow, or which rises to the surface in springs, and is diffused over the surface of the ground. Underground streams, as distinguished from percolating waters, within the law relating to subterranean waters, are those, and only those, which flow in fixed and definite channels, the existence and location of which are known or ascertainable from surface indications or other means without some surface excavations for that purpose. "Percolating waters" may be defined as those which ooze, seep, filter, or percolate through the ground under the surface without a definite channel, or in a course that is uncertain or unknown and not discoverable from the surface without excavation for that purpose. The term "spring" means a place where water issues from the earth by operation of natural forces. A "well" may be defined as an excavation or hole dug, bored, or drilled into the earth for the purpose of obtaining water from subterranean sources.

"Riparian rights" are those belonging to a riparian proprietor, who is one whose land is bounded or traversed by a natural stream. Riparian rights are those which such proprietor has with respect to the stream and its use and enjoyment. Although the terms "riparian rights" and "riparian proprietor" are frequently applied to ownership on the shores of a sea or lake, the more accurate terminology here is "littoral proprietor" or "littoral rights."

Water rights are sometimes treated as easements, either in gross or appurtenant. As a general proposition, in the absence of statutory restrictions, all rights to water, riparian or otherwise, may be severed from the lands to which they are attached, and separately conveyed. Water rights which are appurtenant to land will pass under a conveyance of such land unless expressly excepted or reserved.

§ 18:40. Rights and duties of landowners as to various types of waters.

Am Jur 2d References: Waters (1st ed, §§ 6–34, 50–84, 90–144, 149–176, 273–339).

It is a general principle of the law of waters, subject to qualifications noted below, that a riparian proprietor has the right to have the water of a stream flow by or through his premises in its natural mode, course, and volume. This does not mean, however, that he has an absolute right to the flow of all the water in its natural state; and his right is subject to the right of the upper owners to make reasonable use of such waters. A reasonable diminution, obstruction, or detention of water, necessary for the full enjoyment of the stream and not seriously diminishing the lower riparian owner's enjoyment thereof, is permissible.

A landowner has the right to divert or change the course of a stream flowing through his land, provided he returns it to its original or natural channel before it reaches the land of the lower owner and provided he does not interfere with the rights of an adjoining proprietor, either above or below or on the opposite side of the stream. It is generally held that a riparian owner may restore to its former channel a stream which has formed a new channel upon his land, provided he does so within a reasonable time.

While an upper proprietor has no right unreasonably to interrupt or retard the natural flow of a stream to the injury of lower owners, and a lower proprietor does not have the right to throw the water back upon the proprietors upstream, the right of a riparian owner to make reasonable use of the water entitles him to interrupt, to some extent, the natural flow of the stream. The reasonableness of the detention or obstruction by the upper proprietor depends on the circumstances of each case. The mere fact that some detriment or inconvenience results to other riparian owners is not necessarily decisive.

One of the rights of a riparian owner is the reasonable use of the stream for power or other lawful purposes by means of dams built in the stream. This right and the limitations thereon are discussed in § 18:43, infra.

There is some conflict of authority as to the ownership of and rights in lakes and ponds. The weight of American authority follows the English common-law rule that freshwater lakes and ponds belong to the owners of the soil adjacent. Some states, however, have engrafted various modifications upon this rule; and some jurisdictions make an exception in the case of navigable lakes. It is settled, however, that a lake or pond which is entirely within the boundaries of a single tract of land belongs to the owner of that land. Some New England states make an exception in the case of "great ponds," a pond covering over 10 acres. And title to and dominion over the lands covered by the waters of the Great Lakes of America belong to the several states bordering these lakes, in trust for the public. The rights and privileges of proprietors on lakes and ponds are in most respects the same as those of riparian proprietors generally.

A landowner has the right to use or retain any and all surface water coming upon his land. There are two distinct rules with respect to the right of a lower proprietor to repel, obstruct, or divert surface water flowing from the land of a higher proprietor. One is called the civil-law rule and the other common-law rule or the "common enemy" doctrine. According to the doctrine of the civil law, which prevailed as the common law in England and is the rule in many American states, the owner of the upper or dominant estate has a legal and natural easement or servitude in the lower or servient estate for the drainage of surface water, flowing in its natural course and manner; and such natural flow cannot be interrupted or prevented by the servient or lower owner to the detriment or injury of the dominant proprietor, unless the right to do so has been acquired by grant or prescription. According to the other view, the so-called "common law" or "common enemy" doctrine, no natural easement or servitude exists in favor of the higher land for the drainage of surface water, and the proprietor of the lower tenement may lawfully obstruct or hinder the flow of such water thereon, and in so doing may turn it back or away from his own lands and onto and over the lands of other proprietors, without liability. In other words, the "common enemy" doctrine gives each landowner the right to fight off surface water and dispose of it as best he can. Both of these doctrines are subject to qualifications which vary in the several jurisdictions.

Rights and liabilities in respect of underground streams are governed, so far as practicable, by the rules applicable to surface watercourses. The owner of land through which such a stream flows may make reasonable use of the water of the stream, but he may not divert, waste, destroy, or pollute it to the injury of other riparian owners. Percolating waters which underlie the surface of land (and it is presumed that all subterranean waters are percolating waters unless they are satisfactorily shown to be underground streams) belong to the owner of the land in which the waters are found. There is a tendency among modern authorities, however, to limit the landowner's right to the use of such waters to a reasonable use, subject to similar rights of other landowners. Similar rules govern the use of water from artesian basins.

A spring belongs to the owner of the land on which it is located. However, where the water flowing from a spring establishes a permanent stream or watercourse upon or across the lands of others, riparian rights attach thereto in favor of the owners of such other lands. The owner of a well has a right to the unlimited use of water therefrom, free from interference or pollution by others, subject to the general principles governing subterranean waters.

Riparian rights exist as inherent incidents of the ownership of riparian land. Such rights do not depend upon the ownership of the bed of the stream or body of water. The rights of riparian proprietors on both navigable and unnavigable streams are to a great extent mutual, common, and correlative. The use of the stream or the water by each proprietor is therefore limited to what is reasonable, having due regard for the rights of others above, below, or on the opposite shore. Land, to be riparian, must be in actual contact with the water.

Riparian rights may be transferred by grant, and they pass with the transfer of land without any mention thereof in the conveyance. Generally, riparian rights may be severed from the ownership of the land to which they are appurtenant, either by grant of such rights to another or by reservation thereof in the conveyance of land. Such rights may be lost by prescription or adverse user, but not ordinarily by mere nonuser.

In some jurisdictions, especially in the arid or semi-arid regions of the American West, riparian rights are qualified by the doctrine of "prior appropriation." Under this doctrine the one who first diverts and applies to a beneficial use the waters of a stream has a prior right thereto, to the extent of his appropriation. The subject is discussed in connection with irrigation in § 18:44, infra.

§ 18:41. Navigable and public waters.

Am Jur 2d References: Waters (1st ed, §§ 177–239, 241).

Applying what was supposed to be the English common-law rule, some of the early American authorities stated that navigable waters were those only in which the tide ebbed and flowed; and the confusion of navigable water with tide water prevailed for a while in this country, notwithstanding the great differences existing between the size and topography of the British Island and that of the American Continent. The tidal test is no longer applied in the American states, however, where some of the greatest streams and bodies of water are tideless.

The prevailing rule in this country is that navigable waters are those which are capable of being navigated; that is, navigable in fact. A general definition or test is that rivers or other bodies of water are navigable when they are used, or susceptible of being used, in the ordinary condition, as highways for commerce, over which trade and travel are or may be conducted in the customary modes of trade and travel on water. It is not necessary that the waters be navigable in all their parts in order that the public may have a right of navigation, where a substantial part is of sufficient depth and fitness for such use. Obstructions or obstacles do not necessarily destroy the navigability of the entire stream. Nor is it necessary that the stream be capable of navigation at all seasons of the year or at all stages of the water. Some jurisdictions recognize another class of streams, generally referred to as "floatable," which, while not navigable by vessels, are usable for the transportation of certain things, such as logs, by floatage. Such streams are held to be subject to a public easement for such purposes.

Each state has the power to regulate and control the navigable or public waters within its own boundaries, subject to the paramount powers of the federal government under its constitutional power to regulate interstate and foreign commerce. The ownership of navigable waters is generally vested in the public, or in the state in trust for the public.

The owners of land adjacent to navigable waters are generally accorded certain riparian rights in addition to those which they enjoy in common with the general public. For example, such owners have the right of access to the waters. The riparian rights of landowners is subject, however, to the paramount right of the public to use the waters for the purpose of navigation. No private individual has the right to erect any structure or do any act which would obstruct or interfere with the navigation of such waters. Conversely, the public right of navigation does not include the right to use shorelands held in private ownership.

§ 18:42. Pollution.

Am Jur 2d References: Pollution Control, §§ 53–99; Waters (1st ed, §§ 112, 136, 345, 383–401, 405–421).

A riparian proprietor has the right to make reasonable use of a stream or other waters for domestic, agricultural, or industrial purposes, even though such use necessarily results in some degree of pollution of the water. In opposition to these rights is the basic right of other riparian owners to have the waters come to them in a condition fit for their use.

And apart from the riparian rights, the public has a vital interest in maintaining the purity of navigable and public waters. The accommodation of these conflicting rights and interests has become more difficult and complex with the great growth of population and industry along the waterways of the country. The trend of modern decisions and legislation to restrict the riparian right of the individual to contaminate waters is the result of the vast increase in the number and magnitude of the contaminators and contaminants and of the aggregate effect thereof upon the public health and welfare.

Liability for pollution of waters frequently results from the exercise, in an excessive or improper manner, of a well-established riparian right. Thus, riparian owners generally have the right to use a stream or body of water for the disposal of waste, refuse, or sewage, provided such use does not materially interfere with the rights of other persons in respect of the use of the water. But if such use renders the water unfit for the uses to which other persons have the right to put it, liability in damages or for the creation of a nuisance may result. The ordinary domestic or agricultural use of a stream or its reasonable use in connection with an industrial establishment, will necessarily add some contaminants and impurities to the water. But other owners are not entitled to have the waters come to them in a state of absolute purity and free of any contamination whatever. Liability arises when the pollution is such as to deprive persons of their right to use the waters for reasonable and proper purposes. The right of any riparian owner to use a stream in its purity must yield to the right of every other riparian owner to make reasonable use of the same stream. The determination of liability for pollution always depends upon all of the circumstances of the case, including the size and nature of the waters, the uses to which it is ordinarily put, and the character and extent of the contamination.

Municipalities are generally accorded a more extensive use of a stream or other water than are individual riparian owners. This results from the public interest involved and from the necessities of the case. However, even a municipality may not with impunity unreasonably defile a stream so as to render it unfit for its primary use or so as to create a nuisance, without the payment of just compensation to other riparian owners.

The remedy for an unlawful pollution of waters is an action for damages, a proceeding to abate a nuisance, or a suit for injunction. The prevention and correction of the pollution of public waters, and the regulation of the uses of such waters, are the subjects of an increasing amount of legislation, both state and federal.

One who pollutes percolating waters or subterranean streams, causing injury to the wells or springs of another, may be liable to the latter.

A prescriptive right to pollute waters may be acquired where the person claiming the right meets the strict requirements of the law that the use must be adverse, under claim of right, uninterrupted, continuous for the time prescribed by law, and with the knowledge of the party whose right is invaded. But no such prescriptive right may be acquired where the pollution or the use constitutes a nuisance.

§ 18:43. Dams and other obstructions; water power.

Am Jur 2d References: Waters (1st ed, §§ 13, 18–32, 36, 155–163, 166, 170, 171, 266–268, 346, 382, 402, 433).

Water flowing in a natural watercourse may be detained for the development and utilization of power. Subject to public regulation, a dam may be constructed and maintained across a stream by a riparian proprietor, provided he does not unreasonably diminish the amount of water which would naturally flow to the lands of lower proprietors, or materially affect the continuity of flow, or wrongfully throw back upon upper proprietors. However, such a dam and the mill and machinery in connection therewith must be in proportion to the capacity or volume of the stream, and the detention or diminution of water by this means must not be unreasonable. And a person constructing a dam or any other structure in a stream must take due precautions against injury to other lands by floods. The right to dam streams is frequently regulated by statute.

As against other riparian proprietors, the right to maintain a dam or other obstruction may be acquired by adverse user where the usual requirements of a prescriptive right are satisfied.

The most important use of water power today involves hydroelectric plants for the generation of electricity. Such projects usually involve the impoundment of great lakes by the erection of dams; and, unless the flooded lands are public lands, calls for the exercise of the power of eminent domain.

A person who stores water on his land by means of reservoirs, tanks, or other means of impoundment is held to a high degree of care to avoid injury to others by the escape of the water. Some jurisdictions even make him a quasi-insurer against injury by applying the doctrine of Rylands v Fletcher (discussed in the topic Torts).

§ 18:44. Irrigation.

Am Jur 2d References: Irrigation, §§ 1–72.

The common-law rights of a riparian owner include the right to divert and use water from a stream or other waters for the purpose of irrigation. The riparian right to use waters for this purpose is generally limited to riparian lands. This right must be exercised with due regard for the equal rights of other riparian proprietors. The amount of water diverted from a stream and the manner of its use are limited by the general principle that the use must be reasonable, and this is dependent upon the facts and circumstances of each case and is frequently affected by legislative provisions. A riparian owner diverting from a stream for irrigation purposes is generally required to return to its accustomed channel water not needed or used for that purpose.

In some of the arid and semi-arid regions of western America, the common-law riparian right to divert water for irrigation purposes has been largely replaced by the doctrine of "prior appropriation." Under this system, originating in the customs of the early settlers in the west, he who first changed the course of a natural stream flowing through public lands and appropriated the water so diverted to some useful purpose in connection with the operation of mines and the cultivation of farms, orchards, and vineyards, thereby acquired a superior right to continue the use thereof, without regard to ordinary riparian rights. While this doctrine appears to have been applied originally to operations and waters on public lands, it has been given general application in some jurisdictions, even to the exclusion of ordinary riparian rights. The right based on prior appropriation is generally limited to the amount appropriated and also to the amount actually needed by appropriator, he not being permitted to waste or misapply waters.

Companies are frequently organized for the purpose of constructing and operating irrigation works. Such companies are subject to strict regulation and control by the states. And the statutes of many states authorize the organization of irrigation districts to provide for the irrigation of certain areas.

B. Rights in Submerged Land, Banks, Shores, and Islands

§ 18:45. Title and rights of riparian or littoral proprietor, generally.

Am Jur 2d References: Waters (1st ed, §§ 448–475).

Under the English common law at the time of the American Revolution the title to the bed of the sea below high-water mark, and to the bed of all rivers as far as the flow of the tide extended, was in the Crown, but the title to the bed of all fresh-water rivers above the ebb and flow of the tide, whether navigable or nonnavigable in fact, where the river formed the boundary between adjoining proprietors, was in the riparian owner to the thread of the stream. Many states still follow this rule, holding that the title to the bed of navigable rivers which are tideless, or above the point where the tide ebbs and flows, is vested in the riparian proprietors. Other jurisdictions, however, take the view that this doctrine is not appropriate for application to the great fresh-water navigable rivers of this country, and hold that the riparian owners do not take to the middle of such a stream and that the state is the owner of the subjacent soil thereof. As to nonnavigable streams and bodies of waters, as well as the so-called "floatable waters," it is the general rule that the lands underlying such waters belong to the proprietors of the adjoining uplands.

In the case of a grant of land bordering on tide water or upon a navigable stream, to the bed of which the grantee does not take title, there is a conflict of authority as to whether the grant conveys title to the high-water mark or to the low-water mark in the absence of a specific provision in that regard. As to navigable and tidal waters, the adjoining landowner's rights are always subject to the superior rights of the public in the use of such waters for navigation, and subject also to governmental regulation for the protection of the public rights in such waters.

§ 18:46. Accretion, alluvion, reliction, erosion, and avulsion.

Am Jur 2d References: Waters (1st ed, §§ 476–503).

Accretion is the increase of riparian land by the gradual deposit by water, of solid material, whether mud, sand, or sediment, so as to cause that to become dry land which was before covered by water. The term "alluvion" is applied to the deposit itself, while accretion denotes the act or process, the two terms frequently being used synonymously.

"Reliction" or "dereliction" is the term applied to land made by the withdrawal of the waters by which it was previously covered, as distinguished from the building up of the bottom by deposits displacing the waters. It is to be noted, however, that mere temporary or seasonal diminution of water does not ordinarily constitute reliction for the purposes of riparian ownership.

"Avulsion" is a sudden and perceptible loss or addition to land by the action of water, or a sudden change in the bed or course of a stream. The term "erosion," as used in this connection, means the gradual washing away of land bordering on a stream or body of water by the action of the water.

It is a general rule that where the location of the margin or bed of a stream or other body of water which constitutes the boundary of a tract of land is gradually or imperceptibly changed or shifted by accretion, reliction, or erosion, the margin or bed of the water, as so changed, remains the boundary of the tract, which is extended or restricted accordingly. The owner of riparian land thus acquires title to all additions thereto or extensions thereof by such means and in such manner, and loses title to such portions as are so worn away or encroached upon by the water. However, while the change takes place suddenly and perceptibly either by reliction or avulsion, as where a stream from any cause suddenly abandons its old and finds a new bed, such a change works no change of boundary or ownership. These general rules are independent of the law respecting the title to soil under water, and in most jurisdictions their application does not depend upon whether the water is tidal, navigable, or otherwise.

The foregoing rules generally apply to changes in the shores of lakes, ponds, and oceans, as well as to the banks of streams.

§ 18:47. Islands.

Am Jur 2d References: Waters (1st ed, §§ 275, 276, 489, 504–507).

The title to islands is ordinarily vested in the owner of the bed of the waters out of which they rise. Where the riparian or littoral proprietors have title to the bed of the waters, each is ordinarily the owner of such islands or portions thereof as lie on his side of the thread of the stream or channel and within his side lines. Where the boundary line of riparian proprietors extends only to the margin of the water, the title to islands arising out of the adjacent waters is ordinarily vested in the state or its grantee. The ownership of an island carries with it the usual riparian rights. Where the riparian proprietor has title to the thread of the stream, the title of the owner of an island extends to the center of the channel between the island and the opposite tract on either side.

As a general rule, where the title of the owner of riparian or littoral lands extends to the center of adjacent waters, a grant or conveyance of such lands will include any islands owned by the grantor within the outer boundaries of the grant, in the absence of any reservation or exception. And this rule has been applied to grants of public lands.

VI. ADJOINING LANDOWNERS

§ 18:48. Generally.

Am Jur 2d References: Adjoining Landowners, §§ 1–36, 118–136; Fences, §§ 6–19.

The basic right of a landowner to make every reasonable and lawful use of his property is subject to the corresponding right of adjoining landowners to enjoy their own properties without injury. The maxim "sic utere tuo ut alienum non laedas" (so use your own property that you do not injure others) is applicable in determining the rights and liabilities of adjoining landowners inter se. Under this principle a property owner may put his property to any reasonable and lawful use, so long as he does not thereby deprive an adjoining owner of any right of enjoyment of his property which is recognized and protected by law, and so long as he does not create a nuisance. While the rightful use of one's own land may diminish the value of an adjoining estate, or prevent its being used with the comfort and freedom which might otherwise have been anticipated, this is damnum absque injuria, for which the law affords no redress.

The test of the permissible use of one's land is whether the act or use is a reasonable exercise of the dominion which the owner of property has by virtue of his ownership, having regard to all interests affected, his own and those of his neighbors, and having in view also the public policy. One factor to be considered is whether the benefit derived from the use in question exceeds the harm done to the adjoining owner. So long as the acts of the landowner are within his legal rights, the motive impelling him is generally immaterial.

A landowner is, of course, liable for trespass upon the property of an adjoining owner, whether by physical invasion or by other acts constituting trespass. The creation or maintenance of a nuisance to the detriment of an adjoining owner will also give rise to liability. And a use or activity which would otherwise be permissible may give rise to liability to an adjoining owner if negligence is established. In some jurisdictions, under the doctrine of Rylands v Fletcher (discussed under the topic Torts), a person who brings on his land anything likely to do mischief if it escapes is prima facie liable for all damage resulting from its escape. The related doctrine of liability without fault for injuries resulting to adjoining landowners from ultrahazardous activities or from the use of inherently dangerous instrumentalities is also applied in some jurisdictions.

In the construction and maintenance of buildings, walls, and other structures on his land, a landowner must exercise due care to avoid injury to adjoining property, and he is liable for damage resulting from his negligence in this regard. The same rule applies to the maintenance and felling of trees. And the construction of a roof in such manner that it collects water and discharges it on the adjoining land is a violation of the rights of the adjoining landowner. However, the right of eavesdrip or the like may be acquired by prescription or by agreement.

A tree or hedge growing on the division line between proprietors is generally held to be the common property of both, and neither may destroy or injure it without the consent of the other. However, an owner has the right to take steps necessary to protect his property from injury by such trees.

The rights of adjoining landowners with respect to division or partition fences on their boundary are frequently covered by agreement between them, and in some states such matters are regulated by statute.

In the absence of an agreement or easement, no person has a right to erect buildings or other structures on his land so that any part thereof, however small, extends beyond his boundary, either above or below the surface, and thus encroaches on the adjoining premises. Such an encroachment may constitute a trespass and a private nuisance, resulting in liability for damages.

Injunctive relief is also available to prevent encroachments where legal remedies for the recovery of damages are inadequate (as they usually are); and mandatory injunction to compel the removal of encroaching structures is available in a proper case. However, in determining whether a mandatory injunction should issue to compel an adjoining landowner to remove an encroachment, many courts have taken the position that it is proper to consider the balance of convenience or relative hardship which would result from granting or denying the injunction. Thus, if the damage resulting from the encroachment is slight and the cost of removing it would be great, these courts will not grant a mandatory injunction unless the encroachment was intentional or wilful.

A landowner who is injured by encroachments from adjoining property may in many cases remedy the situation by self-help, without resorting to legal proceedings, especially where the encroachment amounts to a private nuisance. Thus, where the branches of a tree on adjoining property overhang his land, or the roots of such a tree encroach upon his soil, he has the right to cut the branches or foliage overhanging his property and to remove the offending roots. However, both the overhanging branches and any fruit thereon belong to the owner of the neighboring tree and must be returned to him.

§ 18:49. Lateral and subjacent support.

Am Jur 2d References: Adjoining Landowners, §§ 37–88.

The owner of land has the right to lateral support from the adjacent soil, and the adjoining proprietor may not remove the earth to such an extent as to withdraw the natural support of his neighbor's soil without being liable for the resultant injury. This right is an incident to the ownership of land, and both the right and the burden pass with a transfer of title to the land without any express mention thereof, although the parties may, by agreement, vary these rights and duties.

The right of a landowner to lateral support is limited to the support for his land in its natural state. He is not generally entitled to have support for the additional weight and burden of buildings and other structures placed on the land, which increase the lateral pressure and contribute to the subsidence of the land. The same principle applies where the natural condition of land has been altered by other activities of the landowner creating or increasing the need of lateral support, as where the owner raises the level of his land above his neighbor's adjoining land by filling.

The right of a landowner to make excavations on his own property is not negatived by the presence of buildings on adjacent property. One excavating next to a building on adjoining land must proceed in a workmanlike manner and must use ordinary care and skill. He is liable for damage to the adjoining property resulting from negligence on his part. Due care generally requires the excavator to notify the adjoining owner of a proposed excavation so as to give the latter an opportunity to shore up or otherwise protect his buildings. Ordinarily the excavator owes no duty to protect adjoining buildings by underpinning or shoring, but there may be circumstances requiring him to do so. Statutes and ordinances frequently regulate excavations and fix the duties and liabilities of the excavator.

Closely related to the matter of lateral support, and governed by similar rules, is that of subjacent support, which means the support of the surface by underlying strata of the earth, or the support of the upper floors of a building by the part below. Where there is a severance of ownership of the surface from the minerals below or the subjacent strata, or a right is granted to tunnel under the land, the owner of the surface has the right to have the superincumbent soil supported from below in its natural state. However, this right generally applies only to the surface in its natural state or its condition at the time of severance of ownership. While it has been held that the subjacent owner or lessee is bound to support buildings or other structures which were on the surface at the time of the creation of the interest in the subjacent stratum, there is generally no right of subjacent support for buildings and other structures which were neither in existence nor planned at the time the subjacent estate was severed from the surface estate, at least in the absence of a showing of negligence.

§ 18:50. Light, air, and view; spite fences and structures.

Am Jur 2d References: Adjoining Landowners, §§ 89–117.

The owner of land has generally no legal right, in the absence of an easement, to the light and air unobstructed from adjoining land. The English doctrine of "ancient lights," by which the owner of land, by an uninterrupted enjoyment for 20 years, acquires a right of action against an adjoining landowner for interfering with ancient windows by the erection of any structure on his own land, is not generally accepted in the United States. Under the prevailing rule, in the absence of statute or of an easement or contract, a landowner has the right, by erecting a building or other structure on his own land, to obstruct, or deprive the adjoining owner of, the light, air, and view which he had before such structure was erected.

Easements of light, air, and view may be created by express grant, reservation, or contract. There is a divergence of opinion as to whether easements of light, air, and view may arise by implied grant or reservation. According to the English common-law rule, where premises are granted on which a building stands with windows overlooking land retained by the grantor, an easement of light and air arises by implication, and the grantor and his assigns cannot erect any structure which would darken those windows. The prevailing American view, however, is to the contrary, although in some states an exception is made in the case of obvious necessity.

One line of authority takes the view that the right of a landowner to erect a structure on his own land is not affected by his motive for doing so, and that he may with impunity erect even a "spite fence" or structure. A spite fence or structure is one which is of no beneficial use or pleasure to the owner but was erected and is maintained by him for the purpose of annoying his neighbor or with the malicious motive of injuring him by shutting out his light, air, or view. There is a tendency in the recent decisions to abandon that rule and to hold that a landowner has a right of action against an adjoining owner who erects or maintains a spite fence or like structure erected for the sole purpose of injuring him in the lawful and beneficial use of his property. And statutes and ordinances in some jurisdictions prohibit the erection of such structures.

§ 18:51. Party walls.

Am Jur 2d References: Party Walls, §§ 1–44.

A "party wall," sometimes designated as a "wall in common," has been defined as a wall that is used, or is intended to be used, by adjoining landowners in the construction or maintenance of improvements on their respective adjoining lands. It is a wall erected on the line between two adjoining landowners for the use and benefit of both tenements. A more detailed definition of a party wall is that it is a division wall between two connected and mutually supporting buildings of different owners, or intended to be between the building actually constructed and a contemplated one, which usually stands half on the land of each, into which each may insert the timbers and connections for his building, and which is maintained at mutual cost.

Party walls are usually created by agreement between adjoining landowners. They are sometimes created, however, through legislative authorization. And a right to an easement of support in a wall may arise by prescription through use for the requisite period. A wall may acquire the status of a party wall upon a conveyance of the land upon which it stands, or to which it is adjacent, and which it serves or is intended to serve for building purposes. Generally, a conveyance that severs the title to two lots with buildings supported by a wall located on the division line operates to make the wall a party wall. For example, where the owner of two adjoining lots erects buildings upon them with a partition wall on the division line for the support of both buildings, a conveyance of either house and lot, with its appurtenances, gives the grantee the right to use the wall as a support for his building.

Although the wrongful destruction of a party wall by one adjoining landowner will not ordinarily terminate the neighbor's party wall rights, the accidental destruction of such a wall is generally held to terminate the rights and easements therein as a party wall and to restore to the adjoining landowners their full ownership of their portion of the premises on which the wall stood.

VII. SALES AND EXCHANGES OF LAND

§ 18:52. Generally; the contract.

Am Jur 2d References: Exchange of Property, §§ 1–28; Vendor
and Purchaser (1st ed, §§ 2–120, 334–353, 407–436).

The formation of a valid and binding contract for the sale of land is governed by the basic rules of law applicable to contracts generally. Such a contract must be founded upon the mutual assent of the parties thereto to all of the material terms of the contract; it must be incorporated in a written instrument or memorandum sufficient to meet the requirement of the statute of frauds; there must be a legal consideration; and the contract must be sufficiently certain in its terms, including the description of the land and the designation of the parties. The necessary assent or meeting of the minds requires an unconditional acceptance of an outstanding offer. And the basic rules of construction under the general law of contracts are applicable to contracts for the sale or exchange of lands. The purchase price and the time and terms of the payment thereof are usually determined by express provisions of the contract or deed.

Contracts for the sale or exchange of real property are subject to the defenses provided by the general law of contracts. Thus, if the agreement is made under a mutual mistake of a material fact, or if it was procured by fraud or misrepresentation as to a material fact or by duress, the contract is at least voidable at the instance of the injured party and may be rescinded by him. And a land contract will not be enforced if it is in violation of the law or public policy.

Contracts for the exchange of properties are governed by the same general principles as apply to ordinary contracts of sale. The distinctive feature of an exchange is that the consideration is the conveyance of land by each party to the other.

A contract for the purchase of real property may generally be assigned by the vendee. And where a vendor, after contracting for the sale of land, conveys it to a third person, other than a bona fide purchaser for value, the conveyance has the effect of transferring to such third person both the rights and obligations of the vendor under the original contract of sale.

§ 18:53. Subject matter of sale; deficit or excess.

Am Jur 2d References: Vendor and Purchaser (1st ed, §§ 11–13, 55, 121–147).

A contract for the sale of land, to be valid, must describe the property which is the subject of the contract, or furnish the means by which the property may be identified with reasonable certainty. What property is to be included in the contract and the amount thereof are to be determined from a proper construction of the terms of the contract. Extrinsic evidence is admissible to apply the contract to its subject matter; that is, parol evidence is admissible to identify the specific property described in general terms in the contract. A sale of land includes, of course, its appurtenances and fixtures and the timber growing thereon.

In determining the right to relief on the ground of mistake as to the quantity of the land which is the subject of a contract of sale, the courts have established two classes of cases: (1) where the sale is of a specific quantity, usually denominated a sale by the acre, and (2) where the sale is of a specific tract described by name or boundaries, usually called a sale in gross. Whether the sale is in gross or by the acre is determined by the intention of the parties as disclosed by the terms of the contract in the light of all of the surrounding circumstances. A sale by the acre is usually indicated where the price is expressly based on a certain amount per acre or other area unit. And a sale of a tract described by name or by metes and bounds, for a lump sum, without mention of acreage, is clearly a sale in gross, in the absence of an agreement to the contrary. In the case of a sale of land by metes and bounds or other definite description as a tract, which is recited to contain a specified quantity, the addition of the qualifying words "more or less," or the like, will usually, but not always, characterize the sale as one in gross.

In the case of a sale in gross, the parties are usually deemed to have accepted the hazard of reasonable difference between estimated and actual acreage, and no relief will be granted for any but great deficiencies or excesses. The relative extent of the excess or deficiency is an important, but not exclusive, test in determining the right to relief in such cases. Where the sale is by the acre, any material discrepancy in the represented quantity entitles the prejudiced party to relief.

Where either party predicates a cause of action upon a mutual mistake as to the quantity of land sold, the court may either adjust the purchase price to cover the deficiency or excess in acreage, or rescind the contract. A cause of action may also, in a proper case, be predicated on a theory of breach of contract, breach of warranty, express or implied, or on the tort theory of fraud. Also, a purchaser may be able to assert a material deficiency by way of defense in an action by the vendor.

§ 18:54. Title of vendor; abstract; conveyance.

Am Jur 2d References: Vendor and Purchaser (1st ed, §§ 148–333).

A contract to sell and convey real estate, in the absence of any provision therein indicating otherwise, ordinarily implies an undertaking on the part of the vendor to convey a good and marketable title in fee simple, clear of all liens and encumbrances. Whether the tendered title meets the requirements of the contract depends upon the conditions existing at the time when a conveyance is due, rather than the time when the contract of sale is made. The title is sufficient if it is free of defects at the time a conveyance is due, although defects existed at the time the contract was made; conversely, defects arising after the contract is made may prevent the vendor from conveying the kind of title contracted for.

The parties may, of course, contract for the conveyance of some special interest or estate or a title less than fee simple, or one subject to encumbrances. Thus, a contract to convey by quitclaim deed, or to convey the vendor's right, title, and interest, does not obligate the vendor to give a perfect title or to convey a fee simple estate. The parties may contract for an insured or insurable title. A provision in the contract that the title should be satisfactory to a third person, usually the vendee's attorney, is valid, but there is a difference of judicial opinion as to whether such a provision requires that the third person act reasonably in rejecting the title as unsatisfactory, or whether it is sufficient that he act in good faith and without fraud, though mistakenly. The obligation of the vendor to furnish an abstract of title depends upon the provisions of the contract of sale.

The vendor's obligation to convey a good title requires not only a title valid in fact, but a marketable title. There have been numerous definitions of "marketable title." It has been said that a marketable title is one that may be freely made the subject of a resale; that a marketable title means a title free from reasonable doubt both as to matters of law and fact, a title which a reasonable purchaser, well informed as to the facts and their legal bearings, willing and ready to perform his contract, would, in the exercise of that prudence which businessmen ordinarily bring to bear upon such transactions, be willing to accept and ought to accept.

To meet the test of marketability, the title must be free of liens and encumbrances, its validity must be clear, and there must be no reasonable doubt as to any fact or point of law upon which its validity depends. A title is considered to be subject to a defect or encumbrance if, at the time when a conveyance is due, there is an outstanding lien, mortgage, or other encumbrance against it, or an outstanding right of dower or curtesy; if the land is subject to a covenant or restriction which affects its full enjoyment by the purchaser; if the land is burdened with an easement which materially affects or interferes with the full enjoyment thereof; or if there is a substantial encroachment on the land of buildings or other improvements on adjoining land, or if buildings or improvements on the land sold encroach to a substantial extent upon adjoining premises.

If nothing is said in the contract as to the time for conveyance by the vendor, the law requires performance within a reasonable time after a demand. The purchaser is entitled to a deed sufficient in form to convey title to the land and to entitle the instrument to be admitted to record. In the absence of a provision in the contract specifying the kind of covenants to be incorporated in the deed, there is a difference of opinion in this country as to whether the vendee is entitled to a covenant of general warranty. In most American jurisdictions, the vendor has the duty of preparing the deed.

§ 18:55. Loss or deterioration of property; insurance.

Am Jur 2d References: Vendor and Purchaser (1st ed, §§ 389–406).

The question of who, as between the vendor and the vendee in an executory contract for the purchase and sale of real property, bears the risk of loss from injuries to the land and the deterioration or destruction of buildings thereon, pending the performance of the contract, is the subject of some conflict of authority. Since the purchaser is regarded as the equitable owner after the making of an unconditional contract for the sale of realty and before conveyance is made, the majority of jurisdictions hold that he assumes the risk of destruction or deterioration of the property from the date of the making of the contract, caused by accident and not by the fault of either of the parties. In a number of jurisdictions, however, the courts have declined to follow this rule, and hold that where buildings constituting a material part of the purchase are accidentally destroyed or substantially and materially damaged before the time for the delivery of the deed to the purchaser, the loss must fall upon the vendor, and that the purchaser may, if he chooses, withdraw from the contract. The application of this rule is sometimes made to depend upon whether the vendor retains actual or constructive possession or has placed the vendee in possession. If the loss or damage is the result of an act amounting to waste or negligence on the part of one of the parties, he must bear the loss. The loss must fall on the vendor, under either view, where it occurs at a time when he is in default in the performance of the contract.

The parties may, by express provision in the contract of sale, determine who shall bear the risk of loss by fire or other casualty; and where valuable improvements exist on the land, common prudence recommends the inclusion of such a provision in the contract.

Where the vendor carries insurance in his own name on the property, and under the terms of the contract or by operation of law, he must bear the burden of any loss or damage to the property, he is not obligated to account to the purchaser for the proceeds of policies of insurance in case of loss. On the other hand, where the loss would, in the absence of insurance, fall upon the purchaser, it is generally held that he may require the insurance money to be used toward the reduction of the unpaid purchase money, although the contract is silent as to insurance.

§ 18:56. Remedies and protection of vendor.

Am Jur 2d References: Exchange of Property, §§ 40–52; Vendor and Purchaser (1st ed, §§ 438–446, 509–527, 617–642).

In the event of the purchaser's breach of a contract for the purchase of land, the vendor has a choice of several remedies.   He may bring an action at law for damages for breach of contract if the contract is executory, or to recover the contract price if the contract is executed; he may sue in equity for specific performance of the contract, or he may elect to declare the contract at an end and then institute action to recover possession where the purchaser has been placed in possession under the contract.   As a general rule, the election by the vendor of one of these remedies waives the others.

The vendor may, by provision in the contract of sale, preserve title in himself until payment of the purchase price, or he may, in the conveyance, retain a vendor's lien; and in many jurisdictions the vendor has an implied lien as security for the unpaid purchase money.   (As to vendor's liens, see § 18:79, infra.)   The vendor may, of course, secure the payment of the purchase price by means of a mortgage on the property, as to which see the topic Mortgages in this work.

Where a vendor elects to bring an action for damages for breach of an executory contract of sale of real estate, the measure of damages is generally the difference between the contract price and the market value of the land at the time of the breach.

§ 18:57. Remedies and protection of purchaser.

Am Jur 2d References: Exchange of Property, §§ 40–52; Improvements, §§ 1 et seq.; Vendor and Purchaser (1st ed, §§ 528–578, 585–616).

The purchaser in a contract for the sale of land has several different legal and equitable remedies against a defaulting vendor.   If the vendor is able but unwilling to convey title to the land according to the contract, the vendee may invoke the jurisdiction of a court of equity and secure a decree of specific performance, compelling the vendor to make a conveyance, provided that the equitable principles governing the remedy of specific performance (discussed under the topic Equity) are complied with.   And even though the vendor may not be able to convey the full title or all of the property which he contracted to convey, the vendee may, at his election, compel the vendor to perform the contract so far as he is able, with an abatement of the purchase price to compensate for the defect in title or deficiency in quantity.

Instead of seeking relief in equity, the purchaser may bring an action at law for damages where the vendor breaches his contract to convey.   The measure of damages in such cases is generally held to be the difference between the actual value of the land and the agreed price, although in some jurisdictions it is held that where the vendor has acted in good faith, the measure of damages is the amount of the purchase money paid, with interest, thereby denying to the purchaser any recovery for the loss of his bargain.

Where the vendor is in default under an executory contract, or where the contract is invalid for mistake, fraud, misrepresentation, or other reason, or where the property has been destroyed or so materially injured as to relieve the purchaser from the contract, the latter may ordinarily recover payments or deposits made under the contract, where he himself is not in default.

A purchaser of land who is induced to enter into the contract by fraud or misrepresentation by the vendor may generally either rescind the contract and recover back any consideration paid, or maintain an action for damages sustained by reason of the fraud or misrepresentations. The purchaser's election to rescind the contract is usually a waiver of his right to sue for damages based on fraud. In an action for damages for fraud, the great weight of authority makes the measure of damages the difference between the actual value of the property at the time of making the contract and the value that it would have possessed if the representations had been true. In other words, the defrauded purchaser is entitled to recover the difference between the real and the represented value of the property, and is thus given the benefit of the bargain. However, some courts, applying the "out of pocket" doctrine, do not allow the purchaser the benefit of the bargain, but limit his recovery to the difference between the actual value of the property acquired by the plaintiff, at the time of the making of the contract, and the purchase money or other consideration parted with by him.

Where the purchaser has been placed in possession under an executory contract for the sale of land, and he is in default and the vendor exercises his right to terminate the contract and retake possession, the vendee is not, as a general rule, entitled to reimbursement for improvements made by him on the land during the period of his possession. Under some circumstances, however, the failure to complete the purchase is due to the fault of the vendor, and equitable considerations require reimbursement for such improvements. And where the vendor elects to rescind the contract, the vendee is entitled to a return of any part of the purchase price paid by him, and the vendor waives his right to recover any of the unpaid purchase money.

§ 18:58. Claims of third persons; bona fide purchasers.

Am Jur 2d References: Vendor and Purchaser (1st ed, §§ 649–684, 735–766).

It is a general rule that a vendor can, as against third persons having superior legal or equitable interests, convey only such interest as he himself has, and a purchaser can acquire from him no greater legal interest than the vendor possesses, and he takes subject to the interests of such third persons. However, a purchaser may be entitled to protection against outstanding equitable interests or against unrecorded conveyances of legal interests where he can establish that he is a bona fide purchaser for value.

A subsequent grantee of the vendor will take free from the rights of a purchaser under a prior executory contract if he is entitled to protection as a bona fide purchaser; if he is not entitled to this protection, he takes subject to the interest of the prior purchaser. A purchaser of land, even though he is not entitled to protection as a bona fide purchaser, will take free of an earlier deed which is absolutely void.

In determining priority as between the original vendor and a person claiming through a purchaser from him, the general rules governing bona fide purchasers prevail, so that an equitable interest of the vendor in the property may be cut off by transfer by the purchaser of his legal interest to one entitled to protection as a bona fide purchaser. Where the deed from the original vendor is merely voidable, and not void, on the ground of fraud, duress, or undue influence, a bona fide purchaser from the grantee therein is protected against the rights of the original grantor. However, a forged deed is a nullity and ineffectual to pass title, even to a subsequent innocent purchaser from the grantee named in such deed. Also, even a bona fide purchaser for value is not protected where his purchase is from one who claims under a deed which was never delivered to him, as where possession of the instrument was secured surreptitiously or by fraud.

The protection accorded a person as a bona fide purchaser of real estate does not apply to one who acquires no semblance of title; and if his vendor had no title, the purchaser acquires none. General creditors are not entitled to protection afforded to bona fide purchasers, and this rule is applied to judgment creditors.

To be entitled to protection as a bona fide purchaser, the purchase must have been made in good faith and without notice. A purchaser with notice of outstanding interests or claims takes subject thereto, and is not regarded as a bona fide purchaser, even though he parted with a valuable consideration. There must, however, be the additional showing that the purchase was for a valuable consideration, a mere volunteer not being entitled to protection as a bona fide purchaser. Good faith or want of notice, without valuable consideration, is not sufficient. The mere fact that there is a good consideration which would support an ordinary contract does not necessarily establish that there was a valuable consideration sufficient to give the purchaser protection as a bona fide purchaser. The adequacy of the consideration is not always determinative of this question, and the fact that the purchase price was less than the market value of the real estate does not necessarily preclude the purchaser from the position of purchaser for value. However, protection has been denied where the amount paid was so insignificant in comparison with the value of the property as to be deemed unsubstantial or nominal and to have played no material part in the transactions. A person is entitled to protection as a bona fide purchaser only where the consideration has been paid or performed, and an unperformed obligation is not value sufficient to entitle the obligor to this protection. Hence, if the purchaser receives actual or constructive notice of the outstanding interest before payment of the obligation he has assumed, he will not, even though he thereafter pays such obligation, be entitled to protection as a bona fide purchaser.

A remote purchaser of real estate who does not fulfil the requisites for protection as a bona fide purchaser may nevertheless be accorded protection because of his purchase from one who is entitled thereto. And a purchaser who himself acted in good faith, without notice and for value, may be entitled to protection as a bona fide purchaser against a prior interest in the property, although his vendor or any prior grantor in the chain of title was not entitled to such protection.

§ 18:59. — Good faith and absence of notice.

Am Jur 2d References: Vendor and Purchaser (1st ed, §§ 685–734, 763).

In order to be protected as a bona fide purchaser, one must establish not only that he has parted with a valuable consideration, but also that he has proceeded in good faith and without notice of prior conveyances or outstanding interests. Notice which will charge a subsequent purchaser with knowledge of a prior interest may be either direct information of the prior right or information of facts from which actual knowledge may be inferred; the notice need not be actual, but may be constructive or implied. Where he has actual notice of an outstanding interest, the purchaser is charged with notice of all information that an inquiry would have disclosed. Notice, to be effective to deprive a person of protection as a bona fide purchaser, must be communicated before the transaction is completed. Proper notice to the duly authorized agent of the purchaser constitutes notice to the latter.

Notice of prior interest which will be effective to charge a subsequent purchaser with knowledge of its existence may consist of information concerning facts from which actual knowledge may be inferred, and constructive or implied notice may result from the fact that the purchaser had means of knowledge which he did not use. Where the subsequent purchaser had knowledge of circumstances which, in the exercise of common reason and prudence, ought to put a man upon particular inquiry, he will be presumed to have made that inquiry and will be charged with notice of every fact which such investigation would probably have disclosed had it been properly pursued. To charge a purchaser with constructive notice under this principle, however, the circumstances relied on as putting him on inquiry must be such as would raise a suspicion in the mind of a reasonably or ordinarily prudent man, so that a failure to pursue an inquiry may be characterized as negligence.

Under the recording laws of the several states, a proper recording of a transfer of an interest in real estate constitutes constructive notice to purchasers and others acquiring interests subsequently to the recording. A purchaser is also charged with notice of all that appears in the deed to him and in the deeds or muniments in his grantor's chain of title.

Possession of land is a fact putting all persons on inquiry as to the nature of the rights of the occupant. Hence, possession of real estate is generally considered constructive notice of the rights of the possessor. A purchaser of such land is charged with the duty of making an investigation concerning the nature of such possession and the title or rights claimed by the occupant.

VIII. CONVEYANCES

§ 18:60. Generally.

Am Jur 2d References: Deeds, §§ 1–17, 41–60.

The method of conveying freehold estates under the early common law of England was by livery of seisin. This was a formal and ceremonial delivery of possession or seisin by the feoffor to the feoffee. It was usually accomplished by the parties going upon the land, or within sight of the land, in the presence of witnesses (usually neighbors), and the delivery to the feoffee of a bit of earth, a twig, a hasp of a door, or other article symbolizing the land and dominion thereof, accompanied by the speaking of words of feoffment such as "give and grant," and by transfer of possession. Sometimes a deed or charter was read; but no writing was necessary to convey land prior to the enactment of the Statute of Frauds in 1676. The conveyance of real property in the United States has been accomplished from the earliest times by means of deeds of conveyance or deeds of bargain and sale. Indeed, a mere livery of seisin, without a writing, would not be effective under the statute of frauds.

In order to be effective as a conveyance of land, a deed must be executed by a grantor who has the mental and legal competency to execute such an instrument, and it must name a grantee who is in existence at the time of the conveyance. A grant to a deceased person is void at common law, although statutes in some states provide that the grantee's heirs shall take the estate in such a case. The grantor and the grantee must be so designated in the deed as to be identifiable with certainty. As a general rule, a purported deed in which a blank is left for the name of the grantee is inoperative as a conveyance so long as the blank remains unfilled. However, a deed executed in blank as to the grantee becomes valid and effective if the blank is filled in by the grantor or his duly authorized agent. And in some jurisdictions the validity of a deed is not affected by delivery to the grantee himself with a blank for the insertion of his name, the delivery of such a deed being deemed to carry implied authority to insert the name of the grantee.

It is sometimes difficult to determine whether an instrument in the form of a deed is actually a deed or a will. If the instrument, though postponing its effect until after the death of the grantor, is construed as passing a present irrevocable interest in the grantee, the instrument is a deed. Where, however, the provision postponing its effect until after the death of the grantor is construed as passing an interest not to take effect until the death of the maker, so that the instrument is revocable, it is testamentary in character and must be executed with the formalities required of wills.

§ 18:61. Execution and formal requisites.

Am Jur 2d References: Acknowledgments, §§ 1–7; Deeds, §§ 18–40.

The "execution" of a deed connotes all acts which are necessary to the effectiveness of the instrument, including signing, sealing when necessary, attestation and acknowledgment when required by statute, and delivery to the grantee or to someone in his behalf. In the early days of conveyancing, a deed was authenticated by the seal of the grantor, with the addition of his signature if he could write.

Today it is generally recognized that the signature of the grantor is essential to the validity of a deed of real property; and the acknowledgment of the deed will not cure the omission to sign it, in the absence of statute. It is not essential, however, that the grantor's signature be in his own handwriting; another may sign for him or he may sign with the assistance of another. And he may sign the deed by his mark, attested by witnesses. In the absence of a statute requiring that the instrument be "subscribed," it is not essential to the validity of a deed that the signature appear at the end of the instrument. It is generally sufficient if the signature appears in some place in the instrument and is written for the purpose of giving authenticity to the instrument.

At common law, sealing a deed was essential to its validity. And a vestige of this practice remains in the custom in some states to append a printed scroll or the printed or typewritten word "seal"—which, of course, adds nothing to the authentication of the deed. In most jurisdictions now the necessity of seals has been dispensed with by statutes.

Attestation by witnesses is not generally essential to the validity of a deed, although statutes in some states require attestation, at least as a prerequisite of recordation. And manifestly, attestation is necessary where the deed is signed by a mark, unless the mark has such distinctive features as to be recognized as the signature of the grantor.

Statutes in practically all jurisdictions provide for the acknowledgment of deeds before an officer authorized to take acknowledgment, usually in order that the deed may be recorded. Under such statutes, an unacknowledged deed is usually binding between the parties thereto, their heirs and representatives, and persons having actual notice of the instrument; but under some statutes acknowledgment is a prerequisite to the validity of the deed, even as between the parties.

A deed must contain such language as to show who is granting the property, to whom it is granted, and what the property is, and it is usual for the conveyancer to set forth the provisions of the deed in a formal and traditional manner. It is not essential to the validity of the instrument as a deed, however, that it follow any exact or prescribed form of words, provided it expresses the intention to convey. Deeds are traditionally regarded as consisting of a number of formal parts, the first of which is known as "the premises," which consists of the preliminary recitals, the names and descriptions of the parties, the consideration, the words of grant, and the description of the property conveyed. Other parts of a deed include the habendum, the reddendum or reservation, the conditions upon which the estate is granted, the warranty and other covenants of title and the covenants relating to the use of the property, the testimonium, and the attestation clause. The date of the deed is one of its formal parts, but is not essential to its validity. The most essential part of a deed is the granting clause. In order to transfer title, the instrument must contain apt words of grant which manifest the grantor's intent to make a present conveyance of the land by his deed, as distinguished from an intention to convey it at some future time. The usual words employed for this purpose are "grant," "convey," "assign and set over," "transfer," and "give." In formal deeds the habendum is the provision setting forth the estate to be held by the grantee, as "To have and to hold unto the said grantee and his heirs and assigns forever." However, in most jurisdictions today no words of inheritance are necessary to pass a fee simple estate; and where the estate conveyed is clearly defined in the granting clause, the habendum is not really essential.

§ 18:62. Delivery and acceptance.

Am Jur 2d References: Deeds, §§ 76–135.

A deed is not effective as a conveyance of real property until there has been a voluntary delivery thereof by the grantor to the grantee, or to someone in behalf of the grantee, and an acceptance thereof on the part of the grantee, with the mutual intention of the parties to pass title to the property or interest described in the deed.

The intention of the parties is a controlling element in determining whether there has been an effective delivery of a deed. There must be a mutual intention of both parties that the instrument shall be immediately effective to pass title to the grantee. An effective delivery occurs only when the grantor parts with his dominion over the deed with the intention to pass title. Hence, where possession of a deed is obtained without the consent of the grantor, or by force, theft, or fraud, or surreptitiously, there is no valid delivery. While delivery may be by words, or acts, or both combined, and while it is not always essential to legal delivery of a deed that physical possession of the instrument be transferred from grantor to grantee, it is essential to legal delivery that the grantor relinquish all dominion and control over the instrument. There is no delivery where the grantor keeps the deed in his own possession with the intention of retaining it, particularly where he remains in possession of the property. Modern law requires no particular formula of words or acts to effect a delivery of a deed. All that is required is that by his words or by his acts, or by both words and acts, the grantor manifests an intention to deliver the deed beyond recall.

The mailing of a deed by the grantor to the grantee operates as a delivery to the latter as of the time the deed left the control of the grantor. While the fact that a deed is recorded is prima facie evidence of delivery, it is not necessarily conclusive. However, a delivery of the deed by the grantor, with the grantee's acquiescence, to the proper officer for recording, with the intention that it shall pass the title, constitutes an effective delivery, the recording officer being deemed the grantee's agent.

The delivery of a deed to a third person with instructions to pass it on to the grantee, and without any reservation by the grantor of a right to recall it, is a sufficient delivery. Where a deed purports to convey title to several grantees, the delivery of the instrument to one of the grantees is generally regarded as a delivery in favor of all of them.

While a grantor's possession of a deed raises a presumption that the deed was never delivered, it may be shown by evidence that a delivery was completed and that the deed is operative notwithstanding the grantor's subsequent custody thereof.

Valid delivery of a deed requires that it pass beyond the control and dominion of the grantor during his lifetime. Where a grantor retains in his possession and control until his death a deed which he executes without doing anything to indicate an intention to deliver it, it is invalid for want of delivery. Such an instrument can be effective only as a will, if at all. However, it is competent to show by evidence that a deed in the custody of the grantor at the time of his death had, in fact, been delivered. And it is generally recognized that an effective delivery may be made by the grantor's manual delivery of a deed to a third person, with directions to the latter to hold the deed during the lifetime of the grantor and upon the latter's death to deliver it to the grantee, where the grantor intends thereby to part forever with all right or power to recover control of the deed. Such a delivery is effectual to convey title to the grantee upon the grantor's death, even though the grantee is not aware of the delivery until after the grantor's death, since the grantor cannot after such a delivery recall or revoke the deed without the consent of the grantee.

A presumption of delivery of a deed arises from its possession by the grantee or one claiming under him; and a deed in the possession of the grantor is presumed never to have been delivered. However, these presumptions are rebuttable.

While a delivery of a deed must be accepted by the grantee to make it effective, acceptance may be manifested by the grantee's conduct as well as by his words. His intention to accept may be inferred from such conduct as retaining possession of the deed, conveying or mortgaging the property, recording the deed, or otherwise exercising the rights of an owner. The fact that a deed is beneficial to the grantee and imposes no obligation upon him will under some circumstances create a presumption of acceptance by him. Such a presumption may arise where a deed beneficial to the grantee is delivered to a third person for the grantee or is placed on record by the grantor. The presumption of acceptance is especially applicable to beneficial conveyances to infants.

§ 18:63. — Delivery in escrow.

Am Jur 2d References: Escrow, §§ 1–43.

An escrow is a written instrument which by its terms imports a legal obligation and which is deposited by the grantor, promisor, or obligor with a third party, to be kept by such depositary until the performance of a condition or the happening of an event specified in the escrow agreement, and then delivered over to the grantee, promisee, or obligee. In addition to deeds, various other types of instruments may be subjects of an escrow, such as bonds, mortgages, leases, contracts for the sale of real or personal property, promissory notes and other commercial paper, and money. There is no escrow unless the delivery of the instrument by the depositary to the grantee or obligee is conditioned upon the performance of some act or the happening of some event. The condition must be part of a valid contract between the parties.

The terms of the escrow must be agreed upon by the parties, and the escrow agreement must be communicated to and accepted by the depositary or escrow agent. The condition upon which the depositary is to deliver a deed placed in escrow need not be expressed in writing, but may rest in parol or be partly written and in part oral. The parties to an escrow may, of course, withdraw or cancel the same by mutual consent. But there can be no escrow without an irrevocable delivery of the instrument to the depositary. The death of either party does not abrogate a true contract of escrow. Where there has been an actual deposit of a deed in escrow and the death of either party is not contemplated as a condition, the escrow is not affected by the death of either or both of the parties before the actual condition is performed or before final delivery.

A deed placed in escrow does not become effective or pass legal title until the condition has been performed or the event has happened upon which it is to be delivered to the grantee or until delivery by the depositary to the grantee. And a purported delivery by the depositary in violation of the escrow agreement is inoperative and confers no right upon the grantee.

Although the depositary is frequently referred to as the agent of both parties, his actual status is that of fiduciary or trustee of an express trust. The depositary is bound by the terms and conditions of the escrow agreement and is charged with a strict execution of the duties voluntarily assumed. He is liable if he improperly parts with the deed held in escrow, or if he fails to deliver it upon the performance of the condition or happening of the event upon which it is required to be delivered.

According to the prevailing view, a deed held in escrow becomes operative and vests title in the grantee upon the happening of the event or the performance of the condition upon which manual delivery should be made by the depositary to the grantee, although manual delivery is not made at that time. Upon the delivery of an escrow instrument by the depositary, or upon the performance of the condition of the escrow agreement, the deed will be treated as relating back to, and taking effect at, the time of the original deposit in escrow, where a resort to this fiction is necessary to give the deed effect, to prevent injustice, or to effectuate the intention of the parties.

§ 18:64. Validity.

Am Jur 2d References:　Champerty and Maintenance, §§ 11–13; Deeds, §§ 61–75, 136–158.

A deed may be invalid and inoperative by reason of matters discussed in the preceding sections, such as defective execution or lack of the formal requisites as to the contents of the instrument, incapacity or incomplete designation of the parties, or an absence of a proper delivery and acceptance of the instrument. A deed may be either void or voidable, and there is an important distinction between these terms. A deed that is merely voidable is generally operative to convey title to the property and is generally good until annulled by a court of equity, subject to the protection of an innocent purchaser from the grantee. On the other hand, a deed that is void is invalid and inoperative for all purposes and as to all persons.

A forged deed, or one that has been the subject of a material alteration without the consent of the grantor, is absolutely void and ineffectual to pass title, even to a bona fide purchaser from the grantee under such deed. And the recording of such a deed gives it no effect as a conveyance of title. Fraud in the procurement of a deed may render it invalid. Whether the deed is void at law or only voidable in equity depends upon the character of the fraud. Where the fraud is in the factum or act of execution of the deed, as where the nature, identity, or contents of the instrument are misrepresented or falsely read to the grantor, and he is induced to execute the instrument by such fraud without negligence on his part, the deed is generally held to be void, although some courts extend protection to innocent purchasers from the grantee in such cases. Other kinds of fraud inducing the grantor to enter into the sale and to execute the deed render it merely voidable as between the parties. A deed procured by duress or undue influence practiced upon the grantor, or executed pursuant to a mistake, may be voidable in equity, but is not void.

Under the old English doctrine, followed in some states, an attempted conveyance of land in the adverse possession of a third party under color of title is champertous and invalid.

§ 18:65. Construction, operation, and effect.

Am Jur 2d References: Deeds, §§ 159–219, 236–241, 282–313.

When the meaning of a deed is uncertain or ambiguous, courts resort to the established rules of construction. The primary and paramount rule of construction is that the real intention of the parties, particularly that of the grantor, is to be sought and carried out wherever possible, when contrary to no settled rule of property which specifically engrafts a particular meaning upon certain language, and when not violative of any statute or settled principles of law. The intention of the parties is to be gathered from the language of the deed itself, the circumstances attending and leading up to its execution, and the subject matter and the situation of the parties at that time. In arriving at the intention of the parties, the court will consider all clauses and parts of a deed, and then the instrument will be scrutinized as a whole. If possible, effect will be given to every clause and word of the instrument. Where uncertainty or ambiguity remains after the application of the usual rules of construction, doubts will be resolved against the grantor, and that construction will be adopted which is more favorable to the grantee than to the grantor.

While written and printed portions of a deed are equally binding upon the parties, yet if there is inconsistency or conflict as between the printed and the written or typewritten words, the latter will control, since words thus specially inserted are deemed to be peculiarly indicative of true intent. Where two clauses of a deed are inconsistent and totally repugnant to each other, the early common law followed the arbitrary rule that the first clause would be received and the second rejected. Modern authorities, however, tend to disregard the technical distinctions between various parts of a deed and the order in which the conflicting provisions occur, and to determine the primary or dominant intent as disclosed by the instrument as a whole.

Where there is a conflict between the granting clause and the habendum in respect of the quantum of the estate conveyed, the rule most frequently applied by modern authorities is that the real intention of the parties to the deed, if ascertainable from the instrument as a whole, will prevail. The alternative rule is that where there is an irreconcilable conflict between the two clauses, the granting clause will prevail over the habendum. Courts which follow this rule, however, will still attempt to reconcile the two clauses. And whichever of the rules is followed, it is generally agreed that a granting clause which is merely general in form or is indefinite or obscure will be controlled by a specific and clear habendum.

After the vesting of title by the delivery and acceptance of a deed, the instrument itself is important only as evidence of the transaction. The loss, destruction, or surrender of the deed does not affect the grantee's title, although a court of equity may give effect to a contract evidenced by a return or surrender of the deed to the grantor.

An instrument in the form of a deed, although inoperative as a transfer of the grantor's title, may be enforceable as a contract between the parties.

§ 18:66. Property and rights conveyed; description.

Am Jur 2d References: Deeds, §§ 220–261, 289–309.

In order to be effective as a conveyance of land, a deed must describe the property intended to be conveyed with sufficient definiteness and certainty to locate and identify it. Courts are very liberal in their approach to this problem, however, and a deed will not be declared void for uncertainty or lack of description if it is possible by any reasonable rules of construction to ascertain from the description, aided by extrinsic evidence, what property is intended to be conveyed. It is sufficient if the description in the deed furnishes a means of identification of the land; and the courts apply the maxim, "that is certain which can be made certain." As indicated, parol or extrinsic evidence is admissible for the purpose of identifying the property intended to be conveyed, where the deed is ambiguous.

Land may be effectively described in a deed in terms of any of the various elements of description, such as monuments, courses and distances (metes and bounds), and by quantity, adjacent boundaries, by lot, street, and house number, or by the name by which the property is generally known. Land may also be described by reference to a map, another deed, patent, or other such instrument which sufficiently identifies the property. Such a reference has the effect of incorporating the other instrument in the deed by reference.

Certain general rules of construction are applied in determining the identity and extent of the property conveyed by a deed. All such rules are directed to the primary purpose of ascertaining the intention of the parties. Conflicts in description will be reconciled, if possible, but where there are irreconcilable inconsistencies, that construction will be adopted which best comports with the manifest intention of the parties as shown by the whole deed and the surrounding circumstances. Where a particular and a general description of the land are repugnant to each other, the particular description will prevail unless a contrary intention is manifested by the deed as a whole. Another rule of construction applied in doubtful cases is that courts will favor a construction against the grantor with respect to the quantity of land conveyed. Description by quantity or acreage will usually yield to calls for monuments or description by courses and distances, unless there is a clear intent to convey a certain quantity.

In the absence of language in a deed indicating a contrary intention, everything that is properly appurtenant to the land granted thereby—that is, everything which is essential or reasonably necessary to the full beneficial use and enjoyment of the property and which the grantor has the power to convey—will pass to the grantee. This is true even though appurtenances are not mentioned in the deed, although it is customary to include appurtenances by express mention. Included in a conveyance of land are all easements and similar rights appurtenant to the land, and all buildings and other improvements on the land.

A complete and delivered deed has the effect of transferring the grantor's title, or so much thereof as the deed purports to convey, to the grantee, and of divesting the grantor thereof. This is true whether the deed is in the form of a quitclaim deed, purporting to convey only the grantor's right, title, and interest in the property, or is in the form of an unlimited conveyance. A deed may also have the effect of passing to the grantee a title subsequently acquired by the grantor. A grantor who executes a deed purporting to convey land to which he has no title or to which he has a defective title at the time of the conveyance will not be permitted, when he afterward acquires a good title, to claim in opposition to his deed as against his grantee or any person claiming title under the latter. This rule as to after-acquired title is most clearly applicable where the grantor's conveyance was with covenants of general warranty of title. The courts differ as to whether a special warranty will estop the grantor from asserting after-acquired title. There is also some difference of opinion where the deed contains no warranty at all, express or implied, although most courts take the view that if the intention of the parties was to convey the fee or if the deed recited or imported that the grantor had the seisin, the grantee will be entitled to any title subsequently acquired by the grantor. It is settled, however, that a mere quitclaim deed, by which the grantor professes to convey only such interest as existed in him at the time of the execution of the instrument, without more, will not pass to the grantee any title or right acquired by the grantor after the execution of the deed.

§ 18:67. Exceptions and reservations.

Am Jur 2d References: Deeds, §§ 262–281.

There is a technical distinction between a "reservation" and an "exception" in a conveyance of land. A reservation is the creation in favor of the grantor of a new right issuing out of the thing granted, something which did not exist as an independent right before the grant. An exception, on the other hand, operates to withdraw some part of the thing granted which would otherwise pass to the grantee under the general description, which was in esse at the time of the conveyance and which until such conveyance and severance was included in the thing granted. An exception excludes some part of the thing granted from the conveyance and the title to that part remains in the grantor by virtue of his original title, while a reservation creates a new right out of the subject of the grant and is originated by the conveyance.

Any part of the real property, or any interest therein, which may be severed from the whole by conveyance thereof may be excepted from the property conveyed. Among the particular things which may be reserved or excepted from a conveyance of land are growing crops, minerals and mineral rights, growing timber, water rights, and fixtures and improvements. The grantor may reserve an easement or a life estate or a lesser interest for himself. Land embraced in an exception must be described with the same definiteness and certainty that is required in describing the property granted. In construing an exception or reservation, the intention of the parties, as disclosed by the deed and the attendant circumstances, is the controlling factor. When the language of an exception or reservation is ambiguous, doubts will be resolved against the grantor in favor of the grantee.

Most jurisdictions follow the rule that a mere reservation in favor of a stranger to the deed gives him no right or interest in the property conveyed. Under this rule, the effect of a reservation, which cannot operate as an exception, is that the grantee's rights are not qualified or affected by it, and he may disregard it for all purposes. However, such a reservation may be sufficient to give notice of the stranger's claim to that which is purportedly reserved.

The general rule is that an exception attempted to be made in a deed in favor of a stranger thereto, without more, is not effectual to vest any title or interest in him, since the interest in question, where not already in the stranger, remains in the grantor. Such an exception is effectual, however, to prevent the title to the excepted land or interest from passing to the grantee, and it will preclude the latter's interfering with the stranger's enjoyment of that which was excepted, even though the exception itself fails to convey any new right to the stranger. Also, an exception of this kind may operate as notice of the stranger's existing rights and interests. A purported reservation, although not operative as such, may be effective as an exception so as to prevent the passage of the property or interest in question to the grantee.

§ 18:68. Covenants of title; warranty.

Am Jur 2d References: Covenants, Conditions, etc., §§ 43–164.

There are several kinds of covenants of title: the covenant to warrant and defend the title; the covenant of seisin, or of good right to convey; the covenant against encumbrances; and the covenant for further assurance. The contract for the sale of land usually stipulates for the inclusion of certain covenants of title in the deed.

A covenant of warranty is the most common of the covenants of title. Such a covenant is an undertaking by the warrantor that upon the failure of title which the deed purports to convey, either for the whole estate or part only, he will make compensation for the loss sustained. It is an assurance or guaranty of title. The obligation is not that the covenantor is the true owner or that he is seized in fee with the right to convey, but that he will defend and protect the covenantee against the rightful claims of all persons thereafter asserted. A covenant of warranty is a real covenant rather than a personal one, and it passes with the land to the heirs and assigns of the grantee.

A special warranty is one limited to certain persons or certain claims. As a general rule, a vendee receiving a special warranty or a quitclaim conveyance takes title subject to all the infirmities to which it was subject in the hands of the vendor. A special warranty deed warranting title only against claims held by, through, or under the grantor does not warrant the title generally against all persons.

A covenant of general warranty is prospective in nature and is broken only by an eviction under a paramount title existing at the time of the conveyance, or where the grantee yields to an actual hostile assertion of an adverse paramount title. The mere existence of a paramount title which has never been asserted does not amount to a constructive eviction which will support an action for breach of a covenant of general warranty.

A covenant of seisin or a covenant of good right to convey is an undertaking that the grantor is lawfully seized of, and has the right to convey, the property at the time of the execution of the conveyance. Such a covenant, as distinguished from a covenant of warranty, operates in the present, and it is broken, if at all, when it is made. The existence of an outstanding paramount title constitutes a breach, without any eviction of the grantee.

A covenant against encumbrances is a stipulation by the covenantor that there are no outstanding rights or interests in the estate conveyed or any part thereof which will diminish the value of the estate, although consistent with the passing of the estate. Such a covenant relates to things in existence at the time it was made; and, if broken at all, it is broken at the moment it is made. Not only liens and charges against the land, but easements and servitudes to which the land is subject, are within the purview of the term "encumbrances" as used in such covenants.

The covenant of quiet enjoyment is largely supplanted in this country by the covenant of warranty, so far as concerns conveyances of land. Its use is generally confined to leases. It relates to possession and not to the title transferred. It amounts to an undertaking that the covenantee will not be evicted or disturbed by good title in the possession of the premises in question. The covenant is broken only by an eviction or ouster of the covenantee, actual or constructive, by title paramount.

A covenant for further assurance is a covenant that the vendor will perform all acts, deeds, conveyances, and assurances which may be necessary to perfect and confirm the title. It operates prospectively only, and generally is breached only on disturbance or eviction of the covenantee.

The measure of damages for breach of a covenant of title, where there has been a complete failure of title to the entire estate conveyed, is generally held to be the value of the property at the time the covenant was made, and this value is usually fixed by the amount agreed upon and paid as consideration for the purchase. In some states, however, the correct measure of damages for a total breach of warranty of title is held to be the value of the land at the date of the eviction, without regard to the consideration expressed in the deed.

IX. BOUNDARIES

§ 18:69. Generally; descriptions.

Am Jur 2d References: Boundaries, §§ 1–11, 54–76.

Where a deed or other instrument involving real property is ambiguous or uncertain as to the boundaries of the land, the intention of the parties, as illuminated by the surrounding circumstances, will control. Boundaries are indicated by various descriptive elements, such as monuments, courses, distances, quantity, adjacent boundaries, and references to other instruments or maps.

A "monument," when used in describing land, is any physical object on the ground, either natural or artificial, which is of permanent nature. Natural monuments include such things as mountains, streams, trees, etc. Artificial objects and monuments consist of marked lines, stakes, roads, fences, buildings, etc. Where the monument is such an object as a tree, wall, or stone, the boundary is the center line of the monument. And this rule is frequently applied where the boundary monument is a watercourse or highway.

Where land is conveyed with reference to township, range, and lot, the government survey generally establishes the boundaries; and where the conveyance is with reference to maps or plats and lot number, the boundaries will be determined according to such map or plat.

Surveys of the Federal Government are run according to the true meridian, due allowance being made for declination or variation of the compass; and this rule prevails in some states. In other states boundaries are usually run according to the magnetic meridian.

All parts of the description in a conveyance should be given effect if possible. But where the calls for the location of boundaries are inconsistent, other things being equal, resort is to be had first to natural and artificial monuments, then to adjacent boundaries (which are considered a sort of monument), and thereafter to courses and distances. In other words, calls for courses and distances, quantity, etc., will, in case of conflict, be controlled by and will yield to calls for natural objects or landmarks or permanent artificial monuments. As between natural monuments, such as mountains, streams, rocks, etc., and artificial or manmade monuments, preference will be given to the former. As between courses and distances called for in the description of a boundary, the courses are usually considered to be the more reliable guide. Quantity is the least reliable of all descriptive particulars in a conveyance and the last to be resorted to. It yields to calls for monuments as well as to courses and distances, unless there is a clear intent to grant a certain quantity.

§ 18:70. References to waters, streets, and highways.

Am Jur 2d References: Boundaries, §§ 12–53.

Where the description in a conveyance of land calls for a stream or body of water or a street or highway, the location of the boundary generally depends upon the pre-existing ownership of the fee in the street or highway or underlying the waters (as to waters, see §§ 18:45, 18:47, supra). In the absence of an indication of a contrary intention, a person conveying land bounded by streets, highways, or waters is presumed to include his rights and title in and to the street, highway, and the land underlying the waters, in the absence of a clear indication to the contrary.

A reference to a nonnavigable stream locates the boundary along the "thread" or middle of the stream. If the stream referred to is navigable, the boundary is the bank of the stream. Where the description in a conveyance calls for the ocean or a tidal stream, the boundary will normally run along the water's edge. In some states such boundary is at the high-water mark, while in others (particularly in the New England states) the boundary is at the low-water mark.

In surveying land adjacent to a stream, lines are often run from one point to another along or near the bank or margin of the stream so as to leave a quantity of land between these straight lines and the thread or bank of the stream. These are called "meander lines," and they define the sinuosities of the stream constituting the boundary. Such lines are useful for ascertaining the quantity of land to be paid for by the purchaser; but a grant in accordance with such a survey ordinarily makes the water, and not the meander line, the boundary.

Ordinarily, the public does not own the fee of land devoted to highway purposes, but has merely an easement of passage over it. Where such is the case, a grant of land abutting on a highway, under a description with reference to the highway, conveys title to the center line of the highway, unless a contrary intention sufficiently appears. On the other hand, where title to the fee of a highway or street is vested in the public, a reference thereto locates the boundary along the edge of the public way.

§ 18:71. Establishment by agreement or judicial determination.

Am Jur 2d References: Boundaries, §§ 77–118.

Where the boundary line dividing lands of adjoining owners are uncertain or disputed, such owners may establish the line either by written instrument, conveyance, or parol agreement. A parol agreement fixing or locating an uncertain line does not pass title to real property, and hence the agreement does not contravene the statute of frauds. Such an oral agreement, when executed and actual possession is taken under it, becomes conclusive against the owners and those claiming under them. In order for a parol agreement establishing a boundary line between adjoining owners to be effective, however, the location of the true line must be doubtful or in dispute. The courts are divided in their opinions as to the necessity of continued acquiescence of both parties in a boundary line established by parol agreement, and also as to the period of time for which such acquiescence must continue.

An uncertain boundary line may be made certain by acquiescence of the adjoining landowners. If they occupy their respective premises up to a certain line which they mutually recognize and acquiesce in for a long period of time (usually the time prescribed by a statute of limitations), they are precluded from claiming that the line thus recognized is not the true one.

Questions of disputed boundaries may arise and be determined in various kinds of judicial proceedings, such as an action in the nature of ejectment, where title is in dispute, or trespass, where there has been no dispossession of the plaintiff. And special statutory proceedings are provided in most states for the ascertainment and settling of disputed boundaries. This procedure usually calls for the appointment of "fence viewers," commissioners, or processioners upon the application of the landowners, for their report to the court appointing them, and for the establishment of the boundary by the court.

X. DEDICATION

§ 18:72. Generally; mode of dedication.

Am Jur 2d References: Dedication, §§ 1–40, 56–65.

Dedication is the intentional appropriation or donation of land, or of an easement or interest therein, by its owner for some public use. Statutes govern the subject in some states. Dedication of land may be made for its use as highways, streets, alleys, parks, squares, or commons. The essence of dedication is that it shall be for the use of the public at large, and not for one person or a limited number of persons or restricted groups of individuals. However, the theory of dedication has been invoked to uphold gifts for pious and charitable uses, as for churches, schools, and cemeteries. Any person capable of making a grant may make a dedication. There need not be any specific grantee, such as an individual or corporation or municipality. A dedicator of land to the public may impose reasonable terms, restrictions, and limitations on which the land is given, provided such limitations are not inconsistent with or repugnant to the grant and are not contrary to law or public policy.

To effect a dedication of land for public use, it is essential that there be an offer of dedication by the owner, as by express declaration of the dedicator or by his acts, by deed, or by plat. The intention of the owner to set apart lands for the use of the public is the foundation of every dedication, and such an intention must be clearly manifested to establish a dedication. Under the common law, no particular formality is necessary to effect a dedication. It may be established by written instrument, but it need not be made in writing, as the statute of frauds is not applicable to dedications of land to the public. An intention to dedicate may be shown by the acts or conduct of the owner, without any express statement of dedication. Dedication is frequently made by map or plat. The sale of lots shown on a map or plat indicates an intent to dedicate streets, alleys, parks, and other such places designated on the map or plat for public use, unless a contrary intent is shown, as where references to streets or other places on the plat or map are clearly for the sole purpose of description. The dedication is ordinarily held to be irrevocable as between the vendor and the purchasers of lots with reference to such a map or plat. However, such a dedication is not final as between the vendor and the general public until there is an acceptance thereof by or on behalf of the public.

Generally, any offer to dedicate land to public use may be revoked or withdrawn, in whole or in part, at any time before it is accepted by or on behalf of the public, provided the rights of private persons have not intervened. Once a dedication has been accepted and completed, however, it is irrevocable.

§ 18:73. Acceptance, rejection, or abandonment.

Am Jur 2d References: Dedication, §§ 41–55, 66–68.

An offer to dedicate land to public use does not become an effective and complete dedication until there has been an acceptance thereof by or on behalf of the public. Statutes in some states require that the acceptance of a dedication be by public authorities. In the absence of statute, however, an offer to dedicate land may be accepted by the general public. Attempts to accept part of the property offered for dedication and to reject the remainder have resulted in considerable conflict in judicial decisions. Many courts have taken the view that an offer to dedicate streets shown on a map or plat may be accepted in whole or in part, and that a partial acceptance is not ipso facto a total acceptance, while other courts take the view that an acceptance of a part of a number of streets offered for dedication by plat amounts to an acceptance of all of the streets so offered. It is generally (though not universally) held that the acceptance of part of a single street amounts to a total acceptance of the entire street.

The right to accept an offer of dedication will ordinarily continue until the wants and the convenience of the public require the use of the land, or until the offer is withdrawn or revoked. It is indicated in some decisions, however, that the acceptance must come within a reasonable time.

Acceptance of an offer of dedication may be evidenced in various ways. It may be either express or implied, by formal action taken by a municipality or other public body, by the acts and conduct of public authorities, or by public use. For example, the fact that public authorities exercised a control over land offered as a public street, as by improving or paving it, will generally establish acceptance of the dedication offer, especially when accompanied by use on the part of the public. It is frequently held that use by the public may amount to an acceptance of an offer of dedication, especially as against the dedicator, though some courts hold that mere public use of a street or highway offered for dedication is not enough to impose on a municipality the duties and expenses incident to ownership.

An easement created by a dedication may be abandoned, so that, by operation of law, the land reverts to the original dedicator or to his heirs or assigns. Mere misuser or nonuser of land for the public use to which it was dedicated does not, however, work a reverter thereof, except where the sole use to which the property has been dedicated becomes impossible of execution, or so highly improbable as to be practically impossible.

XI. RECORDING OF TITLE INSTRUMENTS; REGISTRATION OF TITLE

§ 18:74. Recording instruments.

Am Jur 2d References: Records and Recording Laws, §§ 47–97, 156–188.

From the early days of America, it has been the practice here (differing from that prevailing in England) to maintain public records of deeds and other instruments affecting title to real property. Recording statutes now exist in all states providing for the recording of such instruments, and thereby protecting all parties against possible loss or destruction of a title instrument, and providing a means by which an intending purchaser or encumbrancer can safely determine what kind of title he is obtaining and protecting him against secret grants and liens.

Although the statutes of the several states vary in their provisions as to what instruments may or must be recorded, most of them provide for the recording of deeds and other conveyances of real property, mortgages, deeds of trust, leases for long terms, etc. Executory contracts for the sale and purchase of land are usually included. Special provisions are usually made for recording lis pendens notices, mechanic's liens, judgment liens, tax liens, and other charges against real property.

The manner and place of recordation are usually specified in the recording statutes. A deed or other instrument affecting title to land must usually be recorded in the county or district where the land lies. And the instrument must be of such nature as to be entitled to recordation, and it must be executed and authenticated with the formalities required by law, in order that the record may constitute constructive notice. In order to be admitted to record, it is ordinarily required that the instrument be properly acknowledged or proved, and in some states statutes require that the execution of deeds be attested by witnesses who subscribe their names thereto as such. Payment of a fee, and sometimes of a tax, may be a condition of the right to record an instrument.

Provision is usually made for the recording of maps and plats of tracts of land proposed to be sold in separate lots. Such a map or plat may aid in identifying land conveyed with reference thereto, and it may also establish a dedication (§ 18:72, supra) of streets and other public places.

The failure to record an instrument affecting title to land does not generally affect its validity as between the parties thereto and their heirs and personal representatives. The persons protected ordinarily against a failure to record such instruments are bona fide purchasers and encumbrancers. Under the recording acts, an unrecorded deed or other instrument required to be recorded is not valid or effective against a subsequent bona fide purchaser for value without notice of such instrument. Purchasers at execution or judicial sales are generally entitled to the protection of the recording statutes. The statutes and the judicial interpretation thereof vary in the determination of the question whether creditors are entitled to the protection of recording statutes. It is elementary, however, that actual notice of an unrecorded instrument is equivalent to the recording thereof, and that a subsequent purchaser taking with notice of the existence of such an instrument is not a bona fide purchaser and is not entitled to the protection of the recording acts.

§ 18:75. Effect of record; notice.

Am Jur 2d References: Records and Recording Laws, §§ 98–155.

The main purpose of recording instruments of title under the recording statutes is to give constructive notice to subsequent purchasers and encumbrancers, so that a person, in dealing with another in relation to real estate, may rely on the record title to the property. The recording of a deed, mortgage or other recordable instrument is constructive notice to anyone who claims any right under the grantor or mortgagor subsequent to such recording. Persons purchasing or encumbrancing property must examine the record and are charged with notice of the state of the title as disclosed by the record.

The recording statutes affect only persons who are required to search the records in order to protect their own interests, and the record of an instrument is constructive notice only to subsequent purchasers and encumbrancers, and does not affect prior parties. Hence, the owner of real estate, or a remainderman, is not required to watch the records to see whether a life tenant or someone else assumes to convey or encumber the property.

In most jurisdictions, the record of an instrument not in the record chain of title is not constructive notice to a person claiming under such chain of title; that is, the record of an instrument is constructive notice only to those who claim through or under the person executing it. Hence, the record of a conveyance by a person not connected with the record title is not notice to a subsequent purchaser or encumbrancer from one who holds the record title. Difficult problems, and conflicting judicial decisions, result from the situation where a conveyance is made and recorded prior to the time when the grantor obtains title.

No legal effect is produced upon the rights of the parties, or of subsequent purchasers or encumbrancers, by the recording of a void instrument, such as a forged deed. Nor does the record of an instrument constitute constructive notice if the instrument is not such as is authorized to be recorded. In some states, the statutes make the grantee or mortgagee responsible for any error or default on the part of the recording officer. In other states, a person who has properly deposited an instrument for record will be protected against the intervening rights of third persons even though the recording officer fails to record the instrument or records it improperly.

§ 18:76. Registration of land titles.

Am Jur 2d References: Registration of Land Titles, §§ 1–9, 19–22.

The "Torrens system" for the registration of land titles, introduced in Australia, provides for the establishment of a system of registration of titles to land, whereby the official certificate will always show the state of the title and the person in whom it is vested. The object of the system was to create absolutely indefeasible and unquestionable titles. However, as a foundation of the system, the title must first be established; and in this country this must be done in judicial proceedings. The system is in effect to some extent, usually on an optional basis, in a few states; and the statutes of these states vary.

XII. ADVERSE POSSESSION

§ 18:77. Generally; elements and requisites.

Am Jur 2d References: Adverse Possession, §§ 1–128, 236–244.

Title to property may be acquired by adverse possession thereof for the prescribed period and under the requisite conditions. Such a title is based upon the running of the statute of limitations applicable to the recovery of property. The running of the statute not only precludes the former owner from maintaining an action to recover the property, but it gives the adverse possessor a new title which he may assert against any person. Some courts have rationalized this result by stating that title by adverse possession rests upon a presumed grant or conveyance or upon the presumption of a lost grant, following the analogy of the basis of the acquisition of easements by prescription. A resort to this fiction is not necessary, however, either to invoke or to justify the application of a statute of limitations.   Unlike the rights arising under most statutes of limitation, which may be used only defensively, a title acquired by adverse possession may be asserted either defensively or offensively, either as a weapon or as a shield, in any kind of proceeding.

In order to ripen into a good title by adverse possession, the possession of a disseisor must have continued uninterrupted for the whole period prescribed by the statute of limitations; it must have been actual, open, visible, notorious, and hostile to the true owner's title and to the world at large; and the possession must have been held under a claim of right or title.   After a title by adverse possession matures and becomes vested, it relates back to the beginning of the adverse holding.   And such a title is not affected by recording statutes.

The length of time for which the adverse possession must be continued depends upon the terms of the statutes, which vary in the several states.   The claimant of title by adverse possession must show that he was in actual possession.   This means that he must have actual dominion and control of the land without subserviency to any other person.   What constitutes such actual possession depends upon the circumstances of the case, including the nature of the land and the uses to which it is adapted.   Unless the possession is maintained under color of title, such as a purported deed, there must be actual possession of all the land claimed.   Where the adverse possession is under color of title, however, it is ordinarily sufficient if part of the premises described in the color of title are actually occupied, the adverse possessor being deemed to be in constructive possession of the entire tract described in the instrument under which he claims.   On the other hand, where several tracts are described in the color of title, constructive possession can only extend to the whole of that which is partially occupied, and it does not ordinarily extend to other and distinct parcels separately described.

The possession of the disseisor must be hostile as against the true owner and as against the world.   Hostility of possession simply means that the possessor claims the exclusive right to the land and denies the title of any other person. The statute of limitations does not commence to run until there is a demonstration of the hostile or adverse character of the possession; and the hostile character of the possession must continue throughout the statutory period.

Considerable confusion has arisen on the question of the adverse character of occupancy of land under a mistake as to the true boundary.   It is generally held that where a person, in ignorance of his actual boundaries, takes and holds possession by mistake up to a certain line beyond his limits, in the belief that it is his true line and with intention to claim title up to that line, such possession, maintained for the requisite period, will ripen into title. On the other hand, where the person, by mistake or inadvertence, occupies up to a given line beyond his actual boundary, because he believes it to be the true line, but with no intention of claiming beyond the true line, there are many decisions to the effect that an indispensable element of adverse possession is wanting, in that the intent is conditional and not absolute.   The difficulty lies in determining the true intent of the possessor.   In the absence of an express disclaimer or understanding during the period of occupancy, the intention of the occupant should be determined by his acts and the nature and extent of his occupancy; and if he exercises possession, control, and dominion, permissible only by an owner, up to certain lines which encroach on his neighbor, his possession should be deemed hostile and adverse, even though he acted under a mistake as to his true boundary. The same principles apply to the occupancy of a building or other permanent structure which, through mistake as to the true boundary line, was erected so as to project over the property of an adjoining owner.

The requisite that the possession of the disseisor must be open and notorious means that his claim of ownership must be evidenced by acts and conduct sufficient to put a man of ordinary prudence on notice of the fact that the claimant holds the land as his own. The requirement that adverse possession must be exclusive means that there must be an ouster or disseisin of the true owner and that the disseisor must show an exclusive dominion over the land and an appropriation thereof to his own use and benefit.

In order that adverse possession may ripen into title, it is necessary to show that such possession has been continuous and uninterrupted for the full statutory period. Such continuity is interrupted where the occupant recognizes the title of another, or by his own ouster by the true owner by entry on the land or under a judgment.

In order to meet the requirements as to continuity of possession, it is not necessary that an adverse possession should be maintained for the statutory period by one person. Under the doctrine of "tacking," continuity may be shown by successive possessions of several different persons between whom the requisite privity exists. Where the successive possessions of those in privity with each other, when tacked together, constitute one continuous adverse possession for the statutory period, it will be sufficient. There must, however, be some privity of estate or connection of title between the several occupants. Such privity exists as between a grantor and his grantee, an ancestor and his heirs, a testator and his devisees, a tenant for life or years and the remainderman or reversioner, between landlord and tenant, between tenants in common, and between principal and agent.

In some jurisdictions an effective adverse possession must be not only under claim of right, but also under color of title. The two requirements are quite different. "Claim of right" or "claim of title" means merely that the possession is hostile and that the possessor is claiming the land as his own against the whole world. Color of title, on the other hand, is that which gives the semblance or appearance of title, but is not title in fact; that which, on its face, professes to pass title, but fails to do so because of want of title in the person from whom it comes or because the instrument is invalid and ineffective as a conveyance. There is a sharp conflict among the authorities on the question whether good faith is a necessary element where claim of right or color of title is relied on in cases of adverse possession.

The payment of taxes by the adverse occupant is frequently a factor affecting the acquisition of title by adverse possession. It is always evidence that the occupant claimed title; and in some states the payment of taxes by an adverse claimant is a prerequisite to establishing title by adverse possession.

§ 18:78. By and against whom title acquired; properties and estates affected.

Am Jur 2d References: Adverse Possession, §§ 129–235.

As a general rule, all persons, artificial as well as natural, may acquire title by adverse possession. And title by adverse possession may be acquired against all persons who are not excepted from the operation of the statute of limitations; but possession of real property is not ordinarily considered adverse as to one who, during its continuation, did not have a right of entry, as, for instance, a remainderman or a reversioner. And statutes of limitation generally except from their operation persons who are under disabilities such as infancy or insanity. Where the owner is thus under disability, the period of the statute does not begin to run in favor of an adverse possessor until after the removal of the disability. As a general rule, an adverse possession cannot be predicated on the possession of a parent as against a child, or on the possession of a child as against its parent. And the same rule ordinarily applies as between husband and wife.

The possession of a vendee under an executory contract of sale, prior to a conveyance to him, is deemed to be subservient to the title of the vendor; and where a grantor continues in possession of land after the execution and delivery of a deed thereto, he is regarded as holding the premises in subserviency to the grantee. The possession of a tenant is deemed to be that of the landlord, and is not ordinarily adverse to the latter; but a tenant may under some circumstances acquire title by adverse possession, where he clearly and openly repudiates the relationship of landlord and tenant and claims title in himself. Some authorities, however, doubt the power of the tenant to initiate adverse possession during the term. The possession of land by one cotenant is not deemed to be adverse to other cotenants. However, where one tenant in common actually and clearly ousts his cotenant and holds adversely for the statutory period, he may, under some circumstances, acquire title by adverse possession.

During the existence of a trust, the trustee may not assert an interest or title antagonistic to the beneficiary. The possession of a trustee is not adverse to the title of the cestui que trust. By repudiating and ending the trust, however, and openly and notoriously setting up title in himself, the trustee may initiate adverse possession which will ripen into title.

Ordinarily, in the absence of legislation providing otherwise, statutes of limitation do not run against the government, and title by adverse possession cannot be acquired as to public property.

Adverse possession of the surface of land, before severance of the title to the minerals thereunder, may ripen into title to the minerals underlying the land, if all of the requisites of a title by adverse possession otherwise exist. After severance of the title to the underlying minerals, title thereto cannot be acquired by the adverse possession of the surface alone. There is a conflict of authority as to whether the severance of the mineral estate will affect an adverse possession initiated prior to the severance. Title to severed mineral estates may be acquired by adverse possession, if there is actual, open, notorious, exclusive, continuous, hostile, and adverse possession of such minerals under a claim of right for the statutory period. Generally speaking, mining operations are necessary in order to constitute adverse possession of a severed mineral estate. This consists of actual taking possession of the minerals by drilling wells or digging mines and capturing or taking possession of the minerals to the exclusion of the mineral title holder.

It it a general rule that the possession of a life tenant, as such, cannot be adverse to the remainderman or reversioner, since the latter has no right of entry and possession during the existence of the life estate. The life tenant may, however, acquire adverse possession under certain circumstances. To establish a possession in himself adverse to the remainderman or reversioner, however, the life estate must first be extinguished, as by renunciation, repudiation, disavowal, disclaimer, or abandonment of that estate and all right of possession referable to it. The life tenant's conduct must demonstrate a clear purpose to oust the remainderman or reversioner and to bring home to the latter the adverse or hostile character of his possession.

A third person may acquire title to the interest of a life tenant in lands in which there is a life estate and remainder, by adverse possession for the statutory period and under the requisite conditions; but the title thus acquired does not affect the estate in remainder or reversion. Where there is adverse possession of land subject to a life estate, the statute of limitations does not generally run against remaindermen until the life estate has terminated, although exceptions to this rule are made by statutes in some states.

XIII. LIENS

§ 18:79. Generally; vendor's lien.

Am Jur 2d References: Vendor and Purchaser (1st ed, §§ 447–508).

Where a vendor of land reserves title until payment of the purchase price and the purchaser is to have immediate possession, it is usually held that the title is held merely as security for the debt and that the vendor has a lien to secure the payment of the purchase price.

The rule was established in England at an early date and it is followed in a majority of the American jurisdictions that a grantor of real estate has an implied equitable lien upon the lands conveyed as security for the unpaid purchase price. In some states the existence of such an implied equitable lien is not recognized, and in other jurisdictions statutes have modified the rules governing the lien. The vendor may waive the implied lien, either expressly or by acts, such as taking a purchase money mortgage or other additional security for the purchase price.

The vendor's implied equitable lien is generally good against all persons except bona fide purchasers for value. The lien is good against a purchaser with notice, actual or constructive, and against a grantee in a voluntary conveyance. The lien will not be enforced, however, against a subsequent bona fide purchaser or encumbrancer for value. The usual remedy to enforce a vendor's lien is by way of a suit in equity for a sale of the land and the application of its proceeds to the satisfaction of the unpaid purchase money.

Real-estate mortgages are treated in this work under the topic Mortgages.

§ 18:80. Mechanics' liens.

Am Jur 2d References: Mechanics' Liens, §§ 1–48, 238–338.

A mechanic's lien is a statutory security made available to persons who furnish labor or materials for the improvement of real estate. It exists only by virtue of statute, as the common law did not provide any lien on real property corresponding to the artisan's lien on personal property. The lien usually protects not only mechanics or laborers, but also materialmen, contractors, and subcontractors. Although their overall objectives are similar, mechanics' liens differ in important respects from maritime liens, from the security afforded laborers, materialmen, and subcontractors under contractors' bonds, and from the rights of laborers and materialmen with respect to the withholding of payments by the owner to the contractor.

Although the main purposes of mechanic's lien laws are the same in all states, the provisions of such statutes and their application and operation vary greatly from state to state. The statutes are generally divided into two basic classes, known as the "New York system" and the "Pennsylvania system." Under the New York system, the lien of a laborer, materialman, or subcontractor depends upon and is limited by the amount remaining due to the general contractor after service on the owner of notice that labor and materials have been or will be furnished. Such statutes give a derivative lien, the claimant being substituted to the rights of the general contractor. Under the Pennsylvania system, laborers, materialmen, and subcontractors are given a direct lien, not dependent on the existence of any indebtedness due from the owner to the contractor.

The general rules governing the interpretation of statutes apply to the mechanic's lien laws, the primary object being to ascertain and carry into effect the intention of the legislature as disclosed by the statute as a whole. There is a conflict of authority on the question whether such statutes should be given a strict or a liberal construction, the modern tendency of the courts supporting the view that such statutes, being remedial, should be liberally construed in favor of the claimant.

Mechanics' liens ordinarily cover both the improvement and the land improved, and usually are limited to real property to the exclusion of personal property. According to the prevailing view, public property may not be subjected to a mechanic's lien in the absence of express statutory provision therefor. A mechanic's lien may attach to any interest in land that is transferable. Thus, it may attach not only to an estate in fee simple, but also to a lesser estate, such as a life estate or an estate for years or a leasehold. However, the lien affects only the interest of the person who created the lien or for whom or at whose instance the labor was performed or the materials furnished.

The question of the time of the accrual of a mechanic's lien depends upon the terms of the statute creating the lien. In a few jurisdictions the lien does not attach until it is actually perfected by filing and complying with all statutory requirements. In most jurisdictions, however, the right to a mechanic's lien attaches prior to the time of actual filing or giving notice. Under such statutes, the right to a lien remains inchoate until there is a filing or giving of notice; but when the statutory requirements are complied with, the lien relates back to and is effective from the time the right accrued under the statute, and it is not affected by intervening changes in the owner's title. Under various statutes a mechanic's lien is held to attach at the date of the contract for improvement, at the commencement of the work, or at the time when labor is begun or the first materials are furnished. Special provisions are made in some statutes with reference to bona fide purchasers from the owner.

The priorities as between mechanics' liens and other liens and encumbrances, and between mechanics' liens of different claimants, depend upon the terms of the statutes. Ordinarily a lien created after a mechanic's lien has attached is subordinate thereto, while a lien existing on property before a mechanic's lien has attached is protected. Some statutes, however, give a mechanic's lien preference over all other encumbrances of which the lienholder had no notice at the time he commenced the labor or commenced to furnish the material.

Different rules and statutes prevail in the several states on the question whether an inchoate mechanic's lien, or the right to perfect a mechanic's lien, is assignable. However, a perfected lien may generally be assigned and the assignee may enforce it in his own name.

The right to a mechanic's lien may be lost or extinguished in several ways, as by failure to take the proper and timely steps to perfect or to enforce a lien, by waiver or release of the right in the required form, or by acts or conduct estopping the claimant from asserting a lien. A mechanic's lien, or the right to such a lien, may be discharged and extinguished by payment of the claim or obligation upon which the lien is founded, by giving a bond for the discharge of the lien, and, in some jurisdictions, by the removal or destruction of the improvements giving rise to the lien.

A contractor or subcontractor may bind himself in advance by agreement with the owner not to file or assert a mechanic's lien. Different results have been reached in different jurisdictions on the question of the effect upon a laborer, materialman, or subcontractor, not a party to such agreement, of a provision in the principal contract that the property shall be kept free of mechanics' liens or that no lien shall be asserted.

§ 18:81. — Right to mechanic's lien; nature of work or claim.

Am Jur 2d References: Mechanics' Liens, §§ 49–166.

Since a mechanic's lien is a creature of statute, the right to such a lien depends upon the terms of the statutes of the particular jurisdiction and upon the claimant's compliance with the statutory requirements.

The persons usually designated as being entitled to mechanics' liens for their contributions to the improvement of land are laborers or "mechanics," persons furnishing materials, subcontractors, and contractors. A corporation is deemed to be a "person" as regards entitlement to a lien. Persons supplying materials to a materialman or to a subcontractor are generally too far removed from the owner to be entitled to a mechanic's lien unless the statute expressly includes them. The lien is given for work done or materials furnished in the construction of improvements of realty, and under many statutes the privilege of the lien is extended to repairs, alterations or additions, demolitions, clearing or grading of land, excavation, landscaping, and the like. The statutes of some states provide for a mechanic's lien for any improvement constructed on any lands with the knowledge of the owner unless he shall, within a specified time, give or post notice that he will be responsible therefor.

Under the statutes of many jurisdictions, it is held to be necessary, in order to be the basis of a mechanic's lien, that materials be not only delivered on the premises but that they also become a part of the structure or improvement. In other jurisdictions, a lien may be acquired for materials furnished although it has not actually been incorporated in the building or improvement, provided the materials have been delivered upon the premises or there has been an implied assent by the owner. The trend of modern authority recognizes the right to a lien for materials furnished for temporary use in the process of construction, such as lumber used in making forms, especially where such material is entirely or substantially destroyed by such use. There is conflict among the decisions on the question whether a materialman is entitled to a lien for materials which are specially fabricated and designed for use in a particular improvement, where it is not actually incorporated therein.

One who does not furnish labor or materials but only furnishes money for an improvement or for the payment of a laborer or materialman is not entitled to a mechanic's lien, in the absence of an assignment from the laborer or materialman.

As a general rule, a mechanic's lien may be asserted only where there is a valid contract with the owner of some estate or interest in the real property to be subjected to the lien, or where the work was done or materials were furnished with or by his consent. The contract may be made by the owner's duly authorized agent or representative; and it need not be directly with the person furnishing the labor or material, as they are entitled to liens for labor and materials furnished to the principal contractor.

The contractor may not assert a mechanic's lien where he is in substantial default in the performance of his contract. The effect of such a default upon the rights of subcontractors, laborers, and materialmen varies in the different states, depending largely upon whether the lien rights of such persons are direct and independent of the rights of the principal contractor, or are derivative and measured by the rights of such contractor.

§ 18:82. — Obtaining, perfecting, and enforcing mechanic's lien.

Am Jur 2d References: Mechanics' Liens, §§ 167–237, 339–433.

The mechanic's lien statutes in many states require a notice to be given or served on the owner or his agent, within a specified time, in addition to the filing of what is variously called a claim, statement, or notice of lien. Under the various statutes, the pre-lien notice informs the owner that a subcontractor, materialman, or laborer has furnished, commenced to furnish, or is about to furnish, labor or materials, or that he intends to claim a lien, or both.

In order to perfect or enforce, and in some states in order to obtain, a mechanic's lien, the lienor must file a verified statement with some designated public official for record within a time prescribed by statute, and in a form sufficient to satisfy the statutory requirements. This statement is variously referred to as "the lien," "claim," "statement," "notice," "certificate," or "affidavit" of lien. The requirements and particulars of such statement or notice vary in the several states. The statutes generally require that this statement or notice be filed within a specified time after the completion of the work or the performance of the contract or from the time the last material was furnished or the labor last performed. The statutes usually declare what the claim, statement, or notice of lien shall contain, such as the name of the owner, the description of the premises, allegations as to the work performed or materials furnished, the amount due, for whom and for what it is due, the name and address of the lien claimant, and a proper verification. Statutes in some states authorize an amendment of a defective notice or statement of lien.

The procedure for the enforcement of a mechanic's lien is determined by the statutes of the individual states. Enforcement or foreclosure of the lien usually involves the sale of the property subject to the lien. The lienor may proceed to enforce his lien and simultaneously bring an action to recover a personal judgment for the amount due. The mechanic's lien statutes usually fix the time within which an action must be brought to enforce the lien.

XIV. REMEDIES TO PROTECT PROPERTY RIGHTS

§ 18:83. Generally; forcible entry and detainer.

Am Jur 2d References: Forcible Entry and Detainer, §§ 1–57.

The owner of real property has several different remedies, given by the common law and by statute, to protect his rights and interests in his property. These remedies include ejectment, trespass, waste, quieting title, and forcible entry and detainer. Each of these remedies is adapted to obtaining relief of a particular nature and from a particular kind of wrong.

The modern remedy of forcible entry and detainer is of statutory origin and was adopted from the criminal or quasi-criminal process of the same name prevailing under the common law. The remedy is summary in nature, and is based on an element of force on the part of the defendant in wrongfully taking or withholding the plaintiff's property. The entry must have been by force or with the threat of force and menace to life or limb. The modern trend, however, is to lessen the emphasis on the necessity of actual physical force. In some jurisdictions it is sufficient to sustain a charge of forcible detainer that the party unlawfully in possession refuses to vacate the premises on notice to do so; and, as in summary proceedings against tenants holding over, the statutes of some states eliminate the question of force altogether in both the entry and the detainer, and make the question turn solely on the right to possession.

The title to the property is not in issue in a forcible entry and detainer proceeding. The plaintiff's possession and right to possession are the matters before the court. Hence, a tenant in actual possession may maintain an action of forcible entry and detainer against a stranger, or even against his lessor, who wrongfully and forcibly dispossesses him.

In the absence of statute expressly authorizing it, damages cannot be recovered by the plaintiff in a forcible entry and detainer action; but statutes in a number of states expressly authorize the assessment of damages in such cases, and some statutes permit the assessment of double or treble damages.

§ 18:84. Ejectment.

Am Jur 2d References: Ejectment, §§ 1–56, 125, 127, 141, 143, 148.

Essentially, ejectment is a form of action in which the right of possession to land may be tried and the possession obtained. Even as modified by statute and though based upon title, the action is still of that essential nature. As developed under the early common law, the action of ejectment involved many fictitious elements, including John Doe as a fictitious party. The action has been greatly simplified by modern statutes, however, and some states have substituted simply actions for the recovery of real property or to determine the title thereto, or actions designated as trespass to try title.

The estate or interest sought to be recovered in an action of ejectment must be of a tangible or visible character; the property sued for must be a corporeal hereditament. The owner of an interest in minerals in situ may maintain ejectment to recover the same; but ejectment is not usually a proper remedy for the disturbance of a mere easement, which is an incorporeal right.

In order to maintain the action of ejectment, the plaintiff must have title to the property with a present right of possession. The plaintiff can recover only on the strength of his own title and not on the weakness of his adversary's. The defendant can defeat the action by showing an outstanding title in a third person or in himself. And the plaintiff can recover in ejectment only on his legal title as it existed at the commencement of the action. However, prior possession by the plaintiff or those under whom he claims is prima facie evidence of title sufficient to maintain ejectment as against a mere trespasser or intruder without even color of title. The plaintiff in an action of ejectment must show not only that he has a present right to possession, but that he has been ousted or deprived of possession, or that possession is wrongfully withheld from him by the defendant.

A judgment in the original common-law action of ejectment did not have the effect of determining the title, and a recovery was not a bar to another and similar action between the same parties for the same land. This rule, or the rule with only slight modifications, still exists in some jurisdictions. However, in many states the judgment has the same conclusiveness and effect as judgments in other cases and will bar a subsequent action between the same parties or their privies for the same land. In states having statutes making former judgments in ejectment conclusive, the defeated party is often given one or more new trials in order to avoid the chance of defeating a good title through surprise or mistake.

Under the old fictitious action of ejectment only nominal damages were allowed and actual damages measured by the profits of the land accruing during the tortious holding thereof by the defendant could not be recovered in such action. Under the modern practice of a number of states, however, mesne profits may be recovered in an action in the nature of ejectment.

§ 18:85. Trespass.

Am Jur 2d References: Trespass (1st ed, §§ 2, 11–20, 25–29, 49, 82).

The common-law form of action for recovery of damages for an intrusion upon the plaintiff's real property was known as "trespass quare clausum fregit." The gist of a trespass to realty lies in the disturbance of possession, which may take place in a variety of ways. At common law, every man's land was deemed to be inclosed, so that every unwarranted entry on the land necessarily carried with it some damage for which the trespasser was liable. Any entry on land in the peaceable possession of another is deemed a trespass, unless the entry is warranted, and neither the form of the instrumentality by which the close is broken nor the extent of the damage is material except as to the amount of the recovery. The intention of the trespasser is not ordinarily material. Thus, a person cutting timber on the land of another is liable in trespass, although his act resulted from a mistake as to the boundary. A breaking of the close may be accomplished without actual entry by the wrongdoer, as by the casting of substances or objects upon the plaintiff's property from without its boundaries. And trespass may result from entry upon the land of another below the surface or into the air space above the land, as by mining operations or by the projection of structures over the boundary.

Actual possession of real property, even without good title, is sufficient to sustain an action of trespass quare clausum fregit against one having no superior right or title. But possession, actual or constructive, at the time of the trespass is essential to the maintenance of the action.

The doctrine of trespass ab initio is of ancient origin. Where a right of entry, authority, or license is conferred by law, and it would not otherwise exist, an abuse of such authority will destroy the privilege and render the act done in excess of authority a trespass ab initio. In such cases the law operates retrospectively to render wrongful all acts done under color of lawful authority when the authority is exceeded. This doctrine is applied both to public officers and to private citizens acting under authority or license of law. Thus, one becomes a trespasser ab initio where he enters an inn lawfully if, after his entry, he commits an assault on the owner.

A judgment in an action of trespass quare clausum fregit is conclusive upon the parties and their privies as to all matters put in issue in the action, including title to the property.

§ 18:86. Waste.

Am Jur 2d References: Waste (1st ed, §§ 2–36).

Waste, as considered here, is a species of tort, which may be briefly and very generally defined as the destruction, misuse, alteration, or neglect of premises by one lawfully in possession thereof, to the injury and prejudice of the estate or interest of another. It has also been variously defined as the destruction or material alteration of any part of a tenement by a tenant for years or for life, to the injury of the remainder, reversion, or inheritance; as an unlawful act or omission on the part of the tenant which results in permanent injury to the inheritance; and as any spoil or destruction done or permitted with respect to land, houses, gardens, trees, or other corporeal here-ditaments by the tenant thereof, to the prejudice of the reversion, remainder, or inheritance. The subject has been generally discussed in connection with life estates, in § 18:7, supra. By these definitions, an act to constitute waste must be wrongful and must be prejudicial to the inheritance or to those entitled to the reversion or remainder.

Waste is classified as voluntary or commissive, and permissive or negligent waste. Voluntary waste is committed by such acts as destroying, altering, or removing buildings, or cutting timber. Permissive waste results from the failure of the tenant to exercise the ordinary care of a prudent man for the protection and preservation of the estate, as by permitting buildings to fall into decay.

Acts or conduct which would otherwise constitute waste may be author-ized and legalized by an appropriate provision in the instrument creating the tenancy, so as to relieve the tenant of liability therefor. The phrase "without impeachment of waste" is commonly employed for this purpose. Author-ization by the person whose estate or interest is affected thereby may also absolve the tenant from liability for acts which would otherwise constitute waste.

Under modern practice, an action for waste may be maintained not only by the person owning the immediate estate of inheritance, but also by a person having an estate in remainder or reversion, notwithstanding any intervening estate for life or years. Injunction to prevent waste will be granted in a proper case in favor of the person who would be injured thereby. The owner of a contingent remainder or of a defeasible future interest in the premises is not ordinarily entitled to maintain an action for damages for waste, but he may maintain a suit for injunction to prevent it. Under the early common law, a tenant committing waste was not only liable for treble damages, but was subject to the loss or forfeiture of property where the waste was commit-ted. The right to enforce a forfeiture, as well as the right to multiple dam-ages, still exists in some of the states of this country.

§ 18:87. Quieting title.

Am Jur 2d References: Quieting Title, §§ 1–65.

A suit to quiet the title to property or to remove a cloud on title is a form of proceeding originating in equity jurisprudence and having for its purpose an adjudication that another's claim of title to or of an interest in property, adverse to that of the complainant, is invalid, so that the complainant and those claiming under him may be free from the danger of the hostile claim. Jurisdiction to grant relief by way of quieting title or removal of cloud from title is inherent in a court exercising equity powers. In many states statutes have been enacted enlarging the jurisdiction of courts in suits to remove cloud or quiet title and providing for actions to determine any adverse claim, interest, or estate in land, or to determine the title thereto.

A cloud on title, which may be the subject of removal in a suit to quiet title, is an outstanding instrument, record, claim, or encumbrance which is actual-ly invalid or inoperative, but which may nevertheless impair or affect inju-riously the title or marketability of the property. Such a cloud may be created by anything that may be a muniment of title or constitute an encumbrance. Among the instruments, records, and proceedings which may create clouds on title, removable in equity, are deeds, leases, wills, mortgages, contracts, options, judgments, and tax and assessment proceedings, which are invalid or unenforceable.

It is generally agreed that a cloud on title is created by an invalid or inoperative instrument, record, or proceeding if the invalidity or ineffectiveness is not apparent on its face but must be proved by extrinsic evidence. On the other hand, most authorities hold that an instrument, record, or proceeding which is invalid and without effect on its face, or which will be shown to be invalid and inefficacious by the evidence necessary to support it, does not constitute a cloud on title. However, there is authority to the contrary on the latter proposition. While it is generally held that a cloud is not created by the fact that the determination of the validity of a pretended title or lien involves a question of law, some courts take the view that a cloud does exist if the invalidity of a claim is such that legal acumen is required to disclose or determine it. A cloud on title is generally held not to be created by a mere verbal or parol assertion of ownership or interest in property; but there are exceptions to this rule, as in the case of claim of title by adverse possession.

A court of equity has jurisdiction to prevent the casting of a cloud on title as well as to remove an existing cloud. Injunction may issue to prevent any wrongful act which, if performed, would create a cloud on title.

A party seeking the aid of a court of equity to remove a cloud on title must comply with the principles and maxims of equity jurisprudence; he must come into equity with clean hands, and he must satisfy the maxim, "he who seeks equity must do equity." And he is generally subject to the equitable principle that the court will deny the relief if the complainant has an adequate remedy by action at law. Courts frequently take jurisdiction of suits to remove clouds on title for the purpose of preventing a multiplicity of suits, excessive litigation, or circuity of action.

A suit to quiet title may be maintained although it is based only on a title by adverse possession. However, some jurisdictions require that the complainant first establish his legal title by action at law. A remainderman or reversioner, although obviously not in or entitled to immediate possession, is usually permitted to maintain an action to remove a cloud from his title. The court, as a condition of quieting the complainant's title, will usually require the complainant to restore any benefits he has received from the defendant, or reimburse the latter for any expenditures which inure to the complainant's benefit, such as taxes or assessments paid by the defendant.

The court taking jurisdiction of a suit to quiet title may, by its decree, adjust all the equities of the parties to the action and determine the status of all claims to and against the property. The court will decree such relief as is necessary for the complete and final disposition of the controversy, and may cancel any instrument constituting a cloud on title. And in a proper case and under the proper pleadings, the court may quiet the title of the defendant as against the plaintiff or grant the defendant other relief to which he is entitled.

*

RESTITUTION, QUASI-CONTRACTS AND IMPLIED CONTRACTS

I. IN GENERAL

I. IN GENERAL

§ 19:1. Generally; quasi-contracts and implied contracts.

Am Jur 2d References: Restitution and Implied Contracts, §§ 1–4.

Where a person has received money, services, or other benefit from another under such circumstances that in equity and good conscience he should return it or make compensation to the person from whom he received it, the law imposes upon him an obligation to make restitution or to pay the reasonable value of the benefit received. Formerly this obligation was frequently said to be based on a contract "implied in law"; but this terminology involves a mere legal fiction, and resulted in confusion with actual contracts implied in fact. This kind of obligation is more properly called "quasi-contract" or "constructive contract." In modern usage, however, all of these terms have been largely supplanted by the terms "unjust enrichment" and "restitution."

The obligation under a quasi-contract or the doctrine of unjust enrichment has no reference to the intentions, assent, or expressions of the parties. The liability exists from an implication of law that arises from the facts and circumstances independently of agreement or presumed intention. Although they are remediable by the contractual remedy of assumpsit, quasi-contracts lack many of the essentials of an actual contract, such as promise and privity, and the obligation of a quasi-contract arises, not from consent of the parties as in the case of contracts express or implied in fact, but solely by operation of law to accomplish justice and equity.

The phrase "unjust enrichment" characterizes the result or effect of a failure to make restitution of, or for, property or benefits received under such circumstances as to give rise to a legal or equitable obligation to account therefor. It expresses the legal principle that one person should not be permitted to enrich himself unjustly at the expense of another, but should be required to make restitution. Thus, it is clear that "unjust enrichment" and "restitution" are correlative terms, and generally unjust enrichment is a prerequisite of the right to restitution.

§ 19:2. Elements and requisites of unjust enrichment and restitution.

Am Jur 2d References: Restitution and Implied Contracts, §§ 3–10, 166–172.

Generally, quasi-contractual liability for unjust enrichment depends upon whether, by the receipt of money or other benefits from the plaintiff, the defendant was enriched at the loss and expense of the plaintiff, and whether such enrichment was unjust in equity and good conscience under all of the circumstances of the case. In other words, recovery under this doctrine requires a showing that there has been an enrichment of the defendant by some benefit conferred by the plaintiff, and that a retention of such benefit without compensation or restitution to the plaintiff would be unjust or inequitable. Good faith or absence of wrongdoing does not necessarily relieve a party of the duty of restitution, but it may entitle him to notice and opportunity to restore, and may also affect the extent of his liability.

As a general rule a person who officiously confers a benefit upon another is not entitled to restitution therefor, since a person is not liable for benefits forced upon him by a mere volunteer. However, there are circumstances under which restitution will be allowed on account of a benefit voluntarily conferred, where such action was necessary for the protection of the interests of the defendant or of third persons.

The right to restitution from one unjustly enriched at another's expense is terminated or diminished if the circumstances have so changed that it would be inequitable to require full restitution, unless the change occurred after the defendant had knowledge of the facts entitling the plaintiff to restitution and had an opportunity to make restitution. A person may be prevented from obtaining restitution because of his own criminal or other wrongful conduct in connection with the transaction on which his claim is based, the equitable doctrine of "clean hands" being generally applicable. With certain exceptions, the right of a person to restitution for a benefit conferred upon another in a transaction which is voidable for fraud or mistake is dependent upon his return or offer to return to the other party anything which he received as a part of the transaction. One who rescinds or voids a voidable contract or transaction must restore to the other party that which he has received under the transaction, before he is entitled to restitution of that which he parted with.

Since the primary aim of restitution is to restore the plaintiff to the position he occupied before the defendant received the benefit which gave rise to his obligation to restore, the general rule is that the plaintiff is entitled to receive that which he parted with, or more specifically, that which the defendant received. This may be the specific property or the value thereof, or the amount of money which he has paid, or the value of work, labor, services or materials furnished, or the value of a performance under a contract, plus interest.

§ 19:3. Grounds for restitution, generally.

Am Jur 2d References: Restitution and Implied Contracts, §§ 11–18.

The principles governing quasi-contracts and restitution are applied in a great variety of situations and instances and in many fields of the law. The doctrine applies to situations where there is no legal contract but where the person sought to be charged is in possession of money or property which in good conscience and justice he should not retain but should deliver to the plaintiff. Among the more common applications of the doctrine are actions to recover for work, services, or materials (infra, §§ 19:4–19:6), and actions for the recovery of payments made (infra, §§ 19:7–19:9). Already considered (supra, § 19:2) is the acquisition of property or other benefits under contracts which are invalid and unenforceable for various reasons. Other situations in which the doctrine is invoked involve benefits resulting from the partial performance of an agreement; services rendered or payments made under contracts violating the statute of frauds; liability for support of a person; liability of an infant for necessaries, or of a parent or husband for necessaries furnished his child or wife; the liability of incompetent persons in quasi-contract; compensation for improvements constructed on the land of another; benefits from an unauthorized loan to a third person purporting to act as agent; payments and advances made to an agent through mistake, fraud, or other wrongful conduct; deposit of money with an auctioneer where the principal's title proves defective; overcharges by a common carrier; rent paid under mistake or in advance and unearned; unauthorized or improper insurance payments; and usurious interest paid.

Under some circumstances a right to restitution arises, on the ground of unjust enrichment, where a party has partly but imperfectly performed an actual contract. If the other party accepts the benefit of such part performance he is accountable therefor. A right to restitution arises also where one person confers a benefit upon another through mistake of fact or of law. And relief by way of restitution is frequently granted for the recovery of that which has been parted with on account of fraud, duress, or undue influence. A person may even waive the tort and recover in assumpsit, on the basis of a quasi-contractual obligation, for a trespass upon real property, where the trespass results in some benefit to the trespasser, as where he cuts and removes timber or wrongfully takes minerals from the land.

II. RECOVERY FOR WORK, SERVICES, AND MATERIALS

§ 19:4. Generally.

Am Jur 2d References: Restitution and Implied Contracts, §§ 19–28.

A promise to pay the reasonable value of services performed by one person for another, without any express agreement as to compensation, will be implied where the circumstances warrant an inference of a promise to pay for such services. And although there is no contract in fact, either express or implied, recovery for services rendered or materials furnished to another may be had in a proper case on the principle that the defendant has been unjustly enriched at the expense of the plaintiff. The performance of services or furnishing of materials at the request of another confers a benefit upon the latter within the principle that a person who has been unjustly enriched at the expense of another is required to make restitution to the other. In the absence of circumstances indicating otherwise, where services are rendered or materials are furnished upon request, it is ordinarily a reasonable inference that the parties understand that they are to be paid for, and the person rendering the services or furnishing the materials may therefore recover in quantum meruit for the value thereof. However, a person requesting another to render services to a third person is ordinarily under no duty to pay for the services, in the absence of an agreement therefor, unless the person requesting the services was under obligation, by family relationship or otherwise, to provide the services for the third person.

The circumstances may be such as to negative any obligation to pay for services rendered, as where the person rendering the service has a strong self-interest in the transaction, or where such services when rendered under like circumstances are customarily given without compensation. Clearly there can be no recovery where it was intended, understood, or agreed that the services were to be gratuitous and that no payment should be made therefor. And there can be no recovery for services rendered without request solely in reliance on the recipient's generosity, in expectation of a gift inter vivos or by will. A person who voluntarily or officiously renders services to one who neither requests the services or accepts the benefits thereof may not ordinarily recover therefor. There may be circumstances of emergency, however, where a person is entitled to restitution for services rendered, without request, for the protection of another. If the services are beneficial to the party to whom they are rendered and he accepts their benefit, he is required to make restitution therefor under the doctrine of unjust enrichment.

§ 19:5. Effect of relationship of parties; kinship.

Am Jur 2d References: Restitution and Implied Contracts, §§ 29–57.

The relationship between the parties may preclude the idea of any legal duty to pay for personal services. If there is such a relationship between the parties as to create a moral or legal obligation upon the claimant to render personal services for the other, it is presumed that such services were rendered in response to that obligation, and not for pay. The general rule is that where persons live together as one family, a promise to pay for services of one to another is not implied from the mere rendition of the services, and the services are presumed to be gratuitous. This rule is applicable where a claim for compensation is made against the estate of a person who has died after the rendition of the services. The family relationship, for the purposes of this rule, need not necessarily be one of blood kindred. The rule rests upon the idea of the mutual dependence of those who are members of one immediate family, and such a "family" may exist although composed of remote relations, and even of persons between whom there is no tie of blood. For the purposes of this rule, the term "family" means a collection of persons who form one household, under one head and one domestic government, and who have reciprocal, natural, or moral duties to serve and care for each other. However, the degree of relationship is an important factor in this matter, and the more distant the relationship between the parties, the weaker the presumption that services rendered by one to another were gratuitous.

The presumption that services rendered for close relatives and family members are intended to be gratuitous may be overcome by evidence of circumstances showing an understanding or intention that payment was to be made for the services. Clearly an express contract or promise to pay for services creates an obligation to pay, regardless of the closeness of the relationship of the parties, and an express agreement may have the effect of rebutting the presumption that the services were rendered gratuitously, even though the agreement, as such, is unenforceable as within the statute of frauds. For example, although an oral promise to leave property by will, in return for certain services, is unenforceable under the statute of frauds, it may be effective to rebut the presumption that the services were gratuitous, so as to permit a recovery on a quantum meruit basis of the reasonable value of the services.

Services rendered by a child to his parent, or to one standing in loco parentis, or by a parent to his child, are generally presumed to be gratuitous. This applies to both minor and adult children, although some courts make a distinction where the services are performed by or for a child after he has left the family and established a separate home. The presumption of gratuity applies as between stepparent and stepchild and foster parent and child, so long as the child is a part of the family of the stepparent or foster parent. The same is generally true as between parent-in-law and child-in-law where the parties are living together as members of the same family, but not otherwise. Similar principles apply as between grandparent and grandchild. Other relationships, such as those existing between brothers and sisters, uncles and nephews and nieces, cousins, etc., are generally too remote to give rise to a presumption that services rendered as between them are gratuitous, unless the parties live together as a family.

§ 19:6. Effect of express contract.

Am Jur 2d References: Restitution and Implied Contracts, §§ 58–82.

It is a general rule that where an express contract is in force, the law does not recognize an implied one. Therefore, when services are performed under an express contract, the action to recover for such services must be under the express contract unless that contract has been waived, abandoned, or terminated, or the plaintiff has been prevented by the defendant from completing the work thereunder. However, the law implies a promise to pay for extra work rendered upon request. Ordinarily, for all work done beyond the express contract by request, recovery may be had as if no special contract had been made.

Where a person has performed services for another under a contract that is invalid or unenforceable, he may recover for those services upon quantum meruit, or on the basis of an implied promise to pay the reasonable value of the services. As in other cases of implied contracts, however, it is usually required that some benefit must have been conferred by the services. In an action to recover compensation for services rendered under an unenforceable agreement, the limit of recovery has been variously said to be the contract price, the value of the services regardless of the agreed price, and the benefit to the recipient of the services. The foregoing principles have been applied where services are performed in reliance upon an agreement which is unenforceable because of indefiniteness, or where the amount of the compensation is not stated in the contract.

It is a general principle that there can be no recovery of compensation for services performed under an express contract which provides for the commission of an illegal act which is malum in se, either under the contract or on quantum meruit. However, if the services are not themselves illegal, either intrinsically or by reason of the circumstances under which they are rendered, the prevailing view permits a recovery on quantum meruit for their reasonable value, although the contract is for other reasons illegal and unenforceable.

Where one has entered into a contract to perform work for another and to furnish materials, and the work is done and the materials are furnished, but not in the manner stipulated, so that he cannot recover on the contract, it is generally held that if the work and materials are of any benefit to the other party or if he accepts the same, a recovery may be had on a quantum meruit for the work and on a quantum valebant for the materials. This principle would seem especially clear where the claimant has made an effort in good faith to perform the contract or where there has been substantial performance thereof. Where full performance of an entire contract for services is prevented by the other party to the contract, it is clear that compensation may be recovered for the services rendered. There is a conflict of authority on the question whether an employee who has, without cause, abandoned an entire contract for the performance of services is entitled to recover for the services actually rendered.

III. RECOVERY OF PAYMENTS

§ 19:7. Generally.

Am Jur 2d References: Restitution and Implied Contracts, §§ 91–
115, 151, 152.

The fact that a claim or demand which a person has paid was invalid and that he was not legally liable thereon is not, standing alone, a ground on which he can recover back the payment. The general rule is well settled that a person cannot recover back money which he has voluntarily paid with full knowledge of all of the facts and without fraud or duress. This means that the party must assert his defense in the action brought to enforce the claim against him, if and when such an action is instituted.

A payment is deemed to be voluntary when it is made intentionally, by choice, and by free exercise of the will. Although the character of a payment as voluntary depends upon all of the facts in each particular case, it may be stated as a general rule that where a person pays an invalid or illegal demand, with full knowledge of all the facts, without an immediate and urgent necessity therefor, unless it is to release his person or property from detention or to prevent an immediate seizure of his personal property, such payment is voluntary. Stated in another way, a payment is not regarded as compulsory unless it is made to free the person or property from an actual and existing duress, imposed by the parties to whom the money is paid; and if a payment is otherwise voluntary, the mere filing of a written protest at the time of payment does not change its character.

If the payment of an invalid or illegal claim or demand is "involuntary," restitution may be compelled. What constitutes the compulsion or coercion which the law recognizes as sufficient to render a payment involuntary is difficult to define in precise general terms. The very word "involuntary," however, implies something which overcomes the will and imposes a necessity of payment in order to escape other ills. According to some authorities, in order to constitute duress, there must be such constraint as is sufficient to overcome the mind and will of a person of ordinary firmness. Under the modern doctrine of duress, however, the courts take into consideration the mental condition of the person acted upon, so that compulsion or duress may be sufficient to render a payment involuntary if it, in fact, overcomes the will of the person against whom it is applied. A rule frequently applied is that to constitute the coercion or duress which will render a payment involuntary, there must be some actual or threatened exercise of power possessed, or believed to be possessed, by the party exacting or receiving the payment, over the person or property of another, for which the latter has no other means of immediate relief than by making the payment. The ultimate fact to be determined in every case is whether or not the party making the payment had a real choice.

Under the modern doctrine of "business compulsion," where a person, because of the peculiar facts and acting as a reasonably prudent person, finds it necessary in order to protect his business interests, to make a payment which he does not owe and which in good conscience the receiver should not retain, the payment may be recovered.

A threat of legal proceedings, or even the actual commencement of such proceedings to recover a demand, does not, in the absence of an actual seizure of the person or goods of the alleged debtor, or of any menace of such seizure, constitute such compulsion as to enable the defendant to recover a payment made under the influence thereof. However, arrest, imprisonment, or prosecution on a criminal charge, and according to some authorities, threats and fear of imminent arrest and imprisonment, constitute such duress as will render involuntary a payment not justly or lawfully due, made to avoid such consequences. A fine or penalty thus illegally exacted and involuntarily paid in criminal proceedings may be recovered back.

§ 19:8. Payment by mistake.

Am Jur 2d References: Restitution and Implied Contracts, §§ 118–144.

It is well settled as a general rule that where a person makes a payment of money that is not legally or equitably due, under the inference of a mistake of fact, he may recover back the payment in an action for money had and received. In order to recover under this rule, the party must show a mistake as to an existing fact of a substantial nature and material to the transaction, and that his mistake induced him to make the payment. A payment made when one is conscious of his lack of knowledge of material facts or is doubtful or speculative concerning them does not meet this requirement.

Although some courts have held that if a person might, by the exercise of reasonable diligence, have ascertained the true facts, he may not, on the ground of ignorance or mistake, recover back payments made, the prevailing view is that in the absence of a change of position to the prejudice of the payee, the failure of one paying money to another under a mistake of fact, to use ordinary care to avoid such mistake, will not defeat his right to recover back in an action for money had and received.   In other words, in such a case the plaintiff's negligence is no defense if the negligence caused the defendant no harm.   And mere forgetfulness or oversight may be a mistake of fact warranting a recovery back of the payment, as where the payment is made through forgetfulness of the fact that the debt has already been paid.

The right to recover back money paid because of a mistake of fact may be lost where the payment has caused such a change in the position of the party receiving it that it would be unjust or prejudicial to require him to refund.

A mistake of law is an erroneous judgment or conclusion as to the legal effect of facts of which a party has full knowledge.   It is a mistaken opinion or inference, arising from an imperfect or incorrect exercise of the judgment on facts as they really are.   The question whether money paid under a mistake of law may be recovered back has long been disputed, but the prevailing view is that money voluntarily paid on a claim of right, with full knowledge of all the facts, and in the absence of fraud, duress, or compulsion, cannot be recovered back merely because the party at the time of payment was ignorant of or mistook the law as to his liability.   The invalidity of the demand paid constitutes, of itself, no ground for relief.   Some courts have regarded this rule with disfavor; and recovery has been permitted in some cases where to refuse it would result in injustice and unjust enrichment.

§ 19:9. Effect of fraud, illegality, or invalidity.

Am Jur 2d References: Restitution and Implied Contracts, §§ 116, 117, 145–150.

The general rule (supra, § 19:7) precluding the recovery of payments voluntarily made presupposes bona fides on the part of the person exacting payment. It has no application when the money is obtained by the fraud of the person receiving it, and payments exacted by fraud may generally be recovered back.

The general rules governing the recovery of payments made under an illegal contract are these: If the agreement is executed and the parties are in pari delicto, neither of them can recover from the other any money paid; but if the contract continues executory and the party paying the money wishes to rescind it, he may do so and recover back his payments in an action for money had and received.   Also where the parties are not in pari delicto, as where the transaction is made illegal for the protection of the party who made the payment, or where the payee was the principal offender and the party making the payment merely acquiesced, the courts frequently permit a recovery of payments.

Money paid on a contract the consideration for which has failed may be recovered back in an action for money had and received, unless the failure of consideration is due to some fault on the part of the person making the payment, or other circumstances would render such recovery inequitable.

SALES

§ 20:1. General matters; nature and elements of sale.

Am Jur 2d References: Sales, §§ 6–18, 27–39, 118–140, 210–226.

The present topic is concerned with sales of personal property. Sales of real estate are discussed in the topic Real Property; and the transfer of commercial paper is covered in Bills and Notes. The law of sales is largely embraced in the Uniform Commercial Code, which replaced the Uniform Sales Act and which has been almost universally adopted in this country. Sales of certain kinds of personal property, such as intoxicating liquors and drugs, are generally regulated by special statutes, as is the transfer of title to some kinds of property, such as automobiles and corporate securities.

A sale is the transfer of ownership of personal property by agreement. A contract for the sale of goods is a contract whereby the seller agrees to transfer the property in goods to the buyer for a consideration called the price. A sale is the actual passing of ownership or title to the buyer pursuant to the contract. No particular form is required of a sales contract, and it need not be in writing except where the statute of frauds or some other statute so requires. Seals are without effect under the Uniform Commercial Code (§ 2–203). However, if the contract or a part thereof is set forth in a writing intended as a final expression of the agreement of the parties, such writing may not, under the Uniform Commercial Code (§ 2–202), generally be contradicted by evidence of a different agreement. Under the Uniform Commercial Code (§ 2–304), the price may be made payable in money or otherwise. The assignability of sales contracts generally is recognized by the Uniform Commercial Code (§ 2–210).

The general principles of contract law governing the formation and requisites of contracts are applicable to contracts of sale. There must be an offer, followed by an acceptance thereof, and there must be a valid consideration. As in the case of other contracts implied in fact, a contract of sale may be implied from the facts and circumstances of the case and the conduct of the

531

parties, so as to create an obligation to pay for goods received from another. The Uniform Commercial Code provides (§ 2–204) that a contract for the sale of goods may be made in any manner sufficient to show agreement, including conduct by both parties which recognizes the existence of such a contract. The Code also provides (§ 2–205) for "firm offers" by merchants to buy or sell goods, in a signed writing, which shall be irrevocable for a stated or reasonable time, not exceeding 3 months. Unless otherwise indicated by the language or circumstances, an offer to make a contract is construed as inviting acceptance in any manner and by any medium reasonable in the circumstances. (UCC § 2–206.) Under the Code (§ 2–207) "a definite and seasonable expression of acceptance or a written confirmation which is sent within a reasonable time operates as an acceptance even though it states terms additional to or different from those offered or agreed upon, unless acceptance is expressly made conditional on assent to the additional or different terms," and the additional terms are treated as proposals for addition to the contract. As between merchants, such terms become a part of the contract unless the offer expressly limits acceptance to the terms of the offer, or they materially alter it, or notification of objection to them has been given or is given within a reasonable time. This section of the Code also provides that "conduct by both parties which recognizes the existence of a contract is sufficient to establish a contract for sale although the writings of the parties do not otherwise establish a contract."

A valid and enforceable contract of sale may not be rescinded or modified without the assent of both parties, in the absence of a default by one party which gives the other party a right to rescind. The Uniform Commercial Code provides (§ 2–209) that an agreement modifying a contract of sale needs no consideration. This section further states that "a signed agreement which excludes modification or rescission except by signed writing cannot be otherwise modified or rescinded, but except as between merchants such a requirement on a form supplied by the merchant must be separately signed by the other party." It also provides that the requirement of the statute of frauds must be satisfied if the contract as modified is within its provisions. However, although an attempt at modification or rescission does not satisfy these requirements, it may operate as a waiver.

A contract of sale may include an agreement by the seller to repurchase the property at a stated price, at the option of the buyer, or may give the seller the right to repurchase the property upon stated terms.

§ 20:2. Validity of sales contract.

Am Jur 2d References: Sales, §§ 57–117.

A contract for the sale of personal property, like any other contract, must meet certain requirements of the law in order to be valid and enforceable. Such a contract must be based upon a valid offer and acceptance, and there must be mutual assent to its terms. There must be reasonable definiteness and certainty as to the terms and obligations of the contract, including the description of the property sold. And the contract must be based upon a good consideration according to general contract law. A sales agreement, like any other contract, may be vitiated by fraud, by misrepresentation of a material fact, or by a mutual mistake affecting the essence of the agreement. Fraud may be a ground for the rescission of a contract of sale and recovery of the consideration paid, or it may be a defense to, or setoff or counterclaim against, a claim for the purchase price, or it may be a ground for recovery of damages in an action for deceit. To be actionable or to constitute a defense, the fraud or misrepresentation must relate to a material fact known to be untrue or recklessly made for the purpose of inducing the sale, and it must have been relied upon by the other party to his injury or damage, and he must have had the right to rely thereon. Under the common-law doctrine of caveat emptor, the buyer must rely either on a warranty or fraud to be entitled to relief because of the unsoundness of a chattel sold to him. But the tendency of modern decisions is to restrict the area in which this doctrine applies. However, a purchaser still has no right to rely upon, or to obtain relief because of, mere "trade talk," "dealer's talk," or "puffing" in the form of statements by the seller extolling the virtues of his goods or exaggerating their value. As in the case of agreements generally, contracts for the sale of personal property are invalid if they are based upon an illegal consideration or are violative of public policy or the law. A sales agreement which is otherwise sufficiently definite is not invalidated by the fact that it leaves particulars of performance to be specified by one of the parties. (UCC § 2–311.)

Applying equitable principles, the Uniform Commercial Code provides (§ 2–302) that if the court finds the contract or any clause thereof to have been unconscionable, it may refuse to enforce the contract, or may enforce the remainder of the contract without the offending clause, or may limit the application of such clause so as to avoid any unconscionable result.

Although contracts for the sale of goods are not ordinarily required to be in any particular form, the statute of frauds does require that such a contract be in writing where the price of the goods exceeds a specified sum. Under the Uniform Commercial Code (§ 2–201), a contract for the sale of goods for the price of $500 or more is not enforceable by way of action or defense unless there is some writing sufficient to indicate that a contract for sale has been made between the parties and signed by the party against whom enforcement is sought or by his authorized agent or broker. As between merchants, a written confirmation of the contract by one party brought to the attention of the other party satisfies the requirements of the statute against such party unless he gives written notice of objection to its contents within 10 days after it is received. And a contract which does not meet the requirements as to a writing, but which is valid in other respects, is enforceable with respect to goods that are to be specially manufactured for the buyer and are not suitable for sale to others in the ordinary course of the seller's business, to the extent that the seller has made either a substantial beginning of their manufacture or commitments for their procurement. Such a nonconforming contract is also enforceable with respect to goods which have been received and accepted or for which payment has been made and accepted.

§ 20:3. Construction and effect.

Am Jur 2d References: Sales, §§ 141–209.

The construction and effect of contracts for the sale of personal property are governed largely by the same principles as are applied in construing contracts generally. The cardinal principle to be followed is to ascertain and give effect to the intention of the parties as disclosed by the contract and the surrounding circumstances. The contract of sale is to be construed as a whole and effect given where possible to all the provisions thereof. Where there is inconsistency between a part of a sales contract which is written or typed and a part which is printed, the written or typed parts will generally control. As between written and typewritten provisions of a contract, the former will prevail in the absence of any indication of intention to the contrary. Where the sales contract leaves particulars of performance to be specified by one of the parties, the Uniform Commercial Code (§ 2–311) requires that any such specification be made in good faith and within the limits of commercial reasonableness.

The meaning and effect of an agreement for the sale of certain goods to the extent of the buyer's requirements, or an agreement for the sale of the seller's entire output, depend upon all of the language of the sales agreement in the light of the surrounding facts and circumstances. The same is true of contracts for exclusive dealing in the particular kind of goods. The subject is broadly covered by Uniform Commercial Code § 2–306, which provides: "(1) A term which measures the quantity by the output of the seller or the requirements of the buyer means such actual output or requirements as may occur in good faith, except that no quantity unreasonably disproportionate to any stated estimate or in the absence of a stated estimate to any normal or otherwise comparable prior output or requirement may be tendered or demanded. (2) A lawful agreement by either the seller or the buyer for exclusive dealing in the kind of goods concerned imposes, unless otherwise agreed, an obligation by the seller to use best efforts to supply the goods and by the buyer to use best efforts to promote their sale."

Where the sales agreement does not specify the time, manner, or the place of delivery of the goods sold, the Uniform Commercial Code (§ 2–307) provides that "unless otherwise agreed all goods called for by contract for sale must be tendered in a single delivery and payment is due only on such tender, but where the circumstances give either party the right to make or demand delivery in lots the price if it can be apportioned may be demanded for each lot." In the absence of agreement to the contrary, the place for delivery of goods is the seller's place of business, or if he has none, his residence; but where the sale is of identified goods which, to the knowledge of the parties, are in some other place, that place is the place for their delivery. (UCC § 2–308, which also provides that documents of title may be delivered through customary banking channels.) The time for shipment or delivery, or any other action under a sales contract, if not specified in the agreement, is a reasonable time, both at common law and under the Uniform Commercial Code (§ 2–309). Under the Uniform Commercial Code (§ 2–310), unless it is otherwise agreed, payment is due at the time and place at which the buyer is to receive the goods, even though the place of shipment is the place of delivery. This section of the Code also provides for the time of payment where delivery is made by way of documents of title.

The parties may, under the provisions of the Uniform Commercial Code (§ 2–305), conclude a valid contract of sale even though the price is not settled. Where there is no provision as to price, the price is a reasonable price

at the time for delivery. The same is true if the price is left to be ag
the parties and they fail to agree, or if the price is to be fixed according to
some agreed market or other standard and no such price is set or recorded
thereby. A price to be fixed by the seller or by the buyer means a price
fixed by him in good faith. Where there is a failure to fix a price under such
a contract through the fault of one party, the other may, at his option, treat
the contract as canceled or himself fix a reasonable price. However, where the
parties intend not to be bound unless the price is fixed or agreed upon, there
is no contract.

The Uniform Commercial Code defines and states the effect of a number of
abbreviations and terms commonly used in commerce and trade in connection
with the shipment and delivery of goods under contracts of sale. Among these
terms are F.O.B. ("free on board") and F.A.S. ("free alongside" vessel) (UCC
§ 2–319); C.I.F. ("cost, insurance, and freight") and C. & F. ("cost and
freight") (UCC §§ 2–320, 2–321). Also provided for in the Code are agreements for delivery of goods "ex-ship" (UCC § 2–322) and contract terms
such as "no arrival, no sale" (UCC § 2–324), and the form of the bill of
lading required in overseas shipments (UCC § 2–323).

In considering the admissibility of extrinsic evidence to aid in the interpretation of sales contracts, the Uniform Commercial Code (§§ 1–205, 2–202,
2–208) follows generally the settled common-law principles applicable to all
contracts. Evidence of extrinsic facts, such as evidence of a prior or contemporaneous oral agreement, is not admissible to vary or contradict a written
contract for sale which was intended by the parties to be the final and complete
expression of the agreement. However, where the written contract is ambiguous or uncertain, extrinsic evidence is admissible to explain its meaning.
Thus, the contract will be interpreted in the light of a course of dealing or
course of performance between the parties, acquiesced in by them, as indicating
their own understanding of the contract or their agreement to a modification
thereof. And a usage or custom of the trade or business in which the parties
are engaged, of which usage they are charged with knowledge, may be admitted
to aid in the interpretation of their agreement.

§ 20:4. Passing of title.

Am Jur 2d References: Sales, §§ 227–277.

The time, place, and manner of the passing of title or property in goods and
chattels under a contract for the sale thereof depend primarily upon the intention of the parties as indicated by the terms of the contract in the light of
the attendant circumstances, the conduct of the parties, and the usages of
trade. This general principle is recognized by both the Uniform Sales Act and
the Uniform Commercial Code. The parties may by agreement provide for
the passing of title or property, as between themselves, at any stage of their
sales transaction. And title to personal property may be transferred by the
execution of a document of title, such as a bill of sale or a bill of lading. In
the absence of agreement to a different effect, a sales contract remains executory, and title does not pass to the buyer, so long as something required by
the contract remains to be done by either party. Such unperformed phases
of the contract may be the determination of the price or quantity, the weigh-

ing, measuring, or counting (unless this is to be done by the buyer alone), the identification of the goods to the contract, and the segregation thereof from a general mass or bulk. In the case of goods to be manufactured or produced by the seller, title does not generally vest in the buyer until the property is completed.

Under a contract for the sale of specific goods in a deliverable state, the property in the goods passes to the buyer when the contract is made, although there is no delivery, in the absence of some provision or apparent intention as to delivery. If the contract calls for delivery by the seller at the buyer's residence or other specified place, or by carrier F.O.B. the latter place, title passes only upon delivery at such place. Where delivery is to be by carrier F.O.B. the point of shipment, a proper delivery to a carrier, consigned to the buyer, passes title to the buyer at that time and place, the carrier being deemed the bailee of the buyer for the purpose of transportation. Where the terms of a sale are for cash, title does not ordinarily pass, as between the parties, until payment of the price. However, this requirement may be waived by the seller, as by delivering without requiring payment, or by extending credit to the buyer.

The Uniform Commercial Code (§§ 2–401—2–502) deals with matters relating to the passing of title in terms of the rights of the parties affected, at each step or stage of performance or nonperformance. It provides (UCC § 2–402), that "[t]itle to goods cannot pass under a contract for sale prior to their identification to the contract," and prescribes (UCC § 2–501) what constitutes such identification generally, as well as where the contract is for the sale of "future goods," crops, or unborn animals.

The rights of unsecured creditors of the seller [secured transactions are discussed herein under the topic Personal Property] are subject to the right of the buyer to recover goods which have been identified to a contract of sale, unless the sale is fraudulent as to such creditors under governing state laws. (UCC § 2–402.) And a buyer who has paid a part or all of the price is entitled to such identified goods upon the insolvency of the seller, even though delivery has not been made, if the insolvency occurs within 10 days after receipt of the first instalment on the price and if the buyer pays any balance of the price. (UCC § 2–502.)

Under the general principle that a person cannot transfer a better title to a chattel than he himself has, a purchaser from one who acquired the property by theft or conversion does not ordinarily acquire title as against the real owner, even though he is a bona fide purchaser for value. However, a bona fide purchaser from one who obtained the property by sale induced by fraud may obtain a good title as against the original seller, since the sale by the latter, while voidable as against his buyer, was not absolutely void. As provided by the Uniform Commercial Code (§ 2–403), "a person with voidable title has power to transfer a good title to a good faith purchaser for value; and when the goods have been delivered to the purchaser he has such power even though there was deception as to the identity of the purchaser, or delivery was in exchange for a check which was later dishonored, or the delivery was procured by fraud punishable as larcenous under the criminal law."

The fact that the owner of personal property entrusts possession thereof to another does not, of itself, enable the possessor to transfer good title to the property. However, the owner may be estopped to deny the right of the possessor to sell the property. If the owner entrusts another with both possession and the indicia of ownership and with apparent authority to transfer title, a bona fide purchaser for value from the possessor, without notice of any defect in the latter's title, may acquire title superior even to that of the original owner. The Uniform Commercial Code (§ 2–403) provides that the entrusting of possession of goods to a merchant who deals in goods of that kind gives him power to transfer all rights of the entruster to a buyer in the ordinary course of business.

§ 20:5. Contracts of sale or return; sales on approval.

Am Jur 2d References: Sales, §§ 278–307.

Contracts of sale or return, delivery of goods to another for the purpose of sale by the latter on commission, and contracts for the sale of goods on approval, although bearing some superficial similarities, are quite distinct from each other, and each type of transaction has legal consequences not attached to the others. A sale made under a contract of sale or return is conditional, being defeasible upon conditions subsequent. Title to goods thus sold passes to the purchaser subject to being divested and revested in the seller by a return of the goods according to the terms of the contract. Property in the goods passes to the buyer, but subject to an option in him to return them by his arbitrary choice, without reference to the quality of the goods. If the goods are not returned within the time specified, or within a reasonable time if no time is specified, the sale becomes absolute. As title vests in the buyer, the risk of loss or destruction of the goods prior to the exercise of his option to return them falls upon him, and the goods are subject to the claims of his creditors. In these respects, a contract of sale or return is essentially different from a delivery of property to a person with a privilege or option to purchase, since in the latter case title does not pass until the option is determined. The delivery of goods to another on consignment for sale, usually on commission or allowing the consignee to retain any sums realized over and above a specified amount, is not a sale at all, and title does not pass to the person receiving the goods.

A sale on approval, as distinguished from a contract of sale or return, is subject to a condition precedent. Where personal property is delivered under an agreement that if it is satisfactory or suitable to the recipient, he will keep it and pay for it, but if it is unsatisfactory he will return it, title to the property does not pass to the buyer until he exercises his option to accept the goods.

The Uniform Commercial Code (§§ 2–326, 2–327) states the general requisites and incidents of a contract of sale or return and a sale on approval, and it also provides (§ 2–326) that "unless otherwise agreed, if delivered goods may be returned by the buyer even though they conform to the contract, the transaction is (a) a 'sale on approval' if the goods are delivered primarily for use, and (b) a 'sale or return' if the goods are delivered primarily for resale." After stating that goods held on approval are not subject to claims of the buyer's creditors until acceptance, but that goods held on sale or return are subject to such claims, the Uniform Commercial Code, § 2–326, provides: "Where goods are delivered to a person for sale and such person maintains a place of business at which he deals in goods of the kind involved, under a name other than the name of the person making delivery, then with respect to claims of creditors of the person conducting the business the goods are deemed to be on sale or return," even though an agreement purports to reserve title to the person making delivery until payment or resale or uses such words as "on consignment" or "on memorandum." This particular provision is not applicable if the person making the delivery complies with an applicable law providing for a consignor's interest or the like to be evidenced by a sign, or if the person conducting the business is generally known to his creditors to be substantially engaged in selling the goods of others, or if the person making delivery is protected by the provisions relating to secured transactions.

§ 20:6. Warranties.

Am Jur 2d References: Sales, §§ 425–513.

A warranty in connection with a sale of personal property is an undertaking by the seller to be responsible in damages for the falsity of an assurance of a fact relating to the property sold.   While the words "warranty," "guaranty," and "guarantee" are of the same origin, and in popular usage are frequently employed indiscriminately, "warranty" is the proper term for this kind of undertaking with relation to sales, and "guaranty" relates to the undertaking by which one person is bound to another for the fulfilment of a promise or undertaking of a third person.   While usually a warranty is a part of a contract of sale and is supported by the consideration on which the main contract is based, it is in a sense a collateral undertaking.   A warranty may be either express or implied.   An express warranty may arise, without the use of the word "warrant," from terms and undertakings to which the law attributes the effect of a warranty.   An implied warranty arises under various circumstances, by operation of law and as a conclusion or inference of law, irrespective of any actual intention of the seller to create it.   In some circumstances the distinction between express warranties and implied warranties becomes very obscure, and the importance of the distinction has diminished under modern law.

Under the Uniform Commercial Code (§ 2–312), reflecting the prevailing view of modern authorities, a sale imports a warranty of good title and a warranty that there is no lien, encumbrance, or security interest of which the buyer has no knowledge; and this is true even though the goods are not in the possession of the seller at the time of sale.   This warranty may be excluded or modified only by specific language or by circumstances charging the buyer with notice that the seller does not claim or purport to sell absolute title.   Where the seller is a merchant regularly dealing in the kind of goods involved, there is also a warranty against claims of infringement or the like, unless it is otherwise agreed or the goods are supplied in accordance with specifications furnished by the buyer.

The Uniform Commercial Code, § 2–313, specifies the circumstances under which an express warranty will arise, even without the use of formal words such as "warrant" or "guarantee," and even without any specific intention on the part of the seller to make a warranty.   "(a) Any affirmation of fact or promise made by the seller to the buyer which relates to the goods and becomes part of the basis of the bargain creates an express warranty that the goods shall conform to the affirmation or promise. (b) Any description of the goods which is made part of the basis of the bargain creates an express warranty that the goods shall conform to the description. (c) Any sample or model which is made part of the basis of the bargain creates an express warranty that the whole of the goods shall conform to the sample or model." However, a mere affirmation of the value of the goods or a statement purporting to be merely the seller's opinion or commendation of the goods does not create a warranty. This latter provision is declaratory of the pre-existing general rule relating to "puffing" and "dealer's talk."

An implied warranty that the goods shall be merchantable arises from a contract for their sale, under the Uniform Commercial Code (§ 2–314), if the seller is a merchant with respect to goods of that kind. To be merchantable, goods must be at least such as "(a) pass without objection in the trade under the contract description; and (b) in the case of fungible goods, are of fair average quality within the description; and (c) are fit for the ordinary purposes for which such goods are used; and (d) run, within the variations permitted by the agreement, of even kind, quality and quantity within each unit and among all units involved; and (e) are adequately contained, packaged, and labeled as the agreement may require; and (f) conform to the promises or affirmations of fact made on the container or label if any." Other implied warranties may arise, under this section of the Code, from a course of dealing or usage of trade.

As to warranty of fitness for a particular purpose, the Code (§ 2–315) provides that "where the seller at the time of contracting has reason to know any particular purpose for which the goods are required and that the buyer is relying on the seller's skill or judgment to select or furnish suitable goods, there is unless excluded or modified under the next section an implied warranty that the goods shall be fit for such purpose." On the subject of the exclusion or modification of warranties, the Uniform Commercial Code (§ 2–316) provides that words or conduct relevant to the creation of an express warranty and words or conduct tending to negate or limit a warranty shall be construed as consistent with each other, wherever this is reasonable, but that negation or limitation is generally inoperative to the extent that such a construction is unreasonable. To exclude or modify the implied warranty of merchantability, the language must mention merchantability, and, in case of a writing, the language must be conspicuous; and to exclude or modify any implied warranty of fitness, the exclusion must be by a writing and conspicuous. It is provided that all implied warranties of fitness may be excluded, for example, by a statement that "there are no warranties which extend beyond the description on the face hereof." And, unless the circumstances indicate otherwise, all implied warranties are excluded by expressions like "as is," "with all faults," or other language clearly excluding warranties. Where the buyer, before entering into the contract, has examined the goods or a sample or model, or has declined an opportunity to do so, there is no implied warranty with regard to defects which an examination should have revealed to him. And an implied warranty may also be excluded by course of dealing, course of performance, or usage of trade.

Warranties are construed as consistent with each other and as cumulative, unless such construction is unreasonable, in which case the intention of the parties determines which warranty is dominant. The Code prescribes (§ 2–317) certain rules for ascertaining the intention of the parties in such cases: "(a) Exact or technical specifications displace an inconsistent sample or model or general language of description. (b) A sample from an existing bulk displaces inconsistent general language of description. (c) Express warranties displace inconsistent implied warranties other than an implied warranty of fitness for a particular purpose."

Matters relating to liability for injuries from defects in articles sold or manufactured, whether based on warranty, negligence, or other grounds, are treated in the topic Products Liability.

§ 20:7. Performance or breach.

Am Jur 2d References: Sales, §§ 308–424.

Performance of a contract for the sale of personal property requires compliance with the terms of the contract, including provisions with respect to delivery, payment, and the quantity, quality, and kind of property delivered. A determination of the sufficiency of a proffered performance involves in every case a construction of the agreement between the parties and is frequently affected by their subsequent conduct and dealings. The manner and sufficiency of performance is dealt with in considerable detail in the Uniform Commercial Code.

A tender of delivery requires that the seller, in the manner and at the time and place agreed upon, put and hold conforming goods at the buyer's disposition and give the latter any notification reasonably necessary. A tender of delivery may require a tender of documents of title. (UCC § 2–503.) A proper tender of delivery is a condition to the buyer's duty to accept and to pay for the goods involved; and, conversely, tender entitles the seller to acceptance of the goods and to payment according to the contract (UCC § 507). The seller is entitled to a reasonable opportunity to correct a nonconforming tender or delivery which has been rejected by the buyer (UCC § 508). The buyer has a right, before payment or acceptance of goods, to inspect them at any reasonable place and time and in any reasonable manner, in the absence of an agreement to the contrary, such as a contract for delivery "C.O.D." (UCC § 2–513). If the buyer is required by the contract to make payment before inspection, such payment does not constitute an acceptance of the goods or impair his rights or remedies with respect thereto (UCC § 2–512).

Unless it is otherwise agreed, if the goods or the tender of delivery fail to conform to the contract, the buyer may reject the whole, accept the whole, or accept any commercial unit or units and reject the rest (UCC § 2–601). Rejection of goods by the buyer must be within a reasonable time after their delivery or tender, and seasonable notice of the rejection must be given to the seller. If the buyer has taken possession of the goods before rejection, he is under duty after rejection to hold them with reasonable care subject to the seller's disposition (UCC § 2–602). Where the buyer is a merchant, the Code (§ 2–603) requires him, on rejection of goods in his possession or control, to follow any reasonable instructions from the seller with respect to the goods or to make reasonable efforts to sell them for the seller's account if they are perishable or the like. In the absence of instructions from the seller within a reasonable time after notification of rejection, the buyer may store the rejected goods, or reship them to him, or resell them for the seller's account (UCC § 2–604). The buyer may be required to state the nature of the defects causing him to reject goods (UCC § 2–605).

Acceptance by the buyer occurs when, after an opportunity to inspect the goods, he signifies that they are conforming or that he will retain them in spite of nonconformity, or if he fails to make an effective rejection (UCC § 2–606). The buyer may, under certain circumstances, revoke his acceptance of goods (UCC § 2–608). After acceptance of goods, a buyer must notify the seller of any breach or of any suit against the buyer for breach of warranty or for infringement or the like which the seller would be obligated to defend or to indemnify against (UCC § 2–607).

Under an instalment contract requiring or authorizing the delivery of goods in separate lots to be separately accepted, the buyer may reject any instalment which is nonconforming, if the nonconformity substantially impairs the value of that instalment, and cannot be cured, or if the nonconformity is a defect in the required document. Where nonconformity or default with respect to one or more instalments substantially impairs the value of the whole contract, there is a breach of the whole, unless the aggrieved party accepts the nonconforming instalment without notifying of cancellation or demands performance as to future instalments (UCC § 2–612).

Unless otherwise agreed, tender of payment is a condition to the seller's duty to deliver. "Tender of payment is sufficient when made by any means or in any manner current in the ordinary course of business unless the seller demands payment in legal tender and gives any extension of time reasonably necessary to procure it"; but payment by check is conditional and is defeated by dishonor of the check (UCC § 2–511).

The doctrine of anticipatory breach of an executory contract, amounting to an unequivocal and absolute renunciation of the contract and refusal to perform, prior to the time for performance, is applicable to contracts for the sale of personal property. This doctrine is recognized by the Uniform Commercial Code (§ 2–610), which provides that upon such an anticipatory repudiation, the aggrieved party may for a commercially reasonable time await performance by the repudiating party, or resort to any remedy for breach, and, in either case, suspend his own performance. The Code (§ 2–611) also affirms the principle that "until the repudiating party's next performance is due he can retract his repudiation unless the aggrieved party has since the repudiation canceled or materially changed his position or otherwise indicated that he considers the repudiation final."

The Uniform Commercial Code also recognizes the right of parties to a sales contract to adequate assurance of performance (§ 2–609). An obligation is imposed on each party that the other's "expectation of receiving due performance will not be impaired," and when reasonable grounds for insecurity arise as to performance by either party, the other may in writing demand adequate assurance of due performance and suspend performance on his part if the assurance is not given.

Where the agreed manner of shipping or delivery by carrier becomes unavailable or commercially impracticable, the Code (§ 2–614) requires that a commercially reasonable substitute, if available, be tendered and accepted. And if the agreed means or manner of payment fails because of domestic or foreign governmental regulation, the seller may withhold or stop delivery unless an equivalent means of payment is provided, and if delivery has already been made, payment by the means or in the manner provided in the regulation usually discharges the buyer's obligation.

The effect of the impossibility or impracticability of performance is dealt with by the Uniform Commercial Code (§§ 2–615, 2–616). It is provided that delay in delivery, or nondelivery, by a seller is not a breach of his duty under the contract if performance as agreed has been made impracticable "by the occurrence of a contingency the non-occurrence of which was a basic assumption on which the contract was made," or by compliance with any foreign or domestic governmental regulation. Where such causes affect only a part of the seller's capacity to perform, he must allocate production and deliveries among his customers, including regular customers not then under contract, but he must notify the buyer of such delay, nondelivery, or allocation. Upon receipt of notice of such delay or allocation, the buyer is given the option to terminate the unexecuted portion of the contract or to take his available quota in substitution.

§ 20:8. Remedies, generally.

Am Jur 2d References:　Sales, §§ 514–551.

The remedies available for the protection of parties to contracts for the sale of personal property are outlined in the Uniform Commercial Code. Under the Code (§ 2–719), the parties may by their agreement provide for remedies in addition to or in substitution for those provided in the Code; and they may limit or alter the measure of damages, as by limiting the buyer's remedies to a return of the goods and refund of the price or to the repair and replacement of nonconforming goods or parts. They may also limit or exclude consequential damages, unless such provision is "unconscionable"; and limitation of consequential damages for injury to the person in the case of consumer goods is prima facie unconscionable. Resort to the remedy provided for in the contract is optional unless the remedy is expressly made exclusive; and where circumstances cause the contractual remedy to fail of its essential purpose, remedy may be had as provided in the Code.

The Code (§ 2–718) recognizes that "[d]amages for breach by either party may be liquidated in the agreement but only at an amount which is reasonable in the light of the anticipated or actual harm caused by the breach, the difficulties of proof of loss, and the inconvenience or nonfeasibility of otherwise obtaining an adequate remedy. A term fixing unreasonably large liquidated damages is void as a penalty."

Expressions of "cancellation" or "rescission" of the sales contract or the like will not be treated as a renunciation or discharge of any claim in damages for an antecedent breach, unless the contrary intention clearly appears (UCC § 2–720). Remedies for misrepresentation or fraud include all remedies available under the Code for nonfraudulent breach, and neither rescission, rejection, nor return of goods will bar a claim for damages or other remedy (UCC § 1–721).

When the prevailing price or value of any goods regularly bought and sold in any established commodity market is in issue in an action between the parties to a sales contract, the Code (§ 2–724) provides that reports in official publications or trade journals or in newspapers or periodicals of general circulation and published as the reports of such market shall be admissible in evidence. The circumstances of the preparation of such a report may be shown to affect its weight, but not its admissibility. In an action for damages based on anticipatory repudiation, coming to trial before time for performance, the market price will be determined as of the time when the aggrieved party learned of the repudiation (UCC § 2–723).

The Uniform Commercial Code (§ 2–725) embodies a statute of limitations for actions on contracts for sale. "(1) An action for breach of any contract for sale must be commenced within 4 years after the cause of action has accrued. By the original agreement the parties may reduce the period of limitation to not less than one year but may not extend it. (2) A cause of action accrues when the breach occurs, regardless of the aggrieved party's lack of knowledge of the breach. A breach of warranty occurs when tender of delivery is made," except, in the case of a warranty extending to future performance, when the cause of action accrues when the breach is or should have been discovered.

Matters relating to liability for injuries from defects in articles sold or manufactured, whether based on negligence, on breach of warranty, or on other grounds, are treated in the topic Products Liability.

§ 20:9. Seller's remedies.

Am Jur 2d References: Sales, §§ 552–663.

The numerous principles developed under the common law defining the rights and remedies of the seller under a contract for the sale of personal property have been generally reaffirmed in the Uniform Commercial Code (§§ 2–702—2–710). An unpaid seller has the right to withhold delivery where payment by the buyer is a condition of the seller's obligation to deliver goods. And an unpaid seller has a lien on the goods and the right to retain them for the price so long as he has possession of them, even though title to the goods has passed to the buyer. Upon the buyer's insolvency, the seller has the right of stopping the goods in transitu after he has delivered them to a carrier or other bailee and before delivery to the buyer. And the seller may retake possession where the delivery of goods was conditional on payment by the buyer and payment has not been made. Other remedies available to the seller in various situations are an action to recover the purchase price; a resale of the property, followed by an action to recover the difference between the contract price and the amount realized on the resale; an action for damages to recover the difference between the contract price and the market value of the property at the time and place the goods should have been accepted by the buyer; and a cancellation of the contract.

Upon discovery that the buyer is insolvent, the seller may not only stop delivery of goods in transit (UCC § 2–705), but he may refuse delivery except for cash, including payment for goods theretofore delivered under the contract;

and where the buyer has received goods on credit while insolvent, the seller may reclaim them within a certain time and under the prescribed conditions.

Upon a breach or repudiation of the sales contract by the buyer, the seller may resell undelivered goods covered by the contract and may recover the difference between the resale price and the contract price, together with any incidental damages, such as expenses of the resale, less any expense saved in consequence of the buyer's breach. Unless it is otherwise agreed, such resale may be at public or private sale, and a purchaser who buys in good faith at such a resale takes the goods free of any rights of the original buyer, even though the seller fails to comply with the requirements of the Code in making the resale (§§ 2–706, 2–710).

Where the seller elects to sue for damages for nonacceptance or repudiation by the buyer, the measure of damages under the Code (§ 2–708) is the difference between the market price at the time and place for tender and the unpaid contract price, together with any incidental damages, less expenses saved in consequence of the buyer's breach. However, under this section of the Code if the measure of damages thus provided "is inadequate to put the seller in as good position as performance would have done then the measure of damages is the profit (including reasonable overhead) which the seller would have made from full performance by the buyer, together with incidental damages . . . , due allowance for costs reasonably incurred and due credit for payments or proceeds of resale."

Where the buyer fails to pay the price as it becomes due, the seller may recover, together with any incidental damages, the price of goods accepted by the buyer, and the price of goods identified with the contract if the seller is unable to resell them at a reasonable price. Where the seller sues for the price, he must hold for the buyer any goods which have been identified to the contract and are still in his control, and the net proceeds of any resale by the seller must be credited to the buyer (UCC § 2–709).

§ 20:10. Buyer's remedies.

Am Jur 2d References: Sales, §§ 664–775.

Several remedies are available to the buyer, at common law and under the Uniform Commercial Code (§§ 2–711—2–718), upon the seller's default under a contract for the sale of personal property. Among these remedies are the right of action for damages for wrongful failure or refusal of the seller to deliver the property; the right of action for damages for breach of warranty; the right to rescind or cancel; and the right, under some circumstances, to recover possession of the specific property.

After a breach or default by the seller, the buyer may "cover" by making a reasonable purchase of goods in substitution for those due from the seller; but failure to do so does not bar him from any other remedy. Where the buyer does pursue this course, he may recover from the seller as damages the difference between the cost of "cover" and the contract price, together with any incidental or consequential damages, less expenses saved in consequence of the seller's breach (UCC § 7–712). Where the buyer does not "cover," the measure of damages for nondelivery or repudiation by the seller is the difference between the market price at the time when the buyer learned of the breach and the contract price, together with any incidental and consequential damages, less expenses saved in consequence of the seller's breach (UCC § 2–713).

Where the buyer has accepted the goods and has given notification of breach or nonconformity, he may recover as damages for such nonconformity of tender the loss resulting in the ordinary course of events from the seller's breach, as determined in any manner which is reasonable. In an action for breach of warranty, the measure of damages is the difference at the time and place of acceptance between the value of the goods accepted and the value they would have had if they had been as warranted, unless special circumstances indicate a different amount as the proximate damages. And incidental and consequential damages may be recovered in a proper case (UCC § 2–714).

The "incidental" damages recoverable by the buyer in a proper case include expenses reasonably incurred in inspection, receipt, transportation, and care of goods rightfully rejected, reasonable expenses and commissions in connection with effecting "cover," and any other reasonable expense incident to the delay or other breach. "Consequential" damages resulting from the seller's breach include any loss resulting from general or particular requirements and needs on the part of the buyer of which the seller knew or had reason to know at the time of contracting and which could not reasonably be prevented by "cover" or otherwise, and injury to personal property proximately resulting from any breach of warranty.

The buyer may, upon notice to the seller of his intention to do so, deduct the damages resulting from any breach of the contract from any part of the price remaining due under the contract (UCC § 2–717). As pointed out above (§ 20:8), liquidated damages may be provided for in the sales agreement for breach by either party.

Specific performance may be decreed under § 2–716 of the Code, "where the goods are unique or in proper circumstances." And the decree for specific performance may include proper terms and conditions as to payment of the price, damages, or other relief. The buyer also has a right of replevin for goods identified to the contract if he is unable to effect "cover" for the goods.

Remedies afforded the buyer for misrepresentation or fraud include all remedies available under the Uniform Commercial Code for nonfraudulent breach; and a rescission of the contract or a rejection or return of the goods is not inconsistent with a claim for damages or other remedy (UCC § 2–721).

§ 20:11. Auctions.

Am Jur 2d References: Auctions and Auctioneers, §§ 1–68.

An auction is a public sale of property to the highest bidder. The auctioneer conducting such a sale has considerable discretion in the details of the proceeding and in the acceptance of bids and in determination thereof. As agent of the owner of the property, the auctioneer's authority is limited. He may not generally extend credit where the terms of the sale are for cash. In the absence of express authority or of a statement by the owner to the contrary, an auctioneer has no authority to warrant the property sold. Although the auctioneer is for most purposes the agent of the owner or seller, if the transaction comes within the statute of frauds, requiring payment, delivery, or a memorandum in writing, the auctioneer is regarded as the agent of both parties in executing a memorandum of the sale.

The owner of property sold at auction may prescribe the manner, conditions, and terms of the sale; and this may be done either in the advertisement of the auction or by announcement at the sale. If the owner wishes to fix a minimum price below which the property will not be sold, or to reserve to himself the right to bid, in person or through another, he must make an express announcement thereof.

A bid at an auction constitutes an offer, and the acceptance thereof by the auctioneer as the highest bid consummates a sale, unless the owner has reserved the right to reject any or all bids received. As a general rule, unless the sale is "without reserve," a seller of property at auction or the auctioneer may withdraw the property from sale at any time before the acceptance of a bid. Such right does not exist, however, where the sale is "without reserve." Although a bidder at auction may not generally withdraw his bid after it has been accepted, he may withdraw it at any time before the hammer falls or the property is knocked off to him. A bidder's retraction of a bid does not, under the Uniform Commercial Code (§ 2–328), revive any previous bid.

The Uniform Commercial Code, § 2–328, provides that a sale by auction is complete when the auctioneer so announces by the fall of the hammer or in other customary manner. Where a bid is made while the hammer is falling in acceptance of a prior bid, the auctioneer may in his discretion reopen the bidding or declare the goods sold under the bid on which the hammer was falling. This section of the Code also governs the subject of sales with or without reserve; and it provides that if the auctioneer knowingly receives a bid on the seller's behalf or the seller makes or procures such a bid, and notice has not been given that liberty for such bidding is reserved, the buyer may avoid the sale and take the goods at the price of the last good-faith bid prior to the completion of the sale. This provision does not apply, however, to a forced sale.

TORTS

I. GENERAL CONSIDERATIONS

II. NEGLIGENCE

III. AUTOMOBILES AND OTHER MOTOR VEHICLES

IV. WRONGFUL DEATH

V. PREMISES LIABILITY; ATTRACTIVE NUISANCES

VI. HIGHWAYS, STREETS, AND BRIDGES

VII. FRIGHT, SHOCK, AND MENTAL DISTURBANCE

VIII. OTHER WRONGS AND INJURIES BASED ON NEGLIGENCE

IX. MASTER AND SERVANT

A. EMPLOYER'S LIABILITY FOR INJURY TO EMPLOYEE

B. WORKMEN'S COMPENSATION

C. FEDERAL LIABILITY AND COMPENSATION ACTS

D. EMPLOYER'S LIABILITY FOR ACTS OF EMPLOYEE

TORTS

X. ASSAULT AND BATTERY

XI. FALSE IMPRISONMENT AND ARREST

XII. MALICIOUS PROSECUTION AND ABUSE OF PROCESS

XIII. FRAUD AND DECEIT

XIV. INTERFERENCE

XV. LIBEL AND SLANDER

XVI. PRIVACY

XVII. NUISANCES

XVIII. TRADE OR BUSINESS PRACTICES

XIX. OTHER WRONGS AND INJURIES INVOLVING WILFUL ACT OR VIOLATION OF LAW

§ 21:97. Violation of civil rights
§ 21:98. Injury from intoxicating liquor; Dramshop or civil damage acts
§ 21:99. Miscellaneous

I. GENERAL CONSIDERATIONS

§ 21:1. Definitions.

Am Jur 2d References: Torts (1st ed, §§ 1–33).

The term "torts" is a very general label designating a vast variety of non-contractual legal wrongs.   A tort may be defined as a private wrong or injury to person or property, or other violation of a right not dependent upon contract, for which a legal remedy is afforded.   Generally and for the purposes of the present topic, it may be stated that any wrongful act or omission not predicated on contract and giving rise to a legal cause of action is a tort.   The existence of a legal right and its violation by one under a legal duty are prerequisities to a cause of action in tort.   A wrongful act may be both a tort and a breach of contract, at the election of the injured party.   And crimes are also torts if they affect the persons, property, or rights of individuals.

§ 21:2. Who is liable.

Am Jur 2d References: Charities, §§ 152–172; Torts (1st ed, §§ 95–100, 110–118).

Any person joining in the commission of a tort is jointly and severally liable with his joint tortfeasors.   And liability in tort may be predicated on instigation or ratification of the acts of another.

On various theories, many courts formerly took the position that charities, such as hospitals, although operated by private corporations, were immune from liability in tort.   There has been a fast erosion of this view, however, as reflected and aided by the annotation at 25 ALR2d 29; and at the present time this immunity is recognized, within increasing limitations, in only a minority of jurisdictions.

The question of governmental immunity is discussed in § 21:3, infra.   Liability for the torts of infants and incompetent persons is discussed in the topic "Persons and Domestic Relations."

§ 21:3. Governmental immunity.

Am Jur 2d References: Municipal, School and State Tort Liability, § 1 et seq.; United States (1st ed, § 136).

It was formerly well settled that no government or governmental agency, including the United States, the several states, and their subdivisions, was liable for the torts of their officers, agents, or employees.   There was never any sound basis for this, and, as pointed out in the annotation at 75 ALR 1196, and as developed in the later decisions, it is clear that the states are fast repudiating this doctrine, either by statute or judicial decision. As pointed out in § 21:4, infra, the United States Government has waived a major portion of this immunity by enactment of its Federal Tort Claims Act.

§ 21:4. —Federal Tort Claims Act.

Am Jur 2d References: Federal Tort Claims Act, §§ 1–145.

By the Federal Tort Claims Act, the United States has waived its governmental immunity from liability for torts and its sovereign immunity from suit, within the limitations stated in the Act. Before judicial action, the claim must be presented to the appropriate federal agency for administrative determination.

For the torts of its officers and employees, the United States is liable under the Act in the same manner and to the same extent as a private individual. The ordinary common-law rules prevailing in the states, such as the doctrine of contributory negligence, are generally applied in actions under the Act. The tort on which the action is based must have been within the scope of the office or employment of the person committing the Act.

Certain types of claims are excluded from the operation of the Federal Tort Claims Act. Among these are claims based on an act or omission of a government employee exercising due care, on the ground of such employee's exercise of, or failure to perform, a "discretionary function"; claims based on the loss or miscarriage of mail and those arising out of government fiscal or financial operations; claims relating to the assessment or collection of a tax or customs duty; claims relating to intentional torts of employees, assault and battery, false arrest or imprisonment, abuse of process, libel or slander, misrepresentation or deceit, and interference with contract rights; and claims arising out of combatant activities of the Armed Forces during time of war.

§ 21:5. Rights as between tortfeasors; contribution and indemnity.

Am Jur 2d References: Contribution, §§ 33–57; Indemnity, §§ 20–26.

For various reasons which seemed sufficient to the courts of the last century, the general rule was followed in England and America that there could be no contribution between joint wrongdoers or tortfeasors and that one of several persons who became liable to another for a tort could not enforce contribution from his co-wrongdoers, although he was compelled to discharge the whole of the liability for the wrong.

Apart from statutes, the courts have engrafted so many exceptions upon the rule against contribution, that the operation of the rule is confined within very narrow limits. As a result of all of the exceptions made, it may be said that all that is left of the original general rule against contribution is that as between conscious, wilful, malicious, or intentional joint tortfeasors who are in pari delicto, neither the law nor equity will enforce contribution.

Exceptions to the rule against contribution are recognized by many courts where there was no concert of action between the tortfeasors; where the wrong involved was not a known or intentional one and the party seeking contribution acted in good faith; where the person seeking contribution was liable only secondarily or vicariously as under the doctrine of respondeat superior; and (probably the most important exception) where the tortfeasors are not in pari delicto and the fault of the tortfeasor seeking contribution is not equal to that of the other. An increasing number of courts apply an exception to the general rule against contribution in cases where the joint tortfeasors are guilty of nothing more than negligence.

A number of states have adopted statutes, such as the Uniform Contribution Among Tortfeasors Act, permitting the enforcement of contribution among joint tortfeasors.

II. NEGLIGENCE

§ 21:6. Definitions and degrees of negligence.

Am Jur 2d References: Negligence, §§ 1–4, 94–107.

Negligence in the legal sense, as a tort for which an action at law may be maintained, is essentially a violation of a duty to use care. Attempts to define negligence comprehensively have resulted in a great variety of language. Any valid definition of negligence must include the element that it depends upon the particular circumstances surrounding the parties at the time and place of the occurrence.

Negligence has been defined as the failure to exercise the care which an ordinarily prudent person would use under the circumstances in the discharge of the duty then resting upon him. Stated more particularly, actionable negligence is the failure of one, owing a duty to another, to do what a reasonable and prudent person would ordinarily have done under the circumstances, or doing what such a person would not have done, which omission or commission is the proximate cause of injury to another.

The concept of degrees of negligence, such as "slight," "ordinary," and "gross," has been disapproved in most common-law jurisdictions in cases involving torts based on negligence. The degree of negligence does become relevant, however, in certain classes of cases, such as those arising under automobile guest statutes, or where exemplary damages are sought, or in jurisdictions where the comparative negligence doctrine is applied. "Gross negligence" may also preclude the defense of contributory negligence.

"Gross negligence" has been defined as the want of even slight care. There may be "gross negligence" without actual wilful or intentional wrong, but the term is broad enough to include wanton acts and even acts done with intent to injure another. To constitute wilful injury, there must be design, purpose, and intent to do the wrong and inflict the injury. To constitute "wanton negligence" there must be an act done intentionally with a reckless indifference to the injurious consequences likely to result therefrom and with knowledge that the conduct will naturally or probably result in injury. According to strictly proper terminology, wilful, malicious, or intentional misconduct is not comprehended in the term "negligence."

§21:7. Nature and elements of actionable negligence.

Am Jur 2d References: Act of God, §11; Negligence, §§10–65, 234–273.

Although negligence, as a ground of legal liability, does not contemplate any intent or motive on the part of the defendant, it does require some fault on his part, that is, some act or omission inconsistent with his duty of care. Some injuries, such as those caused by an act of God or by unavoidable accident, are said to be "damnum absque injuria," for which no action lies. The very definition of actionable negligence negatives liability for injury or damage resulting from an act of God or from an unavoidable accident not contributed to by any default of the defendant.

Actionable negligence contemplates a duty on the part of the defendant, a corresponding right on the part of the plaintiff, and a breach of that duty by the defendant resulting in injury to the plaintiff. The legal concept of duty, imposed upon all persons, is not necessarily the same as one's moral duty. For example, although ethical and humanitarian considerations may require one to render assistance to another in distress or danger not contributed to by the former, there is ordinarily no liability for failure to render such assistance, in the absence of a special relationship imposing such a duty. However, a good Samaritan who volunteers assistance must use due care and is liable for injuries resulting from his negligence in his attempts to help.

An injury is not actionable if it was not foreseen and could not have been foreseen or reasonably anticipated. Actionable negligence must be predicated upon the foresight of an ordinarily prudent person and upon the facts as they appeared at the time, and is not determined by the actual consequences. It is not a necessary element of negligence that one charged therewith should have been able to anticipate the particular consequences of his act or omission or the precise injury sustained; it is sufficient that he should have foreseen that his conduct would probably result in injury of some kind to some person.

There is some diversity of results, and much variation in language, among the decisions dealing with the effect to be given the violation of a statute in determining liability in a negligence action. In a majority of cases, the violation of a penal or criminal statute is actionable negligence or "negligence per se" or "negligence as a matter of law." Under this doctrine, where a statute imposes upon any person a specific duty for the protection of others, his neglect to perform that duty renders him liable to those for whose protection or benefit it was imposed, for any injuries of the character which the statute was designed to prevent and which were proximately produced by such neglect. Not all courts, however, go to this length, some holding that violation of a statute is merely prima facie or presumptive evidence of negligence or that it is merely evidence of negligence.

The mere violation of a penal statute enacted for the protection of the general public and not in the interest of special classes or individuals does not constitute actionable negligence merely because injury ensues. Only those for whose benefit and protection the law was made have a right of action for injuries resulting from its violation. As in all cases predicated on negligence, there can be no recovery unless there is a causal connection between the negligent or unlawful act and the injury or damage to the plaintiff.

There is much conflict of authority on the question of liability for injuries caused by the violation of municipal ordinances. Some courts give ordinances the same or almost the same force as statutes in this respect, while others distinguish sharply between statutes and ordinances.

§ 21:8. Degree and standard of care.

Am Jur 2d References: Negligence, §§ 9, 66–74, 77–93, 108–126.

The duty imposed by the law upon all persons is to use ordinary or reasonable care to prevent injury to others. The standard by which the conduct of a person is judged in determining whether he was negligent in a particular situation is the care which an ordinarily prudent and careful person would exercise under like circumstances. The degree of care required depends upon all the circumstances and upon the danger attendant upon the activity and instrumentalities involved. The greater the danger, the greater the degree of care required.

The criterion of due care and negligence is objective. This is clearly essential to the practical administration of justice, since if the standard of care depended upon the mental or moral condition of the individual defendant, the tests would be of infinite variety and impossible to apply. The standards of the ordinarily prudent man are usually applied in common-law negligence cases even though the person charged with negligence is mentally incompetent or defective or is intoxicated. There is some disposition on the part of the courts, however, to make some allowance in judging the conduct of infants charged with negligence.

One of the circumstances to be considered in determining the degree of care owed is the status, capacity, and age of the person to whom the duty is owed. Persons who are known to be deficient in mind or body, or who are young and inexperienced, are entitled to a degree of care proportionate to their incapacity to protect themselves.

Another circumstance which may affect the legal standard of care is an emergency or sudden peril not occasioned by the defendant's fault. Generally, one who, in a sudden emergency, acts according to his best judgment, or who, because of want of time in which to form judgment, omits to act in the most judicious manner, is not chargeable with negligence, although the injury might have been avoided had he selected another course of conduct, if in the emergency he acted as a reasonably prudent person might be expected to act under like circumstances.

§ 21:9. Strict or absolute duty; Rylands v Fletcher.

Am Jur 2d References: Adjoining Landowners, § 11; Electricity, § 39; Negligence, § 8.

The English case of Rylands v Fletcher (1868) LR 3 HL 330, precipitated a flood of controversy, both in the courts and among commentators, which has not completely subsided after more than a hundred years. This famous decision merely held a landowner liable where water from a reservoir constructed on his property found its way through old mine workings on adjacent property into the coal mines of the plaintiff under remote property. The decision assumed that the defendant was not "negligent" in the ordinary sense in constructing the reservoir. The decision of the House of Lords in this case was predicated on a "non-natural" and extraordinary use of his land by the defendant. In the absence of negligence or "fault" on either part, it was concluded that the public interest required the protection of the mine owner as against the surface owner.

Under the ordinary principles of negligence, the degree of care required varies according to the risk or danger incident to the activities or instrumentalities involved. Where the peril is sufficiently great or the activity or instrumentality involves an unusual and extraordinary use of property, it has been said that there is an absolute duty to prevent injury to others, or that there is "strict liability," or liability "without fault," for any resulting injury or damage. Obviously, "liability without fault" is a contradiction in terms. Instances in which the courts have imposed a strict or absolute duty upon persons engaged in unusual and dangerous activities include the keeping of dangerous animals or substances. If the activity is sufficiently dangerous, its mere undertaking may constitute a "fault" or even a nuisance forming the basis of legal liability.

§ 21:10. Proximate cause.

Am Jur 2d References: Negligence, §§ 127–175.

Liability for negligence must be predicated upon a causal connection between the negligence of the defendant and the injury or damage suffered by the plaintiff. The law refers the injury to the proximate, not to the remote, cause, and establishes proximate cause as an essential element of liability for negligence.

The concept of proximate cause, as applied in particular cases, is a complex one, and any definition of the term must be interpreted and applied to fit the case at hand. The following definition is perhaps as reliable as any: The proximate cause of an injury is that cause which, in natural and continuous sequence, unbroken by any efficient intervening cause, produces the injury, and without which the result would not have occurred. Proximate cause is the primary or efficient cause of an injury.

The proximate cause of an injury is not necessarily the immediate cause nor the cause nearest in time, distance, or space. Assuming that there is a direct, natural, and continuous sequence between an act and an injury, through which the force of the act operated without the interposition of a separate force other than that which the act itself might have set in motion, the act can be accepted as the proximate cause of the injury regardless of its separation from the injury in point of time or distance. Obviously, however, all of these factors must be considered in determining proximate causation.

To establish the element of proximate cause, it must be made to appear that the injury was not only the natural but also the probable consequence of the negligence. This depends upon whether, viewing the events in retrospect, the injury appears to be the reasonable rather than the extraordinary consequence of the negligence.

If the consequences of a negligent act were actually foreseen by the actor, there is no problem of proximate causation. The question whether proximate cause requires a showing that the negligent person anticipated, or reasonably might have foreseen, the injurious consequences of his act or omission, is the subject of much conflict and confusion. Some courts take the position that in order to warrant a finding that negligence, not amounting to a wanton wrong, was the proximate cause of an injury, it must appear that consequences injurious to another were foreseen, or reasonably might have been foreseen, by the wrongdoer. Other courts take a contrary view; and the modern trend of judicial opinion seems to be in favor of eliminating foreseeable consequences as a test of proximate cause, except where an independent, responsible, intervening cause is involved. The test of foreseen or foreseeable consequences, even where applicable, does not require that the negligent person should have been able to foresee the particular injury or the injury in the precise form in which it occurred, or to anticipate the particular consequences which actually flowed from his negligence. It is sufficient that the injuries are the natural, although not the necessary and inevitable, result of the negligence.

§ 21:11. —Intervening and concurrent causes.

Am Jur 2d References: Negligence, §§ 176–233.

The negligence of the defendant, in order to render him liable, need not be the sole cause of the injury. If the negligence was operative at the time of the injury, it may constitute the proximate cause of the injury notwithstanding the fact that it concurred with the act of a third person or other agencies to produce the injury. The fact that the negligence of a third person concurred with the defendant's negligence does not relieve the latter from liability if his negligence was an efficient cause, without which the injury would not have occurred. And the fact that the ultimate consequences are immediately or directly brought about by an intervening cause does not relieve a defendant of liability if the intervening cause was set in motion by his negligence.

Where a person has been put in sudden peril by the negligent act of another, and, in an instinctive effort to escape from the peril, either suffers injury himself or does injury to a third person, the original negligent act is the proximate cause of the injury and the intervening acts are deemed to have been set in motion by the original negligence. In the famous Squib Case (2 WBL 892, 96 Eng Reprint 525) the defendant was held liable for having thrown a lighted squib into a market where several persons successively picked it up and threw it from them until it exploded and injured the plaintiff. Here, however, the original act of the defendant was intentionally mischievous rather than negligent.

An intervening cause is material in determining legal causation only insofar as it supersedes a prior wrong as the proximate cause of the injury, by breaking the sequence between the prior wrong and the injury. The test in such cases is whether the alleged intervening efficient cause was a new and independent force, causing the injury and superseding the original wrong complained of so as to make it remote in the chain of causation. Clearly, a wilful, malicious, or criminal act of a third person causing an injury not intended or foreseeable by the defendant breaks the causal connection between the defendant's negligence and the injury.

Where an injury occurs through the concurrent negligence of two persons and would not have happened in the absence of negligence of either person, the negligence of each is deemed to be a proximate cause of the injury, and both are answerable.

As regards liability to a person attempting to save another exposed to peril, it is held that negligence that imperils life may be a wrong to the rescuer as well as to the imperiled person. Where one person is exposed to peril of life or limb by the negligence of another, the latter is liable for injuries received by a third person in a reasonable effort to rescue the one imperiled, the proximate cause being the negligence which created the peril. This principle is applied by the majority of courts in cases involving injuries resulting from attempts to save property imperiled by the negligence of the defendant.

§ 21:12. Res ipsa loquitur.

Am Jur 2d References: Negligence, §§ 474–520.

Under the doctrine of res ipsa loquitur (the thing speaks for itself), a mere showing of the cause and occasion of an injury may permit an inference of negligence on the part of the defendant and thus permit recovery without evidence of specific acts or omissions constituting negligence. The doctrine is frequently stated in these terms: proof that the thing which caused the injury to the plaintiff was under the control and management of the defendant, and that the occurrence was such as, in the ordinary course of things, would not happen if those having such control and management used proper care, affords sufficient evidence, in the absence of an explanation, that the injury was caused by the defendant's negligence. As otherwise stated, the doctrine instructs that where the circumstances of the occurrence that caused the injury are of a character to give ground for a reasonable inference that if due care had been used by the party charged with the care of the premises or thing, the occurrence would not have happened, negligence may be inferred in the absence of any explanation. The doctrine merely permits, and does not compel, an inference of negligence.

By definition, it is a prerequisite of the doctrine that the instrumentality which produced the injury was at the time of the injury under the management or control of the defendant or of his agents and servants.

The doctrine of res ipsa loquitur is based in part upon the theory that the defendant in charge of the instrumentality which causes the injury either knows the cause of the accident or has the best opportunity of ascertaining it, and that the evidence of the true cause is practically accessible to the defendant but inaccessible to the injured person.

Although technically the doctrine is a procedural rule, merely permitting an inference of negligence in cases falling within its scope and thus carrying the case to the jury without proof of specific acts or omissions, the practical results of the application of the rule are tantamount to a rule of substantive law, insofar as the doctrine permits recovery under circumstances in which recovery could not be had without the application of the rule.

Where all of the facts attending the injury are disclosed by the evidence, and nothing is left to inference, the doctrine of res ipsa loquitur has no application. There is a conflict of authority as to whether pleading a specific act of negligence forfeits the pleader's right to rely upon the doctrine of res ispa loquitur.

§ 21:13. Contributory negligence, generally.

Am Jur 2d References: Negligence, §§ 288–294, 317–351, 378–385.

The contributory negligence of the plaintiff is a defense to an action based on negligence of the defendant. There can be no recovery of damages for negligence if the injured person, by his own negligence, proximately contributed to the injury. Even though the defendant did not exercise due care, he is not liable if it appears that the injury would have been avoided if the plaintiff had exercised due care. The standard by which the conduct of the plaintiff is judged is the conduct of an ordinarily prudent person under like or similar circumstances. In order to bar recovery, there must be a direct causal connection between his negligence and the injury complained of; the plaintiff's negligence, in order to bar recovery, must have contributed proximately to the injury.

Contributory negligence is not a defense to an action based upon wilful, wanton, or intentional wrongs. Whether gross negligence comes within this exception to the rule of contributory negligence is the subject of a conflict of authority, as is the question whether the defense is available to a person charged with the violation of a statute or ordinance.

An essential element of contributory negligence is that the person to be charged therewith knew, or by the exercise of ordinary care should have known, of the circumstance or condition out of which the danger arose. A plaintiff will not be held guilty of contributory negligence if it appears that he had no knowledge or means of knowledge of the danger.

One who is forced to act under the stress produced by a peril confronting him is not expected to act with the coolness and prudence that under other circumstances might be considered an essential of due care. Although a plaintiff confronted by an emergency or sudden peril may not have taken the safest course, he may yet recover for injuries sustained if he was compelled by the defendant's negligence to act without opportunity for deliberation.

Voluntary exposure of one's self to danger does not constitute contributory negligence on his part where the exposure is justified by the ordinary standards of human conduct. A person who sees another in imminent and serious peril caused by the negligence of the defendant cannot be charged with contributory negligence as a matter of law in risking his own safety in attempting to effect a rescue, provided the attempt is not recklessly or rashly made. A similar doctrine applies in some jurisdictions, with modifications, to risks encountered in attempts to protect property.

§ 21:14. —Age and physical or mental condition of injured person.

Am Jur 2d References: Negligence, §§ 352–360.

Since knowledge and appreciation of the peril are essential elements of contributory negligence, an inquiry into the age, experience, and mental capacity of the plaintiff is material where contributory negligence is invoked as a defense. A young child is not required to exercise the same standard of care for its own safety as would be exacted of an adult. A child is held only to such care as may reasonably be expected of a child of its maturity and capacity. The standard by which to measure the conduct of a child, as regards the question of contributory negligence, is that degree of care ordinarily exercised by children of the same age, capacity, discretion, knowledge, and experience, under the same or similar circumstances.

The intelligence and capacity of the particular child, rather than its age, is the important factor in determining whether the infant in question may be charged with contributory negligence. There is an age, of course, at which it would be absurd to attribute contributory negligence to a child. Up to the age of 4 or 5, it is generally assumed, and sometimes conclusively presumed, that an infant is incapable of contributory negligence, although some decisions indicate that a child, even of these tender years, may be guilty of contributory negligence under some circumstances. Similar observations apply to children from 5 to 7 years old. Between the ages of 7 and 14, children may or may not be guilty of contributory negligence, depending upon their mental development and other circumstances. After a child has reached the age of 14 years, it is chargeable with contributory negligence and is required to exercise such care for its own safety as is usual and normal for children of its age, experience, knowledge, and discretion.

There is no different standard of care for one who is aged, feeble, blind, halt, deaf or otherwise impaired in capacity, from that applied to one in good physical and mental condition. The conduct of the ordinarily prudent person under the circumstances is the standard to be applied in determining whether the plaintiff has been guilty of contributory negligence even though he is physically disabled. A person whose senses or faculties are impaired is bound to take extraordinary precautions.

Voluntary intoxication does not relieve one from contributory negligence. One who has voluntarily disabled himself by reason of intoxication is held to the same degree and care for his own safety that is required of a sober person.

§ 21:15. —Last clear chance.

Am Jur 2d References: Negligence, §§ 386–389, 392–396, 398–402, 404–406, 408–413, 440.

The doctrine of last clear chance, sometimes referred to as the doctrine of discovered peril, the doctrine of supervening negligence, or the humanitarian doctrine, is that the negligence of the plaintiff does not preclude a recovery for the negligence of the defendant, where it appears that the defendant by exercising reasonable care and prudence might have avoided injurious consequences to the plaintiff notwithstanding the latter's negligence. Under this doctrine, a negligent defendant is held liable to a negligent plaintiff, if the defendant, who was aware of the plaintiff's peril or (according to many authorities), although actually unaware of the plaintiff's peril, should, in the exercise of due care, have been aware of it, had in fact a later opportunity than the plaintiff to avoid the accident. The person who has the last clear chance or opportunity of avoiding an accident, notwithstanding the negligent acts of his opponent, is considered solely responsible for the consequences of the accident.

The doctrine of last clear chance is traced to the English case of Davies v Mann, 10 Mees & W 546, 152 Eng Reprint 588, in which it was held that the negligence of the plaintiff in leaving his donkey on a highway so fettered as to prevent its getting out of the way of carriages did not preclude recovery against the defendant who negligently drove his carriage against the animal. This old decision, handed down in 1842, did not employ the phrase "last clear chance" or any other of the modern terminology, nor did anything about the case foreshadow its emergence as a landmark case.

Although there is some difference of opinion, many of the best-considered modern authorities take the view that the doctrine of last clear chance, in its origin and in essence, is nothing more than an application of the rule of proximate cause to the situation where both the defendant and the plaintiff have been negligent.

The doctrine of last clear chance presupposes negligence on the part of the plaintiff which, in the absence of the doctrine, would constitute contributory negligence precluding recovery. The thing that obviates the negligence of the plaintiff is what the defendant did or failed to do after the plaintiff was imperiled, constituting the breach of duty for which the defendant is held liable.

It is generally agreed that the doctrine permits a recovery notwithstanding the original or antecedent negligence of the injured person in getting into his predicament, where it appears that the danger was discovered and plaintiff's peril was appreciated by the defendant in time to have enabled him to avoid the accident, and that the plaintiff was physically unable to escape. The same rule is applied in many cases where the danger was actually discovered by the defendant, although the plaintiff was physically able to escape the danger at all relevant times and was guilty of continuing and concurrent negligence in failing to discover or appreciate his own danger. A different situation is presented where the plaintiff was not oblivious of his danger but had actually discovered the fact of his peril.

There is considerable conflict of authority on the applicability of the doctrine to permit a recovery by a plaintiff whose original negligence has placed him in a position of peril from which he is unable to extricate himself, as against a defendant who could have avoided injuring the plaintiff if he had exercised reasonable care in discovering the plaintiff's danger, although he did not discover it. The weight of authority denies the application of the last clear chance doctrine where the defendant did not actually discover the danger to the injured person, although he was under duty to discover it, if the injured person was physically able to escape from the peril at any time up to the moment of the accident.

§ 21:16. Comparative negligence.

Am Jur 2d References:　Negligence, §§ 292, 426, 427, 429–453, 455.

The rule of comparative negligence means that even though the plaintiff was guilty of negligence which operated concurrently with the negligence of the defendant as the proximate cause of the injury to the plaintiff, he may recover if the degree of his negligence was slight as compared with that of the defendant. Under this doctrine, the plaintiff's negligence operates not to relieve the defendant entirely from liability, as under the common-law rule of contributory negligence, but merely to diminish the damages recoverable.

The comparative negligence rule is generally rejected in common-law jurisdictions, although there has been much criticism of the harshness of the all-

or-nothing common-law rule of contributory negligence. During recent years, however, statutes have been enacted in a number of jurisdictions adopting the comparative negligence doctrine or a variation thereof. Such statutes ordinarily provide in effect that the negligence of the plaintiff will not bar recovery if such negligence was not as great as the negligence of the defendant, but that the damages recoverable will be diminished in proportion to the amount of negligence attributable to the plaintiff.

§ 21:17. Imputed negligence.

Am Jur 2d References: Negligence, §§ 456–473.

The term "imputed negligence" refers to the rule which visits upon one person responsibility for the negligence of another. The doctrine may be invoked either to defeat liability to the plaintiff in a negligence action by charging him with the concurrent negligence of a third person, or, by imputing to a person the negligence of another, to charge the former with affirmative liability to a third person injured through the negligence.

The doctrine of imputed negligence is more frequently invoked to defeat a negligence action by imputing to the plaintiff, as "contributory negligence," the negligence of a third person. Generally, however, in order to impute the negligence of one person to another to defeat in action of negligence by the latter, there must exist between them some relation of master or superior and servant or subordinate, or some other relation akin thereto. The relation between the plaintiff and the negligent person, as regards authority, control, and the like, must be such as to make the plaintiff responsible at common law for the negligent conduct of such third person.

For example, a principal or master cannot recover for injury or damage inflicted by a third person if the injury was proximately contributed to by the negligence of the former's agent or servant. The negligence of the agent or servant is imputed to the principal or master in such cases. A similar rule is applied as between the parties to a joint enterprise, although this rule does not prevent one member of the enterprise from holding another liable for the latter's negligence.

It is generally held that the negligence of one spouse is not to be imputed to the other, in the absence of some relationship of agency or common enterprise, other than the marital relationship itself. However, in actions by a husband for loss of the services of his wife through the negligence of others, her contributory negligence may be a defense.

Although the failure of a parent to exercise reasonable care for the protection of a child non sui juris may be a defense to an action by the parent for his own benefit against a third person causing the injury, the weight of authority holds that the negligence of the parent or custodian of a child is not to be imputed to the latter so as to defeat an action by the child or for its benefit against a third person whose negligent act has injured the child, if the child itself was not capable of exercising the proper degree of care for its own safety.

§ 21:18. Assumed risk.

Am Jur 2d References: Negligence, §§ 274–286.

It is a well-established defense to an action based on negligence that the plaintiff voluntarily assumed the risk of injury. The doctrine is expressed in the maxim, "volenti non fit injuria," or that to which a person assents is not a legal injury. As otherwise stated, the rule is that one who knows and deliberately exposes himself to a danger assumes the risk thereof.

The defense of assumption of risk is closely associated with contributory negligence. There are distinctions, however, and assumption of risk may be available as a defense in some cases where contributory negligence would not be. Assumption of risk involves a more or less deliberate choice made by the plaintiff and negatives liability without reference to the fact that the plaintiff may have acted with due care after his choice.

Knowledge and appreciation of the danger is an essential element of the defense of assumption of risk. The doctrine is based upon voluntary exposure to danger and is applicable only where the injured person might reasonably elect whether or not he would expose himself to the peril. If the exposure was due to his inability to escape after he became, or should have become, aware of the danger, the doctrine does not apply. The application of the doctrine requires that the plaintiff not only knew and appreciated the danger, but voluntarily put himself in the way of it.

III. AUTOMOBILES AND OTHER MOTOR VEHICLES

§ 21:19. Duty of care in operation, generally.

Am Jur 2d References: Automobiles, etc., §§ 349–360, 364–374.

Rights and liabilities in connection with injuries growing out of the operation or ownership of motor vehicles are generally governed by the principles of negligence discussed above. Negligence in cases involving motor vehicle accidents, as in negligence cases generally, is the failure to exercise ordinary or reasonable care so as to avoid injury to others. This means that one must exercise that degree of care which an ordinarily careful and prudent person would exercise under the same or similar circumstances. This depends upon all of the circumstances, including the place, conditions, and surroundings attending the accident.

The perils necessarily attending the operation of automobiles upon public highways obviously require a higher degree of care than would be required of the driver of a yoke of oxen. In other words, the care required in connection with a motor vehicle takes into account the inherently dangerous nature of these vehicles and the gravity of the injuries likely to result from the negligent operation thereof. This does not mean, however, that the operator of an automobile is an insurer of the safety of others, or that he is subject to the strict liability of one who keeps ferocious animals or uses dynamite or other dangerous substances.

Ordinary care requires that the operator of a motor vehicle must keep it under control at all times so as to avoid injury to others. What constitutes such control depends upon all of the surrounding circumstances. He must anticipate the presence of others upon the highway and must maintain a lookout and vigilance in accordance with all of the circumstances.

The operator of any vehicle has the right to assume that other travelers upon the highway will exercise reasonable care and will obey applicable traffic regulations and the rules of the road. A motorist is not required to anticipate negligence on the part of another motorist, in the absence of anything to indicate otherwise. But this rule has no application to a motorist who sees, or in the exercise of ordinary care should see, that another motorist will not obey the traffic rules or is unable to do so.

Emergency vehicles, such as police cars, fire department vehicles, and ambulances, are generally exempted from the operation of traffic regulations or rules of the road. However, the operators of such vehicles are required to exercise due care under the circumstances to avoid injury to others, the measure of due care in such cases including the emergency under which the vehicle is operated. The rights and duties of the operators of such vehicles are frequently regulated by statute.

The general rule of "sudden emergency" has frequent application in cases involving motor vehicle accidents. Where the operator of such a vehicle is suddenly confronted with an emergency not produced or contributed to by his own negligence, and is compelled to act instantly to avoid a collision or injury, he is not held guilty of negligence if he makes a choice which a person of ordinary prudence in such a position might make, even though he does not make the wisest choice and even though he may not have exercised the very highest degree of good judgment.

The question whether the violation of a statute or ordinance regulating the operation of motor vehicles constitutes negligence per se, or merely evidence of negligence, is determined by the general rules of negligence discusssed above, and these rules vary in the several jurisdictions. In no event, however, will the violation of such a statute or ordinance impose liability upon the operator of a motor vehicle unless the violation is the proximate cause of the injury complained of. The mere fact that the vehicle was not licensed or registered as required by law, or that the operator thereof did not have the required driver's license, is generally held not sufficient, of itself, to render the driver liable for all injuries in the operation of the vehicle, nor to preclude his recovery for his own injuries.

The general principle of the law of negligence, that in order to impose liability for a negligent or wrongful act, it must appear that such act was the proximate cause of the injury complained of, is fully applicable in cases involving motor vehicle accidents. Equally applicable to automobile accident cases are the principles governing concurrent and intervening causes, and liability for acts in attempting to avert injuries or to rescue imperiled persons or property.

§ 21:20. Injuries to particular persons; pedestrians.

Am Jur 2d References: Automobiles, etc., §§ 380–428, 457–464.

The duty of the operator of a motor vehicle is not limited to the care owed to other motorists and vehicles traveling upon the highway. This duty of care extends also to other occupants of his own vehicle, to pedestrians, children, persons boarding and alighting from public conveyances, and to any other persons lawfully using the way.

The law exacts of a motorist a higher degree of care for those who are unable to care for their own safety, such as blind, deaf, aged, crippled, or intoxicated persons, when such physical disability is known or should have been known to the motorist, but not otherwise.

The operator of a motor vehicle must anticipate the presence of pedestrians lawfully using highways and streets, and he owes to a pedestrian walking along or crossing a highway or street, or on a sidewalk, the duty to exercise reasonable or ordinary care to avoid injuring him. In the absence of an applicable statute or ordinance, a person has the right to walk longitudinally along a street or highway, and is not guilty of contributory negligence as a matter of law in doing so, although, of course, he must exercise reasonable care for his own safety. The operator of a motor vehicle must anticipate the presence of pedestrians along the side of a highway or street and must exercise reasonable or ordinary care to avoid injuring them, including, under certain circumstances, the giving of a timely warning of his approach.

Motorists have the duty of exercising ordinary or reasonable care to avoid injuring pedestrians who are crossing the highway or street, including those crossing between intersections or diagonally. On the other hand, the pedestrian is required to exercise ordinary care for his own safety under the circumstances, including the place of crossing and the condition of traffic. The fact that the pedestrian crosses between intersections or at an unusual place may diminish the degree of care owed by the motorist, and it may impose on the pedestrian the duty to exercise more diligence and greater care than when he crosses at a place provided for pedestrians.

Both the motorist and the pedestrian have a right to assume that others will obey any traffic signs or signals, in the absence of circumstances which would put a reasonable person on notice that such an assumption is unwarranted. A motorist who enters a highway or street intersection against the direction of a traffic light, sign, or officer's gesture, and injures a pedestrian crossing the intersection, is ordinarily guilty of negligence and liable to the pedestrian. On the other hand, a pedestrian crossing a highway or street in disregard of such signs or signals will ordinarily be held guilty of contributory negligence precluding recovery by him for his injuries.

A motorist is generally held not liable for injuries received by a pedestrian who collides with the side of the vehicle, or for injuries to pedestrians who suddenly dart or step into the path of the vehicle.

§ 21:21. —Children.

Am Jur 2d References: Automobiles, etc., §§ 429–456.

Where a motorist knows of the presence of a child or children in or near a street or highway, or should know that they may reasonably be expected to be in the vicinity, he is under a duty to exercise reasonable and proper care for the safety of the children. He is required to be alert and vigilant and to maintain a lookout. He must maintain control of his vehicle and not drive at a speed which may be excessive under the circumstances. The standard of care exacted of the motorist as regards children is higher than in the case of adults. Moreover, the degree of care required of the motorist varies with the age, intelligence, and maturity of the child and with the latter's ability to take care of himself. The motorist must anticipate childish conduct. The circumstances may be such as to require him to sound a warning of his approach.

The degree of care required of children, and their capacity for contributory negligence, are questions discussed above under the general principles of negligence.

A very high degree of care is required of a motorist approaching a school bus discharging or taking on children. In most jurisdictions there are statutes requiring a motorist to stop for a school bus which has stopped for this purpose. The duty of the motorist to maintain caution and vigilance is greater in areas near schools and in thickly populated areas.

Where a motorist is driving carefully, at a reasonable rate of speed, and is obeying the rules of the road, he is not, as a general rule, liable for injuries received by a child who darts in front of his vehicle so suddenly that the motorist cannot stop or otherwise avoid injuring the child. This rule presupposes, of course, that the motorist had no warning that the child might dart into the place of danger.

§ 21:22. —Bicyclists and motorcyclists.

Am Jur 2d References: Automobiles, etc., §§ 549–559.

The operator of an automobile or truck is required to exercise ordinary or reasonable care to avoid collision with bicycles or motorcycles or other small vehicles upon streets or highways. At the same time, bicyclists and motorcyclists are required to exercise reasonable care for their own safety, and to obey legal regulations and the rules of the road; and motorists have the right to assume that they will do so and will not negligently expose themselves to danger.

As a general rule, a motorist is not under a duty to stop when he sees children on bicycles on a highway unless it is apparent that they are in a position of peril, although circumstances may require additional precautions against the possibility that the child, through fright or bewilderment, may place himself in a position of peril.

§ 21:23. — Occupants of vehicle; guests.

Am Jur 2d References: Automobiles, etc., §§ 465–548.

The duty and liability of the owner or operator of a motor vehicle to an occupant of the vehicle depends largely upon the status of the occupant, that is, whether he is an invited guest, an occupant at sufferance, a trespasser, or a passenger for hire.

As to invited guests, the rule followed in most jurisdictions prior to the adoption of statutes to the contrary, was that the owner or operator of a motor vehicle owed the duty to such a guest to exercise ordinary or reasonable care in the operation of the vehicle. In a few states, however, the view was taken, independently of statute, that gross negligence must be shown in such cases.

The general common-law rule requiring the exercise of ordinary or reasonable care to avoid injuring an invited guest has been abrogated in most states by the enactment of so-called "guest" statutes. These statutes, by phraseology varying in the several jurisdictions, limit the liability of the owner or operator for injury to or death of an invited gratuitous guest to cases where the injury or death was intentional on the part of the owner or operator, or resulted from his reckless disregard of the consequences, or from reckless or wilful or wanton acts, or wilful or wanton misconduct, or gross negligence, or gross and wanton negligence, or intoxication. These statutes relieve the owner or operator of a motor vehicle who, without any benefit to himself, transports another, from the consequences of ordinary negligence causing injury to the occupant.

The question of who is a "guest" within the contemplation of a guest statute, or of a comparable common-law rule, depends largely upon the circumstances of the particular case. A "guest" may be defined generally as one who is invited, either directly or by implication, to enjoy the hospitality of the owner or operator of a motor vehicle, and who accepts such hospitality and takes a ride either for his own pleasure or on his own business, without making any return to, or conferring any benefit upon, the owner or operator of the vehicle other than the mere pleasure of his company. If the rider's transportation contributes such a tangible and substantial benefit as to promote the mutual interests of both passenger and owner or operator, or is primarily for the attainment of some tangible and substantial objective or business purpose of the owner or operator, he is not a guest within such statutes. If payment is made or compensation is given for the transportation, the guest statute does not apply.

Actual payment of money for a ride is not necessary to negate the guest relationship. For example, one who accompanies the owner or operator of a motor vehicle for the purpose of guiding or pointing out his route is not deemed to be a guest under such statutes. While the mere fact that an occupant assists with the driving does not change his status from that of a guest to that of a passenger, if it appears that the driving assistance was the inducing reason for transporting the occupant, such services will be regarded as compensation or payment within the meaning of the statutes.

Where there is an arrangement before the start of a trip that an occupant of a motor vehicle should contribute to the cost of operating the vehicle, it is generally held that there is "payment" or "compensation" for the transportation under a guest statute, making the occupant a passenger for hire rather than an invited guest. However, a mere incidental or gratuitous contribution to trip expenses will not constitute such payment or compensation.

The question whether the occupant of a motor vehicle under a "share a ride" arrangement or a "car pool" occupies the status of an invited guest or of a passenger for hire within the meaning of guest statutes depends upon the facts of the particular case.

The mere fact that an occupant of a motor vehicle stands in a family relationship to the owner or operator does not of itself prevent him from being a guest under a guest statute. A child may be a guest within such statutes, and so may an intoxicated person.

Although a different result has been reached under some circumstances and some statutes, it is generally held that the owner of a motor vehicle, or one having general possession and control so as to be practically in a position of ownership, cannot, while riding in his own vehicle, be regarded as the guest of the person permitted to drive, so as to restrict his right to recover for injuries under a guest statute.

Although a simple protest by a guest as to the manner in which the vehicle is being operated is insufficient to terminate the guest status, where he protests because of real and reasonable fear and demands to be let out of the vehicle, the guest's status changes to that of a passenger against will or by duress, avoiding the application of the guest statute.

Whether the acts or omissions of the owner or operator of a motor vehicle amount to gross negligence, wilful or wanton misconduct, heedlessness or reckless disregard of consequences, or intentional injury, depends upon the circumstances of the particular case and is ordinarily a question of fact for the jury, although it may become a question of law for the court where fair-minded men cannot differ as to the conclusion.

A person riding in a motor vehicle driven by another is not absolved from all personal care for his own safety. Apart from guest statutes, such occupant is under the duty of exercising reasonable or ordinary care to avoid injury. However, a different standard of conduct is imposed upon the guest under the guest statutes of some states. The general rule that ordinary contributory negligence on the part of the plaintiff will not bar his recovery in an action based upon the defendant's recklessness or wilful and wanton misconduct, has been applied in several jurisdictions under automobile guest statutes. But in some states, even though ordinary contributory negligence on the guest's part may not bar recovery under a guest statute, no action will lie where the guest's lack of care for his own safety amounts to recklessness of willfulness equal to that of the host, under a doctrine sometimes characterized as that of "comparative misconduct."

Moreover, some courts have rejected entirely, in guest statute cases, the rule that the plaintiff's ordinary contributory negligence does not bar recovery for injury resulting from the defendant's recklessness or willful or wanton misconduct. And under guest statutes specifying "gross negligence" of the host as the actionable conduct, contributory negligence on the part of the guest has been held a good defense.

In jurisdictions which recognize a rule of assumption of risk as distinct from the defense of contributory negligence, it is generally held that assumption of risk by the guest is available to the host charged with wilful or wanton misconduct or recklessness under an automobile guest statute, even though the guest's contributory negligence would not bar his recovery. There is, however, some dissent from this view.

In many states it is held that the duty of care owed to a permissive guest or a guest at sufferance is the same as that owed to an invited guest, while some states hold that the only duty owed to such an occupant is to refrain from wantonly or wilfully injuring him. The duty owed by the owner or operator of a motor vehicle to a trespasser in or on the vehicle is to refrain from injuring him wilfully or wantonly. In some states, however, this rule is applied only to undiscovered trespassers.

§ 21:24. Liability for act of another.

Am Jur 2d References: Automobiles, etc., §§ 560–570.

While an owner who entrusts his motor vehicle to another, knowing him to be an incompetent or careless driver, may be held liable for such person's negligence in the operation of the vehicle (see § 21:25, infra), the courts have been reluctant to extend this principle so as to impose liability on one who has given a motor vehicle to an allegedly incompetent, unfit, or reckless driver. A contrary result has, however, been reached in some cases.

The mere fact that a motor vehicle is owned jointly or in common by two or more persons does not render one of the co-owners liable for the negligent operation of the vehicle by another co-owner, in the absence of agency, employment, partnership, or joint enterprise. A partnership is, of course, liable for the negligent operation of a motor vehicle by one of the partners while engaged in the partnership business. And all occupants of a motor vehicle who are engaged in a joint enterprise are liable for its negligent operation by one of them, irrespective of the ownership of the vehicle.

As a general rule, an occupant of a motor vehicle other than the driver is not liable for injuries to a third person due to the negligence of the driver, in the absence of evidence that such occupant had some control over the driver or that there was some relationship of employment or joint enterprise. A licensed driver accompanying a learner is not liable for the negligence of the learner, but he may be held liable if he is instructing and fails to exercise reasonable care as an instructor.

In some states, by statute, a parent or custodian of a minor is required to sign the latter's application for license to drive a motor vehicle and to assume liability for the licensee's negligence in the operation of the vehicle.

Under the doctrine of respondeat superior, an employer is liable for the negligent operation of a motor vehicle by his employee in the course of his employment.

§ 21:25. Owner's liability where vehicle is operated by another.

Am Jur 2d References: Automobiles, etc., §§ 571–614.

In the absence of statute, it is generally held that the owner of a motor vehicle is not liable for its negligent operation by another using it with his permission, unless the operator was acting as his agent or servant (actually or under the "family purpose" doctrine), or unless the vehicle was dangerously defective, or unless the owner was present in the vehicle and maintained some control over its operation, or unless the owner and driver were engaged in a joint enterprise or partnership activity, or unless the person to whom the vehicle was entrusted was an incompetent or unfit person. In other words, under this common-law principle, liability for the negligent use of a motor vehicle cannot be predicated solely upon ownership of the vehicle.

The mere presence of the owner in a vehicle while it is being driven by another in a negligent manner does not necessarily make him liable for an injury caused thereby, unless the owner maintained some control over the operation of the vehicle. However, many jurisdictions follow the rule that the presence of the owner in the vehicle creates a rebuttable presumption or inference that he was in control of its operation and of the driver.

The owner of a motor vehicle who loans or entrusts the vehicle to an incompetent or unfit person, knowing, or from the circumstances being charged with knowledge, that such person is incompetent or unfit to drive, may be held liable for an injury negligently inflicted by that driver and proximately caused by the driver's incompetence or unfitness. This rule applies to the entrustment of an automobile to a child or to a person who is intoxicated.

According to the general common-law rule, the mere fact of family relationship, such as that of parent and child or husband and wife, between the owner of a motor vehicle and the person driving it does not impose liability upon the owner for the negligence of the driver.

A number of jurisdictions follow the so-called "family purpose" doctrine, under which the owner of a motor vehicle maintained for the use or pleasure of his family is liable for injuries inflicted by the negligent operation of the vehicle while it is used by members of the family for their own pleasure, on the theory that the vehicle is being used for the purpose of the business for which it is kept, and that the person operating it is acting as the owner's agent or servant. However, the family purpose doctrine has been rejected in many jurisdictions.

In a number of states, statutes have been enacted which render the owner of a motor vehicle liable for the negligence of anyone operating his vehicle with his permission, express or implied, whether in the business of the owner or otherwise. Such statutes impose liability upon the owner irrespective of any business or family relationship between the owner and operator; but liability on the part of the owner is dependent upon some fault, such as negligence, which would render the operator liable.

§ 21:26. Contributory negligence, assumed risk, and imputed negligence.

Am Jur 2d References: Automobiles, etc., §§ 361–363, 375–379, 667–681.

The general common-law rule that there can be no recovery for injuries where the person injured was himself guilty of negligence contributing to his injury, is fully applicable in cases involving injuries by motor vehicles. Persons using the highways and streets must be alert to perceive danger and they must exercise reasonable care for the safety of themselves and their property. The general doctrine of assumption of risk also applies to motor vehicle accidents.

The doctrine of last clear chance, permitting a plaintiff in a negligence action to recover notwithstanding his own contributory negligence where the defendant had ample opportunity to be aware that the plaintiff was in danger and to avoid injuring him, is generally applicable in cases involving motor vehicle accidents.

The negligence of the driver of a motor vehicle is not imputable to an occupant thereof so as to prevent a recovery by the latter for damages from a negligent third person, unless the occupant had some control or authority over the operation of the vehicle or was engaged in a joint enterprise with the driver, or otherwise participated in the negligent acts. And this rule is not changed by the fact that the driver and the occupant are husband and wife or parent and child.

However, negligence of the driver is imputable to an occupant, so as to bar recovery by the latter for injuries resulting from the negligence of a third person, where the occupant has some control or authority over the operation of the vehicle. Although there is some authority to the contrary, it is held by most courts that the presence of the owner in his motor vehicle while it is being driven by a member of his family creates a rebuttable presumption or inference that he has or retains control over its operation, so that the contributory negligence of the driver is imputable to him in his action against a third person. This presumption may be overcome, however, by showing that the owner had relinquished all right of control over the driver. And the driver's negligence is not imputed to the owner, in the absence of statute or of some relationship invoking the doctrine of respondeat superior, where the owner was not present in the vehicle at the time of the accident. A statute imposing liability upon the owner for the negligent operation of a motor vehicle by anyone using it with his permission does not have the effect of imputing the negligence of the driver to the owner so as to bar an action by the latter against a third person.

Where an occupant of a motor vehicle is engaged in a joint enterprise with the driver and is injured by the concurrent negligence of the driver and a third person, the driver's contributory negligence is imputed to such occupant and will preclude a recovery by him against the third person. This does not apply, however, to one merely riding as a guest, without any voice in directing the operation of the vehicle.

§ 21:27. Particular circumstances of injury.

Am Jur 2d References: Automobiles, etc., §§ 682–698, 789–797, 839–842.

The condition or physical features of a road, such as hills, curves, slippery condition, or roughness, may impose a duty of additional care upon a driver of a motor vehicle.

The operator of a motor vehicle emerging from a private road or driveway onto a public highway must exercise due care under the circumstances, bearing in mind that vehicles proceeding along the public highway have the right of way. The driver of a vehicle on the public way has the right to assume compliance with this rule unless there is something to warn him that it is not safe to do so.

While the backing of a motor vehicle is not negligence in and of itself, a person backing a car along a public street or highway must exercise due care for the safety of others, and must maintain a careful lookout and give a warning if the circumstances indicate its need. And one backing from private premises onto a public street or highway must exercise even greater care. A driver towing or pushing a vehicle along a public highway must exercise the degree of care which a reasonably prudent person would exercise in this extraordinary use of the highway.

The fact that the operator of a motor vehicle is handicapped by physical deficiencies does not excuse him from the consequences of an accident caused by his lack of skill in handling his vehicle. Such deficiencies do not, however, per se make him guilty of negligence or contributory negligence, although they may be considered with other circumstances in determining these issues. An intoxicated driver is held to the same standard of care in the operation of a motor vehicle as is a sober person. And by statute, the operation of a vehicle by an intoxicated driver may be negligence per se. Although the question is not clearly settled, it would seem that the youth of the operator of a motor vehicle should not affect his duty of care as against a person involved in an accident with a vehicle driven by him upon a public highway. The same is true of a mentally defective driver.

A driver is not ordinarily chargeable with negligence merely because he suddenly becomes ill, faints, or loses consciousness from an unforeseen cause. But if he knows that he is subject to such seizures, his loss of control of his faculties is not a defense. The fact that a driver falls asleep at the wheel without premonition does not, as a matter of law, constitute negligence. However, as there are normally some preceding warnings, such as extended lack of sleep or drowsiness, falling asleep while driving a motor vehicle may be deemed prima facie evidence of negligence.

§ 21:28. — Condition and equipment of vehicle.

Am Jur 2d References: Automobiles, etc., §§ 699–715.

While the owner or operator of a motor vehicle is not liable for injuries resulting from a defective condition of the vehicle, in the absence of negligence on his part, unless a statute imposes such liability, he is required to exercise reasonable care, by inspection and otherwise, to see that the vehicle is in safe condition, and he is liable if he knew, or in the exercise of reasonable care should have known, that the vehicle was in such unsafe condition as to endanger others, and if the defective condition was the proximate cause of injury to another. This duty regarding the safety of the vehicle extends to its equipment, such as brakes, tires, and lights.

Many states have statutes setting forth specific requirements as to brakes, lights, and other equipment on motor vehicles. It is generally held that violation of such a statute, at least if the violation is without legal excuse, is negligence per se.

§ 21:29. — Speed.

Am Jur 2d References: Automobiles, etc., §§ 716–722.

Apart from speed limits fixed by statute or ordinance, a motorist must drive at a reasonable rate of speed in view of all of the conditions encountered, which will enable him to keep his vehicle under control and avoid injury to others. What is a safe speed depends upon all of the circumstances and conditions, such as the condition of the vehicle, the road, and the weather, and the presence of hills or curves or other topographical features. A motorist who drives at a speed which is excessive under all of the circumstances is liable for injuries inflicted upon another, provided such negligent speed was the proximate cause of the injuries.

The violation of a statute or ordinance relating to the speed of motor vehicles, which is the proximate cause of an injury to another, constitutes negligence per se, according to some cases. According to other decisions, it is evidence of negligence. Conversely, the fact that a motorist was not exceeding the legal speed limit at the time of an accident does not necessarily absolve him of a charge of negligence in connection with his speed.

In many cases it has been held to be negligence or contributory negligence to drive a motor vehicle at such a rate of speed that it cannot be stopped in time to avoid an object discernible within the driver's range of vision, or within the assured clear distance ahead. This rule has been held applicable at night as well as in the daytime, so that it is negligence to drive the vehicle so fast at night that it cannot be stopped in time to avoid a collision with objects within the area lighted by its headlights, that is, within the "radius of lights." Some courts have declined to apply a hard and fixed "assured clear distance ahead" rule and take the view that each case must be considered in the light of its own peculiar facts. On many superhighways, on which high speed is not only customary but legal, the operation of a motor vehicle at an extremely low speed may be more dangerous than an excessively high speed, both to the driver and to others upon the highway. Minimum speeds are fixed by law for many highways.

Racing between two motorists on a public highway constitutes negligence which will render them liable for injuries proximately resulting to others, but it does not create any liability as between the participants in the race.

§ 21:30. — Obstruction of vision; weather conditions.

Am Jur 2d References: Automobiles, etc., §§ 723–734.

Where the vision of a motorist is obstructed for any cause, the law requires that he exercise care commensurate with the situation. Under some circumstances, this rule requires him to stop until the obstruction is removed, while in other circumstances he may proceed, but with the exercise of more caution than is required in driving under normal conditions.

The foregoing principle applies where the driver's vision is interfered with by dazzling or glaring lights, whether from other vehicles, from the sun, or from other sources. A motorist whose vision is obscured by unfavorable atmospheric or weather conditions, such as fog, rain, mist, snow, sleet, ice, or frost, or by cloudy conditions, or by smoke, dust, or smog, must exercise care commensurate with the situation.

§ 21:31. — Intersection accidents.

Am Jur 2d References: Automobiles, etc., §§ 735–757.

Reasonable care in the operation of a motor vehicle requires more precaution and vigilance when approaching or entering a street or highway intersection than when driving elsewhere in a street or highway, particularly where the intersection is a blind or obstructed one. A motorist approaching an intersection is under a duty to have his vehicle under such control as to be able to stop upon short notice.

A motorist who has the right of way at an intersection may assume, in the absence of something to put him on notice to the contrary, that nonfavored travelers will yield the right of way to him. However, the fact that a motorist has the right of way at an intersection does not excuse heedless or reckless conduct on his part or exempt him from the duty of keeping a lookout for other vehicles entering the intersection. Where it would be apparent to a reasonable man that the nonfavored motorist does not intend to yield the right of way or to obey a traffic sign or signal, then it becomes the duty of the favored motorist to do what a reasonable man would do in such a situation to protect himself and others from harm.

While a motorist entering an intersection with a traffic light, sign, or signal in his favor is normally entitled to assume that cross traffic will obey the unfavorable light or signal facing it, he is not relieved of all duty of care. A favorable traffic light does not absolve a motorist of the duty to exercise ordinary care in operating his vehicle. In most cases, however, the fact that one charged with negligence or contributory negligence entered the intersection where the accident occurred, with a traffic light in his favor, will result in a decision absolving him of negligence.

A motorist who enters a street or highway intersection against the direction of a traffic light, traffic sign, or traffic officer is, under ordinary circumstances, guilty of negligence or contributory negligence.

§ 21:32. — Meeting vehicles.

Am Jur 2d References: Automobiles, etc., §§ 758–767.

In meeting and passing vehicles approaching from the opposite direction, the operator of a motor vehicle is required to obey the fundamental rule of the road that he keep to the right, and to exercise reasonable care under the circumstances to avoid a collision. This may require, when the way is narrow, that he slow down or yield the right of way, as the circumstances may indicate. Motorists approaching from opposite directions at night generally are under statutory duty to dim their lights, and the failure to do so may constitute negligence.

A motorist who is proceeding on the proper side of the highway, even after he sees an approaching vehicle coming toward him on the wrong side, is generally entitled to assume that the other motorist will return to his proper lane of traffic, at least until he becomes aware or should become aware that the other motorist cannot or will not do so. And the sudden-emergency doctrine may protect the motorist's decision on whether to turn right or left in such a situation.

§ 21:33. — Proceeding in same direction.

Am Jur 2d References: Automobiles, etc., §§ 768–788.

The general rule of reasonable care governs the reciprocal rights and duties of motorists proceeding in the same direction. A motorist to the rear is under duty to watch for and observe signals by the preceding motorist of his intention to stop.

The sudden stopping of a motor vehicle, resulting in a collision between his vehicle and one following behind, may constitute negligence, particularly where such stopping is unsignaled. Apart from statutory requirements, ordinary care may require the motorist to give a signal of his intention to stop. A motorist coming to a sudden or unsignaled stop to pick up or let off a passenger is frequently held guilty of negligence, primary or contributory. In some circumstances, the fact that the stopping motorist was confronted with a sudden emergency has been held to justify him in coming to an abrupt stop without signaling.

A motorist is under duty to drive a reasonable and safe distance from the motorist ahead so as to be able to avoid a collision. He must exercise reasonable care under all the circumstances. The mere occurrence of a rear-end collision is not, however, conclusive of the negligence of the following motorist in driving too closely to the vehicle ahead.

In overtaking and attempting to pass another vehicle proceeding in the same direction, a motorist is required to exercise ordinary care and skill, depending upon the condition of traffic and other circumstances. The passing driver may be required, by statute or by the circumstances, to give warning of his intention to pass.

Generally, it is the duty of a motorist to pass to the left of other vehicles proceeding in the same direction, and passing on the right may constitute negligence. There may be circumstances, however, which justify passing on the right, such as where the preceding driver has indicated his intention to make a left turn or where there is a separate and ample lane to the right of the preceding motorist.

Where a motorist becomes aware that a following motorist wishes to pass, he is generally required to give way and not to increase his speed or otherwise subject the passing motorist to danger.

Passing at an intersection or on hills or curves where the vision of the driver is obstructed or limited may constitute negligence, and is sometimes expressly prohibited by statute or ordinance. Cutting back too soon or too sharply after overtaking and passing another vehicle may render the passing driver liable for a collision with the other vehicle or for forcing it off the road.

Although a leading motorist is not generally under a duty to give a following motorist warning or signal of conditions ahead, if he does undertake to signal the following motorist that it is safe to pass, he may be held liable for injuries resulting from his negligence in giving such signal.

§ 21:34. — Turning.

Am Jur 2d References: Automobiles, etc., §§ 798–810.

The general duty of a driver of a motor vehicle to exercise ordinary or reasonable care for the safety of others using a public way applies to his action in turning his vehicle from the course or direction in which it has been proceeding. A motorist turning left across traffic is required to exercise care commensurate with the situation and to look for approaching motorists. And motorists nearing an intersection where another motorist is turning left are also required to exercise care commensurate with the situation so as not to collide with the turning motorist. Motorists making right turns are required to keep as close as practicable to the right-hand edge of the roadway.

Statutes and ordinances generally require a motorist to give a signal of his intention to turn either left or right. Apart from such positive regulations, however, it is generally held that the failure of a motorist making a left turn to give a proper signal or warning of his intention will render him liable for injuries proximately caused by such negligence. Similar rules govern right-hand turns, and a motorist who veers to the left and then makes a right turn without signaling will usually be held liable for a collision which ensues when a following motorist attempts to pass on the right.

§ 21:35. — Parking and standing.

Am Jur 2d References: Automobiles, etc., §§ 811–838.

One who leaves a motor vehicle parked or standing in a public street or highway must use reasonable care for the safety of others. If he parks in an improper or illegal place, such as the traveled portion of a street or highway, or too far from the curb, or in a double-parking situation, or within or too near an intersection, or on the wrong side of the street or highway, he is generally guilty of negligence rendering him liable for injuries proximately resulting therefrom. He is also under a duty to take proper precautions against the movement of the vehicle accidentally or through the intervention of third persons, and to provide proper light or flares.

One who drives a motor vehicle from a parked or standing position must exercise reasonable care to avoid collision with other vehicles, objects, or persons. And other motorists, passing or approaching, are required to use due care to avoid collision with the emerging vehicle.

IV. WRONGFUL DEATH

§ 21:36. Right of action; beneficiaries.

Am Jur 2d References: Death, §§ 1–83.

At common law no civil action lay for wrongfully causing the death of a human being. An action by the personal representative of the decedent's estate was barred by the rule that personal causes of action died with the person. And no action could be maintained by or on behalf of the decedent's family or dependents based on the death.

At the present time, statutes almost universally provide for the survival, for the benefit of the decedent's estate, of his cause of action for the injury resulting in his death. And, beginning with Lord Campbell's Act, which was enacted in England in 1846 and which was the model for most American statutes on this subject, a cause of action exists for the wrongful death itself.

Such statutes typically provide that when the death of a person is caused by the wrongful act, neglect, or default of another in such a manner as would have entitled the party injured to have maintained an action if death had not ensued, an action may be maintained, if brought within a specified time, in the name of his executor or administrator for the benefit of certain relatives.

Although some death statutes have been given a different interpretation, in most states such statutes have been held to create a new cause of action, distinct from any that the deceased might have had if he had survived, the wrongful death action not being derivative and not being brought to recover for the injuries to the decedent but to compensate the survivors or beneficiaries for loss occasioned by the death.

The wrongful death statutes of the several jurisdictions vary considerably in their designation of the beneficiaries of the recovery in an action thereunder. The original Lord Campbell's Act, which is followed closely in many American states, authorized an action for the benefit of the wife, husband, parent, and child of the decedent.

§ 21:37. Defenses and matters in bar.

Am Jur 2d References: Death, §§ 84–114.

Ordinarily, all defenses that would have been available to the defendant if the injured person had survived and brought an action himself are available to the defendant in an action for wrongful death. Such defenses include assumed risk, self-defense, contributory negligence, or negligence on the part of the sole beneficiary or of all the beneficiaries, although contributory negligence by a part of the beneficiaries is not a defense against the other beneficiaries.

There is a difference in the results of the decisions, based in part on differences in the statutes, on the question whether a recovery or adverse judgment in an action by the decedent for his injury will bar an action for wrongful death by his representative. The same lack of uniformity in result appears in cases involving the effect of a compromise, settlement, or release by the injured person prior to his death.

In both instances, it would seem that a prior adjudication or a settlement and release would bar an action after the death of the injured person based upon his cause of action for his injury and brought under a statute merely providing for the survival of such causes of action. On the other hand, if the action is predicated on a wrongful death statute creating a new cause of action arising only upon the death of the injured person, there is some reason and authority for the view that a settlement or release by the injured person during his lifetime does not operate as a bar to an action for the loss resulting to the beneficiaries from his death.

V. PREMISES LIABILITY; ATTRACTIVE NUISANCES

§ 21:38. Generally.

Am Jur 2d References: Premises Liability, §§ 12–22; Railroads, §§ 402–609.

Mere ownership or occupancy of real estate does not render one liable for injuries sustained by persons who have entered thereon. The owner or occupant is not an insurer against accidents on the premises. Liability must depend upon negligence on his part.

The status of the person on the premises determines in a large degree the owner's duty of care toward him. Clearly, there is a distinction in this respect between trespassers and persons rightfully upon the premises. As pointed out in the next following section, most courts purport to recognize a distinction between licensees and invitees, although both are persons who come rightfully upon the premises. In actual practice, the distinction between licensees and invitees is often vague or arbitrary. The thing that actually influences the court in determining the duty owed by an owner or occupant to a visitor is the nature and purpose of the visit.

§ 21:39. Status of injured person.

Am Jur 2d References: Premises Liability, §§ 62–96; Railroads, §§ 405–429.

One who enters upon premises at the invitation of the owner or occupant has a more favored position than one who enters by the mere sufferance of the owner or occupant. The owner or occupant of lands or buildings who directly or impliedly invites others to enter for some purpose of interest or advantage to him, owes to such persons a duty to use ordinary care to have the premises in a reasonably safe condition for use in a manner consistent with the purpose of the invitation, not to expose them to an unreasonable risk, and to give them adequate and timely warning of latent or concealed perils which are known to him but not to them. There is no liability for injuries from dangers that are obvious, reasonably apparent, or as well known to the person injured as to the owner or occupant. In order to be entitled to the duty of care owed to an invitee, the person injured must be in a place on the premises covered by the invitation and must be using the premises for a purpose contemplated by the invitation.

One is not deemed to have been upon premises by implied invitation unless his purpose was one of interest or advantage to the owner or occupant or in pursuance of an interest or advantage which is common or mutual to him and the owner or occupant. An invitation to come upon the premises is not implied from the mere toleration or sufferance of trespassers.

It is generally held that a social guest, though present by invitation of the owner or occupant, or persons visiting or interviewing employees of the owner or occupant, or policemen or firemen on the premises in their official capacity, are mere licensees rather than invitees.

A licensee is one who enters upon the property of another for his own convenience, pleasure, or benefit, pursuant to the express or implied permission of the owner or occupant. No duty is imposed upon an owner or occupant to keep his premises in a safe condition for a licensee. Generally speaking, a mere licensee assumes whatever risk of injury there may be because of the condition of the property. He cannot generally recover for injuries sustained from defects, obstacles, or pitfalls upon the premises, except where they were caused by the active negligence of the owner or occupant, or where the licensee was needlessly exposed to danger through the failure of the owner or occupant to warn him of dangers known to the owner or occupant and which the latter realized were unknown to the licensee.

A trespasser is a person who enters premises of another without license, invitation, or right. An owner or occupant owes trespassers, including children, no duty to keep his premises in a safe condition for their use, and as a general rule, he is not held responsible for an injury sustained by a trespasser from a defect in the premises. Trespassers must accept the existing condition of the premises as they find them and they must proceed at their own peril so far as dangers from defective premises are concerned.

The observance of due care by an owner or occupant toward a trespasser requires no affirmative conduct to render the premises safe, but only that he shall refrain from injuring the trespasser unnecessarily by wilful, wanton, or reckless conduct, and shall use reasonable care not to injure him by any affirmative act or force set in motion on the premises after he has or reasonably should have become aware of the presence of the trespasser.

§ 21:40. Stores and other places of business.

Am Jur 2d References: Elevators and Escalators, §§ 5–61, 67–69, 78–89; Garages, etc., §§ 81–134; Hotels, etc., §§ 87–106; Premises Liability, §§ 186–198.

The proprietor of a store, hotel, restaurant, garage, parking lot, or other place of business kept open for public patronage owes to customers and guests who enter the premises the duty of exercising ordinary care to keep in a reasonably safe condition all parts of the premises that are ordinarily used by patrons transacting business, and to warn them of dangerous conditions which are known, or which reasonably should be known, to him but not to them. Such customers or guests are deemed to be present by invitation of the proprietor. It is frequently held that one rightfully accompanying a primary invitee upon business premises is also an invitee.

The duty of the proprietor of a place of business opened to public patronage to use ordinary care to make the premises reasonably safe extends to all parts of the premises designed, adapted, and prepared for the accommodation of customers or other invitees, or to which such person may reasonably be expected to go, including interior and exterior lighting, steps or stairways, floors, aisles and passageways, and equipment, fixtures, and appliances intended for the use of customers or guests. A frequent ground of liability of the operator of a store is the presence of obstructions or slippery substances on the floor of which the proprietor has notice or which have been there for such time as will charge him with knowledge of their presence.

One maintaining a passenger elevator or escalator is required to exercise a high degree of care in the maintenance and operation thereof, the duty sometimes being stated in terms approximating that of a common carrier.

§ 21:41. Attractive nuisances.

Am Jur 2d References: Premises Liability, §§ 137–185; Railroads, §§ 431–433.

The duty of the owner or occupant of real estate has been extended for the protection of uninvited and trespassing children by the so-called attractive nuisance or turntable doctrine. Under this doctrine, one who maintains on his premises a condition, instrumentality, or object which is dangerous to children of tender years because of their inability to appreciate the peril thereof, which may reasonably be expected to attract children, at a place where he knows, or reasonably should know, such children are likely to resort or to be attracted by the condition, is under a duty to exercise reasonable care to protect them against the dangers of the attraction and is guilty of actionable negligence if he fails to do so. The attractive nuisance doctrine has been rejected in a number of jurisdictions; and the trend seems to be to limit rather than extend its scope.

To invoke the attractive nuisance doctrine, it must appear that the condition or instrumentality was alluring to youth, appealing to childish instincts of curiosity and amusement. Attractiveness alone, however, is not enough. The tendency of the courts is to exclude from the operation of the doctrine things and conditions which are not in their nature dangerous or peculiarly alluring to children, natural conditions, obvious perils, common or ordinary objects, simple tools and appliances, and conditions arising from the ordinary conduct of business. None of these tests or requirements is absolute, however; they depend upon the circumstances, such as the location of the condition and the age and intelligence of the child.

The existence of conditions which might invoke the doctrine of attractive nuisance does not make the owner an insurer of the safety of children, but requires only that he take reasonable precautions to prevent injury to them. Ordinarily a warning to a child will relieve the owner or occupant from liability for its injury.

To charge a defendant under this doctrine, it must appear that he knew, or reasonably ought to have known, that the structure, instrumentality, or condition was alluring to children and endangered them. It must be shown that he should reasonably have anticipated the presence of children. This requirement may be satisfied by showing that the place or condition possessed an inherent quality calculated to attract children generally, or that, to the defendant's knowledge, children were in the habit of frequenting the place.

While some authorities hold that it is essential to liability under the doctrine of attractive nuisance that the presence of the child on the premises in the first place should be due to the attraction, the preponderance of authority seems to be that the original reason for the child's presence upon the premises is unimportant so long as it appears that the owner or occupant had reason to anticipate the presence of children and the peril that they would encounter.

The attractive nuisance rule is intended for the protection of children of tender years who are peculiarly susceptible to the attraction of certain conditions and are incapable of appreciating the dangers thereof. Accordingly, the maturity, intelligence, and capacity of the injured child must be taken into consideration in determining whether the doctrine is applicable in view of the nature of the condition causing the injury.

A factor which pervades all of the requisites of the attractive nuisance doctrine is the general policy of balancing the importance to the owner or occupant of maintaining the condition in question and the difficulty of safeguarding against injury to trespassing children, as against the risk involved.

VI. HIGHWAYS, STREETS, AND BRIDGES

§ 21:42. Duty and liability of public authorities.

Am Jur 2d References: Highways, Streets and Bridges, §§ 16–20, 340–358, 372, 374–516, 524, 526, 528, 529, 546, 547, 549–578.

The common-law immunity of the sovereign from liability for torts, in the absence of statute, exempts the state and generally its political subdivisions, such as counties, towns, and townships, from liability for injury or damage resulting from defects or obstructions in highways, streets, and bridges. Whether or not this immunity extends to cities and other municipal corporations has never been universally settled. Without the aid of statutes, many jurisdictions invented various grounds for exceptions to the immunity doctrine and held municipalities liable for injuries resulting from their failure to use due care to keep in safe condition the streets, highways, and bridges entrusted to their control.

By statutes in many jurisdictions, governmental immunity in connection with torts relating to highways has been waived, so that the states and their subdivisions and municipalities are liable, under various restrictions and conditions, for injuries resulting from defects in public ways under their jurisdiction.

There is a conflict of authority as to the personal liability of a highway official for injuries resulting from defects in highways or bridges.

The public authority is not an insurer against injury on public ways. It does not warrant its streets and highways to be free from defects at all times so as to make them safe. The extent of its duty, in the absence of statute imposing a higher duty, is to exercise reasonable diligence to put and keep them in a reasonably safe condition for the uses for which they are established and to which they are properly subject.

The responsible public authority is under duty to exercise reasonable care to warn travelers of defects, obstructions, and unsafe places in its streets, highways, and bridges, of which it has or is chargeable with notice, by barriers or guardrails, lights, warning signs, or other means.

Generally, in order to render the public authority liable for injuries resulting from defects or unsafe conditions of highways or bridges which it did not itself create or authorize, the authority must have had knowledge or notice of the condition or defect for a sufficient length of time before the accident to have remedied the condition or to have taken precautions against injuries. Requirements as to notice of defects are embodied in statutes in many jurisdictions.

§ 21:43. Duty and liability of private person.

Am Jur 2d References: Highways, Streets and Bridges, §§ 359–370, 373, 374, 409, 411, 459, 465, 498–500, 517–522, 525, 530–544, 548.

A person who, without special authorization, creates or maintains a dangerous condition in a public highway, street, or sidewalk, is liable for injuries proximately resulting therefrom. If the condition is created under license or permit from a public authority, the person exercising such permit or license must exercise due care for the safety of the public. And contractors for the construction or repair of highways, streets, or bridges are liable for their negligence in the performance of the work contracted.

In the absence of statute to the contrary, an abutting owner is not responsible for the safety of an adjacent street, sidewalk, or highway, if he has not contributed to defects or dangers therein. And he is not liable for injuries resulting from snow or ice on a sidewalk or street.

An abutting owner, though operating under a permit, may be liable for injuries sustained by a pedestrian by reason of the owner's negligence in failing to safeguard an opening or excavation in or under a sidewalk or street. And an abutting owner is liable for injuries to a traveler on a street or sidewalk resulting from the fall of a building or other structure as a result of the failure of such owner to exercise the degree of care required by the circumstances.

VII. FRIGHT, SHOCK, AND MENTAL DISTURBANCE

§ 21:44. Generally; disturbance without physical effect.

Am Jur 2d References: Fright, Shock, etc., §§ 1–12.

There is much conflict among the authorities on the right to recover for a mental or emotional disturbance apart from other injuries. The law on the subject is still in the process of change and development. This confusion and uncertainty in the law reflect the mystery and darkness surrounding the human mind and emotions. The present trend is to enlarge the area in which recovery is permitted, and this is sometimes accomplished by the invention of exceptions or qualifications based upon rather tenuous reasons and distinctions.

It may be stated as a general rule that liability may not be predicated upon the negligence of the defendant where the resulting damage is merely a mental or emotional disturbance. This rule is applicable, and frequently limited, to cases where the mental or emotional disturbance is not accompanied by a bodily impact, and is not attended or followed by an injury to the person or body of the plaintiff, and where there is no other legal injury or cause of action or other element of recoverable damages upon which a cause of action might be predicated.

The rule denying the right to recover for mental or emotional disturbance alone is most frequently applied in cases of negligence. It is usually held that a defendant is liable for a severe mental disturbance which he causes intentionally or by a wilful, wanton, or malicious act, even though there is no physical or bodily impact.

Where actual physical impact is a prerequisite to the right to recover for mental or emotional disturbance, fright, or shock, a very slight impact or physical disturbance is usually held sufficient.

§ 21:45. Disturbance causing bodily injury or illness.

Am Jur 2d References: Fright, Shock, etc., §§ 13–24.

The right to maintain an action for a bodily injury or illness resulting from a mental or emotional disturbance caused by the defendant's negligence, is the subject of a sharp conflict in the authorities. In many cases the courts have denied the right to maintain such an action if the disturbance was not accompanied by a contemporaneous physical injury or physical impact. But in many other cases, including a majority of the recent decisions, one who negligently caused a mental or emotional disturbance resulting in an illness or bodily harm was held to be liable, even though the disturbance was not accompanied by any contemporaneous bodily impact or outward injury. Some courts which deny recovery for mental distress alone will allow recovery for the physical consequences of such distress.

The conflict of authority on this question does not extend to cases involving intentional or wanton conduct. One who does an act with the intention of producing a severe mental or emotional disturbance is liable, even in the absence of any contemporaneous bodily impact or injury, where he causes such disturbance and it results in an illness or bodily injury. The same is true where the act or wrong may be characterized as wilful, wanton, malicious, or grossly reckless.

In order to recover damages for an illness or physical injury resulting from a mental or emotional disturbance, it must appear that the defendant's wrongful act or omission was the proximate cause of the illness or injury. Whether or not the particular illness or injury must have been foreseeable in order to render the defendant liable is the subject of some conflict of authority.

§ 21:46. Particular circumstances and instances.

Am Jur 2d References: Fright, Shock, etc., §§ 25–57.

There is considerable uncertainty concerning liability for conduct causing a mental disturbance or a resulting illness or injury to another, where the latter was especially or peculiarly susceptible to such disturbance or injury. It is frequently held that one whose negligence causes mental distress is not liable where the distress is due to a pre-existing susceptibility to distress and the misconduct would not have caused substantial harm to a normal person. This does not, however, prevent the inclusion of damages traceable to his susceptibility, where he has a cause of action without consideration of the harm arising from the peculiar susceptibility. Where the actor's misconduct was intentional, or where he had knowledge of the susceptibility, the injured person's peculiar susceptibility is no defense.

Where the defendant causes mental or emotional distress to the plaintiff by negligently causing a physical injury to a third person or by placing the third person in great danger of physical injury, there is a conflict of authority on the right of the plaintiff to recover for such distress. The prevailing view is that there is no liability in such a case. The rule is otherwise, however, where the defendant's act was intentional or wanton.

Although there is considerable authority to the contrary, the prevailing modern view appears to be that a cause of action may arise, even in the absence of a contemporaneous bodily impact or injury or acts constituting an assault, where the actor causes a mental or emotional disturbance or a bodily injury or illness resulting therefrom, by disturbing or offensive utterances, such as a threat, false statement, or insulting, humiliating, scandalous, violent, or abusive language.

VIII. OTHER WRONGS AND INJURIES BASED ON NEGLIGENCE

§ 21:47. Amusements and exhibitions.

Am Jur 2d References: Amusements and Exhibitions, §§ 52–100, 104–106.

The proprietor or operator of a place of public amusement or entertainment is not an insurer of the safety of patrons. His duty is to exercise ordinary or reasonable care, such as an ordinarily prudent person would exercise under the same or similar circumstances. He must keep the premises, appliances, and devices in a reasonably safe condition for the uses for which they are intended.

He is also under a duty to maintain order on his premises, and he may be held liable to a patron for injuries resulting from the dangerous activities of third persons, as by assault, pushing, crowding, or other disorderly conduct, if he does not take appropriate precautions to prevent such occurrences.

The degree of care required of the proprietor of a place of public amusement is commensurate with the risk involved, and this obviously varies according to the nature of the particular amusement place, instrumentality, or device. For example, an exhibitor of dangerous wild animals is held to a very high degree of care for the safety of spectators. And the operator of roller coasters, airplane swings, and other "thrill" rides must take precautions and exercise care commensurate with the dangers involved. The doctrine of res ipsa loquitur is frequently applied in cases involving injuries from such devices.

The doctrine of contributory negligence or assumed risk may be applicable in a case involving injuries resulting from amusement and sports activities. For example, a voluntary participant in a lawful game, sport, or contest assumes all risks ordinarily incident to the particular activity, although this does not apply to an injury resulting from an intentional or unlawful act by an opponent or another participant.

§ 21:48. Animals.

Am Jur 2d References: Animals, §§ 80–145.

According to one view, supposed to represent the original common-law rule, the owner or keeper of a wild animal is absolutely liable for any injuries inflicted by such animal, regardless of the absence of any negligence on his part. Other courts hold that the liability of the owner or keeper of a wild animal depends upon negligence in failing to properly restrain the animal or keep it securely. Under either view of liability, the injured party cannot recover if he brought the injury upon himself, even though contributory negligence, as such, is not available as a defense.

In the case of a domestic animal of a kind not naturally vicious, the owner is not answerable for injuries done by it unless it was, in fact and to the owner's knowledge, vicious or dangerous. One who keeps a vicious or dangerous domestic animal with knowledge of its vicious character is generally liable for injuries inflicted by it. Such knowledge or notice on the part of the owner is established if he has seen or heard enough to convince a man of ordinary prudence of the animal's inclinations, the question in each case being whether an ordinarily prudent man should have anticipated the injury inflicted by the animal. By statute in some jurisdictions, the owner of a dog or other domestic animal may be liable for injuries inflicted by it even though he did not know of its vicious propensities.

Stricter rules of liability are generally applied in determining liability for injury or damage to person or property by an animal that is trespassing or illegally running at large.

A person is generally liable for the wrongful injury or killing of an animal, and such liability may exist even though the animal is trespassing at the time, unless the killing is in defense of person or property.

§ 21:49. Aviation.

Am Jur 2d References: Aviation, §§ 27–30, 64–105.

In the absence of special statute to a different effect, the general rules governing tort liability and negligence apply broadly in aircraft accident cases, including the rules relating to proximate cause. Apart from the care owing by an air carrier to its passengers, the measure of care required in the actual operation of aircraft is ordinary care under the circumstances, that is, the care which an ordinarily prudent and reasonably careful and skilful pilot or operator would use under the same or similar circumstances.

It is generally held that the liability of the owner or operator of an airplane to a guest injured or killed therein will be determined under ordinary rules of negligence, and that the degree of care owed such guest is ordinary care. In some jurisdictions, however, "guest statutes" have been enacted, similar to the automobile guest statutes (see § 21:23, supra), limiting recovery by the guest to those cases where there is gross negligence, recklessness, or the like.

A carrier of passengers by airplane is not an insurer of the passengers' safety. A common carrier of passengers for hire by airplane is generally held to be under the duty to exercise either a high or the highest degree of care for the safety of its passengers, not only with respect to the operation of the plane, but also with respect to the maintenance, inspection, and condition of its equipment. Some authorities hold a private carrier by airplane to the same measure of care as that required of a common carrier, but it is more frequently held that the private carrier's duty is only to exercise ordinary care.

The proprietor or operator of an airport or airfield is under a duty to see that it is safe for such aircraft as are entitled to use it.

§ 21:50. Boats.

Am Jur 2d References: Boats and Boating, §§ 32–68.

Tort actions involving boats, ships, or vessels, whether brought in a court of law or of admiralty, are governed in large measure by the substantive principles which determine the rights and liabilities of parties in other civil cases at law. Admiralty proceedings in rem may be brought against a boat, as well as proceedings in personam against the owner or operator thereof.

In accordance with the general rule of maritime law, persons in charge of boats and other vessels must at all times exercise due diligence and maritime skill to avoid injury or damage to others by collision or otherwise. They must exercise the care of a reasonably prudent mariner and they must keep a proper lookout and exercise of the highest watchfulness to detect approaching vessels or other perils. The operator of a motorboat must exercise the care which a reasonably prudent person would exercise under the circumstances to avoid injury to swimmers or water skiers.

A person engaged in navigation in any kind of vessel is under a duty to see that the vessel is seaworthy and properly equipped and manned, and he is liable for injury or damage resulting from the defective condition or unfitness of the vessel.

The use of any boat or vessel as a carrier imposes upon the operator the higher degree of care exacted of all carriers.

The status of a person on board a vessel, as an invitee, licensee, or trespasser, may determine the degree of care owed to him by the operator (§§ 21:38–21:40, supra). Automobile "guest" statutes (§ 21:23, supra) do not generally apply to vessels operating upon waterways.

The owner of a boat is not generally liable for injury or damage resulting from the negligence of one to whom he entrusted the boat, unless the owner was negligent in placing it in the hands of an incompetent or improper operator; and this rule applies to the operation of a motorboat by the owner's minor child. The courts have not extended to such cases the "family purpose" doctrine (§§ 21:24, 21:25, supra) applied in some jurisdictions to automobiles maintained for the pleasure or use of the owner's family.

The ordinary principles of proximate cause apply to boating accidents. Even the violation of a statute, ordinance, or regulation does not render the operator liable for every accident if he can show that such violation had nothing to do with the accident.

Under federal statute, the owner of a vessel, regardless of its size, may institute proceedings to limit his liability to the value of his interest in the vessel. But this statute applies only to the operation of vessels in waters under the general admiralty and maritime jurisdiction of the United States, and does not extend to waters which are not navigable waters of the United States.

It is generally held that where a maritime tort action is tried in a state court or on the law side of a federal district court under the "saving to suitors" clause of the federal statute, it is governed by the comparative negligence doctrine applied in admiralty, under which contributory negligence is not a total defense, but the fault is apportioned, and the amount of damages recoverable is reduced, according to the degree of negligence on each side.

§ 21:51. Electricity and gas.

Am Jur 2d References: Electricity, Gas and Steam, §§ 39–268.

A person who generates, produces, stores, transmits, or supplies electricity or gas must exercise due care to prevent injury or damage to person or property, and is liable for his negligence in this respect. However, he is not generally held to be an insurer against injury from these substances and agencies. The degree of care required in the production, distribution, and use of electricity or gas is stated in various terms by the courts, the requirement varying from reasonable or ordinary care and diligence to a close approximation to the view that the persons responsible are insurers, or that they owe high, or the highest, or the utmost degree of care.

The general principle of negligence, that the degree of care required varies with the danger involved in the particular activity, is properly applicable to gas and electricity. The inherent deadliness of these things calls for a correspondingly high degree of care in dealing with them. The degree of care and the nature of precautions required, being commensurate with the danger involved, may be affected by such circumstances as the voltage of the current transmitted, and the location and accessibility of the lines.

§ 21:52. Explosives and fireworks.

Am Jur 2d References: Explosions and Explosives, §§ 4–91.

One who uses, stores, or transports explosives is under a duty to exercise care commensurate with the danger involved. The degree of care required depends upon such circumstances as the nature of the explosive and its location and accessibility to others. It is frequently stated that the highest degree of care must be used to prevent injury to persons or property by explosives; and in some cases injury from explosives has invoked the doctrine imposing absolute liability, irrespective of negligence, where ultrahazardous substances or activities are involved. The duty to protect children from injury, even though they are trespassers, is especially applicable to the danger from explosives.

In most cases, in order for a person to be held liable for injury or damage from an explosion, he must be shown to have been negligent, unless his conduct constitutes a nuisance, or is in violation of a statute or ordinance, or is an activity of an ultrahazardous nature.

One who blasts on his land and thereby throws rock, earth, or debris beyond his boundaries is generally answerable for the damage caused, on the theory of either negligence, trespass, or strict liability. Cases involving damage by concussions or vibrations resulting from blasting present a conflict of authority on the question whether negligence must be shown.

Both the promoter and the operator of a fireworks exhibition must exercise reasonable care to protect the safety of spectators. And irrespective of negligence, a person is liable for injury or damage from the use of fireworks in such manner as to constitute a nuisance or violation of law.

§ 21:53. Fires.

Am Jur 2d References: Fires, §§ 7–45, 51, 52.

In the absence of statutory provisions establishing a different basis of liability, civil liability for injury or damage resulting from fire is predicated on negligence or upon some tortious act or omission. Reasonable care, proportionate to the risks and dangers to be apprehended, is required of one who employs fire for any purpose, although the circumstances may require extraordinary care and caution.

§ 21:54. Firearms.

Am Jur References: Weapons and Firearms (1st ed, §§ 22–32).

By its very nature and purpose a firearm is a dangerous instrumentality. A person using such a weapon, for sport or other purposes, must use a very high degree of care, a degree of care commensurate with the nature of the instrumentality involved, to avoid injury to others. Due care in the use of a firearm in hunting requires a reasonable knowledge of the nature and operation of the particular weapon and also extreme care in its use.

§ 21:55. Hospitals.

Am Jur 2d References: Hospitals and Asylums, §§ 14–37.

Except where the concept of governmental or charitable immunity is applicable (see §§ 21:2, 21:3, supra), the operator of a hospital or similar institution is liable for any injury or damage proximately caused by the negligence of its agents or servants, such as physicians, nurses, interns, ambulance drivers, and other persons employed by it. Where, however, the individual whose negligence causes the injury, such as an independent physician or a nurse employed by the latter or by the patient and not by the hospital, is an independent contractor and not a servant of the hospital, the hospital is not liable.

§ 21:56. Physicians, surgeons, and dentists.

Am Jur 2d References: Physicians and Surgeons, §§ 105–223.

A physician or surgeon is under a duty to use reasonable care and skill for the safety and health of his patient and is liable for an injury to the patient resulting from his failure to possess and use the requisite knowledge, skill, and care. He must possess and apply in practice that reasonable degree of learning and skill which is ordinarily exhibited by others of his profession. The standard of duty and care exacted by the law takes into account such matters as differences in the several schools of medicine, the existing state of medical knowledge and established modes of practices, the locality, and the limitations attending the practice of a limited or specialized branch or system of the healing art.

It is the general rule that in determining what constitutes reasonable care, skill, and diligence, the test is that which physicians and surgeons in the same general neighborhood, or in similar communities, have and exercise at the time in like cases.

The foregoing principles apply not only to physicians and surgeons, but to practitioners of the kindred branches of the healing art, such as dentists, occulists, and operators of X-ray equipment or the like.

§ 21:57. Prenatal injuries.

Am Jur 2d References: Infants, § 2; Prenatal Injuries, §§ 3–17; Torts (1st ed, § 98).

While the weight of authority holds that there can be no recovery by the personal representative for the wrongful prenatal death of a viable child in ventre sa mere, there is some authority to the contrary. The recent trend of the decisions is to permit a recovery by a child for prenatal injuries wrongfully inflicted on it at a time when it was viable, although the numerical weight of authority is still to the contrary.

IX. MASTER AND SERVANT

A. EMPLOYER'S LIABILITY FOR INJURY TO EMPLOYEE

§ 21:58. Generally.

Am Jur 2d References: Federal Employers' Liability and Compensation Acts, §§ 43–45; Master and Servant, §§ 139–223; Shipping, §§ 220–235.

At common law and in the absence of statute, an employer is liable to an employee for injuries received by the latter in the course of employment, only where the injury results from negligence on the part of the employer. The employer's duty to the employee is to use ordinary or reasonable care to provide the employee with safe tools, appliances, and working places and conditions. What constitutes reasonable care depends, as in other negligence cases, on all of the surrounding circumstances. And the negligence must be the proximate cause of the employee's injury.

Apart from any consideration of the principles of assumed risk or contributory negligence, the liability of the master for injury to a servant may depend upon whether the latter's knowledge of the perils of the employment were equal to that of the master. A discrepancy in knowledge in this respect may require extra precautions on the part of the employer, including warning and instruction.

In order to invoke the principles governing the master's duty and liability to the servant, it must be shown that the latter was in fact an employee of the former and that at the time of the injury he was engaged in the employer's business and acting within the scope of his employment.

By ancient rule of maritime law, a seaman is entitled, at the expense of the ship or her owners, to treatment and cure of sickness or injury sustained in the ship's service. This right is not dependent upon any negligence or fault on the part of the shipowner, and ordinary contributory negligence of the seaman or of a fellow servant does not defeat the right to maintenance and cure, although wilful misconduct on the seaman's part may have this effect.

§ 21:59. Defenses; contributory negligence; assumption of risk; fellow servant doctrine.

Am Jur 2d References: Federal Employers' Liability and Compensation Acts, §§ 43–45; Master and Servant, §§ 218–340.

In an employee's common-law action for injuries received in his employment, the employer may avail himself of any defense ordinarily applicable in negligence cases. Thus, the contributory negligence of the employee bars his recovery even though the employer also was negligent. And the doctrine of assumed risk applies on the theory that by entering the employment the employee assumes such risks as are ordinarily incident thereto. The assumption of risk as an incident of employment embraces such perils and hazards as are ordinarily and normally incident to or a part of the employment in question and of which the employee has knowledge, actual or implied.

Distinctive to common-law actions between master and servant (and probably the most weighty cause for statutory reform in this field) is the fellow servant doctrine. Under this rule, an employer is not liable to an employee for injuries suffered solely as the result of the negligence or misconduct of others who are in the service of the employer and who are engaged in the same common or general employment as the injured employee.

However, if the employer has been guilty of negligence contributing to the injury, the contributory fault of the fellow servant does not defeat the right of recovery. Such negligence on the part of the employer may consist of his hiring or retaining an incompetent servant. And there are certain duties, such as to provide employees with safe and suitable tools and places and conditions of work, which cannot be delegated for the purpose of invoking the fellow servant rule. Many courts make an exception to the fellow servant doctrine where the negligent coemployee was the superior of the injured employee.

B. WORKMEN'S COMPENSATION

§ 21:60. Purpose, scope, and effect of acts.

Am Jur 2d References: Workmen's Compensation (1st ed, §§ 1–191, 281–582).

"Workmen's compensation" is a general term applied to statutes providing for compensation for injury, disablement, or death of workmen through industrial accident, casualty, or disease. Workmen's compensation legislation has arisen out of conditions produced by modern industrial developments, and is based upon the idea that the common-law rule of liability for personal injuries incident to the operation of industrial enterprises, predicated as it is upon the negligence of the employer and subject to the defenses of contributory negligence, fellow servant's negligence, and assumption of risk, is not properly applicable to modern conditions of employment in the complex and hazardous industries of modern times. Such statutes are generally given a liberal construction as being remedial in character.

Under such acts, the theory of negligence as the basis of liability is discarded, the common-law defenses are eliminated, and a right to compensation is given for all injuries incident to the employment, with some exceptions, the amount of which is limited and determined in accordance with a definite schedule, in a summary and informal method of procedure.

Many of the workmen's compensation statutes limit their scope to employment in some trade, business, occupation, or vocation, and exclude from their operation certain occupations, such as agricultural labor and domestic service. And the application of the acts is frequently made to depend upon the employment of a specified minimum number of persons. The right to workmen's compensation is generally limited to employees or workmen, and this excludes independent contractors and their employees.

The statutes frequently provide for other benefits in addition to money compensation, such as medical and surgical treatment, hospitalization, and prosthetic appliances. And compensation is usually provided for the dependents of the employee in case of the latter's death from an injury within the coverage of the statutes.

Workmen's compensation laws are usually administered by boards or commissions of administrative character, rather than by the courts, although provision may be made for appeal to the courts from administrative decisions. The administrative procedure is simplified and less formal than in ordinary judicial proceedings.

§ 21:61. Injuries compensable.

Am Jur 2d References: Workmen's Compensation (1st ed, §§ 192–280).

The Workmen's Compensation Acts define in varying terms the injuries or disabilities compensable thereunder. They employ such terms as "personal injuries accidentally sustained," "accidental injury," or merely "injury" or "personal injury." An "accident" in this connection is generally construed to mean an occurrence which is neither expected, designed, nor intentionally caused by the workmen. An injury sustained during the course of work by the wilful act of a fellow employee may be compensable, but injuries sustained as a result of "horseplay" or practical joking are not. Proximate causation between the accident or injury and the employee's disability must be established.

The statutes usually require that the injury arise out of and in the course of the employment, in order to be compensable. The construction of "course of employment" and the several statutory variations thereof has been the source of much litigation and difference of opinion.

As employed in the statutes, "arising out of" is not always synonymous with "in the course of" employment. The words "arising out of" involve the idea of causal relationship between the employment and the injury, while the term "in the course of" relates more particularly to the time, place, and circumstances under which the injury occurred. It may be stated as a general proposition that an injury occurs "in the course of" the employment when it takes place within the period of the employment, at a place where the employee reasonably may be in the performance of his duties, and while he is fulfilling those duties or doing something incidental thereto or engaged in the furtherance of the employer's business.

While injuries incurred off the premises of the employer are not ordinarily compensable, the result is different if the terms of the employment contemplate the performance of duties outside such premises. Generally, the hazards encountered by employees going to and from their regular place of work are not incident to the employment, and injuries resulting from such hazards are usually held not to be compensable as arising out of and in course of the employment. This general rule is subject to exceptions, however, where the employer provides the transportation or remunerates the employee for the time or expense involved, or where the employee performs or expects to perform some duty in connection with his employment at home or en route.

There is much conflict and confusion in the decisions as to whether and when a disease contracted by an employee may be considered a compensable injury. Recovery depends upon many factors, including the provisions of the particular statute, the circumstances of the particular case, and the policy of the court of the particular jurisdiction.

If the employee's injury was caused solely by his own serious and wilful misconduct, he is generally barred from recovery of compensation. However, such terms as "serious and willful misconduct" or "culpable negligence" used in this connection contemplate a degree of fault on the part of the employee much graver than ordinary contributory negligence.

C. FEDERAL LIABILITY AND COMPENSATION ACTS

§ 21:62. Railroad employees: Federal Employers' Liability Act.

Am Jur 2d References: Federal Employers' Liability and Compensation Acts, §§ 1–38.

The Federal Employers' Liability Act renders a common carrier by railroad liable in damages, in an action at law for the injury or death of an employee employed in interstate commerce, where such injury or death results proximately in whole or in part from the negligence of any officer, agent, or employee of the railroad company or from its violation of the Safety Appliance Acts.

Although the Act requires a showing of negligence on the part of the railroad company and provides for actions thereunder in the federal or state courts, rather than enforcement through administrative proceedings, it abrogates the common-law defenses ordinarily available to an employer in the absence of statute. Thus, if it appears that the injury or death was proximately caused by negligence on the part of the railroad company, the defense of assumption of risk or the fellow servant doctrine is not available to the company. And contributory negligence on the part of the employee does not bar recovery under the Act, unless it was the sole cause of the injury. But contributory negligence may be a factor, as damages are diminished by the jury in proportion to the amount of negligence attributable to the employee, as under the doctrine of comparative negligence.

As the Act provides for recovery of damages only for injuries or death of employees resulting in whole or in part from the negligence of a carrier, there can be no recovery thereunder if the employee's negligence was the sole and direct cause of his injury. This rule precludes recovery where the employee's injury or death was caused solely by his violation of a statutory rule or a company regulation or instruction; but where such violation was not the sole cause of injury but merely contributed to it, the misconduct may be considered only in reduction of damages.

§ 21:63. Seamen: Jones Act.

Am Jur 2d References: Federal Employers' Liability and Compensation Acts, §§ 1–4, 39–55.

The Jones Act extends the provisions of the Federal Employers' Liability Act to seamen and confers a right of action upon seamen or their representatives for injury or death resulting from the employer's negligence, and the

Act abrogates the usual common-law defenses of contributory negligence, assumed risk, and the fellow servant rule. Contributory negligence may be shown, as in actions under the Federal Employers' Liability Act, to reduce the amount of damages recoverable.

The Jones Act applies only to seamen who are employed by the defendant and who are members of the crew of a vessel plying navigable waters. Thus, while the term "seaman" is flexible and will be construed according to the circumstances of each case, it is generally held that such workers as long-shoremen and stevedores are not within the purview of the Act unless they are engaged in performing duties traditionally performed by seamen.

The standard of care contemplated by the Jones Act is governed by the general principles of maritime law. Thus, the shipowner must provide seamen with reasonably safe appliances, equipment, living quarters, and places to work; and he must maintain a seaworthy vessel.

§ 21:64. Federal compensation acts.

Am Jur 2d References: Federal Employers' Liability and Compensation Acts, §§ 83–147.

Several federal compensation acts have been enacted, similar in general scope and purpose to the state workmen's compensation acts, providing compensation to various classes of workmen injured in the course of their employment. These statutes are administered by administrative bodies.

The Longshoremen's and Harbor Workers' Compensation Act provides for the payment of compensation, together with medical and hospital services, to employees for disability or death from injury occurring upon the navigable waters of the United States, including any dry dock, if recovery therefor is not available under state workmen's compensation laws. The Act covers persons engaged in maritime employment other than those on board a vessel primarily in aid of navigation, and it applies to such persons as longshoremen, stevedores, and persons working in various other capacities as maritime employees.

The Defense Base Act makes the provisions of the Longshoremen's and Harbor Workers' Compensation Act applicable to persons employed at military, air, or naval bases outside the United States and to persons employed in public work in any territory or possession outside the continental United States, if such person is so engaged under the contract of a contractor with the United States.

Another federal statute provides for payment of compensation in certain circumstances for injury, death, or detention of various classes of persons employed abroad by the United States or by government contractors, where injury or death results from a war risk hazard or by detention by a hostile force or person.

The Federal Employers' Compensation Act provides for compensation for the injury or death of an employee of the United States while in the performance of his duties. In scope and purpose, this Act is similar to the state workmen's compensation acts. It is administered by the Secretary of Labor.

D. Employer's Liability for Acts of Employee

§ 21:65. Generally.

Am Jur 2d References: Automobiles, etc., §§ 615–645; Master and
Servant, §§ 404–425, 441–445.

A master is liable for injury to the person or property of third persons
caused by the tortious act of his servant or agent in the course and within
the scope of his employment. This is a vicarious liability based upon the doctrine of respondeat superior, and it is predicated on fault or wrongdoing of
the servant, without regard to any negligence or other wrong on the part of
the master.

The employer may be liable under this doctrine not only for the negligence
of his employee, but also for wilful or malicious wrongs committed by the
latter, such as libel or slander, fraud, theft or conversion, trespass, assault or
battery, or false imprisonment or arrest, if the wrongful act is done in the
prosecution of the employer's business and within the scope of the servant's
employment or authority.

The early decisions sometimes rationalized the doctrine of respondeat superior
on the theory of implied authorization by the master of the act of the servant.
But this theory would exclude liability for wilful or malicious torts committed
by an employee, for which the employer may be liable under modern law.
The real basis of the employer's vicarious liability is the idea that in the modern
world, sound policy requires that the master assume responsibility for the acts
of those chosen by him to carry on his business and affairs. The concept is
one of social justice and economic necessity.

Liability of the master is subject to the general prerequisites of tort liability:
the act of the servant must have violated some legal right of the plaintiff and
must have been the proximate cause of injury to the plaintiff; and the active
wrongdoer must have been an employee of the defendant at the time of the
wrongful act, and this relationship must have existed in reference to the
very act complained of.

An employer is not generally liable for wrongful acts of an assistant procured by an employee, unless the employee had authority, express or implied,
to employ help. If the employee was given authority to employ assistants,
or such authority may be implied from the terms of the employment or the
nature of the work to be performed, the master may be held liable for the
torts of an assistant or subagent.

§ 21:66. Scope of employment.

Am Jur 2d References: Automobiles, etc., §§ 617–630, 634–642;
Master and Servant, §§ 426–440.

To charge an employer with liability to a third person for the tortious act
of his employee, it is not necessary that the particular act be expressly authorized or approved, so long as it was done by the employee when he was
engaged in the service of the employer and acting for him in the prosecution
of his business.

The liability of an employer under the rule of respondeat superior extends,
and is limited, to tortious conduct of the employee acting within the scope

of his employment. The difficult problem is to determine whether the particular act was within the scope of the employee's employment, and this is determined by all of the surrounding facts and circumstances, the character of the employment, and the nature of the wrongful act.

If an employee who is delegated to perform certain work for his employer turns aside from the master's work or business to serve some purpose of his own not connected with the employer's business, or if he deviates or departs from his work to accomplish some purpose of his own not connected with his employment, the relation of master and servant is thereby temporarily suspended, and the master is not liable for his acts during the period of such suspension. To render the employer liable, the employee must have been engaged in the former's business at the very time of the act complained of. Not every slight deviation by the employee, however, will excuse the employer from liability. In order for an employer to escape liability for his employee's act on the ground of the latter's deviation or departure from the employer's business for a purpose of his own, it must appear that the employee abandoned and turned aside completely from the employer's business to engage in some purpose wholly his own. The effect of any deviation or detour by an employee must be determined under all of the circumstances of the case.

An employer may be liable for the wrongful act of his employee committed while acting in the employer's business and within the scope of his employment, although the employer had no knowledge thereof, or had disapproved it, or even expressly forbidden it. And he may be liable for a wilful or malicious act of his employee if the act was committed while the servant was acting in the execution of his authority and within the course of his employment or with a view to the furtherance of the employer's business, and not for a purpose personal to the employee.

Although the wrongful act of an employee was unauthorized and outside the scope of his employment, the subsequent approval or ratification of the act or transaction by the employer with full knowledge of the surrounding circumstances may render the latter liable.

§ 21:67. Independent contractors.

Am Jur 2d References: Independent Contractors, §§ 1–47.

An independent contractor is one who, in exercising an independent employment, contracts to do certain work according to his own methods, without being subject to the control of the employer or contractee except as to the product or result of his work. Such a contractor is not deemed to be a servant or employee within the doctrine of respondeat superior, and generally the employer or contractee is not liable for the torts of an independent contractor, or of the latter's servants, committed in the performance of the contracted work.

There are several tests or indicia of the status of an independent contractor. The most important of these tests is the right to control the performance of the work. Other factors which may throw light on the character of the relationship are the existence of a contract for the performance of a certain piece of work at a fixed price, the independent nature of the contractor's business or calling, his employment of assistants with the right to supervise their activities, his obligation to furnish tools, supplies, and materials, the method of payment, whether by time or by job, and whether the work is part of the regular business of the employer. The control of the work reserved to the contractee which indicates a master-servant relationship is control of the means and manner of performance of the work, as well as of the result; the independent contractor relationship usually exists where the person doing the work is subject to the will or control of the employer only as to the result and not as to the means or manner of accomplishment.

The existence of the independent contractor status of the principal wrong-doer does not necessarily excuse the contractee from liability, where the latter has been guilty of some negligence or other fault contributing to the injury. Thus, the contractee may be liable for the torts of an independent contractor if he failed to exercise due care to secure a competent contractor for the work. He may also be liable for injuries resulting from the dangerous condition of the premises. And the owner or contractee may be subject to a nondelegable duty from which he cannot escape by the employment of an independent contractor. Thus, a person has a nondelegable duty with respect to the taking of precautions during work which is dangerous in the absence of such precautions, which is inherently or intrinsically dangerous, or which from its nature is likely to render the premises dangerous to invitees. The same is true with respect to the conduct of ultrahazardous work.

X. ASSAULT AND BATTERY

§ 21:68. Generally.

Am Jur 2d References: Assault and Battery, §§ 109–145.

Assault, for which a civil action for damages will lie, is a demonstration of an unlawful intent by one person to inflict immediate injury on the person of another then present, or an intentional attempt, by force or violence, to do an injury to the person of another, or any attempt to commit a battery, or any threatening gesture showing in itself or by words accompanying it an immediate intention, coupled with a present ability, to commit a battery. Physical contact is not an essential element of assault, if there is an immediate offer or threat of violence. The American Law Institute's Restatement of the Law of Torts defines assault as an act, other than the mere speaking of words, which directly or indirectly is a legal cause of putting another in apprehension of an immediate and harmful or offensive contact, where the actor intends thereby to inflict a harmful or offensive contact upon the other or a third person or to put the other or a third person in apprehension thereof, and where the act is not consented to by the other and is not otherwise privileged. This definition is widely followed.

Battery is the unlawful touching or striking of the person of another by an aggressor himself or by any substance put in motion by him, done with the intention of bringing about a harmful or offensive contact or appre-hension thereof which is not legally consented to by the other and not otherwise privileged.

It is held, in some jurisdictions, that the tort of assault and battery may be committed despite the absence of an intention to inflict harm, if the act complained of is an unlawful act. In many jurisdictions it is held that the present ability of the actor to inflict the bodily contact that his act apparently threatens is an essential element of the tort of assault.

A sexual assault or indecent assault may be committed without actual rape or physical contact. An actionable assault may be committed by the firing of a gun or by pointing it in a threatening manner.

§ 21:69. Defenses.

Am Jur 2d References: Assault and Battery, §§ 146–177.

Various circumstances may give rise to a "privilege" or defense in connection with an act which would otherwise constitute actionable assault and battery. Thus, a peace officer cannot be held liable in an action for assault and battery for the use of force reasonably necessary in the enforcement of law and in the preservation of order. And reasonable corporal punishment as a disciplinary measure by a teacher or a person in loco parentis is "privileged" and does not give rise to a cause of action.

In the absence of statute, it is generally held that mere words or acts that do not amount to an assault, even when spoken or performed for the purpose of provoking an assault, are no defense to a civil action for assault, although such provocation may affect the amount of damages recoverable. The defense of contributory negligence does not apply in actions for assault and battery.

The general rule that a person cannot recover damages for a wrong occasioned by an act to which he has consented applies in civil actions for assault and battery. This rule applies to persons who voluntarily participate in sports or athletic contests, to persons agreeing to surgical operations, and to those who agree to certain sexual offenses. However, this rule does not apply where the consent was obtained by fraud or duress, or where the act consented to amounts to a breach of the peace or is otherwise unlawful. Thus, the agreement of the parties to engage in mutual combat is not generally a defense to an action by either of them to recover damages for personal injuries inflicted upon him by the other, although the consent of the plaintiff may be shown in mitigation of damages.

The right of self-defense, or defense of a third person, is applicable in civil actions for assault and battery, subject to the qualifications generally affecting this defense. Under this principle, a person may use the force necessary to protect himself from bodily harm which is threatened and which he reasonably believes to be imminent. The degree of force justifiable depends upon all of the circumstances, including the danger and the degree of force which must be repelled.

The defense of property also may justify the use of force. The owner of land or chattels may use such force as may be reasonably necessary under the circumstances to protect his possession thereof, but he may use only such force as is reasonably necessary to protect the property. And many courts hold that a person entitled to personal property is not justified in committing an assault or battery upon another to regain possession unlawfully withheld by a third person.

XI. FALSE IMPRISONMENT AND ARREST

§ 21:70. Generally; elements of wrong.

Am Jur 2d References: False Imprisonment, §§ 1–49.

False imprisonment, as a tort for which a civil action lies, is defined as the unlawful restraint by one person of the physical liberty of another. False arrest is practically indistinguishable. A person who is falsely arrested is at the same time falsely imprisoned, although there may be false imprisonment without an arrest. The essential elements of a cause of action for false imprisonment are (1) the detention or restraint of a person against his will, and (2) the unlawfulness of such detention or restraint. The termination of the prosecution is not essential to the maintenance of an action for false imprisonment, nor is it necessary that the wrongful detention or restraint be under color of any legal or judicial proceeding. And, as a general rule, lack of malice, the presence of good faith, or the existence of probable cause for the imprisonment do not affect the cause of action where the detention is unlawful.

Mere loss of freedom does not constitute false imprisonment, unless the imprisonment is unlawful. The ultimate acquittal of a person in a criminal prosecution, or his discharge upon some question of law, does not render his arrest or detention false imprisonment.

While it is essential to the tort of false imprisonment that there be some restraint of the person, the restraint or detention may be brought about by the imposition of either actual or apparent physical barriers. It is not necessary that there be confinement in a jail or prison. The wrong may be committed by acts or by words, or both, and by merely operating upon the will of the individual or by personal violence or both. The confinement or detention may be in a mental institution, a hospital, a restaurant, an office, a store, or even in a public street.

The detention or confinement may be effected by threats as well as by actual force, and the threats may be either conduct or words, if they are such as to induce a reasonable apprehension of the use of force.

Even though an arrest was lawful, an action for false imprisonment may be predicated on an unreasonable delay in taking the person arrested before a magistrate, or upon the wrongful denial of an opportunity to give bail.

Persons other than those who actually effect an imprisonment may be so related to the act or proceeding as to be liable. Those who aid, direct, advise, or encourage the unlawful detention of a person, such as a private citizen at whose request or direction a police officer makes an arrest without a warrant, may be liable for an arrest or detention which turns out to be unlawful.

§ 21:71. Defenses; immunity.

Am Jur 2d References: False Imprisonment, §§ 50–81.

Certain classes of persons, by virtue of the positions or offices they hold, are immune from liability for causing a detention or arrest of another when they are acting within the scope of their offices or positions. Thus, a judicial officer having jurisdiction of the person and of the subject matter is exempt from civil liability for false imprisonment, so long as he acts within that jurisdiction and in a judicial capacity, even though he may commit an error of judgment. Such an officer may be liable, however, where he proceeds in causing the arrest or detention of a person in a proceeding in which he acts wholly without jurisdiction, as distinguished from cases in which he merely exceeds his authority. It is generally held that the invalidity of a statute or ordinance under which a judicial officer acts does not render him liable for false imprisonment. Prosecuting attorneys and other attorneys acting in good faith are entitled to a similar immunity as quasi-judicial officers.

Military personnel are protected against liability for their acts in the reasonable performance of their duties, as are parents and schoolteachers in imposing reasonable restraints upon children.

An arrest or commitment by virtue of process regular and legal in form, duly issued by a court, magistrate, or body having authority to issue it, and executed in a lawful manner, does not constitute false arrest or imprisonment. This principle protects both the person who sued out the process and the officer who executed it. If the process is regular and valid on its face, an officer executing it in good faith is not rendered liable by an irregularity, unknown to the officer, which makes the process voidable.

An owner of property is justified in restraining another who seeks to interfere with or injure the property, where the restraint or detention is reasonable in time and manner. Thus, the owner of a store or other place of business has a right to detain a customer, patron, or other person for a reasonable time for a reasonable investigation, who he has reasonable grounds to believe has not paid for goods or is shoplifting or attempting to take goods without payment. However, there is liability for false imprisonment if there are insufficient grounds to justify the detention or if the detention is for an unreasonable length of time or is imposed in an unreasonable manner.

XII. MALICIOUS PROSECUTION AND ABUSE OF PROCESS

§ 21:72. Generally; elements of cause of action for malicious prosecution.

Am Jur 2d References: Malicious Prosecution, §§ 6–55.

A cause of action in tort for malicious prosecution arises against one who institutes or continues a legal proceeding without success or probable cause, and with actual or implied malice, resulting in damage to the defendant in that proceeding. According to the prevailing view, the same principles govern regardless of whether the alleged malicious prosecution consisted of a criminal prosecution or a civil or administrative proceeding. Some jurisdictions limit liability for the prosecution of civil suits to actions in which the present plaintiff was deprived of his personal liberty or suffered injury to his property or business.

In any event, the plaintiff in a malicious prosecution action must show that the defendant therein was responsible for the institution or continuance of the proceeding complained of. It is a general rule that before one can maintain an action for malicious prosecution, he must show that the original proceeding was terminated in his favor.

While malice, actual or constructive, is a basic element of an action of malicious prosecution, malice alone is not enough. In order to recover in such an action, the plaintiff must show a want of probable cause for the institution of the original proceeding, whether criminal or civil. Want of probable cause is the gist of the action of malicious prosecution and must be affirmatively established by the plaintiff therein. Probable cause for a criminal prosecution may be defined as a reasonable ground for suspicion, supported by circumstances sufficiently strong in themselves to warrant a cautious and prudent man to believe that the party is guilty of the offense with which he is charged.

In any case, civil or criminal, the question of probable cause does not depend upon the actual state of the case in point of fact, but upon the honest and reasonable belief of the party commencing the prosecution or action. The question of the presence or absence of probable cause for a criminal prosecution does not depend upon the guilt or innocence of the accused, although a conviction upon the charge or proof of his actual guilt is ordinarily conclusive evidence of probable cause.

§ 21:73. Defenses; immunity.

Am Jur 2d References: Malicious Prosecution, §§ 56–91.

The fact that a prosecution or action was instituted in reliance in good faith on advice of counsel, given after a full and fair statement of the facts to the attorney, is a complete defense to an action for malicious prosecution. And, as pointed out in the preceding section, any circumstance showing probable cause for the action or prosecution, or showing the absence of malice, will defeat an action of malicious prosecution.

An attorney is not liable for advising or prosecuting a proceeding for his client in good faith, even though the client may be liable for malicious prosecution. And judicial officers, including prosecuting attorneys, are accorded immunity from liability for malicious prosecution, where they acted within their jurisdiction and pursuant to their official duties, even though they acted maliciously and without probable cause. This immunity is based upon considerations of public policy.

§ 21:74. Abuse of process.

Am Jur 2d References: Abuse of Process, §§ 1–19.

Abuse of legal process, for which an action in tort will lie, consists in the malicious misuse or misapplication of such process to accomplish a purpose not warranted or commanded by the writ. It is the malicious perversion of a regularly issued civil or criminal process for a purpose and to obtain a result not lawfully warranted or properly attainable thereby. The action for abuse of process differs from an action for malicious prosecution in that the latter is concerned with maliciously causing process to issue, while the former is concerned with the improper use of the process after it has been issued.

To support such an action, there must be proof of a wilful and intentional abuse or misuse of the process for the accomplishment of some wrongful object or ulterior purpose not intended by the law. In an action for abuse of process, as distinguished from one for malicious prosecution, it is not ordinarily necessary to establish that the action in which the process issued has terminated unsuccessfully.

Actionable abuse of process usually involves the use of the process for some ulterior purpose or unlawful collateral end, as where a warrant of arrest or the criminal process is used not to bring a criminal to justice but to enforce the collection of an alleged debt.

XIII. FRAUD AND DECEIT

§ 21:75. Generally; elements of the tort.

Am Jur 2d References: Fraud and Deceit, §§ 1–40, 144–222.

The basis of the tort action of deceit is fraud resulting in damage. The essential elements of a cause of action for deceit are that a representation was made as a statement of fact, which was untrue and known to be untrue by the party making it; that it was made with intent to deceive and for the purpose of inducing the other party to act upon it; and that the latter did in fact justifiably rely on it and was induced thereby to act to his injury or damage. The same fraud as gives rise to the tort action of deceit will usually be a ground for equitable relief, as by a rescission, with respect to any transaction tainted by the fraud. In order to constitute the basis of an action for fraud or deceit, the facts misrepresented or concealed must have been material facts which substantially affect the interests of the person defrauded. It is not necessary that the person perpetrating a fraud should have derived any benefit from his deception, if the defrauded person suffered damage.

While mere silence does not ordinarily constitute actionable fraud, the active concealment of material facts which one is under a duty to disclose may give rise to a cause of action. And when there is a duty to speak and to disclose material facts, as when a confidential or fiduciary relationship exists between the parties, mere silence or nondisclosure may constitute fraud. A confidential or fiduciary relationship between the parties requires a higher standard of good faith and full and truthful disclosure of material facts than would be exacted of persons dealing at arms' length.

The rule is settled in most jurisdictions that there is no liability in a tort action of deceit unless the defendant had knowledge of the falsity of his representations or the circumstances give rise to a presumption of such knowledge. In some jurisdictions, however, the element of scienter is not regarded as essential. And even where the majority rule prevails, actual knowledge of falsity is not essential to the maintenance of the action where the defendant made the false statements recklessly, without knowing or caring whether they were true or false, and without regard to the consequences. One who makes an unqualified statement which implies personal knowledge on his part, when in fact he has no knowledge as to whether his statement is true or false, is as culpable for the falsity of the representation as though he had actual knowledge of the falsity.

§ 21:76. Nature and subject matter of representations.

Am Jur 2d References: Fraud and Deceit, §§ 41–143.

In order to constitute actionable fraud, a false representation must relate to a matter of fact which either exists in the present or has existed in the past, and the mere expression of an opinion, estimate, or guess which is or reasonably should be understood by the other party to be only that, cannot be the basis of an action of fraud or deceit. The determination of whether a statement is one of opinion or one of fact is sometimes difficult and must be determined in view of the subject matter, the form of the statement, the surrounding circumstances, and the respective knowledge of the parties.

The general rule that actionable fraud cannot be predicated upon the mere expression of an opinion is subject to several qualifications. Thus, an expression of opinion may amount to fraud where it is a part of a fraudulent contrivance or where the other party had a right to rely upon what was stated. And a statement may be so expressed, though in the form of an opinion, as to import that the speaker knows of the existence of facts which support his conclusion. In such a case, the form of the statement as an opinion will not relieve the party from liability. There is much modern authority for the view that the expression of an opinion not actually entertained may constitute actionable fraud where it is stated falsely and with intent to deceive. In support of this rule it is said that by the expression of an opinion the speaker affirms a fact, namely, that he truly entertains that opinion. And the expression of opinion may amount to fraud where there is a relation of trust and confidence between the parties.

It is a general rule that fraud must relate to a present or pre-existing fact, and cannot ordinarily be predicated on representations, statements, or assurances of things to be done or events to occur in the future. Thus, a tort action for fraud cannot ordinarily be based on statements solely promissory in nature and relating to future actions or conduct. In some circumstances, however, the courts decline to apply these general principles and take the position that a person's intention or belief is a matter of fact and that a misrepresentation thereof is one of fact. According to this theory, a misrepresentation of purpose or intent may constitute a misrepresentation of fact. Although some courts hold that fraud cannot be predicated on a mere promise even though it is made with a present intention not to perform it, the weight of authority is to the contrary. The difficulty in applying these principles lies in the necessity of showing a misrepresentation of an actual existing intent, as distinguished from a subsequent change of mind.

Although there is some authority to the contrary, it is generally held that it is an act of fraud to purchase or obtain goods or service with a preconceived intention not to pay for them. This rule is especially applicable where the purchaser is insolvent and conceals that fact from the other party.

The broad generalization is frequently stated that commendatory language is not to be construed as importing a representation upon which a charge of fraud may be based. Thus, general commendations of property sought to be sold, commonly known as "dealers' talk" or "puffing," even though involving exaggerated statements as to quality, value, etc., do not amount to actionable misrepresentations where the parties deal at arm's length. The nature of such statements are understood and properly discounted by reasonable men, and the maxim "caveat emptor" applies. This rule has no application, however, to false representations of material facts which are, in their nature, calculated to deceive and are made for that purpose.

A wilful misrepresentation of the nature, terms, or contents of a contract or other instrument constitutes actionable fraud.

Statements concerning domestic law are ordinarily regarded as expressions of opinion rather than representations of fact, and as a general rule an action for fraud cannot be predicated upon misrepresentations of law. However, there is some authority for the view that a statement of law may have the effect of a statement of fact, and hence may be actionable. Foreign law is generally regarded as a matter of fact, and a fraudulent misrepresentation thereof may be actionable if the other elements of the cause of action are present.

§ 21:77. Reliance and right to rely.

Am Jur 2d References: Fraud and Deceit, §§ 223–282.

A person seeking any kind of civil redress based upon fraud must show that he relied upon the fraudulent statement or representation as an inducement to his action or injurious change of position. The representations must have been relied upon by him and must have deceived him. To meet these prerequisites, it must be shown that the complaining party had knowledge of the representation and believed it to be true. It is not essential to a right of action for fraud that the conduct complained of was the sole cause of the plaintiff's loss; it is enough to show that it was an essential or inducing cause.

The fact that the representee conducts an independent investigation and consults means of information other than the representations made tends to negative—though not conclusively or necessarily—his actual reliance upon the representations.

Actual reliance upon the fraudulent representation, though essential to any relief on the ground of fraud, is not necessarily sufficient. The person asserting the fraud must also establish that he had a right to rely upon the representation in question. Whether or not reliance in a particular case was justifiable, what constitutes reasonable prudence and diligence with respect to such reliance, and what conduct constitutes a failure to exercise such prudence, depend upon the various circumstances involved, such as the form and materiality of the representations, and the respective intelligence and experience of the parties, as well as their relationship and respective knowledge and means of knowledge.

A party clearly has no right to rely upon misrepresentations which relate to facts of which he has knowledge equal to that of the party making the representations, or where he is aware of the falsity of the representations, or has reason to doubt the truth thereof, especially where he conducts an independent investigation of his own, unimpeded by the other party.

The principles relating to the right of reliance are closely connected with the duty on the part of a representee to use some measure of precaution to safeguard his interest. It is frequently stated that a person to whom false representations have been made is not entitled to relief because of them if he might readily have ascertained the truth by ordinary care and attention, and his failure to do so was the result of his own negligence. However, this principle will not be applied where active fraud has lulled the representee into a sense of security or where the latter is fraudulently induced to forego inquiries or investigations which he otherwise would make. And the modern trend is to limit the application of the doctrine of negligence as it affects the right to rely upon fraudulent representations.

XIV. INTERFERENCE

§ 21:78. Generally; interference with contract, business, or employment relationships.

Am Jur 2d References: Interference, §§ 1–21, 38–65.

The tort generally denominated "interference" consists essentially of the violation of the right of another to be secure in his business, contract, and employment relationships.

In order to maintain an action against a third person for interference, it must be shown that the latter acted maliciously and without legal justification. Malice in this connection does not necessarily mean actual malice in the popular sense of personal hatred or spite; it will be imputed whenever there has been an intentional and unjustified interference with the business or contractual relationships of another, resulting in injury or damage to the latter. It is generally held that an intent to interfere, with knowledge of the rights or relationships interfered with, is a prerequisite of a cause of action for interference. And the frustration of the contractual or business right or relationship must have resulted from the act of the defendant. In other words, the act complained of as interference must have been the proximate cause of the plaintiff's injury. If the end result is not justifiable, the means by which an actionable interference is accomplished may be fraud, coercion, defamatory statements, or mere persuasion.

The existence of a valid contract or business relationship is a primary element of liability for interference therewith. Although there is a conflict of authority on the point, it is held in some jurisdictions that there may be a cause of action for maliciously procuring the breach of a contract, although the contract was legally unenforceable because of formal defects, such as lack of mutuality or noncompliance with the statute of frauds.

Interfering with the performance of a contract between others may be actionable, although the defendant does not actually induce a breach of the contract. And interference with precontractual relations, preventing the consummation of a contract which otherwise would have been entered into, has been held to be actionable.

One who maliciously entices an employee to quit the service of an employer may be liable to the latter for the damages suffered by him. But this does not mean that a person may not, in good faith and in his own interest or for the benefit of the employee, employ a person who is in the employment of another. There may also be a right of action in an employee for malicious interference with his right to pursue his employment or for maliciously procuring his discharge.

Irrespective of any contractual relationships, malicious interference with the business relationships of another, by inducing third persons not to deal with him or otherwise, may constitute actionable interference. The same is true of interference with a person's right to pursue his occupation, trade, or profession.

The ordinary remedy for tortious interference is the recovery of damages; and in a proper case injunctive relief will be granted.

§ 21:79. Defenses.

Am Jur 2d References: Interference, §§ 22–37.

Most of the defenses to actions for interference are based upon limitations or qualifications implicit in the basic definition of this tort. The right to interfere under particular circumstances usually depends upon a balancing of conflicting interests, as determined from the viewpoint of the general public interest.

It is frequently stated that absolute rights, including rights incident to the ownership of property, rights growing out of contractual relations, and the right to enter or refuse to enter into contractual relations, may be exercised without liability for interference, without regard to the motives of the person exercising such rights. But the determination of the question whether a right is absolute is frequently a difficult problem, depending upon all of the circumstances of the case and a balancing of the opposing interests.

It is generally held that liability of a third person for procuring a breach of contract is not affected by the fact that the contract is terminable at will, if the other elements of a cause of action for interference are present. And liability for wrongfully inducing a breach of contract is not affected by the fact that the injured party also has a right of action in contract against the defaulting party to the contract.

Immunity from liability for interference is frequently stated in terms of "justification." This, however, is of little help, as the term "justification" is not susceptible of precise definition but depends upon all of the circumstances. Although there is some conflict of authority and the result may be affected by various circumstances, it is frequently held that justification for interfering with the business or contractual relations of another exists where the actor's purpose and motive are to benefit himself and protect his own interests, but that it does not exist where his sole motive is to cause harm to the other. Thus, competition in business may be justifiable interference with another's business relations, and is not actionable, so long as it is carried on in furtherance of one's own interests and by means that are not unlawful or unfair.

XV. LIBEL AND SLANDER

§ 21:80. Generally; definitions and distinctions.

Am Jur 2d References: Libel and Slander, §§ 1–26, 137–145,
                        311–348.

The gist of a tort action for defamation is injury to the plaintiff's reputation by false statements or imputations.

The basic distinction between libel and slander is the means of communication of the defamation. If it is published in the form of printing, writing, pictures, or the like, it is termed libel. If the defamation is communicated orally or by acts or gestures, it is termed slander. Whether the transmission of defamatory matter by radio or television is slander, or constitutes libel, is a problem yet to be settled.

A determination of whether a defamatory statement constitues libel, or is slander, may be important in jurisdictions which make a distinction between libel and slander in determining whether the statement in question was actionable per se, so as to require no allegations or proof of extrinsic matter, or merely actionable per quod or because of extraneous circumstances or special damages pleaded and proved.

In the case of defamation by spoken words, some courts hold that it is actionable per se, without any showing or special harm or loss of reputation, only if the words impute a crime. However, in most jurisdictions slander is actionable per se if it imputes to another a criminal offense, an existing loathsome and communicable disease, conduct, characteristics, or a condition incompatible with the exercise of a lawful business, trade, profession, or office, or, in some states, the unchastity of a woman. Some jurisdictions add to this list imputations tending to cause a person to be disinherited.

Some courts apply the same rules to libel. Other courts, however, consider libel to be broader than slander, being more permanent in form and usually more widely disseminated than spoken words. The latter view holds actionable per se libelous imputations which tend to degrade another person, impeach his honesty, integrity, or reputation, or bring him into contempt, hatred, or ridicule or cause him to be shunned or avoided.

So long as the meaning and intendment of the language is clear, the form of the defamatory statement is unimportant. Thus, a mere implication or insinuation, the statement of a belief or suspicion, or even a question may be actionable if it has a plain defamatory meaning.

It is generally held that if defamatory words are used broadly with respect to a large class or group of persons, and there is nothing that points to a particular member of the class or group, no member has a right of action for libel or slander.

A private corporation can maintain an action for libel or slander respecting its business, integrity, solvency, or credit. The same is true of business partnerships.

Under the common law, the defamation of a deceased person does not give right to a right of action in favor of the surviving spouse, family, or relatives who are not directly reflected upon.

In construing statements alleged to be defamatory, the courts will interpret the words in the sense in which they would be understood, and in which they appear to have been used, and according to the idea which they are adapted to convey, to those who hear them or to whom they are addressed. The ordinary signification in popular parlance of the statement in question is the vital question in each case. The language is given the meaning which the persons to whom it is addressed would ordinarily give to it. In determining the sense in which an alleged defamatory statement is employed, it is proper to consider the cause, occasion, and circumstances of its publication, as words which are harmless in themselves may become actionable in the light of surrounding circumstances. The entire statement or document should be considered, and the meaning of an alleged defamatory statement must be gathered not only from the words singled out as libelous, but from the context. All parts of the publication must be considered in ascertaining the true meaning.

Defamatory words are actionable only if they refer to the plaintiff. It is not necessary that the person defamed be named in the publication if, by intrinsic reference, the allusion is apparent, or if the publication contains matters of description or reference to circumstances from which others may understand that he is the person referred to, or if he is identified by extraneous circumstances so that persons knowing him can and do understand that he is the one referred to. It is not necessary that all the world understand the reference, but it is sufficient if those who know the plaintiff will reasonably believe that he is the person meant.

Every person who, directly or indirectly, publishes or assists in the publication of an actionable defamatory statement is liable for the resultant injury. One who merely distributes a publication containing defamatory matter is not liable, however, if he shows that he did not know and could not reasonably have known that the publication contained defamatory matter. An action for defamation by means of a motion picture may be maintained against its producer or an exhibitor. Where the defamation is by radio or television, the action may be maintained against the owner or operator of the station or any person who procures or participates in the making of the defamatory statements.

A master or principal, whether a natural person or a corporation, is liable for defamation of a third person published or uttered by an agent or servant acting within the scope of his employment and in the actual performance of the business of the master or principal touching the matter in question.

§ 21:81. Imputation of crime or immorality.

Am Jur 2d References: Libel and Slander, §§ 27–70.

A printed or written statement which falsely charges another with the commission of a crime is actionable per se, where the offense imputed involves moral turpitude or brings upon the person degradation in his society. An oral imputation of crime is actionable per se if the crime charged involves moral turpitude or an infamous or ignominious punishment. Some courts extend this rule to the charge of any crime that is indictable.

It is well settled that written words charging a woman or a man with unchastity or sexual immorality are actionable per se, as such a charge tends to degrade the reputation of the person, even though the act charged does not constitute a crime. A different rule is applied in some jurisdictions to oral imputations of unchastity or immorality not amounting to a crime. But even where such slander is not actionable per se, recovery may be had therefor where there is proof of special damage.

§ 21:82. Imputation exposing person to ridicule, contempt, aversion, or disgrace.

Am Jur 2d References: Libel and Slander, §§ 71–95.

For written statements to be actionable as libel, it is not necessary that they impute an offense punishable as a crime, or immoral conduct. It is sufficient that they tend to expose the plaintiff to hatred, ridicule, contempt, or aversion. The publication need not injure the plaintiff's standing with the public or entail universal hatred, if it injures him in the estimation of a considerable and respectable class of the community.

Written words of this kind are generally held to be actionable per se. Many courts, however, recognize a distinction between oral and written defamation and hold that an oral imputation of this nature is actionable per se only if it comes within one of the recognized categories that are so actionable. According to this view, such imputations are not actionable without a showing of extrinsic facts or the allegation and proof of special damage.

Since they tend to bring him into disrepute, to degrade him in the estimation of the community, and to deprive him of public confidence, written or printed charges against another of fraud, rascality, dishonesty, or of being a "crook" are actionable per se; but it is held by many courts that oral charges of this nature are not actionable unless special damage is shown.

It is actionable per se to impute to another in writing disloyalty to his country or subversive activity or conspiracy against his country, particularly in time of war. Although it ordinarily is not defamatory to impute to another support of political or sociological doctrines which are not generally recognized as complete anathema and which do not constitute disloyalty to the country or to the fundamental social order, it is generally held to be actionable per se, as subjecting the person charged to ridicule, contempt, shame, and disgrace, to state in writing that a person is a Communist, a Nazi, or the like.

If the fair import of false written statements as to race or nationality is such as to damage the plaintiff's community or professional standing, they are actionable per se. Accordingly, a written statement that a white person is a Negro or mulatto, or is tainted with Negro blood, is frequently held to be actionable per se. Some courts, in view of prevailing social customs and standards, hold that an oral statement that a white person is a Negro is actionable per se, while other courts hold that such a statement is actionable only where there is a showing of special damage.

An action will lie, without proof of special damage, for imputing, orally or in writing, that another has a loathsome or contagious disease, such as leprosy or a venereal disease. And a false written imputation of insanity, impairment of mental faculties, or confinement in a mental institution is actionable per se. Where the false statement is oral, however, most courts hold that an action will not lie without proof of special damage or unless the charge directly affects the person in his business, profession, or office.

§ 21:83. Imputation affecting business, trade, profession, or financial standing.

Am Jur 2d References: Libel and Slander, §§ 96–136.

False oral or written words that tend to prejudice another in his business, trade, or profession are actionable without proof of special damage if they affect him in a manner that may, as a necessary consequence, or do, as a natural consequence, prevent him from deriving therefrom that pecuniary reward which probably otherwise he would have obtained. False imputations are actionable per se if they have a direct tendency to alienate from the plaintiff's business a large class of customers, although other patrons may not be likewise affected. To be actionable under this principle, it is not necessary that the words impute to the plaintiff illegality, immorality, fraud, or dishonesty, or that they expose him to hatred, contempt, or aversion. The same rule applies to imputations which injuriously affect the profession, business, trade, or employment of another by imputing to him a want of capacity or fitness for engaging therein. Imputations of intoxication, mental incapacity, unfairness or unfriendliness to labor, or of dishonest, fraudulent, or unethical practices, are held to be actionable per se if they affect another in his business, trade, or profession.

The foregoing principles have been applied to a wide variety of businesses and callings. Thus, an oral or written imputation to a clergyman of moral or mental unfitness or of irreligious or immoral conduct which is irreconcilable with a proper discharge of his duties and which tend to prove him unfit to continue his calling, is actionable per se. And any statement published of an attorney at law with respect to his profession is actionable if it tends to injure or disgrace him as a member of his profession. Oral or written words which impute to him a want of the requisite qualifications to practice law or which charge him with improper or unethical practices in the performance of his duties as an attorney are actionable per se. Similarly, words, written or spoken, which impute to a physician, dentist, or the like, a want of professional knowledge or skill, or charge him with malpractice, gross negligence, or serious misconduct, are actionable per se.

Although false defamatory statements concerning a public officer or employee, or a candidate for public office or a politician, are actionable if the necessary requirements are met, the right of such persons to recover is strictly circumscribed by the general privilege accorded criticism of such persons and by the constitutional guaranty of freedom of speech and of the press. Under this constitutional guaranty, comments upon and criticism of a public officer relating to his conduct as such are actionable only upon a showing of malice, which is defined as knowledge that the statement was false or made in reckless disregard as to whether or not it was false.

It is actionable per se to publish a false statement directly imputing insolvency to a merchant or trader, including a corporation or an unincorporated association. Thus, it is actionable per se to charge that a person in business has failed, is bankrupt, is in the hands of the sheriff, or has made an assignment for the benefit of creditors.

Many cases hold that a writing stating merely that a person who is not a trader or merchant or engaged in a vocation wherein credit is necessary has defaulted in the payment of debts is not actionable per se and does not render the author or publisher of the statement liable without proof of special damage. However, there are a number of cases holding that a statement that a person is unwilling or refuses to pay his debts is actionable per se, even though he is not engaged in a vocation in which credit is an essential qualification.

It has frequently been held to be actionable for a creditor to employ methods to coerce payment which hold the debtor up to public disgrace and ridicule. Thus, the publication of an advertisement or the posting of conspicuous placards to enforce the payment of debts has frequently been held to constitute libel actionable per se.

§ 21:84. Publication.

Am Jur 2d References: Libel and Slander, §§ 146–172.

Publication or communication to a third person is an essential ingredient of actionable defamation. Publication in this sense means communication intentionally or by a negligent act to one other than the person defamed. The defamatory language, if oral, must be heard and understood by a third person. Where the communication of defamatory matter was not intended, and the defendant was guilty of no fault or neglect in connection therewith, it is generally held that no actionable publication results from its communication to a third person by accident. And a publication or communication of a defamatory statement or writing will not support an action if it was invited, instigated, or procured by the plaintiff. It is not necessary that the defamatory matter be made known to the public generally, or even to a considerable number of persons. It is sufficient if it is communicated to only one person other than the person defamed.

Publication sufficient to make defamatory imputations actionable may be effected in a wide variety of ways, including the distribution of circulars or handbills, the posting of notices or placards, or the delivery of a speech over an amplifier. A frequent means of publication is the mailing or delivery of a letter which is read by a third person. And defamatory imputations may be published by telegraph. And obviously, actionable libels may be published by means of newspapers, books, and magazines which are placed in circulation or sold. Publication may be effected by means of radio or television broadcasting, a well as by motion pictures, either silent or sound.

A defamatory imputation may be published by its communication to the plaintiff's family or relatives. Thus, there is a sufficient publication where defamatory words spoken or written concerning one spouse are addressed or communicated to the other spouse. However, it has been held in a number of cases, on the basis of the fiction that husband and wife are one in law or on the ground of public policy, that a communication from one spouse to another is not a sufficient publication unless it is made in the presence of a third person.

There is a conflict of authority on the question whether a communication to the defendant's employee or business associate, such as the dictation of defamatory matter to a stenographer, constitutes a publication which will render the defendant liable in an action for libel or slander. There is also a difference of opinion among the courts as to the effect of intracorporate communications between officers or employees of a corporation, and on the question whether communication of defamatory matter to the agent or attorney of the plaintiff constitutes a sufficient publication.

Each communication of a defamatory statement to a third person constitutes a new publication giving rise to a cause of action. The utterer or publisher of a defamation is liable if he republishes it or if he is a responsible for its republication by another. And under the modern view, a person repeating or republishing a defamatory statement is liable, even though he is only repeating what he has heard or read, and names his authority.

According to the common-law rule, each communication of written or printed matter is a distinct and separate publication of a libel contained therein, giving rise to a separate cause of action. This is referred to as the "multi-

ple publication" rule.   Other jurisdictions have adopted the "single publication" rule, under which any single integrated publication, such as one edi-
tion of a newspaper, book, or magazine, or one broadcast, is treated as a
unit, giving rise to only one cause of action, regardless of the number of
times it is exposed to different people.

§ 21:85. Defenses; justification.

Am Jur 2d References: Libel and Slander, §§ 178–191.

In order for the author or publisher of defamatory matter to be exonerated,
he must justify the publication or bring himself within an absolute or conditional privilege.   The pleas of privilege and justification are separate and distinct defenses, and one may be relied on without the other.

One who provokes or consents to a defamatory remark or publication cannot recover damages for the injury resulting therefrom.   And it is held that
where parties to an action for defamation have engaged in mutual vitupera-
tion and abuse, neither can recover.

In the absence of a statutory or constitutional provision to the contrary, it is
well settled that a plea and proof of the truth of the words or other matter
relied on as being defamatory is a complete defense in an action for libel
or slander.   This is true regardless of whether the defamatory matter otherwise would be actionable per se or per quod, nor is it material that the defendant did not know at the time of his publication that he was speaking the
truth.

It is said to be axiomatic that the justification of a libel or a slander must be
as broad as the statement sought to be justified.   And it is frequently held
that the truth of the precise charge must be proved, that is, that the truth of
the defamation must be strictly proved.   However, many authorities hold
that a showing that an imputation is substantially true suffices, and that it is
not necessary to prove the literal truth of a defamatory imputation in every
detail, slight inaccuracies of expression being immaterial.

The defendant's belief that a false statement made by him is true is not
a defense, although it may be shown in mitigation of damages.   This rule applies even though the publication in question purports to be made on information given by another.   A defamatory imputation is not justified by a
showing that it was made in good faith, with laudable motives, and without
a desire to injure another.   Conversely, the fact that malicious or evil motives
prompted the defendant to publish the truth does not generally deprive him
of the defense based on the truth of the publication, in the absence of legislation to the contrary.

It is a general rule that whatever a man publishes, he publishes at his peril.
Although such matters may be shown in mitigation of damages, it is no defense to an action for libel or slander that a defamatory imputation resulted
from mistake, negligence, or from an error of a clerk or workman for whose
conduct the defendant is responsible.   In many cases liability has been predicated on the publication of matter which is untrue because of a mistake in
naming or describing the plaintiff as the person to whom the publication
refers.

A retraction is the withdrawing of an accusation or charge.   Although it
may be shown by way of mitigation of damages, in the absence of statute the

retraction of a libel or slander is not a defense to an action for defamation. However, it has been held that a retraction of slanderous words at the time they were spoken, or before the separation of the persons who heard them and as a part of the same conversation, is a defense. The mere fact that a retraction is published on request does not make it an accord and satisfaction barring the right of action for libel; nor will an apology and an acceptance thereof bar such an action.

In a number of jurisdictions, statutes ordinarily referring to newspapers and periodicals, but sometimes including radio and television broadcasters, have been enacted, providing in substance that if a libel is promptly and fully retracted, only actual damages may be recovered, or that only special damages are recoverable, or that punitive damages may not be awarded. There is some conflict in the authorities on the constitutionality of such statutes. Statutes of this kind sometimes provide for a notice by the libeled person to the libeler, specifying the material complained of, so as to permit the publisher to take advantage of the statutory retraction privilege.

A retraction, to be sufficient, must be fair, frank, and unequivocal. It must be of such nature as to manifest an honest endeavor to repair the wrong done by the defamatory imputation, and should not contain lurking insinuations or hesitant withdrawals. It should clearly refer to and admit the publication of the matter complained of and should retract and recall the statement without any uncertainty, evasion, or subterfuge. Generally, the retraction must be published in as public and prominent a manner as that in which the defamatory statements were made, and it must be made within a reasonable time.

§ 21:86. — Privilege; fair comment or criticism.

Am Jur 2d References: Libel and Slander, §§ 192–310.

The law recognizes certain communications as privileged and so not within the rules imposing liability for defamation. Such a communication or statement is one which, except for the occasion on which or the circumstances under which it is made, would be defamatory and actionable.

Privilege in the law of libel and slander is sometimes attributed to the right of free speech, but its real basis is the public or social interest, superior to the right of the individual to be free from defamation, in assuring the free communication of matters of public interest and the performance of public duties and the efficient administration of justice, without risk of liability for defamation.

Privileged communications are divided into two general classes: those which are absolutely privileged and those which are qualifiedly or conditionally privileged. The difference is that complete protection is afforded by absolute privilege, whereas a qualified or conditional privilege affords protection only in the absence of evil motive or malice in fact.

An absolutely privileged communication is one in respect of which no remedy is afforded in a civil action, even though it is defamatory, false, and made maliciously. To make the defense of absolute privilege available, the communication must be made on a privileged occasion; it is the occasion, determined by the circumstances under which the defamatory language is used, that is privileged.

Absolute privilege is confined within narrow limits, and the courts do not extend such limits unless public policy demands it in new situations. Unless otherwise specifically provided for by statute, and except for communications between husband and wife, the application of absolute privilege is generally limited to legislative and judicial proceedings, and other acts of state.

A communication enjoying a qualified or conditional privilege is one made in good faith on a subject matter in which the person communicating has an interest, or in reference to which he has a right or duty, and made to a person having a corresponding interest or duty. The essential elements thereof are good faith, an interest to be upheld, a statement limited in its scope to this purpose, a proper occasion, and publication in the proper manner and to proper parties only. In the absence of a material dispute as to the facts, the question as to the existence of a privileged occasion is one of law for the court, but the question whether or not a conditionally privileged occasion was abused or whether malice existed is one of fact for the jury.

The existence of a conditional or qualified privilege depends upon the bona fides of the communication. The privilege attaches only if the communication was made in good faith to serve the interests of the publisher and the person to whom it was addressed, and it does not exist if the privileged occasion was abused.

In the absence of malice and if there has been no abuse of a privileged occasion, the defense of conditional or qualified privilege may extend to a communication that is false. The defense is not available, however, if the publisher does not honestly believe in the truth of the defamatory statement or if he has no reasonable grounds for believing the statement to be true.

If a communication or publication is absolutely privileged, the question of malice is not a subject of inquiry, as this kind of privilege is not affected by malice. However, malice becomes an issue where the defendant invokes a conditional or qualified privilege as a defense. This kind of privilege is not available where the publication is motivated by actual malice or if there is such gross disregard of the rights of the person injured as to be equivalent to malice in fact.

A qualified privilege attaches to communications relative to family matters, such as the conduct of a child or spouse, if made in good faith to the proper parties by members of the family, intimate friends, or third persons under a duty to speak. It is also generally recognized that statements in regard to school matters, such as statements by a school official concerning the character or conduct of a teacher, are qualifiedly privileged if made by persons having a duty or interest in the premises and acting in good faith. A similar qualified privilege attaches to statements in connection with the activities of such organizations as lodges, societies, and labor unions. The same is true of communications between church members and authorities in respect of organizational and administrative matters, including charges of misconduct on the part of a minister, officer, or member.

If made in good faith and without malice, statements made in an honest endeavor to vindicate one's character or to protect one's interests, and statements and reports made in the course of mutual controversy, are usually regarded as qualifiedly privileged, even though they are false. And as a general rule, defamatory matter published in response to inquiries made by the one defamed or by his authorized agent is qualifiedly privileged if it does not go beyond the scope of the inquiries and is honestly stated.

Communications to public officers or boards, including petitions or memorials seeking the redress of a grievance or the adoption of a particular policy, and complaints filed with a public officer or board against an inferior officer or employee, are protected by at least a qualified privilege. Members of Congress and members of state legislatures enjoy an absolute privilege with respect to defamatory matter published in the performance of their legislative function. A similar privilege (or, in some jurisdictions, a qualified privilege) applies to subordinate legislative bodies, such as municipal councils.

The heads of state, cabinet officers of the United States, and corresponding state and territorial officers, when engaged in the discharge of duties imposed upon them by law, are immune from civil suits for damages arising from official communications in respect of matters within their authority, even though such communications are prompted by personal or even malicious motives. This is an absolute privilege. And under the federal rule, which is followed in a number of states, the same privilege extends to inferior or subordinate officers or employees; and even in jurisdictions not going to this extent, such communications enjoy a qualified privilege.

It is a general rule that judges, counsel, parties, and witnesses are absolutely exempt from liability for defamatory words uttered or published in judicial proceedings. This rule of absolute privilege is subject, in many American jurisdictions, to the qualification that the statements must be pertinent or relevant to the case. Even where not entitled to an absolute privilege, statements in judicial proceedings are conditionally or qualifiedly privileged. Although it is held by some authorities that an absolute privilege may be invoked only where the court had jurisdiction of the controversy, this view is not universal; and the broad policy underlying the privilege would not seem to be promoted by a rule requiring parties, witnesses, and other participants in judicial proceedings to determine, at their peril, questions of jurisdiction, at least where the proceeding is held under color of jurisdiction. Whether the rule of absolute privilege accorded judicial proceedings applies in administrative proceedings is the subject of a conflict of authority. It is settled, however, that such proceedings are attended by at least a qualified privilege.

Newspapers, periodicals, and radio and television broadcasters, in dispensing news, enjoy no privilege that may not be claimed by the public generally. However, such news-dispensing media, like other persons, may in proper circumstances claim a qualified privilege to report accounts of public proceedings and meetings and the facts as to crimes and criminal charges, and to make fair comment and criticism as to matters of public interest.

Many classes of business communications are regarded as qualifiedly privileged if they are made without malice and in performance of a duty or in promotion of a mutual interest. If made in good faith and in the usual course of business, intercompany communications, including communications between stockholders of a corporation, officers of a corporation, officers and employees, and between employees or agents, are regarded as qualifiedly privileged. This privilege applies also to communications between attorney and client and those between principal and agent.

It is a general rule that a communication respecting the character or competency of an employee or former employee is qualifiedly privileged if made in good faith by a person having a duty in the premises to one who has a definite interest therein. There is considerable uncertainty in the decisions in respect of the privilege attaching to reports issued to or by credit associations.

Matters of public interest and concern are legitimate subjects of fair comment and criticism, and such comment and criticisms are not actionable, however severe in their terms, unless they are made maliciously. Some courts consider this right to comment on matters of public interest as simply an application of general principles of qualified privilege, but others treat this as a separate defense, governed by different principles. To support a plea of fair comment, the statement must be in whole or in part a matter of comment or opinion rather than an assertion of a fact, and the publication must (1) relate to a matter of public interest; (2) relate not to a person, but to his acts; (3) generally be based on facts clearly stated; and (4) be an honest and fair expression of opinion. The defense of public interest is frequently invoked in relation to publications dealing with political matters, public officers, candidates for office, and governmental matters generally.

§ 21:87. Slander of title or of property.

Am Jur 2d References: Libel and Slander, §§ 539–551.

Slander of title is defined as a false and malicious statement, oral or written, made in disparagement of a person's title to real or personal property, causing him injury. Slander or disparagement of property, as distinguished from slander of title, is defined as intentional words or conduct which disparage or reflect upon the quality, condition, or value of another's property, causing him pecuniary damage.

One who maliciously publishes false matter which brings in question or disparages the title to property, thereby causing special damage to the owner, may be held liable in a civil action for damages. Liability may be predicated on the filing or recording of a false instrument purporting to affect the title to property, such as a deed, an affidavit, a lien, a mortgage, or a lease. The publication of any false and malicious statement which tends to disparage the quality, condition, or value of the property of another, and which causes him special injury or damage, is actionable.

As indicated in the definitions, malice, express or implied, in the making of a slanderous statement is an essential ingredient of a cause of action for slander of title or of property. However, this does not mean malice in the ordinary sense of the term. Malice, within the meaning of this rule, is an intention to vex, injure, or annoy. An action will not lie for a statement which, though false, was made in good faith with probable cause for believing it, or where the statement was made under circumstances giving rise to a qualified privilege. Other essential elements of a cause of action for slander of title or of property are that the defamatory words must be false, and that special damage proximately resulted to the plaintiff from the slander uttered.

XVI. PRIVACY

§ 21:88. Generally; existence, definition, and nature of right.

Am Jur 2d References: Privacy, §§ 1–9.

The right of privacy is concisely defined as the right to be let alone; as the right of a person to be free from unwarranted publicity; and as the right to live without unwarranted interference by the public in matters in which the public is not properly concerned. It is apparent that these definitions are couched in the most general terms, which is to be expected in view of the diversity of the situations in which the right of privacy has been applied, and of the relatively undeveloped state of the law. An analysis of all of the authorities on the subject suggests the following as a fairly comprehensive definition of what constitutes an actionable invasion of the right of privacy: the unwarranted appropriation or exploitation of one's personality, the publicizing of one's private affairs with which the public has no legitimate concern, or the wrongful intrusion into one's private activities, in such manner as to outrage or cause mental suffering, shame, or humiliation to a person of ordinary sensibilities.

While invasions of the right of privacy frequently assume a form similar to libel, there are important differences between the two wrongs. In actions for the infringement of the former right, truth is not a defense, and it is not necessary to allege or prove special damages. The right of privacy concerns one's own peace of mind, while right to freedom from defamation concerns primarily one's reputation.

After its first formulation and definition as an independent right in 1890, the right of privacy has been recognized in most of the jurisdictions that have considered the question. Although only the roughest outlines of its nature and extent have as yet been sketched in judicial decisions, the great preponderance of authority supports the view that, independently of common-law rights of property, contract, reputation, and physical integrity, there is a legal right of privacy, the invasion of which gives rise to a cause of action in tort. Statutes have been enacted in some states creating rights equivalent to a limited right of privacy.

§ 21:89. Extent of and limitations upon the right.

Am Jur 2d References: Privacy, §§ 11–27.

A proper delimitation of the right of privacy consists in balancing conflicting interests, the interest of the individual in privacy on the one hand against the interest of the public in news or information on the other. It is a matter of harmonizing individual rights with community and social interests.

The right of privacy is relative to the customs of the time and place, and it is determined by the norm of the ordinary man. The protection afforded by the law to this right must be restricted to ordinary sensibilities, and will not be extended to supersensitiveness. In order to constitute an invasion of the right of privacy, an act must be of such nature as a reasonable man can see might and probably would cause mental distress and injury to anyone possessed of ordinary feelings and intelligence, and situated in like circumstances as the complainant.

Truth is not a defense to an action for an invasion of the right of privacy. It has been held that the motives of the defendant are unimportant in determining whether there has been an invasion of the right of privacy; and the presence or absence of malice does not affect liability in this field.

The right of privacy does not prohibit the publication of matter which is of legitimate public or general interest. At some point public interest in obtaining information becomes dominant over the individual's desire for privacy. However, the phrase "public or general interest," in this connection, does not mean mere curiosity. It has been suggested that the right of privacy does not prohibit a publication that would be privileged under the law of libel and slander.

The right of privacy is a purely personal one, and the plaintiff must show an invasion of his own right of privacy before he can recover. Since this right is primarily designed to protect the feelings and sensibilities of human beings, rather than to safeguard property, business, or other pecuniary interests, it would seem proper to deny the right to corporations and institutions.

The right of privacy, like other rights that rest in an individual, may be waived by him. And a waiver or relinquishment of this right, or of some aspect thereof, may be implied from the conduct of the parties and the surrounding circumstances. A person who, by his accomplishments, fame, or mode of life, or by adopting a profession or calling which gives the public a legitimate interest in his doings, his affairs, and his character, may be said to have become a public personage, and he thereby relinquishes at least a part of his right of privacy. A person may relinquish some part or phase of the rights that ordinary citizens possess to live private lives, without losing entirely the right of privacy or exposing all the intimate details of his private life to exploitation for the amusement of the public. The questions whether a particular individual is a public personage and the extent to which he has lost his right of privacy, are frequently difficult ones, depending upon all of the circumstances of the case. The same is true of the question whether, how, and to what extent a public personage may, by retiring from public life, regain the right of privacy which belongs to private citizens.

§ 21:90. What constitutes violation of the right.

Am Jur 2d References: Privacy, §§ 26–42.

The unwarranted publication of a person's name, or the unauthorized use or publication of his photograph or other likeness, constitutes the most common means of invasion of the right of privacy. The exploitation of another's personality for commercial purposes, as by the unauthorized use of his name or picture for advertising purposes, is a flagrant and common means of invasion of privacy, actionable in all jurisdictions recognizing the right of privacy, and by statute in some other jurisdictions.

The publication of a person's name or picture in connection with a news or historical event of legitimate public interest does not constitute an actionable invasion of the right of privacy. But the unauthorized use of a person's name in a petition, remonstrance, or a political or governmental matter has been held to amount to an actionable invasion of the right of privacy.

Radio, television, and motion pictures are common media for the invasion of the right of privacy. The invasion may consist of the unwarranted use of a person's name or likeness for advertising purposes or in a dramatization of his life or experiences.

It is generally held that the customary photographing, fingerprinting, and measuring of a prisoner for purposes of police records do not amount to an invasion of the prisoner's right of privacy.

The false impersonation of a person for the purpose of obtaining business or trade secrets, or for other improper purposes, has been held to constitute an invasion of such person's right of privacy. And the intrusion upon the privacy of another by eavesdropping, tapping telephone lines, or installing a secret listening and transmitting device in the plaintiff's living quarters, constitutes a clear invasion of the right of privacy, although the defendant does not communicate to anyone else the information thus obtained.

Recovery has been permitted in several cases on account of oppressive treatment of a debtor by a creditor in attempting to collect debts. The giving of undue publicity to private debts may constitute an invasion of the debtor's right of privacy. Thus, the posting of a notice in a public place stating the amount of the plaintiff's debt to the defendant has been held to constitute an actionable violation of the plaintiff's right of privacy; but the contrary view has also been taken.

The right of privacy secures one in the right to obtain medical treatment at home or in a hospital without personal publicity. A physician or hospital may be liable for exposing a patient to unwarranted publicity or publishing pictures showing an operation or other treatment performed upon the patient.

One whose right of privacy is unlawfully invaded is entitled to recover substantial damages, although the only damage suffered by him resulted from mental anguish. Punitive damages may be recovered where the element of malice appears. In jurisdictions which extend equitable remedies to enforce purely personal rights, as distinguished from property rights, injunction has been held available as a remedy to protect the right of privacy.

XVII. NUISANCES

§ 21:91. Generally; definitions and classifications.

Am Jur 2d References: Nuisances, §§ 1–18, 48–60.

The law relating to nuisance operates as a restriction upon the right of an owner of property to make such use of it as he pleases. The term "nuisance" is applied to wrongs which arise from the unreasonable, unwarrantable, or unlawful use by a person of his own property, in such manner as to produce material annoyance, inconvenience, discomfort, or hurt to another. Literally, the term "nuisance" means anything that produces hurt or injury, and in a broad and general sense, nuisance has been defined as anything that works an injury, harm, or prejudice to an individual or the public or which injures or unduly annoys another in the enjoyment of his legal rights. Nuisances are classified on several different bases. There are public nuisances and private nuisances; nuisances per se and nuisances per accidens; and a nuisance may be temporary or permanent.

The difference between a public or common nuisance and a private nuisance is that the former affects the public at large while the latter affects an individual or a limited number of individuals only. The distinction does not relate to any difference in the nature or character of the thing itself, but to the extent or scope of its injurious effect. A public nuisance is defined as an act, omission, or condition that injuriously affects the safety, health, or morals of the public generally or of such part of the public as comes in contact with it, or which works some substantial annoyance, inconvenience, or injury to the public. Closely related to public nuisances is the purpresture, which is an encroachment on or appropriation of land or waters which are common or public, such as highways, rivers, or parks. As stated above, a private nuisance affects only the individual or a limited number of individuals.

A nuisance per se, as distinguished from a nuisance per accidens, is an act, occupation, structure, or condition which is a nuisance at all times and under any circumstances and which cannot be so conducted or maintained as to be lawful. A nuisance per accidens or nuisance in fact is commonly defined as an act, occupation, structure, or condition which is not a nuisance per se, but which becomes a nuisance by reason of circumstances, location, or surroundings. According to some authorities, whether a thing is a nuisance per se depends upon the surrounding circumstances, including the location, and each case depends upon its own facts for classification as a nuisance per se, per accidens, or neither; and under this rule, an act or condition may be perfectly lawful in some localities, a nuisance per se in other localities or under other circumstances, and a nuisance in fact in still others.

Generally speaking, one who creates a nuisance is liable for the resulting damages as long as the nuisance continues. And a person who adopts and continues a previously existing nuisance also becomes liable for its continued maintenance. It is generally held that the creator of a nuisance does not, by conveying or transferring his property to a third person, release himself from liability for the continuation of the nuisance. The grantee or other transferee of land upon which there exists a nuisance created by his predecessor in title is not responsible therefor merely because he becomes the owner or tenant of the premises. To become liable, he must knowingly continue the nuisance, and generally he is not liable for continuing it in its original form unless he has been notified of its existence and requested to remove it, or has actual knowledge that it is a nuisance and injurious to the rights of others. This principle applies also to an heir or devisee succeeding to an estate in property on which a nuisance exists.

§ 21:92. What constitutes nuisance; requisites of cause of action.

Am Jur 2d References: Amusements, §§ 35–50; Funeral Directors, §§ 20, 21; Garages, §§ 5–11; Highways, §§ 274–310; Hospitals, §§ 46–48; Nuisances, §§ 19–47, 61–97.

While generally a person may do what he will with his own, this right is subordinate to the principle embodied in the maxim "sic utere tuo ut alienum non laedas" (so use your own that you do not injure that of another). Generally, a person has a right to use his own property for any lawful purpose which does not deprive others of any right of enjoyment of their property which is recognized and protected by law. The precise limits of one's right to do as he pleases with his own property are difficult to define. The use must be a reasonable one, and the right implies and is subject to a like right in every other person. What is a reasonable use and whether a particular use is a nuisance depends upon the facts of each particular case, such as location, character of the neighborhood, nature of the use, extent and frequency of the injury, and the effect upon the enjoyment of life, health, and property.

In order to give rise to a cause of action, the acts of the defendant must be the proximate and efficient cause of the creation of the nuisance complained of, and the nuisance must be the proximate cause of the injury and damage for which recovery is sought. A thing or condition which results wholly from accidental or natural causes, without the act or agency of man, is not generally a nuisance. However, the fact that other sources besides the nuisance created by the defendant may have contributed to the injury complained of does not relieve him from liability if the nuisance contributed materially to the injury. According to the weight of authority, the intent or motive with which an act is done is not material in determining whether it constitutes a nuisance.

Liability for a nuisance does not depend upon negligence. A nuisance does not rest on the degree of care used, but on the degree of danger existing even with the best of care. However, a nuisance may be a consequence of negligence, or the same acts or omissions which constitute negligence may give rise to a nuisance.

The injury resulting from a nuisance may be either to the person or the property of the complaining party or to both. In general, anything is a nuisance that endangers life or health or disturbs physical comfort to an injurious extent. A thing may be a nuisance because it gives offense to the senses. Anything is a nuisance which causes substantial injury to the property of another or obstructs the reasonable and comfortable use or enjoyment of the property. The fact that a thing is unsightly, on that it offends the esthetic sense, is not in itself sufficient to make it a nuisance. The criterion for determining whether a particular annoyance or inconvenience is sufficient to constitute a nuisance is its effect upon an ordinarily reasonable man, that is, a normal person of ordinary habits and sensibilities—and not its effect upon either supersensitive persons or those of extremely fastidious tastes or, on the other hand, those who are hardened or inured to annoyances of the kind in question.

While noise is not generally a nuisance per se, it may be of such character as to constitute a nuisance in fact, even though it arises from a lawful business or occupation, if the condition is such as to cause actual physical discomfort to persons of ordinary sensibilities or to injure the health of persons residing in the vicinity. In determining what noise constitutes a nuisance, the location and surroundings must be considered. Jarring or vibration may amount to a nuisance where it injures property or interferes with the comfortable occupation or enjoyment thereof.

The pollution of the air by the infusion thereof with artificial impurities or contaminants frequently gives rise to an actionable nuisance. While the right of every person to have the air in its natural state is relative to his locality and the character of his community, and while pollution of the air so far as is reasonably necessary to the enjoyment of life and indispensible to the progress of society is not actionable, the right to add any contamination to the atmosphere must not be exercised in an unreasonable manner so as to inflict injury upon another unnecessarily. While smoke, soot, or dust do not constitute a nuisance per se, any of them may constitute a nuisance in fact where they injure neighboring property or interfere with its use or enjoyment by persons of ordinary sensibilities. The same is true of noxious fumes, gases and vapors, and of foul and offensive stenches and odors emitted from the defendant's premises.

Any unauthorized and unnecessary or unreasonable use of a highway, such as an obstruction or encroachment which materially impedes or interferes with its use by the public for travel and transportation, is a public nuisance. As in other cases of public nuisances, however, a private individual or property owner has no right of action for such a nuisance unless he suffers some peculiar or special injury not common to the general public.

§ 21:93. Defenses.

Am Jur 2d References: Nuisances, §§ 25, 212–234.

The cases are in substantial agreement that the ordinary rule of contributory negligence, which defeats recovery altogether in actions based on negligence, does not apply in the case of an absolute nuisance. According to some courts, however, where the nuisance has its origin in negligence, contributory negligence may be a defense. And the fact that the nuisance was due in part to the fault of the plaintiff may prevent him from obtaining relief in equity. The general unavailability of the defense of contributory negligence does not preclude the defendant from preventing or reducing recovery by showing that the damage sustained by the plaintiff was due, in whole or in part, by his own acts or conduct.

Under the principle expressed by the maxim "volenti non fit injuria," one who voluntarily places himself in a situation whereby he suffers an injury will not be heard to say that his damage is due to a nuisance maintained by another. And it is held by the weight of authority that one who consents to, commits, or acquiesces in the erection of a structure with knowledge of the purpose to which it is to be put and the consequences of its erection and use, will not be heard to say that the building or its uses are a nuisance, unless he can show that he had no reason to believe that a nuisance would result. A right to maintain a private nuisance may rest in a license from the individual affected by the licensee's conduct, and authorization from the plaintiff to the defendant to create the condition alleged to be a nuisance is a defense to an action based on nuisance.

As a general rule, it is no justification for maintaining a nuisance that the party complaining of it came voluntarily within its reach. According to the weight of authority, the fact that a person voluntarily comes to a nuisance by moving into the sphere of its injurious effect, or by purchasing adjoining property or erecting a residence or building in the vicinity after the nuisance is created, does not prevent him from recovering damages for injuries sustained therefrom or from enjoining the maintenance of the nuisance.

The fact that other persons, or the plaintiff himself, maintained similar nuisances in the vicinity is no justification for creating or maintaining a nuisance.

As a general proposition, nuisances cannot be justified on the ground of necessity, pecuniary interest, or convenience to the defendant. At times, however, private interests must yield to the public good, and conditions which would otherwise constitute a nuisance must be tolerated by individuals for the general welfare.

Although it has been said that courts will not hold conduct to constitute a nuisance where authority therefor exists by virtue of legislative enactment, and some cases have applied such a principle to private nuisances, the weight of authority holds that a thing may be a private nuisance although it is authorized by law, and that legislative authorization does not affect the claim of a private citizen for damages or for injunction if he has suffered special inconvenience and discomfort or damage not experienced by the public at large. Constitutional provisions against taking or damaging private property without compensation has been held to prevent the legislature from authorizing a nuisance without compensation to individuals whose property is destroyed or injured thereby.

In the case of private nuisances, prescription is generally recognized as a good defense. In other words, prescription or lapse of time, accompanied by the elements of adverse and continuous user under claim of right, may be relied on to establish a right to maintain a private nuisance.

§ 21:94. Remedies.

Am Jur 2d References: Highways, Streets and Bridges, §§ 311, 313–317, 324–328; Nuisances, §§ 98–211.

The usual remedies for a nuisance are an action for damages, a suit in equity or an injunction (which may or may not include a demand for past damages), a summary abatement of the nuisance without judicial proceedings, and, where the nuisance is a public one, a criminal prosecution. The original common-law remedies against a public nuisance were by indictment and summary abatement by public authorities.

The state, county, municipality, or other political subdivision may maintain a suit to abate or prevent a public nuisance. A private individual may bring an action on account of a public nuisance when, and only when, he can show that he has sustained therefrom damage of a special character, distinct and different from the injury suffered by the public generally. According to the weight of authority, the injury sustained by the plaintiff must differ not merely in degree but in kind from that suffered by the public generally.

A person who has suffered injury to person or property as a result of a nuisance may maintain an action at law for damages. Whether he has a single cause of action for both past and future damage or successive causes of action arising upon the accrual of each separate injury, depends chiefly upon whether the nuisance causing the injury is permanent or temporary. Generally, if the nuisance is permanent in character, a single action may and should be brought for the entire damages, both past and prospective, which will bar a subsequent action. But if the nuisance is temporary or continuing in character, each repetition of it gives rise to a new cause of action for which successive actions will lie. The determination of this question of permanency is sometimes very difficult. The abatable character of the nuisance is a test frequently applied. According to many authorities, a nuisance is temporary or continuing where it is remediable, removable, or abatable.

Courts of equity have jurisdiction to give relief against either public or private nuisances by compelling their abatement or preventing their creation. This is true even though the act constituting the nuisance is also a crime.

And the court may enjoin a threatened or anticipated nuisance, as well as an existing one, where it clearly appears that a nuisance will necessarily result from the contemplated act or thing which it is sought to enjoin.

The issuance of injunctions against nuisances is governed by the equitable principles which control the granting of injunctions generally. These principles involve the application of the maxim "he who seeks equity must do equity" as well as the maxim "he who comes into equity must come with clean hands," under which a court of equity will not interfere if it appears that both parties are at fault. Also, it must generally be shown that the plaintiff has suffered or will suffer irreparable injury from the nuisance, or an injury for which he has no adequate remedy at law. The right to equitable relief may also be lost by laches or acquiescence.

The summary abatement of nuisances without judicial process was well known to the common law from the earliest times. In the exercise of the police power, the state may authorize its officers or agencies summarily to abate public nuisances without resort to legal proceedings, without notice or hearing, and without compensation. A person who suffers injury from a private nuisance may abate it without resort to legal proceedings, provided he can do so without a breach of the peace. While the early decisions recognized the right of a private citizen to abate a public nuisance without suit, the present trend of authorities is to limit this right to instances where the individual has suffered some special injury by reason of the public nuisance. An individual having the right to abate a nuisance may do all that is necessary to accomplish the purpose of protecting his own property and interests, even to the destruction of the property that has become a nuisance. This drastic remedy must be limited, however, to doing that which is necessary to abate the nuisance. And the person exercising this right must use ordinary care to prevent unnecessary damage to the property; and he acts at his peril, in that he is liable in damages if it is subsequently determined that the thing abated was not a nuisance in fact.

XVIII. TRADE OR BUSINESS PRACTICES

§ 21:95. Unfair competition or trade practice.

Am Jur 2d References: Trademarks, Tradenames, and Trade Practices (1st ed, §§ 86–88, 93–149).

Unfair competition, as a justiciable wrong under the common law, is difficult to define precisely. The concept is in process of expansion or extension in modern times. Basically it is a species of fraud or deceit. In its most common form, unfair competition is the simulation by one person of the name, symbols, or devices employed by a business rival, so as to induce the purchase of his goods under a false impression as to their origin or ownership and thus secure for himself benefits properly belonging to his competitor. The essence of this particular wrong is the sale of one's own goods for those of another person, conduct tending to pass or "palm" off one's own merchandise, services, or business as that or those of another.

While some authorities limit the doctrine of unfair competition to this type of conduct, others, especially in the more recent decisions, extend it to other acts done or practices employed for the purpose of pirating the trade of a competitor, and apply the doctrine so as to afford protection and relief against the unjust appropriation of, or injury to, the good will or business reputation of another, even though he is not a competitor.

While it is the injury to a competitor caused by fraudulent conduct or deception that is the ground upon which courts of equity usually act in affording relief from unfair competition, there has been an increasing tendency on the part of the courts to mold the legal remedy in this field to conform to ethical business standards and, rather than on competition alone, to place the emphasis on the injury suffered by the complaining party and the public from the confusion resulting from the defendant's acts.

Simulation of the peculiar or distinctive design, dress, packaging, or combination of features of an article produced or sold by another may be actionable by the latter as unfair competition where it is calculated to mislead the public and result in passing the defendant's product as that of the plaintiff. Unfair competition may consist in the substitution by a dealer of his own or another's goods in the place of those called for by a purchaser. And the act of a vendee in changing the form or composition of an article or commodity sold under a trademark, brand, or tradename, and reselling it under the original mark, brand, or name, may be enjoined where it is likely to result in imposition upon the public or an injury to the good will connected with such mark, brand, or name.

A misrepresentation by a tradesman with respect to his status or identity, for the purpose of pirating the trade of a competitor, constitutes unfair competition.

The sale of goods produced by a secret process or prepared in accordance with a secret formula discovered, invented, or originated and used by another does not of itself constitute unfair competition, where knowledge of the process or formula has been lawfully obtained and the use thereof does not violate any obligation of trust or confidence. But the rule is otherwise where knowledge of the process or formula has been obtained in violation of the rights of the original producer. The use or disclosure of the trade secrets of a competitor, or of confidential information relating to his business, under such circumstances as to constitute a breach of trust or confidence, may constitute unfair competition.

The ordinary remedies for unfair competition are an action at law for the recovery of damages and equitable relief by injunction and an accounting of profits. Equity jurisdiction to grant an injunction against unfair competition is commonly predicated upon such grounds as the protection and preservation of rights of property, the prevention of fraud, the avoidance of a multiplicity of suits, the prevention of irreparable injury, the inadequacy of the remedy at law, and the difficulty of establishing the extent of the injury.

§ 21:96. Actions under antitrust laws.

Am Jur 2d References: Monopolies, Combinations, and Restraints of Trade, §§ 250–417.

A person who has been injured in his trade or business by the activities of an unlawful monopoly, combination, or restraint is generally held to be entitled to recover damages in an action at law for the loss suffered, recovery being sustainable both at common law and under the various antitrust statutes. Many state antitrust statutes expressly confer a right of action for the full amount of damages sustained in consequence of any violation of the provisions thereof. Some permit the injured party to recover twofold or threefold the damages sustained by him. The Federal Antitrust Statute (the Sherman Act) provides that one who has been injured in his business or property by reason of an act forbidden by the antitrust laws may recover threefold the damages which he has sustained. In order to recover under these statutes, the plaintiff must establish that his injury was attributable to the illegal conduct of the defendant. Participation in a monopolistic or restrictive combination or transaction may preclude a party from recovering damages; to constitute a defense to such an action, however, the plaintiff's participation must have been such as to invoke the doctrine of "in pari delicto."

Where irreparable injury is threatened as a result of activities of an unlawful monopoly, combination, or association, injunctive relief may be granted. The federal antitrust laws expressly provide that any person, firm, or corporation may have injunctive relief against threatened loss or damage by a violation of such laws.

XIX. OTHER WRONGS AND INJURIES INVOLVING WILFUL ACT OR VIOLATION OF LAW

§ 21:97. Violation of civil rights.

Am Jur 2d References: Civil Rights, §§ 1, 63, 65–75.

In its general connotation, the phrase "civil rights" is broad enough to include all private legal rights of individuals. In recent times, however, the term is usually employed in a more restricted or particularized sense, referring to the rights created by various state and federal constitutional and statutory provisions designed to prevent discrimination in the treatment of persons by reason of their race, color, or religion. The term is so limited in the present discussion. Numerous state and federal constitutional and statutory provisions prohibit discrimination based on race, color, religion, or national origin, in connection with education, voting, transportation, employment, housing, and places of public accommodation or amusement.

State civil rights laws vary considerably in the type of relief or sanctions for which they make express provision. Some give the aggrieved person a right to recover a forfeiture or penalty in a specified amount; some give a right to recover damages; some give the right to recover both damages and penalty; others are strictly penal in form providing only that the violator shall be fined or imprisoned; and still others do not expressly provide either for civil remedies or for criminal sanctions. Statutes providing no sanctions or remedies whatever have been held to confer upon an aggrieved person the right to recover damages from the violator in a civil action. The same result has been reached under statutes expressly providing only criminal sanctions; but under the type of statute providing that the violator shall pay a stated penalty, the recovery of the penalty has been held to be the aggrieved party's exclusive remedy. Injunction and mandamus have been held available to the aggrieved party under state statutes although they do not expressly provide for these types of relief.

A person aggrieved by a violation of a federal civil rights law may usually maintain an action for damages, injunction, or declaratory relief. A suit for injunction, however, is subject to all of the federal rules governing the grant of injunctions by federal courts.

Class actions are permitted in federal courts in cases involving civil rights. For example, class actions have been successfully prosecuted on behalf of all Negro minors in a school district, similarly situated because of race or color, for relief against racial segregation in public schools, and for declaratory and injunctive relief against the enforcement of bus segregation laws, and against racial segregation in public recreational facilities.

§ 21:98. Injury from intoxicating liquor; dramshop or civil damage acts.

Am Jur 2d References: Intoxicating Liquors, §§ 553–592.

In the absence of statute changing the common-law rule, there can be no cause of action against one furnishing intoxicating liquor in favor of a person injured by the intoxication of the person to whom it was furnished. Liability has been imposed in some cases, however, where the liquor was furnished in violation of a statute prohibiting the sale of liquor to an intoxicated person, to a minor, or to a habitual drunkard. Nor can the consumer recover, in the absence of statute, against a person furnishing him with intoxicating liquor, for personal injuries sustained by him as a result of intoxication.

Many states have enacted statutes, commonly known as "civil damage acts" or "dramshop acts," giving a right of action to persons injured in person, property, or means of support, by an intoxicated person or in consequence of the intoxication of any person, against the person selling or furnishing the liquor. Clearly within the contemplation of such a statute is an intoxicated person's assault upon his wife or other person, or injuries received as a result of a collision with a vehicle driven by an intoxicated person. There is a conflict of authority on the question whether the purchaser of liquor may recover for injuries resulting from drinking the liquor; and there is some conflict on the question whether a civil damage act creates a right of action for damages for the death of an intoxicated person.

Although dramshop or civil damage statutes usually provide for the recovery of damages from "any person" giving or selling intoxicating liquor, it is generally held that such statutes are not intended to and do not create a right of action against one who gives another the beverage as a mere act of hospitality or social courtesy, without any connection with the business of selling liquor.

In order to recover damages under a civil damage or dramshop act, the plaintiff must show that the gift or sale of liquor was a cause of the intoxication of the person to whom it was furnished, or that it materially contributed to such intoxication. Liability for the unlawful sale of intoxicating beverages under a civil damage act is limited to damages caused by the intoxication of the immediate buyer, and if the latter transfers the beverage to another who drinks it and causes damage, the original seller is not liable.

Whether intoxication must be the proximate cause of injury or damage under a civil damage act usually depends upon the phraseology of the statute.

In an action brought for an injury inflicted "by an intoxicated person," that is, by the affirmative act of an intoxicated person, the courts generally hold that it is not necessary that the intoxication be the proximate cause of the injury, so long as the injury was inflicted by the intoxicated person. Where the action is brought for injuries inflicted "in consequence of, or by reason of, or on account of," the intoxication of a person, it has been held that there can be no recovery unless the intoxication was the proximate, or at least a contributing proximate, cause of the injury, although there is authority to the contrary.

§ 21:99. Miscellaneous.

Am Jur 2d References: Abortion, § 37; Conspiracy, §§ 43–55; Rape, § 118; Seduction, §§ 34–60

There is a conflict of authority as to whether a civil action may be maintained to recover damages for injury to or death of a woman who consents to or procures an abortion. The reasoning of the courts denying a recovery is based on the premise that the female was either an accomplice in the crime of abortion or was a willing and consenting participant therein. Many courts permit an action for damages to be maintained against one who performed an illegal operation to produce an abortion, either by the woman, if she survived, or by her personal representative, if death resulted, even though she consented to the act.

A woman who has been raped may maintain an action against her ravisher to recover the damages suffered, and a husband may maintain an action for damages for the rape of his wife. The consent of a female under the age of consent is no defense to a civil action for damages against one committing the crime known as statutory rape.

The common law permitted a civil action by a parent or master for the seduction of his daughter or servant. The basis of this cause of action was the loss of the female's services. The female herself could not recover for her own seduction, in the absence of special circumstances such as the use of force or the existence of a confidential relationship. By statute and by changes in the standards of society and of the courts, the element and nature of the tort action for seduction have changed. Loss of services has generally ceased to be of paramount importance. And some jurisdictions give the seduced female a right of action for her own seduction.

Although the essential elements of civil seduction vary from jurisdiction to jurisdiction as a result of statutory modification and enlargement of the common-law remedy, the presence of the following factors is regarded as essential to the maintenance of an action to recover damages for seduction: (1) enticement, persuasion, or solicitation of some nature; (2) sexual intercourse as a result of the enticement; and, in an action by the female herself (3) chastity of the female at the time of her seduction. The nature and extent of the enticement, persuasion, or solicitation necessary to support an action for seduction is difficult to define, and undoubtedly depends in some degree upon whether the plaintiff is a parent of the seduced female or is the female herself. Although seducers frequently accomplish their purpose by means of a promise of marriage, such a promise is not a necessary element in seduction.

A civil conspiracy is a combination of two or more persons by some concerted action to accomplish some criminal or unlawful purpose, or to accomplish some purpose not in itself criminal or unlawful by criminal or unlawful means.   The primary purpose of the conspiracy must be to cause injury to another.   The gist of a civil conspiracy, giving rise to a cause of action, is not the unlawful agreement, but the damage resulting from that agreement or its execution.   The cause of action is not created by the conspiracy, but by the wrongful acts done by the defendants to the injury of the plaintiff.   The principal function and effect of a conspiracy in a civil action is to bring into play certain rules of evidence and to show unlawful motive or purpose, such as a malicious intent.

*

TRUSTS

---

§ 22:1. Definition, nature, and history of trusts.

Am Jur 2d References: Trusts (1st ed, §§ 1–14).

As the term is used here, a "trust" is a legal relation between two or more persons by virtue of which one is bound to hold property to which he has the legal title, for the use or benefit of the other or others who have an equitable title or interest. It is a right, enforceable in equity, to the beneficial enjoyment of property, real or personal, of which the legal title is in another. The person so holding the legal title or interest is called the "trustee," and the one having the equitable interest and entitled to the benefit is the beneficiary or "cestui que trust." The person creating the trust is called the "trustor" or "settlor." An essential feature of trusts is the division of the title to property, the vesting of the legal title in the trustee and of the equitable title or beneficial interest in the cestui que trust.

The term "trust" is also frequently used in a more general sense to mean confidence or any fiduciary relationship. The word is also used loosely to designate a monopolistic organization which may or may not be effectuated by means of a true trust.

The modern trust is an offshoot of the old English "use," which was extensively employed as a means of avoiding various common-law and statutory restrictions and disadvantages, such as the Statute of Mortmain, forfeiture for treason, subjection of property to the debts of the owner, and the rule against disposing of property by will. Performance of his obligations under a use was entrusted to the conscience of the trustee, as supervised by the ecclesiastical courts, until courts of equity began to assume jurisdiction of matters relating to trusts. By a series of English statutes most of these devices became either ineffectual or unnecessary; and the Statute of Uses abolished uses which merely separated the legal title from the beneficial ownership, those in which the trustee had no interest or duty except to hold the legal title, as in the case of a "dry trust." The Statute of Uses converted the beneficial interest or equitable title into a legal title in such cases, so that the use was said to be "executed." This statute did not, however, apply generally to active uses under which the trustee had duties of management or control. This kind of use became known as a "trust"; and the other kind of use or "dry trust" is still sometimes called a use.

The law of trusts was largely developed by the chancery courts, and matters relating to trusts are still governed by the principles of equity jurisprudence except where these have been changed by statute.

"Springing" and "shifting" uses played an important part in the development of the modern law of estates, particularly future interests and executory devises, but they are of only limited significance in the modern law of trusts. A springing use is an equitable interest that arises on a future condition without a preceding limitation; and a shifting use is one which, after it comes into existence, shifts on a future condition from one beneficiary to another.

§ 22:2. Creation, existence, and validity of trusts.

Am Jur 2d References: Trusts (1st ed, §§ 12–92, 136–146).

The owner of property may create a trust therein by means of his will, deed, declaration of trust, or other instrument establishing his intention to do so. The general rules of construction of written instructions apply to the construction of trust instruments, the cardinal rule being to determine the intention of the trustor or settlor from the language of the trust instrument as a whole in the light of the surrounding circumstances at the time of the execution of the instrument. A writing is generally necessary for the creation of a trust involving real property, and many jurisdictions have statutes specifically requiring a writing for the creation of any trust, whether the property involved is real or personal. The formalities necessary for a trust instrument are those required by the statute of frauds, the statute of wills, or other pertinent statute.

Trusts may be created for any purpose that is not in contravention of law or public policy. Among the purposes for which trusts are frequently created and employed are the following: the holding and management of property for the benefit of a cestui que trust; the collection and receipt of income, profits, and rent; the sale, mortgage, lease, or management of property to satisfy charges thereon or for the payment of creditors; the protection of beneficiaries against creditors; and the creation and preservation of equitable or future estates or interests.

The purpose of a trust must be an active one, and the duties of the trustee must not be merely passive. If the only function or duty of the trustee is to hold the legal title, the trust is said to be passive or dry and is "executed" by the Statute of Uses and similar American statutes, so that the beneficiary is immediately vested with the legal title in his own right.

A trust reserving to the trustor or to some other designated person the power of revocation may be validly created, provided the legal title vests in a trustee, the equitable interest vests in beneficiaries, and the trust possesses the other requisites of a trust. A trust with the reservation of power of revocation may be valid although the trustor may receive some benefit, such as income during his lifetime, and although it is provided that the trust shall terminate or take effect upon the death of the trustor, and the instrument is not executed in accordance with the statute of wills. The validity of a trust with a power of modification or amendment reserved to the trustor or to others is also generally recognized, although the matter is regulated by statute in some jurisdictions.

The essential elements which must occur in the creation of a valid express trust, irrespective of the mode or character of instrument by which it is created, may be summarized as follows: a trustor who is legally competent to make disposition of the legal title of his property and to create the trust; a sufficient indication of his intention to create a trust; the existence, description, and identification of property to which the trust may and does pertain; a definite and complete present disposition of that property, although to take effect in enjoyment in the future; some provision for the office of trustee; and a person capable of holding the equitable interest in the property as beneficiary, although such person may be undetermined or unborn. It is also essential that the purpose be an active one, as pointed out above, to prevent the trust from being executed into a legal estate or interest, and that the purpose be one that is not in contravention of some prohibition of statute or rule of public policy. A declaration of the terms of the trust is essential, and these must be stated with reasonable certainty in order that the trustee may administer, and that a court may enforce, the trust.

A trust may, under some circumstances, be predicated upon precatory language, which consists of words of request, recommendation, suggestion, or expectation. The real test as to the creation of a trust by precatory words is whether the wish, desire, or recommendation expressed by the trustor is meant to govern the conduct of the one to whom it is addressed, or whether it is merely an indication of what the trustor thinks would be a reasonable exercise of the discretion of such person. In other words, it must appear that the precatory words were used in an imperative sense to the exclusion of any option of the devisee, legatee, or donee as to whether or not the expressed wish shall be given effect. The ultimate test is whether an intent to create a trust is sufficiently manifested.

A valid and existing trust may generally be modified, amended, or terminated only according to its own terms, without the consent of all parties in interest. The trustor may validly reserve the power to modify or terminate the trust, but without such reservation no such power exists. The duration of a trust is determined by its terms and by the accomplishment of all of its purposes. A trust may usually be terminated by agreement of all of the beneficiaries; and under some circumstances it may be terminated or set aside by a court.

§ 22:3. Spendthrift and other protective trusts.

Am Jur 2d References: Trusts (1st ed, §§ 147–185).

There are several methods by which the creator of a trust can give another the use and benefit of property and at the same time secure the property and its income against the improvidence of the beneficiary and the claims of his creditors. These trusts preclude the voluntary or involuntary alienation of the trust res by the beneficiary. The most common form of trust for this purpose is called a spendthrift trust. Such a trust is created by an instrument expressly providing against alienation by the cestui que trust and against liability for his debts, or by any language clearly indicating the intention of the trustor to create such a trust. An intention to create a spendthrift trust which the beneficiary cannot assign, nor any of his creditors disturb, is manifested by a provision to the effect that all moneys paid to any beneficiary shall be paid into his hands and not into the hands of any other person, without the right of anticipation; a provision for payment to the beneficiary for his support, with the further instruction that the beneficiary shall have no power to charge, encumber, or anticipate the income; or by a provision that the beneficiary shall not be entitled at any time to alienate, anticipate, or encumber his share of the income or principal, and that the same shall not be liable for his debts.

The validity of spendthrift trusts is recognized in an overwhelming majority of American jurisdictions. This rule is based on the fundamental right of a donor to condition his bounty as he pleases, so long as he violates no law in so doing. The law is concerned with the rights of the donor rather than with the protection of the beneficiary. Although the power to alienate is requisite to a legal estate, it is not an essential quality of an equitable estate, so that the absence of such power cannot be advanced as a valid objection to a spend-thrift trust. However, a few jurisdictions, by judicial decision or statute, follow what is called the English rule and deny the validity of a true spendthrift trust. But even in these jurisdictions the courts recognize the validity of other forms of protective trusts, such as support and discretionary trusts and trusts on a condition subsequent or conditional limitation, as discussed below.

The fact that a spendthrift or similar protective trust leaves the corpus of the trust to the beneficiary or to his heirs upon the termination of the trust does not affect the validity of the trust.

The protection of the beneficiary against voluntary or involuntary alienation may be effected by protective trusts other than technical spendthrift trusts. Thus, the interest of a beneficiary may not be liable for his debts because it is of a personal character or for a specific personal use, because it is inseparable from the interests of other beneficiaries, or because it is indefinite and contingent. And a trust may be made protective against grantees or assignees and against creditors of the beneficiary by means of a provision vesting discretion in the trustee to determine the time, amount, or manner of payments to a beneficiary. Trusts immune from the claims of creditors frequently take the form of a provision for the support or education of the beneficiary.

A trust may validly be protective against grantees or assignees and creditors of a beneficiary by a provision making the solvency of the beneficiary a condition precedent to his receipt of benefits under the trust. And it is well settled, even in jurisdictions which do not recognize the validity of spendthrift trusts, that the terms of a trust may validly provide for termination, cesser, or forfeiture of the interest of a beneficiary upon an attempt to alienate it or upon an attempt of his creditors to reach it or in the event of his insolvency or bankruptcy. Such a trust, involving a condition subsequent, a conditional limitation, or a provision of cesser, has the effect, different from that of a true spendthrift trust, of terminating the interest and rights of the beneficiary upon an attempt at alienation, voluntary or involuntary. Such provisions are discussed also in Real Property, §§ 18:13, 18:14.

In some jurisdictions, by virtue of statutes or otherwise, the surplus of a spendthrift or support trust, beyond what is necessary for the support and education of the beneficiary, is subject to the claims of his creditors. And generally such trusts protect the income due the beneficiary only until he actually receives it from the trustee, so that property or income actually received by the beneficiary is thereafter liable for his debts.

Spendthrift and similar trusts do not protect the beneficiary's interest against all kinds of claims. The protection has been held not to extend to claims of the state or its subdivision for taxes, or claims for the support and maintenance of the beneficiary's wife and children. Whether or not such a trust is protective against the claim of a divorced wife for alimony may depend upon the terms of the trust, different results being reached in the cases involving this question.

It is well settled that a person cannot settle upon himself a spendthrift or other protective trust which will be effective to protect either the income or corpus against the claims of his creditors, or to free it from his own power of alienation.

§ 22:4. Trusts by operation of law; resulting and constructive trusts.

Am Jur 2d References: Trusts (1st ed, §§ 186–247).

The traditional classification of trusts recognizes two main divisions: (1) express or direct trusts, and (2) trusts by operation of law. The latter are frequently referred to as involuntary trusts or implied trusts. However, the use of the term "implied" in this connection may be confusing, since it is also used in connection with express trusts where the law presumes or implies the intention of the testator with respect to the creation and terms of the trust.

From a practical viewpoint, a resulting trust involves primarily the operation of the equitable doctrine of consideration, the principle that valuable consideration, and not legal title, determines the equitable title or interest resulting from a transaction. A constructive trust, on the other hand, generally involves primarily an element of fraud, in view of which equitable title or interest is recognized in some person other than the taker or holder of the legal title. Another distinguishing feature is that a resulting trust involves a presumption, implication, or imputation of an intention to create a trust, whereas a constructive trust is entirely independent of any actual or presumed intention of the parties and is frequently imposed against the intention of the trustee.

Statutes limiting or executing express trusts, such as the English Statute of Uses and similar legislation, do not generally apply to trusts created by operation of law. Nor are such trusts affected by the requirements of the statute of frauds or the statute of wills.

Trusts by operation of law are generally created to prevent fraud or inequity, and such a trust will never be raised where it would result in fraud or the violation of law or public policy.

Broadly speaking, a resulting trust arises from the nature or circumstances of the consideration involved in a transaction by which one person thereby becomes invested with a legal title but is obligated in equity and good conscience to hold that title for the benefit of another, the intention of the former to hold in trust for the latter being implied or presumed as a matter of law. There is usually no element of fraud in a resulting trust, and the presence of fraud makes the trust a constructive one. The two most important groups of resulting trusts are those arising on a failure of an express trust or purpose, and those arising on a conveyance to one person upon a consideration from another.

The failure of a trust based upon a consideration does not generally give rise to a resulting trust in favor of the grantor or his heirs or next of kin. The rule is different, however, in the case of an attempted trust which is not based upon any consideration.

It is a general rule that where a donor conveys, either by will or deed, without consideration, property on a certain trust or for a certain purpose, and the trust or purpose fails, a resulting trust arises for the benefit of the donor or his heirs or next of kin; but such a resulting trust may be rebutted by the showing of a contrary intention in the will or deed or by evidence. This rule applies where the trust fails because of its indefiniteness, uncertainty, or vagueness as to the designation of beneficiaries, or in other respects, and it applies where the trust is illegal or void on other grounds.

A resulting trust arises in favor of the person from whom the consideration comes for a conveyance of property, real or personal, to another, where the parties are strangers to each other in the sense that there is no domestic relationship giving rise to a meritorious consideration; but the existence of such a trust is rebuttable by proof of a contrary intention on the part of the person from whom the consideration comes. This kind of trust arises only in the same transaction in which the legal title passes and on a consideration advanced before or at that time, and not from matters thereafter occurring on consideration thereafter advanced. However, where the person to whom property is conveyed is the wife, child, or other natural object of the bounty of the purchaser who furnishes the consideration, a resulting trust does not arise in favor of the latter in the absence of evidence rebutting the presumption that a donation or gratuity settlement was intended. A typical and frequent example of a resulting trust in favor of the person furnishing the consideration occurs where he purchases property and takes the conveyance in the name of another.

A constructive trust (frequently referred to as a trust ex maleficio or ex delicto) is a trust arising by operation of law and contrary to intention, against one who, by fraud, actual or constructive, by duress or abuse of confidence, or by any form of unconscionable conduct, artifice, concealment, or wrongful or inequitable means, has obtained or holds the legal title or right to property which he ought not, in equity and good conscience, hold and enjoy. A constructive trust is an appropriate remedy against unjust enrichment, which is discussed generally in the topic Restitution, Quasi-Contract, and Implied Contracts.

The forms and varieties of constructive trusts, and the situations in which they may arise, are practically unlimited. An abuse of confidence rendering the acquisition or retention of property by one person unconscionable against another is sufficient ground for the declaration and enforcement of a constructive trust; and such abuse of confidence may be an abuse of either a technical fiduciary relationship or of an informal relationship existing where one person trusts in and relies upon another. The abuse of a confidential relationship by acquiring property through the employment of knowledge or interest obtained in such relationship may be the ground for the declaration of a constructive trust in such property in favor of the person wronged. And a purchase, on his own account or for his own benefit by a fiduciary or confidant, of property constituting the subject matter of the confidence or fiduciary relationship may give rise to a constructive trust in favor of his principal or confider. Also, a fiduciary may be held as a constructive trustee in respect of secret profits or commissions obtained by violation of confidence or duty.

The general rule is that, in the absence of any element of fraud or mistake or anything to indicate the existence of a confidential relationship between the grantor and the grantee, a constructive trust does not arise merely from a breach of an agreement by a grantee to hold property conveyed to him in trust for the benefit of the grantor or another. However, if there is a confidential relationship which is violated or if the grantee has been guilty of fraud, duress, concealment, or undue influence, a constructive trust may be decreed.

A constructive trust is held to arise where an heir, devisee, or legatee violates a promise to the testator, expressly made or inferable from words or conduct, to hold an inheritance, devise, or legacy for another or to give it to another, upon which promise the testator relied in making or changing his will in order to favor such other person. The proof to establish this kind of trust must, however, be clear and strong. In cases involving this kind of frustration of ancestral or testamentary intention, some courts require a showing of fraud on the part of the constructive trustee in addition to his breach of promise made to the testator or ancestor.

A wrongful taking of property of another, followed by its conversion into another or different form, is ground for the declaration and enforcement of a constructive trust with respect to the new form or species, so long as the property or its product or proceeds can be traced and identified and has not come into the hands of a bona fide purchaser for value.

§ 22:5. Trust property and rights therein.

Am Jur 2d References: Trusts (1st ed, §§ 93–111, 248–273).

The question of what property is included in a trust is determined by the terms of the trust and by the description or designation thereof in the trust instrument. A trust may include either real or personal property or both. The estates and interests that may be held in trust have been molded in an almost perfect analogy and correspondence with legal estates at common law. Equity follows the law with respect to the nature and incidents of the several estates and interests, which are discussed in the topic Real Property §§ 18:4–18:27.

It is a basic rule in the law of trusts that a trustee is vested with the legal, as distinguishable from the equitable, estate, and he is compelled to use this estate in accordance with the terms of the trust for the benefit of the beneficiaries. The legal title and estate of a trustee are not, as a general rule, liable for his private debts and obligations, as distinguished from those of the trust estate. Upon the creation of a trust, the trustor usually parts with all title and interest in the trust property, although he may make himself a beneficiary or may have an interest by way of a reserved power of revocation or a reversionary interest under a condition or conditional limitation.

The estate and interest of a cestui que trust are determined by the terms of the trust. His title or estate is equitable, and not legal, in nature, and consists essentially in a right to performance of the trust. Unless there are restrictions on alienation in the trust itself or by statute, the beneficiary has the right to alien or transfer his rights under the trust and in the trust property, and his rights and interest are subject to seizure by his creditors. As noted above (§ 22:3, supra), the settlor may, by means of a spendthrift trust or otherwise, limit the alienability of the beneficiary's interest, and statutes sometimes have the same effect.

Equity will pursue property that is wrongfully converted by a fiduciary, or otherwise compel restitution to the beneficiary. Under the trust pursuit rule a trust will follow property through all changes in its state or form, so long as such property, its product, or its proceeds, are identified. It will follow the property into the hands of a transferee other than a bona fide purchaser for value, or restitution may be enforced, at the election of the beneficiary, through recourse against the trustee or the transferee personally or by compelling the transferee to perform the trust. As implied in the statement of the rule, it is necessary to identify trust property or funds or the product or proceeds thereof in order to follow and enforce the trust against the same. This principle applies where trust property or funds are commingled by a trustee with other property or funds; and where there have been withdrawals from the commingled fund or mass, for purposes not related to the trust, it is presumed that the withdrawals were from property or funds other than those belonging to the trust, so that any remaining part of the mingled mass or funds are subject to the trust.

Where the property or funds of several different trusts have been commingled in a fund which is insufficient to satisfy them all, the courts have generally followed what is known as the rule in Clayton's Case, to the effect that the first withdrawals are to be charged against the first deposits, so that the claimants are entitled to be paid in the inverse order in which their moneys went into the account. An alternative rule is that withdrawals made by the trustee for his own benefit, or for the benefit of others not beneficiaries of the trust, are to be charged to the several trusts in proportion to their interests in the cash credit or other property at the time of withdrawal.

§ 22:6. The trustee; appointment, tenure, bond, accounting, and compensation.

Am Jur 2d References: Trusts (1st ed, §§ 112–135, 497–556).

The trustee is that person in the trust transaction who holds the legal title to the property subject to the trust, for the benefit of the cestui que trust, with certain powers and subject to certain duties imposed by the terms of the trust, equity jurisprudence, or statutory provision. There may be one or several trustees of a trust. Any person sui juris may in general be a trustee, and certain persons, such as infants, may act as trustees, although they are not sui juris for many purposes. A settlor of a trust may in general make himself the trustee of it; but the sole beneficiary of a trust cannot be its sole trustee, as this would defeat the essential requisite of a separation of legal and equitable estates. A corporation may act as trustee where its charter and the statutes of the state empower it to do so. And a municipal corporation may hold and administer property in trust if the trusteeship is germane to the objects of the municipality and otherwise within its charter powers.

The trustee is usually appointed by the creator of the trust; but a court of equity has jurisdiction to appoint a trustee whenever it is necessary to the administration of a trust or to prevent a failure of the trust, whether the necessity arises from failure of appointment, from nonacceptance or disqualification of a trustee, or from other cause. One who has been named as trustee may decline to accept the office, or he may resign. And a court of equity has jurisdiction in a proper case to remove or discharge a trustee for good cause. Where the terms of the trust do not provide the manner of substitution, selection, and succession of trustees in the administration of the trust, the court makes the new appointment. The terms of a trust sometimes give the trustee the power to appoint his successor.

Unless a statute or the terms of a trust require that a trustee give a bond for the faithful performance of his duties, the necessity for such a bond is left to the discretion of the court having jurisdiction of the trust. The terms of the trust or statutes frequently provide that a trustee shall be required to furnish bond. The trustee may be relieved of a statutory requirement by the terms of the trust, or he may be relieved of the requirement of security on his bond. The liability of the surety on a trustee's bond is governed by the terms of the bond, the governing statutes, and the general law of suretyship.

A trustee is under duty to keep and render a full and accurate record and accounting of his trusteeship to the cestui que trust. The records and accounting of a trustee should constitute a complete, accurate, and distinct report and disclosure in detail of the administration of the trust, showing all receipts and their sources, payments by him, and the balance remaining. Such an account is generally required to be filed with and approved by the court having jurisdiction of the trust. However, the accounting of a trustee may be settled or excused out of court by the beneficiaries, so as to release the trustee, provided the latter has made a full and fair disclosure to the beneficiaries in conformity with the high measure of fairness required of a trustee.

As between a trustee and the trust estate, the latter is obligated to bear the cost of all expenses and liabilities properly incurred by the trustee in the administration of the trust. If the trustee advances his own money or uses his own property in discharging such properly incurred obligations, he is entitled to reimbursement out of the trust estate; if he discharges such obligations from trust funds or property, he is entitled to credit therefor in his accounting. The trustee is entitled to reimbursement or indemnity not only where he enters into a contract which is proper in the administration of the trust and is binding on him personally, but also where, without personal fault on his part, he is subjected to liability in tort in the administration of the estate. A trustee thus entitled to reimbursement is generally regarded as having a security interest in or lien upon the trust estate, and he may retain control thereof until he receives reimbursement.

It is the general rule in this country, embodied in statutes in many jurisdictions, that a trustee is entitled to an allowance as compensation for his services in administering the trust. The amount of such compensation may be fixed by the terms of the trust or by statute, and where it is not so fixed it is determined by the court.

§ 22:7. Administration of trust; powers, duties, and liability of trustee and the estate.

Am Jur 2d References: Trusts (1st ed, §§ 274–496).

The administration of a trust according to its terms is primarily the responsibility of the trustee, subject to the supervisory control of the courts. Courts of equity have general jurisdiction over trusts and the administration thereof. A court may exercise this jurisdiction upon application by the trustee for guidance or directions of the court in construing the trust instrument and determining other questions arising in the course of the administration of the trust. And the court may exercise its jurisdiction over the administration of the trust upon a proper application of beneficiaries and other interested parties.

In an extreme case, in order to meet an emergency not anticipated by the settlor, to carry out his ultimate purpose and to preserve the trust estate and prevent a failure of the trust, a court may authorize or direct the trustee to deviate from the literal terms of the trust instrument or to perform acts which would otherwise not be within his power. However, a court will permit a deviation of this kind only in extreme cases and never as a substitution of its judgment for the wishes of the trustor. The theory and result of such a deviation from the terms of the trust are not the same as where a resulting trust arises because of the failure of an express trust (supra, § 22:4); the present principle is more closely related to the cy pres doctrine as applied to charitable trusts (infra, § 22:8).

The administrative powers of a trustee are in general governed by the terms of the trust, the statutes of the state, and the rules of equity jurisprudence governing trusts and trustees. In determining the limit and extent of these powers, the intention of the trustor will be given effect. A power, though not expressly granted, will be implied where it is essential to carry out the terms of the trust and the intent of the trustor. Powers involving mere ministerial duties may be delegated by the trustee to others, but duties requiring the exercise of his discretion may not be so delegated. And some powers of the trustee are personal to him and a matter of special confidence and trust in him, so that they may be exercised by no one else. When the administration of a trust is vested in several cotrustees, they all form but one collective trustee, and they must jointly exercise all powers that call for their discretion or judgment, unless the trust instrument authorizes an apportionment of powers or action by a majority or the like. The surviving cotrustees can generally exercise trust powers. In some instances, by the terms of the trust, the trustee's exercise of certain powers is made dependent upon the advice or consent of others, such as disinterested persons, an executor, the beneficiaries or the trustor.

The duties of the trustee in the administration of a trust may be thus summarized: he must carry out the trust according to its terms; he must use care and diligence; and he must act with the utmost good faith and fidelity. A breach of any of these duties makes him personally liable to the beneficiaries. However, the terms of the trust may limit or preclude such liability; and a beneficiary who is sui juris may release the trustee from liability. Third persons who knowingly participate in a trustee's breach of trust may become liable to the beneficiaries.

The requirement of good faith in the administration of a trust means that the trustee must act honestly and with the highest degree of undivided loyalty to the trust. He must act exclusively in the interests of the trust or the beneficiaries, and may not act in his own interest or in the interest of a third person. He is under duty to avoid situations in which his own interests are brought into conflict with those of the trust. He may not engage in personal trafficking or private use of trust funds or property, and may not engage in any activity in connection with the trust which amounts to self-dealing. He may not obtain any personal benefit or profit from his administration of the trust or from his relation to the trust estate, except such lawful compensation as may be allowed him for his services as trustee. Any such benefit or profit obtained by the trustee inures to the trust estate.

A trustee is required to exercise due care, diligence, and skill in the administration of the trust, and he is liable for all losses resulting to the trust estate from his negligent or wilful failure to meet these requirements. He is not, however, an insurer of the trust estate against losses arising in the administration thereof from errors or mistakes of judgment or from other causes beyond his control, if he meets the standard of care and diligence required of him. The standard usually applied to a trustee is that degree of care, diligence, and skill which an ordinarily prudent man would exercise in the conduct of his private affairs under similar circumstances and with a similar object in view.

It is the duty of a trustee to collect, take possession of, and hold and protect the trust property and assets, and to manage and apply the same to effect the purposes and objects of the trust. In the collection of assets and debts and in the protection of trust property, the trustee has the power to prosecute and defend any actions where such becomes necessary. Where a trust charges the trustee with the continuance and operation of a business, the trustee has the power and duty to carry on the business. The trustee also has the power and duty to make contracts and expenditures requisite to the administration of the trust, although, according to the prevailing general rule, such contracts are made by the trustee on his own responsibility and not as an agent of the trust estate, and the primary liability on such contracts rests upon the trustee. However, he is entitled to exoneration or indemnity from the trust estate for his outlays under proper contracts made by him; and there is a growing tendency to permit recovery directly against the trust estate by the other contracting party.

A trustee is under duty to keep trust funds properly invested. Generally, he may not permit trust funds to lie dormant for a long period. He is under duty to invest such funds in some manner so that they produce income or interest for the benefit of the trust. The question of what are proper investments of trust funds has been the subject of much litigation and of differences of opinion among the courts. Generally speaking, the objectives of trust investments are safety and income for the trust estate, or income consistent with safety, safety being of prime importance. Statutes sometimes specify the permissible or authorized investments for trusts; and the trust instrument may contain directions in this regard and may even authorize the making or retention by the trustee of nonlegal investments.

The terms of a trust may, either expressly or impliedly, give the trustee power to sell trust property, or such power may be conferred by statute, by the court having jurisdiction of the trust, or by consent of the beneficiaries.

In the absence of such an authorization, however, a trustee has no power or duty to sell trust property, and an unauthorized sale by him is generally void, or at least voidable. Similar rules apply with respect to the power of the trustee to mortgage or encumber trust property. The authority of a trustee to lease trust property, which is often the subject of statutory provisions, is commonly found to exist either by virtue of express provisions of the trust instrument or by implication from other powers or duties imposed on the trustee.

It is a well-settled general rule that a trustee is personally liable for injury or damages resulting from a tort committed in the administration of a trust. He is generally held liable also for the torts of agents and servants employed by him. According to the historic rule, still representing the majority view, the trustee's liability for tort is in his individual, and not in his representative, capacity, so that recovery may not be had by the injured person directly against the trust estate. However, the modern tendency is to invent exceptions to this rule and to permit actions against the estate, to avoid circuity of actions. A trustee has the right to reimbursement or indemnity out of the trust estate for sums exacted of him on account of tort liability in connection with the administration of the trust, where the tort did not involve any personal fault or wrongdoing on the part of the trustee. The terms of the trust instrument sometimes relieve the trustee of liability in this regard.

§ 22:8. Charitable trusts.

Am Jur 2d References: Charities, §§ 5–144.

A charitable trust may be broadly defined as one for the benefit of a class of persons indefinite as to identity or number, constituting some portion or class of the public, and in which the property is limited to some kind of public use or benefit. The factor of public benefit is vital to the classification of a trust as charitable.

To guard against the susceptibility of persons in the apprehension of impending death, and against the danger of their being unduly influenced to make charitable gifts which would exclude the natural objects of the donor's bounty, statutory restrictions on the right to make charitable bequests have been enacted in many jurisdictions. Such statutes usually either (1) declare a gift to a charity that is made within a specified time prior to the death of the testator to be invalid, or (2) provide that a testator under certain conditions shall not have the power to give by will more than a certain proportion of his estate for charitable purposes. A gift to a charity which violates such statutes is either void or voidable.

One distinctive feature of a charitable trust is the application thereto of the cy pres doctrine. This doctrine permits a gift for a charitable purpose which cannot, for one reason or another, be carried out as directed by the donor, to be applied as nearly as may be to the fulfilment of the underlying charitable intent. As applied to charities in the United States, the doctrine of cy pres is a doctrine of approximation, and applies or is closely akin to the rule of judicial construction designed to aid the court in ascertaining and carrying out, as nearly as may be, the intention of the donor. The cy pres doctrine is recognized and applied in most American jurisdictions. Even where the doctrine, as such, is not recognized, the courts may still reach substantially the same result by giving effect to the general charitable intention of the trustor. The doctrine may not be invoked unless it is necessary; and it may never be applied to defeat the purpose or intention of the donor. And it is always essential to the application of the cy pres doctrine that a general charitable intent on the part of the donor appear, something beyond the specific terms used in designating the beneficiary or the purpose of the gift or the details as to how it shall be carried into effect.

Where the main charitable purpose is disclosed, directions as to the management of the trust and the precise manner of its application may be regarded as directory rather than mandatory, and the main purpose of the trust may be carried out under the doctrine of cy pres as nearly as possible according to the plan prescribed by the trust instrument. If, however, the charitable purpose is confined to a specific project, objective, or institution, no deviation is permissible under the cy pres doctrine to prevent the gift from failing or the legacy from lapsing. The applicability and administration of the doctrine is always determined by the court having jurisdiction of the trust, and is not left to the discretion of the trustee.

*

WILLS, DESCENT, AND DECEDENTS' ESTATES

I. WILLS

III. ADMINISTRATION OF ESTATES; EXECUTORS AND ADMINISTRATORS

I. WILLS

A. In General; Testamentary Character and Validity

§ 23:1. Generally.

Am Jur 2d References: Wills (1st ed, §§ 2–52, 62, 148–165, 572, 573, 671–679).

A will is an instrument executed by a competent person in the manner prescribed by statute, whereby he makes a disposition of his property (or in some cases merely names an executor), to take effect upon his death. The characteristics of a will are that it manifests the donative intent of the maker, that it neither confers nor evidences an intent to confer upon the donees any property, right, or benefit during the life of the maker, that it has no binding effect during his life, and that it is ambulatory and is revocable in whole or in part at his pleasure. Another requisite of a testamentary instrument is that the maker must have executed the instrument with an intent to make a will. This intent, the animus testandi, may exist even though the testator did not consciously understand that he was making a will, if the instrument contains the essentials of a testamentary disposition and if it is apparent from the instrument that the maker intended to make a disposition of his property to be effective at his death. It is essential to the validity of a will that the testator have known and understood the substance of the contents thereof. The testamentary character of an instrument is determined by its substance and contents, rather than by its form, the name given it by its maker, or the use of technical or legal terms.

The right to dispose of property by will exists in all American jurisdictions. It is a privilege subject to legislative regulation and control, however, and may be exercised only in the manner and subject to the limitations prescribed by statute. A testator may make any disposition of his property not contrary to the law or public policy of the state. The courts will not reject a will on the ground that it is unreasonable or unnatural or because it excludes persons who would inherit in case of intestacy. The right or power to take under a will is subject to regulation by the state. At common law as well as by statute, a person who feloniously kills a testator is not permitted to take any beneficial interest under the will.

In many states, a will is not effectual as to a child born after the execution of the will or one not named or provided for therein, such child taking by inheritance as though the will did not exist.

A will may be valid in respect to some devises or bequests and invalid as to others. Where an invalid gift or clause in a will may be expunged without essentially changing the scheme of the whole will or the particular testamentary disposition in which it appears, the valid portions of the will are upheld and given effect. However, if a rejection of the invalid, and a retention of the valid, provisions would defeat the testator's wishes or result in manifest injustice, or if the valid and invalid provisions are so interdependent that the invalid portions cannot be disregarded and the will given effect without doing violence to the general scheme of the testator, the whole will or the entire disposition in question will be regarded as ineffective.

A will may, by its terms, be conditional or contingent. Such a will is one which is dependent for its operation upon the happening of a specified condition or contingency. If the condition fails, the will is inoperative and void, unless it is republished. Examples of such wills are those to become effective upon the death of the testator from a certain peril or during a certain contemplated trip or voyage. A will is construed to be unconditional in case of doubt on that score. The statement of a contingency as the occasion or inducement for making the will does not render the instrument conditional.

The owner of property may make a binding contract, either to make a will disposing of property in a specified way (see § 23:4, infra), or not to dispose of the property by will but to permit it to descend according to the laws governing intestacy.

§ 23:2. Testamentary capacity.

Am Jur 2d References: Wills (1st ed, §§ 50–147).

The power and capacity to dispose of property by will are subject to legislative regulation by each state. It may be stated generally that any person of legal age and sound mind may make a will. The early disability of married women in this respect has been removed by statutes. The testamentary power of an infant and the age at which a person is competent to make a will depend upon statutory provisions, which vary in the several states. Illiteracy does not disqualify a testator who is mentally competent. The common-law rule by which a felon or traitor forfeited his property to the crown has never been applied in this country, and a convict is as competent as anyone to dispose of his property by will.

The capacity of a person to make a will may be affected by his mental condition, but attempts to establish a universal test of the mental acumen essential to testamentary capacity have not been successful. Not every degree or kind of mental weakness or unsoundness will destroy this capacity; but, on the other hand, incapacity may exist without absolute imbecility or complete insanity. Mental capacity to make a will is not always governed by the same tests that apply to the capacity to make a contract or deed, or to the conduct of one's business. Nor are rules governing criminal responsibility applicable in determining testamentary capacity.

The testator must be able to understand the business in which he is engaged when he makes his will, and to appreciate the effect of the disposition made of his property. If he knows his estate, the object of his affections, and to whom he wishes to give his property, he has sufficient capacity to make a will. A disposing mind and memory is one in which the testator has a full and intelligent consciousness of the nature and effect of the act he is engaged in, a knowledge of the property he possesses, and an understanding of the disposition he wishes to make of it by will, and of the persons and objects he desires to participate in his bounty, or as it is often expressed, a knowledge of the natural objects of his bounty.

There is some difference of opinion as to whether a testator may have capacity to make a simple will disposing of an uncomplicated estate, and yet not have capacity to make a will with complex provisions or one disposing of extensive properties. However, the testator need not comprehend the legal significance of the technical terms in which a will is written by his attorney under his instructions.

Neither old age, physical weakness and infirmity, nor disease is necessarily inconsistent with testamentary capacity, although evidence thereof is generally admissible on the issue of capacity. To a person in such condition, the usual tests as to testamentary capacity will be applied, that is, whether the testator knows the nature and amount of his property and the natural objects of his bounty and understands what he is doing. Blindness, deafness and mutism, or weakness of memory, do not incapacitate a person to make a will. Eccentricity in conduct, appearance, or beliefs, or the existence of unjustified prejudices against particular persons, does not of itself establish testamentary incapacity, unless the condition amounts to an insane delusion.

The time to be looked to in determining the mental capacity of a testator to make a will is the time when the will was executed, although evidence as to his mental condition at other times may be admissible as bearing upon his condition at the time the will was executed. Temporary incapacity does not invalidate a will if it was executed in a lucid interval or at a time when the testator was competent.

Partial insanity invalidates a will which is the direct product thereof. A will which is the result of an insane delusion is invalid for lack of testamentary capacity. Insane delusion, in this connection, may be defined as a belief in things which do not exist, and which no rational mind would believe to exist. The essence of an insane delusion is that it has no basis in reason, cannot be dispelled by reason, and can be accounted for only as the product of mental disorder. To invalidate a will on the ground that the testator was possessed of an insane delusion, it must be shown that the will was the product or offspring of the delusion, and that the delusion influenced him at the time he executed the will, in his determination of the manner in which he should dispose of his property. Religious beliefs and views, no matter how strange or contrary to those generally recognized in the community, cannot alone be the basis of a finding of testamentary incapacity. However, a person may be insane on religion as well as upon any other subject, where a religious belief unsettles the judgment and becomes an insane delusion which usurps the place of reason in making a will.

§ 23:3. Undue influence, fraud, and mistake.

Am Jur 2d References: Wills (1st ed, §§ 349–453).

Undue influence or fraud exerted on a testator and affecting his disposition of his property is a ground for attack on the validity of a will, unless there has been a re-execution or republication of the will. Undue influence in this connection is that which substitutes the wishes of another for those of the testator. To establish undue influence it must appear that as a result of such influence the testator acted not as a free agent, but under the control of another. Undue influence sufficient to invalidate a will is such as overcomes the free volition of the testator and substitutes the purposes of another. It must be such as to control the mental operations of the testator in making his will, and to oblige him to make a disposition of his property which he would not have made if left to act freely according to his own wishes.

Undue influence presupposes pressure brought to bear directly upon the testamentary act with the purpose of procuring a disposition of property in favor of a particular person. No influence upon the testator is sufficient to invalidate a will unless it was directly connected with the execution of the instrument by the testator and was present and operating on his mind at the time of the execution of the will, so as to control the disposition of his property. A general influence over the testator will not invalidate a will unless it is brought to bear upon the testamentary act. The time when the undue influence was exerted is not material if it was present and operating on the mind of the testator at the time the will was executed.

Although any discussion of undue influence presupposes testamentary capacity, it is obvious that the mental condition of the testator may affect the determination of the question of undue influence. It requires less influence to control the will of a person of weak mentality or infirm in health or purpose than one of unimpaired body and mind.

While there is some authority to the contrary, the prevailing rule is that part of a will may be held valid although other parts are invalid because of undue influence exercised upon the testator, provided the parts so affected are separable so that the will remains intelligible in itself if the invalid parts are deleted, and provided the valid and invalid parts are not so interdependent that they cannot be separated without defeating the testator's general intent and scheme of distribution.

Undue influence is closely associated with fraud in the contest of a will. Fraud is frequently a means of exercise of undue influence, which may include both fraud and coercion. However, there may be undue influence invalidating a will without fraud in the legal sense; and fraud may be an independent ground for invalidating a will without any undue influence. As in the case of undue influence, parts of a will may be held valid although other parts have been affected by fraud and are invalid, provided the parts not so affected are separable and comprise a complete will in themselves. Fraud invalidating a will may be an intentional misrepresentation of any fact which influences the testator in the disposition of his property, such as false accusations against one who would be a natural recipient of the testator's bounty. But the fraud must have been operative upon the testator at the time he executed the will, although the fraud may have been practiced at some other time.

A malicious interference with the execution of a will whereby the intention of the testator to name a third person as beneficiary is frustrated is a tort which will sustain an action for damages by the intended beneficiary against the person who interfered.

The general rule in the absence of statute is that the validity of a will is not affected by a mistake of law or fact on the part of the testator, unless fraud or undue influence was perpetrated upon him. This principle has been modified by statute, however, in some jurisdictions. Under the prevailing rule, a will is not invalidated by the fact that the testator was mistaken in the effect of the language thereof or as to the relationship between him and the beneficiaries or other persons.

While a will is not generally subject to reformation on the ground of mistake, under the equitable principles applicable to instruments inter vivos, courts do effectually correct errors in wills as a part of the process of interpretation; and in some states the probate court may strike out severable provisions inserted by a mistake of the scrivener; and where a mistake of an intending testator leads to the execution of the wrong instrument, there is a want of the necessary testamentary intent, and the instrument so executed is not a valid will.

§ 23:4. Agreement to make will.

Am Jur 2d References: Wills (1st ed, §§ 166–216).

A person's right to dispose of his property by will in any way he wishes may be relinquished by contract to devise or bequeath the property in a specified manner, as well as by contract to convey the property. The owner of property may make a valid and binding agreement to dispose of the property by last will and testament to a particular person or in a particular manner, or he may bind himself by contract not to make a will depriving a designated individual of a share in the estate, or not to alter or revoke a will already made. Such a contract is not testamentary in nature and need not be executed with the formalities required of a will. It must, however, meet the prerequisites of valid contracts generally: there must be a mutual assent to the terms of the agreement; there must be a legally sufficient consideration; and the agreement must not contravene the law or public policy.

A contract to devise or bequeath property to a particular person or in a particular way is generally irrevocable by the promisor, so long as the promisee is not in default; and a will executed pursuant to such an agreement cannot be revoked or changed so as to defeat the rights of the promisee.

An action at law will lie against the personal representative of the promisor's estate to recover damages for breach of a contract to devise or bequeath property. An action on the quantum meruit lies to recover on an implied or express agreement to compensate by will for services rendered pursuant to the agreement, the measure of recovery being the reasonable value of the services.

Ordinarily, equity has jurisdiction to enforce an agreement to devise or bequeath property. While such an agreement is not susceptible of execution by the promisor, since he cannot be compelled to make a will during his lifetime and he is beyond the reach of a court after his death, the equivalent of specific performance of such an agreement may be decreed by a court of equity after the promisor's death by ordering those upon whom the legal title to the promisor's property has descended to convey it in accordance with the terms of the agreement. Equity enforces such contracts by impressing a trust upon the property in favor of the promisee, and by following it, after the death of the promisor, into his estate in the hands of his heirs, devisees, personal representatives, and even grantees who are not protected as bona fide purchasers.

In order to obtain equitable relief with respect to a contract to devise or bequeath property, the promisee must comply with the general principles of equity: he must come into equity with clean hands and must offer to do equity; he must show a valuable consideration for the promise to make a will; and it must appear that he has no adequate remedy at law.

§ 23:5. Joint, mutual, and reciprocal wills.

Am Jur 2d References: Wills (1st ed, §§ 680–742).

A "joint" will may be defined as a single testamentary instrument which contains the wills of two or more persons, is executed jointly by them, and disposes of property owned jointly, in common, or in severalty by them. "Mutual" wills are defined as wills executed pursuant to an agreement between two or more persons to dispose of their property in a particular manner, each in consideration of the other. Mutual wills may be in separate instruments or in the same instrument. A joint will may be mutual, but is not necessarily so. "Reciprocal" wills are those in which the testators name each other as beneficiaries under similar testamentary plans. Wills may be strictly reciprocal, each testator leaving his or her entire estate to the survivor, or they may depart from strict reciprocity by including bequests to third persons, without losing their character as reciprocal wills. A joint will may be reciprocal, but is not necessarily so.

By the great weight of modern authority, an instrument is not to be denied probate as a will for the reasons that it was executed by two or more persons purporting to sign as testators, contains bequests which are reciprocal, and was executed pursuant to contract, provided the instrument is not dependent upon the death of the survivor for effectiveness of the will of the first to die, but can be admitted to probate successively upon the death of each testator, as his separate will. If, however, the instrument requires a combination of testamentary dispositions in order to be effective, so that it is inoperative until the death of the survivor, it is invalid as a will. Separate wills whereby each testator bequeaths his property to the other are not invalid, although executed pursuant to a contract or arrangement between the testators.

The general rule is that a will jointly executed by two persons, being in effect the separate will of each of them, is revocable at any time by either of them. And either testator under separate wills with reciprocal bequests can revoke his or her will at pleasure, at least in the absence of fraud or of a contract against revocation. Also, in the absence of a definite agreement not to revoke wills or of circumstances giving rise to a trust, either testator under reciprocal wills has a right to revoke even after the death of the other testator. Although there is some conflict of authority on the question of the effect of a contract against revocation of a joint or reciprocal will, the prevailing view is that such a will may be revoked by either testator, notwithstanding the contract. This does not mean that the obligation of the contract is escaped by revoking the will, but merely that the instrument so revoked will not be admitted to probate as a will. Liability for breach of the contract is generally of no concern to the probate court. A joint or reciprocal will may be revoked by operation of law, as by the marriage of one of the testators.

B. Formal Requisites; Execution, Attestation, and Publication

§ 23:6. Generally.

Am Jur 2d References: Wills (1st ed, §§ 20, 21, 217–348).

In determining whether an instrument is a valid will, the form of words or expressions is unimportant, except as indicating testamentary intent. The statutes of the several states do prescribe certain formalities in the execution of wills, however, and these statutory requirements must be complied with in order to give an instrument validity as a will. Most modern statutes require that a will be in writing, except in some instances of nuncupative wills and informal wills of soldiers and seamen. So long as a will is in writing, it may be upon any kind of material. It may be typewritten or written by hand, with pen and ink or by pencil, or it may be printed. It may be written on two or more sheets of paper, and it may be comprised of two or more separate documents.

A separate instrument may become an integral part of a will under the doctrine of incorporation by reference. A duly executed will may incorporate into itself by appropriate reference a written paper or document which is in existence at the time of the execution of the will, irrespective of whether such document is one executed by the testator or by a third person, whether it is executed or attested as a will, or whether it is in itself a valid instrument, provided the document referred to is identified by clear and satisfactory proof. So incorporated, the extrinsic paper takes effect as part of the will and is admitted to probate as such. To come within this principle, however, the extrinsic document must be in existence at the time the will is executed, and there must be a definite and certain reference to the document so as to permit its identification and to manifest the intention of the testator to incorporate it as a part of the will. The doctrine of incorporation by reference permits the incorporation in a will of a prior will of any person, a contract, a promissory note, a deed, or an informal writing, such as directions written in a book or a list or schedule, provided such document is in existence when the will is executed.

The doctrine of incorporation by reference has been rejected or narrowly restricted in some jurisdictions.

It is generally held that a will must be signed by the testator, although the signature may be by mark, and by statute in some states the signature may be written by a person other than the testator in the latter's presence and at his direction. The statutes of most states require that the signature be at the foot or end of the will.

Attestation consists in witnessing the execution of the will by the testator. The publication of a will consists in the communication by the testator to the attesting witnesses at the time they attest the instrument of his intention that it shall take effect as his will. Publication is required in some states and is unnecessary in others. Attesting witnesses are required by the statutes of most states. The number of such witnesses varies in the several states. It is generally required that the witnesses attest or subscribe the will at the request of the testator. The signatures of attesting witnesses are usually appended to an attestation clause. Statutes frequently provide that the witnesses shall be "credible" or "competent." A person who is interested as a legatee or devisee under the will, or is to derive pecuniary benefit from the will, is generally disqualified to act as an attesting witness. It is generally required that the witnesses subscribe their names in the presence of the testator; and in some jurisdictions it is required that the witnesses subscribe their names in the presence of each other.

§ 23:7. Holographic, nuncupative, and soldiers' and seamen's wills.

Am Jur 2d References: Wills (1st ed, §§ 632–670).

A type of will known as a "holographic" or "olographic" will is recognized under the statutes of many states as a valid testamentary instrument. Such a will is one that is entirely written and signed by the testator in his own handwriting. Where such a will is recognized, the whole thereof must be in the handwriting of the testator, including the date, where a date is required by statute. If any essential part of the will is typewritten (even by the testator himself) or printed, the instrument is not a valid holographic will. Statutory requirements as to attestation and publication do not apply to holographic wills. An informal document, such as a letter, may constitute a valid holographic will if there is clearly a testamentary intent on the part of the writer.

A nuncupative will or testament is one that is not in writing and is made where the testator declares his will orally before witnesses. Such wills were valid under the early common law, at least as regards bequests of personal property; and some states still permit the making of a will by nuncupation, although the statutes limit the privilege of making such a will in respect to the circumstances under which it can be exercised and the kind of property which can be bequeathed thereby. It is generally held that an oral or nuncupative will can be made only when the testator is in his last illness; and according to some authorities, but not all, the requirement as to last illness means that the testator must be in extremis.

The wills of soldiers and sailors have from early times been excepted from the formalities required in the execution of wills generally. Under most statutes such wills may be either oral or written. The circumstances under which such wills may be made, and the necessity that the testator be in active service or at sea at the time the will is made, vary under the statutes of the several states. A soldier's or seaman's informal will, oral or written, remains in effect after the testator's return from the sea or from military service, until actual revocation by him.

C. Revocation or Change

§ 23:8. Generally; revocation by later instrument.

Am Jur 2d References: Wills (1st ed, §§ 454–492, 517).

A will or a part thereof may be revoked in several different ways. A revocation may result from a later will containing an express revocation clause or making an inconsistent disposition of property. A will may be revoked by the intentional destruction thereof by the testator. And revocation may result by operation of law because of changes in the circumstances of the testator after the execution of the will. The revocation of wills is largely a matter of statutory regulation. Where a statute specifies the manner in which a will may be revoked, the terms of the statute must be followed in order to effect a revocation. Generally, a written will cannot be revoked by parol statements. Revocation depends upon the intention of the testator and requires an overt act accompanied by an intent to revoke. One lacking testamentary capacity cannot revoke a will made when he possessed such capacity.

A will may not only be revoked by an express statement of revocation in a later will, but by implication where the later will is completely inconsistent with the earlier one, as where the later will makes a different disposition of all of the testator's property. An implied revocation by later will may affect only part of the earlier will or part of the testator's property. This results where there is inconsistency between some but not all of the provisions of the wills. In such cases, both instruments may be probated together as the will of the testator.

The doctrine of dependent relative revocation, discussed in § 23:9, infra, may be applied to a revocation effected by a later document as well as to revocation by cancellation or destruction. This doctrine is a rule of the presumed intention of the testator. The question whether a will containing dispositive provisions and a clause revoking a prior will should be held to revoke the prior will, where the dispositive provisions fail for some reason other than the manner of execution of the instrument, depend upon the intent of the testator determined from the whole will.

A will is revocable notwithstanding an express provision therein against revocation, or a contract binding the testator to make the will, although there may be liability on the contract.

§ 23:9. Destruction or alteration of will.

Am Jur 2d References: Wills (1st ed, §§ 493–516).

A later testamentary act is not the only means by which a testator may revoke his will. The statutes of the several states provide for revocation by various acts physically destructive of the will, performed by the testator or in his presence and by his direction, and with the intent to revoke the will. Such revocation may be effected by burning, tearing, canceling, or obliterating a will. In order that an act shall have the effect of revoking a will, however, the intention to revoke must clearly appear. A destruction or mutilation which is done accidentally or by mistake does not operate as a revocation. However, the intent to revoke may be inferred from the nature of the testator's act, or it may be shown by extrinsic evidence. Statutes in some states provide for revocation in this manner either in toto or as to certain parts of a will.

A testator cannot vary the terms of his will after it has been executed and attested, by additions, interlineations, obliterations, erasures, or other changes made upon the face of the instrument which give a new meaning to the part altered or to other provisions of the will, unless such changes are executed and attested in the manner provided by law for the making of the will, or unless the will is republished in its amended form. The interlineation by the testator of a word, name, paragraph, clause, or a new and independent bequest, after the will has been executed and attested, does not work a revocation of the will.

Under the so-called "doctrine of dependent relative revocation," which is also termed "provisional," or "conditional," revocation, the established rule is that if a testator cancels or destroys a will with a present intention of making a new one immediately and as a substitute, and the new will is not made, or if made, is not effective, it will be presumed that the testator preferred the old will to intestacy, and the old testament will be admitted to probate in the absence of evidence overcoming the presumption, provided its contents can be ascertained. The doctrine is a rule of presumed intention rather than a substantive rule of law, and the presumption will not prevail as against actual evidence of the testator's intention. The doctrine of dependent relative revocation applies to a partial as well as to an entire revocation.

§ 23:10. Revocation by operation of law.

Am Jur 2d References: Wills (1st ed, §§ 521–571).

The doctrine of revocation by operation of law is to the effect that the revocation of a will is to be implied from certain changes in the family or domestic relations of the testator, or in his property or estate, or involving the beneficiaries of his will, from which the law infers or presumes that he intended a change, either total or partial, in the disposition of his property. The doctrine is expressly affirmed by statute in some states, but it is not recognized in all jurisdictions. At common law, a change in the testator's property or estate, no less than a change in his family, revoked his will by operation of law, the theory being that the interest which the testator had when he made the will must continue until his death if the will is to be effective. But a mere increase in the estate or change in its relative value is immaterial in this connection. This common-law rule has been changed in many jurisdictions by statute. It is clear, of course, that where a testator, subsequently to the execution of a will specifically devising lands, voluntarily conveys the lands by an absolute conveyance, the will is revoked to that extent.

At common law the will of a man was not revoked merely by his subsequent marriage, but the marriage of a woman generally revoked any will that she had previously made. However, statutes in many states expressly provide that the will of a man is revoked by his subsequent marriage; and statutes have modified in various ways the rule with respect to women.

A divorce of the testator or testatrix from the bonds of matrimony does not in itself revoke his or her previously executed will. However, statutes have altered this rule in some jurisdictions; and it is generally held that a property settlement in connection with divorce proceedings revokes a prior will of one of the spouses.

§ 23:11. — Revocation upon birth of child.

Am Jur 2d References: Wills (1st ed, §§ 572–604).

Under the rule prevailing at common law, the birth of a child after the execution of a will by its father does not revoke the will where the will was executed after the marriage of the testator. However, the marriage of a man and the birth to the union of a child capable of inheriting from him, both events occurring after the execution of his will, revoked the will so as to permit the after-born child to take his share as an heir of the testator, in the absence of a provision for the benefit of the child, or of anything in the will to indicate that it was made in contemplation of marriage. The birth of a posthumous child is within this rule. A similar rule is applied to the will of a woman, under modern statutes removing the disabilities of married women.

In many states the effect of the birth of issue, on a will previously made, is controlled by statute. While the statutes vary in phraseology, they provide in effect that where the testator has a child born after the making of his will, either in the lifetime or after the death of the testator, such birth operates as a revocation of the will, thereby permitting the child to share in the testator's estate, unless the child is named or provided for by the will, or the will was made in contemplation of the contingency of a birth of a child to the testator, or it clearly appears that it was the intention of the testator to disinherit such child. Some statutes provide that a child of the testator shall share in the estate as though the testator had died intestate, unless the child was named in or provided for by the will, or it is apparent that the testator intended to omit him; and after-born children, as well as those living at the time of the execution of the will, may be within the protection of such a statute. In the absence of special statutory provisions, the question whether a will is revoked by the subsequent birth of an illegitimate child would seem to depend largely upon whether the illegitimate child would share in the estate as an heir in the absence of a will.

§ 23:12. Revival and republication.

Am Jur 2d References: Wills (1st ed, §§ 615–631).

A will which has been revoked may be revived. Some authorities hold that a revival can be effected only by a new testamentary act on the part of the testator in re-executing or republishing the will, at least where the will has been revoked by a will containing an express revocation. And where a will has been revoked by operation of law, as by marriage or the birth of a child, it can be revived only by a valid re-execution or republication. A will which has been revoked by a second will may be revived by a third will which revokes the second will, provided the intention to revive it clearly appears. And apart from questions of revival, the contents of the revoked will may be incorporated by reference in a third will.

Conflicting views are expressed on the question whether the revocation of a later will, effected by the destruction thereof, operates to revive an earlier will which was revoked by the will so destroyed. Some authorities hold that the first will, which has been preserved by the testator, is revived by the destruction or cancellation of the second will which revoked the first one, at least where the second will contains no revocation clause and its effect as a revocation is implied. Other authorities hold that the revocation of a subsequent will, effected by its destruction, does not revive a prior will, at least where the subsequent will contains an express revocation clause. Some authorities hold that the question of revival of an earlier will under such circumstances depends upon the intention of the testator, although there are diverse views as to the necessity and manner of showing such intention. The courts are not agreed on the question whether the provisions of a will which are modified or revoked by a codicil are restored to their original form and effect by the destruction of the codicil with intent to revoke it.

As already observed, the re-execution or republication of a will is essential in various situations to validate alterations in the will or to revive a revoked will. Under the prevailing rule, such a republication may not be effected by parol, but must be made with the same solemnity and formality as was required in the execution and attestation of the original will.

A duly executed codicil operates as a republication of the original will and makes it speak from the new date, insofar as it is not altered or revoked by the codicil. The weight of authority supports the rule that such a codicil amounts to a republication of a prior will or codicil which was invalid because defectively executed. A will which was invalid as originally executed, for want of testamentary capacity or because of fraud or undue influence, is validated and republished by the execution of a codicil thereto by the testator at a time when he had testamentary capacity and was not subject to fraud or undue influence. A will which has been revoked by the testator but is still in existence is republished and revived by the execution of a codicil thereto. And a will which has been revoked by operation of law, consequent upon the subsequent marriage of the testator or birth of a child to him, is revived by republication accomplished by the execution of a codicil thereto subsequent to the marriage or birth of the child. Generally, the republication of a will is a revival of codicils to the will, in the absence of a manifest intention of the testator to the contrary.

§ 23:13. Codicils.

Am Jur 2d References: Wills (1st ed, §§ 605–614).

A codicil is some addition to or qualification of a will. It is not necessary that codicils be actually attached to the will, but when it is a separate document the codicil must refer to and identify the will with reasonable certainty. A codicil may republish or revive a will which has been revoked or is otherwise ineffective.

A will and a codicil thereto are to be regarded as a single and entire instrument, taking effect at the time of the testator's death. They are to be construed together as if they had both been executed at the time of the making of the codicil, in the absence of a manifest intention to the contrary. A codicil republishes the will, and the several parts of a will and codicil should, if possible, be harmonized if this can be done without contravening the general intent and purpose of the testator as disclosed by the entire instrument. Where a will and codicil are inconsistent, the codicil, being the latest expression of the testator's desires, is to be given precedence, provisions of the will which are inconsistent with those of the codicil being deemed revoked by implication.

However, a disposition made by the will is not to be disturbed further than absolutely necessary to give effect to the codicil.

D. PROBATE AND CONTEST

§ 23:14. Generally.

Am Jur 2d References: Wills (1st ed, §§ 743–968, 995–1019).

Statutes in all states provide procedure for the probate of wills. Probate consists of proving, establishing, and recording an instrument as a last will and testament. Although the common law was otherwise, statutes today generally require that wills be probated, so that a will may not be admitted in evidence as the foundation of a right or title unless it has been duly probated. The person having the custody of a will is generally under obligation to produce the instrument for probate upon the death of the testator. Suppression or concealment of a will by a person under obligation to produce it for probate may result in criminal punishment or forfeiture of rights under the will.

It is generally held that a will probated in the court of one state or country is not effective as a muniment or conveyance of title to property situated in another state or country until the will has been proved and recorded in the latter jurisdiction, unless a statute dispenses with the necessity of ancillary probate in such jurisdiction. There is, however, some authority to the contrary; and the necessity and manner of ancillary probate are subject to regulation by local statutes.

Jurisdiction to probate wills is conferred upon courts denominated probate courts, surrogate courts, orphans' courts, or special courts, or upon district courts, county courts, circuit courts, or other courts of general jurisdiction acting as probate courts.

The purpose of a proceeding to contest a will is to divest the legatees and devisees of rights in the estate of the testator, and to vest the property in his heirs at law or in the beneficiaries named in another will. In this country, the right to contest a will is based upon statute and must be exercised in accordance with the provisions of the statute. The issue to be determined where an application to probate a will is opposed by proper pleading, or where it is sought to contest the will after probate, is whether the instrument offered is the valid last will and testament of the decedent. The questions arising in such proceedings concern the testamentary character of the instrument propounded; the testator's knowledge of the contents of the instrument and his intent to execute it as his will; the question of the factum of the will, executed and attested in the manner and form required by statute, at a time when the testator had the requisite power and capacity to make a will; whether the will is invalidated by mistake, fraud, duress, or undue influence; and whether the will has been revoked. In some jurisdictions, the grounds upon which a will may be contested are specified by statutes.

Statutes generally specify the persons who have a right to contest a will. Under statutes permitting the contest of wills by persons interested or claiming to be interested in the decedent's estate, the general rule is that the contestant must have some pecuniary or beneficial interest in the estate of the decedent that is detrimentally affected by the will. A person may be estopped to contest a will: such an estoppel may arise from unreasonable delay in exercising the right to contest the will; by the assumption of an inconsistent position which renders it inequitable for him to contest the will; or by the acceptance of benefits under the will.

Persons having or claiming an interest in a decedent's estate may compromise by valid agreement. A person contesting a will may make his separate peace with legatees or propounders, and a beneficiary under a will may make such settlement as he sees fit with one or more of the contestants. And a bona fide agreement by one interested in the estate of a testator to refrain from contesting the will is valid if it is based upon a good consideration and is not tainted by fraud or duress. Family settlements of will controversies are favored and encouraged by the law, even though such a settlement involves the withholding of the will from probate.

§ 23:15. Lost or destroyed wills.

Am Jur 2d References: Wills (1st ed, §§ 969–990).

Wills that have been lost or destroyed may, in some circumstances, be probated by following the procedure and conditions prescribed by statutes. The loss of a will or its destruction under conditions not effecting its revocation do not preclude the probate of the will. Statutes providing for the proof of such wills impose various conditions, such as that the will be shown to have been destroyed without the knowledge or consent of the testator.

Parol or other secondary evidence is admissible to prove the due execution and the contents of an alleged lost or destroyed will. This includes testimony of the subscribing witnesses and declarations of the testator. However, the proof of the execution, loss or destruction, and contents of the will, must be clear and convincing.

E. Construction and Interpretation

§ 23:16. Generally; rules of construction.

Am Jur 2d References: Wills (1st ed, §§ 1020–1039, 1120–1164).

It is the function of a court, in the construction of a will, to ascertain the intention of the testator as to the disposition of his property and to carry it into effect, not to reconstruct or reform the will. Unless a will is ambiguous or its meaning is uncertain, there is no occasion to invoke the rules of construction.

Among the canons of construction generally recognized and applied by the courts are the following: The law favors that construction of an ambiguous will which conforms most nearly to the general law of inheritance applicable in cases of intestacy; the court should, if possible, adopt a construction which will render the will valid and effective, rather than one which would make it illegal or invalid; where a will contains provisions which are apparently inconsistent or repugnant, every effort should be made to construe the instrument so as to harmonize the conflicting parts; and effect should be given, if possible, to all words, clauses, and provisions of the will unless this is inconsistent with the intent manifested by the instrument as a whole.

The "ejusdem generis" rule is applicable, under the proper circumstances, in the construction of wills. This means that where certain things are enumerated and a more general description is coupled with the enumeration, the general expressions are understood to cover only things ejusdem generis, that is, of a like kind, with those specifically enumerated. However, this principle must yield to the testator's intention as expressed in the whole instrument.

The paramount rule in the interpretation of wills, to which all other rules of construction are subordinate, is that the intention of the testator is to be ascertained and given effect. All other canons of construction are designed to ascertain and give effect to the intention of the testator. However, the testatorial intention, even where clearly ascertainable, must yield to an established rule of law or public policy if it is in conflict therewith, as where the terms of a will disregard the rule in Shelley's Case or the rule against perpetuities.

The intention of the testator is to be ascertained from the language of the will, considered in its entirety, read in the light of all of the circumstances surrounding the testator and the execution of the will, including the condition, nature, and extent of the testator's property, his relations with his family and the beneficiaries named in the will, the financial condition of various beneficiaries, and the relative amounts of advancements made to different beneficiaries.

In construing a will it should be read in the ordinary and grammatical sense of the words employed, and the words will be given their ordinary and natural meaning, unless a different meaning is indicated by the context. Technical words in a will should be construed according to their technical meaning, as established by reference to the science or art to which they are peculiar, unless it appears from the will that they were used in a different sense. Allowances will be made, however, for the fact that a will was drafted by a layman.

Although the testator's punctuation and capitalization may be taken into consideration in construing his will, they must give way whenever they interfere with the proper and reasonable construction of the will, and conflict with the natural sense in which the words are used.

Certain legal principles governing the interpretation of wills are commonly laid down in the form of presumptions—all of which are subject to the controlling effect of the testator's manifest intention. Where a will has been executed, the reasonable presumption is that the testator intends to dispose of his entire estate and does not intend to die intestate as to any part thereof. In cases of doubt, there is a presumption against an intention on the part of a testator to disinherit his legal heirs. And it is frequently stated that the testator is presumed to have been acquainted with the rules of law that might have some bearing upon the devolution of his property at his decease.

§ 23:17. Extrinsic evidence to aid interpretation.

Am Jur 2d References: Wills (1st ed, §§ 1040–1119, 1144).

The admissibility of extrinsic evidence to aid in the construction of wills is broadly governed by three basic rules: (1) Extrinsic evidence is not admissible to vary, contradict, or add to the terms of a will, or to show a different intention on the part of the testator from that disclosed by the language of the will.

(2) Where a will contains no ambiguity, latent or patent, and can be carried into effect without the aid of extrinsic evidence, such evidence is not admissible to show the intention of the testator or to give the language of will a meaning different from that which the law attributes thereto. (3) Extrinsic evidence is admissible to explain, interpret, or apply an ambiguous will. Although the extensive literature of the law in this field involves many amplifications and refinements of these principles, and the manner of their application must vary with the circumstances and problems involved in the particular case, these three fundamental rules ultimately govern the admissibility of parol or extrinsic evidence in the interpretation of wills.

The admissibility of extrinsic evidence is often made to depend upon the nature of the ambiguity sought to be resolved. If the ambiguity is patent, such evidence, according to this view, is not admissible; if the ambiguity is latent, it is. A patent ambiguity, within the meaning of this principle, is one which appears upon the face of the will; a latent ambiguity is one which is not discoverable from a perusal of the will but which appears upon consideration of the extrinsic circumstances, as, for example, a bequest to "my cousin John," it appearing that the testator has two or more cousins named John. In view of the numerous cases admitting some extrinsic evidence where the indefiniteness, inaccuracy, or ambiguity was apparent on the face of the instrument, it is clear that the above statement of the rule with respect to patent ambiguities is too broad. A more accurate statement of the rule is that extrinsic evidence is admissible to show the situation of the testator and all the relevant facts and circumstances surrounding him at the time of the making of the will, for the purpose of resolving even a patent ambiguity.

It is frequently stated as a corollary of the broad doctrine that extrinsic evidence is not competent to vary or add to the terms of a will, that an unintentional or inadvertent omission of a provision, word, or name intended to be inserted in a will cannot be shown or supplied by such evidence in a proceeding involving the construction of a will, in the absence of fraud; and extrinsic evidence is not generally admissible to show or correct a mistake in an unambiguous will, since the evidence in such a situation would operate to contradict the will. It is a general rule that extrinsic evidence is not admissible to fill a blank appearing on the face of a will or to determine the person or property intended by the testator, where there is a total failure to designate any. If, however, there is a sufficient description in the will to identify the legatee or devisee, the mere existence of a blank in the place left for his name does not defeat the gift or preclude extrinsic evidence to aid the description. And under the doctrine of false demonstration or "falsa demonstratio non nocet," parol evidence may be received to enable the court to strike out or disregard the false or erroneous part of the description in a will and to apply the remaining part to determine the person or property designated thereby, where enough remains of the description to form the basis of such identification.

Where the circumstances are such as to permit the introduction of extrinsic evidence to aid in the interpretation of a will, any kind of written or parol evidence, not excluded under the general rules of evidence, will be admitted if it throws light upon the meaning of ambiguous language in the instrument or upon the situation of the testator and the circumstances surrounding him at the time of the making of the will. Thus, to aid in resolving an ambiguity in a will, the habits, custom, or usage of the testator with respect to the use of words, names, nicknames, or descriptions, and the testator's relations, affections, and feelings toward persons affected by the will, may be shown by extrinsic evidence to aid in determining the testator's intention.

It is frequently stated by the courts that extrinsic evidence is not admissible to prove directly the intention of the testator, as an independent fact and without reference to the language of the will. However, where the will contains a latent ambiguity or equivocation, so that its terms are applicable indifferently to two or more persons or properties, it is generally held that direct evidence of the testator's intention is admissible. The same principles are generally applicable to declarations of the testator himself, the great weight of authority supporting the rule that declarations of the testator, to the scrivener or another person, are admissible where there is a latent ambiguity or equivocation as to the person or property intended.

§ 23:18. Particular interpretive problems.

Am Jur 2d References: Wills (1st ed, §§ 1165–1398).

The interpretive problems which may confront the court in connection with wills are of almost infinite variety. As observed in the preceding sections, the solution of such problems involves a determination of the intention of the testator.

Although, for purposes of interpretation, a will must be considered with reference to the circumstances existing at the time of its execution, it is well settled that a will speaks as of, and takes effect only upon, the death of the testator. Hence, property acquired by the testator after the execution of a will passes under a devise or bequest otherwise broad enough to include it, unless a contrary intention of the testator is shown.

The use of precatory words in a will, that is, words whose ordinary significance imports entreaty, recommendation, or expectation rather than any mandatory direction, such as "desire," "request," "wish," etc., frequently raises a question as to whether they were intended to be testamentary and dispositive in nature and tantamount to such outright words of gift as "devise" or "bequeath." Such language in a will is sometimes held to create a precatory trust, although the courts are generally reluctant to adopt such a construction unless it clearly appears to have been the testator's intention.

Questions as to the scope and meaning of numerous words and phrases used in describing testamentary beneficiaries have come before the courts. One of these is the term "children," which is a technical word, primarily one of purchase, not of limitation, and imports only immediate descendants. However, it may be construed as a word of limitation and as the equivalent of "heirs" where the will requires such a construction. In the absence of a contrary context or statute, it is generally held that the word "child" or "children" as used in a will should not be construed as including adopted children; but the intention of the testator to the contrary, as shown by the will as a whole in the light of the circumstances surrounding him, may require the inclusion of adopted children. The term "child" or "children" does not generally include grandchildren. In the absence of an apparent intention of the testator to the contrary, these words will apply to children born after the making of the will, including the testator's posthumous children.

The word "heir" or "heirs," while technically a term of limitation, may be treated as a word of purchase where such appears to have been the intention of the testator. The primary and presumptive meaning of the word "heirs," as used in a will, denotes those persons who would have taken the property of the testator if he had died intestate. However, if it is clear that the testator used the word in a different sense, "heir" may be interpreted as equivalent to "child" or "next of kin." Whether the term "heirs" includes adopted children ultimately depends upon the testator's intention; but in the absence of any clear indication of such intention, the applicable statute relating to the adoption of children or descent of property in intestate succession may be determinative of the question.

While the term "next of kin," as used in a will is ordinarily construed as including only blood relatives of the testator or other propositus, where the intention of the testator to include other persons, such as a surviving spouse, is made to appear, such intention will be respected. The term "issue," as used in a will, is primarily a word of limitation, but it will be treated as a word of purchase where the will indicates that such was the intention of the testator. The word generally includes descendants of every degree, unless the will and the surrounding circumstances show an intention to limit the term to mean "children," "grandchildren," or the like. The term "issue" includes a child conceived but not born at the time when the class is to be determined. Whether the term includes adopted children or stepchildren depends, of course, upon the intention of the testator, as shown by the will and the surrounding circumstances.

Many difficult interpretative problems arise in connection with gifts to a class. A widely accepted definition of a class gift is that of Jarman: "A gift of an aggregate sum to a body of persons uncertain in number at the time of the gift, to be ascertained at a future time, who are to take in equal or some other definite proportions, the share of each being dependent for its amount upon the ultimate number" of the persons—although there is some criticism of the requirements of "a body of persons uncertain in number" and of an "aggregate sum." Many refinements of theory have been applied to the determination of when a gift is one to a class and to the question of membership in a class. However, these questions depend ultimately upon the intention of the testator. The primary incidents of a class gift are survivorship and the admission of after-born members. Thus, the death of a person coming within a group designation prior to the death of the testator will not result in a lapse of such person's share but will merely augment the shares of the other members of the class; and the birth of other persons who come within the group or class designation has the effect of reducing the portions of the original members of the class so as to assure to the new members their designated portion of the total gift.

It is often both important and difficult to determine whether beneficiaries under a will are to take per capita or per stirpes. If they take per capita they share by heads, share and share alike. Those who take per stirpes take in the aggregate and by representation or substitution the share of their deceased ancestor. It has been frequently stated that where the intention of the testator is not clear from the language of the will and the circumstances surrounding its execution, distribution of a gift per stirpes rather than per capita is favored. However, the intention of the testator is always the controlling factor.

F. Legacies and Devises

§ 23:19. Generally; classification.

Am Jur 2d References: Wills (1st ed, §§ 1399–1423, 1503–1525, 1574–1578, 1606–1618).

Testamentary gifts are classified broadly according to whether their subject is land or personal property, those involving land being designated "devises," and those involving personalty, "legacies" or "bequests." Legacies are commonly classified as "specific," demonstrative," or "general," each type having certain recognized incidents, which are discussed in the sections which follow.

These incidents may be thus summarized: specific legacies do not abate in the event of a deficiency of assets, but are subject to ademption in the event of the disposal of the subject matter by the testator during his lifetime; general legacies are payable out of the general estate of the testator and hence are not dependent upon the latter's continued ownership of any specific property, but are subject to abatement in the event of a deficiency of assets to pay all of the gifts made in the will; and demonstrative legacies are not subject to ademption in the event of the disposal of the fund designated for their payment, but are payable from the general assets of the estate, and do not abate with the general legacies except in the event of the disposal by the testator prior to his death of the fund primarily designated for their payment. Specific legacies, unlike general and demonstrative legacies, carry with them any accretions arising after the death of the testator.

A specific legacy may be defined as a bequest of a particular, individualized chattel, fund, or portion of the testator's personal estate, which is set apart from the balance of his property and which is differentiated from all other articles or funds of the same or similar nature. It may be satisfied only by delivery of the specific object, fund, or portion designated, and not by the receipt of some equivalent in money or property. A general legacy is one which is designated primarily by quantity or amount and which may be satisfied out of the general assets of the testator, without the necessity of delivering any particular chattel or fund to the legatee. A demonstrative legacy partakes of the nature of both general and specific legacies. It is a gift of money or property payable out of or charged on a particular fund or other property in such a way as not to amount to a gift of the corpus of the fund or property charged or to evince an intent to relieve the general estate from liability in case of the failure of such fund or property. Two elements are necessary to constitute a demonstrative legacy: (1) it must appear that the testator intended to make an unconditional gift in the nature of a general legacy; and (2) the legacy must be given with reference to a particular fund or particular property as a primary source of payment.

The nature of a legacy as specific, general, or demonstrative is to be determined in accordance with the intention of the testator, as gathered from the will as a whole and the circumstances surrounding the testator at the time of its execution. The inclination of the courts is to construe legacies of a doubtful nature as general or demonstrative rather than specific.

A general residuary clause in a will is one which employs some broad terms such as "property" or "estate" and hence is sufficient to carry all classes and kinds of property; but a residuary gift may be expressly limited to a certain fund or to a particular kind of property. The residue of an estate passing under such a clause is that which remains after discharging all legal and testamentary claim on the estate, or in other words, that which is left after the payment of charges, debts, and particular legacies. While the traditional words for a residuary gift are the "rest, residue and remainder of my estate," or some close variant thereof, it is recognized that no particular language or formula is necessary to create a residuary gift. In determining what property is included in a residuary clause, the courts apply the general presumption that the testator did not intend to die intestate as to any of his property.

A testator may attach to a gift in his will any lawful terms and conditions that he pleases, although his intention to create a condition must clearly appear. Conditions which are regarded as contrary to law or public policy, which are impossible of performance, or which are too vague and uncertain to disclose the actual intention of the testator, will not be enforced. Conditions are of two kinds, conditions precedent and conditions subsequent. A condition precedent is that which must take place before an estate can vest, while a condition subsequent is that which operates on an estate devised and renders it liable to be divested for breach of the condition. A devise of real estate subject to a condition precedent which in its inception is impossible of performance or which has subsequently become impossible to perform fails and is not an effective gift, even though there was no default on the part of the devisee, and the property passes under the residuary clause or as intestate estate, as the case may be. But when a condition subsequent is or becomes impossible of performance, except through the donee's own fault, the gift remains in effect discharged of the condition. The rules relating to the effect of the invalidity of a testamentary condition are similar to those relating to the effect of the impossibility of the performance of a condition. As regards conditions precedent, some courts make a distinction between gifts of real property and of personal property.

A legacy to a creditor of the testator equal to or greater in amount than the indebtedness will be presumed, in the absence of anything to indicate a contrary intention, to have been intended as a satisfaction of the debt. There are situations, however, in which this presumption does not apply, as where the debt consists of an obligation to pay money and the testamentary provision is a legacy of specific chattels or a devise of real estate, or where the will contains an express direction for the payment of the testator's "debts" or "debts and legacies."

§ 23:20. Lapse.

Am Jur 2d References: Wills (1st ed, §§ 1424–1456).

The term "lapse" is used to indicate generally any falling back of a legacy or devise, or its subject, into the testator's estate. While the usual occasion for a lapse is that where a legatee or devisee dies before the testator, the expression "lapse" is frequently employed with reference to other situations, such as the dissolution of a corporate donee prior to the testator's death, the renunciation of a testamentary gift by the legatee or devisee, or the impossibility of the happening of a contingency subject to which a testamentary gift is made.

It is a well-settled general rule that a devise or legacy in favor of a person individually, and not jointly with others, will lapse upon the death of the donee in the lifetime of the testator, unless the testator has indicated a contrary intention or a statute necessitates a different result. Gifts to a class, however, such as gifts to "children," "brothers and sisters," or "nephews and nieces" of a designated person, are generally construed, in the absence of the indication of a contrary intent on the part of the testator, as including only those members of the class who are alive at the death of the testator, so that the death during the testator's lifetime of one or more of the individuals included in the class does not result in a lapse of his or their share, the shares of the surviving members merely being enlarged to that extent. The same result is reached where the language of a testamentary gift is such as to indicate an intention to create a joint tenancy in several people, whether they constitute a technical class or not, the surviving joint tenants in such case taking the whole.

Where a will makes a gift of a life estate followed by a remainder, and the life tenant dies during the lifetime of the testator, it is held, in the absence of contrary context, that the remainder interest is not defeated by the life tenant's death, but takes effect upon the testator's death.

In all situations, the question whether a legacy or devise shall lapse or not is subject to the testator's intention. It is clear that a testator can prevent the lapse of a legacy by providing for the substitution of another beneficiary in case the original beneficiary predeceases the testator. Statutes in many jurisdictions have modified in various respects the common-law doctrine of lapse.

It is well settled that, in the absence of a residuary clause or other indication of the testator's intention to the contrary, the subject matter of a lapsed or ineffectual legacy or devise passes as intestate property to those who would be entitled to take under the statutes of descent and distribution. It is also well established, both at common law and under modern statutes, that the subject matter of a lapsed or ineffectual legacy of personal property will, in the absence of a contrary testatorial intention, pass under a general residuary clause and does not descend as intestate property to the testator's next of kin. At common law, this rule did not apply to lapsed or ineffectual devises of real property, such property not passing under a general residuary clause but descending to the testator's heirs in the absence of any showing of a contrary intention. However, in most jurisdictions today a general residuary clause will, in the absence of an indicated contrary intention, carry lapsed or ineffectual gifts of both real and personal property.

§ 23:21. Abatement; application of assets.

Am Jur 2d References: Wills (1st ed, §§ 1457–1502).

"Abatement" in the law of wills means the reduction of testamentary gifts because of the insufficiency of the testator's estate to pay all of such gifts in full after the payment of debts and charges against the estate. The priority of different classes of bequests and devises in the process of abatement has been established by the courts and in some instances by statutes.

Where the intention of the testator as to the abatement of legacies is not ascertainable from the language of the will, the following principles are generally applied: Residuary legacies must first be exhausted; as between general and demonstrative legacies, the former must be first absorbed, unless the fund designated in the will as the source for the payment of the demonstrative legacies is not in existence at the testator's death, in which event the demonstrative legacies abate pro rata with the general legacies; and specific legacies do not abate in favor of general ones, which, as between the two, must first be exhausted in the payment of debts. As between legacies of the same class, whether general, demonstrative, or specific, abatement is pro rata. The same principles are generally applied in determining questions of abatement as between devises of real property and as between such devises and legacies or bequests of personal property, although some courts, applying the general principle that personal property is the primary source for the payment of indebtedness, hold that specific legacies must abate in favor of specific devises.

All of the foregoing rules are subject to two paramount principles: (1) The intention of the testator, as declared or ascertainable, governs the manner or order of abatement of any kind of legacy or devise; and (2) a legacy to the testator's widow in lieu of dower is given preference and priority over other legacies and devices in determining questions of abatement. An exception to the rule of pro rata abatement of legacies of the same class is required in the case of a legacy given for the support or maintenance of a near relative, or for the payment of a debt of the testator or otherwise founded upon a valuable consideration.

The personal property of a decedent is the primary fund for the payment of his debts, whether he leaves a will or dies intestate. Accordingly, resort will not be had to the real estate until the available personal property has been exhausted. However, real property which passes as intestate estate is to be used for the payment of debts next after the general personal estate, and many authorities hold that such real property is to be invaded even before personalty which is particularly bequeathed. Clearly, personal property undisposed of by the will must be used for the payment of debts before property which is specifically bequeathed or devised; and as between land passing as intestate estate and personalty so passing, the latter must be first used for the payment of debts. All these rules are subject to change by the expressed intention of the testator. A testator may charge his real estate, or particular real property, with the payment of his debts, and he may exonerate his personal property or a designated part thereof, from liability for the payment of his debts, if his real estate is of sufficient value to satisfy the claims of his creditors.

The devisee of real estate subject to a lien created by the testator is entitled, as between himself and a residuary legatee, to have such liens paid from the residuary estate in exoneration of the land devised; but the devisee is not entitled to such exoneration as against specific legatees.

In the absence of a controlling statutory provision or the expression of a contrary testatorial intention, the personal property of a testator is not only the primary, but indeed the exclusive fund for the payment of his legacies, and if the personal estate is not sufficient to pay all the general or pecuniary bequests contained in the will, they must abate. However, the testator may in his will provide that a legacy shall be a charge upon designated property, real or personal. A legacy charged on land is, when the devise is accepted, not only a debt of the devisee enforceable at law, but an equitable charge or lien upon the land devised, enforceable in equity.

§ 23:22. Ademption.

Am Jur 2d References: Wills (1st ed, §§ 1579–1605).

The ademption of a testamentary gift is the extinction or satisfaction thereof by some act of the testator equivalent to its revocation or clearly indicative of an intention to revoke, or by the destruction or disposal of or change in the subject matter of the bequest or devise. The sale or other disposal of real or personal property by a testator after making a specific devise or bequest thereof operates as an ademption of the devise or bequest. The proceeds of the sale, or other property acquired by the testator, cannot be substituted so as to avoid the ademption, unless the proceeds or substituted property come within the description of the devise or bequest. Abatement by disposal or destruction of the subject matter of the gift does not apply as against general legacies or demonstrative legacies, but only against specific legacies.

Where a testator, after the execution of his will, transfers money or property to persons in whose favor he has made general or pecuniary legacies, the question whether such legacies are adeemed is dependent upon the testator's intention. If the legatee is a child of the testator, it is generally presumed that such advances were intended to be in satisfaction of the legacy, and not to constitute a double portion. This presumption does not apply, however, to beneficiaries who are not thus related to the testator. The doctrine of ademption by advancement or gift inter vivos is not usually applicable to devises of real estate.

An ademption, whether by alienation or extinction of the subject matter of a testamentary gift or by an inter vivos gift or advancement to a beneficiary under the will, operates pro tanto only, so that where only part of the subject matter is disposed of or destroyed, or the inter vivos gift or advancement is less in value than the testamentary provision, the legatee is entitled to the balance.

§ 23:23. Election, acceptance, renunciation, and estoppel.

Am Jur 2d References: Wills (1st ed, §§ 1526–1573).

The doctrine of election in connection with testamentary instruments is the principle that one who is given a benefit under a will must choose between accepting such benefit and asserting some other claim he has against the testator's estate or against the property disposed of by the will. One who elects to accept a benefit extended to him by a will is bound to give effect to all the provisions of the instrument and perform the burdens imposed on him therein, including the renunciation of any inconsistent rights or claims. The theoretical basis of the doctrine is usually referred to the principles of estoppel or to the proposition that a testamentary gift is subject to the implied condition that the donee shall conform to the other provisions of the will. It is generally agreed that the principle of election depends upon the intention of the testator, at least to the extent that a testatorial intention that a beneficiary may both accept the provision made for him in the will and assert a seemingly inconsistent right or claim must be respected.

The two commonest situations in which the doctrine of election is invoked are presented where a testator makes a provision for his surviving spouse and the question arises whether the latter must elect between such provision and his or her marital rights in the testator's property; and where a testator leaves property to a designated individual and also attempts to dispose of property owned by such individual or with respect to which the latter may assert some independent claim or right.

The right of a testamentary beneficiary to elect whether to take under or against the will is personal to him. Where he is mentally incompetent, the right to elect may be exercised in his behalf by a court of competent jurisdiction or in the manner provided by statute. The right of election may not be controlled by the creditors of the beneficiary; they can claim no right or interest in the estate contrary to their debtor's election, whether it is exercised affirmatively or negatively.

Statutes regulating the election of a surviving spouse to take under the will of a deceased spouse or to take instead the statutory benefit given a widow or widower usually fix a definite period of time within which the election is to be made. The effect of a failure to make an election is usually determined, expressly, or by implication, by the terms of the statutes, some enactments providing that such failure shall operate to vest the share given the survivor by the will, and others that it shall vest the statutory marital rights.

The question of what constitutes an election to take under or against a will, and the manner and form in which such an election must be made, are matters usually governed by statute. In the absence of an applicable statute, a testamentary election may be express or may be implied by the acts or conduct of the beneficiary, as by the acceptance and enjoyment of money or property given to him under the will. Two things are usually necessary in order that acts of the beneficiary may constitute an election: (1) He must have been cognizant of his rights and must have had knowledge not only of the condition and extent of the testator's estate, but also of his duty to elect between two inconsistent rights; and (2) having knowledge of his rights, he must have intended, as shown by clear and unequivocal acts, to make a choice. Where an election is made by a party bound to elect, either expressly or impliedly, with full knowledge of all the facts, it binds him and those who claim under him, and it may not be revoked, in the absence of fraud or undue influence.

A testamentary beneficiary is not compelled to accept a devise or bequest. He has the right to renounce or decline the gift, however beneficial it may be to him, although he may not accept the benefits of a gift and at the same time reject its burdens. The beneficiary's right to renounce even a beneficial testamentary provision in his favor may not be challenged by his creditors.

II. DESCENT AND DISTRIBUTION OF DECEDENTS' ESTATES

§ 23:24. Generally; basis, nature, and effect of intestate succession or descent.

Am Jur 2d References: Descent and Distribution, §§ 1–36, 69–74, 90, 175–184.

The descent and distribution of property not disposed of by will are determined by state statutes. The descent or inheritance of real estate is governed by the law of the state in which the property is located, while the distribution of personal property, tangible and intangible, is generally governed by the law of the state of the owner's domicil at the time of his death. Where there have been changes in the law of descent and distribution, the law in effect at the time of the decedent's death applies.

The early English common-law canons of descent of real property, which, in accordance with the feudal system, prohibited lineal ascent, admitted the male before the female, and recognized the rule of primogeniture, by which the eldest male inherits, were not accepted in America. Statutes in the United States generally provide a complete system for succession to intestate property, and they frequently provide for the descent and distribution of both realty and personalty in the same course and manner.

Upon the death of the ancestor, title to real property vests immediately, and by operation of law, in the heirs. The interests of distributees in personal property accrue immediately on the death of their ancestor, but they may not claim the property except in the administration and distribution of the estate by the personal representatives.

All interests in property, real and personal, which survive the death of the owner and which are not disposed of by will, pass under the statute of descent and distribution. This applies to future as well as present interests, and includes contingent as well as vested estates. Property which, for any reason, does not pass under a will left by the owner descends and is distributed as intestate property according to the statute; and the testator cannot prevent the operation of the statute even by provision of his will expressly disinheriting an heir or next of kin. Statutes of many states provide, in varying terms, that a child of the testator shall share in his estate as though he had died intestate, unless the child was named in or provided for by the will, or it is clear that the testator intended to omit him.

§ 23:25. Persons who take, and their shares.

Am Jur 2d References: Descent and Distribution, §§ 41–63, 75–89, 103–107; Wills (1st ed, § 573).

The statutes of descent and distribution vary widely in the different states. Generally speaking, they prescribe certain persons who shall take and the order in which they shall take. Children of the intestate and their descendants are usually preferred. In default of children and their descendants, the descent is cast in various ways, sometimes upon collateral relatives and sometimes upon the parents of the intestate. The usual statute of descent, enumerating the persons who are to take, provides that in default of any of the persons enumerated, the estate shall go to the next of kin. A "lineal" descent is one in the direct line of the intestate, as, for example, from father or grandfather to son or grandson, or from son or grandson to father or grandfather. "Collateral" descent is to collateral relatives, as from brother to brother, cousin to cousin, etc.

Relationship by affinity is the tie between one spouse and the blood relations of the other. Under most statutes of descent and distribution, a person cannot by legal succession receive an inheritance from a relation by affinity. Thus, a stepparent is not generally included in the designation of a parent, father, or mother, and a stepchild does not take as an heir of its stepparent, in the absence of specific statutory provision therefor.

The word "consanguinity" imports blood through some common ancestor, irrespective of amount. It may be either lineal or collateral. Although there are exceptions imposed by law, as in the case of a surviving spouse and adopted children, the concept of blood relationship has always been fundamental in the law of descent and distribution. The rule of the common law excluding the half blood has never met with favor in the United States. Most statutes are construed to include the half blood equally with the whole blood.

In determining who is "next of kin" or "nearest of kin" within the meaning of statutes of descent and distribution, the civil-law method of computing degrees of kinship has been adopted in most jurisdictions. Under this method the degree of kinship is determined by counting upward from the intestate to the nearest common ancestor, then downward to the claimant, each generation representing one degree. Under this system, parents and children of a deceased are related to him in the first degree; grandparents, grandchildren, and brothers and sisters of the deceased, are related to him in the second degree; and uncles, aunts, nephews, nieces, and great-grandparents are related to him in the third degree; the fourth degree of relationship includes first cousins, great-uncles and great-aunts, and great-great-grandparents. The common-law or canon-law method of computing degrees of kinship, which has been applied in a few American cases, determines the degree of kinship by the number of generations from the nearest common ancestor to the intestate or to the claimant, taking the longer of the two lines where they are unequal. The difference in the two methods of computation of degrees exists only in relation to collateral consanguinity.

The policy of the common law was to keep real property in the line of the ancestor by whom it was brought into the family. Accordingly, it was the rule that on failure of lineal descendents of an intestate his land descended only to those of his collateral relatives who were of the blood of the first purchaser. Thus, land which an intestate inherited from his father, who had himself inherited it from the intestate's grandfather, would pass, on death of the intestate without issue, only to those collateral relatives who were related to the intestate on the paternal side. This common-law doctrine of ancestral estates is not favored in American law, but it prevails in some states.

Although it is a general rule that persons who are not in being at the death of an intestate do not inherit from him, posthumous children are deemed to be existent from the time of conception, and such children, if born alive, inherit as they would have if they had been born in the lifetime of the intestate and had survived him.

The determination of intestate succession to property in the situation which arises when an ancestor and an heir die in such circumstances that there is no evidence as to which survived the other is generally controlled by the provisions of the Uniform Simultaneous Death Act. The Act provides that where title to or devolution of property depends upon priority of death and there is no sufficient evidence that the persons have died otherwise than simultaneously, the property of each person shall be disposed of as if he had survived.

§ 23:26. — Surviving spouse.

Am Jur 2d References: Descent and Distribution, §§ 108–133.

At common law a surviving spouse of an intestate is not an heir, the dower or curtesy interest not being deemed an inheritance.   Under modern statutes of many states, however, a surviving spouse takes a share of an intestate's property by descent and distribution, as distinguished from dower or curtesy. The share may be the same in both real and personal estate, or a certain share in the real estate and a certain share in the personal property.   The size of the share of the surviving spouse varies greatly from state to state.   This share is usually larger where there are no children or descendants of children, or parents, of the deceased spouse.

Some statutes provide that particular acts of misconduct, such as desertion or abandonment of the deceased spouse by the surviving spouse, or the latter's adultery, bar such spouse from sharing in the estate of the deceased spouse. And the same forfeiture results where one spouse feloniously kills the other. An absolute divorce deprives each spouse of all right and interest in the estate of the other as surviving spouse, under the law of descent and distribution. Remarriage after the death of a spouse does not generally affect the rights of a surviving spouse under such statutes.

§ 23:27. Taking per capita or per stirpes.

Am Jur 2d References: Descent and Distribution, §§ 64–68.

The terms "per capita" and "per stirpes" refer to methods of computing the share of an estate to be allocated to individual members of a class of heirs or distributees.   To take per capita is to take equally with other children, other brothers and sisters, or other kin of the intestate, and in one's own right.   "Per capita" means by the head or individual.   As most commonly employed, the term "per stirpes" signifies a taking, by representation, of a share which a deceased ancestor would have taken if he had survived the intestate.

Where the heirs or distributees of an intestate are his children or his parents— persons who are in the first degree of kinship to him—such persons clearly inherit in their own right and not as representing other persons who would have taken had they survived the intestate.   These heirs take per capita. Similarly, brothers and sisters, being descendants of the same parent or parents, take per capita.   The children of a deceased child or of a deceased brother or sister, where, in the first case, there are surviving children, or where, in the second case, there are surviving brothers or sisters, together take such share as their deceased parent—the stock or root—would have taken had he or she survived the intestate.

If all the intestate's children predecease him, leaving grandchildren among whom the estate is to be divided, the question arises whether the grandchildren share equally or whether they take per stirpes as representatives of their parents. Contrary to the English law, the prevailing rule in the United States is that equally related remote descendants of the intestate, such as grandchildren or great-grandchildren, take per capita.   Where an intestate, all of whose children have predeceased him, is survived by grandchildren, descendants of some

670

deceased children, and by great-grandchildren, whose parents are deceased, different results have been reached as to whether there should be per capita or per stirpes sharing, the results sometimes depending upon the wording of the statutes. Similar principles govern the determination of the shares of collateral or remote kin.

§ 23:28. Forfeiture of right to inherit; killing of ancestor by heir.

Am Jur 2d References: Descent and Distribution, §§ 91–102.

Under the English common law, a person who was convicted of a felony, or who fled after having committed a felony, was deemed attainted, and neither his lands nor his personal property could pass to his heirs or distributees. Such property, through the doctrines of forfeiture and escheat, was taken by the king or by the overlord, depending on the nature of the offense. This ancient doctrine of attainder has been abolished in England, and it was never accepted in the United States. Statutes providing that a person convicted of crime and committed to prison for life shall be deemed legally dead do not generally work a devolution of the convict's property, as in the case of natural death, unless the statute so provides. And such statutes do not usually preclude inheritance by such a person as heir or distributee of another person, although a different conclusion has been reached by some courts.

A potential heir or distributee who feloniously brings about the death of his intestate is not allowed to take and enjoy the property of the person so killed. This result is reached in some states even in the absence of a statute to that effect, and in other states statutes specifically provide that a person who feloniously kills another may not inherit from him. A defense or justification which bars conviction of a felony, such as self-defense, will generally permit the killer to inherit from the victim. Under some statutes there must be a conviction for the killing of the intestate in order to effect a disinheritance. The murderer's heirs or representatives, claiming through him, cannot take the victim's estate; but where they claim the murderer's forfeited share, not through the murderer, but as heirs of the murdered intestate, a different question is presented and is determined by the provisions of the applicable statutes.

§ 23:29. Alienation, release, or renunciation of interest.

Am Jur 2d References: Descent and Distribution, §§ 160–174.

At common law, the expectancy of a prospective heir that he will succeed to the estate of his ancestor is not regarded as an existing interest, and cannot be passed by an assignment and cannot be made the subject of a gift or devise. However, a vested interest which has been acquired by intestate succession, upon the death of the ancestor, is assignable and transferable by the heir or distributee. And it is generally held that a release by an heir or distributee, made to the ancestor before the latter's death, where supported by an advancement to the heir or distributee or other consideration, and freely and fairly made, is binding on the heir or distributee. As the ancestor could accomplish the same result by making a will, there would seem to be no reason why such an agreement should not be given effect. However, some courts have held than an heir or distributee is not bound by his release made to his own sister before the latter's death.

According to the common law, title to the property of a person who dies intestate passes by operation of law, and no voluntary act of the decedent former owner, or of a subsequent owner who takes by intestacy, can vary this result. In conformity with this theory, it is held that, in the absence of statute, a person who takes by intestate succession has no power to prevent the passage of title to himself by renunciation. Under the civil law, and by statutes in some jurisdictions, an heir or distributee may renounce his succession to the property of an intestate decedent, and such renunciation is effective as against the creditors of the heir or distributee.

§ 23:30. Advancements.

Am Jur 2d References: Advancements, §§ 1–101.

The basic definition of an "advancement" is, a perfect and irrevocable gift made by a parent, during his lifetime, to his child, with the intention on the part of the donor that such gift shall represent a part or the whole of the portion of the donor's estate that the donee would be entitled to on the death of the donor intestate. There is a well-defined distinction between an advancement and a debt or loan, an advancement involving a transfer of property without consideration, and no part of an advancement being recoverable from the donee. An advancement is also distinguishable from a gift, in that a gift carries with it no obligation whatever, while an advancement, although a gift in the sense that it need not be repaid, is subject to the doctrine of hotchpot, which requires the donee to account for the advancement before he is permitted to share in the intestate's estate. The rules governing advancements are defined and regulated by statutes in the various jurisdictions.

The definition of an advancement requires that it must be an irrevocable gift. Also, in order that the transfer of property from a parent to his child shall constitute an advancement, it must, in the absence of a statutory provision to the contrary, satisfactorily appear that an intention existed, coincident with the transaction, to treat it as a portion or settlement in life and as an anticipation of the child's share of the donor's estate if the latter should die intestate; and it is the donor's intention that is controlling in determining whether or not there has been an advancement. It is the intention existing at the time of the transaction, and not at a prior or subsequent date, which is determinative of this question.

As the doctrine of advancements is based on the assumed desire of the donor to equalize the distribution of his estate among his children, the doctrine has no application unless the ancestor dies wholly intestate, i.e., intestate as to all of his property, both real and personal. However, statutes in some jurisdictions make the doctrine of advancements applicable where the donor dies partially intestate.

The donee has the option either to accept or reject the advancement. If he accepts it, he is bound by the intention of the donor that it be treated as an advancement. If he rejects it, the property remains the property of the donor.

The process by which the shares of heirs and distributees are equalized, where advancements have been made to some of them by the intestate, is called "hotchpot," "hotchpotch," or "hodgepodge." The hotchpot rule means that the value of advancements is included as a part of the intestate's estate for the purpose of computing the share of each heir and distributee, so that the share of each is charged with and reduced proportionately according to the advancements given to him.   As a general rule, the valuation of the property involved in an advancement is its worth on the date when the advancement was made.

§ 23:31. Liability for debts.

Am Jur 2d References: Descent and Distribution, §§ 37–40, 134–159.

The rule of the early common law was that personal property, but not real property, was liable for the general debts of a deceased owner.   Real property was not an asset of a decedent's estate for the payment of his debts except in the case of specialties which were expressly made binding upon his heirs.   Under modern statutes, however, no such distinction is made between real and personal property, and all property, real and personal, insofar as it is not exempted, is liable for the debts of the deceased owner, and heirs and distributees take the property subject to such debts.   The liability of an heir for debts of his ancestor is limited to the property which descends or is distributed to him.   A vestige of the solicitude of the common law regarding real estate is still evident in the rules governing the order of liability as between real and personal property.   It is the rule in most jurisdictions that personal property is primarily liable for the debts of the ancestor, and that real property may be subjected to such debts only after the exhaustion of personal property for the purpose.

Until the death of an ancestor, the expectancy of an heir apparent or a distributee apparent is not subject to execution or seizure by his creditors. Immediately upon the death of the ancestor, however, the heir's interest in real property is subject to seizure for his debts; and a distributee's interest in personal property may be reached in most jurisdictions by creditors' bills or other processes.

§ 23:32. Escheat.

Am Jur 2d References: Escheat, §§ 1–48.

In its most comprehensive scope, "escheat" means the reversion or forfeiture of property to the government upon the happening of some event or default.   Under the English common law, escheat signified the interest which reverted to or devolved upon the lord of the fee upon failure of heirs of the original grantee.   The Crown took personal property which was without an owner, and "escheat" was not technically a correct term for this succession. In the United States escheat denotes the falling of an estate into the general property of the state because the owner has died intestate without lawful heirs to take the estate by succession, or because of some other legal disability to take or hold the property.   The escheat is to the state, rather than to the Federal Government or some political subdivision of the state, in the absence of contrary statutory provisions.   The states have broad powers, through statutes and constitutions, to regulate escheats.   As between the state or country of domicil and the state or country in which the property is located, real property escheats according to the laws of the latter state or country. As to personal property, there are divergent views as to which law governs.

All kinds of property, real and personal, tangible and intangible, and all kinds of interests and estates therein, are subject to escheat to the state. State laws frequently provide for the escheat of abandoned or unclaimed personal property, including bank deposits, stock dividends, insurance funds, and property in the custody of a court or public officer.

The procedure by which an escheat is effectuated varies in the several states. Under the common law of England a special proceeding for this purpose was known as "inquest of office" or "office found"; and these terms are still sometimes used in this connection. By whatever name it is called and whatever procedural details are prescribed, some kind of judicial proceeding is usually required to establish the absence of legal heirs or other grounds of escheat, and to vest title in the state.

III. ADMINISTRATION OF ESTATES; EXECUTORS AND ADMINISTRATORS

§ 23:33. Generally; scope and manner of administration.

Am Jur 2d References: Executors and Administrators, §§ 1–43, 193–208.

The administration of a decedent's estate involves the collection of assets, the use thereof for the payment of debts, taxes, and costs of administration, and the distribution of the balance to the persons entitled thereto. The administration is conducted by an executor or administrator, the personal representative of the decedent, under the supervision of the proper court. An executor is a person nominated by a testator to carry out the directions of his will and to dispose of his property according to his testamentary provisions. Administrators are persons appointed by a court to administer and settle intestate estates and the estates of testators who have not designated a competent executor.

Formal administration may be dispensed with in many cases by agreement among the interested parties. Such agreements or arrangements are frequently termed family settlements. Compromises and settlements among heirs, distributees, devisees, and legatees of a decedent's estate will be enforced if made between persons having the legal capacity to contract, if containing the elements of a valid contract, such as good consideration, and if not tainted by fraud, duress, or the like. Such an agreement may provide for the distribution of the estate on a plan different from that prescribed by the statutes of descent and distribution, or different from the plan provided for in a will. Such a settlement is binding, of course, only on the persons joining therein; it does not affect the rights of nonconsenting creditors. Also, it has been held that such an agreement may not modify or defeat a testamentary trust.

In many states, special courts, variously designated as probate, surrogate, or orphans' courts, have been established and given jurisdiction of the administration of decedents' estates. In other states, the common pleas courts, county courts, superior courts, or other courts of general original jurisdiction, are given jurisdiction in probate matters. A decedent's domicil at the time of his death is generally the proper jurisdiction in which to obtain domiciliary letters testamentary or of administration. Real property is subject to administration only in the state where it is located. Personal property, though generally having its situs at the domicil of the owner, may, depending upon its nature or upon local statutes, be subject to administration in other jurisdictions.

As a general rule, the real estate of a decedent vests immediately in his heirs or devisees by operation of law, without any intervention of a personal representative, subject to the payment of the decedent's debts in most jurisdictions. Personal property, however, must generally be distributed to the next of kin or legatees by the administrator or executor.

§ 23:34. Appointment, qualification, and tenure of executor or administrator.

Am Jur 2d References: Executors and Administrators, §§ 44–153, 603–639.

The nomination or appointment of an executor in a will is generally binding upon the probate court. In general, a court has no discretion respecting the issuance of letters testamentary to persons nominated in a will, unless the nominees are disqualified by statute or discretion is vested in the court. And a testator may delegate the power to appoint an executor to a person or persons designated in his will; and he may delegate to his executor the power to select a coexecutor or an alternate or successor executor.

An administrator is appointed by the probate court and derives his power solely from this appointment. The right to letters of administration is generally regulated by statutes that designate the priorities of various relatives or other persons. Priorities are based primarily on nearness of relationship and extent of interest. Usually the first right to receive letters of administration on the estate of a deceased person is given to the surviving spouse. Following the surviving spouse, the preference in securing letters of administration is usually given to the next of kin of the deceased. If persons having preferred rights to letters of administration fail to apply, or are incompetent, a creditor may secure appointment as administrator.

A person nominated as executor in a will is not required to accept the appointment. He may elect to renounce his rights, as may one having a preferential right to letters of administration of an intestate estate.

Letters testamentary or of administration are granted on the filing of an application therefor in accordance with statutory provisions. Competency of a particular person or entity, such as an infant, mentally incompetent person, alien, nonresident, or corporation, to act as executor or administrator, is governed by statutes, which vary in the several jurisdictions.

An executor or administrator may be removed from office and his appointment revoked for good cause shown according to the governing statute. A ground for revocation or removal may be a showing that the letters testamentary or of administration were issued illegally or through fraud, where the executor or administrator has been guilty of misappropriation of funds, waste, negligence, or mismanagement, or where he has become unfit to perform his duties because of insanity or other reason. Statutes frequently give an executor or administrator a qualified right of resignation, subject to acceptance in the discretion of the court; but at common law he had no right to resign.

Executors and administrators are required to give bonds, under such terms and conditions as are prescribed by statute, for the faithful performance of their duties and for the protection of all persons interested in the estate.

Where, after appointment and qualification of an administrator, a vacancy occurs in the office before the assets are fully administered, the court will appoint an "administrator de bonis non" to complete the administration of the estate. Where a will fails to nominate an executor or the nominee fails or refuses to qualify and act, the probate court may appoint an "administrator with the will annexed." If a vacancy occurs after an executor has qualified, the court will appoint an "administrator de bonis non with the will annexed."

§ 23:35. Public or special administrators; executor de son tort.

Am Jur 2d References: Executors and Administrators, §§ 640–679.

Statutes of many states have created the office of public administrator for the purpose of administering estates that would otherwise remain unadministered for want of a private administrator. The appointment, powers, and duties of public administrators depend upon the terms of the statutes of the particular jurisdiction, although the provisions of the general probate law are usually applicable to the public administrator where not inconsistent with statutes specifically relating to his office.

A special or temporary administrator may be appointed until an estate can pass into the hands of a person fully authorized to administer it. Such appointments are specifically authorized in a number of jurisdictions. The powers of such an administrator are usually limited to the special purpose for which he is appointed, which is generally the conservation and preservation of the personal estate of the decedent until the appointment of a general administrator.

An executor de son tort is one who, without authority from the deceased or the court of probate, assumes to act as executor or administrator and performs such acts with respect to assets of the estate as can legally be done only by a properly appointed executor or administrator. He is one who intrudes himself into office without legal authority and intermeddles with the property of a decedent. He is subject to all the liabilities of a lawful personal representative, but generally he acquires none of the rights or privileges that belong to that office, although he may be protected in all acts, not performed for his own benefit, that a rightful executor or administrator could properly perform.

§ 23:36. Rights, powers, duties, and liabilities.

Am Jur 2d References: Executors and Administrators, §§ 3, 4, 154–192, 209–215, 713–802.

Both executors and administrators are under the immediate control of the court appointing them and are subject to any proper orders of the court relating to the estate, except, in the case of an executor, where the will manifests an intention of the testator that the executor's discretion shall be free from ordinary judicial control. It is a common practice for an executor or administrator, for his own guidance and protection, to ask the court for instructions with respect to matters relating to the administration of the estate.

The powers of an administrator or executor depend upon the provisions of applicable statutes, and in the case of an executor, upon the terms of the will nominating him. In the absence of statute, court order, or will provision authorizing such act, a personal representative cannot generally make an executory contract binding on the estate. Thus, he generally has no power to purchase real property on behalf of the estate or to encumber real property belonging to the estate.

An executor or administrator, even though he is himself a qualified attorney, may properly employ an attorney to render necessary legal services in the administration and settlement of an estate. An executor generally has the right to select the attorney for the estate, and it is generally held that he is not bound by a provision of a will naming an attorney, although there is some authority to the contrary. An executor or administrator may employ agents for extraordinary services of administration or services that require a degree of skill not within the command of ordinary persons. Thus, an executor may empower a broker to sell real property or to collect rents.

Personal representatives of a decedent occupy a position of trust, and they must exercise good faith, care, and diligence in the management and administration of the estate they represent. This includes the obligation to protect the estate against every demand that is not legally enforceable, and the duty to take charge of all of the effects and personal assets belonging to the decedent and to collect debts due the estate, by means of legal action when necessary. Executors and administrators are usually required to file an inventory of the assets of the decedent's estate, and in many jurisdictions an appraisal of the assets is required in connection with the inventory. The duty of an executor to procure the probate of a will depends upon statute. He is under duty to use reasonable diligence to locate heirs and legatees.

An executor or administrator may maintain an action in his representative capacity to recover or protect the assets of the decedent's estate or to recover on any cause of action in favor of the decedent which survived his death. Personal representatives are also subject to being sued in their representative capacity on claims or causes of action against the estate, where the statutory requirements are complied with.

§ 23:37. Custody and management of estate.

Am Jur 2d References: Executors and Administrators, §§ 216–269.

In the performance of his fiduciary duties, an executor or administrator must exercise the utmost good faith in all transactions affecting the estate. And he must exercise the care and diligence that an ordinarily prudent man would use under like circumstances in his own affairs. While he is not an insurer or guarantor, he must use ordinary care, prudence, skill, and diligence.

The conduct of a business operation is normally outside the scope of administrative functions, and if an executor or administrator continues the operation of a business of the deceased, he does so at his own peril and he is liable for any losses resulting therefrom, unless he is authorized to do so by a provision of the will, an order of court, or a statutory provision. There may be circumstances, however, under which a personal representative is justified in temporarily continuing a business for the purpose of winding it up and liquidating the assets. He may never, however, share in the profits of the business. Authority of an executor or administrator to invest funds belonging to the estate may be conferred by provisions of a will or by statute. The nature of investments which he may make depends in many instances on particular testamentary provisions, and may be governed by statute. He is liable for any loss resulting from an investment made contrary to the direction of the decedent's will or in violation of governing statutes.

In the absence of statute to the contrary, title to personal property of a decedent vests, on his death, in his executor or administrator for the purpose of administration. The personal representative holds the property in trust for the payment of debts and the distribution of the remainder pursuant to the provisions of the will or under the statute of distribution. As to real estate, the general rule is that such property becomes vested on the death of the owner in his heirs or devisees, subject to the right of the personal representative to resort to it for the payment of creditors in case the personal estate is insufficient to pay the debts of the estate and the expenses of administration.

An estate is not generally liable for a tort committed by an executor or administrator in the course of the administration of the estate. Liability for such torts rests upon the executor or administrator personally. This general rule applies whether the injury results from an intentional wrong or from mere negligence. There is some indication of authority, however, for the proposition that the estate is liable, at least to the extent of assets received by it as a result of the personal representative's tortious act.

§ 23:38. Presentation, allowance, and payment of claims.

Am Jur 2d References: Executors and Administrators, §§ 270–311, 316–339, 463–485.

By virtue of statutory provisions, an action cannot be maintained against an executor or administrator on a claim against the estate unless the claim has first been presented to the representative within a specified time for his allowance or rejection. Such statutes are generally referred to as nonclaim statutes. A personal representative's knowledge of the existence of a claim does not dispense with the provisions of statutes requiring presentation. And it is held by the majority of courts that the statutory requirement may not be waived by an executor or administrator. However, in some jurisdictions the institution of suit against the personal representatives is considered a sufficient presentation of the claim to take it out of a statute of nonclaim.

The claims which must be presented to the personal representative under statutes of nonclaim are debts or demands of a pecuniary nature that could have been enforced against the deceased in his lifetime. These statutes are usually held not to apply to a claim that does not arise until after the death of the testator or intestate, such as claims for expenses of administration or for funeral expenses. Whether or not a tort claim must be so presented depends upon the terms of the nonclaim statute. Claims of the Federal Government are not within the scope of such statutes; and it is held in many cases that a claim for taxes may not be barred because of noncompliance with nonclaim statutes. Claims secured by mortgage or a specific lien on property of the decedent need not be presented in order to preserve the right to enforce the lien against the property, although presentation may be necessary in order to enforce payment of the claim out of the general assets of the estate. The time within which claims against a decedent's estate must be presented is prescribed by statute or fixed by an order of the probate court. The power of the court to extend the time depends upon statutory provision.

Statutes generally make it the duty of the executor or administrator to give public notice to all persons having claims against the estate to present them for allowance. The form of the claim is generally sufficient if it states the character and amount of the claim, enables the personal representative to provide for its payment, and serves to bar subsequent claims based on the same subject matter. Particular requirements as to the form and contents of the claim are frequently prescribed by statute. Verification of a claim is generally required. A claim may be amended, even after the time for filing claims has expired, but it cannot be amended after such time so as to substantially change the original claim or to introduce a new or different claim.

Many states have statutory provision for family allowances, the purpose of which is to provide for the daily necessities of the surviving family following the death of the breadwinner, until such time as a final settlement or award can be made. Such an allowance to the widow and children of a decedent is preferred to most other claims and will generally be allowed even though the estate is insolvent.

After proper presentation to and allowance of claims by the personal representative or the probate court, it is the duty of the executor or administrator to pay the claims, in the order of their priority, to the extent of assets of the estate in his hands. In the distribution of the estate, the rights of creditors are superior to those heirs or legatees, and their claims must be paid before distribution is made to legatees or heirs. Statutes ordinarily classify debts of decedents and specify the order in which they are to be paid by the personal representative. High in the order of priority usually accorded such claims are claims of the United States or of individual states, claims for funeral expenses or the expenses of the last illness, allowances to the widow and family, and the expenses of the administration of the estate.

There is considerable variation in both the statutory provisions and judicial decisions on the question of the power of an executor or administrator to waive the bar of the statute of limitations as to debts of the estate, or to toll the running of the statute.

§ 23:39. Sales.

Am Jur 2d References: Executors and Administrators, §§ 340–462.

Under the common law an executor or administrator has almost unlimited power of disposal over the personal estate of the decedent, subject to provisions of the latter's will governing the disposition of the property. In the absence of restrictions by statute or will, the personal representative may sell the decedent's personal property on such terms as he sees fit, at public or private sale, for cash or on credit. However, statutes in many jurisdictions limit this power of sale, and frequently require the previous consent of the court to the sale of the personal estate and prescribe the manner and terms of such sales.

The power of an executor or administrator to sell the real property of a decedent is dependent upon statutory authorization or the provisions of the decedent's will. Statutes usually provide for the sale of the decedent's real estate where this is necessary for the payment of his debts, though usually the real estate is resorted to for this purpose only after the exhaustion of the personal estate. In making such sales, the personal representative must follow the procedural requirements of these statutes, and such sales are usually subject to confirmation by the court. An executor may be authorized by the decedent's will to make a sale of his real or personal property. Where such authority is conferred by will, the executor may make a sale without prior authorization by the probate court. An implied power of sale may be found when a sale is necessary to carry out the provisions of the will, the intention of the testator being the prime consideration in determining whether such a power is to be implied.

§ 23:40. Distribution of assets.

Am Jur 2d References: Executors and Administrators, §§ 550–602.

After having paid the decedent's debts and the expenses of administration, the executor or administrator has the duty to distribute the assets remaining in the estate to those entitled thereto, that is, to those designated in the decedent's will or those specified by the statutes of descent and distribution. It is the duty of the personal representative to identify the heirs or legatees entitled to share the estate, and he may be liable if he makes a distribution to the wrong persons. The time for distributing an estate may be controlled by provisions of a will or by statute. In the absence of any provision in a will as to the time of payment, pecuniary legacies are ordinarily payable one year after the death of the testator, although a statute may provide otherwise. Such a legacy will earn interest at the legal rate from the time when payment was due.

The right to a distributive share in an estate is subordinate to the distributee's indebtedness to the estate. Such indebtedness will be deducted from or offset against the legacy or distributive share of the debtor. There is a conflict of authority on the question whether an indebtedness of an heir may be charged against his inherited share of real estate.

§ 23:41. Accounting, settlement, and compensation.

Am Jur 2d References: Executors and Administrators, §§ 486–549.

An executor or administrator is required to keep and render full and accurate accounts covering the assets of an estate in his hands. The probate court having jurisdiction over the administration proceedings has jurisdiction over the accounts of executors and administrators, with the power to examine the accounts and vouchers and to determine objections which may be made thereto. The resignation of an executor or administrator or his removal from office does not relieve him from his liabilities until he has settled his accounts and delivered the unadministered assets of the estate to his successor. Where an executor or administrator dies without accounting, it is the duty of his personal representative to file an account for him. The time for accounting is generally governed by statute, subject to an extension of time by the probate court. If the estate is not finally settled within a certain time, the personal representative is often required to file an intermediate annual account. It is usually required that notice be given to all interested parties before a final settlement of a personal representative's account, and any person beneficially interested in the estate, or any creditor, may file an objection to items in the account. The probate court has the power to compel the administrator or executor to file his accounts, and any person interested in the estate may invoke the jurisdiction of the court for this purpose.

An executor or administrator is entitled in the settlement of his accounts to a credit for all proper claims against the estate that he has paid, and for all actual and necessary expenses incurred in good faith and with the exercise of reasonable judgment in the care, management, and settlement of the estate. He may be surcharged in his accounts for the amount of losses incurred by the estate as the result of some act or omission on his part which constitutes a breach of trust, and for money or property coming into his hands for which he fails to account.

An executor or administrator is entitled to compensation for his services. The amount to be allowed him is usually fixed by statute as a certain percent of the value of the estate or of the personal property thereof. In the absence of a statute fixing the rate of compensation, the court will make a reasonable allowance to the representative. Under some circumstances, a personal representative may be allowed extra compensation for extraordinary services, such as special services as an attorney or accountant. Conversely, the right of an executor or administrator to compensation has been denied or reduced where he has been guilty of neglect of the estate, or fraud, dishonesty, or misconduct resulting in loss or detriment to the estate.

§ 23:42. Ancillary administration.

Am Jur 2d References: Executors and Administrators, §§ 680–712.

Where a decedent leaves assets in a state other than that of his domicil, ancillary administration may be obtained in the other state for the collection and disposition of property of the deceased within that state. In some states, however, a foreign administrator may be permitted to act by virtue of the power originally granted to him, upon the mere production of his duly authenticated letters. The ancillary administration is auxiliary to the domiciliary administration, which is the principal administration.

An ancillary administrator has authority to collect the debts and receive the assets of the estate found in the jurisdiction where his administration is granted. He is clothed with all powers incident to the administration of such assets. It is his duty to pay creditors within his jurisdiction out of the assets coming into his hands. Any surplus remaining after the payment of claims lawfully allowed in the ancillary administration and the payment of the expenses of that administration should generally be remitted to the domiciliary representative for final settlement and distribution of the estate, although circumstances may be such as to require a distribution of the surplus in the ancillary jurisdiction. Ancillary representatives are required to account to the court having jurisdiction of the ancillary administration.

*

INDEX

ABANDONED PROPERTY
Dedication of real property, mode of, § 18:73

Escheat of, § 23:32

Personal property as, § 16:6

ABANDONMENT OR DESERTION
Criminal offense of abandonment or desertion of wife or child, § 7:71

Divorce as based on, § 9:10

Dower or curtesy as affected by, § 18:20

Inheritance rights as affected by desertion or abandonment of deceased spouse by surviving spouse, § 23:26

ABATEMENT
Wills, legacies and devises, § 23:21

ABDUCTION
Criminal offenses, § 7:63

ABORTION
Criminal offense, § 7:48

Injury or death resulting from abortion, liability for, § 21:99

ABSOLUTE DUTY
Negligence, § 21:9

ABSOLUTE LIABILITY
Products liability, § 17:9

ABSTRACT
Vendor and purchaser, § 18:54

ABUSE OF PROCESS
Federal Tort Claims Act as excluding claims for, § 21:4

Malicious prosecution, § 21:74

Punitive or exemplary damages as recoverable in action to recover damages for, § 8:1

Tort actions involving, recovery of damages in, § 8:8

ABUTTING OWNER
Adjoining Landowners (this index)

Highways, liability of abutting owner for injuries in, § 21:43

ACCEPTANCE
Commercial paper, acceptance of, § 2:6

Contract, acceptance of offer as essential to, § 5:8

ACCEPTANCE—Cont'd
Conveyances, §§ 18:62, 18:63

Gift, acceptance by donee as element of, § 16:9

Lease, requirement as to acceptance of, § 18:30

Legacies and devises of wills, § 23:23

Principal, acceptance of benefits as ratification by, § 1:11

Real property, mode of dedication of, § 18:73

ACCESSION
Personal property, § 16:8

ACCESSORIES
Criminal law, §§ 7:12-7:14

ACCIDENT INSURANCE
Insurance, risks and coverage of, § 13:11

ACCOMMODATION PARTY
Negotiable instrments, § 2:7

ACCOMPLICE
Criminal law, § 7:12

ACCORD AND SATISFACTION
Contractual modification by, § 5:28

ACCOUNTANTS
Corporate books and records, right to assistance of skilled persons in inspection of, § 6:5

Executor or administrator as entitled to extra compensation for services as accountant, § 23:41

Insurance to cover liability of, § 13:10

ACCOUNTING
Books of Account (this index)

Declaratory relief, relief by way of accounting in proceeding for, § 12:1

Executors and administrators, § 23:41

Guardian, accounting of, § 9:50

Partnership affairs, § 15:4

Trusts, § 22:6

Unfair competition, action for accounting as remedy for, § 21:95

683

BANKRUPTCY OR INSOLVENCY
—Cont'd
Partnership dissolution, bankruptcy as basis for, § 15:6

Sales contract, insolvency of seller as affecting delivery of goods under, § 20:4

Seller's remedy on insolvency of buyer, § 20:9

BANKS AND BANKING
Escheat of bank deposits, § 23:32

Lien of bank on securities of customer, § 16:17

BANKS OF STREAM
Waters and water rights, §§ 18:45-18:47

BAR OF DOWER
Real property, § 18:20

BASE FEE
Real property, § 18:6

BASTARDS
Generally, §§ 9:40-9:43

Adoption of illegitimate children, § 9:34

Crime of incest as affected by illegitimate relationship of parties, § 7:62

Deed, rights under, § 9:43

Divorce and separation, generally, § 9:14

Filiation proceedings, § 9:42

Inheritance, rights of, § 9:43

Legitimation, § 9:41

Presumption of legitimacy, § 9:40

Real and demonstrative evidence in bastardy actions, § 11:20

Will, rights under, § 9:43

BATTERY
Assault and Battery (this index)

BELIEF OR OPINION
Capacity of infant to commit crime, § 7:4

Criminal state of mind, § 7:9

Expert or opinion evidence, §§ 11:26, 11:27

Fraud or deceit, expression of opinion as basis of action for, § 21:76

Hearsay evidence rule as applicable to opinion polls, § 11:12

BENEFICIARIES
Wrongful death, right of action, § 21:36

BEST AND SECONDARY EVIDENCE
Evidence, §§ 11:10. 11:11

BESTIALITY
Crime of, § 7:71

BICYCLISTS
Automobiles and other motor vehicles, § 21:22

BIGAMY
Criminal offense of, § 7:53

Religious beliefs as affecting commission of, § 7:9

Validity of marriage affected by, § 9:2

BILL OF EXCHANGE
Defined, § 2:1

BILL OF LADING
Pledge of, § 16:22

BILL OF PEACE
Equitable remedy of, § 10:7

Vexatious or oppressive litigation, obtaining bill of peace as relief against, § 10:16

BILL OF RIGHTS
Constitutional law, generally, §§ 4:12-4:17

BILLS AND NOTES
Commercial Paper(this index)

BILLS OF ATTAINDER
Constitutional provision against enactment of, § 4:18

BILLS OF LADING
Uniform Commercial Code as applicable to, § 2:1

BILLS QUIA TIMET
Equity, relief in, § 10:14

BIRTH
Negligence, wrongs and injuries based on, § 21:57

Will, revocation or change upon birth of child, § 23:11

BLACKMAIL
Criminal offenses, § 7:58

BLASTING
Injuries caused by blasting operation, liability for, § 21:52

BLINDNESS
Crime, blindness as affecting capacity for, § 7:4

Testamentary capacity as affected by, § 23:2

BLOODHOUNDS
Admissibility of evidence as to trailing by, § 11:6

BLOOD TESTS
Admissibility of, § 11:21

Marriage as affected by failure to comply with requirement as to, § 9:2

HIGH SEAS—Cont'd
Piracy, § 7:71

HIGHWAYS
Streets and Highways (this index)

HIJACKING
Constitutional provision against unlawful search and seizure as affected by precaution against, § 4:17

HOLDER OF COMMERCIAL PAPER
Status and rights of, §§ 2:4, 2:5

HOLDING COMPANY
Corporations, § 6:1

HOLDING OVER
Landlord and tenant, § 18:37

HOLOGRAPHIC WILLS
Wills, formal requisites of, § 23:7

HOMICIDE
Criminal offenses, § 7:61

Descent and distribution, killing of ancestor by heir, § 23:28

Dower and curtesy as affected by homicide comitted by surviving spouse on other spouse, § 18:20

Inheritance rights as affected by felonious killing of other spouse, § 23:26

Will, killing of testator as affecting beneficial interest under, § 23:1

HOSPITALS
Negligence, wrongs and injuries based on, § 21:55

Privacy, liability of hospital for invasion of, § 21:90

Tort, hospitals as immune from liability in, § 21:2

HOTCHPOT RULE
Advancements as affected by, § 23:30

HOTEL
Premises liability of proprietor of, § 21:40

HUMANITARIAN DOCTRINE
Negligence, § 21:15

HUNTING
Profit a prendre as including right to hunt on land of another, § 18:26

HUSBAND AND WIFE
Generally, §§ 9:16-9:29

Adoption of wife as child and heir at law by husband, § 9:33

Adverse possession based on possession by husband as against wife or vice versa, § 18:78

HUSBAND AND WIFE—Cont'd
Agency of, § 9:22

Alienation of Affections (this index)

Alimony, suit for, § 9:25

Antenuptial Agreements (this index)

Community property rights, § 9:18

Consortium, loss of, § 9:28

Contracts and conveyances by wife, § 9:19

Criminal conversation, § 9:29

Criminal offense of desertion and nonsupport of wife, § 7:71

Curtesy, §§ 18:19, 18:20

Debts of spouse, liability for, § 9:24

Disabilities of coverture, generally, § 9:16

Divorce and Separation (this index)

Dower, §§ 18:19, 18:20

Embezzlement with respect to property of other spouse, § 7:57

Estate by entireties by, § 18:18

Imputed negligence of one spouse, § 21:17

Marriage (this index)

Partnership, § 9:23

Personal property, estate by entireties in husband and wife in, § 16:5

Postnuptial property settlements, § 9:20

Privileged communications between, §§ 11:9, 21:86

Property rights, generally, §§ 9:17, 9:18

Real property, §§ 18:18, 18:19

Settlements, antenuptial and postnuptial, § 9:20

Status and relationship of, § 9:16

Support of Family (this index)

Third persons, torts of spouses against, §§ 9:27, 9:28

Torts, generally, §§ 9:26-9:29

Transactions between, § 9:21

Witnesses, disqualifications against spouses as, § 11:28

IDENTITY
Criminal law, defense of identity of offenses, § 7:21

IGNORANCE
Criminal state of mind as affected by, § 7:9

ILLEGALITY
Restitution, quasi-contracts and implied contracts affected by illegality, § 19:9

NEWSPAPERS AND PERIODICALS
—Cont'd

Sales contract, admissibility in evidence of reports in newspapers or periodicals as to value of goods in, § 20:8

NEW TRIAL

Double jeopardy, new trial granted for errors in first trial as constituting, § 7:20

NEXT OF KIN

Descent and distribution, determining "next of kin" within meaning of statutes of, § 23:25

Wills, use of term "next of kin" in, § 23:18

NOLLE PROSEQUI

Criminal prosecution as affected by practice of entering, § 7:18

Double jeopardy as affected by entry of, § 7:22

Procedure and remedies of, § 7:40

NOLO CONTENDERE

Generally, § 7:39

Admissions against interest as including plea of nolo contendere, § 11:16

NOMINAL DAMAGES

Damages, classes of, § 8:2

NONEXPERT WITNESSES

Expert and opinion evidence, § 11:26

NOTARIAL ACT

Adoption by, § 9:33

NOTICE OR KNOWLEDGE

Agency
– effect of notice of revocation of, § 1:4
– imputation of agent's knowledge to principal, § 1:16

Bailment contract, requirement of notice for modification of, § 16:11

Commercial Paper (this index)

Due process of law as requiring notice, § 4:25

Insurance, obligations and rights after notice of loss, § 13:13

Leases, notice requirements of, §§ 18:30, 18:36

Mechanic's liens, notice of, §§ 18:80, 18:82

Partnership, liability to third persons as affected by notice of dissolution of, § 15:6

Premiums and assessments, notice as required for payment of, § 13:3

NOTICE OR KNOWLEDGE—Cont'd

Principal, notice of death of, § 1:5

Real property, recording of title instruments affecting, § 18:75

Recording of lis pendns notices, § 18:74

Vendor and purchaser, absence of notice, § 18:59

NOVATION

Contracts, § 5:28

NUISANCES

Generally, §§ 21:91-21:94

Adjoining landowners, liability for nuisance, § 18:48

Attractive nuisance, § 21:41

Cause of action, requisites of, § 21:92

Classifications, § 21:91

Defenses, § 21:93

Definitions, § 21:91

Land, nuisance as based on flight of aircraft over, § 18:1

Pollution of waters, abatement of nuisance as remedy for, § 18:42

Punitive or exemplary damages as recoverable in action to recover damages for, § 8:1

Remedies, § 21:94

What constitutes, § 21:92

NUNC PRO TUNC

Criminal procedure, entry of nunc pro tunc order to correct errors concerning, § 7:44

NUNCUPATIVE WILLS

Wills, formal requisites of, § 23:7

NURSES

Hospital liability for negligence of, § 21:55

Privileged communications, communications made to nurses as, § 11:9

OBSTRUCTION OF VISION

Automobiles and other motor vehicles, § 21:30

OBSTRUCTION OF WATERS

Waters (this index)

OFFER

Contracts, offer and acceptance of, § 5:7

OFFICIAL RECORDS

Documentary evidence, § 11:24

OMNIBUS CLAUSE

Automobile insurance, § 13:12

OPERATION OF LAW

Agency, termination by, § 1:5

INDEX